Teaching and the Case Method

Teaching
and the Case Method

Louis B. Barnes, C. Roland Christensen,
and Abby J. Hansen

Text, Cases, and Readings

Third Edition

HARVARD BUSINESS SCHOOL PRESS

Boston, Massachusetts

Printed in the United States of America

Credits begin on page 333, which constitutes a legal extension of the copyright page.

Library of Congress Cataloging-in-Publication Data

Barnes, Louis B.
    Teaching and the case method : text, cases, and readings / Louis B. Barnes, C. Roland Christensen, and Abby J. Hansen.—3rd ed.
        p.   cm.
    Rev. ed. of: Teaching and the case method / C. Roland Christensen. ©1987.
    Includes bibliographical references.
    ISBN 0-87584-403-0 (alk. paper)
    1. Business teachers—Training of—United States. 2. Case method.   I. Christensen, C. Roland (Carl Roland), 1919– .   II. Hansen, Abby J., 1945– .   III. Christensen, C. Roland (Carl Roland), 1919– . Teaching and the case method.   IV. Title.
HF1131.C48   1994   94-766
650′.071′2—dc20   CIP

Case material of the Harvard Graduate School of Business Administration, the Harvard School of Public Health, the Harvard Graduate School of Education and the Derek Bok Center for Teaching and Learning is made possible by the cooperation of associations who may wish to remain anonymous by having names, and other identifying details disguised while basic relationships are maintained. All cases are prepared as the basis for class discussion rather than to illustrate either effective or ineffective handling of administrative situations.

The paper used in this publication meets the requirements of the American National Standard for Permanence of Paper for Printed Library Materials Z39.48-1984.

To Fritz J. Roethlisberger

Who taught us to listen to thoughts as well as words, feelings beyond ideas, and to ever seek the understandings of both heart and head.

Contents

* Found in the Instructor's Guide

Contents

* Found in the Instructor's Guide

III

Improving Current Practice: Reflection and Reappraisal   283

* Found in the Instructor's Guide

Acknowledgments

This book is the result of the imagination and effort of a great number of people. We wish to take this opportunity to thank, all too briefly, those whose contributions have made its development possible. We are in their debt, as will be the instructors who use this volume to improve discussion teaching at their own institutions.

The cases in this edition are the product of a cooperative venture among the authors of this book, colleagues here at Harvard University, as well as other academic institutions, and seminar participants who shared their classroom experiences. So many will benefit from their generosity. We also acknowledge our debt to the authors and/or publishers of articles included in the reading sections of the seminar outline. Their essays present useful insights for understanding the teaching opportunities described in our case histories.

Our collective efforts to create a teaching program focusing on a case discussion pedagogy gained significant and unique support from the milieu in which we worked. With obvious bias, we believe the Harvard Business School is a great teaching institution. Over the decades, its culture has been supportive of the centrality of teaching to the mission of a professional school; "How did class go today?" is a typical first question at a faculty luncheon. Its promotion-reward system is supportive of superior teaching; senior faculty are expected to mentor younger instructors. Organizational practices insist that faculty invest considerable time in designing and implementing course outlines as well as in planning daily teaching tasks. Research and teaching are linked in numerous ways; central is the expectation that faculty members will develop cases for their own and other courses. We hope this third edition will honor that tradition and help interested colleagues learn more about the artistry of discussion teaching.

Our program to develop a faculty seminar on case method instruction has benefited from the long-term enthusiastic support of the Harvard Business School's leadership. With special appreciation, we note the contributions of former Dean George P. Baker and former Director of Case Development Andrew R. Towl, who were responsible for initiating this effort in 1968, as well as Dean John H. McArthur, who, with his colleagues former Associate Dean Dean W. Currie, Senior Associate Dean William A. Sahlman, Associate Dean Linda S. Doyle, and Associate Dean Ralph James, have provided us with intellectual, financial, and administrative resources essential for the ongoing development of this experiment in teacher education.

We are also in debt for the creative input of Carol Franco, senior editor, and Natalie Greenberg, production editor, both of the Harvard Business School Press, who marshaled the resources of that division in support of this effort. Our associate, Eileen Heath, with skill, devotion, and a sense of humor, managed the complicated task of text and case prepress preparation.

The authors also acknowledge appreciation to David A. Garvin and Ann Sweet, editors, along with C. Roland Christensen, of *Education for Judgment: The Artistry of Discussion Leadership*. The essays in their book are a valuable adjunct for one's study and discussion of the cases included in *Teaching and the Case Method*.

Over the years, a number of managers of large and small business organizations, as well as leaders of not-for-profit institutions, have participated in our teaching seminars. The boardroom and the classroom are not far apart; discussion leadership skills have universal application. The career of the late Joseph Fishelson of Wooster, Ohio clearly demonstrated that conclusion. He was an academic dean, classroom professor, trustee, and corporate board chairman—a great teacher in all those roles. We appreciate his major contributions to the development and publication of this third edition.

This program to learn more about the complexities of case teaching has also benefited enormously from the contributions of a dedicated group of Harvard Business School faculty—James Austin, David Garvin, James Heskett, and William Poorvu. Their leadership of case-discussion teaching seminars throughout Harvard University and at sister institutions has enabled us to gain additional knowledge and insight. We owe them so much.

Within the wider university scene, former President Derek Bok was instrumental in integrating his program to improve teaching effectiveness throughout Harvard College with our similar efforts at the Business School. And we are pleased that President Neil Rudenstine is continuing support for Mr. Bok's vision. Critical to this linkage has been the work of the Bok Center for Teaching and Learning (formerly the Harvard-Danforth Center for Teaching and Learning). We appreciate the cooperation of its director, Dr. James Wilkinson, and its associate director, Dr. Lee Warren. Dr. Warren has played an im-

portant part in our teaching and research program. We acknowledge the major contribution of the assistant to the president and associate dean of the Divinity School, Professor Constance Buchanan. She has been a continuing source of wise counsel on all pedagogical issues.

Other departments within Harvard University, especially the Schools of Public Health, Medicine, and Education have made major contributions by sponsoring teaching seminars and developing case materials that focus on the unique classroom challenges confronting their faculties. We want to give special thanks to Dean Jerome Murphy and Professor Richard F. Elmore of the School of Education.

Beyond this university, we are thankful for the suggestions we received in seminars at Roanoke College, the University of Richmond, the University of Denver, Göttenburg University, and Idaho State University.

We also wish to thank our colleagues at other academic institutions who, on a continuing basis, are experimenting with these materials as part of their faculty development efforts. We appreciate our ongoing association with Dr. John J. Newhauser, dean of the Walter Carroll School of Management, and Dr. Thomas Angelo, director of Academic Development Center, Boston College; Professors Alan Foster, Aneel Karnani, and Andrew Lawlor of the Business School, University of Michigan; Professors Taieb Hafsi and Laurent Lapierre, Graduate School of Business, University of Montreal; Dr. Sol Gittleman, provost, and Professor Robyn Gittleman, associate dean for Undergraduate Education, Tufts University; Dean John W. Seybolt, Associate Dean Debra Scammon, and Professor Gary Grikscheit of the David Eccles School of Business, University of Utah, collaborating with Ian Cumming, chairman of the Leucadia Corporation and member of the Utah State Board of Education; and Professor Selma Wassermann of the School of Education, Simon Fraser University, Burnaby, British Columbia, Canada.

We owe special thanks to the following associates. Over several decades, Mr. Andrew R. Towl, as director of Case Development, was responsible for establishing and putting into practice the school's program for developing and using cases. We are still dependent on his wisdom. Professor John R.N. Gordon, Queen's University, Kingston, Ontario, Canada has not only designed and led seminars throughout North America but has also pioneered in adapting those concepts and cases for use in the international educational scene. Senior Associate Dean William A. Sahlman's commitment to the success of our form of "educational entrepreneurship" has been central to this effort. His firm belief that the skills and attitudes of a practicing manager have much in common with those of a case discussion teacher have encouraged us to "climb higher mountains" and to push further into the unknowns of the teaching-learning process. Professor David Garvin's long-term contributions to our efforts to improve the practice of case discussion teaching are unmatched. His inputs to the design and implementation of the seminar program have been major. This book of cases and readings incorporates many of his suggestions for improving case teaching. And he played a central role in the creation of *Education for Judgment: The Artistry of Discussion Leadership*.

We also acknowledge the participants who, over the past decades, have joined with us in exploring case discussion teaching. They have played an active and important role in the development of seminar concepts and cases. We look forward to their continuing collaboration.

And, we honor the memory of the late Dr. Edmund P. Learned to whom the second edition of this book was dedicated. His 40 years of teaching, leadership of nine courses, and mentoring of dozens of younger associates still influence our institution.

Any ongoing research and teaching initiative requires not only individual author but also wider family interest. This revision would never have been completed without the support of our spouses, Wendy Barnes, Dorothy (Smitty) Christensen, and Thomas S. Hansen. Their interest and belief sustained us; their thoughtful suggestions enriched the final outcome.

Our lives as students of learning have been pro-foundly touched by the person and work of Fritz Roethlisberger to whom this book is dedicated. Fritz began life on October 21, 1898, the son of a Swiss-French mother and a Swiss-German father. The cultural conflicts represented by these parental backgrounds are symbolic of a fascination Fritz developed for all cultural tensions that multiplied in meaning. Fritz went on to spend a lifetime trying to understand the chasms, barriers, and misunderstandings that separated persons, groups, and people in organizations and societies from one another. He began as a student trying to reconcile science and humanities, went from philosophy at Columbia University to industrial engineering at MIT, to the aims of education with Alfred North Whitehead at Harvard, and then on to apprentice under an Australian humanist-psychologist named Elton Mayo and a Harvard biological chemist named Lawrence J. Henderson. Out of these associations eventually came a milestone research publication driven largely by Fritz's zeal for describing humanity as science and science as humanity. It provided one of the first systematic studies of human beings in industrial organizations and depicted the disparate worlds of managers and workers. The book was fittingly called *Management and the Worker*. But that was not all. Somewhere and somehow during the years of living within and alongside a world of contradictions and dichotomies, Fritz, the ever-inquiring student, became a passionate teacher of learning. His courses went by such old-fashioned names as Human Relations. His students were MBA and doctoral students at the Harvard Business School where he became one of the early case teacher masters. But in a much more profound sense, Fritz taught tolerance, curiosity, careful listening, classroom excitement, and a quest for understanding subtle differences. Most important, and the reason we honor him in this book: he taught us what it meant when a teacher cared.

Introduction

This book—text, cases, and readings—is a revision of earlier editions published in 1981 and 1987. It overviews a 25-year experiment conducted by faculty of the Harvard Business School. Our goals had been twofold: to learn more about the skills and knowledge essential to case method teaching and to develop better ways of helping instructors lead case discussions. Robert Frost once remarked that "education is hanging around till you've caught on." Too often, we believed, the same methodology was used to prepare instructors for discussion teaching. The typical sink-or-swim initiation into this complex pedagogy was economically inefficient and, far worse, exacted major human costs. In response to this problem, we developed a seminar program to help case method instructors become more adept in their craft. Not surprisingly, the seminar itself is based on cases describing actual classroom situations.

This edition reviews another phase of our continuing efforts to learn more about the artistry of case teaching. Since our earlier reports, we have made modest progress accompanied, of course, by the usual blunders of any exploratory effort. We would like to bring you up to date on the current status of the project, and we hope that readers will want to experiment with the seminar program found in Part II of this book. Your comments and suggestions will be appreciated.

A revised *Instructor's Guide* for seminar leaders is also available from the Harvard Business School Press. It includes (B) and (C) cases supplementary to those found in this book, teaching notes for all cases, and readings that may be of interest.

Growing Concerns about Teaching

Criticism of education has always been part of our culture. In *The Education of Henry Adams,* Adams put the point quite dramatically: "The chief wonder of education is that it does not ruin everybody concerned in it; teachers and taught." Ralph Waldo Emerson agreed—even more so! In the *New England Reformers* (1844), he complained, "We are students of words: we are shut up in schools and colleges and recitation rooms for ten or fifteen years and come out at last with a bag of wind, a memory of words and we do not know a thing." Matthew Arnold, inspector for schools in the United Kingdom in 1869, pessimistically concluded that "I find in schools, if I compare them with their former selves, a deadness, a slackness and a discouragement which are not the signs of progress."[1]

Arnold's message, with but slightly different words, is repeated by many of the private and governmental study groups currently reporting on the state of education in the United States. A primary conclusion of a good number of those reports is that teaching, in every dimension, must be improved. The Association of American Colleges sums up the point: "The faculty should concern itself with the quality of college teaching in which, after all, the effectiveness of any curriculum depends. We must assure that future college teachers are better prepared to teach."[2] Former President Donald Kennedy of Stanford, in an address to his faculty in April 1990 re-enforces the association's point. "The joint product character of our enterprise has long been a source of strength to us: teaching and research are both important. But the relative weight has shifted over time, as the relatively new term 'research university' suggests. *It is time for us to reaffirm that education—that is, teaching in all its forms—is the primary task, and that our society will judge us in the long run on how well we do it.*"[3]

Why such slow progress in improving teaching? Professor Theodore Sizer of Brown University offers one explanation. In *Horace's Compromise: The Dilemma of the American High School*, he comments, "Current educational reform is not listening to the exceptional teacher. Rather it's laying down more bureaucracy on schools and its thrust is to sand down eccentricity."[4] Fred Heckinger, educational editor of the *New York Times*, reminds us that "the teacher is central to any revitalization of our educational system." He points out that "Education is the teachers you remember after you've forgotten the others." Heckinger also comments that "Changing the way schools are organized and introducing technology to provide much of the instruction may increase the chances for serendipity to provide what

is missing in schools, but the ultimate reform must come through the person of the teacher."[5]

These pleas for more attention to teaching have been accompanied by a questioning of higher education's traditional dependence on lecturing. Both users (students) and producers (teachers) are demanding greater use of active, student-involved teaching methods.[6] The report of The Task Force on Teaching as a Profession, prepared by the Carnegie Forum on Education, recommends that "teaching cases illustrating a great variety of teaching problems should be developed as a major focus of instruction."[7]

Interest in discussion teaching is clearly on the rise throughout the academic community. For example, a special panel convened by the Association of American Medical Colleges (AAMC) urged medical schools to provide more active learning experiences by reducing lecture time, emphasizing independent learning skills, and requiring less factual memorization. Specifically the report recommended that

medical schools should establish programs to assist members of the faculty to expand their teaching capabilities. . . . Faculty members who guide students in independent learning must do more than merely transmit information. They must challenge medical students to be involved actively in their own education rather than being passive recipients of prepackaged information. To create such a learning environment, faculty members will require assistance in developing the skills they need to be effective and stimulating guides and mentors.[8]

1. Reported in the *Spectator Magazine* (London) May 15, 1993, p. 16.
2. Association of American Colleges, "Report of the Project on Redefining the Meaning and Purpose of Baccalaureate Degrees," *Chronicle of Higher Education*, February 13, 1985, p. 13.
3. "Stanford in Its Second Century," an address given to the Stanford community at a meeting of the Academic Council, April 5, 1990.
4. Theodore R. Sizer, *Horace's Compromise: The Dilemma of the American High School* (Boston: Houghton Mifflin, 1985), p. 10.
5. Quoted by B. Claude Mathis in "Faculty Disdain and Poor Schools," *Improving College and University Teaching*, Spring 1984, p. 148.
6. Alexander W. Astiv, "Involvement: The Cornerstone of Excellence," *Change*, July/August 1985, pp. 35–39, and Alvin M. White, "Teaching Mathematics as Though Students Mattered," *Teaching as Though Students Mattered: New Directions for Teaching and Learning* (San Francisco: Jossey-Bass, 1985), pp. 39–48.
7. "A Nation Prepared: Teachers for the 21st Century—The Report of The Task Force on Teaching as a Profession," prepared by the Carnegie Forum on Education, 1986, p. 77.
8. *Physicians for the Twenty-First Century: The GPEP Report*, Association of American Medical Colleges, Washington, D.C., September 1984; see also Peter Houts and Thomas Leamon, *Case Studies in Primary Medical Care* (University Park: Pennsylvania State University Press, 1983).

Under the leadership of Dean Daniel Tosteson, the faculty of the Harvard Medical School has instituted the New Pathways program, which meets many of the needs outlined in the AAMC report. This innovative experiment promises to have a major influence on American medical education.

Other professional fields are also reviewing their instructional modes. The John F. Kennedy School of Government, in cooperation with the Institute for the Study of Diplomacy at Georgetown University, under the direction of John Boehrer and with the support of the Pew Charitable Trust, has established a program "to strengthen and broaden the curriculum at schools of international affairs through the development and use of case studies for instructional purposes." Some 80 different academic institutions are involved.

With the leadership of Associate Dean James Ware and Associate Dean for Professional Education, Dr. Gareth M. Green, M.D., the Harvard School of Public Health has developed an innovative faculty development program. It involves support for individual faculty members who wish to design and implement teaching experiments for their specific courses; a continuing seminar—also involving the faculties of medicine and dentistry—concerned with improving faculty discussion leadership skills and, as well, a program which supports faculty members to develop and teach Public Health-based cases to colleagues. Results to date are encouraging.

The David Eccles School of Business at the University of Utah is initiating a major long-term program to accomplish similar objectives. It is beginning that effort by developing designs for classrooms specially tailored to meet discussion needs while offering faculty seminars in teaching and writing cases.

So many indicators point to increasing pedagogical change within the academy; Messrs. Holmes, Adams, and Arnold would be pleased.

The Teaching Seminar

The Harvard Business School's efforts to improve case discussion leadership through a formal program of teaching seminars mirrors these broader trends. Early experimental seminars focused on the needs of younger faculty; next we welcomed business school faculty from all ranks. Later we were joined by faculty from the arts and sciences—history, literature, music, philosophy, economics, zoology, and computer sciences—as well as colleagues in education, medicine, public health, dentistry, and government plus guests from other regional colleges and universities. These seminars gathered committed teachers to discuss common challenges, learn from other colleagues' experiences, and experiment with case-based teaching—all with the hope of improving their day-to-day classroom practice.

Equally important, these seminars have helped meet another wider university need—a forum where colleagues from different disciplines, using a variety of pedagogical approaches, might get together to talk about the vocation of teaching. Making this point quite dramatically, a participant opened the first session of one seminar by noting that this was the first formal opportunity to talk with colleagues about teaching issues that he had encountered in 17 years in academia. Another participant closed that same program with the following: "Working with these dedicated teachers has reaffirmed my faith in the worth of teaching, its tremendous contributive potential and its centrality to the complete academic life. It has given me impetus for career rededication."

Five theses are central to an understanding of our efforts to help instructors work more effectively in case discussion classes. They are, perhaps, more articles of faith than hypotheses capable of being verified. But is it reasonable to hope for scientific proof when the object of our inquiry is the elusive essence of the fundamental teaching-learning process? We put these propositions directly. At best they will help the reader identify the assumptions and philosophy that support this seminar; they offer windows to the authors' teaching credo. At a minimum they alert you to our biases.

First, we believe that when educational objectives focus on qualities of mind (curiosity, judgment, wisdom), qualities of person (character, sensitivity, integrity, responsibility), and the ability to apply general concepts and knowledge to specific situations, discussion pedagogy may well be very effective. Lectures about judgment typically have limited impact. Reading about problems or memorizing principles does little to prepare the practitioner—architect, doctor, or manager—to apply concepts and knowledge to the complexity of real-life problems. Discussion teaching helps achieve that objective. It puts the students in an active learning mode, challenges them to accept substantial responsibility for their own education, and gives them first-hand appreciation of, and experience with, the application of knowledge to practice.

Second, as our explorations indicate, we believe that the artistry of discussion leadership can be abstracted, articulated, and learned. John Dewey recognized the value of trying to capture the massive unused potential of gifted teachers:

> The successes of such individuals tend to be born and to die with them. . . . The only way by which we can prevent such waste in the future is by methods which enable us to make an analysis of what the gifted teacher does intuitively, so that something accruing from his work can be communicated to others.[9]

Our experience has been that instructors can improve their classroom competency modestly through participation in a formal program similar to the one presented in this book.

Third, the knowledge, skills, and attitudes associated with discussion leadership are universally relevant. The capacity to ask appropriate questions, to listen carefully and respond constructively, to deal with uncertainty, to reward and punish, to create learning environments of openness and trust are common to any discussion, whether the substantive topic be Elizabethan poetry or national military policy, whether the discussion occurs during a board of directors meeting, a church elders council, or the deliberation of a community advisory committee.

Fourth, there is "scholarship in teaching," to borrow the phrase of Harvard Medical School's associate dean of educational services, Myra Bergman Ramos. Too often academics draw a sharp contrast between scholarly research and teaching assignments. But teaching offers many opportunities to use scholarly skills. Evidence of scholarly accomplishment is evident in what Rippey calls "the corpus of artifacts or products developed in connection with instruction"[10]—course syllabi, case analyses, teaching plans, lecture notes, case histories, and examinations. A course syllabus provides opportunities for the exploration and evaluation of the literature of a field or course. A case analysis offers opportunities for systematic inquiry and rigorous

reasoning about the substantive issues in that statement. A teaching plan evidences the instructor's creativity in the process of planning for the discussion, in the use of supplementary readings and exercises and his or her understanding of what is known and what remains to be discovered about the substantive issues raised by the case.

Our fifth thesis is put best by the late Professor Charles I. Gragg in his essay, *"Teachers Also Must Learn,"* when he states:

> Teaching is a social art, necessarily involving a relationship between people; and the success of a teacher in the practice of his art depends upon his possessing that quality or attitude of mind which enables him to make the relationship between himself and his students a reciprocal one. Not all the teaching should be done by the teacher. Not all the learning should be done by the students.

Finally, if an instructor views his or her classroom not simply as physical space but also as a learning laboratory, he or she gains both knowledge and insight. Students, in their naïvete, pose wonderful research questions. Opportunities for experimentation abound. A teacher may use different opening and closure procedures in two sections of the same course or explore different combinations of readings and cases, and various patterns of questioning and responding. So often, effective teachers are clinical researchers of the classroom scene.

This Volume

The third edition of *Teaching and the Case Method* includes text, cases, and readings for a seminar focusing on the knowledge, skills, and attitudes requisite for the effective leadership of a case discussion. It builds on a long-term clinical research effort to understand better the dynamics of case teaching. In addition, it incorporates suggestions gleaned from experimentation with course concepts and materials, the size and composition of participant groups, multiple seminar time lengths, varying from intensive two- or three-day models to semester-long versions, as well as attempting to gauge the impact of the architectural design of the seminar room and the administrative protocols employed on patterns of student contribution.

Building on those experiments, plus constructive suggestions from colleagues, has enabled us to strengthen this edition in several ways. We have substantially increased the number of cases, allow-

9. John Dewey, *Sources of a Science of Education* (New York: Liveright, 1929), pp. 10–11.
10. Robert Rippey, *The Evaluation of Teaching in Medical Schools* (New York: Springer, 1981), p. 99.

ing us to consider fundamental issues in new contexts as well as to include cases dealing with the emerging classroom issues of the 1990s. In addition, we have created a seminar outline that can readily be adapted to meet the needs of institutions ranging from undergraduate and graduate schools, to professional schools and community colleges, and which can be adapted to programs varying in length from short intensive efforts to a year-long format. We have also strengthened the readings which support individual course modules. Finally we have focused many of the essays in Part III on the short-term steps a participant might take to improve his or her classroom practice.

The materials included in Part I, "Teaching and the Case Method: Premises and Practices," will be useful to colleagues as they prepare for a teaching seminar. These five essays are arranged to flow from the philosophic underpinnings of a discussion pedagogy to a very pragmatic mode—What is it like to participate in the give and take of a case discussion?

The Harvard Business School owes a great deal to the intellectual gifts of William James, Alfred North Whitehead, and John Dewey. The first essay, John Dewey's "Thinking in Education," is excerpted from his seminal study, *Democracy in Action,* written in 1915. In it he summarizes the basics of a discussion pedagogy and reasons for its success.

> . . . careful inspection of methods which are permanently successful in formal education . . . will reveal that they depend for their efficiency upon the fact that they go back to the type of situation which causes reflection out of school in ordinary life. . . . They give the pupil something to do, not something to learn, and the doing is of such a nature as to demand thinking.[11]

The second essay, "Teachers Also Must Learn," written by Charles I. Gragg, directs attention to the impact of Dewey's philosophy on the roles of teacher and student. His essay is not only insightful but also a delight to read.

The next essay[12] summarizes the basic premises and associated operational practices central to a discussion pedagogy. First, that teachers and students share as *partners* the responsibilities and privileges of learning. Second, while a discussion class normally begins with a number of individuals being administratively assigned to the course, it needs to become a *learning community* with shared goals, values, and operational responsibilities dedicated to collective as well as personal learning. Third, a discussion teacher needs to forge a primary *alliance with students* as well as subject matter. Subject matter defines the boundaries of the intellectual territory; students' intellects, learning styles, fears, and aspirations shape their paths of inquiry. We need to know and respect each student. Fourth, "Teaching with Cases at the Harvard Business School" overviews the historical evolution of the case method of instruction at our school. In addition, this essay details the objectives and organization of seminar programs found in Part II. The final essay, "Suggestions for Seminar Participants," targets three questions: Why might a colleague want to join a case teaching seminar? What is it like to be a member of such a group? What critical assumptions and articles of faith undergird this course? Ideally, we hope that participants will be able to study all the text in Part I before their first session. If that is impossible, we suggest giving priority to "Teachers Also Must Learn," and the pages on the objectives and organization of the program from "Teaching with Cases at the Harvard Business School," and "Suggestions for Seminar Participants."

Part II presents materials for a case-discussion teaching seminar. Part III offers graduates of that seminar a number of "next-step" suggestions for their consideration. In an operational mode, the first essay proposes that you develop cases for your own teaching seminar; the second urges colleagues to investigate the benefits of being videotaped. In "Student Learning Beyond the Classroom: Implications for a Discussion Methods Teacher," we pose an especially interesting question for a discussion leader—How do we teach outside of the classroom? The essay, "Leading Discussion in a Lecture Course: Some Maxims and an Exhortation," offers suggestions on melding the didactic and discussion pedagogies. Next, we include cases and an accompanying teaching note to emphasize the value of teaching plans for classroom practice. The concluding readings shift from an operational to a reflective mode. Selma Wassermann's delightfully provocative statement, "Memorandum to Michelangelo: Tenure Denied," asks the academy to face up to the problems

11. John Dewey, *Democracy and Education* (New York: The Free Press, 1966), p. 154.
12. C. Roland Christensen, "Premises and Practices of Discussion Teaching," in *Education for Judgment: The Artistry of Discussion Leadership* (Boston: Harvard Business School Press, 1991), pp. 15–34.

of our current tenure process. Parker Palmer's "Good Teaching: A Matter of Living the Mystery" asserts that

> good teaching cannot be equated with technique. It comes from the integrity of the teacher, from his or her relation to subject and student and from the capricious chemistry of it all . . . good teaching requires courage—the courage to expose one's ignorance as well as insight, to invite contradiction as well as consent, to yield some control in order to empower the group, to evoke other people's lives as well as reveal one's own.

The authors and contributors to this book, joined by dedicated educators who have experimented with these concepts and cases in sister institutions, invite your participation in this adventure to improve the quality of case discussion teaching. Doing so may enhance the effectiveness of your present classroom practice. Equally, if not more important, it may encourage you to articulate your own philosophy of the teaching-learning process. Soren Kierkegaard in his statement, "A Point of View on Teaching," summarizes his point of view. Although it was written some 130 years ago, we find his statement refreshingly current. If you were to try your hand at this task, how might yours read?

A Point of View on Teaching

. . . if real success is to attend the effort to bring a man to a definite position, one must first of all take pains to find HIM where he is and begin there.

This is the secret of the art of helping others. Anyone who has not mastered this is himself deluded when he proposes to help others. In order to help another effectively, I must understand what he understands. If I do not know that, my greater understanding will be of no help to him. If, however, I am disposed to plume myself on my greater understanding, it is because I am vain or proud, so that at bottom, instead of benefitting him, I want to be admired. But all true effort to help does not mean to be a sovereign but to be a servant, that to help does not mean to endure for the time being the imputation that one is in the wrong and does not understand what the other understands . . . For to be a teacher does not mean simply to affirm that such a thing is so, or to deliver a lecture, etc. No, to be a teacher in the right sense is to be a learner. Instruction begins when you, the teacher, learn from the learner, put yourself in his place so that you may understand what he understands and in the way he understands it . . .[13]

13. Søren Kierkegaard, *The Journals,* 1864.

PART I

Teaching and the Case Method: Premises and Practices

1. The Essentials of Method. No one doubts, theoretically, the importance of fostering in school good habits of thinking. But apart from the fact that the acknowledgement is not so great in practice as in theory, there is not adequate theoretical recognition that all which the school can or need do for pupils, so far as their *minds* are concerned (that is, leaving out certain specialized muscular abilities), is to develop their ability to think. The parceling out of instruction among various ends such as acquisition of skill (in reading, spelling, writing, drawing, reciting); acquiring information (in history and geography), *and* training of thinking is a measure of the ineffective way in which we accomplish all three. Thinking which is not connected with increase of efficiency in action, and with learning more about ourselves and the world in which we live, has something the matter with it just as thought (See *ante*, p. 147). And skill obtained apart from thinking is not connected with any sense of the purposes for which it is to be used. It consequently leaves a man at the mercy of his routine habits and of the authoritative control of others, who know what they are about and who are not especially scrupulous as to their means of achievement. And information severed from thoughtful action is dead, a mind-crushing load. Since it simulates knowledge and thereby develops the poison of conceit, it is a most powerful obstacle to further growth in the grace of intelligence. The sole direct path to enduring improvement in the methods of instruction and learning consists in centering upon the conditions which exact, promote, and test thinking. Thinking *is* the method of intelligent learning, of learning that employs and rewards mind. We speak, legitimately enough, about the method of thinking, but the important thing to bear in mind about method is that thinking is method, the method of intelligent experience in the course which it takes.

I. The initial stage of that developing experience which is called thinking is *experience*. This remark may sound like a silly truism. It ought to be one; but unfortunately it is not. On the contrary, thinking is often regarded both in philosophic theory and in educational practice as something cut off from experience, and capable of being cultivated in isolation. In fact, the inherent limitations of experience are often urged as the sufficient ground for attention to thinking. Experience is then thought to be confined to the senses and appetites; to a mere material

Thinking in Education

JOHN DEWEY

world, while thinking proceeds from a higher faculty (of reason), and is occupied with spiritual or at least literary things. So, oftentimes, a sharp distinction is made between pure mathematics as a peculiarly fit subject matter of thought (since it has nothing to do with physical existences) and applied mathematics, which has utilitarian but not mental value.

Speaking generally, the fundamental fallacy in methods of instruction lies in supposing that experience on the part of pupils may be assumed. What is here insisted upon is the necessity of an actual empirical situation as the initiating phase of thought. Experience is here taken as previously defined: trying to do something and having the thing perceptibly do something to one in return. The fallacy consists in supposing that we can begin with ready-made subject matter of arithmetic, or geography, or whatever, irrespective of some direct personal experience of a situation. Even the kindergarten and Montessori techniques are so anxious to get at intellectual distinctions, without "waste of time," that they tend to ignore—or reduce—the immediate crude handling of the familiar material of experience, and to introduce pupils at once to material which expresses the intellectual distinctions which adults have made. But the first stage of contact with any new material, at whatever age of maturity, must inevitably be of the trial and error sort. An individual must actually try, in play or work, to do something with material in carrying out his own impulsive activity, and then note the interaction of his energy and that of the material employed. This is what happens when a child at first begins to build with blocks, and it is equally what happens when a scientific man in his laboratory begins to experiment with unfamiliar objects.

Hence the first approach to any subject in school, if thought is to be aroused and not words acquired, should be as unscholastic as possible. To realize what an experience, or empirical situation, means, we have to call to mind the sort of situation that presents itself outside of school; the sort of occupations that interest and engage activity in ordinary life. And careful inspection of methods which are permanently successful in formal education, whether in arithmetic or learning to read, or studying geography, or learning physics or a foreign language, will reveal that they depend for their efficiency upon the fact that they go back to the type of the situation which causes reflection out of school

in ordinary life. They give the pupils something to do, not something to learn; and the doing is of such a nature as to demand thinking, or the intentional noting of connections; learning naturally results.

That the situation should be of such a nature as to arouse thinking means of course that it should suggest something to do which is not either routine or capricious—something, in other words, presenting what is new (and hence uncertain or problematic) and yet sufficiently connected with existing habits to call out an effective response. An effective response means one which accomplishes a perceptible result, in distinction from a purely haphazard activity, where the consequences cannot be mentally connected with what is done. The most significant question which can be asked, accordingly, about any situation or experience proposed to induce learning is what quality of problem it involves.

At first thought, it might seem as if usual school methods measured well up to the standard here set. The giving of problems, the putting of questions, the assigning of tasks, the magnifying of difficulties, is a large part of school work. But it is indispensable to discriminate between genuine and simulated or mock problems. The following questions may aid in making such discrimination. *(a)* Is there anything but a problem? Does the question naturally suggest itself within some situation or personal experience? Or is it an aloof thing, a problem only for the purposes of conveying instruction in some school topic? Is it the sort of trying that would arouse observation and engage experimentation outside of school? *(b)* Is it the pupil's own problem, or is it the teacher's or textbook's problem, made a problem for the pupil only because he cannot get the required mark or be promoted or win the teacher's approval, unless he deals with it? Obviously, these two questions overlap. They are two ways of getting at the same point: Is the experience a personal thing of such a nature as inherently to stimulate and direct observation of the connections involved, and to lead to inference and its testing? Or is it imposed from without, and is the pupil's problem simply to meet the external requirement?

Such questions may give us pause in deciding upon the extent to which current practices are adapted to develop reflective habits. The physical equipment and arrangements of the average schoolroom are hostile to the existence of real situations of experience. What is there similar to the conditions of everyday life which will generate difficulties? Almost everything testifies to the great premium put upon listening, reading, and the reproduction of what is told and read. It is hardly possible to overstate the contrast between such conditions and the situations of active contact with things and persons in the home, on the playground, in fulfilling of ordinary responsibilities of life. Much of it is not even comparable with the questions which may arise in the mind of a boy or girl in conversing with others or in reading books outside of the school. No one has ever explained why children are so full of questions outside of the school (so that they pester grown-up persons if they get any encouragement), and the conspicuous absence of display of curiosity about the subject matter of school lessons. Reflection on this striking contrast will throw light upon the question of how far customary school conditions supply a context of experience in which problems naturally suggest themselves. No amount of improvement in the personal technique of the instructor will wholly remedy this state of things. There must be more actual material, more *stuff*, more appliances, and more opportunities for doing things, before the gap can be overcome. And where children are engaged in doing things and in discussing what arises in the course of their doing, it is found, even with comparatively indifferent modes of instruction, that children's inquiries are spontaneous and numerous, and the proposals of solution advanced, varied, and ingenious.

As a consequence of the absence of the materials and occupations which generate real problems, the pupil's problems are not his; or, rather, they are his *only as* a pupil, not as a human being. Hence the lamentable waste in carrying over such expertness as is achieved in dealing with them to the affairs of life beyond the schoolroom. A pupil has a problem, but it is the problem of meeting the peculiar requirements set by the teacher. His problem becomes that of finding out what the teacher wants, what will satisfy the teacher in recitation and examination and outward deportment. Relationship to subject matter is no longer direct. The occasions and material of thought are not found in the arithmetic or the history or geography itself, but in skillfully adapting that material to the teacher's requirements. The pupil studies, but unconsciously to himself the objects of his study are the conventions and standards of the school system and school authority, not the nominal "studies." The thinking thus evoked is ar-tificially one-sided at the best. At its worst, the problem of the pupil is not how to meet the requirements of school life, but how to *seem* to meet them—or, how to come near enough to meeting them to slide along without an undue amount of friction. The type of judgment formed by these devices is not a desirable addition to character. If these statements give too highly colored a picture of usual school methods, the exaggeration may at least serve to illustrate the point: the need of active pursuits, involving the use of material to accomplish purposes, if there are to be situations which normally generate problems occasioning thoughtful inquiry.

II. There must be *data* at command to supply the considerations required in dealing with the specific difficulty which has presented itself. Teachers following a "developing" method sometimes tell children to think things out for themselves as if they could spin them out of their own heads. The material of thinking is not thoughts, but actions, facts, events, and the relations of things. In other words, to think effectively one must have had, or now have, experiences which will furnish him resources for coping with the difficulty at hand. A difficulty is an indispensable stimulus to thinking, but not all difficulties call out thinking. Sometimes they overwhelm and submerge and discourage. The perplexing situation must be sufficiently like situations which have already been dealt with so that pupils will have some control of the meanings of handling it. A large part of the art of instruction lies in making the difficulty of new problems large enough to challenge thought, and small enough so that, in addition to the confusion naturally attending the novel elements, there shall be luminous familiar spots from which helpful suggestions may spring.

In one sense, it is a matter of indifference by what psychological means the subject matter for reflection is provided. Memory, observation, reading, communication, are all avenues for supplying data. The relative proportion to be obtained from each is a matter of the specific features of the particular problem in hand. It is foolish to insist upon observation of objects presented to the senses if the student is so familiar with the objects that he could just as well recall the facts independently. It is possible to induce undue and crippling dependence upon sense-presentations. No one can carry around with him a museum of all the things whose properties will assist the conduct of thought. A well-trained mind is one that has a maximum of resources behind it, so to speak, and that is accustomed to go over its past experiences to see what they yield. On the other hand, a quality or relation of even a familiar object may previously have been passed over, and be just the fact that is helpful in dealing with the question. In this case direct observation is called for. The same principle applies to the use to be made of observation on one hand and of reading and "telling" on the other. Direct observation is naturally more vivid and vital. But it has its limitations; and in any case it is a necessary part of education that one should acquire the ability to supplement the narrowness of his immediately personal experiences by utilizing the experiences of others. Excessive reliance upon others for data (whether got from reading or listening) is to be depreciated. Most objectionable of all is the probability that others, the book or the teacher, will supply solutions ready-made, instead of giving material that the student has to adapt and apply to the question in hand for himself.

There is no inconsistency in saying that in schools there is usually both too much and too little information supplied by others. The accumulation and acquisition of information for purposes of reproduction in recitation and examination is made too much of. "Knowledge," in the sense of information, means the working capital, the indispensable resources, of further inquiry; of finding out, or learning, more things. Frequently it is treated as an end itself, and then the goal becomes to heap it up and display it when called for. This static, cold-storage ideal of knowledge is inimical to educative development. It not only lets occasions for thinking go unused, but it swamps thinking. No one could construct a house on ground cluttered with miscellaneous junk. Pupils who have stored their "minds" with all kinds of material which they have never put to intellectual uses are sure to be hampered when they try to think. They have no practice in selecting what is appropriate, and no criterion to go by; everything is on the same dead static level. On the other hand, it is quite open to question whether, if information actually functioned in experience through use in application to the student's own purposes, there would not be need of more varied resources in books, pictures, and talks than are usually at command.

III. The correlate in thinking of facts, data, knowledge already acquired, is suggestions, inferences, conjectured meanings, suppositions, tentative explanations:—*ideas*, in short. Careful observation and recollection determine what is given, what is already there, and hence assured. They cannot furnish what is lacking. They define, clarify, and locate the question; they cannot supply its answer. Projection, invention, ingenuity, devising come in for that purpose. The data *arouse* suggestions, and only by reference to the specific data can we pass upon the appropriateness of the suggestions. But the suggestions run beyond what is, as yet, actually *given* in experience. They forecast possible results, things *to do*, not facts (things already done). Inference is always an invasion of the unknown, a leap from the known.

In this sense, a thought (what a thing suggests but is not as it is presented) is creative,—an incursion into the novel. It involves some inventiveness. What is suggested must, indeed, be familiar in *some* context; the novelty, the inventive devising, clings to the new light in which it is seen, the different use to which it is put. When Newton thought of his theory of gravitation, the creative aspect of his thought was not found in its materials. They were familiar; many of them commonplaces—sun, moon, planets, weight, distance, mass, square of numbers. These were not original ideas; they were established facts. His originality lay in the *use* to which these familiar acquaintances were put by introduction into an unfamiliar context. The same is true of every striking scientific discovery, every great invention, every admirable artistic production. Only silly folk identify creative originality with the extraordinary and fanciful; others recognize that its measure lies in putting everyday things to uses which had not occurred to others. The operation is novel, not the materials out of which it is constructed.

The educational conclusion which follows is that *all* thinking is original in a projection of considerations which have not been previously apprehended. The child of three who discovers what can be done with blocks, or of six who finds out what he can make by putting five cents and five cents together, is really a discoverer, even though everybody else in the world knows it. There is a genuine increment of experience; not another item mechanically added on, but enrichment by a new quality. The charm which the spontaneity of little children has for sympathetic observers is due to perception of this intellectual originality. The joy which children themselves experience is the joy of intellectual constructiveness—of creativeness, if the word may be used without misunderstanding.

The educational moral I am chiefly concerned to

draw is not, however, that teachers would find their own work less of a grind and strain if school conditions favored learning in the sense of discovery and not in that of storing away what others pour into them; nor that it would be possible to give even children and youth the delights of personal intellectual productiveness—true and important as are these things. It is that no thought, no idea, can possibly be conveyed as an idea from one person to another. When it is told, it is, to the one to whom it is told, another given fact, not an idea. The communication may stimulate the other person to realize the question for himself and to think out a like idea, or it may smother his intellectual interest and suppress his dawning effort at thought. But what he *directly* gets cannot be an idea. Only by wrestling with the conditions of the problem at first hand, seeking and finding his own way out, does he think. When the parent or teacher has provided the conditions which stimulate thinking and has taken a sympathetic attitude toward the activities of the learner by entering into a common or conjoint experience, all has been done which a second party can do to instigate learning. The rest lies with the one directly concerned. If he cannot devise his own solution (not of course in isolation, but in correspondence with the teacher and other pupils) and find his own way out he will not learn, not even if he can recite some correct answer with one hundred per cent accuracy. We can and do supply ready-made "ideas" by the thousand; we do not usually take much pains to see that the one learning engages in significant situations where his own activities generate, support, and clinch ideas—that is, perceived meanings or connections. This does not mean that the teacher is to stand off and look on; the alternative to furnishing ready-made subject matter and listening to the accuracy with which it is reproduced is not quiescence, but participation, sharing, in an activity. In such shared activity, the teacher is a learner, and the learner is, without knowing it, a teacher—and upon the whole, the less consciousness there is, on either side, of either giving or receiving instruction, the better.

IV. Ideas, as we have seen, whether they be humble guesses or dignified theories, are anticipations of possible solutions. They are anticipations of some continuity or connection of an activity and a consequence which has not as yet shown itself. They are therefore tested by the operation of acting upon them. They are to guide and organize further observations, recollections, and experiments. They are

intermediate in learning, not final. All educational reformers, as we have had occasion to remark, are given to attacking the passivity of traditional education. They have opposed pouring in from without, and absorbing like a sponge; they have attacked drilling in material as into hard and resisting rock. But it is not easy to secure conditions which will make the getting of an idea identical with having an experience which widens and makes more precise our contact with the environment. Activity, even self-activity, is too easily thought of as something merely mental, cooped up within the head, or finding expression only through the vocal organs.

While the need of application of ideas gained in study is acknowledged by all the more successful methods of instruction, the exercises in application are sometimes treated as devices for *fixing* what has already been learned and for getting greater practical skill in its manipulation. These results are genuine and not to be despised. But practice in applying what has been gained in study ought primarily to have an intellectual quality. As we have already seen, thoughts just as thoughts are incomplete. At best they are tentative; they are suggestions, indications. They are standpoints and methods for dealing with situations of experience. Till they are applied in these situations they lack full point and reality. Only application tests them, and only testing confers full meaning and a sense of their reality. Short of use made of them, they tend to segregate into a peculiar world of their own. It may be seriously questioned whether the philosophies (to which reference has been made in section 2 of chapter X) which isolate mind and set it over against the world did not have their origin in the fact that the reflective or theoretical class of men elaborated a large stock of ideas which social conditions did not allow them to act upon and test. Consequently men were thrown back into their own thoughts as ends in themselves.

However this may be, there can be no doubt that a peculiar artificiality attaches to much of what is learned in schools. It can hardly be said that many students consciously think of the subject matter as unreal; but it assuredly does not possess for them the kind of reality which the subject matter of their vital experiences possesses. They learn not to expect that sort of reality of it; they become habituated to treating it as having reality for the purposes of recitations, lessons, and examinations. That it should remain inert for the experiences of daily life is more or less a matter of course. The bad effects are twofold. Ordinary experience does not receive the enrichment which it should; it is not fertilized by school learning. And the attitudes which spring from getting used to and accepting half-understood and ill-digested material weaken vigor and efficiency of thought.

If we have dwelt especially on the negative side, it is for the sake of suggesting positive measures adapted to the effectual development of thought. Where schools are equipped with laboratories, shops, and gardens, where dramatizations, plays, and games are freely used, opportunities exist for reproducing situations of life, and for acquiring and applying information and ideas in the carrying forward of progressive experiences. Ideas are not segregated, they do not form an isolated island. They animate and enrich the ordinary course of life. Information is vitalized by its function; by the place it occupies in direction of action.

The phrase "opportunities exist" is used purposely. They may not be taken advantage of; it is possible to employ manual and constructive activities in a physical way, as means of getting just bodily skill; or they may be used almost exclusively for "utilitarian," i.e., pecuniary, ends. But the disposition on the part of upholders of "cultural" education to assume that such activities are merely physical or professional in quality, is itself a product of the philosophies which isolate mind from direction of the course of experience and hence from action upon and with things. When the "mental" is regarded as a self-contained separate realm, a counterpart fate befalls bodily activity and movements. They are regarded as at the best mere external annexes to mind. They may be necessary for the satisfaction of bodily needs and the attainment of external decency and comfort, but they do not occupy a necessary place in mind nor enact an indispensable rôle in the completion of thought. Hence they have no place in a liberal education—i.e., one which is concerned with the interests of intelligence. If they come in at all, it is as a concession to the material needs of the masses. That they should be allowed to invade the education of the élite is unspeakable. This conclusion follows irresistibly from the isolated conception of mind, but by the same logic it disappears when we perceive what mind really is—namely, the purposive and directive factor in the development of experience.

While it is desirable that all educational institutions should be equipped so as to give students an opportunity for acquiring and testing ideas and information in active pursuits typifying important social situations, it will, doubtless, be a long time before all of them are thus furnished. But this state of affairs does not afford instructors an excuse for folding their hands and persisting in methods which segregate school knowledge. Every recitation in every subject gives an opportunity for establishing cross connections between the subject matter of the lesson and the wider and more direct experiences of everyday life. Classroom instruction falls into three kinds. The least desirable treats each lesson as an independent whole. It does not put upon the student the responsibility of finding points of contact between it and other lessons in the same subject, or other subjects of study. Wiser teachers see to it that the student is systematically led to utilize his earlier lessons to help understand the present one, and also to use the present to throw additional light upon what has already been acquired. Results are better, but school subject matter is still isolated. Save by accident, out-of-school experience is left in its crude and comparatively irreflective state. It is not subject to the refining and expanding influences of the more accurate and comprehensive material of direct instruction. The latter is not motivated and impregnated with a sense of reality by being intermingled with the realities of everyday life. The best type of teaching bears in mind the desirability of affecting this interconnection. It puts the student in the habitual attitude of finding points of contact and mutual bearings.

Summary. Processes of instruction are unified in the degree in which they center in the production of good habits of thinking. While we may speak, without error, of the method of thought, the important thing is that thinking is the method of an educative experience. The essentials of method are therefore identical with the essentials of reflection. They are first that the pupil have a genuine situation of experience—that there be a continuous activity in which he is interested for its own sake; secondly, that a genuine problem develop within this situation as a stimulus to thought; third, that he possess the information and make the observations needed to deal with it; fourth, that suggested solutions occur to him which he shall be responsible for developing in an orderly way; fifth, that he have opportunity and occasion to test his ideas by application, to make their meaning clear and to discover for himself their validity.

The Queen seemed to guess her thoughts, for she cried, "Faster! Don't try to talk!"

Not that Alice had any idea of doing *that*. She felt as if she would never be able to talk again, she was getting so much out of breath; and still the Queen cried "Faster! Faster!" and dragged her along. "Are we nearly there?" Alice managed to pant out at last.

"Now! Now!" cried the Queen. "Faster! Faster!" And they went so fast that at last they seemed to skim through the air, hardly touching the ground with their feet, till suddenly just as Alice was getting quite exhausted, they stopped, and she found herself sitting on the ground breathless and giddy.

Alice looked around her in great surprise. "Why, I do believe we've been under this tree the whole time! Everything's just as it was!"

READING

Teachers Also Must Learn

CHARLES I. GRAGG

In any sensible discussion of teaching, emphasis of course must be upon learning rather than upon teaching. Teaching has no excuse except as it results in learning. Yet everyone who has been a student knows that it is possible, after even the most strenuous classroom exertions, to find, like Alice, that "everything's just as it was." The teacher's art lies in his ability to help his students to reach new positions, or, to put the matter with the utmost triteness, in his ability to help his students to learn.

Teaching is a social art, necessarily involving a relationship between people; and the success of a teacher in the practice of his art depends upon his possessing that quality or attitude of mind which enables him to make the relationship between himself and his students a reciprocal one. Not all the teaching should be done by the teacher. Not all the learning should be done by the students.

No one can learn in any basic sense from another except by subjecting what that other has to offer to a process of creative thinking; that is, unless the learner is actively and imaginatively receptive, he will emerge from the teaching experience with nothing more than a catalogue of facts and other people's notions. Anyone, consequently, who is to teach another must see to it that his pupil listens to him in an attitude of creative receptivity. But the teacher will not succeed in leading his students to receive ideas with a lively and formative spirit unless he, himself, shows toward his students a comparable attitude of being willing to learn from them.

Ideally, the only mark distinguishing the teacher from the student will be the teacher's greater learning.

Professor Whitehead in one of his powerful and compact essays, "The Aims of Education," has pointed out that those who seek to train the young must "beware of 'inert ideas'—that is to say, ideas that are merely received into the mind without being utilized, or tested, or thrown into fresh combinations."[1] In discussing the need for "self-education," or active participation by the learner in the process of learning, A. Lawrence Lowell wrote: "'Self-education' is based on the principle that, beyond the mechanical elements, no one can be really educated against his will, or without his own active effort."[2]

The passive reception of ideas or facts constitutes no education at all. In short, the learner must share actively in the task of learning; he must create for himself the ideas that the teacher seeks to communicate to him. The word "create" is used advisedly. The process is not one of absorption or of fitting pieces of knowledge into a pattern. The process of learning is truly one of creation. No teacher can take a concept, however simple, and place it intact and usable in the mind of another. The art of communication is too imperfect. From what the teacher says or writes or does, the learner must create his own concept. It may approach that of the teacher, but, like all created things, it will be to some extent original. The student has created something and it is his. He has learned, moreover, something of the labors and the joys of such activity. There is no serious doubt in educational circles that this process is desirable. No intelligent person maintains that any amount of listening and remembering will produce an educated man. As Professor Whitehead remarks later in his essay, "A merely well-informed man is the most useless bore on God's earth." If it be accepted that he who is to learn must take an active part in his own education, then from the point of view of the art of teaching the question

becomes one of what the teacher can do to encourage his students to make the necessary exertion. The teacher not only must have a genuine ability and desire to communicate to others the thoughts and concepts which have become his through his own imaginative thinking; he must go farther. He must have a genuine desire and ability to be communicated to, for it is this desire and ability which above all else will encourage, almost force, the student to the exertion necessary to the creation of something which will be his own, to the cultivation of a quality of thinking which ever will stand him and the world in good stead.

Teaching is not only the art of thinking and speaking. It is also the art of listening and understanding. Nor by listening is meant just the act of keeping still. Keeping still is a technique; listening is an art. Most of us, though all too infrequently, have experienced the stimulation of talking with someone whom we have felt to be genuinely willing to listen to us, that is, to exert himself to receive what we were saying and to comprehend it to the full extent of his capacity for imaginative understanding. In the presence of such a person we are carried out of ourselves, our minds become more active, our thoughts more vibrant and original. We see relationships and meanings that before were not apparent to us. We may even end by seeing that our notion was in truth a poor and feeble one. But whatever the outcome, it is something alive and real, not only for us, but also for our friend. Creative intercommunication has taken place though our companion may not have said three words.

In another connection Professor Henderson has stressed the importance of the attitude of receptivity. Speaking of the medical profession, he says:

> The doctors have always found it necessary to take account of what patients tell them. . . . The physician listens, first, to what the patient wants to tell, secondly, for implications of what he doesn't want to tell, and thirdly, for implications of what he can't tell.[3]

1. A. N. Whitehead, *The Aim of Education and Other Essays* (New York: The Macmillan Company, 1929).
2. A. Lawrence Lowell, *Report of the President of Harvard College and Reports of Departments*, 1931–1932.

3. L. J. Henderson, "Introductory Lectures, Sociology 23" (in mimeographed form). (For private distribution only, unpublished paper October 1938, pp. 13–14. In L. J. Henderson Papers, Baker Library, Harvard Business School.)

Also, in the field of employer-employee relations, Professor Roethlisberger has pointed out the importance of the listening attitude: "The first rule is that the supervisor should listen patiently to what his subordinate has to say before making any comment himself. . . ."[4]

Just as everyone has had the invigorating experience of talking with persons of receptive minds, so too we have all had the experience of trying to communicate a thought to someone unwilling to receive it. Such a person, if we are fortunate, may keep quiet while we speak, but he will not exert himself to understand what we are saying. It is not, of course, that we need approval. Approval and disapproval are beside the point. We are never discouraged in our thinking by having our ideas disapproved of or disagreed with by someone we know understands them. But how stultifying is either approval or disapproval when it comes from a person who does not know what we are talking about! Everything such a person says, no matter how weighty, is without pertinence. Naturally so, for we are not talking about the same things. How chilling and futile is such an exchange of words! Our ideas wilt; our imagination retreats. In such an atmosphere nothing can come to life. The criticisms, comments, and suggestions offered by our adversary, for such he insists upon being though we looked for a friend, may be splendid and profound. The trouble is that they have no applicability in the situation. In the presence of such an attitude, creative thought is stifled. Neither we nor our companion have gained anything. Our idea is no different from what it was at the beginning though it now seems less alive to us. Our companion has had the satisfaction of stating his own views, but presumably he has had this satisfaction before and will have it again. Nothing creative has happened in either mind.

Expounders and debaters may thrive in an atmosphere of nonreceptivity. Blind opposition, flat denials, and the introduction of irrelevancies may spur them on. But, they are not thinking; their object is not to communicate with others, but to convince them. There are places in which such activity is valuable, though far fewer than is commonly

4. F. J. Roethlisberger "Understanding: A Prerequisite of Leadership," address before Professor Cabot's Business Executives' Group, Boston, February 9, 1936.

thought. Certainly the classroom is not one of them. Persons of unreceptive minds are sorry sights in halls of learning. There, as in the marts of trade, "no sale is ever made by winning an argument."

Now, if we, who should be somewhat used to the ways of productive thinking, can feel our creative faculties retreating in the presence of a mind which shows itself, to us at least, as opaque, how much greater is the effect of such an attitude likely to be upon the young? They know their ideas are untried and, though they may put up a bold front of confidence, they are easily discouraged. That they should be discouraged in their ideas may not matter, but that they should be discouraged from having ideas matters greatly. It is the teacher's task to establish a basis of communication between himself and his students which will lead them to the only type of mental activity through which they can learn, namely, the imaginative handling of ideas with the aim of creation.

I

It cannot be denied, and the writings of educators are filled with this plaint, that students in general resist "learning." At the same time they crave it. Neither of these tendencies is to be wondered at, for the acquiring of learning is as hard as it is happy. Every creator knows the torments and the joys of his art, and so does every "learner," for he too is a creator. Yet there is more behind the student's resistance to learning than the mere natural difficulty of the process. The unwillingness of students to work freely and wholeheartedly for what is their avowed objective, and for what is surely to their own self-interest, results perhaps from certain typical reactions of parents to their children's early efforts to acquire learning. The basic etiology of what in effect amounts to self-frustration by the student has a vital bearing upon the problem of teaching. It suggests both the attitudes which the helpful teacher must avoid and those which he must cultivate.

The child originally has no resistance to the creative incorporation of ideas or experiences; quite the contrary. He is eager to master the world, to make all knowledge, experience, and achievement his own. Unfortunately, the attitude of his elders is customarily far from encouraging. The child's eagerness for creative learning tends to arouse in his elders one of four commonly observed reactions.

These reactions may be described as: the direct-withholding-of-information reaction; the depreciation-of-the-learner reaction; the drowning-of-the-learner reaction; and the talking-beside-the-point reaction. The withholding-of-information reaction is immediately recognizable.

"Why are my roosters so bad to my hens? They bite them all the time."
"Sh! Never mind. Don't pay any attention to that. You're just imagining things. Run on and play."

"I have answered three questions, and that is enough," said his father. "Don't give yourself airs. Do you think I can listen all day to such stuff? Be off, or I'll kick you downstairs!"

Then there is the depreciation-of-the-learner reaction, which, of course, amounts also to an exaltation of the elder.

"That's all wrong. Here, let me show you. You'll never be a good ball player if you hold the bat like that."
"This way's O.K., Daddy. See how far I can knock them!"
"Now look here. Don't be so *stubborn*. Don't you *want* to learn? I know what I'm talking about. Now watch me and try to do it right."
"I guess I'll play something else."

"I don't know what you mean by *glory*," Alice said.
Humpty Dumpty smiled contemptuously. "Of course you don't—till I tell you. I meant *there's a nice knock-down argument for you!*"
"But *glory* doesn't mean *a nice knock-down argument*," Alice objected.
"When *I* use a word," Humpty Dumpty said in rather a scornful tone, "it means just what I choose it to mean—neither more nor less."
"The question is," said Alice, "whether you *can* make words mean so many different things."
"The question is," said Humpty Dumpty, "which is to be Master—that's all."
Alice was too much puzzled to say anything. . . .

The drowning-of-the-learner reaction is another means for glorifying the adult. The adult, or educationally speaking, the teacher, often is unable to refrain from demonstrating his superior learning in response to a question. For example, an innocent inquiry as to why a flower is red while the leaves of the plant are green may produce a prolonged lecture drawn from ophthalmology, chemistry, and cosmology in the large. The effect of this flood of information quite inevitably is to make the squirming inquirer more cautious in the future about providing a similar opening.

"Oh, it needn't come to that!" Alice hastily said, hoping to keep him from beginning.
"The piece I'm going to repeat," he went on without noticing her remark, "was written entirely for your amusement."
Alice felt that in that case she really *ought* to listen to it, so she sat down and said, "Thank you," rather sadly.

Closely related to the drowning-of-the-learner reaction is the talking-beside-the-point reaction. Seldom is the child, or anyone else for that matter, able to convey by a single question or statement what really is on his mind. Yet how seldom the unlucky little questioner has an opportunity to clarify his position before his elder launches forth on a dissertation based upon faulty assumptions as to what the child wishes to talk about.

"Daddy, I think I'll be a soldier when I grow up because when you're a soldier, you can kill lots of people."

Now it happens that what the child is trying to express is his horror and amazement at the fact that if one is a soldier, it is his duty to kill as many people as he can; and if he is *not* a soldier, but merely a smuggler, or a bank robber, or a mastermind as in *Dick Tracy*, and he kills just one person, all the police and the coast guard and the detectives go after him and never rest until they get him, whereupon they throw him in jail and are very mean to him. But how does Daddy answer? It would not be at all surprising to learn that he replied:

"I've a darned good notion to take those toy pistols away from you and not let you listen to *Dick Tracy* on the radio any more. It's horrible all this gangster stuff they feed the kids. Why don't you listen to some good programs that teach you something, or read a book? I bought you a whole set of. . . ."

"I'd rather not try, please!" said Alice. "I'm quite content to stay here—only I *am* so hot and thirsty!"

"I know what *you'd* like!" the Queen said good-naturedly, taking a little box out of her pocket. "Have a biscuit?"

Alice thought it would not be civil to say "No," though it wasn't at all what she wanted. So she took it, and ate it as well as she could; and it was *very* dry; and she thought she had never been so nearly choked in all her life.

"While you're refreshing yourself," said the Queen, "I'll just take the measurements. Have another biscuit?"

"No, thank you," said Alice. "One's *quite* enough!"

"Thirst quenched, I hope?" said the Queen.

Alice did not know what to say to this, but luckily the Queen did not wait for an answer, but went on.

Very likely this constitutes only a partial explanation of the student's attitude toward formal education. Nevertheless, a continual bumping against attitudes of these types is bound in the ordinary course of events to have a paralyzing effect upon free thought, free expression, and free reception. It produces a state of wariness, a reluctance either to try to give out or to receive. The cumulative effect on the child of the stereotyped reaction of parents, themselves similarly conditioned no doubt, tends toward a conviction, perhaps wholly unconscious, that learning is a curious process made up of helpless frustration, passive reception, unthinking imitation, and acquiescence in the elder's apparent eagerness to talk only about what interests *him*.

II

The teacher, both of elementary and advanced subjects, therefore, faces as a basic problem the need for encouraging, even of re-establishing, in his students the faculty of approaching the task of learning in a spirit of creative receptivity and independent accomplishment. One of the means sometimes suggested for solving the problem of the mental passivity of students is to bring them into contact with stimulating personalities. It is indeed an excellent thing when an institution of learning has upon its faculty teachers who can fill the young with a sense of the beauty and blessing of learning and with a desire to belong to the company of the learned. All good teachers will have this stimulating influence. Unfortunately, a spectacular personality which creates interest in itself is sometimes confused with the personality which inspires interest, not alone or chiefly in itself, but rather in the creative incorporation of knowledge. An ability to inspire students with a desire to listen to you and to learn from you is part of the art of teaching. It is not the whole art.

Inspiration, or stimulation, is a fine starting point for learning, but it needs to be translated into creative thinking. Most of us who have passed our youth can look back upon moments of being "inspired." But all too frequently we shall be able to remember nothing of the episode beyond the sweetness and the thrill of being so inspired. Too often we merely basked in the sensation of inspiration and failed to make our own the body of that inspiration which the teacher possessed and which he was endeavoring to communicate to us. It is sheer pleasure to be inspired. It is hard work to learn. We cannot make ideas our own except through a laborious and painful process. Nor is this process less painful for him who occupies the teacher's chair than it is for those who sit on the student benches.

The imaginative reception of another's thoughts, often only partially created and certainly often poorly expressed, is a grueling task. It is by the performance of this task that the teacher both fulfills his true function and reaches the real reward of his calling—the continual enrichment of his mind. But this is a reward truly earned by the sweat of the brow. That is why many teachers, even those who at one time were making progress in the art of learning, cease their efforts after a bit and become teachers only in the halfway sense of seeking to tell other people something. They do not wish to receive anything from their students except their own notions as little damaged as possible by their journey from teacher to students and back again. These teachers run a sort of lending library of facts, figures, and ideas. They desert the difficult practice of creative interchange of thought and so, while they may fill their students' heads with interesting and valuable ideas and facts, they nevertheless deprive those students, so far as lies in their power, of the precious opportunity to learn how to learn. The teacher who has given up the art of learning from his students should also give up the practice of teaching.

Some may think that if the teacher really wishes to enrich his own mind, he can find better ways of doing it than by listening to his students. He had best engage in original research and conversations with other learned men. There are several things to be said about this view. In the first place enrichment of the teacher's mind is not now under consideration except as such enrichment may be of help to his students. The idea that a man rich in knowledge is necessarily a valuable teacher is mostly poppycock. With the right attitude and little knowledge, a teacher still may be the gateway to great learning for his students. With much knowledge and the wrong attitude, a teacher, so far as his students' mental life is concerned, can be of no more value than a book, perhaps less. President Conant, speaking of the great interest in education in England in the seventeenth century, has said:

> It was not so much the knowledge they acquired as the spirit they encountered which drew the young men. . . .
>
> . . . If I understand the college tradition correctly, therefore, the liberal-arts colleges today should not worry too much about whether to require a knowledge of this or that but should rather direct their energies primarily to providing a Faculty which ensures the continuation of the university spirit. What, after all, determines whether a given course is part of a liberal education or is merely pre-vocational training? Clearly the outlook of the teacher.[5]

In the second place, a man cannot be enriched by contact with other men, no matter how learned, or by research, unless he has the capacity of imaginative receptivity. And this is not something which can be turned on or off at will. It is unlikely that a man who is not receptive where his students are concerned will be receptive in other directions. He may keep quiet longer when his learned associates are speaking than he does when his students speak, but it is doubtful if he will be listening any more in one case than in the other.

In the third place, the good old principle of teaching by example still applies. Most educators agree that students should be encouraged, not to a passive acceptance of ideas with a view to bringing them forth when a pat occasion arises, but rather to an active, imaginative receptivity of knowledge. How better then can the teacher indicate what is

meant by this concept than by demonstrating it over and over again to his students by his own attitude?

And finally, it is by no means certain that for teachers original research or conversation with learned men is a more fruitful source for the enrichment of thought than is communication with students. An attitude of genuine receptivity to another's thoughts presupposes respect for that other; if respect is lacking, listening will be no more than perfunctory. It is impossible for creative interchanges to take place between people who do not respect each other. This barrier is perhaps another reason why teachers sometimes fail to keep their minds open to their students so that the necessary incentive to communication will be present. Many teachers are filled with pride and pleasure when one of their students makes a contribution to their thinking. But all too often the teacher has a patronizing attitude toward his students. Sometimes this attitude amounts to an almost brutal depreciation, leading the teacher to endeavor to trip and embarrass the students. This does not of course refer to that good-natured tripping which uncovers sloth or brings to a halt a rambling medley of rationalization which the unfortunate perpetrator is probably relieved not to be able to get away with. Sometimes the teacher's patronizing attitude takes the form of the beautiful compassion expressed by Professor Palmer in his inspiring essay, "The Ideal Teacher,"[6] when he says:

> In short, I was deficient in vicariousness—in swiftly putting myself in the weak one's place and bearing his burden. . . . Ours it should be to see that every beginning, middle, and end of what we say is helpfully shaped for readiest access to those less intelligent and interested than we.

A patronizing attitude must inevitably interfere with that desirable relationship between teacher and student upon which depends the effectiveness of the teacher as a stimulator of creative thinking. It is true, as Professor Palmer has said, that the teacher, for the time being, is in the stronger position. His then is the responsibility so to respect his students that they will feel free to think in his presence and to strive to communicate *their* thoughts,

5. James Bryant Conant, "The Role of the Privately Endowed College," an address at the celebration of the Fiftieth Anniversary of Bryn Mawr College on November 2, 1935, reported in *Harvard Alumni Bulletin*, November 8, 1935.

6. George H. Palmer, *The Ideal Teacher* (Boston: Houghton Mifflin Company, 1910).

not his, to him. Nor is a mere pretense of respect of any avail. As a matter of fact, when no respect is felt, it is best that none be shown. Young people are no fools, and to add deception to disrespect is to make a bad matter worse.

Since no true intercommunication can exist in the absence of that mutual respect which is a requisite to an open mind, it is clear that, of all those who should not be teachers, the egoist ranks first. For the egoist cannot have a receptive mind; he is impelled to hear only that which flatters him and must value ideas and persons according to how they minister to his egoistic needs. Unfortunately the profession of teaching is one that, while it attracts the noblest and most self-effacing personalities, also attracts egoists. Few other professions hold the promise of such rich rewards for the self-centered. In this high calling the egoist has the opportunity to display himself and his learning to large numbers of young people who by the rules of the game are bound at least to show him the signs of respect and to seek to please him. He usually can have the satisfaction of seeing in print whatever he may choose to write, particularly if he is employed by one of the great universities. Moreover, since accomplishment is peculiarly difficult to judge in the field of teaching, the egoist has an excellent chance of impressing his colleagues. He talks dramatically and firmly. He charges about. This combination is likely to be impressive. As Dean Wallace B. Donham has pointed out in another connection, "action may be esteemed evidence of accomplishment."

How difficult it is to know whether the teacher is fulfilling his high mission of creative intercommunication with his students! "What sort of conditions will produce the type of faculty which will run a successful university? The danger is that it is quite easy to produce a faculty entirely unfit—a faculty of very efficient pedants and dullards. The general public will detect the difference only after the university has stunted the promise of youth for scores of years."[7] Probably no one represents such a danger to the vital life of an educational institution as the egoist. He cannot teach others for he has shut his mind to being taught. Moreover, to whatever extent his influence reaches, he will perpetuate his own mediocrity for he is bound to sympathize with those who are of inferior abilities.

The notion that in order to teach, that is, in order to produce learning in someone else, the teacher must have an attitude of imaginative receptivity to the thinking of his students has a bearing upon the much debated question as to whether the same man can be both a good teacher and a good research man. Professor Philip Cabot has said: "It is a mistake to assume that the researcher and the teacher are always, or even commonly, united in the same person. The qualities needed for success in these two fields are different and are rarely found in the same man."[8] Inasmuch as Professor Cabot usually is right, he may be right in this. However, he is probably using "researcher" in a somewhat narrower sense than it is used by other authorities. It may be, too, that Professor Cabot is thinking of research men as they so often are and not as they sometimes are and always should be. President Conant describes research as "the advancement of learning . . . for I should like to include under one title not only the increase in our positive knowledge, the advances made in all science, but also the study and interpretation of those cultural values which come to us from the past."[9] If Professor Cabot is content to accept this interpretation of research, it will be evident that he, himself, is an excellent researcher and, thereby, a case in point against his own assertion.

Whether it is possible *in general* for men on our university faculties to be productive research workers and sound teachers is a controversial matter. Nevertheless, the same attitude of mind which characterizes the good teacher is also necessary for sound research: namely, an attitude of lively, imaginative receptivity. It is likely that one reason so much of our research, particularly our social and economic research, has been a failure is that it has been carried on by men who lack such receptivity. Professor Henderson has pointed out that: "In certain respects the observation, study, and interpretation of what men say is the characteristic feature of the social sciences."[10] In the pure sciences, the

7. A. N. Whitehead, "Universities and Their Function," *Atlantic Monthly*, May 1928.

8. "Our Times and Your Future," commencement address, Juniata College, June 1, 1936.

9. James Bryant Conant, "The Mission of American Universities," an address before the Cincinnati Chamber of Commerce Forum, reported in *Harvard Alumni Bulletin*, February 26, 1938.

10. L. J. Henderson, "Introductory Lectures, Sociology 23," p. 19.

importance of being receptive to the creative thinking of others is at least not so apparent though the need is nevertheless there.

A laboratory is provided for the teacher by his classroom, his student interviews, and the papers of his students. In this laboratory he will find clues pointing to new hypotheses; will be able to test these hypotheses in order to modify, discard, or accept them. Professor Melvin T. Copeland, equally distinguished for his teaching and for his research work, recently offered a case in point. He had held the view that students entering a certain course understood the meaning of the commonly used business concept of "general management" as something different from "departmental management." Various things which students said to him in the course of individual conferences, called for another purpose, suggested to him, however, that this concept might in fact mean very different things to different students, and that for some it might lack any meaning. Having in this way obtained a number of clues pointing in the same general direction, Professor Copeland undertook to retest his former hypothesis. Lack of alertness to the significance of seemingly irrelevant remarks made during the interviews would have prevented this particular strengthening of the understanding between teacher and students.

There is another implication of the theory of receptivity that should be mentioned. We hear much discussion of the proper age of retirement for teachers. If a teacher is good, he should be begged not to retire until he becomes too feeble to make intelligent motions. If a teacher has a truly receptive mind, he is bound to grow better and better until he totters to his grave. He can never be outmoded, for he is in incessant communication with the thought of the day; he cannot become stale, for he never has allowed his faculty for creative thinking to be dulled by lack of use.

"The crinkled smile on the Dean's kind face is
Gone with a myriad smiles we miss;

So please, dear God, don't fill the places
Quite yet of Kitty and Copey and Bliss."[11]

The attitude of mind of the good teacher forms the bridge between two accepted principles of teaching. The first of these principles is that the teacher needs to have an imaginative and creative mind as well as a store of knowledge. It is deadening to a developing intelligence to come in contact with a mind loaded down with information to which it can give no life for lack of imagination and enthusiasm. While this principle unfortunately is often lost sight of in practice, in theory it cannot be questioned. The second accepted principle of teaching is that the student must recreate imaginatively the ideas and facts communicated to him by the teacher if those ideas and facts are to mean anything to him, if he is to be truly educated.

Given a teacher with a vivid creative intelligence, how can he lead his students to undertake for their own parts the creative interpretation of knowledge? The answer lies in part at least in the ability of the teacher to listen to his students, not with a view to appraising them, correcting their mistakes, and filling in the gaps in their knowledge, but rather in the constant and true expectation of learning something. A properly conducted class, however, is not one in which the teacher sits supinely wide eyed, beaming respect and approval, while his students in crescendoes of oratory pour forth their views as to what is what. Learning is hard, and there is much to be learned. There is no time for mawkish sentiment and backslapping. The teacher is the strong man, the center from which flows a fresh and vivifying stream of knowledge imaginatively conceived.

---

11. Lawrence McKinney, 1912, cited in the Tercentenary Graduates' issue of *The Lampoon*. [Reprinted with permission.] Reprinted in *Notes on the Harvard Tercentenary* (Cambridge: Harvard University Press, 1936), p. 24. (References are to George Lyman Kittredge, 1882, Charles Townsend Copeland, 1882, and Bliss Perry, Litt. D. (Hon.) 1925.)

This book is like a group discussion among experienced, committed discussion teachers. Although we share a common purpose—to lower the barriers to discussion teaching, as David Garvin puts it—our statements will reflect the individuality of personal judgments. We do not speak from some mountain peak of ultimate truth but, like all discussion participants, from vantage points along a path that winds from insight to insight.

That diversity is healthy, and inevitable. As Alexander Pope reminds us, "'tis with our judgments as our watches, none go just alike, yet each believes his own." This essay, which describes some basic hypotheses about discussion pedagogy, is offered in the hope that other teachers will consider my reflections, and then consult their own "watches."

The most fundamental observation I can make about discussion teaching is this: however mysterious or elusive the process may seem, it can be learned. Through collaboration and cooperation with friends and colleagues, and through self-observation and reflection, teachers can master both principles and techniques of discussion leadership. But the task is complex. Discussion teachers' responsibilities are as varied as their rewards. With greater vitality in the classroom, the satisfaction of true intellectual collaboration and synergy, and improved retention on the part of students, the rewards are considerable. The responsibilities may be difficult to appreciate at first. For example, effective preparation for discussion classes takes more time, because instructors must consider not only *what* they will teach, but also *who* and *how*. And the classroom encounter consumes a great deal of energy; simultaneous attention to process (the flow of activities that make up a discussion) and content (the material discussed) requires emotional as well as intellectual engagement. Effective discussion leadership requires competency in both areas; it can only be achieved with patience.

The discussion teacher is planner, host, moderator, devil's advocate, fellow-student, and judge—a potentially confusing set of roles. Even the most seasoned group leader must be content with uncertainty, because discussion teaching is the art of managing spontaneity. Nonetheless, a good chart can help a mariner navigate safely even in fog. The premises and associated operational practices described in this essay are my personal chart, tested over years of practice and found dependable in

Premises and Practices of Discussion Teaching

groups that range in size from twenty to eighty or even a hundred participants. Four principles seem fundamental:

1. A discussion class is a *partnership* in which students and instructor share the responsibilities and power of teaching, and the privilege of learning together.
2. A discussion group must evolve from a collection of individuals into a learning *community* with shared values and common goals.
3. By forging a primary (although not exclusive) *alliance with students,* the discussion leader can help them gain command of the course material.
4. Discussion teaching requires *dual competency:* the ability to manage content and process.

A Partnership between Teacher and Students

Lecturing, which emphasizes the instructor's power over the student, is a master-apprentice relationship of great power when the transfer of knowledge is the primary academic objective. But when the objective is critical thinking (in the liberal arts setting, for example) or problem-solving (in the professional school milieu), and the development of qualities such as sensitivity, cooperation, and zest for discovery, discussion pedagogy offers substantial advantages. To achieve these complex, value-laden educational goals, both teachers and students must modify their traditional roles and responsibilities.

In discussion teaching, partnership—a collegial sharing of power, accountability, and tasks—supplants hierarchy and asymmetry in the teacher-student relationship. The discussion process itself requires students to become profoundly and actively involved in their own learning, to discover for themselves rather than accept verbal or written pronouncements. They must explore the intellectual terrain without maps, step by step, blazing trails, struggling past obstacles, dealing with disappointments. How different from simply following others' itineraries!

Such creative activity cannot be ordered or imposed upon the unwilling. Teachers can police attendance and monitor the memorization of theory and fact by tests. But we cannot order our students to be committed to learning and willing to risk experimentation, error, and the uncertainty of exploration. Such attitudes are gifts from one partner to another.

Professor McGregor of MIT used a story to illustrate the true dependency of superior on subordinates. A young executive arrived at a unionized textile mill and told the union officer, "I am the new manager here, and when I manage a mill, I run it. Do you understand?" The union agent nodded and waved his hand. Every worker stopped; every loom stopped. Then the agent turned to the manager and said, "Go ahead, run it." Students, at least in North America, are not unionized, but they possess the power to turn a discussion class into an academic charade by withholding involvement.

Another force mandating partnership in the teacher-student relationship is the fundamental need for students' input to the leadership of a group—a fact of life that lucky instructors discover in the adolescence of their teaching careers. Students not only teach themselves, and one another, they participate in leadership tasks traditionally counted as the teacher's—such as setting the discussion agenda and determining pacing and emphasis.

When students are unaccustomed to discussion pedagogy, the instructor must take practical steps to promote partnership. Students may greet the notion of sharing power and responsibility with skepticism based on years of contrary experience. To the instructor's promise that "we're all partners here," hardened skeptics may silently respond "fat chance!" But even they may feel a twinge of hope: "What if he really means it?" This twinge can prompt further questions: "I know the rules of the regular classroom game. But now the professor's changing them. To what?"

When students feel uncertain about the rules of the game, they try to resolve their doubts by testing the instructor. They ask—explicitly or indirectly—does this teacher genuinely want my contributions? Is she interested in knowing me as a special person, and will she keep my individuality in mind when she listens to my comments? Does he receive my suggestions with a positive attitude (there are some fascinating ideas here), or a negative bias (I'll find something wrong)? Does she really listen at all, or just pause while I talk? Does he ask for my help, work with my suggestions, demonstrate respect for my judgment? How does she react when I question her methods or conclusions? When we teachers repeatedly pass these tests, we communicate respect and validate our students' role as co-teachers. Our confidence in them encourages cooperation and friendship—and friendship is a marvelous ingredient in partnership.

Partnership is fragile and difficult to regain once lost. It needs continual nourishment, which can be provided in part by operational rituals and procedures. How a professor starts the day's session, for example, sends a message about the working relationship of the whole class. If the instructor lays out a step-by-step outline for the discussion—orally or on the blackboard—the class picks up a clear signal: follow my lead or be lost! Any partnership between a leader and followers is clearly a limited one.

In contrast, when the instructor invites students to set the agenda for the day's discussion, the openness of the invitation communicates a different message: you, the students, bear the responsibility for this discussion. It belongs to you. As the classroom dialogue evolves, the instructor can further underscore the principle of joint ownership by asking students to summarize points or lines of argument, or to suggest the next question the group should discuss.

Direct participation in the leadership of their class enhances students' self-esteem—essential for effective learning—and gives them an opportunity to consolidate what they know by teaching others. Instructors can increase the value of our students' input by publicly acknowledging its importance. We all tend to exert our best efforts when we feel appreciated.

Instructors can also benefit from the sharing inherent in partnership. By bringing unexpected points of view and creative, upsetting questions to material that has become extremely familiar to the instructor, fresh and energetic students play a particularly useful role in class: they wake us up. Moreover, when students function as co-teachers, their growing mastery of discussion leadership can permit the instructor to step back—mentally, and sometimes even physically—to observe the class from their perspective. This opportunity to focus on how students listen, react, make notes, prepare to pounce, or perhaps "tune out" is invaluable. Such observation provides "instant feedback" on the progress, or lack thereof, of individual students as well as the group as a whole. By watching our own classes unfold, we can assess our performance from the most meaningful point of view: that of the students. And when students become skilled partners, their after-class comments can provide sophisticated

assessments to help us answer every teacher's inescapable question: how am I doing?

Partnership is both a window through which students can observe the teaching/learning process and a mirror that reveals them to themselves (surely a major element in any education). In deepening their personal involvement, taking responsibility for the quality of the discussion, and making an emotional investment in the outcome of the course, students claim ownership of their own educational process. This ownership not only stimulates them to excel, it also enhances our effectiveness as instructors.

Finally, partnership makes teaching more joyful. We teachers trade the aloneness and distance of hierarchy for the cooperation and closeness of colleagueship. Partnership with students gives us an incentive to be students again—and what are great teachers if not great students?

A Learning Community

Quality of context—the milieu in which the collective dialogue takes place—is fundamental to effective discussion. Where the context supports rigorous intellectual analyses and group collaboration, where an operational contract defines how teacher and students work together, and where there is mutual respect among all participants, a community dedicated to learning emerges.

Even a casual observer can tell when a group lacks the spirit of community. "If the tone of a class is confrontational, critical, and acerbic," a colleague once noted, "students will retreat—all except those who are red in tooth and claw." Gresham's Law (bad money drives out good) applies to the class that lacks community: the vocally aggressive and personally super-confident "drive out" the contributions of their measured and reflective, but perhaps less articulate, fellow students. In the absence of understood, trustworthy boundaries for appropriate behavior, attack—not exploration—often becomes the predominant activity. When participants compete to score individual points rather than collaborate to build group themes, they damage the fabric of discussion. In such a milieu, students resist modifying early conclusions even when contrary evidence emerges—a particularly dangerous practice for intellectual growth.

In a true learning community, by contrast, diverse backgrounds blend and individuals bond into an association dedicated to collective as well as personal learning. The students seem interested in one another and the academic assignment of the day. And their dialogue has the open-ended quality of exploration. Speakers not only present points of view but test and modify their ideas; instead of doggedly defending personal conclusions, they listen to one another with interest, not fear. Differences of opinion produce inquiries, not disputes. Working as a unit, the class learns to value measured progress without expecting instant gratification.

The basic academic drive to master a body of knowledge, and its application to practice, powers all education ventures, including solo study. But what turns a collection of students into a learning community? Not the mere assignment to the same room and time slot. The instructor must take concrete steps to promote collaboration and comradeship. He or she needs to develop strategies that will reflect the values that enable a group of individuals to work together productively. Here are the basic values I endorse for this purpose:

Civility—courtesy in working with one's associates—is a simple but powerful virtue. In class as elsewhere, politeness sets a cooperative tone and encourages the openness that lets people help one another by sharing experience and insight. *Willingness to take risks*, both individual and collective, not only helps students understand the topic of the day, but encourages daring and innovation. Finally, *an appreciation of diversity*—in backgrounds, personalities, questions posed, learning styles, frames of inquiry, and spectrums of interpretation—ensures that the group will avoid the rigidity of single-track paths to single-point destinations. Instead, the group will feel free to venture into intellectual *terra incognita*, where explorers need one another's help and support. The totality of these values can determine the tone of the group's discussions, and their collective impact creates an ethos that can activate, permeate, and enrich a group's minute-by-minute dialogue.

Instructors who build community reinforce these values by their own behavior. It helps simply to welcome the class to each session before plunging into the business of the day, or to greet individual students by name as they arrive. We can demonstrate our commitment to honest sharing by helping discussion participants who run into difficulties, and by asking for students' help when we find ourselves in an intellectual or procedural quandary.

Reinforcing the values of community can also take the form of being candid about ourselves. Hugh Prather puts the point pragmatically when he notes, "in order to see, one must be willing to be seen."[1] To promote openness in students, we must reveal our own areas of certitude and uncertainty, our dreams and our defeats. And, if we want our students to take the risks that make creativity possible, we must show we are willing and able to assist them when they stumble. To make independence practical, and enfranchise all the members of the group, we must support students when their comments depart from the consensus of the moment or their proposals collide with firmly held convictions of the class. One way I do this is by explicitly including the iconoclast in a "majority of two" to make it clear that I will abet honest exploration, even when the group finds it unorthodox.

When the instructor both endorses and models a set of positive common values, the group will usually adopt them. Physical attendance then is transformed to academic belonging, and the group can achieve high quality in its discussions and its relationships.

We instructors can also strengthen the sense of community by paying attention to our teacher-student learning contracts. As Abby Hansen notes elsewhere in this book, a pedagogical contract is a pattern of understood and accepted ground rules that guide the protocols, rituals, mutual obligations, and standards of behavior of a class. We teachers build contracts with our words and our behavior. As we ask questions and respond to students' contributions, we give them material to form judgments of our leadership style and values. To communicate our genuine appreciation for the knowledge and judgment of our students, we can invite them to join us in defining the terms of our academic collaboration—and then make sure to honor their terms with our practice.

Implementing the teacher-student learning contract is complicated, for three primary reasons. First, since teaching contracts are set both explicitly (by statements) and implicitly (by the often inadvertent accretion of precedents), instructors must attend to both dialogue and behavior. Second, because much of our behavior originates on the intuitive or preconscious level, it can be difficult to know what

1. Hugh Prather, *Notes to Myself* (Moab, UT: Real People Press, 1970), unpaged.

contract we are promulgating. (A hint: students' readings of our actions will provide important clues.) Third, since contracts are organic, they change. Untended, they can either grow wild or decay. As students' interests and command of the course materials evolve throughout the semester, the contract must reflect these sometimes subtle changes.

When we let students share in the governance of their own course, they are less likely to feel like second-class citizens. And since people who contribute to setting standards often feel moved to surpass them, the best teacher-student learning contracts can also transcend themselves. When this happens, they evolve beyond formal procedures, legality, and details of enforcement to become covenants rather than mere contracts: solemn compacts among members of a group to pursue common goals for mutual benefit. Covenants promote the deep commitment that encourages accountability and mutual responsibility. They nurture true community, for who will reveal his innermost beliefs, dreams, doubts, and most adventuresome ideas in an atmosphere of distrust?

One can be a good lecturer without giving these matters much more than minimum thought. But in the extemporaneous face-to-face dialogue of discussion teaching, all parties are vulnerable, and students feel their exposure particularly keenly. Learning means leaving the known for the unknown—an exhilarating, but scary venture. In a discussion class, students often feel they are undergoing a private, even intimate, recreation of their *personae* in public view. A mature student speaks poignantly about this experience:

> It is extremely important for me to be in a classroom where there is acceptance and hospitality, an absolute hospitality of teacher and classmates that will allow ideas to be born for the first time. I feel very vulnerable. The teacher is in the privileged position of knowing me before I change and after. In a way it is similar to being a parent. The teacher holds my continuity because he or she knows me before, yet sees me leave my earlier self behind. School needs to be a safe place to leave my old self behind and change.

While discussion classrooms will never be perfectly safe, instructors can minimize students' vulnerability by promoting trust and respect. It is not enough to espouse these worthy goals in the ab-

stract, for students readily detect empty idea-worship; they believe our actions more than our words. Two skills are especially valuable as teachers attempt to make the discussion classroom hospitable.

First, we can *listen* to students' comments with discipline and sensitivity; second, we can *respond* to them constructively. When discussion participants realize that the instructor treats their comments seriously and takes pains to build them into the discussion, they feel valued. And when this respect is maintained over time, students develop a sense of trust, a *sine qua non* for a true learning community. Disciplined listening elevates students' comments to the status of contributions. A wise instructor once commented that we should give—not pay—attention to what students say. Paying implies a cold, impersonal commercial transaction; giving communicates colleagueship, sharing, community.

As disciplined listeners, we try to hear the unspoken. Perhaps Bob's terse, "Boston isn't moving very fast to integrate public housing" carries messages about his ghetto youth, repeated difficulties in getting good housing for his own family, and aggressive leadership of a tenants' union. If Betty, who has held forth often and forcefully against sending arms to Central America, fails to speak out in today's emotional discussion of the same issue, a disciplined listener will hear her silence and wonder about its cause. Does she expect the teacher to hear yesterday's comments again today? Has she changed her views? The sharpness of questions and responses and the vividness of language employed are useful clues to the intensity of students' feelings.

Treating students' comments with respect does not necessarily mean accepting them at face value. Discussion participants sometimes float verbal trial balloons filled with hot air. When we spot such bloated assertions, the trick is to suppress the tendency (ours or the students') to sarcastic harpoonery and let the discussion bring these balloons gently back to earth.

As teachers, we also build community with our constructive responses to students' comments. If we view all comments as potentially positive contributions to the group's learning process, our task as teachers is to integrate this raw material so as to further the discussion. I have found certain practical mechanisms useful in putting these ideals to work. For example, one can honor participants' contributions by giving speakers time to complete their arguments. Although teachers feel pressed to keep dialogue moving quickly (doodling can spring up at a moment's notice), haste can produce damaging cut-offs that belittle and stymie speakers. A suggestion: after a student finishes talking, watch her eyes. Do they indicate that her thought is now complete? If you feel unsure, wait a few seconds and re-check. A five-second pause often produces a contributor's most insightful thought.

At the most elementary level, an instructor shows respect for a student's statement by making sure that the group has understood its basic analysis. To promote a true community of learning, however, it is also valuable to ensure that a spirit of colleagueship characterizes the way the group will test and explore that analysis. How? By taking care that our comments convey appreciation for the time and effort the student expended to prepare the contribution—and also for his or her courage, if the contribution espoused an unpopular view. A learning community needs brave, as well as adroit, students.

Community is strengthened when we put students' comments to work, immediately if possible. We can use their questions to subject conclusions (both students' and the instructor's own) to scrutiny. We can link their contributions from earlier classes to the current dialogue; we can follow their leads for next-step inquiry; we can build summaries around their formulations and use their words.

Community-minded instructors will be cautious in introducing their own personal judgments into the classroom dialogue, and will state such judgments in a manner that clearly invites students to differ. "Ruth, many experts disagree on the question of increasing the federal gasoline tax. I'm in favor of it, but where do you come out on this question, and why?"

Constructive response appreciates the conditional tense. *Would* this approach seem right? *Might* this be the route to take? *Should* the evidence lead us to this conclusion? Such an approach leaves maneuver room for students and instructor alike. It eschews false absolutes such as, "This is the way to lay out the factory work flow," or "It is wrong to subsidize low-cost housing." It encourages the cultivation of balanced judgment and lets disagreement flourish without confrontation.

Shared values, a mutually understood teacher-student learning contract, and a relationship of mutual trust and respect all nurture community. When discussion groups become communities, instructors can transcend their own uncertainties and vulnerabilities and enter into genuine covenants with their students. Doing so, they can unleash, and then slowly harness, a powerful energy of experience and creativity that students often did not know they possessed.

Alliance with Students

Effective discussion leadership, unlike lecturing, requires instructors to forge a primary alliance with students. We do not bring the material to them, but rather help them find their own ways to it. The subject matter defines the boundaries of our intellectual territory, but the students' unique intellects, personalities, learning styles, fears, and aspirations shape the paths they will take. Students hunger for wholeness. They want recognition, not just as novice learners, but as persons with the competence to contribute to their own education, and that of their fellow students. Alliance with them means learning about them. Students' multiple affiliations—family, social, institutional—affect both the style and content of their discussion contributions. Our personal reward for getting to know students is obvious; the experience of teaching becomes a warmer, emotionally enriched pursuit. But there is a pedagogical reward as well: we become more effective in leading the discussion process.

Of course forging an alliance with students has costs as well as benefits. Learning about them requires an investment of scarce resources—time, emotional energy, and research ingenuity. The more we learn about the complexities of discussion participants, the more daunting our pedagogical task may seem. A colleague once asked, "Can one ever learn enough about a student?" Certainly, there are limits. But where are they? In a formal, but friendly relationship, what is appropriate information? And learning about students can be intimidating too, for the more we understand the many worlds in which they live, the more we appreciate the gulf between those worlds and ours.

Despite these costs, I have found that the rewards prevail. Knowledge of students enables us to meet the first obligation of all instructors—at the very least to avoid injuring those whom we seek to help. I recall, with chagrin, asking a student to comment on a one-page statement I had distributed a few minutes earlier in class. He blushed and declined. After class he explained his frustration: he was dyslexic. And I recall the story of a secondary school science instructor who began his methods class early in the semester by calling on the boy who sat directly in front of him in the first row. The instructor did not know that the boy, although fascinated by science, was shy and clumsy in public speaking. The student stammered some sort of answer, and the instructor handled the ensuing dialogue equally badly. That boy—a Boston Brahmin now ninety years old—still recounts the incident with fresh pain and anger in his voice. Its ultimate impact was a poor orientation in course substance and subsequent avoidance of science in college and career—despite an early, passionate interest in the subject. How easily we can damage students' confidence, scar their spirits.

Many of the techniques of our craft carry some dangers. Role playing, for example, requires us to be particularly sensitive to students' backgrounds. I would not lightly assign a student a role that might give personal offense—ask a devout Mormon to pretend to be the sales manager of a liquor firm, or a member of a minority group to play the role of a bigoted manufacturing executive. It is easy to mistake labels for people, unless we know our students as individuals. One young woman recalled that most of her college instructors had used her as "our Korean resource" because of her name, appearance, and birthplace. In fact, the daughter of a diplomat, she knew little of Seoul, and much about Paris and Madrid.

Knowing students can also help us humanize the all-too-often cold and formal setting of a classroom in which students, as we know from experience, sometimes feel like "necessary nuisances." Nobel laureate Robert Solow has embroidered on the well-known definition of education—a student sitting on one end of a log and a great teacher on the other—by noting that some professors appear to be sitting on their students and talking to the log. How true! Students appreciate our taking an interest in them, and as a result, the whole class has more fun. And when we sense our students' good feelings, our own efforts seem more positive to us. "This is a first-rate group," we say. "The class is really rolling this year." We telegraph our buoyant mood with our step and posture as we enter the classroom. Our eyes sparkle; our energy is high as we lead the discussion. And communication improves. We hear the message in students' comments with greater appreciation when we understand something of their background and current interests. And the

teacher-student dynamic improves, too. As we learn about students, they are encouraged to learn about us. And learning brings appreciation.

Our knowledge of students helps us meet them "where they are." And that is where learning begins. No matter what the curriculum or course plan may assume, students occupy unique intellectual and emotional spaces, and the discussion teacher is well advised to seek out their locations. What sort of a learner is Tim? Does he know when and how to get help, and how to test its appropriateness? Is he frightened or excited by the unknown? Does he cut corners in defending his points of view? Is he self-aware? Does he know his own blind spots and "hot buttons?" How does he work with classmates? Is he willing to have his ideas tested rigorously, to explore a classmate's argument, even though it contradicts a strongly-held conviction of his own? How does he view peer "error," as a chance to demonstrate personal superiority or an opportunity to help a classmate learn? Does he have the leadership skills to contribute to the educational objectives of the day? Does he frame questions that catch the current "drift" and extend its range? Does he truly listen? Can he accumulate and integrate prior comments and construct a unified whole? Wasn't it T.S. Eliot who said that hell is where nothing connects? Does Tim see the connections?

As discussion teachers, we need to see our students on life's wider screen. What academic and work experiences do they bring to the discussion classroom? Have they tutored in secondary school, sold encyclopedias in poor neighborhoods, worked as systems analysts, done research for a state regulatory agency or managed an overseas branch of a corporation? In what other worlds do they live? What current interests, whether social, political or recreational, consume them?

Such knowledge can help us in our minute-by-minute leadership of a discussion. If Carol is at her best when given time to reflect on an issue, I would not "cold call" her. If Sam's father is dying, or if Hal is in the final week of producing the second-year class play, perhaps they should not open the discussion. If Ida has managed a day care center and the topic of the day is child care in the workplace, how should I bring her into the dialogue—as an expert, an advocate, a challenger, or a back-up resource? What will do her, as well as the class, the most good?

Meeting students where they are encourages us

to ask ourselves where *we* are. What are our wider worlds, current interests? How do these affect our leadership of the group? Our own circumstances can have an enormous, inadvertent impact on what we do in class. In planning the course, for example, we may tend to teach first what we, ourselves, learned last. We often want to give priority to our discovery of the moment, because we find it fresh and exciting. But this may not help our students. They may need to learn first what we also learned first, because it is basic.

Knowing where we and our students are, intellectually and emotionally, can help us with the ever present problem of how to choose among several students with raised hands and anxious expressions. Almost inevitably, it is a mistake to be guided by the democratic instinct to favor the person whose hand has been raised the longest. Most likely, that student's comment will be stale because it will address whatever points were in play when the student first raised his or her hand.

Inexperienced instructors often assume it is desirable to recognize the participant whose background experience best matches the current point under discussion. If the class is discussing federal revenue policy and Arlene is an experienced tax accountant, should one call on her? The simple fact of her experience might lead to a boring or intimidating barrage of information. Given a choice between a participant with a specialized background and one skilled in making cogent comments and relating them to the flow of discussion, I would choose the latter. Or I might call on the student who could best profit from tackling the problem under examination and working with the specific comments just made. At points where the flow of discussion has become sufficiently turbulent (or turbid) to warrant summary, the instructor might do well to recognize a participant with a sophisticated command of intellectual synthesis and a talent for clear expression.

Since knowing our students in depth can confer such palpable benefits, why is it not the norm? I have mentioned some of the costs, but there is also a perceptual barrier to be overcome. All too often we see only what we want to see or what we are accustomed to seeing. Marcel Proust wrote, in *Swann's Way*, of the simple act of looking at someone we know:

We pack the physical outline of the creature we see with all the ideas we've already formed about him,

and in the complete picture of him which we compose in our minds those ideas have certainly the principal place. In the end, they come to fill out so completely the curve of his cheeks, to follow so exactly the line of his nose, they blend so harmoniously in the sound of his voice that these seem to be no more than a transparent envelope, so that each time we see the face or hear the voice, it's our own ideas of him which we recognize and to which we all listen.[2]

As Proust suggests, the difference between "our own ideas of him" and a student's ideas about himself can be substantial. We need to ask ourselves how to narrow the gap by obtaining appropriate and useful information.

Let's take a look at my former student "Bob Smith." Like all students, he was a complexity of past happenings, present circumstances, and future aspirations, a melange of roles and responsibilities. The richness of this complexity emerged as I began to understand him in the round. According to the registrar's sheet, he was "Robert W. Smith, 27, graduate of Wainsworth College, candidate for the MBA degree with a major in entrepreneurial management." That was just the tip of the iceberg.

There was Bob Smith, spouse, who lived with his wife and two young children in a mixed industrial-residential area of Boston. Bob belonged to several community service clubs and headed a program for physically disadvantaged inner-city children. And there was the former Lt. Robert W. Smith, U.S. Infantry, veteran of two years' duty in Vietnam. Wounded in combat, Lt. Smith had been awarded the Silver Star medal for bravery. And there was R. Wainsworth Smith, a graduate of the college his great-grandfather had founded, who left school with average grades and a record noting a two-week suspension from classes for having participated in a student protest. And there was Rob Smith, the youngest child in his family, with two older brothers in political and professional careers. There was also Robbie Smith, son of two academic parents, both active in the Society of Friends.

Bob's background—prominent family, social concerns, military experience—made itself felt in the classroom. It conditioned his choice of issues and levels of involvement in the discussion at large, as well as his relationship with peers, students outside the class, and the instructor. Faulkner's *Requiem for*

2. Marcel Proust, *Remembrance of Things Past*, tr. C. K. Scott Moncrieff (New York: Random House, 1935), I, 15.

a Nun puts the point well: "The past is never dead, it's not even past."[3] Students bring their pasts to the classroom, as well as their hopes for the future. We teachers need to understand both of these dimensions in order to teach them well in the present.

But where, and how, can we obtain the "intelligence" we need to turn each student from a cipher to an ally in the learning process? Just around the campus—the classroom, our offices, the local coffee shop or hangout—there is a rich lode of information to be mined. The student newspaper and various campus social functions also offer ample opportunity for teachers to get an informal sense of what's going on, as well as specific information—who just made the dean's list, who was awarded a prize. Coming to class quite early during the first weeks of a semester can prove rewarding. Students who arrive at about the same time as you do—early birds—usually have a song to sing: a personal concern or request for help or understanding. These pleas may not be verbalized at the first meeting, but they are generally communicated soon after that. I have found them inevitably of major significance to working with the individual, and sometimes to working with the whole group. But the discussion class itself is the richest source of all, for it allows us to take continual readings of our students' academic accomplishments, their skill in helping to guide the discussion, and their involvement in specific topics.

The office is but a more intimate classroom, the most appropriate setting for individualized instruction. When students initiate appointments, we can be certain that the topic they raise is important to them. Often the items on their agendas are problems of some sort, and chats about their difficulties with course materials can move on to requests for the instructor's thoughts on career planning or more personal matters. In this regard, we teachers need to be wary of moving too far into areas that are not merely personal, but private. There's a huge difference between knowing that Hans is an avid stamp collector and knowing the details of his current romantic entanglements. We are guides, but not professional counselors. Nonetheless, when professionally handled, personal conversations can provide rich opportunities for insight and, in turn, feed the educational process.

3. William Faulkner, *Requiem for a Nun* (New York: Random House, 1951), p. 92. Gavin Stevens is speaking to Temple Drake.

A colleague observed that a group of students is like a pack of cards face down. To read those cards most accurately, to gain maximum useful personal data, we need to formalize our informational search a bit. I have found it useful to ask students, on a voluntary basis, for personal statements that provide information in three areas. Initially, I inquire about the students' view of the course, asking questions such as, What is your preparation for this course? How do you see it relating to past and upcoming studies? Which of the topics listed in the syllabus hold the most—or least—interest for you? In what areas do you feel most confident, and where might you appreciate special assistance? By what measures and in what ways will you evaluate the worth of this course? How might I make the ritual of academic grading personally useful for you?

Second, I seek to learn about participants' backgrounds. I ask the students to describe, in whatever detail they consider appropriate, two or three particularly meaningful incidents from their academic or professional experience and to explain why they chose these episodes. I ask, What did you learn? What questions do these experiences pose for you now? The "critical incidents" sections of student information statements have proven extremely useful. Almost inevitably they provide some clue to understanding the real person, as well as leads to help link his or her experience to classroom dialogue.

Third, I inquire about the future. What are your academic plans for the remainder of the degree program? What are your plans for a job search? What are your career and life goals at this point? Students' answers to such questions often illumine their motivations.

Experimenting with personal information statements is not complicated. A few administrative suggestions, however, may be in order. I explain the purpose of the statements in class by proposing that students help me so that I may help them. I stress that their cooperation is completely voluntary and that all the information they provide will be held in confidence. I encourage them to modify my questions in any way that seems appropriate to them— and many do this with great creativity. I conclude by asking if there are any physical challenges—sight or hearing problems, for example—with which I might help them cope in this course. I keep the number of questions to a minimum and give no due date for completed statements. Nor do I pressure students who choose not to provide information.

Forging a primary alliance with students means investing intellect, time, energy, and emotion in discovering who they are, where they are, and how they may best find their way to the material. Such efforts help the instructor become a true teacher.

Like the bedrock of partnership and community, alliance with students is both a lofty goal and a matter of everyday practice. All of these converge in the fourth, most practical-minded premise: that discussion teachers must develop skill in managing both the content and the process of the discussion.

Dual Instructional Competency

Most of the rest of the essays in this book focus, from their authors' various perspectives, on the teaching and learning process as it unfolds in the discussion classroom. They assume that discussion teachers must not only (like lecturers) have mastered the content of their courses, but must be equally adept in process. The *what* of teaching (concepts and facts) is no more crucial than the *who* and *how:* knowledge of students and ability to affect the context in which learning takes place. These distinctions, of course, are integral parts of an organic Gestalt; they run together and overlap like freshly applied watercolors.

Taken as a whole, mastery of process and content grant what I call dual competency, the central element in effective discussion leadership. But how does one begin to develop this complex mastery? Concentrating on the most fundamental level, I shall offer suggestions about teaching preparation as grounding for the advice presented in much of the rest of this volume. What better foundation for dual competency than dual preparation? The instructor who takes time to think not only about the material, but also about how to play it with a particular group of students, will enjoy a double advantage of confidence and competence.

Preparation can never completely eliminate anxiety. After all, one is attempting to foresee the unforeseeable. Discussions are group improvisations; how can one possibly know in advance what students will want to say? Although I have no simple answers, I can offer the following well-tested method based on my own experience with case discussions in Business Policy courses. My preparation begins on familiar turf, with a careful review of content, but it also includes assessment of students' and the group's capacity to work in concert, and

speculation about teaching tactics to promote effective collaboration. Taken as a whole, this exercise can give an instructor a running start toward dual instructional competency.

First, I evaluate the academic progress of the class as a whole. How well does this group understand basic course concepts and their application to practice? Where has this class developed mastery; where is it still struggling? What specific topics have been covered? Which remain, and where and how might these materials best be introduced? I make certain that I am in command of the case to be discussed, and I assess it as a learning instrument. What are its strengths, its limitations? Does it include material with the potential to offend? Where is it likely to excite and intrigue? And I try to predict what the students' attitude toward it might be and how well they are likely to prepare it.

Second, I assess the status of the class as a learning group. How does their skill at working together measure up against the challenge of the case? What is their mood—are they having fun or are they glum? What is happening in the wider academic scene that might affect tomorrow's discussions—exams, reports, or important campus events? What "hot button" issues have been highlighted in the school newspaper?

Third, I try to estimate each student's current circumstances, his or her academic strengths and weaknesses as well as abilities to contribute to the discussion process. Who might learn most from the upcoming discussion? Will the case be of special interest to students with particular backgrounds or career interests? Will it offer quiet students a useful entry point into the class discussion? Who might find the case intimidating? Which other students might be good "coaches" to help their peers with their difficulties? Which students are likely to take leadership roles in the anticipated dialogues, and who will probably remain on the sidelines?

Fourth, I consider my own mood. How do I feel about this material? Is this a fun section of the course or an academic chore? Are there some sour apples in the group? Where might my personal biases and prejudices affect my leadership of the discussion? All these considerations—as well as family and personal concerns—influence any teacher's behavior in the classroom.

Fifth, I think about the mode, pace, and flow of the upcoming class. Is it to be a drill in applying analytic techniques to the problem defined in the case of the day, or an open-ended search for stimulating and creative solutions to a broader range of problems? What is an appropriate pace—do I want the dialogue to move briskly, cover a large number of topics, and include the maximum possible number of student contributions? Or do I want to probe a limited number of issues in depth—with fewer students speaking at greater length? In terms of flow, do I want the group to build a single construct of the issues involved, by accretion, or would I hope for a more competitive series of arguments and rebuttals presented by individual students in defense of their positions?

Sixth, I work out a rough-cut process plan for the upcoming discussion. What leadership choices might help the group deal most effectively with this material? How should class time be divided between discussions of analysis and action? How should the chalk board be used—what would I hope to see there at the beginning and end of the class? How active a role do I want to play—should I intervene often or only when changes in direction seem necessary?

Seventh, and last, I think about possible openings and endings for the class. Should I begin with some comment on the previous session and announce my expectations for this one? Should I open with a very narrowly focused question, or a broad one? Whom should I invite to speak? What might the student's response be, and how might the whole group, in turn, react? I give similar attention to the end of the discussion. Should I, for example, offer a prepared general wrap-up, let one evolve extemporaneously, or end the discussion without a summary? What "mind-benders" might I give the students when they leave class? What suggestions, if any, for the next class meeting?

Systematically previewing both content and the major process dimensions—the group dynamic, student needs and ambitions, instructor's interests and biases, and the interplay among material, discussion mode, and larger course concepts—can help any instructor anticipate, at least in a general sense, the paths a class might want to explore. At the minimum, such planning can prevent a few errors (and terrors) and build the confidence and clearheadedness necessary to seeing and seizing teaching opportunities when they arise. Most teachers who work through this, or a similar, protocol several times feel that it sensitizes them to the complexities of discussion teaching. At its best, this preparation can help us harness the power generated by the fusion of process and content.

Conclusion

The territory of discussion teaching has never been well mapped. This chapter's four basic premises and accompanying suggestions for practice are but one instructor's sketch. I still find it richly rewarding to explore this world of wonders, and I hope that teachers who practice other modes of instruction might undertake similar explorations. All of us share a splendid vocation with limitless potential. My observations about one type of pedagogy should, therefore, be placed within the context of a premise that I consider even more basic: there is magnificence in *all* teaching. In any form—tutorial, laboratories, and lectures—our efforts bring bountiful rewards. We enjoy the privilege of lifelong learning, a constant link to youth, growth, search, and the world of ideas, and the knowledge that our work has fundamental worth to others. The potential of our daily routines to create impressive results—some of the moment, the most intriguing of the future, makes our work a service of ever unfolding fulfillment. We are part of something great.

Teaching with Cases at the Harvard Business School

In business education, the case method has been closely identified with the Harvard Business School. Though the approach was not invented on the banks of the Charles River—witness the long Talmudic tradition—the Business School is well known for its commitment to an active, discussion-oriented learning mode, disciplined by case problems drawn from the complexity of real life. It is a pedagogy that supports our fundamental objectives: to train women and men for professional business practice.

Together with colleagues in other professional schools, at the university we urge to "mate" knowledge and action, as Alfred North Whitehead puts it,

> What the faculty have to cultivate is activity in the presence of knowledge. What the students have to learn is activity in the presence of knowledge.
>
> This discussion rejects the doctrine that students should first learn passively, and then, having learned, should apply knowledge. It is a psychological error. In the process of learning there should be present, in some sense or other, a subordinate activity of application. In fact, the applications are part of the knowledge. For the very meaning of the things known is wrapped up in their relationship beyond themselves. This unapplied knowledge is knowledge shorn of its meaning.
>
> The careful shielding of a university from the activities of the world around us is the best way to chill interest and to defeat progress. Celibacy does not suit a university. It must mate itself with action.[1]

The Business School's commitment to linking knowledge and application is supported by a number of programs designed to assist instructors in the effective use of cases, one of which is the teaching seminar presented later in this volume. The faculty has appreciated James Harvey's admonition that "teaching may hasten learning; it may also block it or kill it outright, or sometimes just render it comatose for years." The faculty has acknowledged that a tradition of teaching excellence is essential to the School's accomplishments. Dean John H. McArthur puts it succinctly, "How we teach is what we teach." Before detailing the objectives and organization of our teaching seminar, it may be helpful to review

---

1. Alfred North Whitehead, *Essays in Science and Philosophy* (New York: Philosophical Library, Inc., 1947), pp. 218–219.

its historical development and to present a general overview of the case method of instruction—its origins and evolution at the Harvard Business School, the reasons for its educational success, the changing nature of cases and their classroom use, and the basic pedagogical elements of the method. At a more operational level, we will describe how an instructor evaluates a case discussion. Finally, we will overview our current seminar program.

Much of what the Harvard Business School represents has never been interpreted in words: Our practice, values, and traditions remain oral.[2] Focusing on one individual's observations may involve a possibility of substantial misinterpretation. The risk is especially great when one attempts to interpret the School's intellectual core—the case method of instruction—the still point in our rapidly changing academic world. We acknowledge that danger.

Evolution of the Seminar

Phase I: The Seminar Begins

Forward thinking sometimes starts with a backward glance. On February 1, 1968, Thomas Graves (then assistant dean of Harvard Business School, and Andrew R. Towl (then director of case development at HBS), convened a group of research assistants and instructors interested in learning about teaching with cases. Some more-experienced faculty members were asked to talk about leading case discussions.

During the next several years, these sessions were repeated several times. They enjoyed modest participant acceptance, and the instructors gained from the discipline of preparation and the process of answering questions. We soon knew, however, that our format was inappropriate and that our impact on teaching practice was limited.

The first problem was that we simply could not accomplish our mission in a one- or two-session program. Teaching is a complex activity, requiring considerable skill on the part of the instructor. A lecture can be a work of art, extremely difficult to create and deliver. Discussion teaching is an even more complicated instructional task. We needed time to carry out our mission.

Second, we found we knew little, in any systematic sense, about the dynamics of leading a case discussion. We could not specify precisely what we wanted "old pros" to talk about with their "apprentice" audience. It soon became obvious that good teachers could not necessarily abstract and articulate the skills and techniques they employed in their daily classroom practice.

Critics correctly pointed out that we should have anticipated this age-old problem of the artist as teacher. The dilemma is well illustrated by a story told of Anna Pavlova, the great classical star of the Imperial Ballet. A young ballerina once asked her, "What was the meaning of your dance?" Pavlova replied, "Why, if I could tell you that, I wouldn't have needed to dance." Artists are often inarticulate about both meaning and method.

Finally, we found but a modest amount of helpful literature. Though a great deal of research had been conducted at early childhood, elementary, and high school levels, less had been done to explore the dynamics of large-scale section teaching in professional schools. Much of the research had been directed at developing new theory rather than improving day-to-day teaching.[3] The Harvard Business School had addressed the "why" of case teaching, but said little about how instructors carried out such a complex educational assignment.

While we encountered many a doubting Thomas, other colleagues urged us to continue our efforts. Dean George P. Baker gave us both psychological and financial sustenance at a critical juncture. Andrew Towl, who led a pioneering broad-scale effort involving case teaching and research activities with the Visiting Professor's Case Method Program and with the Southern Case Writer's group, was especially supportive.[4]

Phase II: Investigation

Our efforts to resolve the problems of the early seminar program led us in two major directions. First, in 1973, we developed a multisession seminar on case method teaching for doctoral candidates in

3. For an excellent review of research on teaching, see Arthur S. Bolster Jr., "Toward a More Effective Model of Research on Teaching," *Harvard Educational Review,* August 1983, pp. 294–308.

4. The results of Professor Towl's exploration and experiments are reported in his book *To Study Administration by Cases* (Boston, Mass.: Harvard Business School, 1969). It contains a wealth of information essential to understanding a total case method curriculum.

2. Professor Melvin T. Copeland's history of the school, *And Mark an Era* (Boston: Little, Brown & Co., 1958), is a valuable reference. In particular, Chapter IX, "The Case Method of Instruction," is a rich resource.

the Business Policy area. Simply having more time enabled us to explore a wider range of topics related to case teaching—for example, the development of teaching notes and class teaching plans, the creation of a course syllabus, evaluation of students' classroom contributions, and the use of cases for exams and report writing programs. We still asked "master teachers" to talk about their craft, but this became just one part of a wider program.

A second initiative was an attempt to analyze the dynamics of the in-class discussion process. We needed to understand how an instructor could use a specific case situation to stimulate individual students, as well as the overall section, to engage in constructive educational dialogue. Our focus was on the knowledge, skill, and attitudinal requirements of the discussion leader. We sought to compare the discussion process in classes that seemed to have gone particularly well or badly. Toward these ends, we observed more than 70 case discussion classes over several years and informally interviewed dozens of students and instructors about their experiences with this methodology.

Our attempts to learn more about this teaching-learning process mirrored those of Henry Miller, who noted in *Reflections on Writing:*

> My whole work has come to resemble a terrain of which I have made a thorough geodetic survey—not from my desk with pen and ruler—but by touch, by getting down on all fours, on my stomach, and crawling over the ground inch by inch and this over an endless period of time in all conditions of weather.[5]

As students of teaching, we found this a joyful research experience; it gave us a chance to explore familiar, yet unknown, territory. Over the years we became increasingly interested in the specific instructor decision points that recur over and over again in any discussion situation. For example:

How does the instructor select a student to start off the class?

How does the instructor select one student to answer a question when many others with hands raised, are asking for recognition?

What kinds of questions can be used by the instructor? What type of question is most appropriate at what specific time in class?

How does an instructor decide whether or not to respond personally to a student's comment, ignore it, or refer it to another student for comment?

When does one put a comment on the chalkboard?

How does an instructor obtain high levels of student involvement in a case discussion? Deal with apathy? Work with an angry student?

What should an instructor "know" about a student? How can such information be obtained? What professional considerations govern its use?

In this observational universe—section, student, and instructor engaged in a case discussion—we observed a beautiful and infinitely complex educational endeavor, one that we could not hope to capture in its totality, but could understand in part. Our goal was to learn a bit about this discussion dynamic and the instructor's contribution to its productive outcome.

As our investigative phase moved forward, we turned to Professor Nathaniel Cantor's framework for observing and understanding the discussion process. He asks three fundamental questions: What is happening to the student(s)? What is happening to the instructor? What happens between them?[6] Given the complexity of the territory, the simplicity of this framework was powerful.

Our explorations, although rough cut, reinforced our sense of the power of a pedagogy that emphasized student discovery rather than instructor revelation and, to borrow Professor Gragg's phraseology, those "attitudes of mind" that engendered mutual respect between teacher and student. This research effort allowed us to identify both the everyday decisions an instructor must make and the basic recurring problems encountered throughout a semester. It enabled us to define some of the skills and techniques used by sensitive instructors in leading case discussions—a process whose success depends on an intricate integration of course objec-

5. Henry Miller, "Reflections on Writing," *The Henry Miller Reader,* ed. Lawrence Durrell (New York: New Directions, 1959), p. 249.

6. Nathaniel Cantor, speech to the Visiting Professors Case Method Program, cited in Towl, *To Study Administration by Cases,* p. 153.

tives (substantive knowledge as well as analytic and clinical skills), case problems, and student and section learning needs. Most important, we gained additional appreciation for the complexities of the discussion leader's task and the way those complexities help unleash learning power.

Phase III: Experimentation and Case Development

At the end of our investigation, we summarized our findings in three integrated propositions that became the basis for the seminar's philosophy, organization, and operations:

1. A critical responsibility of the instructor is the leadership of the case discussion *process*. It is not enough to be in command of the substantive knowledge of one's field or the specifics of the case problem. The instructor also must be able to lead the process by which individual students and the overall group explore the complexity of a specific case situation.
2. The key to effective discussion leadership is the instructor's artistry, which consists primarily of mastering detail. The effective instructor, for example, expands the entire section's opportunities for learning by asking the appropriate question of a specific student at the best time during the discussion.
3. The pertinent details (skills and techniques) can be observed, abstracted, and taught. Case discussion leaders can be helped to learn their craft.

Having identified the basic challenges confronting a discussion teacher and the skills and techniques that can be helpful, we could now move forward with a case research program. We began building a bank of teaching cases. Some of the first cases were based on our own teaching experience; others were joint efforts developed with the help of former participants. Most of these early cases were snapshots of a classroom incident that had occurred some time in the past. Later we began to develop more complex case studies that involved detailed study of a section's activities over a period of time. In building our case collection, we aimed to explore important teaching issues in depth and to address some specific kinds of problems we thought should be covered in a basic seminar program.

Simultaneously we began an iterative curriculum development program. We worked through various combinations of topics, cases, and readings with seminar groups that were increasingly catholic in composition. With the support of the Harvard-Danforth Center for Teaching and Learning (now the Bok Center for Teaching and Learning), we began to include participants from other departments of the university. These newcomers contributed to the substantive development of our seminar, sharing experience gained in a wide range of academic disciplines and professional schools, and helped us clarify the assumptions on which the seminar was based.

Because we wished to focus on the process of discussion leadership, we assumed the instructor had intellectual command of his or her professional field or academic discipline, and of particular theories and knowledge relevant to the specific course. We also assumed the instructor had a framework for organizing those constructs so as to encourage student learning. Clearly, knowledge and conceptual understanding lie at the heart of any academic effort. But we were convinced that an important stimulus to learning can be the way in which a class is conducted.

Taking mastery of content for granted, we developed what we called process-dominant cases. They focused primarily on the dynamics of individual and group interaction, but included enough data on the knowledge requirements of the course that one could appreciate the academic circumstances in which the teaching problem had developed.

Another critical assumption was that student growth, not instructor ego gratification, was the goal. There is a bit of the actor in most teachers. In the intensity of the classroom drama, they may seek to play center stage, with the class as but their supporting cast. Emotional electricity must be harnessed to power student learning, not to spotlight the instructor's dreams of glory. We assumed that the instructor had a sincere interest in helping students to learn.

During Phase III we also began to sort out the circumstances under which the Harvard Business School's version of discussion teaching might best be used by other institutions. Though James Garfield thought education required only Mark Hopkins at the other end of a bench, we believe physical facilities are extremely important to the success of case teaching. The traditional academic classroom, with its podium and rows of chairs in military formation, severely limits group discussion. A U-shaped amphitheater classroom helps make any instructor a more effective discussion leader. Scale is also important. Much of our pedagogical approach seems most appropriate in groups of roughly 20 to 100. Group continuity is essential; with stable membership, the class develops a social organization and a group dynamic that can be very helpful.

A central consideration, of course, is the intellectual character and instructional needs of the discipline or applied field of study. Thomas Clough, a seminar participant, observed that case discussion methodology is best applied in certain circumstances:

> Where truth is relative, where reality is probabilistic and where structural relationships are contingent, teaching and learning are most effectively accomplished through discussion. With intrinsically complex phenomena and the limited usefulness of simple theoretical relationships, little of value can be communicated directly from teacher to student. The learning process must emphasize the development of understanding, judgment, and even intuition.[7]

Discussion teaching requires a major change in an instructor's role and classroom responsibilities. Traditional teaching, and the lecture mode with which it is so often associated, gives primacy to the instructor. Classroom activity derives from the teacher's presentation of subject matter and follows his or her class plan. The student's role is clearly subordinate.

Discussion teaching proceeds from a quite different perception of teacher-student relationships and responsibilities, emphasizing student involvement and self-teaching. As Professor Nathaniel Cantor put it:

> A skilled teacher recognizes that all significant learning can only come from creative efforts of the learner. That's another way of saying learning is personal. You cannot learn for anybody. . . . Essentially the student must be the one to raise the significant problem for you to help him find the answer.[8]

Discussion teaching works best when the instructor gives up the relative certitude of a planned lec-

ture and an instructor-dominated question period for the ambiguity of a hard-to-plan, free-flowing discussion driven by student ideas, which may well follow unusual paths and come to unexpected end points. For teachers who like to be in charge, discussion teaching is a most uncomfortable assignment.

Experimentation and Reappraisal: A Continuing Adventure

We continue to make our efforts here at Harvard available for use and review by the wider academy. In 1981, we prepared a preliminary report on teaching by the case method.[9] In 1984, we conducted a colloquium that brought together 80 experienced participants representing all major professional fields and key disciplines from the arts and sciences. In 1987, *Teaching and the Case Method: Text, Cases, and Readings* was published, and in 1994, this revised edition becomes available. In addition, in 1991, with the help of a larger group of colleagues, *Education for Judgment: The Artistry of Discussion Leadership* was published. The essays in that book are designed to be used with the key modules of this edition of *Teaching and the Case Method*.

This seminar-building process is a continuing venture; like any creative experiment, it is inevitably unfinished. Alan Gregg, the great medical educator, once lightheartedly noted that a good education leaves much to be desired. There still is much to be done to help discussion leaders practice their craft efficiently and effectively.

The Case Method of Instruction

Before turning to the seminar program, it may be useful to review the historical development of the case method of instruction at the Harvard Business School.[10] A brief look at the founding and early years of the School will suggest some reasons for the initial adoption of case instruction. Then we may ask why this approach remains the essence of the School's educational efforts in both teaching and research as well.[11] Finally, we will focus on cases

---

7. From a report on Discussion Leadership prepared by Thomas Clough for the Fall 1979 Teaching by the Case Method Seminar.
8. Cantor speech, in Towl, p. 157.

9. C. Roland Christensen, *Teaching by the Case Method* (Boston: Harvard Business School, Division of Research, 1981).
10. See also "The Genesis of the Case Method in Business Administration," *The Case Method at the Harvard Business School*, ed. Malcolm P. McNair (New York: McGraw-Hill, 1954), pp. 25–33.
11. Dean's Report, Harvard University, Graduate School of Business Administration, Dean Lawrence E. Fouraker, 1978–1979.

themselves and their continuing evolution in concept, format, and classroom use.

The Historical Origins of Case Instruction at the Harvard Business School

Like many other Harvard endeavors, the Business School originated in a pragmatic marriage of intellectual challenge, societal need, and practical advantage. President Eliot described the new undertaking to the University Club of Indianapolis on May 6, 1908:

> We are just establishing a school of business administration which is to be for graduates only. That is to say, admission to the school of business administration is to be on the same footing as admission to our Schools of Divinity, Law, and Medicine. No one can enter it, unless he already possesses a preliminary degree. We start that school next October. It is our last contribution to the list of professions for which Harvard prepares.
>
> What does that development mean? It means that the universities propose to supply, in the end, the leaders in business. We do not imagine that the University will be able to produce, through teaching, the peculiar instinct for profitable trade which characterizes some men who have had defective education, and who nevertheless arrive at the height of business success. That class of men will arise in our country independently of all institutional education. We do propose to train systematically in the universities a large class of men who will make a probable success in business, because they know all the administrative methods therein used . . . The motives which determined us to establish this school at Harvard are plain; we observed last June that more than half of our Senior class, then graduating, went into business, and we have also observed for a good many years past that a large proportion of our graduates who have gone into business have attained a high place.[12]

With a bit of "tongue in cheek," Mr. Eliot presumably intended "defective education" to signify non-Harvard. His distinction between professional men and business leaders was probably applauded by those in his community who did not accept business as an appropriate academic field. One such purist

is said to have objected to "Sully[ing] the robes of Chaucer and Shakespeare with seekers of gold. Why should a great university concern itself with the mundane of commercial life, with the way of the trader, with the training of men for business and wealth?" But even without a marketing background, the president knew something about meeting consumer needs; Harvard men were business bound.

The magnificence of Mr. Eliot's vision for a new school was matched only by the boldness of his decision to require a bachelor's degree for admission to a two-year course of study, culminating with the award of a master's degree in business administration. In 1908 only 5% of the nation's 18- to 21-year-old age group enrolled in colleges and fewer than 4,000 master's degrees were awarded by the entire educational system in 1909–1910. Business practice was rudimentary, in some respects approximating the level of medical practice when showmen traveled the West dispensing advice and elixirs from a wagon tailgate. *Safe Methods of Business*, a guidebook popular in 1908, covered topics such as spelling and penmanship, methods of bookkeeping (including a better way to add long columns), a guide to law, and such miscellaneous information as a treatise on the uselessness of lightning rods.[13] Preparation for business typically involved simply going to work for a company or signing on as an apprentice. Some studied law as a background for management; others entered secretarial training courses.

Academic studies in commerce, as business education was then often designated, were limited. Pioneering efforts included the undergraduate program of the Wharton School of Commerce and Finance, established in 1891, and undergraduate and graduate programs of the Amos Tuck School of Administration and Finance (1900).[14] Courses in accounting, finance, commercial geography, and law, along with the emerging field of industrial management, provided an instructional base, but in many respects there just wasn't much to be taught in business education in the early twentieth century! President Eliot's decision was ahead of its time; his vision guided business education for decades to come.

Lacking traditional academic building materials—

12. President Eliot's speech on "The University in a Democracy," before the University Club of Indianapolis, *Harvard Bulletin*, May 6, 1908.

13. J. L. Nichols, *Safe Methods of Business* (Naperville, Ill.: J. L. Nichols & Co., 1899).
14. Copeland, *And Mark an Era*, pp. 15–16.

theory, concepts, an epistemology of practice,[15] faculty trained in specialties, programs of research— the new school faced monumental challenges. It had difficulty even in stating what preparatory work its incoming students should have mastered, suggesting only that applicants should have a command of good English and a reading knowledge of at least one modern foreign language, and that "some knowledge of mechanical drawing is highly useful in almost all branches of business."

The early curriculum was a potpourri of courses, some borrowed from other departments of the University, others specifically constructed for the new venture. There were three required courses: Principles of Accounting, Commercial Contracts, and Economic Resources. Other offerings were German, French, Commercial Correspondence, Fire Insurance, Economic Resources of Eastern Asia, and Railroad Operations (in which, the course description noted, "there will be studied in detail the arrangements of freight and passenger stations, the operations of yards and terminals and the organization of train service"). A surveying course was listed as a useful adjunct.

To convert Eliot's vision into an operational reality, Dean Edwin Gay gathered an academic faculty of seven and recruited a considerable number of visiting lecturers, including F. W. Taylor, father of scientific management, and Henry L. Gantt, a pioneer in the field of industrial engineering. Catholic in composition, divided by background and field of study or practice, the faculty seemed to agree on only one point: that business administration was *not* the study of applied economics. Apart from this negative definition, they were less articulate about just what business administration was. Unable to define their field of study or a logic for curriculum design, the faculty was paradoxically precise in its statement of educational purpose, proposing "to give each individual student a practical and professional training suitable to the particular business he plans to enter." The key words, *practical* and *profes-*

sional, remain central to the Business School's mission.

Dean Gay was clearly determined to achieve that objective with an emphasis on a pedagogy that linked the classroom to the actualities of business and engaged the MBA student in a practice-oriented, problem-solving instructional mode. In the first school catalogue, he stated:

> In the courses on Commercial Law the case method will be used. In other courses an analogous method, emphasizing classroom discussion in connection with lectures and frequent reports on assigned topics— what may be called the "problem method"—will be introduced as far as practicable. Visits of inspection will be made under competent guidance to various commercial establishments in Boston and in the neighborhood manufacturing centres of New England. Similar field work of a more specialized character will form a feature of the advanced work of the second year.[16]

He encouraged faculty to explore not only what they taught but how they taught, a tradition that persists to this day.

The setting was hospitable to Dean Gay's dream: a vocation struggling to take small steps toward formalizing its practice to meet the needs of a complicating society; an absence of interest on the part of traditional academia in meeting these needs; a great university willing to experiment; and a new school committed to creating new ways of educating young people "for the oldest of the arts," to use President Lowell's words, "and the newest of the professions." We underscore the importance of a "new" school for, as Professor Kenneth Andrews reminds us, freedom from traditional academic dogma encouraged major faculty experimentation.

So did the maverick, almost anti-academic nature of the School's early faculty. Professor William James Cunningham, one of the School's first chaired professors, had obtained his academic preparation from the International Correspondence School of Scranton, Pennsylvania. As the late Professor George Albert Smith, Jr., often observed, these pioneers were convinced that traditional means of preparing men for a career in business were ineffective; they were eager to apply new insights to old problems.

---

15. This topic is covered generally in Donald A. Schön, *The Reflective Practitioner* (New York: Basic Books, 1983) and more specifically for the field of business administration in Dr. Schön's paper, "The Crisis of Professional Knowledge and the Pursuit of an Epistemology of Practice," presented at the colloquium on Teaching by the Case Method held at the Harvard Business School, April 1–4, 1984 and found in the Instructor's Guide for this book.

16. Copeland, *And Mark an Era*, p. 27.

Why the Success of the Case Method Approach?

"No question," said George Bernard Shaw, "is as difficult to answer as that to which the answer is obvious." Why has the case method played such an important role in our institution's accomplishments? Why its success?

First and foremost, this pedagogy suits the Business School's mission of training men and women not only to know, but to act. One of the School's first professors, Arthur Stone Dewing, put the point philosophically:

This method [lectures] has great advantages. Above all, it is efficient, it is also economical of the time, energy, and the patience of instructor and student. Further, this method produces brilliant results. A student trained under it seems to possess a sureness, a precision, a firming of grasp remarkable for the relatively short time which he is compelled to spend on acquiring his knowledge . . .

The other method starts with an entirely different purpose and ends with an entirely different result. . . . [Businesspeople must be able] to meet in action the problems arising out of new situations of an ever-changing environment. Education, accordingly, would consist of acquiring facility to act in the presence of new experience. It asks not how a man may be trained to know, but how a man may be trained to act.[17]

In a more pragmatic vein, President A. Lawrence Lowell underscored the relationship between classroom discussions and the day-to-day work of a businessman.

The case method of business training is deemed the best preparation for business life, because the discussion of questions by the banker, the manufacturer, the merchant or the transporter consists in discerning the essential elements in a situation and applying to them the principles of organization and trade. His most important work consists of solving problems and for this he must have the faculty of rapid analysis and synthesis.[18]

17. Arthur Stone Dewing, "An Introduction to the Use of Cases," *The Case Method of Instruction*, ed. Cecil E. Frazer (New York: McGraw-Hill, 1931).
18. Exact citation not available. Believed to have been quoted in the foreword to a Harvard business problem book in the early 1920s.

Professor Bertrand Fox, writing some 35 years later, emphasized the individual learning opportunities in a group's discussion process.

With so many practical business problems the final decisions are reached only after discussion among smaller or larger groups. I have felt that each class is in essence a practical experience in group behavior and in the benefits of group discussions in arriving at business decisions. As a part of this process, but in part distinct from it, each class provides an experience in learning how to express one's self and perhaps to persuade others to one's point of view. The method provides an opportunity to gain confidence in one's own judgement, but also a degree of humility as well. It also provides a most invaluable opportunity to learn how far one can go by rigorous logical analyses of one or another dimension of the problem and the extent to which judgement comes into play when many factors which have no common denominator must be weighed.[19]

Columbia's John Dewey would have given strong support to the Dewing-Fox position, for his theories of learning support a discussion-oriented teaching methodology. As Jonas Soltes notes, Dewey believed the learner is like an explorer who maps in unknown territory:

The explorer like the learner, does not know what terrain and adventures his journey holds in store for him. He has yet to discover mountains, deserts, and water holes and to suffer fever, starvation, and other hardships. Finally, when the explorer returns from his journey, he will have a hard-won knowledge of the country he has traversed. Then, and only then, can he produce a map of the region. The map, like a textbook, is an abstraction which omits his thirst, his courage, his despairs and triumphs—the experiences which made his journey personally meaningful. The map records only the relationships between landmarks and terrain, the logic of the features without the psychological revelations of the journey itself.

To give the map to others (as a teacher might) is to give the results of an experience, not the experience by which the map was produced and became personally meaningful to the producer. Although the logical organization of subject matter is the proper goal of learning, the logic of the subject cannot be truly

19. Copeland, *And Mark an Era*, pp. 264–265.

meaningful to the learner without his psychological and personal involvement in exploration. "Only by wrestling with the conditions of the problem at hand, seeking and finding his own way out, does he think. . . If he cannot devise his own solution (not, of course, in isolation but in correspondence with the teacher and other pupils) and find his own way out he will not learn, not even if he can recite some correct answer with one hundred percent accuracy."

Although learning experiences may be described in isolation, education for Dewey consisted in the cumulative and unending acquisition, combination, and reordering of such experiences. Just as a tree does not grow by having new branches and leaves wired to it each spring, so educational growth does not consist in mechanically adding information, skills, or even educative experiences to students in grade after grade. Rather, educational growth consists in combining past experiences with present experiences in order to receive and understand future experiences. To grow, the individual must continually reorganize and reformulate past experiences in the light of new experiences in a cohesive fashion.[20]

The case method enables students to discover and develop their own unique framework for approaching, understanding, and dealing with business problems.[21] To the extent that one can learn business practice in a classroom, and the limits are substantial, it achieves its goal efficiently.

Equally important, case method teaching is intellectually stimulating for the faculty. In current jargon, it is teacher friendly, affording the instructor opportunities for continuous self-education. In this respect, what's good for the faculty is good for the students. As John Dewey observed, "If teaching becomes neither terribly interesting nor exciting to teachers, how can one expect teachers to make learning terribly exciting to students!"

Every class provides opportunity for new intellectual adventure, for risk taking, for new learning. One may have taught the case before, but last year's notes have limited current value. With a new group of students, the unfolding dynamic of a unique section, and different time circumstances, familiar material is revitalized. Class discussions typically leave

the instructor with new questions about old challenges.

The case method also meets a faculty's teaching and research needs.[22] The development of new field cases links instructors to the world of practice. It encourages them to be in touch with their professional counterparts, maintaining a dialogue that explores current problems and anticipates future issues. Clinical field work provides a faculty with rich data from which to extract new hypotheses and modify current working generalizations.

Also, the case method is supportive of a culture that places high value on review and innovation. Too often, faculties teach change and practice the status quo. Individual course and overall curriculum reviews often depend on the personal initiative of an instructor or the work of faculty committees. But when faculty must prepare teaching cases, their continuing contact with the world of practice provides the institution with an external force for change. Suggestions that a familiar framework be reviewed or new concepts developed are often received more sympathetically when they derive from the impersonal demands of practice rather than from colleagues or departments, with their personal agendas. The case method encourages an adaptive culture.

Finally, the case method as practiced at the Harvard Business School is economically efficient. A distinguished Harvard dean once said that discussion teaching "is not operative in groups larger than seven." Similarly, Professor Theodore Sizer argues that a questioning (discussion) group approach "requires a seminar format, a circle of fewer than twenty people."[23] But case method teaching can work well with much larger groups—given well-crafted cases, instructors trained in large-scale discussion teaching techniques, and physical facilities designed to support this method.

Harvard Business School classrooms have been architecturally designed to minimize physical distance and to maximize psychological togetherness between teacher and student, and to encourage student-to-student rather than instructor-to-student interactions. An 80- or 100-person class has an obvious economic advantage over a traditional

20. Jonas Soltes, *Encyclopedia of Education*, 5th ed., s.v. "Dewey, John."
21. See Pearson Hunt, "The Case Method of Instruction," *Harvard Educational Review*, Summer 1951, pp. 175–192.
22. Professor E. P. Learned wrote an unpublished history of the Business Policy course that provides an in-depth study of this phenomenon.
23. Theodore Sizer, *Horace's Compromise* (Boston: Houghton Mifflin, 1984), p. 119.

small discussion group. Spreading instructional fixed costs over a larger group makes it possible to finance a very expensive case development program.

Skilled teachers are a scarce resource. If they can work with larger student groups, instructional efficiency increases. Moreover, in a large section, the instructor can draw on a wider range of student interest and experience. The need to limit the "air time" of each student encourages the instructor to find ways of helping the class practice the skills of listening, observing, synthesizing, and summarizing. Thus, scale can be an asset, not a liability, in discussion teaching.

Heralded by Dean Gay, and infused with intellectual substance and organizational support by Dean Donham, the case method succeeded because of its educational effectiveness for both students and faculty, its economic efficiency, and its nurturing of an adaptive institutional milieu. First tentatively identified as the "laboratory method," then as the "problem method," the Business School's distinctive pedagogy has undergone substantial changes over the years. Our ideas have changed as to just what constitutes a case, how cases are developed, and how they are taught in the classroom.

The Evolution of the Case Method of Instruction

Originally, cases were just about anything the new faculty could find to provide a basis for provocative classroom discussion: a legal document, a business report, or a business problem with which the teacher was familiar. They preferred the latter for they intuitively saw these problems as a bridge between academia and business. Businessmen had to deal with a daily succession of problems (cases). Why not bring those problems to the classroom for apprentice managers' use? At first businessmen were asked to write up their own company problems and to lead class discussions about their situation. Later the School dispatched researchers into the field. By 1924 the Bureau of Business Research had 20 recent MBA graduates at work preparing cases.

These early efforts are well illustrated by the Badger Manufacturing Company and the Ajax Manufacturing Company cases, shown here:

BADGER MANUFACTURING COMPANY: BUYING HABITS OF CONSUMERS

The Badger Manufacturing Company produces enamelware for kitchen use in a wide variety of articles and styles of several qualities. The company has recently decided to start an extensive advertising campaign in order to increase its sales.

What are the buying habits and motives of consumers purchasing such products, which the advertising manager of Badger Manufacturing Company should take into account in planning this campaign?

AJAX MANUFACTURING COMPANY: FILING RECEIVING CLERK'S COPY OF PURCHASE ORDER

The Ajax Manufacturing Company has, for the past five years, sent a copy of each purchase order to the receiving clerk. The receiving clerk places these copies on a spindle and when the shipment is received, if it is complete, he attaches his copy of the purchase order to the detailed notification of material received report which he makes out.

When this method of placing the copy of the purchase order on a spindle was started this company was producing approximately eight hundred pairs of men's Goodyear welt work shoes per day. During the years 1916–1918, however, it expanded its output to over 3,500 pairs per day. This expansion has necessitated the filing of the copies of the purchase orders in the receiving department, in accordance with some systematic scheme.

Mr. Carney, the receiving clerk, has visited several factories and has found that some receiving clerks file their copy of the purchase order by the date the shipment is due; others file them by the name of the commodity or by the name of the vendor.

What method of filing the copy of the purchase order should Mr. Carney establish in his department?

From these rather simplistic problem statements, cases have evolved into complex educational instruments based on carefully designed research plans and intensive field research.[24] Their content has broadened to include internal company information as well as external industry data, psychological and sociological observations as well as technical and

24. See Raymond Corey, "The Use of Cases in Management Education," HBS Case No. 376–240.

economic material. Whereas early cases were essentially snapshots of a company at a single point in time, students now learn from series cases that report company operations at all levels of management over a period of time. A series on NIKE, Inc., consists of 15 teaching cases tracing that company's managerial challenges as it evolved from a small entrepreneurial firm to a billion-dollar organization. Individual cases have been designed so they can be combined into course modules for senior management, middle management, and MBA groups.

The evolving definition of case studies has been marked by both continuity and change.[25] Professor Gragg's classic statement defines the intended role of case studies in the 1930s:

> A case typically is a record of a business issue which actually has been faced by business executives, together with surrounding facts, opinions, and prejudices upon which executive decisions have to depend. These real and particularized cases are presented to students for considered analyses, open discussion, and final discussion as to the type of action which should be taken.[26]

In the 1950s, Professor Paul Lawrence viewed a case history in a more operational mode:

> A good case is the vehicle by which a chunk of reality is brought into the classroom to be worked over by the class and the instructor. A good case keeps the class discussion grounded upon some of the stubborn facts that must be faced in real life situations. It is the anchor on academic flights of speculation. It is the record of complex situations that must be literally pulled apart and put together again for the expression of attitudes or ways of thinking brought into the classroom.[27]

For seminar development purposes, we found the following definition useful:

A case is a partial, historical, clinical study of a situation which has confronted a practicing administrator or managerial group. Presented in narrative form to encourage student involvement, it provides data—substantive and process—essential to an analysis of a specific situation, for the framing of alternative action programs, and for their implementation recognizing the complexity and ambiguity of the practical world.

This definition reaffirms the traditional elements of a case: real-life business problems confronting business managers at a particular moment. It enlarges on Lawrence's theme of the case as a teaching instrument crafted to create a specific discussion opportunity. In addition, it indicates some of the basic limits of all case studies: they are partial in coverage, and historical distortion is a probability. As our field research methodology becomes more sophisticated, as we expand our cases to include a combination of verbal, numerical, and visual data, one can be certain that the case study of our centennial year, 2008, will be very different from those used today.

The classroom use of cases has also evolved. On the basis of the limited archived documentation available, supported by interviews with emeriti professors and alumni, it is quite evident that the manner in which cases were taught changed substantially in the decade following World War II.

Dean Wallace B. Donham, who led the Business School from 1919 to 1942, often compared its teaching methodology with that of the Harvard Law School. Then as now, however, legal and business cases were quite different. Some faculty members thought the dean's efforts to link the two systems publicly was intended to quiet critics by associating the fledgling Business School with one of Harvard's most distinguished professional schools.

Yet there were similarities. At both schools student sections were large, and instruction centered on a professor's disciplined questioning of an individual student, with little if any group dialogue. The objective of that professorial interrogation, however, was quite different in the two schools. Many Law School instructors utilized the Socratic method;[28] that methodology required a student to

25. See also James Erskine, M. R. Leenders, and L. A. Mauffette-Leenders, *Teaching With Cases* (London, Ontario: School of Business, University of Western Ontario, 1981).
26. Charles I. Gragg, "Because Wisdom Can't Be Told," *The Case Method at the Harvard Business School,* p. 6.
27. Paul Lawrence, "The Preparation of Case Material," *The Case Method of Teaching Human Relations and Administration,* ed. Kenneth R. Andrews (Cambridge, Mass.: Harvard University Press, 1953), p. 215.
28. ". . . questioning of another to reveal his hidden ignorance or to elicit a clear expression of a truth supposed to be implicitly known by all rational beings." *Webster's New Collegiate Dictionary,* 9th ed., s. v. "Socratic."

"boil down" case facts to their essence—in Law School jargon to "state the case." The instructor then interrogated the student and encouraged him to derive appropriate legal principles from the specific case circumstances. The Business School instructors questioned students on the quality of their analysis, the scope of their proposed action plans, and their sensitivity to the managerial challenges inherent in their proposals. The instructor's objective was to help the student develop a way of understanding and contributing to the solution of a corporation's problems. The development of organizational principles was given but modest attention.

A New Pedagogy Emerges

The years after World War II brought major changes to the Business School. A "re-educated" faculty, a new breed of student, a major curriculum revision emphasizing the teaching of administrative skills, and the introduction of new classroom facilities all contributed to the emergence of a "new" case method of instruction.

During the war many senior faculty held defense-related leadership positions in government or business, thereby gaining firsthand managerial experience. Those remaining at Soldiers Field taught senior managers in newly developed executive education programs and engaged in an intensive review of existing academic programs that culminated in the development of a new curriculum. In the early postwar expansion period, younger faculty members brought additional questions and ideas for pedagogical change.

The needs and interests of the student body also changed. Postwar MBA students were very different from their prewar counterparts. Members of the new breed were older, and many were married and lived off-campus. The academic section, rather than the dormitory, became a crucial element in the educational setting. Most postwar students had had substantial military leadership experience. Questioning traditional authority patterns, impatient and independent, these men were confident of their ability to participate in the give-and-take of a group discussion and eager to assume responsibility for their own education.

In 1946 a new first-year curriculum, The Elements of Administration, was introduced; it was a decision crucial to the long-term evolution of the School's educational strategy. The curriculum design was powerfully simple: a single, first-year course integrating all the traditional functional areas into one study program. Three new administratively oriented courses were developed: Public Relations and Responsibilities, Control (a combination of Accounting and Statistics), and Administrative Practices. These courses, particularly Control and Administrative Practices, underscored the faculty's interest in moving the MBA program closer to the practice of management through the development of administrative attitudes and skills and the cultivation of sensitivity to organizational relationships and processes.

This experiment had substantial impact. The day-to-day faculty collaboration required by an integrated curriculum gave instructors firsthand experience with managerial circumstances in functional fields other than their own. The faculty soon discovered that while the tasks of leading a sales department and a production operation differed in substantive knowledge requirements, their managerial dimensions had much in common. As Professor James Culliton observed, "A set of concepts and skills, basic to any functional management position had been identified. More importantly we were beginning to understand better just what was involved in education for management."

Somewhat paradoxically, increasing knowledge about functional management sparked faculty interest in exploring the functions, roles, and skills of the general manager and ways of researching and teaching them. The School had long identified itself as a "school of general management" without specifying very precisely just what was meant by that phrase. Now it was ready to address the question posed by Professor Kenneth Andrews: "Just what is the specialty of being a generalist?" In seeking an answer, the Business Policy course (a second-year required course focusing on general management functions) began a series of research and teaching programs that led to the adoption of the concept of corporate strategy as the unifying theme for that course and later for the entire MBA program.

Greater knowledge at both the functional and generalist levels reinforced the faculty's intuitive conviction that management was a field of academic study separate and distinct from its supporting discipline. In a sense they had answered the 1908 question, What is education for business if it is not applied economics? The key word in the School's name became *administration*, not *business*.

In June of 1953, as these developments were unfolding, Aldrich Hall opened. Its parabola-shaped classrooms were an architectural breakthrough. For the first time the faculty had facilities designed to support large-scale discussion teaching.

All of the forces for change—faculty, student, curriculum, and facilities—were now in play. While the large-section format remained constant, the instructional scene had changed dramatically. No longer was the student section simply an administrative convenience, an agglomeration of individuals assigned to a course and a room at a designated time. It became the center of the MBA's intellectual and social life with a powerful dynamic of its own.[29] With process teaching goals becoming more important, the group discussion format provided an excellent way to sensitize students to administrative problems and processes and allow them to practice managerial skills.

The impact on the instructor was significant. His new role was less to question a series of individual students than to direct a process by which the section explored a complex case situation. Symbolically, the older Baker Library classroom had enthroned the professor on a platform separated from the students he overlooked by brass railing and curtain. In the new classroom, the professor sat at a desk from which he looked up at the members of his section. The power balance between teacher and student shifted perceptibly; students gained increased opportunity for personal learning and group contribution.

Thus a new case method of teaching was born, quietly, over time and in some measure without the faculty's full appreciation of the magnitude and magnificence of the change.

Basic Pedagogical Elements

A case history provides only the foundation for the learning process we call the case method of instruction—a complicated interaction of case situation, individual student, overall class section, and discussion leader. Education theorists would describe the method as an effort to blend cognitive and affective learning modes. Any attempt to capture this dynamic, the subtle ebb and flow of interacting ideas between teacher and student, is difficult at best, perhaps impossible. This may be why the phenomenon of class discussion has so seldom been analyzed or even described.[30]

A few snapshots may give a useful view of this process. Writing about a case class in the late 1920s, Professor Arthur S. Dewing noted that

> teaching by the case method is class discussion of possibilities, probabilities, and expedients—the possibilities of the combination of very intricate facts, the probabilities of human reactions, and the expedients most likely to bring about the responses in others that lead to a definite end. . . . Cases should be used with clear consciousness that the purpose of business education is not to teach truths—leaving aside for a moment a discussion of whether there are or are not such things as truths—but to teach men to think in the presence of new situations. There should not be a single problem [case] in use which is not capable of at least two intelligent solutions.[31]

Donald R. Schön and Philip Sprague, reflecting on their personal experience as MBA students during the early fifties, commented:

> The initial atmosphere of the classroom does little to restore a feeling of certainty. The behavior of the professor is strangely disconcerting. There is an absence of professional dicta, a surprising lack of "answers" and "cold dope" which the student can record in his notebook; rather he is asked what *he* would do, and what problems *he* feels are important. Similarly he finds that today's problems cannot necessarily be solved by yesterday's solutions. Every time he feels that he has arrived at generalizations or principles which will apply in all cases, he is confronted with a set of variables which will not yield to such analysis. The plea that he has insufficient evidence or data on which to make a decision is more or less ignored; he is told to do the best he can with what is available.

> As he airs his views, feelings, reactions, attitudes

29. See also Charles D. Orth III, *Social Structures and Learning Climate: The First Year at the Harvard Business School* (Boston: Harvard Business School, Division of Research, 1963); and John Van Maanen, "Golden Passports: Managerial Socialization and Graduate Education," *The Review of Higher Education* 6, no. 4 (Summer 1983): 435–455.

30. See Selma Wassermann, *Put Some Thinking in Your Classroom* (Chicago: Benefic Press, 1978) and Clark Bouton and Russel Garth, eds., *Learning in Groups* (San Francisco: Jossey-Bass, 1983).

31. Arthur Stone Dewing, "An Introduction to the Use of Cases," *The Case Method at the Harvard Business School*, pp. 3–4.

and prejudices and sees them reinforced or rejected by thinking individuals around him, he has an opportunity to re-evaluate and re-appraise his own character and personality. Preconceived notions and handed-down attitudes examined in an atmosphere of reality and with a focus on effectiveness can be seen for what they are.[32]

Robin Hacke described her experience during the 1980s:

I entered the battle of the case method unarmed. The routines and tools that had allowed me to survive years of schooling no longer helped me; my old study habits were useless—counterproductive, in fact. For example, I had always been a diligent student, priding myself on completing the assignments I was given. If I was expected to read pages 220–256 of a book, I read them. As a student in a case class, though, my assignments were open-ended: prepare the case and develop recommendations. I was supposed to decide how to approach the material, but it was hard to know how much to do, hard to know where to stop. Was I supposed to consider two alternatives or six? Was I supposed to consult outside sources (textbooks, classnotes, the business library)? I had always been an outliner, finding that outlining helped me see the structure of the material. But cases by their very nature could not be outlined. They were not books, logically organized by the author to facilitate my understanding. Just because a particular aspect of the case situation occupied the first three pages of the case booklet did not mean it was more important than an aspect mentioned in one small paragraph on page 17. Just because certain data was not provided did not mean it was not necessary.

Like a "real" manager in a "real" business situation, it was now my job to impose a meaningful framework on the unruliness of case facts. I had to search for the key nuggets of data, distinguishing central facts from peripheral ones. I had to sort out the conflicting explanations and alternatives presented to me, and arrive at a reasonable recommendation for action.

I understood the importance of these skills in the real world. But that understanding didn't make the skills any easier to develop. When I tried to ignore six pages of a case in order to focus on one crucial ex-

hibit, a little voice inside me would ask, Why did they give you this if it's not important? Every time I needed to make an assumption, particularly one involving numbers, I hesitated and thought, How would I defend my assumption? How could I know what was reasonable? I rarely could walk into class secure in the knowledge that I had "cracked" the case. The uncertainty was frightening.[33]

A review of the fundamental principles underlying case method teaching may help explain its extraordinary power to involve the student in a highly personal learning experience. Keeping Occam's razor in mind, let us note the five we believe to be most important.

1. The primacy of situational analysis. For both administrators and students of administration, the primary consideration is "the law of the situation," to use Mary Parker Follett's pithy phrase.[34] Analyzing a specific situation forces the student to deal with the "as is," not the "might be." He or she must confront the intractability of reality: an absence of needed information, the ever-present conflict of objectives, and the imbalance between needs and resources. The manager must and can act effectively under those circumstances; the intern manager is also expected to do so.

This situational orientation, moreover, insistently reminds the student of the vast gap between simplistic, global prescriptions and what can be said to a specific manager, at a specific time, on a specific issue. The goal of the case discussion is to help students develop the capacity to deal with the situation-specific, not to deliver commentaries on the general. From experience garnered in many case discussions, the student will in fact derive generalizations, but they are stated tentatively, tested frequently, and always used with care.

2. The imperative of relating analysis and action. The traditional academic accomplishment has been to know; the practitioner's necessity has been to act. The case method of instruction seeks to combine these two activities. The application of knowledge, always partial, to the complexities of an administra-

32. Donald R. Schön and Philip R. Sprague, "The Case Method as Seen by Recent Graduates," *The Case Method at the Harvard Business School*, pp. 80–81.

33. Robin Hacke, *The Case Method: A Student Perspective*, unpublished working paper, Harvard Business School, 1985.
34. M. P. Follett, *Creative Experience* (New York: Longmans, Green and Co., 1924), p. 152.

tive problem, never capable of complete solution, is the manager's primary task.

A case discussion is a crude mirror of that reality. The class considers action in tandem with analysis whenever possible. The minimum end product of a case discussion is an understanding of what needs to be done and how it can be accomplished. At its best, the case discussion will include an exploration of how a plan can be translated into the committed behavior of a group of managers.

The importance of action influences the entire case discussion, which focuses on the practical and doable, the partial but accomplishable, and the necessity of dealing with first-step accommodations rather than waiting for complete solutions.

3. *The necessity of student involvement.* The active intellectual and emotional involvement of the student is a hallmark of case teaching. That involvement offers the most dramatic visible contrast with a stereotypical lecture class.

In education for management, where knowledge and application skills must be related, student involvement is essential. One does not learn to play golf by reading a book, but by taking club in hand and actually hitting a golf ball, preferably under a pro's watchful eye. A practice green is not a golf game, and a case is not real life. Fortunes, reputations, and careers are not made or lost in the classroom. But case discussion is a useful subset of reality; it presents a microcosm of actual administrative life. It also allows students to practice the application of real-life administrative skills: observing, listening, diagnosing, deciding, and intervening in group processes to achieve desired objectives.

Case discussion demands total participant involvement in a variety of ways, first and foremost in the give-and-take of class discussion—with mind as well as vocal cords. It insists that students practice managerial skills both in class and in all other academic activities, taking responsibility for their own self-education and for the development of their colleagues. For managers are both teachers and students in their everyday work.

4. *A nontraditional instructor role.* A teacher thoroughly experienced in traditional methodologies may well find case teaching difficult to understand. "As far as I can see, the instructor's job is to give an intelligent grunt of approval or disapproval, ask some questions, and make a summary statement,"

said one. Another commented, "It's a blinking bit of intellectual chaos and so darned inefficient! Why let a class 'muck around' for an hour trying to work through a point when I can explain it in a few minutes. They call that teaching? Just what's the instructor doing?" Guiding a process of discovery, an advocate of the method might reply.

Some instructors, unfortunately, use the case method in masquerade form. While espousing openness and collaboration, they require students to follow their teaching plan point by point, with drumbeat cadence. It may seem as if the students' assignment were to come up with the missing words in an academic crossword puzzle—the instructor's teaching plan. Such pedagogical failures give ammunition to our critics, for a badly executed case discussion can be a disaster: inefficient in use of time and ineffective in student motivation.

Even when the teacher is a master of case method instruction, it is difficult to say just what he or she is doing.[35] We all appreciate the difficulty of describing what an artist "does." Witness the story attributed to Antal Dorati's three-year-old daughter. After watching her first rehearsal, she explained the mystery of conducting: "Daddy," she said, "you are the only musician who makes no noise."

What conductors or instructors do or don't do, when and how, may be as important as what they know. The artistry of teaching may be arcane, but some of its mystery can be clarified. Professor Kenneth Andrews has thoughtfully described the case instructor's role:

> The instructor provides the impromptu services which any group discussion requires. He keeps the proceedings orderly. He should be able to ask questions which invite advance in group thinking and at the same time reveal the relevance of the talk that has gone before. He needs the ability to weave together the threads of individual contribution into a pattern which not only he but his class can perceive. He needs the sense of timing which tells him that a discussion is not moving fast enough to make good use of available time or is racing away from the comprehension of half the class. He knows what to do on such occasions. He exercises control over an essentially "undirected" activity, but at the same time he keeps out of the way, lest he prevent the class from

35. See Pearson Hunt, "A Professor Looks at Teaching and Himself," *Harvard Business School Bulletin,* January–February 1964.

making discoveries new also to him. Since unpredictable developments always distinguish real learning, he examines his class rather than his subject.[36]

This approach to teaching has its parallels in a variety of fields, as these comments on the teaching of drawing suggest:

> The job of the teacher, as I see it, is to teach students, not how to draw but how to learn to draw. They must acquire some real method of finding out facts for themselves lest they be limited for the rest of their lives to facts the instructor relates. They must discover something of the true nature of artistic creation—of the hidden processes by which inspiration works.
>
> My whole method consists of enabling students to have an experience. I try to plan for them things to do, things to think about, contacts to make. When they have had that experience well and deeply, it is possible to point out what it is and why it has brought these results.[37]

The instructor's role in this kind of learning process differs in several respects from traditional practice.[38] First, the task is not so much to *teach* students as to encourage *learning*. This shift in mission affects a wide range of instructor activities, from preparing class material and planning class sessions to measuring what the course has accomplished.

Second, the teacher must be willing to forgo the role and status of a center-stage, intellectually superior authority figure.[39] As a discussion leader, he or she is simply a member of a learning group, albeit one with a unique position. Professor Gragg puts the point well in his classic piece, "Teachers Also Must Learn." In addition to providing information and monitoring the quality of student analysis and presentation, the instructor must facilitate a process of joint inquiry. A primary responsibility, therefore,

is the maintenance of the quality of those paths of inquiry.

Third, the instructor must be both teacher and practitioner. Students will accept that one can legitimately discuss the battle of Waterloo without having the capacity to command a brigade of infantry. But an instructor who tries to develop students' skills of observation, listening, communication, and decision making will be expected to practice what he or she preaches. Failure to do so brings swift retribution.

5. A balance of substantive and process teaching objectives: the development of an administrative point of view. When successful, the case method of instruction produces a manager grounded in theory and abstract knowledge and, more important, able to apply those elements. At the Harvard Business School, that accomplishment has traditionally been summed up as the development of an administrative point of view.

While the faculty has always agreed that the development of this professional competence was its primary educational goal, only limited efforts have been made to define and articulate its educational components. A young instructor, many years ago, asked a senior colleague to define the administrative point of view. The curt reply has been long remembered, "If you have to define it, you will never understand what it is. If you know what it is, you don't need to define it. Give your students an opportunity to discover it for themselves."

This advice, whether good or poor, was a bit disquieting. Clearly, however, it reflected the normal operating mode of the school's faculty. The Business School's tradition, then and now, has been to devote its intellectual resources to teaching, to practice, to accomplishment; pedagogical theorizing is given short shrift.

The research of Professor F. J. Roethlisberger, however, made a major contribution to our understanding of the skill components of an administrative point of view. His definition of "skill" underscored the complicated nature of our educational mission:

> Skill is the response of a whole organism, acting as a unit, that is adequate to a particular point in a given situation. A skill is always manifested at a particular point as a complex capacity acquired by experience in

36. K. R. Andrews, "The Role of the Instructor in the Case Method," in *The Case Method at the Harvard Business School,* pp. 98–99.
37. K. Nicolaides, *Introduction to the Natural Way to Draw* (Boston: Houghton Mifflin, 1941).
38. See also Ronald T. Hyman, *Improving Discussion Leadership* (New York: Teachers College Press, Columbia University, 1980).
39. A delightful sketch of one such experiment is detailed in Donald W. Thomas, "The Torpedo's Touch," *Harvard Educational Review,* May 1985, pp. 220–222.

responding appropriately to particular, concrete, and whole situations.[40]

That definition, together with his emphasized distinction between "knowledge about" and "knowledge of," pinpointed the skill competence we hoped our students might achieve:

Although related, we assumed that there were two kinds of knowledge that needed to be different. One is the kind of knowledge that is associated with the scientist who is seeking to make verifiable propositions about a certain class of phenomena. The other is the kind of knowledge that is associated with the practitioner of a skill in relation to a class of phenomena. . .

The difference between these two kinds of knowledge can be readily seen by contrasting the aim of the scientist with the aim of a practitioner of a skill. The aim of the scientist is to discover and make verifiable propositions about a certain class of phenomena; the aim of the practitioner is the immediate "control" of the phenomena with which he deals. Although the "knowledge of acquaintance" which the practitioner acquires from the practice of skills often remains intuitive and implicit, it serves his immediate purposes well. A skillful carpenter who works with many kinds of woods, for example, has a great deal of "acquaintance with" the properties of different woods. He "knows" what different woods will and will not do for certain conditions—at least sufficient for his purposes of fashioning them into useful objects. He does not have, however, that kind of analytical "knowledge about" phenomena sought by the scientists. He does not "know" about the relative tensile strengths of different kinds of building materials.[41]

Although the faculty may not have been able to define the administrative point of view, it knew that it wanted to train carpenters—albeit carpenters who drove Cadillacs and wore Brooks Brothers' suits—and not to create wood theorists. And it knew how to train these practitioners.

The Administrative Point of View: Its Complexities

As the Harvard Business School approaches its 100th anniversary, the faculty still has not articu-

lated a neat definition of the administrative point of view, although all of us have our own working explanations. Perhaps we might think of it as a manager's skill in ordering his relationship to an organization, understanding how that organization functions, what its needs are, and how to intervene constructively in its affairs to achieve desired change.

Clearly the administrative point of view is a composite of many elements whose successful application depends on the skill with which they are combined. We can now identify some of the critical elements in that fusion; such a listing may clarify the kinds of in-class experiences we hope to create for our students.

A focus on understanding the specific context. What are the unique circumstances that differentiate this situation from others? Or, as one colleague asked at the beginning of each class, "What's the nature of the beast?" The manager's choice of problems to work on, and the manner and sequence in which he deals with these challenges, depend very much on whether the company is a textile converter, a film producer, or an integrated steel operation. Equally important, what are the key challenges facing this manager, at this time, with these resources and limits?

A sense for appropriate boundaries. Problems do not come to the manager in neatly delineated form. Some boundaries are established by external forces, others by organizational structure and financial limits. A key managerial skill is to define the boundaries of any issue so as to balance the need for breadth (to include all essential factors) with the need for sufficient focus (to enhance the probability for constructive improvement).

Sensitivity to interrelationships: the connectedness of all organizational functions and processes. An organization is like a tangle of rubber bands: tugging on one affects all the others. In dealing with a specific issue, the manager must recognize that it will always influence and be influenced by the general situation. How he or she deals with a problem in the sales department, for example, may affect overall company operations. The effective manager must think about the organization holistically and behave accordingly.

40. F. J. Roethlisberger, *Training for Human Relations* (Boston: Harvard Business School, Division of Research, 1954), p. 8.
41. Ibid., pp. 6–7.

Examining and understanding any administrative situation from a multidimensional point of view. The manager must consider not only the present circumstance of any issue but also its historical legacy and future perspective. He or she must accept that any problem may well be understood differently by individuals and groups, and that perceptions change dramatically by organizational level. Presidents and foremen have different agendas. An awareness of this multidimensional context and the capacity to deal with the inevitable conflicts it creates is the hallmark of a manager.

Accepting personal responsibility for the solution of organizational problems. Much of academic life revolves around the role of commentator and critic. The successful administrator, in contrast, is one who defines problems in ways that encourage their solution and then accepts personal responsibility for the accomplishment of that objective.

An action orientation. The ultimate contribution of any manager is to help the organization deal with problems and exploit opportunities, to move it from an imperfect present to an improved future. Action is the core ingredient in an administrative point of view.

The last point is critical. Professor John Dewey put it succinctly: "Saints engage in introspection while burly sinners run the world."

Action: Its Main Ingredients

The manager's primary contribution is to lead the organization—to get things done. We can identify some important ingredients of this action orientation:

- A sense for the possible. A willingness to accept compromise, accommodation, and modest forward motion instead of a fruitless search for the perfect solution. A willingness to view action as a spectrum of potential possibilities, not simply as a few go or no-go intervention points.
- A willingness to make firm decisions on the basis of imperfect and limited data and, despite the omnipresent risk and uncertainty, to have the courage and self-confidence to carry out the proposed action.
- A sense for the critical, the jugular. Managers must set the right priorities for attention—select action points essential to their organization's resolution

of its crucial problems.
- The ability—marrying analytic discipline with personal creativity—to create a vision of what the undertaking is all about. Such a scenario for the future enables the manager to tie actions taken in a specific context to a larger conception of what is to be accomplished.
- The skill of converting targets into accomplishments. Managers do not confuse intent with impact. They understand the complexity of implementation, the process of converting abstract goals into the committed behavior of the organization's members. Action requires skill in carving out doable tasks and sequencing these initiatives for maximum effectiveness, as well as a sense for when objectives and plans need to be reappraised.
- An understanding that almost all management challenges are grounded in the human and organizational context. Technical, financial, or conceptual issues usually become "people problems" as they move toward the action stage. They can be dealt with only when those human issues are resolved.
- An appreciation of the major limits of managerial action. The complexity of the general manager's problems rules out "solutions" in the conventional sense of that word. Instead, the manager must settle for accommodations, knocking off the rough edges of the problem, knowing that it will never disappear and, even if managed successfully, will recur.

We have identified five basic dimensions of the case method of instruction. It is not the individual elements in isolation that give force to the method, however, but their fusion into an operational gestalt. When this blend of the cognitive and affective is built into the preconscious, it has a unique capacity to prepare a student for continuous learning, growth, and administrative maturity throughout his or her career.

Evaluating Case Discussions

As in many other professional fields, it is difficult to evaluate the overall effectiveness of management education.[42] Our tests measure only partial ele-

---

42. See Martin R. Lip, *The Bitter Pill: Doctors, Patients and Failed Expectations* (New York: Harper & Row, 1980) and Greer Williams, *Western Reserve's Experiment in Medical Education and Its Outcome* (New York: Oxford University Press, 1980).

ments of practice, perhaps the less important ones. Christine McGuire puts the point dramatically: "After thirty years of research we do not have a satisfactory methodology for evaluating professional habits and attitudes. Perhaps a radical new approach is required to achieve any progress in this arena. . . . Work on the development of an acceptable theory or unifying conception of competence is urgent."[43] Grade designations do little more than sort out individuals who perform well and less well in academia. As J. Sterling Livingston and others have pointed out, there is little direct relationship between academic and practical accomplishments.[44] Perhaps Howard Gardner's concept of multiple kinds of intelligence offers us at least a partial answer.[45]

Nathaniel Cantor offers another explanation. Implicitly he asks us to consider whether our curriculum is not shaped by our sense of what we can teach well rather than by the needs of practice:

> Logic and mathematics do not begin to exhaust the nature of reality. Yet most of us have grown up in the tradition that the solution to human problems is found in statements, logical propositions. Our formal education is primarily intellectual. We learn answers, general propositions, abstract concepts. We accumulate facts but continue behaving pretty much the same as the generations of biblical times. Knowledge does not seem to make much difference.[46]

Whether or not Professor Livingston is correct, it is undoubtedly difficult to predict long-term results of any educational effort. To paraphrase Amy Lowell, teaching is like dropping ideas into the letterbox of the human unconscious. You know when they are posted but you never know when they will be received or in what form.

In the third phase of the seminar development effort, we attempted to learn more about this "post-

ing and delivery" process by comparing classes evaluated as "effective" and "poor" by students, instructor, and researcher. This rough-cut evaluation did not tell us anything about long-term educational results, but did give us some understanding of how students and teachers evaluated short-term case-course efforts. At a minimum it provided instructors with a profile of questions to ask about their current teaching situations.

One early finding departed somewhat from conventional wisdom. Instructors often judged a class "good" if there were numerous hands in the air, impressive verbal pyrotechnics, and a great deal of student excitement and laughter. Students, however, indicated that those classes, while enjoyable, often were not particularly useful and tended to be forgotten. Our inquiries identified several characteristics of a successful case discussion class and course.

1. The section functions as a learning group. Students are usually assigned to a specific discussion section. They may or may not already know their sectionmates. Productive case discussions typically developed only after that agglomeration of individuals had been converted into a cohesive learning community.

In some sections, after weeks of togetherness, the class was still an assemblage of individuals; students sitting next to one another were distant neighbors. Individual interests dominated the discussion patterns, and the overall group accepted few responsibilities. Other sections had gone through an acculturation process that enhanced the possibilities for effective discussion. Individual students behaved so as to make contributions to the section's learning requirements. The section as a whole was sensitive to the specific learning needs of individual members and maximized the opportunities for them to contribute. The section took responsibility for the setting of academic standards; the discovery, exploration, and resolution of case issues; and the enforcement of appropriate standards of discussion behavior.

Productive case discussions were much more likely to occur in such a cohesive learning group and were typically characterized by a high level of student-to-student discussion. Where instructor-to-student interactions dominated, it was often an indication that the section had not yet made the transition to a learning group.

43. Christine H. McGuire, "Evaluation of Student and Practitioner Competence," Chapter 12, in Frank Stritter, ed., "Faculty Evaluation and Development" in *Handbook of Health Professions Education* (San Francisco: Jossey-Bass, 1983).
44. See J. Sterling Livingston, "The Myth of the Well-Educated Manager," *Harvard Business Review,* January–February 1971, pp. 79–89.
45. Howard Gardner, *Frames of Mind* (New York: Basic Books, 1985).
46. Nathaniel Cantor, *The Learning Process for Managers* (New York: Harper & Brothers, 1958), p. 85.

2. *High levels of student involvement.* Involvement is the hallmark of any case discussion, but in certain class sessions extraordinary levels of involvement developed.

Discussion dialogue can develop at three levels. At the first level, students explore a problem by sorting out relevant facts, developing logical conclusions, and presenting them to fellow students and the instructor. The students discuss someone else's problem; their role is that of a commentator-observer in a strictly academic sense.

The second level of discussion may be achieved by assigning to students roles in the case under discussion. Their comments then tend to reflect a sense for the organizational and personal circumstances of the company managers whose robes they wear. Their analyses and recommendations embrace both academic logic and company dynamics. When the role-playing session is completed, the section resumes a regular case discussion pattern, but the dialogue usually is more firmly rooted in practical realities. The section has moved away from the external observer's role toward that of an involved insider.

The third discussion level is reached when students, on their own initiative, project themselves into the situation. The classroom and case meld together, with the students vicariously acting as the firm's executive group (an unusually large one). Problems are not discussed as abstract topics, but as issues inextricably bound up in a manager's career and power circumstance. Student comments reflect a personal commitment to the arguments advanced. This level of discussion comes as close to real life as can be achieved in an academic situation. Learning opportunities and risk, however, are high for all.

3. *Instructor direction, not domination, of the discussion.* Instructor direction, as opposed to control, of the class is critical. In classes controlled by instructors, the students' obligations were simple: They had only to follow a predetermined teaching plan, question by question. The instructor decided issues to be discussed and determined when these points had been adequately covered. There was little room for student-initiated exploration or discovery. Students knew that once they had worked through the instructor's teaching plan, they would be given his or her summary of significant conclusions.

This instructional style may be comfortable for the instructor, but it provides thin educational gruel for a student. Kenneth Eble makes a similar point:

> I once had an intense argument with an English teacher who took me to task for saying offhandedly that a teacher could be too well organized. That seemed to me a simple truth implicit in Melville's remark that "there are some enterprises in which a careful disorderliness is the true method." But to her my statement assailed revealed truth. Organization was on an ascending scale, the highest organization, I presume, approximately of being heaven. For me, organization, like other principles that rule our lives, is more like temperature, offering a range in which humans can live: comfortably but with extremes where discomfort begins. Surely students, from primary school classes to graduate seminars, are familiar with teachers who are simply too organized. It may be a passion for organization distorts the actual relationships among a collection of diverse particulars. Or the organizing power of the teacher may leave too little for the student to do and offer too few possibilities for seeking a structure closer to the student's own understanding. Teachers can be, as one student told me, "beautifully organized but dull as hell."[47]

In other discussion classes we observed a free-flowing, instructor-student collaborative exploration that we categorized as leadership via direction. This "directional" style of leadership was fostered by a complex of factors, of which two seemed most important. First, the instructor provides the students with a path of inquiry—a conceptual framework for understanding the complexities of the problems being studied.[48] Second, he or she develops a teaching plan that considers both what is to be taught and *how* the discussion may unfold.

In the classroom, the instructor shapes and molds the discussion flow so as to make certain that critical case issues are covered in a disciplined way. Direction may take the form of questions, often derived from prior student comments; suggestions of alternative approaches to the problems; the highlighting of neglected information and its possible consequences; a request for clarification of assumptions;

47. Kenneth E. Eble, *The Craft of Teaching* (San Francisco: Jossey-Bass, 1976), p. 159.
48. See F. J. Roethlisberger, *The Elusive Phenomena*, ed. George F. F. Lombard (Boston: Harvard Business School, Division of Research, 1977), pp. 69–71.

or a strategically timed proposal for a summary by a section member or the exploration of alternative programs of action. In this way, the instructor can achieve discipline and productive discussion with a maximum of student input and freedom.

In summary, our observations suggested that case discussions were most productive when sections functioned as learning groups, students were personally involved in the discussion, and instructors directed the discussion process skillfully. These objectives, difficult to achieve, became the basis for the later development of our teaching seminars.

Some further clues to the personal impact of a well-taught case class emerged as students reviewed case discussion experiences with us. Here are some of their perceptions:

I learned something about myself; I really uncovered a blind spot in the way I deal with others.

Learning how to prepare a funds flow statement was a real mystery until Jill James explained it in class. Professor Abbot never could. I may go into banking now.

I didn't realize there were so many different ways of dealing with this "situation," and there are lots of "situations" in every case. I'm going to get away from "single track" thinking.

The module on cost accounting taught me a lot. It isn't just that I can understand variance analysis; more important, I could stand the pressure of not knowing—not making any progress for weeks. They were hell, but I didn't quit. Funny, I've gotten a lesson in patience and perseverance.

I went into class with one point of view; it came under attack! In the old days I would have dropped my idea immediately, but I stuck in there, gave ground where I saw I was weak, and came away having convinced most of my section that our plan was right. I can do it!

I'm now confident that I have a framework of understanding; how to understand and get things done in a company. That case gave me the final know-how on ways of working in complicated production circumstances.

I sure goofed! My plan was a good one and I had spent hours working it through. Yeah—but I ignored the key element: How was I going to convince others that doing it was the best plan?

You'll think it funny, but I came out of that class with a greater respect for Dad. I'd always figured he was nuts to spend his life at the office working his butt off. But business is a challenge; strategy makes a difference for workers too. Business can be done professionally.

These comments illustrate the rich and varied nature of student learning experiences in a case setting. They do not do justice to students' substantive learning experiences, however, emphasizing instead the development of personal insight into individual strengths and weaknesses, reaffirmation of the importance of qualities perhaps not fully appreciated—patience and persuasion, and confidence in one's own capacities to endure stress. Instructors must wonder how much of this can be planned or even predicted. Few of us set out to teach students patience or filial piety. We tend to assume, understandably and appropriately, the primacy of our academic objectives. What and when students learn is often only indirectly related to formal teaching plans.

Instructors commenting on productive discussion experiences believed that ideally students took the conceptual framework of the course, modified it to meet their personal requirements, and then practiced its application until use became intuitive. Their evaluations, however, tended to focus on the group rather than on specific students, and on the course as a whole rather than individual class sessions. A "good" section, with self-discipline, worked through cases—incorporating individual contributions into a unified discussion that produced not only situational diagnosis but pragmatic action suggestions. Where that process unfolded with a maximum of student-to-student interaction and student direction of the dialogue, the class was doubly successful. Instructors gave high marks to sections that understood both the power and the limits of course concepts, that noted not only conclusions but questions for further reflection.

As the course moved along, instructors evaluated progress by the section's ability to draw on previous sessions in analyzing the case of the day. When such linkages gradually built up a matrix of concepts and case problems that students could use to formulate summary operating generalizations, instructors believed course objectives had been substantially achieved.

The ultimate class, in their judgment, occurs

when section discussion imperceptibly melds academic dialogue with intense student involvement, mirroring the reality of organizational struggle and danger. The student confronts the circumstances of corporate life at close range. Cantor describes this well:

> What one wants to do, however, is not simply a matter of knowledge or analysis. What one *does* occurs in a complicated context of hope, fear, risk, courage, resistance, guilt, rationalization, confusion, ambivalence, and so on (dimensions of norms, ethical beliefs, and personal needs). It is a spectrum of feeling which eventuates in the drive or will or motivation which is the decision. To escape from the discomfort of struggle, to avoid the disagreeable feelings of uncertainty, inadequacy, and self-responsibility, we turn to the expert, the formula, the book, the superior or *the* verbal answer. Thus we think we avoid the heartache and the headache of assuming responsibility for our own decision. . . . Answers are, by definition, verbal propositions, statements, abstractions. The application of the answer requires a commitment, a bit of living with its accompanying disturbance, risk, and recognition of feelings.[49]

Amy Lowell was correct; we do not have a good way of understanding or evaluating how people learn. But in our brief excursion into this complicated area, we found a good bit of agreement between teachers and students as to the elements of an effective case class. Both felt the ultimate teaching objective was the student's development of a personally tested, intuitive pattern of understanding and acting in complex administrative situations.

While all of us hope for that ultimate case discussion, a more practical challenge is to improve our everyday teaching contribution. A central theme of these teaching seminars is that case instruction calls for a dual competency: command of the basic conceptual and knowledge component of one's field, and an ability to lead the class discussion process.

To emphasize the importance of process is not to denigrate the value of knowledge. It is the relationship of knowledge to practice that is critical for any practitioner. Sir William Osler, the great physician, makes the point well:

> To study the phenomena of disease without books
> Is to sail an uncharted sea
> While to study books without patients
> Is not to go to sea at all.[50]

For a teacher of management, the interplay of knowledge and the discussion process is critical. Like two scissor blades, both elements must work together for incisive learning. Not all instructors appreciate that reality; most students do.

The Seminar Program

Our seminar rests on a premise so basic that it must be stated: all of our teaching cases assume that the instructor has command of his or her professional field or academic discipline. Although we realize that, in most classroom circumstances, instructors must work with both the content and process dimensions of teaching, these cases and their associated case discussions tend to downplay content and emphasize process—often dramatically. This point understood, the following overview of the seminar program will give a brief account of the rationale for this organizational plan, the suggestions that inspired it, and a section-by-section introduction to the units into which we have divided this model curriculum.

Organization of Materials

The enterprise of organizing case materials into a formal curriculum is more complicated than a cursory glance might suggest. Every time the aspiring instructional architect thinks he or she has built a solid model, rotating it just a few degrees under the light of intellectual scrutiny reveals yet another unexpected facet. A case that seemed to fit the ethics module perfectly now shows characteristics that would go awfully well in the contract section. As colleague Abby J. Hansen has observed, good cases don't hold still. The attempt to pin them down not only is doomed to partial success, at best, but also is likely to deprive one of the opportunity to see them in the round.

Four characteristics of cases make them particularly challenging to organize:

49. Cantor, *The Learning Process for Managers*, pp. 86–87.

50. Sir William Osler, "Books and Men, Remarks," *Boston Medical and Surgical Journal*, 144 (January 17, 1901) 60–61. Reprinted with permission.

1. Cases are holistic. They are drawn from practice, which typically involves multiple problems and issues. The same case narrative can promote disciplined speculation about subjects as diverse as what information about students is appropriate for an instructor to have and what challenges are implicit in humor and game playing in class.

2. Not only do multiple problems coexist in the same case, but each problem can be discussed on a number of different levels of meaning. In our seminars, we often use the image of the "abstraction ladder" to suggest the possibility of considering any given case issue along a continuum that ranges from theory to "nuts and bolts" practicality. For example, one can treat the "Case of the Dethroned Section Leader" as a problem of how to deal with a disruptive student or use it to discuss ideas about power in the classroom.

3. Cases flow together. The discussion of a case is not a separate, discrete event, to be mentally filed away. Wednesday's discussion may continue, in greater breadth and depth, the questions raised in Monday's case. Or it may preview the problems that will come up for fuller consideration on Friday.

4. Participants almost always come to a case with their own agendas, based on the priorities of their own personal interests. These agendas will determine the areas that they wish to investigate—and they may or may not match the agenda of the syllabus. Even when these do match, the correlation is rarely precise.

In addition to the complexities noted above, the seminar organizer must remain mindful of the local situation, time available, faculty schedules and other commitments, and physical teaching facilities. All of this suggests that there is no single neat way to organize a case-based seminar. All the same, the seminar outline that follows is neither random nor arbitrary. We have ordered these materials to reflect a series of themes vitally important to the discussion teaching process, in a sequence that participants can grasp and instructors manage as their knowledge of how to work with one another increases and deepens, and the whole group gains sophistication.

How the Seminar Program Arrived at this Form: Learning by Doing

The seminar format that follows in Part II of this book is the result of more than a decade of experimentation. Participants from almost every major discipline and profession have contributed to our discussion groups, and we have developed a cohort of colleagues within our university and in other sister institutions. This network of talented, insightful participants and colleagues has provided the authors with invaluable suggestions for improvement, on a continuing basis, and helped the seminar design evolve—as we hope it will continue to do.

We have responded to participants' suggestions about course organization in a number of ways. One was to reflect the normal trajectory of a course, beginning with start-up procedures and the challenges of novice, or younger, instructors. Another was to provide material and suggestions to help make the introductory sessions welcoming, exciting, and fun. Our seminar "graduates" have helped us realize how important it is to intrigue, not intimidate, participants, and to give them some indications of the unique and special aspects of using a case discussion pedagogy.

We have also developed a small number of powerful cognitive tools or approaches that are critical to discussion leadership—ways to approach the day-to-day complexities of a discussion. Underlying this idea is the activity of building a common language system for talking about the challenges of discussion leadership. By suggesting concepts like the "teaching-learning contract" and the fundamental skill triad of "questioning, listening, and responding," we invite seminar participants from very different disciplines to use common terminology. This shared language system, in turn, helps specialists from diverse backgrounds not only communicate and help one another, but also see how much common ground they share as teachers. To promote this intellectual collaboration and cross-pollination further, we have included cases from a wide variety of different teaching settings.

We have arranged our cases to flow from a more focused type ("The French Lesson" or "The Day the Heat Went On") through materials that highlight a wider range of problems, to materials that pose even wider questions for the academy as a whole ("Who Should Teach?"). And we have also tried to organize our materials into a series of intellectual building blocks, or modules, with enough material to permit a prospective instructor to design a seminar to suit his or her own needs. One reason that we have fashioned a prototype seminar of this length is to honor participants' observations that the enterprise of learning new skills, attitudes, concepts, and approaches to a problem takes time.

A bird's-eye view of the seminar will show that the first section sets the scene and introduces the notion of learning by reading stories and discussing their meanings, interrelations, theoretical implications, and applicability to one's own professional challenges. The seminar group has the chance to view familiar territory from new perspectives and see the unsuspected richness that others' points of view can reveal in seemingly mundane events. Section 2 introduces the multiple, sometimes conflicting, roles that teachers assume when they take up discussion pedagogy. Sections 3 ("contract"), 4 ("key skills"), and 5 (leadership style—"control and guidance") help seminar participants improve the way in which they approach and act on some inevitable challenges that discussion teaching presents. (In these sections, in particular, the seminar group has a chance to work at building a language system for communicating with colleagues on this extraordinarily complex subject.)

Section 6 ("operational challenges"), the longest, stands alone. It can be used as a "case bank" from which to select modules that seem appropriate to one's own department or institution. Sections 7 ("ethical dilemmas") and 8 ("wider questions") form a pair; they exist on a more philosophical level than the preceding units.

Some Fundamental Characteristics of the Seminar

First, the seminar emphasizes the *universality* of the basic knowledge, skills, and attitudes required for effective discussion teaching. Instructors from diverse disciplines and professional fields like literature, astronomy, religion, music, architecture, medicine, and business share common premises and principles for dealing with the challenges and opportunities presented by this pedagogy. In our seminars, instructors from widely different academic specialties and types of institutions have learned from one another because of, not despite, their diversity.

Second, the seminar is primarily *practice-oriented*, not theoretical, in nature. It aims to help any participant, from a doctoral candidate or teaching fellow to a senior professor with decades of experience, to sense, understand, and respond effectively to the challenges of the discussion setting.

Third, the seminar is *case based*, presenting some 35-plus incidents drawn from actual practice and

crafted by clinical researchers to provide learning opportunities. A good case looks at a deceptively simple event and describes its complexity—thus providing ample opportunity for a discussion group to confront, explore, and learn from the stubbornness of practice. It gives life to James Russell Lowell's aphorism, "One thorn of experience is worth a whole wilderness of warning."[51] Cases are rich in what Professor Jerome Bruner calls "predicaments," puzzles without neat and simple answers, packed with opportunities for "discovery rather than learning about it."

Despite inevitable stylistic differences—these cases were developed over time, at different institutions, with the objective of exploring a spectrum of teaching challenges—each case will enable you to experience the learning of the whole in the particular; each will provide you with a contained, bounded teaching instrument that encourages an expansive, even constructively explosive, learning opportunity. As colleague Abby J. Hansen reminds us, cases, if taught effectively, generate an abundance of questions, a variety of next-step options, and a multiplicity of wider issues that link the discussion of the hour to past and future dialogue.

Some of these cases are stand-alone, single-teaching instruments. Others have been divided into multiple segments to enhance learning. Some 20-plus readings, encapsulating the wisdom of master practitioners, provide useful support in our efforts to provide intellectual nourishment for members of the seminar.

Major Goals of the Seminar

The seminar's overarching aims are to help instructors become more skillful and professional in their discussion leadership, to encourage seminar participants to view class as both a teaching and a research opportunity, a chance to learn more about the barriers and gateways[52] to effective discussion learning and, finally, to gain additional respect for the complexity and creativity involved in case dis-

51. James Russell Lowell, "Shakespeare Once More," *Among My Books* (Boston: Fields, Osgood & Co., 1870).
52. David Garvin suggests some of the institutional, cultural, and personal barriers to "active learning," and some fundamental changes in approach that can open the gateway to this pedagogy in "Barriers and Gateways to Learning," in *Education for Judgment: The Artistry of Discussion Leadership*, edited by C. Roland Christensen, David A. Garvin, and Ann Sweet (Boston: Harvard Business School Press, 1991), pp. 3–13.

cussion teaching. These objectives, however, are only a means to the ultimate goal of any teacher: the development of educated, creative men and women who will contribute their talents to society's needs.

We subscribe enthusiastically to Sir Richard Livingstone's statement of an educator's fundamental mission:

> For the teacher to have clearly in his mind this distinction of means and ends, and the need for higher ends, to feel that he is training his pupils to live a life that is a symphony and not a series of disconnected noises—even if they are beautiful noises—to see that while they acquire the means which they need for the practical purpose of life, they should also form an idea of the end at which they should aim. If that could be done, we should have cured the chief disease of our times. If you want a description of our age, here is one: The civilization of means without ends; rich in means beyond any other epoch, and almost beyond human needs; squandering and misusing them because it has no overruling ideal; an ample body with a meager soul.[53]

The conversion of this lofty goal into day-to-day practice is the ultimate end of our teaching seminars.

The Course Materials

SECTION 1. TEACHING AND THE CASE METHOD OF DISCUSSION: OPPORTUNITIES, DILEMMAS, AND RISKS. Although content is always important, in this opening section of the course, the social goal of creating a cohesive, inclusive group culture overshadows a rigorous concern for covering all the issues that the material might suggest. At this point in the curriculum, it is less important to dwell on categories of problems than to experience and examine the *process* by which an assemblage of individuals transforms itself into a learning group in partnership with an instructor, in pursuit of academic goals. It is as much the instructor's task in this section to set a welcoming, supportive tone as to promote incisive commentary.

The cases in this group describe incidents from the early stages of courses, when the classroom culture has not yet been set into some definitive mold. (One class, in fact, was a start-up.) In unsettled environments like these, events like a walkout, a wolf whistle, and a student's indiscreet comment about another's private life have the potential to create major disruptions—and learning opportunities as well.

As an initiation to the case discussion process, these cases give the seminar group a chance to experience how a discussion class really works with an instructor. The participants can see the pattern of a discussion flow, which tends to move from analysis ("What's going on?"), to action ("What should the case character do?"), to reflection ("What wider issues does this suggest?"). This group of materials also opens the door to the critical issue of the teaching-learning contract, which we consider in more depth in section 3, and which will recur over and over in the participants' professional experiences.[54]

Like most enterprises that provide opportunities for real rewards, discussion teaching also contains risks and dilemmas. These opening cases show teachers who encounter unexpected problems during classroom dialogue with students. The instructors differ from one another. One is male, the others female; two are in liberal arts disciplines, one in a professional setting. Their courses and academic subjects differ as well: two are in the humanities, and one in a more technical subject. But the teachers also have much in common. All are relatively inexperienced, and encounter jarring challenges in class. All seem anxious to help their students learn, but are not necessarily aware of all the subtleties involved in balancing the students' needs with their own. None of these instructors appears humorless or rigid, but, on the other hand, none seems willing to forgo the students' respect. All face a dilemma: How to balance good feelings in the classroom with order, seriousness, and decorum.

The cases in this module highlight the element of

---

53. Sir Richard Livingstone, *On Education* (New York: Cambridge University Press, 1956), p. 99.

54. Abby J. Hansen, "Establishing a Teacher/Student Learning Contract," in *Education for Judgment*, edited by Christensen, Garvin, and Sweet, makes three basic points about the contract: although omnipresent, it is often overlooked because of the subtlety of many of its elements; it consists of explicit (stated) and implicit (behaved) aspects; and, despite the elusive nature of its implicit component, it may be examined and influenced with a degree of conscious choice.

surprise. In each story, the instructor has an unexpected experience. Moreover, the experiences have the potential to damage the fabric of the classroom relationship and the mutual respect of teacher and students. Although the protagonists in these cases happen to be relatively young instructors, it is useful to remember that the potential for surprise never truly deserts the classroom.

This group of cases gives the seminar participants an early opportunity to discover by experience how a case works as a document—what it means to read and prepare an (A) segment, discuss it, and then be given the (B) and, perhaps, (C) portions to read and discuss in class. Going through this process, the group will begin to develop operating patterns. It will consider analyses, actions, and wider questions and start to link cases. Members of the class will start to see the relationship between who one is and how one operates in a group setting. They will begin to learn by considering other people's interpretations of experience (both in the case and in the class) and, through that lens, gain new perspective on their own interpretations.

At this early stage of the seminar, the group will begin to experience the power that multiple minds can bring to a common intellectual exploration. To students familiar with theoretical analysis of clearly defined problems, the storm of inquiry unleashed by what had seemed, just hours earlier, to be a very simple question can come as a shock. One lesson of this introductory portion of the seminar is that, in group discussion, there is virtually no such thing as an "open and shut" case. The richness, depth, and complexity of the case data illustrate Nietzsche's observation that "all that is profound wears a mask." The faces that our cases reveal may seem easily readable at first, or even second, glance. But the process of engaged group discussion generally exposes layers of complexity and ambiguity.

Participants often comment that they find this discovery both exhilarating and unsettling, in proportions that vary, of course, from person to person. But the energy of this discovery can help fuel a simultaneous process of great importance: the building of a partnership that will allow the group to become a learning community. This process will continue (becoming ever more complex) throughout the course.

In the opening sessions of the seminar, the instructor has the responsibility to discover as much as possible about the students—how they think, their strengths, weaknesses, and interests—and to give them the chance to learn about her or him. This is the point in the life cycle of the course when the students can absorb the lesson that the discussion leader respects them as partners in a joint adventure in which all parties bear responsibility.[55] It is also the time when teachers can begin to set behavioral boundaries (the "go" and "no-go" in this class), and to present visions of collective objectives—beyond improving one's discussion leadership skills and techniques—for the seminar.

To promote these goals and permit the group to discover its own pace, we have included short, terse cases in this portion of the model syllabus. Alert discussion leaders will let their discussion groups enact their own versions of the rites of introduction without rushing them. These cases require no major investments of time to read and reread. Their central problems are of the common garden variety, readily accessible and familiar to most teachers. They portray no exotic misadventures, just teachers biting down on that unexpected bit of grit in the salad of classroom life. The familiar material in these cases will help participants see the multilayered nature of the problems that they contain.

All of the apparently simple problems in these cases have roots in the fundamental dynamic of all teaching, which involves respect, community, and cooperation, and which takes place within the context of a behavioral contract among all concerned. These cases give participants and instructors a chance to glimpse some universals that shape all discussion leadership, not just case method teaching. They foreshadow abiding themes (respect, community, and cooperation don't die away; they grow more complicated) and permit students and instructors to begin to construct a conceptual model that shows the links among not only the cases in this section, but all of the course materials *and* their own daily practices.

Last, and perhaps most important, these cases give participants a chance to experience how it feels

55. Compare the discussion of the unique qualities of the give-and-take relationship among students and teachers in the discussion setting in C. Roland Christensen, "Every Student Teaches and Every Teacher Learns: The Reciprocal Gift of Discussion Teaching," in *Education for Judgment*, edited by Christensen, Garvin, and Sweet, pp. 99–119.

to be a student again—more precisely, a student in a discussion setting—and to appreciate the intellectual complexity of what we, as instructors, are asking our students to do in discussion classes.

SECTION 2. THE ROLES, RESPONSIBILITIES, AND SKILLS OF THE CASE DISCUSSION LEADER.

In moving from lecturing to discussion leadership, one exchanges a fairly straightforward classroom role—primary authority, explainer, or elucidator of knowledge—for one with so many facets that it may be most easily grasped as a collection of roles, rather than one. Lecturers bear a different relationship to their students than discussion leaders do. Lecturers need to gauge their audiences in order to pitch the material to their interests and level of sophistication and adjust the pace to suit their needs. But the simple fact that lecturers do almost all of the talking in class gives them more power in the instructor-student relationship than discussion leaders command. We do not intend to suggest that students are powerless in lectures. On the contrary, they can signal lack of interest in many subtle and unsubtle ways. But their general acceptance of the task of listening while the lecturer speaks gives the lecturer virtually sole control of the "air time" (and, with it, the overall quality) of the class.

Discussion teachers experience a very different balance of power in class: their students talk more than they do and, thus, "run" much of the class. This alone suggests that discussion teachers must become their students' partners. In practice, discussion teachers and their students experience an ever shifting balance of rights and responsibilities that is often difficult to perceive and evaluate, let alone fine tune. Instead of playing one major role, as a lecturer does, discussion teachers play many—musical conductor, moderator, tour guide, cheerleader, traffic cop, sounding board, summarizer, fellow learner, resource center, and, occasionally, sphinx.[56]

If one chooses to move to a case discussion pedagogy (it doesn't work for every subject matter) and accept the multiplicity of the roles that one will play, one must also expect to shoulder new and more complex responsibilities.[57] Lecturers must pay attention to the quality of an audience's response and its apparent absorption of their expositions of material. But discussion leaders must also be concerned about group dynamics and how this aspect of a class helps or hinders the learning process. The ability to lead a group in discussion requires shifting from primary (although not, of course, exclusive) allegiance to the material to primary alliance with students. Crudely put, the lecturer brings the material to the students, while the discussion leader does the reverse. The responsibility of the discussion leader is, then, to work toward dual competency: mastery of the techniques of discussion leadership as well as of the content of the course.[58]

In this portion of the syllabus, the group has a chance to begin to consider the changing skill requirements that accompany the change in roles. As discussion leader, sharing the floor with students and encouraging them to question one another, the instructor must be concerned with a core triad of skills: questioning, listening, and responding. (The seminar addresses these at length in section 4.)

The cases in this group share the theme of movement from the didactic to the discussion mode—thus providing the group with opportunities to examine the myriad implications of the changes in roles, responsibilities, and skills that this shift implies. When instructors change from lecturing to discussion leadership, they often sense a loss of power. The paradox of this phenomenon is that, by ceding a measure of control (or, rather, exchanging a central leadership role for one of partnership and shared power), they may trigger even more potent learning experiences for their students and, of course, themselves.

Assuming the role of discussion moderator introduces uncertainties into the teaching process. There is a world of difference (and danger) between delivering a prepared analysis of, say, Shakespeare's im-

56. For a fuller discussion, compare Richard F. Elmore, "Foreword" (pp. ix–xix) and C. Roland Christensen, "Premises and Practices of Discussion Teaching" (pp. 15–34), in *Education for Judgment*, edited by Christensen, Garvin, and Sweet.

57. Compare Elmore on the distinction between transferring knowledge and transforming students, and David A. Garvin "A Delicate Balance: Ethical Dilemmas and the Discussion Process" (pp. 287–303) in *Education for Judgment*, edited by Christensen, Garvin, and Sweet on issues like the multidimensional character of concepts like fairness in a discussion setting.

58. For a fuller discussion of this topic, see Christensen, "Premises and Practices of Discussion Teaching," premise 4: "Discussion teaching requires dual competency: the ability to manage content and process."

agery of defeat in *Richard II* and asking a student to kick off an educational discussion by commenting on a passage from the play (as Bea Benedict discovers in "The Case of the Dethroned Section Leader"). A discussion leader does not play the role of sole expert on the course content. Nor can he or she simply order students to do things in the classroom. The discussion leader shares power with the students in a seamless give-and-take of reciprocity.[59]

In "Look at the Fish!," the student Karen Prentiss gives us some detailed glimpses of the beginning of one discussion course (providing a natural bridge back to the first section of this syllabus, in which we concentrate on start-ups). She describes one teacher's discussion-leading style and its effect on her personal uncertainties at this point in her career (her second day of graduate school).

"How Do You Expect Us to Get This. . . ?" offers a glimpse of what happens when one moves, in mid-course, from telling students the facts about a discipline to letting them discover them for themselves. Mary Ann Demski's adventures portray, from the instructor's point of view, the disruption in the balance of power that results when a teacher takes a step toward introducing discussion-based teaching into a lecture-based, content-oriented course.

We then continue this theme in "Trouble in Stat. 1B," where the problem gains further complexity: Dan Shea wants to shift a whole course to a case discussion model, in a setting where this hasn't been done before. This attempt poses unexpected challenges for the teacher who must forge a partnership with his students when other teachers in the same course aren't working with them in this way.

Finally, we move to "The Case of the Dethroned Section Leader," which briefly portrays a young teacher (unlike the more experienced Dan Shea of "Stat. 1B,") trying to learn how to start a discussion group and facing some issues of control (coverage of the material), responsibility (who should lead the discussion?), and power. This case opens the way for fundamental questions: What rudimentary steps must any discussion leader take in using cases?

59. See Christensen, "Every Student Teaches and Every Teacher Learns," *Education for Judgment,* on the measure to which students control the process of their own learning in discussion teaching.

SECTION 3. ESTABLISHING, MONITORING, AND MODIFYING A TEACHING/LEARNING CONTRACT.

Three primary aspects of the teacher-student learning contract stand out in high relief. First, contracts are ubiquitous, although subtle and often difficult to appreciate. Second, they consist of two components: explicit elements, such as course descriptions, grading policies, and syllabi; and implicit elements, such as how people address and respond to one another in class. Third, contracts can be evaluated and, when necessary, changed—often with help from a sympathetic and keen observer. In the absence of a written document stipulating norms of conduct, many teachers and students fail to realize that a behavioral contract exists, let alone appreciate its power. But, in practice, the behavioral and attitudinal aspects of the contract often overwhelm the explicit, stated parts. This makes the unwritten aspects of contracts all the more important to recognize and control. The effort, although complicated, can be worth the trouble.

Teachers who treat students sarcastically set contracts of belittlement and abuse, not support and nurturing. Students who skip class and miss assignments set contracts of mistrust and disappointment. Teachers who "spoon feed" students set contracts of dependency. Every aspect of how teachers and students deal with one another, both in and outside of the classroom, plays a part in the teaching/learning contract.

Contracts can, of course, vary considerably from teacher to teacher, and from culture to culture. Cultures that reward verbal agility and outspokenness will have very different teaching and learning contracts from cultures that prize silence and public self-effacement. (The cases that we group under the heading of "Diversity" in the seminar section, "The Case Discussion Leader in Action: Operational Challenges and Opportunities," provide some opportunities to examine the special challenges of teaching/learning contracts among people from different cultures who speak different languages.)

Whatever its initial assumptions, however, every teaching-learning contract changes over time. This happens partly because students learn more and more of the material, and thus narrow the gap between their competence and the instructor's, and partly because they grow to appreciate the centrality of their role in the teaching and learning process. Teachers converse differently with beginners than they do with intermediate or advanced students. And experienced discussion participants both ask and respond to questions differently than neophytes do. As the contract changes, the proportions of teacher-student versus student-student dialogue tend to change. All through the course, the vocabulary, level of intellectual complexity, and dynamics of the relationships change—and, with them, the contracts. For example, a teacher who waits patiently for a class to comprehend a fairly simple calculation in the first week of a statistics course may well become irritated if the pace hasn't picked up several weeks later. And the students who listen avidly to the teacher's step-by-step explanations of introductory problems in the first weeks are likely to doodle, yawn, and pass sarcastic notes if she continues this approach in the eighth week.[60]

Although the issue of the teaching-learning contract is universal, the cases in this section highlight it with particular clarity. A few of the basic issues that these cases raise are: How does one define a contract? Why is it important? How can instructors establish a contract? What happens when they pay no attention to it? How does one modify an unsatisfactory one? What is the difference between the explicit and implicit components of a contract? How can one appreciate the implicit contract since so much of behavior is unconscious? How much influence should students have on the contract? Should an instructor have one contract for all students or make exceptions?

SECTION 4. QUESTIONING, LISTENING, AND RESPONDING: THE KEY SKILL REQUIREMENTS. The materials in this section of our prototype syllabus share a dominant motif: They all focus on aspects of the three activities to which discussion teachers devote most of their classroom time: questioning, listening, and responding.[61] There is some betrayal

60. Abby Hansen has discussed this subject more fully in "Establishing a Teaching/Learning Contract," in *Education for Judgment*, edited by Christensen, Garvin, and Sweet, pp. 123–135.

61. C. Roland Christensen's "The Discussion Teacher in Action: Questioning, Listening, and Response," in *Education for Judgment*, edited by Christensen, Garvin, and Sweet, pp. 153–172, explores the complexities of these aspects of discussion leadership, revealing some of the many types of questions that a discussion leader can employ at different stages of a class, and for different purposes, the special challenges of active listening—and some techniques with which one can improve this often undervalued skill—and the multiplicity of responses that are available to a discussion leader.

in naming these skills separately, for they flow into one another and form a holistic triad. One listens and responds to a seminar group, and to individuals, even as one mentally prepares, formulates, and poses the next question. And the act of responding to a participant's contribution certainly requires listening. But it would be a mistaken—or at least greatly oversimplified—assumption that the ideal discussion is nothing but a chain of questions and responses. And an even more dangerous mistake to assume that the seminar leader bears sole responsibility for fielding every answer and flinging a question back in response. Responding can be quite different from replying; body language can be more eloquent and effective than words. Genuinely engaged, productive discussions aren't volleyball games, with the discussion leader on one side and all the participants on the other. They tend to run like streams, in ebbs, flows, eddies, bends, and even occasional moments of stillness.

Although the prime focus of the most sophisticated group discussions tends to fall anywhere but on the leader, leaders do spend a lot of their classroom time at the physical focal point of the room—a position that, along with the many other invisible trappings of leadership, attracts attention and symbolizes power. This centrality of position confers a certain responsibility on the discussion leader: even when talk centers on a "hot spot" in a distant part of the room, the students notice the leader's responses (even the subtle, unconscious ones), and these affect the discussion.

All these observations suggest that the often overlooked skills of questioning, listening, and responding are so central to the art of discussion leadership that even minor improvements in instructors' awareness and command of them are likely to enhance the quality of the discussion as a whole. In questioning, the key is to realize the potentially infinite variety of questions and the implications of how one poses them. In listening, it is helpful to be selective and decide what aspects of what one hears are likely to be the most telling. In responding, the point is to become aware of body language, breadth of options, and, as always, the overtones and implications of what one does (and says) for the culture of the classroom. How can one put such insights to work? By doing things as fundamental as developing and operationalizing one's own typology of questions. For example, when would you use a challenge question? When would you ask a predictive question? When do your questions become more abstract, and when more personal and detailed?

While the cases in this part of the syllabus invite exploration of many facets of this triad of skills, they tend to stress the operational aspect. How does one choose which student to recognize? Does one make a random selection? Does one call on the student whose hand has been raised longest? (Our experience suggests not. A raised hand often stops thought. The hand-waving student usually has a comment left over from an earlier moment in the discussion.)

Sensitive listening is the bridge between questioning and responding. Our approach highlights five practical rules of thumb:

First, in early sessions of a seminar, we ask numerous "checking questions." "Is that what you said, Elaine? Did Mike hear your point?" When miscommunication occurs—and the first law of communication is to expect miscommunication—we explore the reasons for the breakdown. These interchanges serve as a continuing reminder that listening is hard and that, as a class, we have to keep working to overcome this problem and improve our communication.

Second, we emphasize the fundamental distinction between listening for content and listening for underlying feelings: the hidden agenda. Instructors must make continual split-second decisions about which level to address.

Our third principle relates closely to the second: Effective listening is difficult under any circumstances, but easier when you know something about the person. Knowing a participant helps the instructor hear what she is really saying, especially when her unvoiced feelings are critical to the discussion.

Fourth, constructive listening requires that one understand not only what the other person has said, but also what he or she might have been expected to say—but did not. We need to keep in mind what the class has been talking about and what it may be talking about in the next few minutes, in the next few classes.

Our final working proposition can be expressed by an old Swiss proverb, "When one shuts one eye, one does not hear everything." Observations of the entire classroom scene, its hot and cool spots, the speaker's manner in making a point, and the reaction of the other person, or people, to whom the message is being sent—all contribute to the teacher's understanding.

The crafting of questions, practice in sensitive listening, and delivery of constructive responses are the key skill requirements for effective discussion teaching. Our ability to stimulate meaningful classroom dialogue, with multiple individual insights and points of view, and to create circumstances in which individual students may practice seminar skills and gain in knowledge, maturity, and wisdom depend in large measure on our ability to carry out these tasks.

SECTION 5. THE CRITICAL INSTRUCTIONAL CHOICE: GUIDANCE VS. CONTROL. A reliable predictor that an instructor is on the way to playing every discussion participant's least favorite game—"What's on Teacher's Mind?"—is his or her impulse (conscious or not) to control every facet of the discussion. One simple way to monitor the proceedings for this cardinal instructional sin is to listen to proportions of "air time." Are you outtalking your students?

In a healthy discussion, satisfying to teacher and participants alike, the teacher neither knows in advance what questions the participants will answer nor even necessarily understands all of the implications of their answers as they are presented. Probing implications is the business of the group as a whole, and understanding, a highly personal matter, may not take shape until long after the last voice in this discussion has faded.

We propose that, while the discussion leader is fundamentally responsible for the success of the proceedings, he or she will get better results by guiding than by controlling. And we hope to focus discussion, not on issues of discipline, although these surely do arise, but on the management of the discussion process itself. We suggest that guiding the proceedings leaves students room to answer freely, playfully, and creatively, while controlling them creates artificial and stifling attempts at compliance (which can lead to resentment and mutiny). We also suggest that, in a genuine discussion class, where students feel secure and supported by the instructor, surprising and often ground-breaking contributions can emerge—unplanned, unanticipated, and unforced. Instructors who attempt to control students' responses risk not only creating a stultifying atmosphere, but also boring themselves. In a true discussion class, teachers learn, and it is impossible to learn what one already knows.

We hasten to note that we do not endorse anarchy. Faced with a clearly unacceptable situation—an attack on a weak member of the group, a comment so insulting that no one in the class mistakes its hurtful intent, or a chain of logic so faulty that it must lead to a preposterous conclusion—the instructor will have to face the fact that he or she is in charge. A smoothly functioning discussion section can, at times, appear leaderless, but, in times of crisis or extreme dysfunction, the responsible leader can and should take control. We recommend that, whatever form this control may take, its roots lie in the most important control of all: *self*-control. And we further recommend that control be exerted only when guidance fails.

What do we mean by guidance? A host of activities, all rooted in an attitude of collaboration, cooperation, partnership, and respect. Guidance is subtle; it works by modeling, prompting, supporting, and showing respect by occasionally turning over the reins of leadership. A guide exerts power benevolently, protecting the weaker and slower members of a group and encouraging the stronger to do the same. The connotations of control are harsher. Guidance can and should involve humor; control often tends to sarcasm. Guidance gives shape and direction to a discussion, but never dominates. Control, by contrast, tends to stifle the more tentative members of the group and inhibit their participation.

In our experience, it is difficult, at best, to create and sustain a relationship of reciprocal trust and respect with a group of students. Gentle guidance makes the bond; harsh control cracks it. We offer the cases in this section to give participants an opportunity to sharpen their appreciation of distinctions between guidance and control, and begin to improve their skills as guides.

SECTION 6. THE CASE DISCUSSION LEADER IN ACTION: OPERATIONAL CHALLENGES AND OPPORTUNITIES. This section as a whole is organized into four modules. The first two cluster around fundamental complexities of teaching that have always been recognized as important, no matter what the pedagogy, but which gain special complexity in case discussion teaching. The teacher-student relationship is fundamental to any learning situation. It is hard to imagine a teacher who will find these problems totally unfamiliar. It is also hard to imagine a teacher who will find them comfortable, uncomplicated, or easy to deal with. The second module deals with one of the most persistent, and all too often painful, chores of academe: evaluation and grading.

The next two modules—suggested by former participants as central to the emerging classroom scene—involve issues of gender and diversity (in its broadest sense). These issues promise to test, in new ways, our abilities to be effective discussion leaders in a rapidly changing world. They also offer participants a host of ways to become even more creative in their day-to-day practice.

These cases present operational issues and challenges that appear over and over again in the push and tug of real classroom practice, in cases so rich in everyday detail that they might be considered as imaginative *practica,* or fieldwork. These cases contain many demands for action. While the instructors in all of our cases have options for action, some of them have fairly restricted choices. In these cases, there is a multiplicity of options to consider and weigh.

In studying and discussing these materials, seminar participants have an opportunity to polish and refine their diagnostic skills and to give increased time and attention to an action mode. How is the teacher going to get things to happen in these situations, given stubborn reality, with its annoying tendency to interfere with teachers' high-minded plans? In these cases, neither the teachers nor the readers have every bit of information that they might want. Reading them, the student learns a lot about how people spoke, moved, and acted. But—as in real life—even these data are insufficient to explain everything. These case characters are as imperfect as we are and equally undersupplied with time and resources to make perfect decisions and do the best possible job. This aspect makes these cases particularly likely to stimulate complex—and, we hope, personally involved—discussions.

Given the mix of cases and the seminar's process design (proceeding from a diagnostic mode to greater emphasis on operations and "getting things done"), one may expect a change in the way the classroom dialogue shapes up in this section. The instructor might open with an action question—"Margaret, how would you deal with this situation?"—and then shift back to a diagnostic mode—"Frank, why do you think Margaret made that recommendation?"—for a "check-up." A sequence of this sort is one way to link these two dimensions of thinking about teaching practice. One would also expect increased use of predictive questions in this section: "What do you think would happen if the principal character in this case did this or that?"

As a rule, by the time a seminar group has completed a substantial portion of the syllabus, classroom dialogue highlights the links between previous cases and the current case. Participants also tend to devote more attention to the wider challenges of both individual instructors and the academy as a whole. Our seminar materials also gradually turn to these wider challenges.

SECTION 7. ETHICAL DILEMMAS AND THE CASE DISCUSSION PROCESS. Colleague David Garvin reminds us that ethical choices—perhaps more complex than many of us realize—face all discussion teachers

> Ethical choices are unavoidable in discussion settings. Because they are normally embedded in routine decisions about classroom management and the flow and direction of discussion, with few obvious ethical overtones, heightened awareness is the critical first step toward ethical discussion leadership. Most of us need to develop greater sensitivity to the ethical implications of our in-class behavior, and must learn to think harder about the trade-offs we face among various forms of fairness. One way or the other, these decisions will be made. A conscious weighing of values will undoubtedly accomplish more than decisions made by default.[62]

As Garvin points out, our values may seem clear—We're all in favor of "fairness," aren't we?—but they have multiple implications in a discussion class that make them anything but simple. Under the heading "fairness," Garvin distinguishes five potentially conflicting categories: fairness to individuals, to the group, to the process, to the material, and to the teacher's own ethical beliefs, among the discussion leader's challenges and recommends that all discussion teachers cultivate "heightened awareness" to these issues.

Discussion leaders often find themselves on the firing line in class. Faced with an ethical dilemma, they must act swiftly, often with little more than impulse to shape what they do and say. The cases in this module of our syllabus feature interactions in which ethical issues—considerations of right and wrong—lie particularly close to the surface. And so do the emotions that ethical issues almost invariably stir up.

62. David A. Garvin, "A Delicate Balance: Ethical Dilemmas and the Discussion Process," in *Education for Judgment*, edited by Christensen, Garvin, and Sweet, pp. 287–303.

Discussion teaching always opens the classroom door to emotion. Case teaching intensifies this process by portraying real people and real events: Participants rarely fail to identify, positively or negatively, and this identification often results in the recounting of personal experience, which can be painful. All cases carry the potential to explode in unexpected ways, but perhaps none more powerfully than these, in which the teachers themselves probed painful emotional tissue. Given our explicit goal to improve quality of discussion teaching and learning, we cannot turn our backs on ethical questions, however uncomfortable some of them may be.

A badly delivered lecture may create problems. But the personal pain of a bungled discussion—perhaps a shy student has been "hung out to dry" by sharp-tongued public criticism, or an expert student has writhed in frustration while others wring the last drops of illogic from erroneous hypotheses—can cause real destruction. Should a teacher slight a student for the sake of a group, a point of logic, a needier student? Surely, questions like these lie at the very heart of discussion teaching.

The cases in this module progress in the level of detail and density of data, but all revolve around explicitly ethical dilemmas that teachers confronted, with varying degrees of success. These cases permit students and colleagues to focus on several issues, such as how a teacher manages her own personal ethical beliefs in dealings with individuals or small cohorts of students whose ethical systems may well differ from hers. They also provide a window through which to survey a whole area of ethical terrain: rules of courtesy and conduct. Like tufts of grass on quicksand, these can turn out to be less solidly grounded than they appear.

In the second two cases, issues of fairness come to the fore. To what extent should discussion teachers—in their capacity as nurturers and protectors—be expected to sacrifice their own personal opportunities to those of their students? And what rights and responsibilities do discussion leaders have to impose their own cherished ethical systems on groups? Where is the line between freedom of conscience and unacceptable behavior? And how can a teacher interpret the ethical implications of students' actions and words in class?

One of the purposes of this section is to remind discussion teachers that, if misunderstandings, arguments, and accusations can crop up in discussions about seemingly bland cases, then cases that deal with socially volatile topics are probably much more likely to generate heat. There is no way to predict fully the degree of heat, or when flames will burst out, but the preliminary exercise of thinking through—and testing—one's basic values will help ground one's response and, perhaps, make it possible to contain or douse the blaze. What sorts of exchanges are permissible? How can one tell if a student, or group of students, is being insulted? Who should act to remedy the situation, and how? All of these questions relate to basic value systems. None is easy or simple, and all depend on the cultural context in which one operates. What they have in common is a potential to wake up and roar at a teacher in the classroom. Instructors, be warned.

We have placed the cases in this section at this point in our model syllabus as a possible bridge linking operational issues to broader considerations that, in turn, relate the enterprise of discussion leading to the interests of society as a whole.

SECTION 8. SOME WIDER QUESTIONS. In this part of the course, we spiral back to some of the elements that marked the start of the seminar. As a rule, we slow the pace (which can both quicken and heat up during the action-oriented and ethically charged portions of the course). At this point, we give attention to the administrative, philosophical, and personal details of closure. We ask students for formal and informal feedback. And we suggest next steps for them: that they reflect on all that has taken place, including the cases, discussions, relationships, and their own reactions; that they think about what the seminar has meant to them; that they dwell not only on the cases, but on the readings that have impressed them; and that they take time to link their thoughts to the details of their own practice.

We also hope to broaden our focus to a social perspective and remind participants that teaching is one of the least isolated phenomena. Who teaches? Far more people than actually write "teacher" under the heading "occupation" on their income tax forms. And they teach in many more places than classrooms. Doctors teach patients; clergy teach parishioners; executives teach their staffs and clients; parents teach children; older siblings teach younger siblings; supervisors teach workers. Anyone who tries to "get something across" to someone or help another human master a skill is a teacher.

The case in this section, "Who Should Teach?," addresses some of these issues. It contains the usual issues of diagnosis and action—should Paul Warburton be allowed to continue in the teacher training program; why or why not?—but more important, it addresses both wider and more fundamental questions. How do we prepare teachers? Is teaching a vocation or a profession? What is the role of certification, for good or ill? Who should set and apply standards, and how? How does teaching differ (and how is it the same?) in kindergarten compared to medical or law school? What about postgraduate and adult education classes? Who should decide whether John or Mary is fit to teach?

We end our materials with one of the most beautiful teaching stories ever written—a story so moving that we recommend that people share it with spouses, friends, colleagues, and students. In the best tradition of Robert Coles's *The Call of Stories*, the brief narrative called "Winter Oak" has become one of the "cases" most frequently commented on in all of our seminar programs. The story is set in a small country school in Russia. There are two characters, Anna Vasilyevna—the new teacher, all beans and vinegar—and Savushkin, the gentle, marginal student who doesn't quite "fit." What one sees in the story of their hour-and-a-quarter's walk is the preciousness of the reciprocal gift that teachers and students can give. Every student has his or her Winter Oak, an imaginative place where it is safe to take risks, a place where learning can somehow, magically, come alive. The questions for great teaching are, Can one create a Winter Oak classroom for a group, and how?

Some Next Steps

Whether your current academic interest is music or marketing, some of you may want to continue with this experiment after completing your current seminar program. We have three suggestions. First, why not try your hand at teaching a module selected from one of the seminar programs? Each module has been designed so that it can be taught independently. Readings are suggested, although you may wish to substitute others more appropriate to your own interests. We suggest teaching a module (e.g., "The Case Discussion Leader in Action: Operational Challenges and Opportunities"), rather than a single case. In our experience, setting educational objectives that are too narrow may force you into stating points rather than letting them emerge from the give-and-take of discussion. Give yourself maneuvering room: Don't fill up every space in your discussion outline.

Find a colleague who might be willing to observe and offer feedback on your classroom practice in return for similar assistance. A sensitive observer, genuinely interested in helping rather than "grading" your classroom leadership, can provide invaluable assistance. You will learn not only from suggestions but also from the discipline of having to design and implement a scheme for observing and analyzing the classroom instructional dynamic.[63] Many instructors are using videotape as an observational tool and debriefing with an experienced, sympathetic colleague or educational specialist.

Finally—since it is our belief that the true definition of a "case" is a teaching instrument *plus* its discussion—we suggest that you try writing a teaching note, as an imaginative projection of how a seminar group might work with your story. What decision points do you see in your case? What details would you target for specific questions? Where would you shine the spotlights of analysis, action, and reflection? Are there places in the case where a reader might be tempted to skim—thinking that she had identified and solved the problem—when you, the writer, know that multiple layers lie under the surface, rich with ore? What questions might you prepare to help a group sift the gravel and see the gold?

Conclusion: Independent Ideas Out of Actual Experience

So much of teaching is the artistry of encouraging discovery. This concept is central to the educational philosophy that underlies the case method of instruction. Discussion teaching, in contrast to the lecture mode, assigns both student and teacher nontraditional roles and relationships. Students are asked to assume primary responsibility for their own learning and for the education of others. The instructor must provide not only necessary theory and knowledge, but also an appropriate learning milieu and pedagogical skills that maximize the stu-

dent's opportunities for personal discovery and learning.

We share this educational philosophy with colleagues in other professional schools and academic disciplines and it provides us with an opportunity to participate directly in the birth of learning. A most magnificent example of this process was Helen Keller's experience in learning about the relationship between reality, W-A-T-E-R, and language systems.

You will recall that Miss Keller was deaf and blind. Through the genius of her teacher, Annie Sullivan Macy, she became not only an educated person but also a scholar and leader of her times. With the assistance of Michael Anagnos, director of the Perkins Institute for the Blind, the two women influenced the then current practices for teaching blind students.

Helen Keller reports "her lesson" with beauty:

As the cool stream gushed over one hand, she, Annie, spelled into the other the word *water*, first slowly, then rapidly. I stood still, my whole attention fixed upon the motions of her fingers. Suddenly I felt a misty consciousness as of something forgotten—a thrill of returning thought; and somehow the mystery of language was revealed to me. I knew then that W-A-T-E-R meant that wonderful cool something that was flowing over my hand. . . . I left the wellhouse eager to learn. Everything had a name, and each name gave birth to a new thought. As we returned to the house every object which I touched seemed to quiver with life.[64]

Annie Sullivan Macy summarized her philosophy in a letter to Michael Anagnos:

If the child is left to himself, he will think more and better, if less showily. Let him go freely, let him touch real things and combine his impressions for himself instead of sitting indoors at a little round table while a sweet-voiced teacher suggests that he build a stone wall with his wooden blocks or make a rainbow out of strips of colored paper or plant straw trees in bead flower pots. Such teaching fills the mind with artificial

63. James Austin, Ann Sweet, and Catherine Overholt, "To See Ourselves as Others See Us: The Rewards of Classroom Observation," in *Education for Judgment*, edited by Christensen, Garvin, and Sweet, pp. 215–229, list practical suggestions: to focus on specifics—specific techniques or skills, particular junctures in the process, students' reactions, and the like— as well as to give and receive criticism in a spirit of helpfulness, not judgment.

64. Joseph P. Lash, *Helen and Teacher* (New York: Delacorte Press/ Seymour Lawrence, 1980). An excellent review of this book, in the Radcliffe Biography Series, is by L. A. Waltch, *Radcliffe Quarterly*, June 1980.

associations that must be got rid of before the child can develop independent ideas out of actual experiences.[65]

All teachers will be moved by these vignettes; they enable us to share in the joy of student discovery, in the victory of our philosophy of teaching under circumstances far more difficult than we encounter in our daily classroom routines. We applaud both Helen Keller and Annie Sullivan Macy; we can learn from both!

Teachers at the Harvard Business School and other schools have a community of interest with these two remarkable women; we too try to provide an academic setting in which our students can develop "independent ideas out of actual experiences." Our academic circumstances, however, are a bit different. We cannot bring the spring, wellhouse, and water into our classroom. Much as we applaud the "reality" of our cases, they are second-order reporting, not first-hand experience.

Even more challenging is the nature of our teaching goals. Helen Keller could touch and feel water, and when her teacher spelled out W-A-T-E-R, she immediately experienced the joy of learning. Our students cannot touch and feel decisions. Instructors cannot give immediate feedback when the hoped-for educational output is student maturity, wisdom, and judgment. As Amy Lowell reminded us, it may be years before we know what we have or have not achieved.

Yet it is the imperfectness of what we are doing that promises such an exciting future. While new dimensions of education unfold, there is much to be done to improve present ways of teaching with cases. Our seminar program attempts to make a small contribution to that undertaking. We hope you will want to participate in this adventure, experimenting in ways meaningful to you and your institution.

65. Ibid.

1. What is a Case-based Teaching Seminar?

Any seminar is a gathering—usually with a leader—of people who apply their collective wisdom and energy to a subject that perplexes, intrigues, and touches them all in some way. At the Harvard Business School seminars, our special subject is the process of teaching by holding discussions (as opposed, for example, to labs or lectures). One source of the uniqueness of our approach is that seminar discussions reproduce, in concentrated form, the process they study. They are conducted among groups of teacher-participants analyzing other teachers' classroom experiences, probably under the guidance of another teacher. The effect can be prismatic: our discussions are tinted by the reality they analyze.

A second unusual characteristic of our approach is the use of *teaching cases* to help focus discussions that might otherwise degenerate into rambling group conversations. Teaching cases are condensed accounts of thought-provoking events from the professional lives of real instructors. As the seminar, or workshop group, tackles each set of occurrences, designations of role within the group may begin to blur. It is often difficult to say precisely who is "leading" in case method instruction, because teacher and students form an organic conversational continuum. Much of the direction of the discussion derives from the teacher's questions—only some of which are prepared—but its energy also feeds on the students' responses. At every stage in a case discussion, both teacher and students contribute. Furthermore, our approach encourages students not only to generate their own questions but to address them to each other (often with increasing frequency as the group gains cohesion, sophistication, and mutual trust). When skill and sophistication characterize a case discussion, the leader's interventions may be so subtle as to challenge detection.

In an academic group where all involved are likely to be colleagues, it seems inappropriate to call the person who moderates the discussion "teacher" and all the rest "students." All have gathered to study in one another's company, and, as a rule, all are teachers. This might suggest that, because all have similar backgrounds, all should play similar roles in the proceedings (that the discussion should, in effect, be leaderless). But we have found it most effective to have one person assume the role of leader—first among equals. This means that he or

Suggestions for Seminar Participants

she will attend to the continuing details of the group's organization, oversee the distribution of reading materials, and guide the discussions with the twofold goal of encouraging analytical thoroughness and the participation of as many group members as possible. Chaos—even cheerful chaos—is not among our goals. Our preferred designation for the person who undertakes these guiding tasks is "discussion leader." We refer to the rest of the group as "participants," aware that these roles are flexible. At times, the leader will hand the baton, as it were, to the participants and let the group take the lead. But the final responsibility for the discussion process as a whole will rest with the discussion leader. It is another unusual aspect of our approach that we hold that even a neophyte discussion leader can successfully shepherd experienced colleagues through a case discussion—provided that the leader takes primary responsibility for overseeing the discussion process itself.

Consider a moment—any moment—of a classroom discussion. Someone is probably talking; others are listening; but all are reacting intellectually and emotionally, emitting subtle, almost subliminal signals—facial expressions, changes in posture, small nonverbal sounds. Furthermore, all are in some way absorbing what has gone before and projecting what may come. Learning begins somewhere in this tapestry of thought and feeling. We offer our materials as a means to improve one's own weaving techniques by unraveling others' webs.

Given our dynamic approach to the discussion process, we recommend that participants view case discussions as voyages of exploration. Primed by our teaching notes and other supporting materials, the discussion leader may be expected to offer each class a battery of questions rather than a rigid agenda of points to make and memorize. As a rule, discussions should be fluid, cordial, collaborative, and fun. Participants should read and study each case before class (using our appended study questions for convenience if they wish), with an eye to presenting and defending opinions and helpfully criticizing those of their colleagues. Each participant's deepest allegiance will, of course, be to his or her own professional needs. As a participant, you should determine what each case says to you. But we also hope that, as the group meshes its strengths, your loyalty to the other members will grow along with your ability to help them, and theirs to help you.

Some people have assumed that the purpose of a case-based seminar must be to prepare case method teachers. Not so. Because our materials encourage emphasis upon process, the insights our teaching cases can trigger apply to almost the whole spectrum of teaching disciplines.

2. Why Join a Case-based Teaching Seminar?

In addition to its most obvious benefit—the intellectual synergy that can arise when many minds work on a common problem—case discussion offers a significant fringe benefit: it tends to be fun, and fun has a rejuvenating effect on even the most jaded. Not that case discussions are all levity. On the contrary, some of the situations we portray in our teaching materials awaken distressing memories. Speaking of a misunderstood, frustrated, or misinterpreted case character, participants often say, "I *was* that character." Perhaps it is more appropriate to speak of emotional engagement than either fun or sorrow. But both contribute to making case discussions involving and memorable.

We cannot promise that every case discussion will be intense, whether hilarious or touching. But we do suggest that a case-based teaching seminar will provide a novel opportunity for surveying your craft from multiple vantage points in order to learn more about what it is you really do when you teach. The experience of hearing how other people, from other backgrounds, react to situations that one initially considers open-and-shut rarely fails to open minds.

The prevailing philosophy of recent years could be described as follows: Most teaching beyond the secondary school level is still a sink-or-swim affair. Quite a few graduate students simply become teachers the day they find themselves facing undergraduates in a classroom because their fellowships require it. Sometimes serendipity results from the confrontation: a natural teacher emerges, to everyone's delight and profit. At other times the encounter causes pain for all concerned. Many teachers experience both at various times. When things go well, they sigh and dive into the next day's preparation. When things go wrong, they may corral a sympathetic pal for a few teaching tips, but just as often they muffle their misery for fear of seeming incompetent. Once a discussion group has reached a solid rapport, instances of gloom and glee may surface and provide substance for objective, constructive analysis. In teaching, the difference between success and maladroitness often resides in some deceptively small detail. Extraordinary power lurks, for example, in the way a teacher moves in the classroom. Some teachers persistently frustrate fully half of each class by failing to make eye contact with students on one side of the room during discussions. Others intimidate students by speaking too fast, or too loudly. Still others overprotect students with condescending questions that effectively obstruct the students' progress. Small failings, perhaps—yet potentially devastating, and fairly easily corrected. Our cases deal with issues like these, and the teaching notes we offer discussion leaders suggest ways to focus the group's attention upon just such practical details along with more general and theoretical formulations of policy.

Our basic mission is to familiarize teachers with the potentially vast array of choices open to them in order to produce insights that lead to practical improvements. The case discussions are meant to provide a safe testing ground for the participant's evolving ideas, because our emphasis on cooperation stresses the value of all contributions to the process. Not that we consider all opinions equally "correct." On the contrary; most of our discussions tend toward a consensus that finds some approaches to be "righter" than others, but few worthwhile goals can be reached without the exploration of a blind alley or two along the way.

Prospective participants sometimes challenge our stress upon the discussion process, raising the issue of content. Our answer—"For present purposes, we shall assume that the teacher has mastered the course material"—sometimes inspires skepticism. We tend to avoid discussions of content, not because we consider it unimportant, but because it is too specialized to yield useful, broadly applicable insights that will cut across disciplines. When the issue is the selection of a textbook, even a very experienced teacher of Urban Real Estate Development will have little useful advice for an instructor of French Romantic Poetry. But these two may very well enlighten each other and provide effective ways to encourage shy students or probe overly dogmatic opinions in class without giving offense. Content imbues the teaching and learning process with significance. Issues such as the choice of primary readings, design of research assignments, and the timing and design of examination questions (to mention a few topics that we do not generally discuss) make huge differences. But the breadth of our intended public forces us to concentrate on the few

virtually universal factors of discussion teaching: the discussion process, its preparation and evaluation, and the teacher's power to influence it. We hope to reveal the amplitude of choices available to teachers on every level and the rich possibilities in activities often considered mundane: preparation, questioning and responding to participants' answers, selecting students to speak in class, judging their work, and many more.

3. What, Exactly, Is a Case?

There are many thumbnail definitions of the word "case," none perfectly satisfying, and none sufficient to tell you what a case is before you have read, studied, discussed, and learned from one. Cases have long been in use, for example, in schools of business administration and medical schools. And the word will sound familiar to readers of detective fiction, social workers, and law enforcement officials. The word has broad, and not always cohesive, connotations, for its meanings are varied and the world of cases is wide. Our task is to describe our little corner of the territory.

To some, a teaching case is a description of episodes of practice, a selection of reality,[1] a slice of life, a story designed and presented as study material, an exercise, a puzzle, or a problem. All these kinds of cases have a common purpose: to teach. But this statement brings a further complication of terminology. The expression "teaching case" has the power to confuse as well as communicate because it has at least two meanings. On the one hand, it designates any case designed for discussion. On the other hand, a teaching case is a case *about teaching*. Our cases are both.

Our cases have something in common with fiction and journalism, but they are really a *genre* in themselves. Like fiction, they portray emotion, character, setting, and dialogue. And, like fiction, they were not written simply to engross or fascinate the reader (although, at their best, they do). They are the product of long, probing interviews between researchers and people to whom the case events really happened (although it is our customary practice to present both the characters and their settings disguised for confidentiality).

A good case is not just a history; it relates an event—or sequence of events—that contains

---

1. "McNair on Cases," *Harvard Business School Bulletin*, July/August, 1971.

enough perplexities to inspire a rich educational discussion. The goal of a good case is to present rich data coherently. The researcher usually interviews a few principal "informants"—in our materials, the teacher and other involved participants—to review the central episodes with them in order to get a textured picture of reality. Then the case writer attempts to distinguish foreground from background data, and present it all in a readable document that students can contemplate the night before the discussion. In addition to the case, the researcher develops suggested study questions, and a parallel set of discussion questions for the discussion leader, to indicate a path through the brambles and make reasonably certain that most of the participants will have considered similar issues before the discussion.

An important note: although some of the events we depict are dramatic, our cases portray normal people—sometimes under pressure, but still in reasonably familiar situations. Even when our cases portray outbursts, or socially unexpected (and, to some, offensive) behavior, we strongly urge student-readers to resist the urge to label the case characters with phrases like "neurotic," "acting out," or the like, and leave the analysis at that. Although under pressure and sometimes stretched beyond the limits of generally acceptable behavior, our case characters are not meant as a gallery of curiosities. On the contrary, their very normalcy is the reason that we have included them in our materials. We have selected the episodes that we present for group exploration, however superficially odd or *sui generis* they may seem, because they have the potential to lead to broadly applicable insights into the process of discussion teaching and learning. We suggest that, in a teaching seminar, it is most fruitful to examine the dynamics that produced the irritation in the characters' situations, with an eye to finding ways to help within the normal boundaries of most academic institutions. What might the teachers in these cases have foreseen or forestalled? Given similar early warning signs, what might you do? Another point: our cases are neither set up nor contrived. They all really happened—often to the surprise and discomfort of the teachers—and we suggest that, as you read them and burrow beneath their surfaces, you focus your search on the universal elements that glimmer, masked, behind the specific details. The process of a case method discussion is less specialized and technical than many

people assume. Its focus upon the interpretation of a central document recalls the classic *explication de texte* (or close reading) of literary studies. Its analytical component should be familiar to art critics, musicologists, physicians, historians, sociologists, students of politics—in short, anyone whose discipline involves reading or observing, analyzing, and presenting one's insights to a group for criticism and refinement.

Cases attempt to digest reality, with all of its deceptions, contradictions, discrepancies of perception, and general resistance to orderly analysis. Their irreducible core of ambiguity is one reason that they are usually fun to discuss. In fact, fun, with its concomitant energy, is a major advantage of the case method. Controversy is another. Study questions are always open-ended, and frequently involve judgments. They are not meant to entrap or breed hostility, but rather to help participants clarify their own and each other's unspoken assumptions because, as one woman put it, "People don't know what they think until they see what they say." Case discussions that include controversy can jostle participants into statements of principle that sometimes surprise them. One strength of the case method is that it encourages participants to defend their positions—which may result in jettisoning them. But effective teaching and learning have few worse enemies than complacency. If a focused, well-moderated discussion lures biases into the light for examination and assessment, it will have served a useful purpose.

What the case method absolutely will *not* do is offer a code of rules or techniques. Its suppleness precludes such rigidity. Each case is a slice of someone's life. The lessons it suggests will vary for each reader. To put it differently, each case is a kaleidoscope: what you see in it depends on how you shake it.

We present our teaching materials in the form of cases partly to generate empathy, both for the teachers and the students we describe. Empathy can supply leaven and spice to the discussion process. It is also the trait most students miss in their worst teachers. We do not confuse this quality with pity or softheartedness. On the contrary, empathizing with a student's true predicament (insofar as one human being can truly appreciate another's situation) might conceivably suggest a strict course of action. We suggest that teachers make the attempt to understand their students' points of view in order to assess their goals, strengths, and weaknesses as fairly as possible. To do less is to risk alienation, even hostility.

4. For Whom Do We Intend These Materials?

Anyone who teaches by means of a method other than straight "transfer of knowledge" (where a fly-paper memory is often the student's best friend) may benefit from working with our teaching cases, either in a full-length seminar or briefer workshop. We will *not* help teachers choose textbooks or primary readings, write watertight exam questions, ferret out plagiarism, or develop podium charisma. But we do believe that we can stimulate insight into the complex of small skills that constitutes effective discussion leading. Time and again, such insight has stimulated practical improvement. Our materials invite attention to the discussion process as it occurs in the classroom. We take up basic questions such as how to choose an opening speaker, how to deal with belligerent, recalcitrant, retiring, or bored students, how to establish and maintain rapport with a group. These challenges face all teachers, regardless of their years in the classroom. Whether this is your first or fortieth year as a teacher, you will probably meet several groups of expectant strangers in the next year, attempt to involve them in your chosen subject, guide them from ignorance to sophistication, and, ultimately, evaluate them. Over the years, students' culture changes; teachers' personalities and attitudes alter as well. Experienced instructors may find that sure-fire material of a few years ago blows up or, perhaps worse, fizzles when they use it this year. We offer these materials to help newcomers conquer their insecurities, and old hands, their boredom. Each new class is an adventure and an opportunity. Growth is always possible.

5. What Might Participation in a Case-based Teaching Seminar Be Like?

Be warned: preparing to discuss a teaching case is not the same as preparing to teach. It is not necessary to develop a fully defensible, "expert" analysis before class. To prepare for discussion, first, of course, you read the case. Then you try to "feel" your way into it, emotionally, from the major case character's point of view, and from as many other vantage points as you can discern. How might this teacher have felt in this situation? What might have been going on in the students' minds? How

might a dean have viewed the whole sequence of events? What advice would you have given at different points in the case if you had been a good friend of one of the characters? For the purposes of preparing to discuss a case, it is probably more valuable to stockpile questions than answers. Heartfelt perplexity can kindle valuable insights.

Preparing for a case-based teaching seminar also differs from preparing for an examination or a discussion of an article or textbook chapter. A case is not a collection of maxims of tenets to be memorized and recapitulated. Nor is it simply a story, to be analyzed from a purely aesthetic point of view. It is a version of real events, which require some sort of action, and which have been selected because the manner of their unfolding possesses the potential to reveal some underlying process or principles at work. This is not to say that every reader or interpreter will necessarily detect the same dynamic. Our cases are grounded in reality, which always resists perfect analysis, and in which two or three equally sincere and perspicacious observers can make very persuasive arguments for mutually exclusive interpretations.

To prepare for a case method discussion, it is a good idea to read the case several times, getting deeper and deeper into the narrative each time. When the story is sufficiently vivid (for some, this happens when they can hear the characters' voices, imagine their settings, and begin to feel something of what they might have been going through at critical moments), it is time to ponder some simple questions. What are the most significant points in the narrative? What might be some explanations for why things happened as they did? If you were a case character, how would you feel? What would you be thinking? What would you do? What underlying process with broader implications do you discern?

The point of preparation is not to "nail" a single, perfect analysis, but to begin to define paths that may lead to enlightenment—in the full understanding that even a thorough discussion will not exhaust all of the potentially convincing answers to the questions that the case raises. (It may not even exhaust all of the interesting questions!) The goal of preparing for a case discussion is to come furnished with thoughtful preliminary hypotheses and questions that can help others see deeply into the details of the case. Honest perplexity may draw attention to obscure (and therefore rewarding) moments in the narrative. Because good cases are the stuff of life—not *schema* constructed to illustrate theories *about* life—they are rich in perplexing moments. This is why, in case discussions, great questions are more valuable than great answers.

The discussion itself usually begins with the leader posing questions—generally by asking one or two opening speakers to mark some terrain for further exploration. How can this be done? By asking the lead speakers to present overviews of the case that raise central issues for the rest of the participants to explore. Those who open accept the discussion leader's offer to set the initial focus on what they consider to be the most important aspects of a case, then tend to continue to play active roles in the whole session. After the first few presentations, the discussion leader may probe for greater depth or breadth, call for opposing views, or even slide into role-playing, but the overall goal of the first section of the discussion will probably be to cover the events of the (A) case. The (A) case usually ends with the main character facing some decision. The leader will probably ask the group for suggestions or predictions, and then if the case is so organized, distribute the (B) case, which details what did happen. As a rule, after evaluations of these events, the group turns to considerations of principle. After assessing the appropriateness of the main character's actions, the group applies whatever rules of general significance it has extracted from the case to its own concerns. Some of our cases continue with further segments—perhaps giving the case character's reflections upon the events or the researcher's analysis.

Many participants experience a sort of double consciousness as they "play student" and watch someone else do what they have done for years: teach. Often they click in and out of single-minded participation, sometimes feeling playful and childlike, and at other times detached and superior to the proceedings. This is natural; sometimes, participants even interrupt the flow of discussion to challenge the leader's handling of some particular sequence, and a new line of inquiry emerges, to the benefit of all.

The least desirable activity that one can pursue during a case discussion is copious note-taking, which kills dialogue as it flies. The point of the exercise is to loosen up, collaborate, let the mind roam free, and react with emotions and intellect to others' contributions. Many experienced teachers

(adults, all) find it frustrating after years or decades at "center stage," to play the role of student again. How ignominious to wave one's hand at the teacher for five minutes, only to be ignored. How annoying to formulate and reformulate a brilliant rejoinder, only to have it grow staler and staler as the talk progresses to other topics. But there is a positive side to this frustration: it can stimulate powerful reflection *after* the class.

Many times, our participants have left the seminar room still puzzling over issues from the discussion. Some continue their debates with colleagues outside of class. Others have written their thoughts in brief essay or memo form and circulated them to the group. Many have found that their enthusiasm for talking about teaching has risen, and that they are spending more time with colleagues, friends, spouses, and even their children, talking about their craft. If the frustration of not being called on produces this happy effect, so be it.

Another potential value in playing the student's role is that there are few surer ways to develop empathy for students than by actually filling their shoes. Most experienced teachers find it both frustrating and exhilarating to participate in a discussion group someone else is leading. On one hand, they relish the freedom of not "being in charge," for a change. On the other hand, they sometimes find it painful to re-experience the powerlessness of the student's situation. But this pain, too, can contain a useful lesson. Teachers who feel, anew, the exaggerated impact of the discussion leader's movements in class and experience the heightened effect of the leader's tone of voice, volume, and speed of speech, can gain a new appreciation of the importance of attending to their own manner of speaking and behaving in class. As you watch, and listen and react to, the discussion teacher, compare his or her style to your own. What, if anything, would you like to change?

6. Conclusion: Some Articles of Faith

Certain assumptions about the enterprise of teaching color all of our work. We take for granted that our participants wish to teach effectively, even as we acknowledge the other professional and personal demands, tensions, and pressures in every teacher's life. For us, the measure of good teaching is good learning. Even though we realize that there are no absolute scales to assess students' progress, most teachers and students can feel whether classes are "working" or not. We, for example, tend to value discussions that develop ever more subtle, sophisticated, and insightful questions. One of our most abiding articles of faith is that no one has an exclusive patent on truth in discussion teaching. When our discussions achieve the goal of provoking various participants to formulate questions that address their specific situations, we feel that we are succeeding. But how can one measure success in endeavors like ours? Despite continuing efforts to quantify the results of discussion teaching, we suspect that subjectivity will always color this activity. Whether we can support our judgments with unassailable evidence, we all know teachers who help, teachers who are ineffectual, and teachers who are downright obstructive. We think that one important key to becoming more helpful as a teacher is to recognize the enormous power of the discussion process, and the nature of one's responsibility in that process. The teacher's task is to aid students as they conquer the material, not demonstrate his or her own brilliance. Since the classroom is the prime arena for helping students learn, classroom

practice should occupy a great deal of a teacher's attention. One of our basic beliefs is that almost every fundamental principle of good teaching can be *operationalized*—put into practice—by word or gesture. Principles are of little use if one does not act upon them.

Our materials address perennial issues of discussion teaching—basic, besetting, often deceptively simple matters, but all accessible to improvement, and central, we believe, to success. Our bias is toward formulating practical plans to achieve theoretical goals. We recognize that good teaching is an art that touches the heart as well as the brain. Most important, we consider it to be a teachable art. Our method—cooperating with a group of colleagues to analyze other teachers' challenges, evolve recommendations, and deduce principles—can both create alertness to opportunities and deepen each participant's individual appreciation of the power of the teaching process. We propose to help participants study teaching as a live thing. Mindful of the poet William Wordsworth's warning about scientific practice, we will not *murder* teaching to *dissect* it.

PART II

The Seminar Program

Section 1. Teaching and the Case Method of Discussion: Opportunities, Dilemmas, and Risks

Bert Peters, an assistant professor of French at prestigious Bower College in rural Illinois, had four years of full-time college teaching experience. Today he was leading the twenty students in his 10 A.M. section of Intermediate French Grammar and Composition through an exercise in the subjunctive. They were three weeks into the fall semester and this group had already impressed Bert as outstandingly bright and enthusiastic, even for the generally high-caliber students at Bower.

As usual, Bert was trying to breathe life into the intrinsic boredom of pattern drills. He moved energetically around the classroom—whose movable desk-chairs he always had his students form into a U-shape—and tossed ridiculous sentences at them for translation from English to French.

Bert paused in front of Franny Ellis. "Franny," he said, "if this chalk were a piece of Camembert, I would eat it." He accompanied the sentence with a pantomime of gluttony directed at the chalk. Franny laughed and translated the sentence smoothly. Bert nodded and smiled and moved two chairs farther along the U. He pointed the chalk at Jack Sothern and said, "Jack, here's one for you: 'If I hadn't stolen that Citroen, I wouldn't be sitting in this ugly prison now!'" There was some laughter, but Jack didn't even smile. He grimaced, stared at the ceiling and, after a pause, produced a garbled string of French words. Bert had noticed from the first that Jack seemed nervous and translated more slowly than the others, but this was his worst performance to date. Instead of saying anything critical, however, Bert simply moved a few desks farther along the U and presented the same sentence to another student, who translated it perfectly. Bert nodded and continued the exercise, making up ever more outrageous sentences with similar grammatical structures.

Except for Jack, the students handled their assignments well, laughing and groaning at Bert's jokes with gratifying frequency. But Jack muffed every sentence Bert addressed to him. Finally, Bert stood at Jack's desk and lowered his voice and said, "If you didn't have a chance to study the lesson last night, Jack, tell me and I won't call on you."

Jack didn't answer. He just blushed and stared at his hands. This surprised Bert, who had expected something like a thank you; but instead of pursuing the subject further, he simply resumed the class exercise, trying not to look back at Jack. Soon he noticed that Jack had left the room. The other stu-

CASE

The French Lesson (A)

Abby Hansen wrote this case for the Developing Discussion Leadership Skills and the Teaching by the Case Method seminars. Data were furnished by the involved participants. All names and some peripheral facts have been disguised.

HBS Case No. 9-384-066.

dents noticed, too. About ten minutes later, Jack returned, a bit red-faced, and took his seat. The other students' awareness of his discomfort dampened the formerly jolly mood of the class. Bert's efforts to rekindle the humor became more and more self-conscious.

After class, Bert positioned himself near the door. He wanted to catch Jack and get the matter cleared up as soon as possible. But Jack slid by Bert when his back was turned.

He won't even talk to me, Bert thought. Uh oh, this kid is really ticked off!

Bert considered it essential to accord his students respect in the classroom because he knew that eroding their self-confidence could only destroy rapport and worsen their chances for conquering the complexities of good spoken and written French. He prided himself on putting students at their ease, but here was Jack Sothern acting as if Bert had attacked him! Dammit, Bert thought, he's got me all wrong. What's going on—is Jack an oversensitive baby, or am I just a lead-headed boor?

W hen a malfunctioning heating system sent the classroom temperature up near 90°, Ellen Collins, a first-year assistant professor of Finance at Fleming Graduate School of Business and Public Management in Toronto, encountered an unexpected interruption. Although she always made it a rule to wear a jacket while teaching, the heat had become so stifling that she unobtrusively shed her blazer and draped it over a chair before turning back to the chalkboard. No sooner was Ellen's back turned than, from the rear of the large amphitheater-shaped classroom where sixty students sat, there came a long, loud wolf-whistle.

* * *

The Instructor

Before accepting her tenure track post with the Finance teaching staff at Fleming, Ellen, a recent Ph.D. in Economics from the University of Chicago, had already done two years of postdoctoral research in International Banking at the school. She was married, thirty years old, 5'4" tall, and slim, with collar-length brown hair, blue eyes, and a soft speaking voice. "Many of my male colleagues try to be tough," Ellen told the researcher, "and a few are really rough. But I don't admire that style and it wouldn't work for me anyway. I'm not tall; I can't physically dominate a large room; and nobody has ever called my voice 'booming.' I would never 'wipe the floor' with students, as they call it here—grill them so they look stupid in public—but there are teachers who do it regularly."

The School

Fleming Graduate School of Business and Public Management in Toronto enjoyed an admirable reputation for producing successful leaders who assumed influential positions all over the world. Advancement in this faculty was highly prized, as was its well-known master's degree, awarded after a two-year program to 430 students each year—about 25% of them women. The faculty ratio was similar.

At Fleming, the 500 first-year students were divided into units of 80 to 100 students called "learning groups" (LGs). Each LG met daily at 8:30 A.M. in a particular classroom permanently assigned to its use, and took three hour-and-a-half-long case discussion classes in a row with just one break for lunch. The first-year curriculum included nine dif-

CASE

The Day the Heat Went On (A)

Abby Hansen wrote this case for the Developing Discussion Leadership Skills and the Teaching by the Case Method seminars. Data were furnished by the involved participants. All names and some peripheral facts have been disguised.

HBS Case No. 9-384-098.

81

ferent courses, most of them taught by the case method. Class participation usually counted heavily in course grades. Teachers "floated" from classroom to classroom to lead discussions with the LGs. Spending so much time together, and facing the pressure of the heavy workload, the LGs usually developed strong internal bonds. Most instructors described the LGs as self-protective.

The Situation

In her first year at Fleming, Ellen taught Finance to two LGs—III and VI. LG III had another woman teacher, but aside from Ellen, LG VI had only male instructors. These, according to her, constituted a mixed bag of personality types whose net effect was to create tension in the members of the group. Ellen mentioned various teachers whom LG VI thought "distant but cooperative"; some they thought "too strict" or "too lax"; one they thought "brilliant"; and one they thought "a tyrant." The "tyrant," Charlie Brennan, was their instructor in Organizational Psychology (OP). A notable practitioner of the tough style of teaching, Charlie started class on the dot of the hour, held students' presentations to a prescribed number of minutes, and had once made a lasting impression on the women of LG VI by calling a special meeting for them during which he said that because the professional world of bureaucracy had high standards for female decorum, he too, would tolerate "no messy purses, no ungainly leg crossing, no sloppy attire"in his class. According to Ellen, several women in the group described this meeting to her and mentioned how insulted Charlie's message had made them feel.

To make matters worse for Ellen, she usually taught LG VI immediately after Charlie's OP class with them. On these occasions Ellen found the group "so wound up that I had to do something to get them to relax before they could get their minds on the Finance class." To this end, Ellen made it a ritual to give them a few opening minutes for nervous joking. When one fellow began to use these openings for mildly flirtatious humor directed at Ellen, she tried to deflect it with good-humored shrugs. Once he opened the prediscussion joke session by saying, "Now, Ellen, smile if you have a secret crush on me!" Ellen was taken aback, but when she heard the LG laughing she good-naturedly smiled, too. "Aha! I knew it!" the student crowed, but he was laughing and Ellen read the incident as harmless and proceeded with the Fi-

nance discussion. Nonetheless, she considered his sexual undertones inappropriate and was very relieved when the jokes did not escalate any further in the direction of bad taste.

Although Ellen's relations with LG VI were generally satisfactory, she recalled having noticed right away that "the women in the group seemed demoralized. All the student association officers in this LG were male, and the women behaved particularly quietly in class, more so than in my other group, LG III. When one of the women spoke, the males tended to look bored or fidgety, as if Finance was so complex a subject that no female could possibly have anything worthwhile to say about it. I think Charlie Brennan was responsible for this intimidating atmosphere."

Ellen mentioned a further obstacle to her success with LG VI: a peculiarity of the scheduling at Fleming decreed that Finance should start in the spring semester—much later than most other courses—so that the students could accumulate technical background in economics and accounting and learn how to study by the case method before tackling its complexities. For Ellen, however, the late start also meant that she "inherited a section that had already set its social norms in the complete absence of women instructors." Nonetheless, Ellen hoped that LG VI would accept her simply as someone who could lead them through discussions of the Finance cases.

When she agreed to teach at Fleming, Ellen knew that its institutional culture could be very rough on women. Although women were significantly represented in the junior faculty, only five women were tenured out of a senior faculty of 100 members. No one found Charlie Brennan's condescending attitude toward his female students particularly unusual. The master's-degree students at the school had a reputation for playing pranks, and those they sprang on women teachers often had sexual overtones. For example, when one woman teacher discovered that some fellows in her LG had hired a belly dancer to interrupt her class, she managed to intercept the woman and bar her from the classroom. But this lack of taste was quite common in all sorts of joking at Fleming.

Ellen mentioned to the researcher that, after her course with LG VI was over and she spoke less formally to some of the women of the group, they mentioned having been deeply offended by many things in their first year at Fleming—not only Charlie Brennan's speech, but the general level of obscenity in the LG's humor and the tacit assumption of so many male students that women students couldn't possibly say anything useful about public administration. Ellen also mentioned that LG VI had included "three extraordinarily bright women—but oddly enough these three seemed to be having just as hard a time, for different reasons, as the less gifted, more intimidated ones." Ellen described these three as "outstanding and outspoken," but she noticed that when any one of them began to speak, the rest of the group, male and female alike, put on expressions of bored tolerance, and "sarcastic chuckles" could be heard in the room as if to say "there goes old Sue, being so damned brilliant again—ho hum." Ellen felt "sorry to see these three—all of whom later won high honors, by the way—being almost systematically ostracized by their peers. All in all, I think their experience here was pretty negative, despite the honors. That just underlines the fact that women—all women—have a very tough time at Fleming."

Given this strained atmosphere and her late entry into the academic program of LG VI, Ellen worked hard to prepare herself to make a good impression on the group. "It sounds trivial," she smiled, "but women must worry about wardrobe in these public situations. If you look too frilly, you come across as an *airhead*; but if you look too severe, you're a *schoolmarm*. There's another aspect to dress here, too. Most of the male teachers begin class by removing their jackets and rolling up their shirtsleeves. Women can't do that because shedding an article of clothing in front of sixty students in an amphitheater might seem perilously close to some sort of strip-tease. I can't imagine any image less likely to bolster authority!"

* * *

The day the heat went on was a day in early April of her first year teaching at Fleming, during the third week of the Finance course. Ellen had worn a typically conservative outfit: dark skirt, high-necked white blouse, woolen tweed blazer. Unfortunately, by afternoon, the weather had turned unexpectedly warm. At 1:00 P.M. when she entered their classroom, Ellen noticed her LG VI students were all casually dressed; several were in running shorts. It was instantly apparent to Ellen that somehow the heat in their classroom had been turned on by mistake. Ellen got about fifteen minutes into the discussion before beginning to feel extremely uncomfortable. She was putting a student's key points on the board when "the temperature felt as if it had gotten up near 90°. The students were all slumping. I was trying to listen to the speaker, but I, too, was beginning to succumb to the incredibly cloying atmosphere. That room was always stuffy. Now it was dizzyingly hot." As the student continued, Ellen stepped back from the board, shrugged out of her blazer as unobtrusively as possible, and turned to drape it over the chair that stood behind the instructor's desk near the blackboard. Then she turned to walk back to the board. As soon as her back was turned, the wolf-whistle rang out from the top row, where, Ellen knew, "a bunch of drinking buddies sat together." For a split second, anger crashed over Ellen. What nerve! How childish! What an insult! She clutched the chalk tightly and wondered what response to make.

CASE

The Introduction (A)

Well . . . Mike is from Westin, Connecticut. He attended Westin Central High School. So far, he likes his roommate. Mike has a red Firebird which he drives too fast. Mike likes to drink, uses cocaine often, has a 21-year-old girlfriend who is . . . [pause], oh yes, and he can't wait for this boring class to get over.

With only a few minutes of class remaining, freshman Dianne Quinn glanced around the room, appearing to look for approval as she completed her introduction of the twenty-sixth and final student in the first meeting of the English Literature and Composition (ELC) class at Pax Vobiscum College (PVC).

Professor Leslie O'Connor felt her face burn with anger. Using a tried and true exercise to help students get to know one another, she had asked the freshmen to pair up and interview one another. Each student would then introduce the other to the rest of the class. Leslie sensed an uneasiness in the room:

> After a few gasps, no one moved. No one even shuffled a paper. The students appeared to be avoiding any eye contact. Many were looking down at their hands. Dianne had gone from the innocuous, to the inappropriate, to playing dirty pool. I was *really* annoyed. This was the first day of this class's college career.

Pax Vobiscum College

Pax Vobiscum College (PVC) first opened its doors to provide an education for the sons of the swelling Irish and Italian Catholic immigrant population of Metropolis. In time, PVC relocated from its urban beginnings to an idyllic suburban setting resplendent with Gothic spires and green quads. PVC alums were fiercely loyal; many of its students are the second and even third generation of their families to attend.

Students today still come from predominantly Catholic homes, with both parents and student seeking a strong liberal arts program grounded in Christian values. Despite a more geographically diverse and affluent student body, the character and ethos of the school have remained intact. Having marked its first decade of full coeducation in all of its five colleges and academic departments, PVC

*This case was written by **Marina McCarthy** in collaboration with **C. Roland Christensen** for the Developing Discussion Leadership Skills and Teaching by the Case Method seminars. While the case is based on data furnished by participants involved, all names and some peripheral facts have been disguised.*

HBS Case No. 9-386-146.

was also enjoying one of its healthiest applicant pools in years.

Leslie O'Connor

Leslie O'Connor had a fondness for PVC. Although she was not a graduate, she had cross-registered into the English department during her senior year from a nearby secular university. She remained in touch with her PVC professors over the decade that followed, and was eventually invited to join the faculty to teach freshman English. In fact, she had not applied for a position at PVC; rather, a senior professor had telephoned early one summer to ask her if she would like to teach there. Leslie was pleased with the way her ELC classes were going, and was encouraged by her consistently high reviews.

Leslie had always found student introduction a technique useful in breaking down the strained atmosphere of the first day. Since students were often uncomfortable when asked to speak about themselves, Leslie asked each to socialize briefly with a neighbor before introducing him or her to the class. The result was a lighter treatment instead of the previously stilted and awkward recitations.

Leslie's Version of the "Start-Up"

The beginning of that first class was uneventful. My general administrative noises included a welcome to PVC. I jokingly assured the students that they were not "admissions mistakes" and commended the class for making a great choice—coming to PVC. Introducing myself, I explained that I had once been a student in the English department, had been teaching for the past several years, and was now finishing my doctoral work at another institution, where I also had an additional teaching commitment. I then asked the class to break out of rows and form a circle. While the students were moving their chairs I walked over to the instructor's desk on the raised platform at the front of the room where I had left my briefcase and various papers. As I rummaged through my briefcase looking for a folder, I thought, "Who on earth would ever actually sit up here? I'd feel pompous!"

Before distributing the syllabus and course description, I asked the class to fill in their names, local phone numbers, and addresses on the 3x5 cards I was passing out. I also asked them to write down if they had a nickname they preferred to be called. Finally, I asked them to indicate where they had gone to high school.

I waited until the other handouts had made their way around the circle before briefly going over course content and expectations. Although I had pushed a student chair for myself into the circle, I continued to stand as I introduced the course.

Explaining that I was adopting a model that I had used in an upper level course the previous term, I announced that we were going to drop one class meeting per week and lengthen the second by fifteen minutes to make time for individual writing conferences. I thought I heard an "Oh goody!" when I mentioned the canceled class, but I just treated the comment as innocuous and proceeded. . . . It just didn't sound funny or humorous enough to pick up on. . . .

I hoped that the class would share my interest and enthusiasm for the experiment, and related how the students last term had specifically found the one-to-one conferences to be very helpful. If anyone did not feel comfortable with the design of the course, I suggested that he or she see me after class so I could suggest another section in the same time slot.

Since there were no questions about the course design, I proceeded to hold up the texts we would be using for the semester. I joked that Strunk and White's *Elements of Style* would be our bible for the term. A few smiles broke through the intense note-taking. I continued to discuss the syllabus and the course description handout.

To make the transition from texts and syllabi to student introductions, I mentioned the final feature of last term's seminar: two students each week were responsible for bringing refreshments. I asked for a show of hands if they wanted to carry on the tradition. I smiled at the enthusiasm and then reached into my folder to pull out two "sign-up sheets." Chuckling, I said, "I thought you would! There should be enough slots for everyone to sign once; if there are any extra spaces, I'll fill in! Now, to kick off, I'll supply for today. These are store-bought. I don't want anyone to feel the pressure to be fancy." I then retrieved a bag from the desk at the front of the room. Several students began to laugh. One joked, "I *thought* I smelled baked goods!"

As soon as I asked the students to pair up and interview one another, the noise level in the class rose. I was pleased. For all but one student (I had taken a poll), this was their last class of the day (3:00–4:15). It had been a long day for most of them—their first day of college. Since all of the first-year classes are large lectures, the group was in its first and only "small" class of the day. The English department feels strongly about keeping the sections small—"almost like a homeroom," one of my senior colleagues said. Hence, we had 80 sections of freshman English—give or take a few—each year.

The atmosphere was right and the introductions began. I was now seated in the semi-circle, diligently taking notes as each student spoke. All the while I nodded and maintained eye contact to encourage the speaker. I guess I gave them carte blanche to say what they wanted. I urged the students to find out a bit about their neighbor's background—where he or she was from, what high school they attended, any talents—musical, theatrical, athletic.

The group was learning who had played what instrument or what sport in high school, who was from the same section of the same state. A camaraderie was building. I noticed two female students from Florida, who hadn't appeared to know each other, signaling each other to meet after class. Two male students found out that they had both been high school lacrosse players and were going to "walk on" at PVC's varsity tryouts that afternoon.

When Dianne made her inappropriate introduction of Mike, I fumed. Like a high-speed slide carousel, options of what to do flashed through my mind. Part of me wanted to slam my hand on my desk. A little shock value often goes a long way if you reserve it for emergencies. But I wasn't at a real desk. I had taken a student desk and was facing the class.

I couldn't believe someone would make a wise remark like that on the *first* day of college. I was angry at myself for having nodded at Dianne as she began her seemingly innocent introduction. I had smiled and encouraged her to continue. . . . Some of the previous students had been a bit nervous speaking up in class. . . .

Though I was furious at Dianne, what about Mike? His chair was turned to the side so I couldn't see his facial expression or reaction. Maybe Mike and Dianne knew each other before coming to PVC. It might have been an attempt at humor on her or both their parts. *Regardless*—the tone was inappropriate. Maybe Mike was being naive—or perhaps a wise guy—by telling Dianne as much as he did. Perhaps he did not realize that she was naively going to repeat everything. I felt my face getting redder and hotter.

After Class

Back in her third-floor office, Leslie removed her jacket and carefully hung it on the back of her chair.

She gave her skirt a customary check for chalk smudges and muttered how she must remember not to wear navy on "teaching days." Seated behind her desk, Leslie put her feet up and leaned back. Her colleague and friend from across the corridor, Jo Smith, noted Leslie's knit brow and, sensing that she was upset, pulled up a chair and closed the door. Jo and Leslie saw eye to eye on many professional and personal issues. Leslie rose and stood with her back to the window, deliberately tapping a pencil in her left palm. The afternoon sun was streaming into the office; Leslie paused for a moment to adjust the curtains. She leaned forward against the window sill, supporting herself with both elbows. Gazing out onto the quad, she began twisting a stray paperclip as she prepared to recount Dianne's introduction of Mike O'Neil. Irritation filled her voice as she began.

Leslie Confides in Her Colleague

This first class today really hit a raw nerve. One thing I especially enjoy about teaching on the college level is that you don't have to fuss with discipline. The students are here to learn and you don't have to stand on your head to entertain, cajole, and deal with those who don't want to be here. You know, many of the PVC instructors in our department hate to teach freshmen. We often hear them say, "Ugh, a required course. . . . Freshmen are so young and immature. Their skills are getting worse and worse every year." My vantage point is obviously much different. The *course* may be compulsory, but college is not. I enjoy teaching freshmen. I enjoy teaching. I enjoy talking about teaching. In fact, there are several senior faculty members with whom I regularly get together to talk about pedagogy and ideas about teaching. Why, just last week, a senior faculty member referred several students to me who were interested in teaching. He thought I might have some advice for them.

Dianne's inappropriate introduction really took me by surprise; but in retrospect, maybe it shouldn't have. Maybe I should have paid more attention to the reaction to my canceling a class per week. That "Oh goody!" is a bit haunting now. But all had been going along so smoothly at that point. I looked at the clock and had only a few minutes to go. The sudden quiet in the class led me to conclude that the students were concerned as well. What would you have done?

Section 1. Teaching and the Case Method of Discussion: Opportunities, Dilemmas, and Risks

Not so long ago at one of those obligatory social functions, I was superficially engaged in conversation with a rather wearisome creature who inquired as to my profession. "I'm a teacher." Taking a sip of the warm, red punch, he smiled and asked me, "Why?" Confused, I echoed the question: "Why?" "Yes, why do you teach?" I stammered. The first reasons that came to mind were not right. For money. People who teach for money are a minority—poor, blinded souls who have yet to make the acquaintance of a banker, doctor, or mortician. For glory. The few who still teach for the glory tend to be young and idealistic— poor, blinded souls who have yet to read the fine print on promotion and tenure. For the opportunity to do research. Maybe; but unless you have a bevy of graduate assistants, objective tests, and no office hours, even the most elementary cost-benefit analysis reveals this to be a losing proposition. My inquisitor was out of punch, and I was out of time. I had to say something. "I teach for the students."

We parted—he for more punch, I to collect my thoughts. What kind of an answer had I given? Do I teach for the students? I felt myself wanting to smile. I caught myself trying to imagine the sophisticated, tweedy intellectuals among my colleagues admitting to such an unabashedly human reason. But before worrying about them I needed to answer the question for myself. Names and facts—some together, some separate—all flashed through my memory. Suddenly the movie stopped, and I remembered Scott.

I met Scott early in my teaching career one unfortunate semester when the two sections of my beginning speech course had been scheduled to meet at the same time. That meant I had sixty students instead of thirty. I was in no mood to sign overloads. Scott was patient, polite, and insistent. He had to have this course. He was going to be a doctor. "I have to communicate important messages. I want to learn how to do it right." The deepset, brown eyes never wavered. Mine dropped; he had a point. Later, I chided myself for being a pushover. When would I learn a student could feign interest in any course if it fell into the right time slot?

My first mistake with Scott was the assumption his interest was feigned. It turned out to be all too genuine. This error was compounded by a second. I assumed I knew enough about communication to satisfy the intellectual curiosity of my students.

READING

Why Teach?

MARYELLEN GLEASON

Scott's academic appetite was voracious. The course had barely begun and he was asking questions I couldn't answer, raising issues I'd never considered, and reading books I didn't know. Even my best-reasoned, most eloquent response did not settle an issue. It only stimulated more questions.

I was frightened—not just by the questions. It was his answers—to everything. One day on the way to class I wondered out loud why the yellow crocuses always bloomed first. Oh, that was easy, he assured me. It was a matter of dominant genes. The yellow plants had them, which meant they were the hardiest and therefore bloomed first. "Oh." I couldn't really think of anything else to say. I had only been trying to make conversation.

I couldn't help feeling a bit relieved when the semester ended. I didn't know anything else to teach Scott. The experience was humbling, and yet there was exhilaration as well. I was forced to admit here was a student more dedicated and determined about learning than I had ever been. Here too was a student brighter than I. The revelations startled me, but once the admissions were made I was ready to learn something far more significant: Students can teach us if we let them.

The pictures in my mind moved again. This time when they stopped I saw Ron—an average student thoroughly convinced of his ordinariness. Yes, he could play baseball, but that was just about it. "I'm not much of a student," he told me, and that pretty well summed up his less-than-adequate writing skills, his 2.1 GPA, and his general disinterest in anything academic. At the end of his sophomore year, Ron had yet to confront an intellectual idea that mattered.

Ron had also yet to confront a teacher who thought he mattered. I treated him like someone special. It wasn't hard. He was and is a unique human being without duplicate. It seemed like such a simple solution. Ron responded very much like my Swedish ivy when I finally got around to giving it some fertilizer. He started to grow. Almost before I knew what happened both Ron and my ivy were discovering places they had never been before. Ron found out that the nonverbal communication I lectured about in class he actually used when he played baseball. My ivy discovered the window latch around which it proceeded to grow. In both cases the very obvious changes attracted attention and the two continued to flourish.

From Ron I learned teachers have power—power

that can affect and change students. It would be nice if the power was inherently creative. It is not. But then the power is not inherently destructive, either. Rather, the potential for teachers to influence students simply exists. Unfortunately, most teachers neglect to use this influence to accomplish any effect.

Ron was gone. I sighed as I remembered Richie—a black, ghetto kid raised in Watts who used to tell me he did not know ground could be green until he moved to Oregon. Later I wondered if it was a joke.

Richie lived with ignorance. His vocabulary permitted only the most rudimentary and repetitious descriptions of what happened. During one of many study sessions I was struggling, without apparent success, to explain inflation. I permitted a momentary diversion while I tried to brainstorm a better approach. Richie chatted amicably about the bank downtown where he had opened a savings account to keep his tuition for next semester. He was impressed by the size and security of the safe. "Well," he concluded, "That's the way it should be. I don't want nobody running off with my money." "Richie, your money is not in that safe." Feeling the tension, I began cautiously, "Banks are in business to make money. They do that by borrowing money. They've spent yours. You'll get somebody else's when you take yours out." The face was angry. "They can't do that! It's my money. How come they didn't tell me? Bastards!" "They thought you knew, Richie." My answer didn't touch his anger.

Richie astonished me. I had never seen the lonely islands of ignorance that still exist in our advanced, civilized society. Most of my time is spent at the higher levels of learning. My students are interested in actualizing; they want to realize their full potential. Richie was a tangible reminder that not all knowledge is luxury. Some is essential. Deprivation of these basic life facts relegates one to the peripheries of existence.

I wanted to move on. I remembered Eileen—what the professionals called a "nontraditional learner." Eileen was thirty, married, and a mother who wanted a college degree. For some reason she felt inferior—felt as if she had never accomplished much that mattered, at least to her. Get a college diploma and she would have tangible proof of an accomplishment that mattered. It was a noble challenge. Eileen had not been near a classroom since high school. She and her husband were struggling financially with a huge dairy farm, which meant there was no money for college. She financed the venture with a part-time secretarial job. Her arrival in class marked no small accomplishment, but for Eileen that was only the first step. She didn't anticipate the second step would be easier, and it was not.

As the date for the first exam approached, the tension rose noticeably. There were office calls and embarrassed questions asked quietly. "I don't know how to study the texts." "I don't understand things I've written in my notes." The very brown eyes twinkled, but the face was serious. "I tell the cows about what I read in the text. Some of them seem as slow as me."

On the day of the test the anguish was visible. I hoped for the best—so much appeared to be at stake. The best turned out to be a C minus—a shaky two points from a D. Eileen was in my office when I returned from class. She quietly closed the door and sat down. There was stubborn determination as we painstakingly went through the test, question by question. Neither of us mentioned the tears that accidentally spilled on the last page.

By sheer gut determination Eileen made it in my class and many others. From that remarkably strong woman I learned there are values in education I have too long taken for granted.

I suppressed the urge to remember more. It was time to return. I took a sip from my still-full punch glass and smiled. I could live with the answer— even if it did open to public scrutiny my humanity. I owe students a great deal. The debt ought to be acknowledged.

The Dreaded Discussion: Ten Ways to Start

PETER FREDERICK

The only privilege a student had that was worth his claiming, was that of talking to the professor, and the professor was bound to encourage it. His only difficulty on that side was to get them to talk at all. He had to devise schemes to find what they were thinking about, and induce them to risk criticism from their fellows.

THE EDUCATION OF HENRY ADAMS

The conspiracy of silence is breaking up: we are learning to talk more openly about our joys and fears as teachers, our achievements and frustrations in the classroom. As I have listened to my colleagues talk about their students and their classrooms, the one fear and frustration mentioned more than any other, as for Henry Adams, was in leading a discussion. No matter how many articles on technique we read, or workshops we attend, the dreaded discussion continues to bother us more than any other part of our daily teaching lives. Freshman seminar and discussion-based core programs continue to develop. Pressures not only to "do more discussion" but to do it well, reinforced by student evaluations and faculty development centers, do not go away. We are learning, alas, that to walk into class and hold up one's copy of the assigned text, asking, "How'd you like that?" does not necessarily guarantee an enthusiastic, rewarding discussion.

We need, first of all, to acknowledge our fears in facing discussion classes: the terror of silences, the related challenges of the shy and dominant student, the overly-long dialogue between ourself and one combative student, the problems of digression and transitions, student fear of criticism, and our own fear of having to say "I don't know." Worst of all, perhaps, is the embarrassment of realizing, usually in retrospect, that "about half way through the period I lapsed, *again,* into lecture." I suspect that our fears about discussion (and our lapses) have a great deal to do with the issue of who controls the classroom. Although psychologically rooted, the control issue is best dealt with as a nitty-gritty practical question of how to plan and how to begin.

My first assumption is that an effective discussion, like most anything, depends upon good planning. The content goals for any given class period usually suggest employing different teaching strategies. We would like to be able to select from among many discussion possibilities with confidence. The purpose of this article is to expand the range of our options by describing very precisely several different ways of starting a discussion. Like Henry Adams, we "devise schemes" to find out what our students are thinking.

My particular schemes are guided by the following assumptions and principles about discussions:

- because we have much to learn from each other, all must be encouraged to participate
- it is important to devise ways in which each student has something to say, especially early in the class period
- students should be expected to do some (often highly structured) thinking about a text or issue before the discussion class begins
- students should know and feel comfortable with each other and with the teacher. As Carl Rogers and others keep reminding us, learning is aided perhaps most of all by the equality of personal relationships
- those relationships are enhanced by a climate of trust, support, acceptance, and respect: even "wrong" answers are legitimate
- a student's self-image is always affected by his or her participation in discussions: feedback, therefore, is crucial for self-esteem
- the primary goal in any discussion is to enhance the understanding of some common topic or "text" (in the broadest sense)
- different kinds of texts, purposes, and faculty teaching styles suggest using different kinds of discussion schemes.

My hope and expectation is that other teachers will adapt these suggestions and devise schemes for their own texts, purposes, and teaching styles.

(1) GOALS AND VALUES TESTING: The students are asked to pair off and decide together what they think is the primary value of the particular text for the day, and how their consideration of it meshes with course goals. "Why are we reading this?" "Why now?" After five minutes or so, invite reactions. It is not necessary to hear from each pair, but hearing from a few provides a public reality test for the teacher's course goals ("Is this text serving the purpose I had hoped it would?"), as well as providing a mutual basis for further probing into the text. An alternative initial question for the pairs is to ask for a list of relationships (comparisons and contrasts) between this text and another, usually the

most recent one. Make the instructions explicit: "Identify three themes common to both texts," "Suggest the two most obvious differences between the two texts," "Which did you like best and why?" [and] "Make a list of as many comparisons (or contrasts) as you can in ten minutes." In this case, in order to benefit from the richness of diversity, as well as to confirm similar insights, it is probably best to check in with each pair.

(2) CONCRETE IMAGES: It is obvious, of course, that discussions go better when specific references are made. Yet I think we often need help remembering the content of our text. A few minutes at the beginning can guarantee that the sophisticated analysis we seek will be based on specific facts. Go around the table and ask each student to state one concrete image/scene/event/moment from the text that stands out. No analysis is necessary—just recollections and brief description. As each student reports, the collective images are listed on the board, thus providing a visual record of selected content from the text as a backdrop to the following discussion. Usually the recall of concrete scenes prompts further recollections, and a flood of images flows from the students. A follow-up question is to invite the class to study the items on the board, and ask: "What themes seem to emerge from these items?" "What connects these images?" "Is there a pattern to our recollected events?" "What is missing?" This is, obviously, an inductive approach to the text. Facts precede analysis. But also, everyone gets to say something early in class and every contribution gets written down to aid our collective memory and work.

(3) GENERATING QUESTIONS: We have our own important questions to ask about a text. And we should ask them. But students also have their questions and they can learn to formulate better ones. Being able to ask the right questions about a particular text may be the first way of coming to terms with it. There are many ways of generating questions:

a. Ask students ahead of time (Wednesday for Friday's class) to prepare one or two questions about their reading. One can vary the assignment by specifying different kinds of questions: open-ended, factual, clarifying, connective and relational, involving value conflicts, etc.

b. As students walk into the classroom ask them to write down (probably anonymously early in the term) one or two discussable questions about the text. "What questions/issues/problems do you want this group to explore in the next hour about this reading?" Hand all questions to one student (a shy one, perhaps) who, at random, selects questions for class attention. Do not expect to get through all of them, but the discussion of two or three questions usually will deal with or touch on almost every other one. Students, like all of us, ask questions they really want to answer themselves, and they will make sure their point is made somehow.

c. Same as b, except the teacher (or a student) takes a minute or two to categorize the questions and deals with them more systematically.

d. Ask each student to write down one or two questions (either ahead of time or at the start of class), but in this case the student owns his/her question and is in charge of leading the discussion until he/she feels there has been a satisfactory exploration of the issues. Start anywhere and go around the table. This obviously works best in smaller groups with longer periods than 50 minutes.

e. Divide the class into pairs or small groups and charge each group to decide upon *one* salient question to put to the rest of the class.

(4) FINDING ILLUSTRATIVE QUOTATIONS: We do not often enough go to the text and read passages out loud together. Students, we are told, do not know how to read any more. If so, they need to practice and to see modeled good old-fashioned *explication de texte*. Ask each student, either ahead of time or at the start of class, to find one or two quotations from the assigned text that he/she found particularly significant. There are many ways in which the instructions may be put: "Find one quotation you especially liked and one you especially disliked." Or, "Find a quotation which you think best illustrates the major thesis of the piece." Or, "Select a quote you found difficult to understand." Or, "Find a quotation which suggests, to you, the key symbol of the larger text." After a few minutes of browsing (perhaps in small groups of three to four), the students will be ready to turn to specific passages, read out loud, and discuss. Be sure to pause long enough for everyone to find the right spot in their books: "Starting with the middle para-

graph on page sixty-one—are you all with us?" Lively and illuminating discussion is guaranteed because not all students will find the same quotations to illustrate various instructions, nor, probably, will they all interpret the same passages the same way. It is during this exercise that I have had the most new insights into texts I had read many times previously. And there may be no more exciting (or modeling) experience than for students to witness their teacher discovering a new insight and going through the process of refining a previously held interpretation. "Great class today! I taught Doc Frederick something he didn't know."

(5) BREAKING INTO SMALLER GROUPS: No matter the size of a class, sixty or six or one hundred and sixty, it can always be broken down into smaller groups of four, five, eight, fifteen, or whatever. The purpose, quite simply, is to enable more people to say something and to generate more ideas about a text or topic. Also, groups lend themselves usually to a lively, competitive spirit, whether asked to or not. We are interested not only in the few people we are grouped with but also in "what they're doing over there." Furthermore, reticent students often feel more confident in expressing themselves in a larger group after they have practiced the point with a safer, smaller audience. There are three crucial things to consider in helping small groups to work well. First, the instructions should be utterly clear, simple, and task-oriented. Examples: "Decide together which of the brothers is the major character in the novel." "Which person in the *Iliad* best represents the qualities of a Greek hero? Which person, the same or different, best represents a hero by your standards?" "Why did the experiment fail? What would you suggest changing?" "Identify the three main themes of this text." "What is Picasso's painting saying?" "Identify three positive and three negative qualities of King David's character." "What do you think is the crucial turning point in Malcolm's life?" "If you were the company treasurer (lawyer), what decision would you make?" "Generate as big a list as you can of examples of sex-role stereotyping in these first two chapters." "If you were Lincoln, what would you do?" In giving these instructions, be sure to give the groups a sense of how much time they have to do their work. Second, I believe in varying the ways in which groups are formed in order to create different-sized groups with different constituencies. Pair off ("with someone you don't know") one day; count off by fives around the room another; form groups of "about eight" around clumps of students sitting near one another on a third day. And third, vary the ways in which groups report out when reassembled. Variations include:

- each group reports orally, with the teacher recording results (if appropriate) on the board
- each group is given a piece of newsprint and felt-pen upon which to record its decision, which are then posted around the room
- space is provided for each group, when ready, to write their results on the blackboard
- each group keeps notes on a ditto master, which the teacher runs off and distributes to everyone for continuing discussion the next meeting
- no reporting out is necessary or reactions are invited from the several groups, but not necessarily from all of them

Further possibilities for small groups are described in the suggestions that follow:

(6) GENERATING TRUTH STATEMENTS: This exercise develops critical skills and generates a good deal of friendly rivalry among groups. The instructions to each group are to decide upon three statements known to be true about some particular issue. "It is true about slavery that. . . ." "We have agreed that it is true about the welfare system that. . . ." "It is true about international politics in the 1950s that. . . . "We know it to be true about the theory of relativity that. . . ." And so on. I have found this strategy useful in introducing a new topic—slavery, for example—where students may think they already know a great deal but the veracity of their assumptions demands examination. The complexity and ambiguity of knowledge is clearly revealed as students present their truth statements and other students raise questions about or refute them. The purpose of the exercise is to develop some true statements, perhaps, but mostly to generate a list of questions and of issues demanding further study. This provides an agenda for the unit. Sending students to the library is the usual next step, and they are quite charged up for research after the process of trying to generate truth statements.

(7) FORCED DEBATE: Although neither one of two polar sides of an issue obviously contains the whole truth, it is often desirable to force students to select one or the other of two opposite sides and to defend their choice. "Burke or Paine?" "Booker T. Washington or W. E. B. Du Bois?" "Are you for or against achieving racial balance in the schools?" "Should Nora have left or stayed?" "Who had the better argument: Creon or Antigone?" "Capitalism or Socialism for developing nations?" Once students have made their choice, which may be required prior to entering the room for class that day, I ask them to sit on one side of the table or room or the other to represent their decision. Physical movement is important and sides need to face each other. Once the students have actually, as it were, put their bodies on the line, they are more receptive to answering the question: "Why have you chosen to sit where you are?" Inevitably, there may be some few students who absolutely refuse (quite rightly) to choose one side or the other. If they persist, with reasons, create a space for a middle position. This adds a dimension to the debate and, as in the case of deciding between Burke and Paine on whether or not to support the French Revolution, those in the middle find out what it is like to attempt to remain neutral or undecided in heated, revolutionary times. I also invite students to feel free to change their place during a debate if they are so persuaded, which adds still another real (and sometimes chaotic) aspect to the experience.

(8) ROLE PLAYING: This is a powerful learning strategy, guaranteed to motivate and animate most students and to confuse and make nervous many. Role playing is tricky. It can be as simple (deceptively so) as asking two members of the class to volunteer to adopt the roles of two characters from a novel at a crucial point in their relationship, discussing how they feel about it or what they should do next. Or two students can act out the President and an advisor debating some decision, or two slaves in the quarters at night discussing whether or not to attempt to run away, or a male and female (perhaps with reversed roles) discussing affirmative action or birth control. Issues involving value conflicts, moral choices, and timeless human dilemmas related to the students' world usually work best, but role playing need not be so personal. A colleague of mine in biology creates a student panel of foundation grant evaluators, before whom other students present papers and make research proposals. Or, as students walk into class and sit down, they find a card in front of them which indicates the name of a character from a novel, or an historical personage, or even a concept. For the discussion that follows they are to *be* the role indicated on their card. Knowing this might happen is not a bad motivator to make sure students get their reading done.

Any situation involving multiple group conflicts is appropriate for role playing. There are many simulation games for contemporary issues in the social sciences. But for history, I like to create my own somewhat less elaborate "games," putting students into the many roles represented in some historical event or period. One of my favorites is a New England town meeting in 1779, in which a variety of groups (landed elite, yeoman farmers, Tory sympathizers, soldiers and riff-raff, artisans, lawyers and ministers, etc.) are charged with drafting instructions for delegates to a state constitutional convention. Another is to challenge several groups in 1866—defeated Confederates, southern Unionists, northern Radical Republicans, northern moderates, and Black freedmen—to develop lists of goals and strategies for accomplishing them. I play an active role, as moderator of the town meeting or as President Johnson, organizing and monitoring the interactions that follow group caucuses. Our imagination can create many appropriate examples for role playing. You have, I am sure, your own.

But because role playing can be traumatic for some students and because a poorly planned or poorly monitored role play can get out of control, I want to make a few cautionary suggestions that I have found helpful, if not crucial. First, except for finding the cards at the beginning of class which compel playing a role, in most role playing activities students should have some choice in how much to participate, either by deciding whether or not to volunteer or by being part of a group large enough to reduce the pressures on any one individual. Teachers should monitor carefully the unspoken signals of students who may find their role uncomfortable, and intervene, often by skillfully pursuing their own role, to extricate or reduce the pressures on an actor. Generally, however, I have found role playing to be an effective way for the normally shy student, who has said little or nothing in class, to unblock in the new role and participate more readily in conventional discussions afterwards. Second, give students some time (how much depends upon the nature of the particular role play) to prepare themselves for their role. This might mean two days

or more in order to do some research, or fifteen minutes in groups to pool information, or five minutes to refresh one's memory about a character in a novel, or a couple of minutes simply to get in touch with the feelings of a character and situation. Third, in giving instructions the definition of roles to be played should be concrete and clear enough for students to get a handle on who they are playing, yet open enough for the expression of their own personality and interpretation. If the roles are prescribed too clearly, students merely imitate the character described (although sometimes this is the requirement) and have difficulty going beyond it with anything of themselves. If the roles are described too loosely, without a clear context, students will stray too far from the actual situation to be experienced and learned. And finally—and most importantly—in any role play experience, as much (if not more) time should be devoted to debriefing afterwards as for the exercise itself. This is when the substantive lessons of the experience are discovered, explored, and confirmed. This is when those students who may have served as observers will offer their insights and analysis on what happened. Above all, this is when the actors will need an opportunity to talk about how they felt in their roles and what they learned, both about themselves and about the substantive issues involved.

(9) NONSTRUCTURED SCENE SETTING: Most of the ways of starting a discussion described thus far involve a great deal of structure and direction. But inevitably, when teachers suspect that they have been dominating too much ("I blew it again—talked most of the hour!"), it is clearly time to give students an opportunity to take a discussion in *their* directions, and to do most, if not all, of the talking. The teacher, however, has a responsibility for setting the scene and getting class started. There are a variety of ways to do this, some more directive than others. Put some slides on a carousel and, without a word, show them at the beginning of class. Or, as the students walk into the classroom, the teacher plays a piece of music or a speech on a tape recorder. Or, on the board before class the teacher writes a quotation or two, or two or three questions, or a list of words or phrases or names, or even an agenda of issues to be explored. The only necessary verbal instructions are to make it clear to the students that until a defined time (perhaps the last five minutes) you, the teacher, intend to stay out of the discussion entirely. Even having said that, I have still found that I am capable of breaking my own contract and intervening or, more likely, affecting the class by nonverbal signals. I tell my students that I find it extremely difficult to stay uninvolved, and that I need their help in making sure I stay out of the discussion. They are usually happy to oblige. If possible, adopt an utterly nonevaluative observer role and take descriptive notes on the course of the discussion. To read your notes back to the students may be the most helpful feedback you can give them.

(10) A TENTH WAY TO START: As the term progresses students will have experienced many different exciting ways to start a discussion, most of which, we hope, enhance their understanding of a text or issue. Once the expectation of variety has been established, there is even a legitimate place for the following strategy: stroll into class with your book, sit on the edge of the table, hold the book up, and ask: "How'd you like it?"

Although it has not been my primary purpose in this article to extol the many values of discussion, I assume that my bias has been implicitly clear. The key to effective retention of learning, I believe, is in owning the discovery. Emerson wrote in his journals that a wise person "must feel and teach that the best wisdom cannot be communicated [but] must be acquired by every soul for itself." My primary strategy as a teacher is to structure situations in which students have as many opportunities as possible to acquire wisdom for themselves; that is, to own the discovery of a new learning insight or connection and to express that discovery to others. In this way their substantive learning is increased and their self-esteem is enhanced. How we plan the start of class is crucial in achieving this goal. "Hey, roomie, I now know what Emerson meant by self-reliance. What I said in class about it today was that. . . ." Which translated means: "Hey, I'm OK, I understand this stuff. I said something today others found helpful." Which translated means: "Class was good today: he let me talk."

READING

The Gifted Can't Weigh That Giraffe

SELMA WASSERMANN

The turbojet descends from 32,000 feet into the purple air and the rainy-wintry Vancouver morning left far behind is transformed magically into spring. On the freeway the cars wear yellow and blue license plates reading KING NI and M. BENZ and HOT TUBS and you know you are in Southern California.

The school is low and wide-flung and I am led into an attractive room—the "center" for working with gifted children. A group of nine volunteers, ages 10 to 12, are led in to participate in a demonstration of a "teaching for thinking" lesson with this teacher who has just dropped out of the skies. Around the periphery of the room is a large group of teachers who have come to observe teaching strategies that emphasize higher-order cognitive skills.

Perspectives

The pupils are reserved and there is some evidence of anxiety. My attempts to establish rapport are not very successful.

I offer them a piece of wisdom. "How do you suppose birds learn to fly?"

"What do you mean?" asks Chris.

"I don't understand what you want us to do," says Mark, his body shifting uncomfortably.

"We didn't study birds yet," says Ann, explaining the lack of response.

The children are clearly troubled.

I make several attempts, using a variety of different open-ended tasks that have no clear, definitive answers, to tap the creative thinking capabilities of these children, and I am dead-ended every time.

Again and again I encounter responses in which the pupils try to manipulate me into helping them "get the right answer." The more I avoid doing this, the more tense they seem. Their dependency, their rigidity, their intolerance for ambiguity, their inability to take cognitive risks and their anxiety are astonishing.

The pupils I see later that afternoon are representatives of a different group. Although the school has a more benign name for them, they are the low achievers.

"How could you weigh a giraffe?" I begin. They immediately rise to the challenge.

"You put 'em on a bathroom scale," says Maria.

"Dummy, he ain't gonna fit," says Benedetto, smiling at his wisdom. "You gotta put two scales. Put his back feet on one and his front feet on the other."

More and more responses of equally refreshing ideas keep coming. Then Sam offers: "I'd get a big truck and fill it with food that giraffes like to eat. Then I'd weigh the truck. Then, I'd hide inside of it and call, 'Here, giraffe. Here, giraffe.' When he got inside, I'd slam the doors and weigh the truck again."

I am astonished at the difference in responses of both groups, and even more concerned about the "single, right answer" orientation of the pupils identified as gifted. I am flabbergasted at their limited personal autonomy and their difficulty with questions that do not call for single, correct answers. I want to find out more, so I ask for time to talk with small groups of children from both schools.

The children from the gifted classes tell me that they carry with them anxiety that is constant and pervasive. They worry about their school performance and grades.

Pressures from parents and teachers to perform at high levels is subtle, but excessive. The children are *always* on guard. They use their considerable talents to try to figure out what their significant adults demand of them, and their lives are tilted in the direction of performance up-to-expectations.

They are crippled by fears of making mistakes and their anxieties are manifest in a variety of stress-related physical symptoms. Because school tasks are largely of the "single, correct answer" type (e.g., "The sea is made of water"), these children have become gifted lesson learners—excelling at the lower-order cognitive tasks found in traditional textbook and workbook exercises.

Unfortunately, the transfer of these lower-level thinking skills to the higher-order tasks of problem solving, creating, and imagining does not occur magically. There is even evidence to suggest that such activities are counterproductive to higher-order functioning. And so we have a group of gifted children who are exceptionally good at the very narrow tasks of finding single, correct answers to the most mundane questions but who lack experience and therefore expertise in the more intellectually rigorous and more creative stuff.

But what about the low achievers? How is it they were able to outperform the gifted group? Though the in-school experiences are largely similar (lots and lots of textbook and workbook activities requiring single, correct answers), the out-of-school experiences of these children appear to be significantly different. Most of them are out on the streets involved in many activities that require high levels of creative problem-solving capabilities. They have become "street-wise"—experienced and talented problem solvers; while the gifted and talented group attends music lessons and French lessons and does prodigious amounts of homework.

What does it add up to? Can this one event have any educational significance at all? Perhaps not. On the other hand, if you were to look at children's behavior and see excessive anxiety about school performance, considerable dependency, preoccupation with single, correct answers, and inability to think creatively in the face of new problems, then it might be fair to conclude that our teaching is decreasing their autonomy and is substantially disabling them as problem solvers.

Seven Questions for Testing My Teaching

LAURA L. NASH

A friend of mine was made an assistant professor. This fellow—we'll call him Lee—was *very* bright, very nice, sympathetic, also an athlete, a devoted husband, and new father. He was very excited about the undergraduate course he would offer in the fall. The topic was quite interesting. It was a history-of-ideas course of the highest academic integrity and he was writing a book on the subject at the same time.

Well, Lee prepared and prepared and prepared for the course. We talked a good deal with him about what material he wanted to cover and how to acquire it. I must say that he got me very interested in the topic. The semester passed, and Lee—very much worn out from preparation and grading—got through the course. (His mode was to lecture.)

At the end of the year Lee was distinguished in the student newspaper as the most boring professor on campus—a fact which was picked up and reprinted in the wider press.

I suspect his lectures were brilliant, that he was "superstudent," and that he had geared his lectures to the intellectual level of the Society of Fellows with all its Nobel Prize scholars.

As I went over in my mind what went wrong despite all Lee's good intentions and preparation, I began to come up with this idea that he'd overlooked all sorts of basic questions about what he wanted to do and was doing in the course, and that asking them might relieve the catatonic anxiety he now has about teaching. Let's review those questions.

1. *Do all students start equal?*
   Level of Learning. Where do I want to end? Amount of material in the syllabus? If not equal, strengths and weakness of students? How to get this information: class cards?
2. *How am I asking them to learn?*
   Mode of Learning. Programmatic, exploratory, group effort, lecture, attack? Level of uncertainty? Variety of modes? Silent signals, self-referring, teacher-referring?
3. *What's going on in class?*
   Room dynamics; interpersonal dynamics? Are the talkers representative of rest of class? Did they get it? Can I help them next time with a summary?

4. *What's going on outside of class?*
   Chem. 20 midterm, football weekend, recruiting week?
5. *How does my mode of evaluation affect learning?*
   When does it occur; feedback expected? Where does it occur, how often, what forms?
6. *Who do I want to be?*
   Personal Role. Expert, best friend, senior professor, popularity queen, remote, developer, mentor?
   How do these roles affect learning? Do students see me in same role as I see myself? What is an appropriate role?
7. *What do I owe myself?*
   Complete graduate work? Research? Family?
   How to get perspective on what I am doing, teaching included; is this enjoyable?

CASE

"Look at the Fish!":
Karen Prentiss and Professor Lockwood (A)

*This case was developed, researched, and written by **Abby Hansen** for the Developing Discussion Leadership Skills and Teaching by the Case Method Seminar. It is based on data contributed by involved participants. All names, places, and some peripheral facts have been disguised.*

Harvard Graduate School of Education Case No. 1.

Karen Prentiss—a first semester master's candidate at prestigious Farwestern University Graduate School of Education (Ed School) in northern California—sat in the Sunset Cafe and stared into her coffee cup. Across the street was the classroom building where she had just received her first paper grade from Professor Andrew Lockwood.

The grade was a big, red "zero minus." She shook her head in disbelief. Her background was strong: private secondary schools, a good college, two successful years of high school teaching and administration. And her other professors were reacting well to her class contributions. But Lockwood had humiliated her during the first class (a large-group case discussion). And now this grade. She had never seen anything like it.

Karen sipped her coffee and wondered: Should I be in this course? Should I even be at Farwestern?

* * *

The Professor

Andrew Lockwood was in his mid-fifties. Tall and fair-haired, he always taught in a coat and tie. He had come to the Policy Studies Program at the Graduate School of Education from a dual career in law and public administration in which he had gained distinction. A colleague called him "one of the most sought-after, innovative, hardest-working professors at Farwestern University." In an institution where many professors had warm, nurturing teaching styles, Lockwood had a reputation for rigor and formality.

The Student

A 27-year-old woman with shoulder-length blond hair and green eyes, Karen Prentiss dressed casually, often in tailored slacks. She described herself as "from a family of educators. We moved from Chicago to Pennsylvania when I was eight because my father got a job as headmaster and history teacher in a private college preparatory school for boys. He aspired to administrative heights, but never got the jobs he wanted—maybe because he didn't have a doctorate. Or maybe he was just too nice."

Karen studied in private, all-girls' junior high and high schools. She expected to continue at an Ivy League college, but "didn't get into my first choices. Instead, I went to Oberlin—and loved it. I double-majored in History and Political Science, wrote for the school newspaper, worked in Student Services, served on dozens of committees, was student body president and student rep to the Board of Trustees. The experience taught me that I really love college campuses."

Right after college Karen married a "computer engineer, six years older than I. Steve and I met before I left for college. Being apart was hard, but also good for us and our relationship. When we got married, he was a senior program analyst at a company near Philadelphia. We agreed to stay there for three years—after which we would move wherever we had to so that I could go to graduate school."

During those three years, Karen taught history at an independent girls' school and became department chair. "I loved the contact, the controversy, working with kids, and the challenge of messy things—or rather, getting out of messy things. It made me more certain than ever that I wanted a graduate degree."

How Karen Came to Farwestern

Karen "applied to the best schools of education that I could think of—Stanford, Harvard, Columbia, and Farwestern, to 'see if I could play with the big boys.'" Getting into Farwestern's one-year Ed.M. program in Educational Policy and Practices thrilled her: "The program was just what I wanted, and getting accepted meant that I'd finally made the 'major leagues.'"

The preparatory school where she was working offered Karen "a good administrative post." Instead of accepting it, she "did something wild. I persuaded Steve to sell our furniture, drive to California, and find jobs to save up for my graduate school tuition. It wasn't as impetuous as it sounded—Steve's company was laying off computer engineers, and he was one of them, so nothing held us in Pennsylvania. But we both also knew that I have this crazy drive. I couldn't wait to go West. It was scary and very exciting."

In California, Karen and Steve "found an apartment near Farwestern University. Steve spent days looking for computer jobs. At night, from 7 P.M. to midnight, he unloaded milk trucks at a local supermarket. I worked in a furniture store from 7 A.M. to 11 P.M., six days a week. It was a great year: we learned a lot about work, ourselves, and each other." Karen worked "right up until the week before Orientation."

Karen's Orientation Week

Karen recalled, "I was psyched to be studying at Farwestern. Finally! Early in the week, all 650 of us brand-new graduate students assembled in a big theater on campus. While the Dean of the Graduate School of Education addressed us, I scanned the faces of the other students. They all looked smart. I wondered, 'How will classes be? Will I be able to do this?'"

Orientation Week had multiple purposes—to introduce students to the institution, their program requirements, their advisers, their fellow students, their professors, and the course offerings. On the first morning of Orientation, Karen ran into "Paul Schirm, who had interviewed me during my admissions process. He was finishing a doctorate in Educational Policy and Practices and working part-time in the Admissions Office. He greeted me on the street and mentioned Professor Andrew Lockwood right away. He said that Lockwood was a 'big wig,' at the top of his field, incredibly knowledgeable, first rate. Lockwood was teaching an elective course, Educational Policy and Practices, that semester. When we parted, Paul said, 'Check it out.' The meaning I got was: 'Karen, you're a fool if you don't take advantage of this!'"

Later that day, Karen had lunch with Roberta Russell, a student adviser, assigned to help newcomers during Orientation. When Karen mentioned her interest in Lockwood's course, Roberta—who was also a doctoral candidate in Educational Policy and Practices—"raised her eyebrows, put her hand out in a 'Whoa!' gesture, and said, 'Karen, you don't want to do that first semester.' I asked why not, and she said, 'Listen to me—Lockwood is one tough cookie.'"

Karen remembered, "That intrigued me. It's 'typical Karen' to take on challenges. If somebody tells me I can't do something, that's what I want to do. Paul's glowing praise and Roberta's warning made me think, 'I just have to take this course.' So I went to Lockwood's Orientation talk."

Andrew Lockwood's Orientation Talk

During Orientation Week, Farwestern Graduate School of Education faculty gave fifteen-minute talks to introduce themselves and their courses. "They're usually informal, and their purpose is basically to encourage students to take this professor's course. As I listened, I'd be thinking, '$14,000 for eight courses—this had better be good.'"

101

Karen compared Lockwood's talk to the other professors': "Everyone else's was in a little classroom or seminar room. Lockwood's was in the school's only big formal discussion classroom. It's an amphitheater, with curving terraced rows of desks that rise up from the central teacher's area, which has a desk and a set of movable blackboards. Many teachers barely filled a little room, but this guy had people standing in the aisle of the biggest room at the Ed School."

Karen remembered the diverse crowd he drew: "I thought, 'Oh, there are Business and Government School people here. This must be *serious*.'" She recognized a few fellow Ed School newcomers, who seemed to be thinking, "'Hmm, this is something different.'"

Lockwood impressed Karen as "formal and unsmiling. He held a packet of papers. I assumed that these were copies of the course syllabus, and that he would begin, like other teachers, by giving them out. In other introductory talks, professors spoke while we read through the syllabus. But it soon became clear that Lockwood wasn't going to do anything that would distract our full attention from him. He held the packet of papers while he talked."

"Other faculty members opened casually—'Hi, I'm so and so and I teach such and such'—and then they talked about their courses. If a student asked, 'How long is the paper?,' the prof would say, 'Well, I'm flexible.' You got an impression of 'warm, fuzzies.' But Lockwood's opening was different. He said, 'I assume you are all here to learn about Educational Policy and Practices, not How to Groom Your Poodle or How to Have a Relationship.'"

His sarcasm provoked "nervous laughter," and Karen thought, "'He's putting us down, but nobody's leaving the room.' Then he told us, 'This class meets from 8 to 10 A.M. Tuesdays and Thursdays. If you have a problem with that, you should leave right now.'" A few people left. Then he defined a key process that the course would cover: negotiation. "He said that it meant 'solving problems by sitting down and seeing what people can get from each other—with both sides getting what they want.'"

Karen thought, "'Oh boy, this is big league stuff. This is power. This is *it!*'" She recalled that "Lockwood looked around the room and said, 'I see about 150 people here. The course has room for 75, so you'll have to write a paper to get in. I want to know why I should accept you. The paper is to be

one page exactly, single-spaced, due at my office by 8 tomorrow morning—no ifs, no buts, no excuses.'"

Hands went up. In other introductory talks, students had asked, "What if we can't say it all in one page?," or, "I have to pick up a child in day care—can you extend the deadline?" Karen thought, "Oh God, if people question this guy, he'll fry them." He responded the same way to each question, "What did I just say?"

Students had asked other faculty members, "What will your course do for my career?" With Lockwood, they asked, "How will we know if we get into this course?" He said, "I'll pick the first twenty people that I want. If they decline my invitation, I'll go on to the next twenty." Karen's reaction was, "Boy, we'll know right away if we're on his A list, or B list, or what."

When someone asked, "Can we get a syllabus?," Lockwood said, "No. I'm not giving it to people who aren't going to be in the class." Then he handed out the papers he had been holding. They turned out to be directions to his office. Karen looked around: "Some older students, in their forties or fifties, looked enraged, as if to say, 'I can't believe it—I've been a superintendent of schools, or a college president, or whatever . . . why am I putting up with this?'" But nobody left the room. "People were too intimidated to walk out on Lockwood."

That Night

Karen and Steve had worked and saved for a year so that she could go to graduate school. That night—their last night of "freedom" before classes began—they were supposed to attend the big student social event of Orientation Week, a dinner cruise on San Francisco Bay. When Karen got home, she said, "We can't go on the cruise—I have to write a one-page memo to get into Andrew Lockwood's course."

Steve said, "We paid $25 apiece for those tickets!"

"I know," Karen replied, "but I've *got* to get into this course. This is exactly why I came here."

He shook his head, "Oh my God, this is going to be a long year."

But Karen knew that he could see "that excitement, that juice I get when I'm determined."

Karen "spent hours writing the memo for Lockwood that night. I showed Steve a draft that began, 'I have always been interested in academic administration,' and he said, 'No, no. If you don't lay it on the line, he'll know. Tell him what you *really* want.' So I wrote, 'I want to be a college president, and I see that the job involves taking different elements on campus and helping them come to resolution.' I put in all sorts of stuff that I otherwise wouldn't—that I had been student body president in college, that the senior class had dedicated its yearbook to me."

She stayed up all night, "writing draft after draft of that memo for Lockwood." She got her paper in by 8 A.M., knowing that the results would be posted outside his office, "where everyone could see them."

The Course

"Educational Policy and Practices" was an elective case-discussion course that attracted so many students that it was often subdivided into two sections, each the size of other professors' whole courses. The material included policy analysis, conflict resolution, press relations, and many other issues useful to educational administrators and policymakers. Although discussion-based, it also featured a mixture of pedagogical techniques—simulations, role-plays (both planned and impromptu), videotapes, and class visits from practitioners. Requirements included a weekly one-page case analysis and class participation.

Professor Lockwood's final grades conformed to the same A through D scale as the rest of the school, but, as students soon discovered, he had an internal system of his own for everything but final exams and course grades.

The Student Group

Karen reported, "Half the class was from the School of Government. One of them was a general from the Israeli army, who was at Farwestern for a one-year program in administration. There were some Business School and Law School students too. And the rest of us were from the Grad. School of Education. It was an older class than most."

The First Class Meeting

The first session took place on the second day of the fall semester, in the large amphitheater-shaped classroom (bisected by one central aisle) in which Lockwood had given his introductory talk. There were no assigned seats. At 8 A.M. sharp, Karen sat on the aisle in the second row down from the back—far from the teacher's desk down in the center of the room.

Professor Lockwood walked up the aisle to the middle of the room. "He turned to one side of the classroom, then to the other, and announced, 'We have some rules in this classroom.' He held up his thumb. 'One. We do not raise our hands while other people are speaking.' He jabbed his index finger into the air. 'Two, we do not bring up unrelated points—if you have a contribution, it must relate to the point on the floor.' (Karen recalled thinking that this was good—as an undergraduate, she had been frustrated by a lack of focus in discussions.) Lockwood raised his middle finger. 'Three. You all have name cards. Bring them every day. If your card is not there, you will not be called on.' He held up his ring finger. 'Four, you will use each other's names.' He held up his little finger. 'Five. All assignments will be turned in on time.'"

He kept his hand up for a second, then lowered his arm and walked briskly down to the teacher's desk. There he turned to the group and continued, "You might want to form a study group of five to six people to prepare each day's case and readings so that you have time to think about what you're going to say in class." Karen thought, "Right, you don't want us to waste your time with stupid comments." From Lockwood, the words "you might want to" came across like "a command. Everyone knew it, so we formed groups with whoever was around us."

Lockwood had distributed all the cases and readings for the course before the weekend. He asked, "Is there anyone who hasn't gotten a case packet yet?" A few hands went up, mostly those of foreign students. Lockwood looked around and said, "Well, they've been available for 72 hours—you're already behind."

Then he opened the case discussion. He pointed at a woman in the second row and read her name card. "Myra," he said. "Who are the key players in this case?" Waiting for her answer, he moved to the blackboard and picked up a piece of chalk. Karen remembered, "Myra listed every name in the case. Obviously, like most of us in the class, she had no idea what the term 'key players' meant. He let her talk on and on. It seemed interminable. As she said each name, he wrote it on the board. When she finished, he pointed to a name, looked at the whole class, and said, 'Do you *really* think that Ralph is a key player here?'"

The class took Lockwood's tone as a cue to demolish Myra's list. "The people who seemed most confident were School of Government students, who had clustered in the seats down near the teacher's desk. Most of them were male second-years; they'd already had a lot of case discussions. They'd say, 'X isn't a key player,' and Lockwood would erase X's name.'" As the School of Government students spoke, Karen noticed people from other schools "raising their hands, then lowering them. There was a lot of 'should I, or shouldn't I?' in the room. Every time Lockwood erased a name, more and more hands would go down." Karen felt "awful for Myra, but happy that he hadn't called on me."

Finally, Lockwood asked, "Well, who *are* the key players?" More hands went down. To Karen, it seemed that "people were thinking, 'I'd better keep my mouth shut, or he'll erase me!' After a while, Lockwood was left with a core group of talkers, just School of Government students."

He steered the discussion through key players, key events, key problems, and key solutions. Near the end of class, Karen gathered courage: "I don't remember the exact point under discussion, but Lockwood had been getting visibly more frustrated for several minutes. He hadn't been writing people's comments on the board—and I had noticed that when he liked a comment, he wrote it down and then said something about it. This case involved a dispute among a superintendent of schools, a school board, the teachers, and the bus drivers. For some reason, I thought that everyone had been on the wrong track and I had the answer."

Karen's hand had been up for some time when he called on her. He was down at the blackboard when she said, "I think the superintendent feels concerned about losing her job." As she recalled, "Job security wasn't mentioned in the text. I thought it was important background."

Lockwood pointed his finger at her and said, "Karen, where in the case do you see that?" Karen's stomach started to clench. "Well, I just think the superintendent feels that way." He started walking up the aisle towards Karen, then paused at someone else's desk, a few rows below where she was sitting.

"Of course, everyone was looking at me by now. Lockwood stabbed his finger on the case that lay open on the other student's desk and said, more loudly: '*Where do you see that?*' I was completely befuddled by this time. I said, 'Well, you can see

that she's worried about her job from the conversation she has with the union leader. . . .'"

Then he walked all the way up to Karen's seat, stood over her, and pointed his finger down at her. "Karen, is that in the fish?" His remark referred to a reading passage that he had assigned with the first case, "an article on Louis Agassiz as a teacher. Agassiz gave his student a fish to dissect, and each time the student thought he had described its structure thoroughly, Agassiz would come back and say, 'Look at the fish.'"

Karen "just looked at Lockwood. He put his hand down flat on top of my copy of the case and said, '*Look at the fish!*'" Turning back to the class, but still pointing down at Karen, he said, "*This* is why you must read the case!"

Then he strode back down to the teacher's desk and class was over. As Karen packed up her things, a few people came over to pat her on the shoulder. The Ed School had a week-long grace period during which one could drop or add courses. Karen was wondering whether she should stay in Lockwood's course.

After the First Class

Karen went to the library alone. "I sat for a while, miserable, and finally said to myself, 'Okay, I didn't read the case well enough. I'll read the next case better.'"

Her study group met the next day. "We had formed the study groups with people sitting near us. My group included five women, all around thirty. We introduced ourselves. I was the only married one. Three of us were from the Ed School; the other two were from the School of Government. I and one other woman were the only ones who didn't live in graduate dorms. After introductions, we immediately started working on the next case. We tried to do what Lockwood had done in class—list key characters and issues. When we were done, there were a couple of comments about Lockwood—'Isn't Lockwood tough? This isn't going to be any picnic.' But people also said that they had learned a lot in the class. Nobody criticized Lockwood's teaching style. We were too scared. We just wanted to study the case and find the 'right' answer, the answer he wanted. We were preparing for discussion and also for the required one-page memo on the case. The memo was supposed to answer specific questions—What are the major

problems here? What is your resolution? I thought,
'I'll do a great job on this memo. *I can do this!*'"

The Second Class Meeting

Karen "spent the whole night before class writing
the case memo. I was exhausted, depressed, and
still wondering whether I should stay in this course.
I turned in my paper as I entered the room. I sat
way in the back and as far to the right as I could.
And I kept my hand—and head—down. I was so
upset that it was hard to focus on what was said.
It all went by in a blur."

The Next Class Session: Papers Are Returned

Karen "entered at the upper door of the classroom
promptly at 8 A.M. the next Tuesday. Our papers
were all fanned out in piles on the upper back row
of desktops. You could see people's names and
grades. The grades were in red, right on top of the
papers. My paper had a big '0−.' That's all; no other
comment. At first I was so stunned I couldn't see
anything else, but then I noticed that maybe a third
of the other papers also had 0−. Others had a check-
mark or a plus." Karen saw "a lot of shocked expressions, a lot of heads down."

Lockwood opened the class: "You'll notice that
you've gotten your papers. A check or plus means
you're in the right direction. Minus means it needs
some work. Zero minus means you missed the
point. Any questions?" Nobody raised a hand.

The day's case involved a company that had been
accused of polluting a river. Lockwood began the
discussion by saying, "Okay, role-play." Karen remembered, "He asked Claire—a shy, soft-voiced
woman from the Midwest—to play the CEO of the

company that had been polluting. Then he called
on others to play members of her staff, environmentalists, a TV reporter, and a camera operator."

Karen recalled the simulation: "Lockwood took
the environmental group out of the room for a moment. When they returned, the leader held a big
paper bag. Then Lockwood had Claire, the CEO,
sit at the teacher's desk. The person playing her
secretary said, 'There's an environmental group to
see you, and the press is with them. What do you
want to do?' Claire said, 'I'll talk to the environmentalists. But no press.' Then—by pre-arrange-
ment with Lockwood—the environmentalists'
leader barged up to her desk, followed by a student
with a prop video camera, which Lockwood had
given him. Another student, who was pretending
to be a newscaster from the six o'clock news, also
rushed up to the CEO's desk. The environmentalist
held the paper bag behind his back and said, 'You're
poisoning our rivers!' Claire made some reasonable
answer. Then the environmentalist emptied his bag
onto her desk. Splat—a big dead fish flopped out."

"Claire just sat there and stared at the fish. And
that was the end of the role-play. Lockwood spent
the rest of the discussion on the power of imagery
with the press."

After class, Karen skulked out of the building
with her shoulders hunched. "I crumpled the paper
with the big red 0−, threw it into a trash can, and
went across to the café. A couple of people I recognized from Orientation were having coffee. I
turned away from them and found a table in the
corner alone. All I could think about was that grade.
What did it mean? Should I be in this course?
Should I be at this school? Should I be in graduate
school at all? I really didn't know what to do."

"How Do You Expect Us to Get This If It Isn't in Your Notes?" (A)

*This case was developed and written by **Abby Hansen** for the Developing Discussion Leadership Skills Seminar. Data were furnished by involved participants. All names and some peripheral facts have been disguised.*

Harvard School of Public Health Case No. 1.

Mary Ann Demski, a second-year assistant professor at Farwestern University School of Public Health in California, stood facing the fifteen students in her introductory "Numerical Analysis in Statistical Applications" class. It was mid-October, about a quarter of the way through an eight-week lecture course that she had taught once before. Today's lecture topic was the Fast Fourier Transform (FFT), a technique widely used by engineers, but rather novel for statisticians.

The textbook explained the FFT, but Mary Ann considered the material complex enough to warrant supplementary explanation. She had spent hours writing a thick packet of notes, which the students picked up as they entered the classroom that day. To motivate them to learn the FFT, Mary Ann had decided to open her lecture by going over a "really messy statistical equation" that the FFT could help solve. She had written this equation in the notes because it included many complicated symbols that the students might get wrong if they copied them down in class. The explanation wasn't in the notes; she intended to go through that quickly and spend the bulk of the lecture on the FFT.

The class proceeded normally as Mary Ann discussed the statistical equation. But before she could finish, Ph.D. candidate Cindy Richardson, one of three advanced doctoral candidates taking the course, ruptured the typically low-key mood of the lecture. Cindy rose half out of her seat, slammed her books and notes down on the desktop, and said, in a voice charged with anger, "I don't understand! How do you expect us to get this if it isn't in your notes?"

The Instructor

One of the youngest faculty members at the school, Mary Ann was also among the most promising. Colleagues described her as "a rising star," "brilliant," "totally in command of her material," and "sincerely concerned about teaching."

Tall and athletic, with long blond hair that she often wore up or in a braid, 29-year-old Mary Ann Demski "knew better than to teach in jeans." Instead, she "dressed up a little bit," in tailored slacks, pullovers, and simple jewelry (small earrings, a plain gold cross on a chain around her neck). Her typical demeanor was friendly and warm. She used expressive hand gestures and sometimes punctuated her conversation with Polish phrases.

Section 2. The Roles, Responsibilities, and Skills of the Case Discussion Leader

CASE
"How Do You Expect Us to Get This If It Isn't in Your Notes?" (A)

Mary Ann's concern for teaching was by no means the norm at this school. In the quantitative disciplines in particular, faculty members tended to make their reputations as researchers, and virtually all instruction was done in traditional lectures. The previous year, when Mary Ann and a fellow instructor had written a proposal to improve math instruction, a friendly older colleague had warned, "This place is about research. Teaching will have no impact on your promotion prospects—as long as you aren't horrendous. Spend a maximum of two hours of preparation for each class hour." Mindful of this, Mary Ann had increased her research hours to "sixty to seventy per week." Even so, she calculated her teaching preparation time as "more like eight hours for every class hour."

Mary Ann's Background

Mary Ann had grown up "near Chicago, on a mile-long road where practically everybody was related to us. My godmother lived kitty-corner to our house; Uncle Casimir's and Uncle John's families lived down the street. My father never finished high school. He worked in a paint factory, starting in the resin department and working his way up into the motor pool where he became a master mechanic. Dad can fix anything; he even built our house."

She described her mother: "She married Dad right after high school and had five kids in six years. All of us, except the youngest, have college educations which we paid for ourselves. Annette, the oldest, also worked at the paint factory while studying accounting full-time in college. I'm the second daughter. Jimmy, the third child, teaches math at Gallaudet College for the Deaf near Baltimore. Eddie, the fourth child, is a journalist for a major company in Orlando, Florida. And Josie, the fifth, still works at the paint factory. She hasn't gotten a college education yet."

Mary Ann recalled high school and college: "I knew that Mom and Dad couldn't help much financially, so I hit the books and got a scholarship to Indiana University." Every summer, like her father, brothers, and sisters, Mary Ann did manual labor. Her first job was in the paint factory, sweeping floors. Then, for two summers, she worked in an ice cream factory, straightening the cookie tops on ice cream sandwiches and packing popsicles on an assembly line. Describing the job, she automatically made the hand motions of popsicle packing.

She commented, "It's probably fair to say that at least some of my desire to be a college professor has to do with wanting to get away from factory work." The first career that occurred to her was teaching math. She earned a provisional teaching certificate in college, interning as a high school math teacher.

In college, all of Mary Ann's math classes were lectures. She observed, "In class, we students expected to understand only about 20 percent of what the professor said. We'd listen and copy what was written on the board. It was like stenography. We'd keep our mouths shut in lecture because we didn't want to appear stupid. Then we'd go away and learn the material on our own."

After graduating near the top of her class, Mary Ann came to Farwestern Graduate School of Public Health for a Ph.D. in statistics. She spent two postdoctoral years there doing research before being hired as an assistant professor. Now in her second year, she considered herself as "known to be making the change from student to faculty member."

A Memorable College Experience

"I still get angry about the way a college professor responded to a question I asked in lecture," Mary Ann recalled. "By senior year, I was frustrated with the passivity of listening to lectures. I had finally decided that I wanted to *think* a bit more in class. It had occurred to me that the professor's job was to help us understand in class."

One day, in an Advanced Calculus lecture, Mary Ann raised her hand and said, "Excuse me, Dr. Liu, I really don't understand this. Could you explain it in some different way?" She was hoping that the professor would convert the equation he was describing into a graph or chart. "I'm a visual learner," she explained. "A graph would be a big help to me." But instead of casting the material in a different form, or asking Mary Ann to clarify her request for help, the professor—whom she described as "very traditional"—just repeated his explanation "in the same words that he had used the first time."

Mary Ann persevered, "I'm sorry, professor, I didn't understand that." This time, she recalled, "He looked really annoyed and said, 'This is very basic, Mary Ann. Why are you so stupid?'"

Retelling the incident, Mary Ann blushed of embarrassment. "Friends came up to me after class and said that the professor had behaved like a louse. I've since thought how much better it would have been if he'd acknowledged that this was difficult material or said something reassuring like, 'Don't worry, Mary Ann, you're just having some kind of block today. You can do this.'"

Mary Ann's Course

Mary Ann's "Numerical Analysis in Statistical Applications" was an eight-week course given in the fall semester, including two 2-hour lectures and a computer lab session each week. Mary Ann assigned weekly problem sets to be done in the computer lab. But she permitted students to work at their own pace and hand in the problem sets whenever they were complete. Mary Ann and her teaching assistant "always showed up at the labs for a while to help students."

The lecture class met from 1:30 to 3:00 P.M. in a somber, gray-walled, gray-carpeted, fluorescent-lit classroom with table-desks at which students sat in twos. The desks all faced the front of the room. Mary Ann faced the class, using a projection screen and overhead projector to show equations and illustrations. Her purpose was to "see people's faces while I talked to them. When you write on the board, you're always turning your back on people."

Because she had earned her own Ph.D. at Farwestern, Mary Ann had a clear idea of how lecturers worked at the school. "The assumption was that the instructor introduced the material in lecture and the students went off and learned it, 'in the privacy of their own rooms', as my department chair put it."

During the first lecture of her numerical analysis course, Mary Ann told her students that, "I wanted them to *think* at least once in each class, so I would introduce some mathematical problems that we would go through together, step by step, with them contributing to the process." At these points in her lectures, Mary Ann recalled, "I might say, 'What do you guys think? How would you go about solving this problem?' Then I would let them react to each other's ideas."

One participatory exercise that she tried in the classroom worked well: "I brought in a big bag of coins for them to sort by denomination and year and write out the method that they used. It was great—the three major types of sorting algorithms all came up in the group."

Another experiment met with less success: "I began the first computer lab session of the course with a group discussion. I handed out an article in class and asked someone to start off the discussion of it and someone else to back them up. I wanted people

to get used to thinking and participating. But the discussion didn't really get off the ground, and there wasn't enough time to follow up. So we dropped that approach in labs. Numerical analysis isn't really a discussion course; it's about computers and algorithms."

The Student Group

Numerical analysis had fifteen students. The majority (twelve) were "first-years—Master's degree candidates right out of college." The other three—"Cindy Richardson, Pete Ziegler, and Cecile Cummings"—were third-year doctoral candidates in statistics. These three advanced students also worked as teaching assistants (TAs) in various other courses. For the sake of the majority, Mary Ann pitched her course at an introductory level.

Most of the people in the class were younger than Mary Ann. "They were about 25 or 26," she reported. "I was 29. At our first meeting, I told them to call me by my first name. I said that I would lecture, but that they should feel free to interrupt. And I let them know that they were welcome to discuss any questions they had during my office hours. They did interrupt—politely—and they did come to see me with questions. Our relationship was good, not at all adversarial."

Mary Ann characterized Cindy Richardson—the student who erupted in class—as "an A student, active on the department's Student Committee, and known to the faculty as having a passion for details. She was about my age. Physically, I would describe her as of medium height, with short, curly red hair and a high, pleasant voice."

"I knew Cindy slightly because TAs have little cubicles; hers was near my office. When we met in the hallway, we would say hello, and she had stepped into my office a few times to ask a question about personal computers."

"During the early weeks of this course," Mary Ann recalled, "Cindy had written me a few long notes after my lectures. Sometimes she asked for clarifications; sometimes she even corrected mistakes I had made. I knew from these notes that she was *thorough*. But her need for thoroughness hadn't shown up in class. She had just sat there and listened quietly, like everyone else."

The Classroom Incident

On the day of Cindy's eruption in class, she sat in the front row, to Mary Ann's left, with the other

Section 2. The Roles, Responsibilities, and Skills of the Case Discussion Leader

CASE
"How Do You Expect Us to Get This If It Isn't in Your Notes?" (A)

two third-year doctoral candidates flanking her. Mary Ann was explaining the FFT:

The FFT has to do with the cyclical nature of frequent occurrences. I explained that it was new and sexy to statisticians, and I would introduce it by showing a complicated statistical operation that it could help simplify. I told the students not to write, just to listen while I explained. Then I started describing something called the characteristic function, which tells you what the distribution is. I was talking about some really messy-looking statistical equations, with lots of thetas, parentheses, superscripts, and subscripts. All the symbols were in the students' notes and on the screen behind me as I spoke.

"When Cindy raised her hand that annoyed me a bit. I didn't want to stop before we got to the FFT. I looked at her and noticed that she seemed pale. Her voice sounded strained when she spoke, *'I . . . don't . . . understand . . . the . . . symbols.'*"

Mary Ann "was really anxious to keep moving, so I answered hurriedly, 'Just plug some sample numbers into the equation and see what happens. You'll see how these symbols work.'"

Mary Ann didn't "want to get into details at that point. I felt that my job was to give the big picture about the FFT in the lecture. This method had been working fine in the course so far. But Cindy didn't look satisfied, so I tried to reassure her, 'I know this is hard stuff. Just pick a few numbers and work the equation with them. I'm sure you'll get it.' I nodded encouragingly and took a breath to continue my lecture."

"That's when Cindy 'lost it.' She half-stood, grabbed her notebooks and my handout, really slammed them down onto the desk-top, and said, with real heat, *How do you expect us to get this if it isn't in your notes?*"

Mary Ann recalled, "Everything about her—the sudden noise, her posture, her voice—made me barely aware of the others in the class at that moment. The first thing I wanted to do was defuse this situation—defuse *her.* But I also wanted to emphasize that this was really difficult stuff. I was faced with a classic example of the need for one-second decision making."

CASE

"Trouble in Stat. 1B" (A)

Dan Shea, a forty-eight-year-old associate professor of public management at Fairchild University Graduate School of Public Policy, puffed on his pipe as he spoke with the researcher in his office:

> Four years ago, in Stat. 1B, an introductory course in regression analysis, a student literally stopped a group problem-solving discussion to complain about my teaching methods. I still think about this incident, not only because it was so unpleasant, but because it raises teaching questions far more profound than how to deal with a classroom confrontation.

Dan's pipe was out. He rummaged in his sports coat for matches as he continued: "How do you get students to learn technical material so they can apply it in real life—not just pass an academic exam? How do you get them to accept an experimental teaching method? And, even more basic, what is the teacher's real job?"

The School

Founded in 1778 on the banks of Connecticut's Avon River, Fairchild University included 11 professional schools and a large, famous coeducational undergraduate division. Its 20-year-old Graduate School of Public Policy (GSPP) had 700 students and 150 faculty members, many with international reputations. The GSPP offered degrees from the master's to the doctorate, and its lectures, conferences, and professional seminars drew participants from all around the world. Dan observed that the GSPP had, in recent years, sought to combine a traditional, lecture-based approach like that of a government department in the arts and sciences branch of a university with the kinds of case-based discussion pedagogies normally associated with professional schools. In fact, the GSPP had two distinct master's programs.

The Pre-Career Master's Program, for students with just a few years of professional experience, included a few discussion-based management courses, mostly in the second year. The bulk of its first-year curriculum was "lecture-flavored," especially the required math courses. By contrast, the Mid-Career Master's Program—for students with ten to fifteen or more years of professional experience—offered mostly case-based discussion courses. Dan explained that the GSPP's mission was "to train policymakers." But he noted a problem particularly

*This case was researched and written by **Abby Hansen** for the Developing Discussion Leadership Skills Seminar. The author thanks Carolyn Briggs Style for her help with the technical material used in this case. The case is based on data contributed by the involved participants; all names, places and some peripheral facts have been disguised.*

Harvard Graduate School of Education Case No. 2.

obvious among the Pre-Career students: "Even after two years of intensive training, they weren't ending up as leaders. They were managing technicians or being technicians themselves—often working for people who hadn't even gotten into Fairchild."

The Instructor

Almost six feet tall, with blue eyes, a moustache, and "dirty-blond hair," Dan Shea usually taught in chinos, white shirt, striped tie, and a tweed sports jacket. Dan and his wife Beth Wilkins, a vice president of an environmental firm, lived with their two small sons in a suburban Victorian house, which Dan was renovating in his spare time.

Originally from greater New York, Dan had earned two degrees (a bachelor's in engineering and a master's in architecture) simultaneously at Stanford. After graduating in 1968, he received a coveted University Scholarship for Ph.D. work in engineering and applied physics.

His experience in public management included a stint, in 1979–1981, as Assistant Secretary of the Environment for the state of Connecticut. During the past five years, he had published books on urban planning, landscaping, and decision theory, and articles on health care, mathematical modeling in social policy, and Italian opera. An amateur jazz pianist, he had also written on Duke Ellington. In addition to teaching, research, and writing, Dan often presented papers at professional conferences.

A colleague described Dan as "original, brilliant, a true searcher, and deeply committed to helping people learn." Dan called himself "a missionary about teaching mathematical skills for real-world applications because it's a way to improve government by indirect means."

When the Stat. 1B confrontation occurred, Dan had been teaching "on and off for twelve years"—as Lecturer in Urban Studies at Cal. Tech., Assistant Professor of Public Policy at Stanford, and, most recently, Associate Professor at Fairchild. He was on tenure track, and his productivity and excellent teaching record in the Mid-Career program put him in the front rank. On the other hand, he noted, "the diversity of my publications made it difficult for specialists in any one field to assess them as a whole."

His current teaching assignment at Fairchild GSPP included case-based Mid-Career management courses as well as Stat. 1B.

The Course

Stat. 1B, "Econometrics," was the second half of the Pre-Career mathematics requirement: "Introduction to Statistics and Mathematical Modeling." The course consisted, in Dan's words, of "a term of regression analysis." (In layman's terms, regression analysis is a set of widely used mathematical techniques that make it possible to predict scores on one measure using scores on other measures with which it is associated. Concepts like standard deviations, sums of squares, slopes, and beta weights form part of the terminology of regression analysis.)

Course requirements included readings in an assigned text; standard, graded problem sets; a midterm; and a final exam. Two-thirds of the graders were teaching assistants (TAs), who had taken the course the previous year. Dan said, "Most students hated the whole Statistics course and treated it like an obstacle between them and their degrees. And professors didn't seem interested in doing anything about it."

Dan's own interest in "doing something about it" stemmed from "two remarkable experiences. In one class, a roomful of students couldn't come up with the idea of using queuing theory in a case that described nothing but people waiting in lines for medical care and hating it. And this group had just experienced two weeks of lectures on queuing theory. In another class, students who had just had a term-and-a-half of lectures on economics couldn't figure out whether a property tax on an asphalt plant was an economic cost or a transfer. These students were smart and they 'knew' the stuff in some sense of the word, but they just couldn't use it."

His successes with case-based management courses at other institutions and in the GSPP's Mid-Career Program—combined with encouragement from highly respected senior colleagues who also taught Mid-Career courses—spurred him to remedy the defect he perceived by introducing problem-based discussion pedagogy. His opportunity to put his ideas into practice arose the year before the incident, when an instructor's unexpected illness created a "teaching gap" in Stat. 1B.

In Dan's first year of teaching Stat. 1B, he tried only modest changes: "I lectured, held brief discussions afterwards, and didn't enjoy a minute of it. Even worse, I didn't feel that I was teaching future policymakers to apply mathematical concepts to real-world problems creatively."

In his second year as a Stat. 1B instructor, Dan took his innovations further. He abandoned lecturing and "grafted on" a series of "Problems of the Day" to focus group discussion on the material in the text. These "messy and complex" problems were meant to approximate the sort of mathematical modeling that students would have to perform in policymaking jobs. Dan observed:

> Unlike the elegant step-by-step solutions you see in math books, real problem-solving involves trial-and-error—plenty of error. I wanted the students to live this process in class because I believed that the new approach would promote the kind of mastery they would need.

Dan distributed all the Problems of the Day for Stat. 1B on the first day of class, along with the pre-existing course materials and a syllabus. The syllabus outlined the course grading policy; all Stat. 1B grades would include 25% for traditional problem sets, 25% for the mid-term exam, and 50% for the final examination. Grading would be done by the Stat. 1 staff (only one-third of whom were faculty) and "curved to the GSPP standard, which was an A−/B+ median." According to the syllabus, students were to tackle the Problems of the Day and bring their partial solutions to class as discussion material. Neither these problems nor discussion participation would receive grades.

The Students

The 150 Pre-Career Master's Program students (about one-third of whom were women) had a median age of 24 with an average of two and a half years' professional experience. They had been accepted to Fairchild because of their very high scores on standardized tests, like the GREQ (Graduate Record Exam—Quantitative), and their section assignments for Stat. 1 reflected this. Dan's 60 students were "those with the highest scores and most years of training; the best." Dan noted, "There was some shuffling of students between sections from first to second semester, so these people hadn't been in a single, consistent group from the beginning of the year. But most of them knew each other and had worked together in some capacity."

In addition to the first-year math course, all the Pre-Career Master's students were taking "one discussion-based management course, plus three lecture courses: Economics, Political Science, and De-

cision Theory." The students in the other two sections of Stat. 1B used only the pre-existing materials and experienced the course as a series of traditional lectures.

Besides the regular class sessions, there were weekly review meetings in which "TAs spooned the stuff out quite expertly, and practically everybody in the course attended," according to Dan.

One Student's Comments

In a separate interview, Frank Preston, who took Stat. 1B with Dan Shea that year noted, "I liked Dan's teaching and learned from him. But I think most people were just interested in getting what they could use, and not everybody expected to use regression analysis in their jobs."

Frank also reported that

> We were taking another quantitative course at the same time, and the other teacher was poor. He just talked about what interested him and if you didn't keep up, too bad, you were a wimp. People's bad feelings about this other teacher spilled over into both math courses.

Frank characterized the lecturer who taught the first half of Stat. 1 as "excellent: he laid out the material step-by-step so you could learn it." Then "along came Dan Shea saying, 'Here's the world, let's look at it.'" Frank observed, "I think Dan's approach annoyed a lot of people. They weren't used to preparing for discussions in quantitative courses, and those Problems of the Day just meant more work."

According to Frank, the Pre-Career Master's students had clear expectations about preparing for a quantitative course. "You didn't have to do the reading. You'd get the stuff in class. People showed up expecting to be taught."

The Incident

Dan Shea described his classroom:

> We met in a horseshoe-shaped room—excellent for discussions. No formal podium; wide aisles so you could walk around fairly freely while people talked. There was a large blackboard and a pretty dysfunctional overhead projector. The room seated seventy-five, so there were some fifteen empty seats in this

class. At this point—about six weeks into spring semester—attendance was still high.

He went on to describe the day of the incident:

We had finished with simple regression techniques.
Now our task was to describe what a mathematical
model said and what it didn't, and understand how
to make it better. In particular, we were working on
minimizing the standard deviation of the slope of a
line summarizing a lot of data points.

The Problem of the Day was "Smoking and Cancer," which presents data on the incidence of cancer
and how long people had smoked before getting sick.
In this class, I wanted the students to find mathematical answers to questions like, "How sure are we that
smoking causes cancer at this rate?" This meant not
only drawing a line on a graph and calculating its
slope but interpreting the standard deviation of that
slope.

A particular, well-known equation describes your
uncertainty about the line on the graph. If you're
going to testify before Congress that we should raise
the tax on cigarettes, people will want to know how
sure you are that smoking really does cause cancer at
such and such a rate before they adopt a policy that
could put a lot of tobacco workers in North Carolina
out of work. You'd use this equation to show that
you were sure enough.

I hoped students would volunteer commonsense
suggestions about maximizing certainty, like taking a
larger sample of data (n) or a wider range of S. One
teaching objective for this class was to discuss the
confluence between common sense and the formula. I
wanted the group to work from instincts and tentative ideas to greater clarity because that's what real
policymakers do.

**Dan's pipe was out again. He got up, fished the
packet of matches out of his pocket, and relit it as
he paced.**

I don't recall exactly what happened that day, but
here's the general picture: I think I opened with a
broad question like, "Well, who has made some progress? How can we increase our certainty that smoking
causes cancer?"

A student—I can't remember much about her except what she contributed, so let's call her Marie—
said, "Well, it seems to me that you would know beta
more certainly if you had more data."
I said, "Okay, how can I write that in mathematical
terms?"
Marie thought a moment, "Well, sigma sub beta
gets smaller if n gets larger."
"That's an interesting idea," I said. I was waiting
for something with an equals sign and the letter n in
it—an equation to write on the board. "What else affects sigma sub beta?"
Marie answered, "Well, obviously, sigma does."
I said, "So we have sigma and n. Can you be more
specific?" She still hadn't given me a formula.
She paused again. "Something like . . ." I waited.
"Something like sigma sub beta equals sigma over n?"

**"'Good, a formula,' I said, hoping that I sounded
as pleased as I was. Her equation was technically
wrong; you could look that up in the textbook. But
she had given us a formula that related sigma−b,
sigma, and n. I started writing it on the board. No
doubt some people in the class were amazed that I
didn't scream, 'No! Wrong!,' but I wanted everyone
to realize that looking mathematical and getting
written on a blackboard don't make a formula correct, but also that it's a good start. Now it was their
job to think it through."**

**Dan continued, "As I finished writing Marie's
equation, a woman's voice called out, *'Wait a minute!
Is that right?'*"**

It doesn't particularly matter who the speaker
was—an average-aged, average-looking, bright
woman student. Let's call her Joan. She was half out
of her seat, waving one hand in the air, palm out, as
if trying to flag down a train. I remember tone of
voice more than anything else. Joan's was furious.

At the time, I was thinking that Joan's technical instincts were on target. But this was a discussion. The
last thing I wanted was to kill it by either damning or
blessing Marie's equation at this point. I stood there,
wondering how to react to two things: Joan's *"wait a
minute!"*—a direct order to stop the class—and her
equally direct question: *"Is that right?"*

CASE

The Case of the Dethroned Section Leader (A)

Abby Hansen *wrote this case for the Developing Discussion Leadership Skills and the Teaching by the Case Method seminars. Data were furnished by the involved participants. All names and some peripheral facts have been disguised.*

HBS Case No. 9-382-177.

Several years ago, when I was a second-year teaching fellow in English Literature," Beatrice Benedict recalled, "I had a painful experience in a discussion class when my authority was directly—and publicly—questioned. I felt quite insulted at the time, and I still wonder how well I handled the situation."

The Instructor

Bea Benedict was a fourth-year graduate student in Renaissance English Literature at Fairchild University, a large and famous institution in Arden, Connecticut. A tall, 26-year-old, Bea had recently begun jogging two miles a day. Like many other graduate students, she dressed almost invariably in jeans, pullovers, and track shoes. After graduating with honors from Fairchild, Bea had spent four years in Chicago and Denver working in journalism and publishing. Although her assignments increased in challenge, she was always an "assistant" of some sort, and she felt that her salary had not advanced satisfactorily. Bea reported:

> There was just one woman editor at the last publishing house where I worked. She answered to the title "Doctor" on the job, and that's partly why I decided to go back to school and get a doctorate in English. The rest of the reason was probably that, after four years in the "real world," I was pretty sick of editing and writing trivia. I felt ready for a good, nourishing drink of great literature.

Early in the year in which this incident occurred, Bea had become a resident adviser (RA) in Falstaff House, one of Fairchild's coeducational dwelling units. She counseled English majors and advised graduating seniors seeking fellowships and other academic awards.

The Course

English 200, "Shakespeare," was a highly popular survey course taught to about 400 students in a large lecture room in Warwick Hall. Professor Owen Glendower, a celebrated scholar and raconteur, gave two formal lectures each week. The third meeting was a discussion section, led by one of the fourteen graduate teaching fellows (TFs) who, like Bea, had received their teaching assignments as a precondition of their fellowship stipends. The TFs led discussions, made writing assignments, and were totally responsible for their students' grades.

Professor Glendower's principal course assistant made up the section assignments under instructions to place 15 students in each group; scheduling problems, however, produced sections inevitably numbering from 8 to 20 students.

Bea had two sections. One—a group of 18—met in a classroom in Warwick on Thursday afternoons. Bea did more lecturing than discussing with this group because 14 of them were freshmen, unfamiliar with literary analysis. Her other class met after dinner the same evening in Falstaff House because, like the half-dozen other section leaders in English 200 who were also RAs, Bea had requested that at least one of her groups be made up of Falstaff residents. This was a much livelier group than Bea's other section.

[Because Bea considered Professor Glendower's lectures entertaining but superficial, she took a few hours each week from her own dissertation research (on Elizabethan political thought) to read literary criticism on the plays and cull excerpts to present to her sections.]

The Setting

Founded in 1778, Fairchild University included eleven professional schools as well as a large, co-educational undergraduate division that enjoyed widespread praise for embodying the ideal of community (i.e., academic) fellowship. After their first year, all undergraduates lived in residential units like Falstaff House, each unit holding about three hundred and fifty students and twenty-five RAs like Bea. RAs ranged from graduate students through senior professors and occasional visiting celebrities—musicians, writers, scientists, and scholars.

Falstaff House, a red brick neo-Tudor compound on the west bank of the Avon River, included a large private dining hall, conference rooms, living suites, common rooms (lounges resembling living rooms), squash courts, a small gym, and a central courtyard where anything from political rallies to frisbee games could occur in good weather.

The Section

Bea's Falstaff House section included five men and three women; all lived in the House. Out of that group, Bea recalled four students especially:

Jack Kesselman, a sophomore from Lake Forest, Illinois, was known on campus as particularly active in political protests. A folk singer and songwriter, Jack had a reputation for cleverness. He would often sit in the House courtyard playing his guitar and singing original ballads about people we all knew. He was also something of an operator: once he told me he had arranged to receive credit toward his degree for private guitar lessons he was taking from an upperclassman in the House.

Elke Gunnarson was a tall, blond woman from Kansas City, a senior in Political Science, and a star of the women's tennis team. She usually dressed either in tennis whites or her varsity sweatshirt when she came to the discussion section. Elke participated in the House Council, organized a formal dance, and served as hostess at sherry hours.

Elke's boyfriend, Cliff Farmer, was also in the group. Cliff was a hockey player born and raised in Rockport, Maine. His major was American History, and he planned to go to law school. I considered him steady—not overly brilliant, but a very reliable and pleasant sort of fellow.

Skip Townsend, a junior from Palo Alto, California, also participated in our group's discussions. He was an odd sort of guy, who wrote "beachcomber" under "Professional Plans, if Any" on the Student Information card I handed out. I recall him as ironic, fairly quiet, but with a sharp sense of humor.

Bea added:

By the way, the Student Information cards were my own idea. Glendower gave us almost no guidance in setting up our discussion groups. I had just started distributing the cards because the previous year I learned a week after the final exam that one of my students had spent the past three summers at the Stratford Shakespeare Festival. She'd understudied their Juliet one year. And I never even asked her to read in class.

Bea's section met just off the Falstaff courtyard in a small room furnished with an enormous rectangular oak conference table and straight-backed wooden chairs. Bea sat in the chair nearest the chalkboard, and the students arranged themselves in two rows along the sides of the table.

The Incident

[In the following section, Bea recalls in her own words the circumstances leading up to the incident.]

It was the fourth session in the semester, and I

thought this group was doing quite well. The informality of meeting in the House after dinner seemed
pleasant for all of us. I used to bring my coffee mug
to class, and the students brought pieces of cake from
the dining hall. My usual opening was to pass out
photocopied excerpts from published criticism about
the play in question. The students then scanned the
handout while I stood at the board to write some key
terms for the evening's discussion or perhaps the title
of a particularly important book from the recommended readings list. Then I'd sit down and run
through a few administrative details—paper deadlines
or in-class report assignments—and then present a
brief summary of some points from Glendower's lectures. After this opening, I'd call on the student
whose turn it was to give a report—an analysis of an
assigned passage—to kick off our class discussion. I
had asked the students in the first two meetings to
choose a date on which they'd like to report, and I
tried to accommodate their choices in my assignments. I had stated at our first meeting that students
should expect to give two reports during the semester. They were to prepare them thoroughly, but not to
read criticism for their analyses. I wanted to hear
their own original ideas so I could form impressions
of their critical abilities that would help me grade
them.

That evening we were discussing Shakespeare's
Richard II. As usual, I sat in the chair nearest the
chalkboard. It was a warm night, and through the
open window of our conference room, the frisbee
players' shouts of "nice catch," and "whoa, boy, look
out for the bushes!" were almost louder than our own
voices. I toyed with the idea of asking the students in
the courtyard to be quiet, but I knew that it would
shortly be too dark to play frisbee, and they would
soon give up their game. Skip sat halfway down the
table from me. Jack sat on my right. Elke and Cliff sat
together just beyond him. (The other students in the
section—Patricia Haley, Bob Connors, Charles
Schwartz, and Lisa Evans—were all present, but I
confess I have nothing in particular to say about
them. In fact, I hardly remember them. I had to look
up their names in my old gradebook.)

It was Jack Kesselman's turn to begin that night. I
sat down, put on my reading glasses, and turned the
pages of my text to the passage I had assigned him.
Then I said something like: "Well, Jack, my syllabus
has your name here under October 18. Could you tell
us what you make of Richard's speech in the second
scene of Act III where we see and hear him grappling

with the idea that he may actually lose his throne?
You remember, as I've mentioned, of course, that the
third act in Shakespeare is pivotal. It's exactly in the
middle of the five-act structure, and it usually gives
the audience the turnaround, the reversal of the
world we meet in the first act. I'm very interested, in
particular, to hear what you think of Richard's rather
pathetic lines 'Not all the water in the rough rude sea/
Can wash the balm off from an anointed king'—especially here in the play, when his enemies surround
him and he is about to be deposed?" Then, I think, I
smiled, took off my reading glasses, and turned to
Jack. "Okay, you've got the floor."

Jack slouched in his seat, looking away from me,
and riffled the pages of his text. Then he said, "Bea,
I'm not sure what I make of Richard's lines. There's
something else on my mind."

That took me by surprise. After all, he knew he
was being graded on his presentation. So I tried to be
encouraging.

I said: "You must have taken some time to think
about the passage. Why don't you just give us your
reactions. Do you think Richard has any idea that he
might lose his power despite his words?"

Jack still hadn't turned to meet my gaze. "Um, I'd
like to make a statement," he said.

"Go ahead," was my reply.

Jack said: "I think something's wrong here. In this
section. Bea, you talk too much. I timed your introduction. Fifteen minutes. Of our time. And you were
just summarizing a lot of stuff we've already heard. It
was pretty boring."

I remember I must have been blushing. I felt attacked. I think I sat there staring at Jack—at the side
of his head, that is. My first instinct was self-defense.

I said, "I don't think you're being fair. I spent a lot
of time preparing for this discussion. I've been studying this material intensively for four years now, and I
really want to convey some of what I've learned to
you. Glendower hired me for a purpose, you know.
Don't you think I've got anything to teach you?"

Now Jack had turned to face me. I remember thinking when I saw him full face how little I had ever
liked him. Now I could hardly stand to look at him.
Elke and Cliff had been exchanging glances. Elke now
telegraphed me a look of embarrassment. Cliff looked
unnerved too. Skip was leaning back on the rear legs
of his chair. He was grinning. I could imagine him
thinking this whole thing a fine joke.

Jack was talking again: "I think we should vote. As
far as I'm concerned, Bea, all your talking only stifles

us. Even if we're full of hot air, we ought to hear each other's ideas and sort of feel our way along with this material."

By this time I was really furious with Jack, but I would have felt tyrannical if I'd refused to let the sec- tion vote. Also, the situation had begun to appeal to my sense of adventure. I was wondering how a lead- erless discussion might turn out.

I stood at the board and faced the group, wonder- ing what to do.

READING

The Professor-Student Barrier to Growth

MARCIA YUDKIN

She sat down in the chair I indicated, unwound her scarf, and unbuttoned her jacket. "I don't know if you remember me," she began. "Of course I remember you!" I was astounded. Linda Harrison had been one of 15 students in a discussion section that had met weekly, just the previous semester—my first as a philosophy professor at Smith College. How could she suppose I wouldn't remember her?

When I thought about it later, my astonishment was tempered by the reflection that when I was an undergraduate I imagined myself part of a fog of names, faces and personalities to my professors, a fog that might clear when I spoke up in class or besieged them during office hours, but would quickly and inexorably descend again. After all, they had so very many other students and such other important things to think about. But later that week I heard my colleagues reminisce about students who had graduated five years previously. So it wasn't true!

That was the first of several startling comparisons I made between the views from the students' and the professors' sides of the desk. Another occurred after having brooded about what seemed to me an epidemic of absences from class. It had to mean that they thought me boring or incompetent. I confessed to a senior in my other class my anxiety over the number of students who skipped my intro course. "Hmmm," she said, "does it meet early in the morning? Or right after lunch? Or in the evening?" My worry dissipated.

I remembered that there were lots of reasons for skipping class, like all-nighters, personal crises, extracurricular commitments and general lethargy—reasons that had nothing to do with me, the professor.

It took another odd experience to make me recall that as a student I would not have believed that a professor could take my absence personally. A student in my intro course interspersed her written responses to assigned "thought questions" with remarks about the class, including one to the effect that she was able to observe me during class while remaining unobserved herself, so that while she knew a lot about me, I knew nothing about her.

"Not true," I wrote in the margin. "Your face is a giveaway." Facial expressions, even in a class of 45, registered vividly. I would pick out resentment, interest, confusion, and happy struggling with new ideas. I would notice who was and wasn't there. I realized that when I was a student, I believed I was

From *The New York Times*, January 4, 1981, Educational Review.

invisible, protected by a sort of one-way screen. That was mistaken too.

When I began teaching, I had a definite conception of my role in the classroom: I would provoke students to take responsibility for our progress through the course by being active participants in discussion. The goal of studying philosophy, I thought, was for them to incorporate the material, issues and questions into their lives. I would keep lectures to a minimum and encourage lively verbal exchanges in class and individual thinking on paper. I warned students at the outset that if they wanted to memorize without getting involved, they should go elsewhere. In my classroom they would be making discoveries. Unexpectedly, I made discoveries there, too.

One day, when everything was going right and there was an exhilarating interchange about whether Descartes' attempt to use reason to prove the existence of God made sense, a student turned toward me and asked, "What do *you* think?" All the other heads turned toward me, and there was silence while I balanced on the horns of a dilemma: if my opinion, as the professor's, carried more weight, I shouldn't give it. But if I held back my view I would be doing what I wanted none of the students to do. I took a deep breath and acted as if I were one of them. *I told.* Forty pencils moved, and the discussion ground to a halt. Anyone looking in would have seen me sitting in the circle, but really I was on the other side of the desk, standing in full academic regalia.

As much as I tried to subvert the traditional role of professor as authority figure, it refused to disappear. It would lurk like a ghost and materialize when I thought I had exorcised it. At evaluation time, I would get some evidence that my strategy worked: "Best course I've had at Smith. We were made to think for ourselves instead of having answers handed to us that we had to regurgitate." But I also got advice like this: "Less discussion by ignorant students and more lectures by the knowledgeable prof."

Why did she think I was knowledgeable? It was an assumption I might have made in her position too, that the Ph.D. after my name in the catalogue meant that I knew something.

I thought my age and appearance would aid me in transcending the traditional image of a professor. At 28 I still look about 20 and dress as I did when a student. Sometimes it does help, but when students cease to think of me as an authority figure, there is another role waiting in the wings: that of a pal. When that comes into play, if I announce firm deadlines for papers I am assumed not to mean it, or if I fail to give an A to someone with whom I have had good rapport, I am reproached: "How could you do this to me?" I have violated our compact as chums.

The upshot is after two and a half years of teaching I see the roles as obstacles I am not capable of removing alone. I can shove the desk into the corner of the room, but then I may be trampled upon by students unaccustomed to its absence. In any case, the struggle to move it away must begin again with each new group of students. The roles of professor and student prevent me, when a whole discussion section clams up, from finding out what is wrong. I also believe the roles prevent many students from developing a questioning habit of mind and self-reliance that would be theirs for life. As a philosopher, I am inclined to pose my concern as a question: wouldn't it be better for everyone if the views from the two sides of the desk were not so different, if the roles of professor and student were broken down?

READING

Bike Riding and the Art of Learning

ROBERT G. KRAFT

If you reach 10 percent of your students, you're a good teacher." In 13 years as a college English teacher, I've heard that too often. Can you imagine your mechanic saying, "If I fix 10 percent of the cars in my shop, I'm a good mechanic"? Or your doctor: "If I heal 10 percent of my patients, I'm a good doctor"? That's a 90 percent kill rate.

For many of my teaching years, I had a 90 percent kill rate. I'd been talking my students to death. It was 1971 when it hit me. I was lecturing to my American literature class about Henry James. After class a student came to me and said, "Something you said I didn't get down right. Would you repeat it for me please? I'm student teaching in the fall and I want to give this stuff to my high school Lit class." I was stunned. This young man wanted to present my words and ideas to his students. He felt no need to stir my lecture into his own understanding. He felt no need to consider what high schoolers would respond to. He would just lecture them my lecture. Where had he gotten such ideas?

Obviously, from me. From all his teachers.

That student confirmed my suspicions about myself and most of my university teachers. We are teaching badly. Horribly, in fact. For me that day in 1971 started an anxious search. There had to be a better way. Since then I've come to some firm answers about these old questions. What is learning? When and how do people learn?

When and how did I learn? I sometimes ride a bike to school. When I think back to how I learned to ride, I remember a heavy green-and-white girl's bike from Sears. I was seven, the youngest in my family, and too small to reach the pedals on my brother's bike. My dad's store, with candy, cookies, and all that, was three blocks away. I went there several times a day, and I was tired of walking. Besides, smaller kids than I could ride two-wheelers.

I straddled the bike and came down hard on the top pedal. I tipped over. I got back on and tipped again. The bike pinned me under and I scraped a thigh on the sidewalk. But I had to learn, so I kept at it. In a week I could ride pretty well. Today I can also read, write, ski, and even fix the clothes dryer in my home. I learned them all the same way.

There is something so simple, so universal in this learning pattern. I needed to know or do something, so I went after it. It was hard and hurt sometimes, but it worked. But when I think about what I learned in classrooms, that bike-riding pattern seldom happened. Often I sat passive, waiting for class to be over. Sometimes I got interested in something and read up on it. Twice I read an abridged *Moby Dick*. I did well on tests and everyone thought I was a good student. I remember some of the things I read in school too. Did you know King James I of England, remembered for the King James Bible, was fascinated by witches and liked to hunt them down? I don't know why I remember that. But mostly I learned how to succeed in school. This is a familiar story. A string of books have come out in the last two decades about our time-killing, dreary schools. But these told me little about college teaching. I had to provide the conditions for learning that made it possible for me to learn to ride a bike.

I started the search with a book of collected essays by reputedly great teachers. I don't remember the title now because the book made little impression on me. These were people students admired, and they came across as warm, witty, and altogether likable. Most were pleased and surprised at having been chosen. But baffled. They had no helpful advice to offer me except—this is one line I remember—"Wear a different tie to school each day."

I had a memorable teacher at the University of Minnesota. Her name was Emeline. She taught Victorian literature. She had a glass eye that fixed on your hairline when she talked to you. Emeline liked my paper on Robert Browning's play *A Blot on the Escutcheon*, and I loved her for liking it. The class smiled and applauded after her brilliant closing lecture. I was awash in admiration.

If I were to ask Emeline today what her teaching secrets are, she too would be baffled. She might say, "Prepare, be yourself, and be civil." As her student, I had a different view; she liked my paper and I liked her. But that was different from good teaching. My infatuation, her glass eye, even her bright and witty lectures were like my brown, leathery school bag. Nice, but only what's inside matters. How much Browning, Tennyson, and Arthur Hugh Clough (rhymes with "rough," I recall) are part of me today? What is still part of me measures Emeline's effectiveness, and only that.

Emeline, I'm sure, thought little about what her Victorian gentlemen would be to me 15 years later. She knew what these gentlemen had to say and

what it meant. There was nothing in her literary Ph.D. studies that told her what would make Dante Gabriel Rossetti live in the hearts of her students. There was certainly nothing in mine. She learned teaching from watching her teachers. And their advice was, "Wear a different tie each day." I was back where I started.

But I pushed the question. How much Victorian literature do I recall? It seemed a fair test. I hadn't taught or read Victorian literature since Emeline's class. My specialty was modern American fiction, and I was barely able to keep up with that. So I asked, "Kraft, what do you know about Victorian literature?"

First, I remember everyone's names. (Roll this name off your tongue: Algernon Charles Swinburne.) I remember some Browning poems because I liked them. "Soliloquy in a Spanish Cloister" I can even recite. It's about monks, you see, and I went to a college that was part of a monastery. I knew about monks. Once I was even going to be one.

But most of all I remember that Browning play I wrote about; it was the paper Emeline liked so well. That play was full of phony love conflict and, above all, grand speeches. I said it was a bad play and Emeline agreed.

That paper set me thinking about other papers I wrote. I remembered one about Edgar Allen Poe's poem "Eureka," which describes how the universe came to be. It was the big bang theory long before scientists hit on the same idea. My teacher thought that was a fine essay. Another, about an early Hawthorne story, went over so well my teacher thought it should be published. I remembered my weaker papers too, but not so well.

I thought then about my other teachers and whether I liked or disliked them. There were good lecturers among them, but I had to admit I couldn't remember anything they'd said. I only remembered a crack a favorite English teacher once pitched at me when I protested the chaos of the class. He said, "Kraft, is your mind so small you have to keep it neat?" And that's what all those lectures came to. What I have left from all those college classes are the papers I wrote.

I have with me now what I did in school, and little of what I was told. That was a first principle I could use as a teacher. Ah, my carefully prepared lectures, useless.

But I was still in trouble. Papers were what we did outside class. Continue the papers, yes, but what do we do in class if not lecture? Discuss? Okay, but three fourths of my students won't discuss. I hadn't been a great discusser myself. I rarely had the confidence to speak in those formal and frightening classes.

One thing I had learned in my Ph.D. studies was how to research, how to track down answers, even if they were other people's. So when I was asked to teach a course called Teaching College English for graduate students, I decided to make that a forum for my search. Developmental psychologists seemed a splendid source of ideas. Psychology pursued answers objectively, using the scientific method. That appealed to me. I wanted the authority of science behind my conclusions. Carl Rogers, a humanistic psychologist, scotched my notions about objectivity and the scientific method. "Experience," he wrote, "is, for me, the highest authority." For Rogers, tests and measurements—science—that supposedly proved something never measured the important changes in people. He trusted only his "inner, nonintellectual sensing," which told him about his success and failure as a therapist and teacher. That made sense to me. I always knew without tests how my students were doing. Every teacher who watches and listens carefully knows. If I could never prove what good teaching was, my sensing would give me good directions. I would test the conclusions of psychologists against my experience.

Rogers's experience told him what mine told me: "I have come to feel that the only learning which significantly influences behavior is self-discovered, self-appropriated learning. Such learning, . . . assimilated in experience, cannot be directly communicated to another." My experience exactly. Since then I've been asking people these questions: "Think about what you know today. Did you learn it from being told? Or did you learn it from experience?" The answers always amount to, "Well, my dad told me lots of things. But I didn't really learn them until I lived a while and found out Dad was right." My dad and my teachers didn't teach me. They guided me and confirmed (or denied) what I learned from living.

A sabbatical gave me a chance to hunt further. There were lots of others I could look to. I had heard their names all my life. John Dewey, Jean Piaget,

Jerome Bruner. If these people confirmed my experience, I would be satisfied.

Though Dewey had gone out of favor, what I read of his always struck me hard. So I went to his original great work, *Democracy and Education*, published in 1916. Dewey spoke confidently, dogmatically in fact, out of his experience. It was a posture I envied. He looked into the same gap I saw between learning and what so often goes on in schools.

"There is a strong temptation," Dewey wrote, "to assume that presenting subject matter in its perfected form provides a royal road to learning. What is more natural than to suppose that the immature can be saved time and energy, and be protected from needless error, by commencing where competent inquirers have left off?" That, to Dewey, was the worst, yet most frequent error. "No matter how true what is learned to those who found it out and in whose experience it functioned, there is nothing which makes it knowledge to the pupils. It might as well be something about Mars."

I needed no more reassurance but began to find it everywhere. Jean Piaget demands that students "undertake authentic work instead of accepting predigested knowledge from outside." Jerome Bruner points to the reasons students go along with their endless lecturers and fake it. "Telling children and then testing them on what they've been told inevitably has the effect of producing bench-bound learners whose motivation for learning is likely to be extrinsic to the task at hand—pleasing the teacher, getting into college, artificially maintaining self-esteem." Most universities continue down Dewey's royal road. That's why my teachers were so little help to me.

Faculty go on doing what they've always done—and blame the students when it fails. Piaget suggests that teachers should do some animal training, "since when that training fails, the trainer is bound to accept that it's his own fault, whereas in education failures are always attributed to the pupil."

Remember the bicycle? Tipping, scraping the thigh? How do we get some of that tipping, scraping, and riding experience into the classroom? Not by just sitting. In the journal *College English*, Vern Wagner of Wayne State University explained why students don't learn to read and write in English classes. "In the classroom no reading and little writing take place . . . we only talk about reading and writing." Carl Rogers put it simply: "Significant learning is acquired through doing."

Yet silence and passivity drift like fog through the classrooms and hallways of colleges. What students learn is to keep their mouths shut and let professors do their thing. A couple of my professors dimly understood that. As a graduate student I once asked a favorite professor at the University of Washington when I should take my final exams. "Look," he said, "get out of here as soon as possible. You won't learn anything until you do." Now that I'm the professor, preparing the classes and writing articles, I'm learning almost as fast as I learned to speak English. And that was before I started school.

Dewey understood that too back in 1916. "Only in education, never in the life of farmer, physician, laboratory experimenter, does knowledge mean primarily a store of information aloof from doing." Piaget echoes: "A truth is never truly assimilated except insofar as it has first been reconstituted or rediscovered by some activity," which "may begin with physical motions" but grows to "the most completely interiorized operations." In discovery, Bruner says, the student learns how to learn more quickly and easily in the future, feels the excitement of learning and rushes to the next learning, remembers without memorizing.

But no real discovery and no learning take place unless the student is genuinely absorbed. He must feel a need to do and to know, and it cannot be for what Bruner calls extrinsic reasons, like passing courses, getting grades and degrees, or pleasing someone else. If such are his only purposes, then how to get high grades, degrees, and approval will be all he will permanently learn. A colleague told me of a student who supposedly learned all about punctuation and sentence structure in remedial English class. Next term, in a more advanced class, the student could no longer punctuate or structure sentences. When asked what had happened, he explained, "But I thought that stuff was for the bone-head class."

Piaget calls interest "that decisive factor." No permanent learning happens without it. The learning must touch the student, engage him in his concerns. So how can I get students interested in literature for its own qualities and use? What concern of students can the grammar teacher tap? Carl Rogers focused on this knotty problem for me: "A person learns significantly only those things which he per-

ceives as being involved in the maintenance or enhancement of his own self." Since most of us want to talk and write to people, even grammar maintains and enhances.

Psychologist Abraham Maslow set up a beautiful scheme that explains what we are all after—his "hierarchy of human needs," a list of everything people need to stay alive, prosper, and be happy. Basic needs must be fulfilled before people turn to higher considerations. Here, oversimplified some, is Maslow's hierarchy:

1. Physiological needs: food, clothing, shelter, self-preservation, sex. A continually hungry person will seek to feed himself. Other needs are pushed to the background.
2. Safety needs: Once physically comfortable, a person will try to protect himself from physical harm. Thus government, laws, etc.
3. Love needs: Once fed and safe, a person seeks love and belonging.
4. Esteem needs: Once fed, safe, and loved, a person needs to respect himself and be respected by others.
5. Self-actualization needs: Once the earlier needs are taken care of, a person seeks to know, to understand, to appreciate. And he seeks to realize his potential.

According to Maslow, fulfilling these needs is what interests us. And it takes a lifetime. Schools, especially colleges, deal mostly with self-actualization. But we know hungry children will not learn to read and write. And the unloved and self-hating cannot lose themselves in literature. A college professor brings his subject to students who are at different stages of need. Younger students are feverishly interested in jobs and sex, love and self-esteem. Adults often make better students, because they've had more time to satisfy first needs.

A teacher can't find jobs or lovers for his students. But he can support their job hunting and treat them lovingly. He can respect them. He can treat his subject and arrange his class activity so that many needs are occasionally filled. He can boost self-esteem by starting his students on activities they can perform and then pointing to their successes. He can encourage them to experiment without threat. He can encourage cooperation, which earns them the respect and friendship of peers. No

123

teacher can choose to ignore the range of student motivations that is part of what Piaget calls the laws of mental development. Ignoring the laws dooms a teacher to only partial, sporadic success and much failure. Honoring the laws won't guarantee success. Teaching is like that.

Not all motivation is personal; the group counts for a great deal, too. There are critics who argue that learning together isn't necessary and that perhaps classes should be done away with. Aside from the impracticality of the suggestion, there are strong reasons for keeping classes. Though we learn much by ourselves, we all like to have other learners around. I did all the reading and writing for this essay alone, but it was stimulating to talk to others about it. I never would have learned to ski if I had gone to the mountain alone.

"The traditional school," says Piaget, "hardly offers scope for more than one type of social relationship: the action of the teacher upon the pupil. . . . The new methods of education, on the other hand, have allotted an essential place to the social life that develops among students. As early as the first experiments of Dewey . . . the students were free to work with one another, to collaborate in intellectual research as much as in the establishing of a moral discipline; this teamwork and self-government have become essential ingredients of active school practice."

As long as the individuals aren't lost in the bunch, bunching learners in classes may be the best part of the traditional school—but only if the groups have a chance to know each other and work together and the teacher can attend to individual needs too.

In the last year, I've been incorporating these principles into my English classes:

- I've cut the lectures. My talk can guide and support. It can awaken and enlighten. It cannot teach. When I talk I try to keep it under twelve minutes and never let it go longer than twenty. Psychologists say people stop listening after that. I don't try to cover everything anymore. When I did I always found I was the only one for whom it was covered. When I have something to say to students that could be especially useful, I write it. In that form they can use it in their activities, much as I have drawn on Dewey, Piaget, and others.

- I arrange for my students to do things, in and out of class. Since I'm an English teacher, I require that they read and write constantly. I don't judge all their writing because if I do they resort to pleasing me rather than trying to discover for themselves.

- I start students working on questions that touch their current interests. I can't motivate by appealing to future needs and concerns. People resist prophets. When my students read *Wuthering Heights*, I ask them why Kathy would fall in love with someone like Heathcliff. This leads them to examining character. The more advanced the students, the more naturally they lead themselves to literary history, mythic criticism, and other sophisticated literary matters. I found such matters fascinating (sometimes) as a graduate student, but not earlier.

- Students like to work together for support and friendship, so I ask small groups to write about questions like the one above and to read and talk to one another about findings and questions. Often they bring those questions to me and seem genuinely interested in my answers. Out of these inquiries they write finished papers, which are graded.

Planning and organizing all this has been demanding. It was easier to lecture, because I love to talk. But students say they like these workshop classes, and now I am convinced their learning will last.

Professor Shaler's Recollections

Agassiz's laboratory was then in a rather small two-storied building, looking much like a square dwelling-house, which stood where the College Gymnasium now stands. . . . Agassiz had recently moved into it from a shed on the marsh near Brighton bridge, the original tenants, the engineers, having come to riches in the shape of the brick structure now known as the Lawrence Building. In this primitive establishment Agassiz's laboratory, as distinguished from the storerooms where the collections were crammed, occupied one room about thirty feet long and fifteen feet wide—what is now the west room on the lower floor of the edifice. In this place, already packed, I had assigned to me a small pine table with a rusty tin pan upon it. . . .

When I sat me down before my tin pan, Agassiz brought me a small fish, placing it before me with the rather stern requirement that I should study it, but should on no account talk to any one concerning it, nor read anything relating to fishes, until I had his permission so to do. To my inquiry, "What shall I do?" he said in effect: "Find out what you can without damaging the specimen; when I think that you have done the work I will question you." In the course of an hour I thought I had compassed that fish; it was rather an unsavory object, giving forth the stench of old alcohol, then loathsome to me, though in time I came to like it. Many of the scales were loosened so that they fell off. It appeared to me to be a case for a summary report, which I was anxious to make and get on to the next state of the business. But Agassiz, though always within call, concerned himself no further with me that day, nor the next, nor for a week. At first, this neglect was distressing; but I saw that it was a game, for he was, as I discerned rather than saw, covertly watching me. So I set my wits to work upon the thing, and in the course of a hundred hours or so thought I had done much—a hundred times as much as seemed possible at the start. I got interested in finding out how the scales went in series, their shape, the form and placement of the teeth, etc. Finally, I felt full of the subject, and probably expressed it in my bearing; as for words about it then, there were none from my master except his cheery "Good morning." At length, on the seventh day, came the question, "Well?" and my disgorge of learning to him as he sat on the edge of my table, puffing his cigar. At the end of the hour's telling,

Louis Agassiz as a Teacher

LANE COOPER

he swung off and away, saying: "That is not right." Here I began to think that, after all, perhaps the rules for scanning Latin verse were not the worst infliction in the world. Moreover, it was clear that he was playing a game with me to find if I were capable of doing hard, continuous work without the support of a teacher, and this stimulated me to labor. I went at the task anew, discarded my first notes, and in another week of ten-hours-a-day labor I had results which astonished myself and satisfied him. Still there was no trace of praise in words or manner. He signified that it would do by placing before me about a half a peck of bones, telling me to see what I could make of them, with no further directions to guide me. I soon found that they were the skeletons of half a dozen fishes of different species; the jaws told me so much at a first inspection. The task evidently was to fit the separate bones together in their proper order. Two months or more went to this task with no other help than an occasional looking over my grouping with the stereotyped remark: "That is not right." Finally, the task was done, and I was again set upon alcoholic specimens—this time a remarkable lot of specimens representing, perhaps, twenty species of the side-swimmers or Pleuronectidae.

I shall never forget the sense of power in dealing with things which I felt in beginning the more extended work on a group of animals. I had learned the art of comparing objects, which is the basis of the naturalist's work. At this stage I was allowed to read, and to discuss my work with others about me. I did both eagerly, and acquired a considerable knowledge of the literature of ichthyology, becoming especially interested in the system of classification, then most imperfect. I tried to follow Agassiz's scheme of division in the order of ctenoids and ganoids, with the result that I found one of my species of side-swimmers had cycloid scales on one side and ctenoid on the other. This not only shocked my sense of the value of classification in a way that permitted of no full recovery of my original respect for the process, but for a time shook my confidence in my master's knowledge. At the same time I had a malicious pleasure in exhibiting my "find" to him, expecting to repay in part the humiliation which he had evidently tried to inflict on my conceit. To my question as to how the nondescript should be classified he said: "My boy, there are now two of us who know that."

This incident of the fish made an end of my novitiate. After that, with a suddenness of transition which puzzled me, Agassiz became very communicative; we passed indeed into the relation of friends of like age and purpose, and he actually consulted me as to what I should like to take up as a field of study. Finding that I wished to devote myself to geology, he set me to work on the Brachiopoda as the best group of fossils to serve as data in determining the Palaeozoic horizons. So far as his rather limited knowledge of the matter went, he guided me in the field about Cambridge, in my reading, and to acquaintances of his who were concerned with earth structures. I came thus to know Charles T. Jackson, Jules Marcou, and, later, the brothers Rogers, Henry and James. At the same time I kept up the study of zoology, undertaking to make myself acquainted with living organic forms as a basis for knowledge of fossils.

Professor Scudder's Recollections

It was more than fifteen years ago [from 1874] that I entered the laboratory of Professor Agassiz, and told him I had enrolled my name in the Scientific School as a student of natural history. He asked me a few questions about my object in coming, my antecedents generally, the mode in which I afterwards proposed to use the knowledge I might acquire, and, finally, whether I wished to study any special branch. To the latter I replied that, while I wished to be well grounded in all departments of zoology, I purposed to devote myself specially to insects.

"When do you wish to begin?" he asked.

"Now," I replied.

This seemed to please him, and with an energetic "Very well!" he reached from a shelf a huge jar of specimen in yellow alcohol.

"Take this fish," said he, "and look at it; we call it a haemulon; by and by I will ask what you have seen."

With that he left me, but in a moment returned with explicit instructions as to the care of the object entrusted to me.

"No man is fit to be a naturalist," said he, "who does not know how to take care of specimens."

I was to keep the fish before me in a tin tray, and occasionally moisten the surface with alcohol from the jar, always taking care to replace the stopper tightly. Those were not the days of ground-glass stoppers and elegantly shaped exhibition jars; all the old students will recall the huge neckless glass bottles with their leaky, wax-besmeared corks, half eaten by insects, and begrimed with cellar dust. Entomology was a cleaner science than ichthyology, but the example of the Professor, who had unhesitatingly plunged to the bottom of the jar to produce the fish, was infectious; and though this alcohol had "a very ancient and fishlike smell" I really dared not show any aversion within these sacred precincts, and treated the alcohol as though it were pure water. Still I was conscious of a passing feeling of disappointment, for gazing at a fish did not commend itself to an ardent entomologist. My friends at home, too, were annoyed, when they discovered that no amount of eau-de-Cologne would drown the perfume which haunted me like a shadow.

In ten minutes I had seen all that could be seen in that fish, and started in search of the Professor— who had, however, left the Museum; and when I returned, after lingering over some of the odd animals stored in the upper apartment, my specimen was dry all over. I dashed the fluid over the fish as if to resuscitate the beast from a fainting-fit, and looked with anxiety for a return of the normal sloppy appearance. This little excitement over, nothing was to be done but to return to a steadfast gaze at my mute companion. Half an hour passed— an hour—another hour; the fish began to look loathsome. I turned it over and around; looked it in the face—ghastly; from behind, beneath, above, sideways, at a three-quarters' view—just as ghastly. I was in despair; at an early hour I concluded that lunch was necessary; so, with infinite relief, the fish was carefully replaced in the jar, and for an hour I was free.

On my return, I learned that Professor Agassiz had been at the Museum, but had gone, and would not return for several hours. My fellow-students were too busy to be disturbed by continued conversation. Slowly I drew forth that hideous fish, and with a feeling of desperation again looked at it. I might not use a magnifying-glass; instruments of all kinds were interdicted. My two hands, my two eyes, and the fish: it seemed a most limited field. I pushed my finger down its throat to feel how sharp the teeth were. I began to count the scales in the different rows, until I was convinced that that was nonsense. At last a happy thought struck me—I

would draw the fish; and now with surprise I began to discover new features in the creature. Just then the Professor returned.

"That is right," said he; "a pencil is one of the best of eyes. I am glad to notice, too, that you keep your specimen wet, and your bottle corked."

With these encouraging words, he added:

"Well, what is it like?"

He listened attentively to my brief rehearsal of the structure of parts whose names were still unknown to me: the fringed gill-arches and movable operculum; the pores of the head, fleshy lips and lidless eyes; the lateral line, the spinous fins and forked tail, the compressed and arched body. When I had finished, he waited as if expecting more, and then, with an air of disappointment:

"You have not looked very carefully; why," he continued more earnestly, "you haven't even seen one of the most conspicuous features of the animal, which is as plainly before your eyes as the fish itself; look again, look again!" and he left me to my misery.

I was piqued; I was mortified. Still more of that wretched fish! But now I set myself to my task with a will, and discovered one new thing after another, until I saw how just the Professor's criticism had been. The afternoon passed quickly; and when, toward its close, the Professor inquired:

"Do you see it yet?"

"No," I replied, "I am certain I do not, but I see how little I saw before."

"That is next best," said he, earnestly, "but I won't hear you now; put away your fish and go home; perhaps you will be ready with a better answer in the morning. I will examine you before you look at the fish."

This was disconcerting. Not only must I think of my fish all night, studying, without the object before me, what this unknown but most visible feature might be; but also, without reviewing my new discoveries, I must give an exact account of them the next day. I had a bad memory; so I walked home by Charles River in a distracted state, with my two perplexities.

The cordial greeting from the Professor the next morning was reassuring; here was a man who seemed to be quite as anxious as I that I should see for myself what he saw.

"Do you perhaps mean," I asked, "that the fish has symmetrical sides with paired organs?"

His thoroughly pleased "Of course! Of course!" repaid the wakeful hours of the previous night. After he had discoursed most happily and enthusiastically—as he always did—upon the importance of this point, I ventured to ask what I should do next.

"Oh, look at your fish!" he said, and left me again to my own devices. In a little more than an hour he returned, and heard my new catalogue.

"That is good, that is good!" he repeated, "but that is not all, go on"; and so for three long days he placed that fish before my eyes, forbidding me to look at anything else, or to use any artificial aid. "Look, look, look," was his repeated injunction.

This was the best entomological lesson I ever had—a lesson whose influence has extended to the details of every subsequent study; a legacy the Professor has left to me, as he has left it to many others, of inestimable value, which we could not buy, with which we cannot part.

A year afterward, some of us were amusing ourselves with chalking outlandish beasts on the Museum blackboard. We drew prancing starfishes; frogs in mortal combat; hydra-headed worms; stately crawfishes, standing on their tails, bearing aloft umbrellas; and grotesque fishes with gaping mouths and staring eyes. The Professor came in shortly after, and was as amused as any at our experiments. He looked at the fishes.

"Haemulons, every one of them," he said; "Mr. —— drew them."

True; and to this day, if I attempt a fish, I can draw nothing but haemulons.

The fourth day, a second fish of the same group was placed beside the first, and I was bidden to point out the resemblances and differences between the two; another and another followed, until the entire family lay before me, and a whole legion of jars covered the table and surrounding shelves; the odor had become a pleasant perfume; and even now, the sight of an old, six-inch, worm-eaten cork brings fragrant memories.

The whole group of haemulons was thus brought in review; and, whether engaged upon the dissection of the internal organs, the preparation and examination of the bony framework, or the description of the various parts, Agassiz's training in the method of observing facts and their orderly arrangement was ever accompanied by the urgent exhortation not to be content with them.

"Facts are stupid things," he would say, "until brought into connection with some general law."

At the end of eight months, it was almost with reluctance that I left these friends and turned to insects; but what I had gained by this outside experience has been of greater value than years of later investigation in my favorite groups.

I wish to present some very brief remarks in the hope that if they bring forth any reaction from you, I may get some new light on my own ideas.

I find it a very troubling thing to think . . . about my own experiences and try to extract from those experiences the meaning that seems genuinely inherent in them. At first such thinking is very satisfying, because it seems to discover sense and pattern in a whole host of discrete events. But then it very often becomes dismaying, because I realize how ridiculous these thoughts, which have much value to me, would seem to most people. My impression is that if I try to find the meaning of my own experience it leads me, nearly always, in directions regarded as absurd.

So in the next three or four minutes, I will try to digest some of the meanings which have come to me from my classroom experience and the experience I have had in individual and group therapy. They are in no way intended as conclusions for someone else, or a guide to what others should do or be. They are the very tentative meanings, as of April 1952, which my experience has had for me, and some of the bothersome questions which their absurdity raises. I will put each idea or meaning in a separate lettered paragraph, not because they are in any particular logical order, but because each meaning is separately important to me.

a. I may as well start with this one in view of the purposes of this conference. My experience has been that I cannot teach another person how to teach. To attempt it is for me, in the long run, futile.

b. It seems to me that anything that can be taught to another is relatively inconsequential, and has little or no significant influence on behavior. That sounds so ridiculous I can't help but question it at the same time that I present it.

c. I realize increasingly that I am only interested in learnings which significantly influence behavior. Quite possibly this is simply a personal idiosyncrasy.

d. I have come to feel that the only learning which significantly influences behavior is self-discovered, self-appropriated learning.

e. Such self-discovered learning, truth that has been personally appropriated and assimilated in experience, cannot be directly communicated to another. As soon as an individual tries to com-

Personal Thoughts on Teaching and Learning

CARL R. ROGERS

municate such experience directly, often with a quite natural enthusiasm, it becomes teaching, and its results are inconsequential. It was some relief recently to discover that Soren Kierkegaard, the Danish philosopher, had found this too, in his own experience, and stated it very clearly a century ago. It made it seem less absurd.

f. As a consequence of the above, I realize that I have lost interest in being a teacher.

g. When I try to teach, as I do sometimes, I am appalled by the results, which seem a little more than inconsequential, because sometimes the teaching appears to succeed. When this happens I find that the results are damaging. It seems to cause the individual to distrust his own experience, and to stifle significant learning. Hence I have come to feel that the outcomes of teaching are either unimportant or hurtful.

h. When I look back at the results of my past teaching, the real results seem the same—either damage was done, or nothing significant occurred. This is frankly troubling.

i. As a consequence, I realize that I am only interested in being a learner, preferably learning things that matter, that have some significant influence on my own behavior.

j. I find it very rewarding to learn in groups, in relationship with one person as in therapy, or by myself.

k. I find that one of the best but most difficult ways for me to learn is to drop my own defensiveness, at least temporarily, and to try to understand the way in which [the other person's] experience seems and feels to the other person.

l. I find that another way of learning for me is to state my own uncertainties, to try to clarify my puzzlements, and thus get closer to the meaning that my experience actually seems to have.

m. This whole train of experiencing, and the meanings that I have thus far discovered in it, seem to have launched me on a process which is both fascinating and at times a little frightening. It seems to mean letting my experience carry me on, in a direction which appears to be forward, toward goals that I can dimly define, as I try to understand at least the current meaning of that experience. The sensation is that of floating with a complex stream of experience, with the fascinating possibility of trying to comprehend its everchanging complexity.

I am almost afraid I may seem to have gotten away from any discussion of learning, as well as teaching. Let me again introduce a practical note by saying that by themselves these interpretations of my own experience may sound queer and aberrant, but not particularly shocking. It is when I realize the implications that I shudder a bit at the distance I have come from the commonsense world that everyone knows is right. I can best illustrate that by saying that if the experiences of others had been the same as mine, and if they had discovered similar meanings in it, many consequences would be implied.

a. Such experience would imply that we would do away with teaching. People would get together if they wished to learn.

b. We would do away with examinations. They measure only the inconsequential type of learning.

c. The implication would be that we would do away with grades and credits for the same reason.

d. We would do away with degrees as a measure of competence partly for the same reason. Another reason is that a degree marks an end or a conclusion of something, and a learner is only interested in the continuing process of learning.

e. It would imply doing away with the exposition of conclusions, for we would realize that no one learns significantly from conclusions.

I think I had better stop there. I do not want to become too fantastic. I want to know primarily whether anything in my inward thinking, as I have tried to describe it, speaks to anything in your experience of the classroom as you have lived it, and if so, what the meanings are that exist for you in your experience.

Section 3. Establishing, Monitoring, and Modifying a Teaching/Learning Contract

It was February, almost a month into the second semester at Farwestern University Graduate School of Education in northern California. Lecturer Allen Hall (J.D., Ed.D.), teacher of a popular course on Higher Education and the Law, sat reading in his office when the phone rang.

"Allen? Hi, it's Eleanor Lund from the Dean's office."

Allen's anxiety level rose. "Any call from the Dean's office would have gotten my attention. I was on a year-to-year contract then, and hiring decisions were under consideration. It flashed through my mind that Eleanor might be about to say, 'Congratulations, we've already decided to renew you for next year.' But it could also be bad news."

Eleanor said, "We've had a student complaint about your Law and Higher Education course."

That was a shock. Allen had taught this course three times before, with fantastic student evaluations. There had never been a formal complaint about his teaching.

He replied, "What's the problem?"

"It's about the cookies you serve."

"The cookies? Someone complained about the cookies?"

"Yes."

"Could you tell me who?"

"Maybe you should talk with the student directly."

"Of course. I'd be delighted to. Why didn't the student come to me in the first place?"

"She was afraid you might be annoyed."

Allen told the researcher: "I *was* annoyed, and anxious. I work hard to be accessible to students, and one had complained to the Dean's office rather than come and talk to me. And this business about the cookies . . . It sounded like a joke. This course met from four to six P.M. In England, it's tea time. People appreciate something to hold them till dinner. I've given out cookies for years, with only two minor complaints. One Law School student said that Hydrox were just cheap imitation Oreos. So I bought Oreos. But then a vegetarian said that Oreos contain animal fat. So I switched back to Hydrox. That was it. Besides, the issues of this course—sexual harassment, school integration, affirmative action—are explosive, and you can get only so mad at someone when you're eating a cookie."

The phone call ended with Eleanor's assurance that she would tell the student that Allen was willing to discuss the matter. She did not give the student's name.

CASE

A Question of Cookies (A)

This case was prepared for discussion purposes, not to illustrate either effective or ineffective handling of any teaching situation. Data were furnished by involved participants. All names and some peripheral facts have been disguised.

Harvard Graduate School of Education Case No. 3.

131

The Instructor

A colleague described Allen as "knowledgeable, genial, a beloved teacher." In his mid-thirties when this case occurred, Allen was nearly six feet tall, of medium build, fair-skinned, with brown hair, glasses, and a quiet voice. He always wore a jacket and tie when he taught. When these events took place, Allen was engaged. His fiancée lived in a distant city.

Allen's parents, who raised him with their other two children in a middle-class suburb of Chicago, had been involved in civil rights causes. During college, Allen worked one summer as a welfare buildings inspector and another as assistant to a black professor at the University of Chicago who taught a course on racial sensitivity. After graduating from Johns Hopkins, Allen took a position teaching English in a high school in rural North Carolina. "Moonshine and stock car races," he reminisced. "I loved it. Initially, I just wanted to learn about literature. But once I got into the classroom, I realized that I also loved teaching."

When high school teaching jobs became scarce, Allen moved back to Chicago, where he did research on desegregation for the school board and later worked as an investigator for the state Equal Opportunity Commission. According to Allen, "The bigoted politicians I encountered made me want to go to law school so I could sue those guys." Allen took two degrees—a J.D. in law and an Ed.D. in education—at Farwestern. After a few jobs litigating civil rights cases in the Midwest, he returned to Farwestern Law School to teach a first-year course on litigation. "When I held office hours, the students said this was the only time they had spoken to a faculty member outside of class."

In his second year as an adjunct lecturer at the Law School, Allen was offered a chance to teach a course on higher education and the law at Farwestern's School of Education. He commented, "The Law School teaches hand to hand combat. Students hate the place, and frankly I was delighted at the prospect of an Ed. School lectureship, even though it was only a part-time position. I hoped that good teaching would help my prospects."

Allen's student evaluations read like the *Hallelujah Chorus.* "The most valuable material in this course was the instructor." "The best course I have taken at Farwestern—bar none." "Lectures were excellent, and I also liked the cookies," "Allen Hall is the best instructor I have ever had for reasons too numerous to mention," "So much thought on Al-

len's part went into creating this course that every component was valuable," "I cannot think of anything negative to say about this class under any circumstances," "Respect and caring for students and the learning process permeate everything he does," and "Nothing short of dazzling—in a very unobtrusive way!"

Despite this spectacular teaching record, Allen was unsettled by the call from the Dean's office. He put it bluntly, "If you haven't won a MacArthur Fellowship or published a lot yet, students' assessments have a proportionately greater weight."

The Student Group

Allen said, "I always try to get about one-third law students and two-thirds educators in this course. I also actively recruit minority students. I appear briefly at a minority student orientation meeting to say that this course has a lot to do with civil rights issues in education. Obviously, I think these issues have relevance to their lives. But I've also noticed that all students speak more freely about issues like racial prejudice when there is a critical mass of minority students in the room. If there are just a few black students, for example, they may not feel comfortable participating, and some white students may be reluctant to disagree with them, for fear of seeming to pick on them. If there's just one Native American, she may fear that whatever she says will be seen as 'the Native American view.' But when there's a significant number of minority students, they can speak as individuals and feel free to disagree with one another. In this course, there were 55 students. About fifteen were blacks or Hispanics and, as I recall, about 60 percent were women."

Allen spent time preparing the law students and educators to work together in this course: "In the first two weeks I ran an extra meeting on educational policy for the lawyers and two meetings on legal terminology and research for the educators." He also put time into getting to know the students: "I went to several social gatherings, including a potluck supper that a woman Ed. School student hosted for the class. And I made a point of speaking with members of the class when I met them around campus, and holding lots of office hours."

One student whom Allen came to admire was Janetta DeForrest, a black woman he described as "a powerful contributor. She was older than I, older than most of the students—in her mid-forties or so—and had had a long career in education and as a civil rights worker in Alabama. This was her last year of doctoral work at Farwestern. After graduation, she went on to become a high-level university administrator in the Midwest. Janetta had an air of quiet authority. She was a thoughtful person. Students came to regard her as something of a sage. She was also someone whose opinion mattered a lot to me. She came to office hours a few times to discuss issues from the classes, and we became friends."

Allen's Guidelines for Working with This Group

At the first class meeting, Allen set a friendly tone by giving out the cookies. "I think I even joked about nourishing the whole student." As people ate their cookies, Allen told them "that graduate school classes can be infantilizing, but I wanted them to participate as the competent adults they were outside of class. I told them that I cared about what they had to say, that my teaching fellows and I actually liked talking with students. I think I quoted an old rock and roll song that says something like 'my friends all tell me that you're using me, but if this is being used, then use me up.'"

Allen recalled, "I also said that everyone has difficulty learning legal language for the first time because it was created to confuse people so that lawyers could get paid to translate. I told them that the educators in the class could expect to struggle for a while, and that we would have extra sessions to help them. I said that, in class, I would consider no question too stupid, and that people would do better by cooperating than competing in this course—I even wanted them to work together on the take-home mid-term and final exams. Finally, I said that I was open to constructive criticism. If people had an objection to the material or anything else, I would be grateful to hear about it. They could come talk with me in person, or do it anonymously."

Then Allen put his office hours on the board: "Four per week, more than most faculty." He added, "Oh yes, I invited the students to bring snacks if they wanted—for themselves or to share with the group. Then we got into our first discussion of a legal case, and after that I ran the course as a group discussion of the cases and articles we were reading."

The Cookie Confrontation

A week after Eleanor's phone call, Allen was working in his office. There was a knock at the open door. It was Mary Kay Compton. Allen described her: "Mary Kay worked in an office at a nearby college. Like a couple of other students in this course, she was taking it for non-degree credit. I remember her as having blonde hair, a pale complexion, and deep-set eyes—as if she might not be sleeping well. She didn't strike me as either thin or fat, but she had a largish frame. She was around thirty-five—my age. I thought her conscientious, sweet, and high strung. But she kept herself apart in class and always sat in the very last row of the classroom, almost at the exit door. I suspected that the other students thought her odd."

Her classroom contributions were certainly different from most. Allen said, "She focused on details, usually far off the point. Once, for example, we were talking about a Wyoming state supreme court decision regarding a professor who had been asked to sign a loyalty oath. People were arguing about how free professors at public institutions are to engage in public advocacy on controversial issues. Mary Kay raised her hand and said, 'Do you know if Wyoming state court judges are elected or appointed?' As usual, several people leaned way back in their seats, rolled their eyes, and gave each other a 'here she goes again' look. I restated her comment in a way that tied it to the discussion, however tangentially, to show that I wanted to include everyone in class discussions if I could."

When Mary Kay appeared in Allen's doorway that day, he expected a question like, "What's an injunction?"

Instead, after taking a seat, she said, "Dean Lund said it was okay to talk to you. About the cookies."

Allen reported, "I had two reactions: I felt genuinely curious to know why anyone would object to something as innocuous as a teacher giving out cookies. At the same time, I also felt put upon. Like many of the other students unfamiliar with legal terms, Mary Kay had been in my office two or three times before this, and I had always treated her cordially. My internal dialogue went something like, 'Mary Kay, you know my door is always open to the class. If you object to my serving cookies, why the hell did you have to complain to the Dean?' But I realized that her reluctance to come directly to me meant that something was really troubling her. The last thing I wanted to do was open our conversation with anything that she might take as a rebuke."

Allen said, "Mary Kay, I'm glad you felt comfortable enough to stop by. What's on your mind?"

She said, "I suffer from an eating disorder. Do you know what that is?"

Allen remembered, "Those words—'eating disorder'—made me think, 'Whoa!, this is serious.' It happens that a former girlfriend of mine had been anorexic before we met. She educated me about anorexia and bulimia. I knew that eating disorders could be devastating, even deadly. And I knew that there were an awful lot of women with eating disorders out there."

I said, "Yes, I know what that is. I'm very sorry to hear that it's a problem for you. I guess my giving out cookies puts you under a lot of stress."

"It sure does."

By then Allen was also thinking of the rest of the class: "I was wondering how I could explain it if I suddenly stopped giving out cookies. I certainly couldn't say, 'We can't eat cookies because Mary Kay here has an eating disorder,' or 'I've run out of money,' or 'The stores weren't selling any cookies today.'"

Recalling his dilemma, Allen shook his head: "I really didn't know how to handle this situation."

On a warm evening in early fall, shortly
before the beginning of a new semester,
Professor Lynn Novak of Great Western
University School of Industrial Relations sat in her
study preparing orientation materials for new
Teaching Assistants (T.A.'s) in her upcoming course
in Labor Economics. Working with new instructors
always brought back memories of Lynn's own first
year as a T.A., now well over a decade in the past.

One particularly upsetting confrontation remained etched in Lynn's memory. Speaking with a
researcher, she reconstructed the event and its background:

> That cold, sunless winter morning at 8 A.M., I
> opened my Statistics lab session in the usual way,
> summarizing major points from Professor Fitzsim-
> mons's lecture of the previous day. Then I presented
> a simple problem for the students to work on.
>
> I put the problem on the chalkboard at the front of
> the room and asked, "Can anyone get started on
> solving this?" When no one volunteered, I looked at
> George Perkins, who sat in his usual place at the
> front, near my desk, and said, "Well, George, why
> don't you give it a try?"
>
> At first he just stared at me. Then he burst out:
> "Look, I'm sick of you women teachers always pick-
> ing on me and I'm not going to take it any more.
> That's just it, you're trying to castrate me and it's
> been that way since I was in elementary school. Well,
> you're not going to get away with it now. Professor
> Fitzsimmons is going to hear what you're trying to do
> to me. You'll be sorry!"
>
> George now stood by my desk. I looked at him,
> then at the class, then back at him. The rest of the
> class was silent. All I could do was think, frantically,
> 'What's going on? What do I do now?'

Background

Great Western University was large and prestigious, with a selective admissions policy. Its 12,000
undergraduates and 3,000 graduate students had
the opportunity to choose among several specialized schools and departments, many of which were
considered leaders in their fields. The school also
offered broad financial support for most graduate
students and provided tuition, fees, and small stipends to cover basic living expenses through two
part-time employment methods: research assistantships to aid professors engaged in critical work, and
teaching assistantships for the large, required lecture courses.

CASE

George Perkins (A)

*This is a rewritten version of a case by **Tamara Gilman**
written under the supervision of **C. Roland Christensen**
with assistance from **Abby Hansen** from data supplied by
involved participants for the Developing Discussion Leadership Skills Seminar. All names and some peripheral facts
have been disguised.*

HBS Case No. 9-394-069.

The Statistics Course

Lynn described the course to the researcher:

Statistics 210 was the introductory statistics course required of all sophomores in Human Ecology and Industrial Relations. There were about 300 captive students each semester, which provided five teaching assistants with half-time work. We taught three two-hour "labs" a week, each with about 24 students at a time. Since many of the students slept or read the college newspaper during the three weekly 9 A.M. lectures by Professor Fitzsimmons, we T.A.s tried to summarize the major points made that week and then hand out a problem set that required use of the new techniques in order to solve the problems. We didn't require attendance in the labs, but attendance was usually pretty high, since this was the only time students could practice doing problems similar to those on the exams. And because we only had a midterm and a final on which to base the course grade, most people showed up on schedule.

The labs were held in one of two rooms called the machine rooms because they contained SCM calculating machines for student use in working out the numerical answers to problem sets. The SCMs were antiquated, even then, compared to the newer electronic calculators. They were incredibly noisy and so big they looked like supermarket check-out machines. They often jammed up so that they either incorrectly calculated or didn't work at all. Each machine sat on a separate grey metal office-sized desk and they were lined up in four rows of six each. Given the drab decor, the lack of any windows, and the noise level when every machine was working, it could be pretty bleak in there.

The purpose of the T.A., as I saw it, was to help the students learn how to do the problems and understand why they were doing them in a particular way or using a particular technique. The concepts weren't simple for people who didn't have a strong background in math, and for most of the students, this was their last quantitative course.

I began my labs by listing the major issues Professor Fitzsimmons had discussed at a theoretical level, and then I spent 15 or 20 minutes on how these could be used in a practical way to solve problems. Simple, somewhat humorous illustrations that somehow related to the particular character and interest of the class work seemed to work best. For example, in the lab I might use a hypothetical distribution of quarts of beer drunk by the various fraternity houses on campus.

I also gave the class the opportunity to work the

problem out, or at least make a stab at it, by asking, "Can anyone suggest any way to go about solving this problem?" If no one raised a hand, I went ahead and worked it out myself, explaining while I did it.

After going over the example, I handed out the worksheet and spent the rest of the period answering questions and helping students do the problems. The instructor's desk was at the head of one row of desks, and I usually just sat there for the next 15 minutes or so drinking a cup of coffee, but after that I wandered around the lab so that people could stop me and show me their problem if they needed help. Primarily, at the beginning of the semester, I try to be enthusiastic and supportive, because I knew so many were overly anxious about the math.

When they completed the problems, the students handed in the finished sheets to me. If there was time left in the period, I checked the answers, and if there were any mistakes we discussed them. However, most students took nearly the full time to do the work and I couldn't check them all at once, so I did that outside of the lab and then handed them back the next week. Often the individual discussions in lab were as much about the mistakes of the prior week as they were about the problems of the current week. The problem sets weren't "graded," but if there were errors I marked them, indicating what mistakes were made so that the student would understand what should have been done.

Besides discussing the problems in lab, I scheduled six hours a week for conference time, so that the students could drop by for a private discussion if they wanted to. Well, it was almost private; although other students weren't around, my two officemates were often there. Most of my students came by infrequently and then only to discuss particularly troublesome problems or concepts. For instance, if a student made the same error on the problems for two or three weeks in a row, I would put a note on the latest paper saying "Why don't you stop by my office and we'll try to clear this up once and for all?"

There were, however, two other types of students who stopped by almost every week. The first group really understood what was going on and just wanted to fine-tune that knowledge so that they would get an A. Students in the second group were usually doing just adequate work and had little mathematical experience. I thought they were frightened by the very idea of a Stat course and in some ways had a mental block against it, not lack of real ability. I tried to encourage them to stop worrying by listening to them, patiently going over the problems—sometimes several times in a row in different ways—and by explaining really elementary operations, like how to take square roots. I could really sympathize with these people because I wasn't in Math or Stat, and I knew how anxious I would have felt if I had been required to take a quantitative course that I thought was over my head.

My officemate, Steve Benson, a master's candidate in Stat, thought I wasn't tough enough. One day I was listening to a young woman, after she had just gotten her midterm back. She said, "I just don't understand it. I worked so hard for this exam and now I've done so poorly. I studied a lot for this. It's really upsetting, getting a grade like this after all that work."

"I know how you feel, Kate," I said. "But I don't think that you did all that badly, and I'm sure if we work together for the next several weeks, you'll be able to do much better on the final. It is hard when you're not used to math. . . ."

Steve was sitting at his desk at the back of the office. At that point in my "sympathy" speech, he practically flew over his desk. He stood in front of us and berated the student for lying and trying to take advantage of me when she obviously hadn't done any work in the course at all. The student left in a hurry, as bewildered as I was! Then Steve, who had taught the course before, told me watching me deal with students during conference hours had convinced him I was "taking too much crap from the students." He said, "You let them push you around with their sob stories," and kept telling me to "get tough with them!" I'm still not convinced that I should have done that, and even if I wanted to be tough, I'm not at all sure how I would go about it. Being tough just isn't my style.

The Instructor's Background

When she taught the statistics lab for the first time, Lynn had just graduated from a midwestern university with a major in economics. She was 22 and a first year student in a master's program in Industrial Relations.

She recounted the events that led to her being an instructor:

At the beginning of my senior year in college, I wasn't at all sure about what I wanted to do after graduation. My mother wanted me to "do something practical," like work or take a computer course. Ever since sophomore year she had been sending me clip-

pings about my high school girl friends that said things like, "So and So appointed Regional Sales Manager of Local Firm." But I was leaning to graduate school, so I guess she thought I hadn't gotten the message. I didn't have the money for school, and she thought I'd be crazy to go into debt for something I'd probably never use.

Well, I decided to apply to graduate school. Although my average was only a B−, it was an A− in economics and I was really interested in labor economics. I also applied for financial aid, but I really didn't hold out any hope. I was ecstatic when I learned that I had not only been accepted, but would receive financial aid. My acceptance letter from Great Western said that I'd be informed later in the summer which professor I'd be working for. When I told my family, the only positive comment my mother made was, "At least it isn't Art History."

I left in June for a research job with a consulting company in Amsterdam. One day at work I received a letter from my mother which enclosed the letter from Great Western. It stated that I would be a teaching assistant for Professor Fitzsimmons in the introductory Statistics 210 course. Was that a shock! I had been hoping for a research assistantship because I had never taught before and don't really like to be in the spotlight. Besides, I'd only had one course in statistics myself, and I only got a C in that. At first I considered forgetting the whole thing. I really didn't think I was up to it. Then some people I was working with convinced me to clamp down and suggested that I get a few Stat books to review. Luckily, English texts are used frequently in Holland and I found two on Statistics, which I went over with the help of several Heinekens!

Lynn's Introduction to the Statistics Department

Lynn's recollected her arrival at the department:

I went to Professor Fitzsimmons's office to find out my office assignment. It was right before registration day and the Stat Department was mobbed. I got in a long, noisy line of students waiting to talk to the department secretary. A tall, somewhat older looking fellow was going up and down the line asking people if he could answer any questions about the course for them—things like that. In those days I had long hair and dressed in sweaters and jeans. That, combined with my short, slight build, must have made me look like a student. He came and asked if I needed help. I told him I was a T.A. in Stat 210, just waiting in line for my office assignment. He looked really surprised and asked my name. When I told him, he looked even more surprised.

He said, "Lynn Novak? I'm Steve Benson. We're going to be officemates." Then he gestured me to follow him to the department secretary's desk. When he introduced me to her, she looked just as surprised as he had. I must have really looked like a kid in those days. The secretary apologized for having let me wait in line with the students. I had been there about twenty minutes, as I recall. Steve helped me take care of all the procedures—the books, assignments, things like that—and I followed him to our office.

We talked a little before I left to see some professors about my own courses. Steve seemed business-like—not impolite, just a little brusque. I told him I was somewhat nervous about teaching Stat because I wasn't getting an M.A. or Ph.D. in Stat like the rest of the instructors and didn't feel all that comfortable with it. I also told him I hadn't taught before. Steve said that he had taught 210 the year before and so had all the other instructors. I got them all together one day before my first lab and grilled them about how they ran a lab and what they did. I even asked them if I should wear a skirt or pants, but they weren't very much help to me on that. They were all guys.

Lynn Recalls Her First Lab

According to Lynn, the first lab had been designed to enable students to develop a "hands on" familiarity with the calculators through a demonstration of how they worked and through a brief, purely mechanical problem set. The following is her description of the first session and the events that followed:

My lab was scheduled for Tuesday at 2:30 P.M. Professor Fitzsimmons was supposed to show me how to run the calculators the day before, but he didn't get around to it until noon of the day that I was to teach. It wasn't difficult to run the machines, but there were certain common mistakes he told me to watch out for. I just hoped I could remember all of them.

At about 2:30, I finally conquered my doubts and walked into the machine room. Actually, I came a little late on purpose so I wouldn't have to stand up in the front of the class waiting for everyone to arrive. The first thing that I noticed was there were no

women in the lab. The second was the size of the guys. They were huge! I found out later that this was the "jock" section, made up of football and hockey players.

After introducing myself and talking a little about the purpose of the labs, I showed them how the SCMs worked and handed out the worksheet. I thought to myself, Well, at least you survived the first day. Was I mistaken!

Suddenly everything seemed to be going wrong. First, there was a rash of machine breakdowns. One machine after another had keys that stuck, a carriage that wouldn't move, multiplied instead of added on command, or wouldn't respond at all. Then there were voices shouting throughout the room, "Hey, Teach, my machine won't work!"—accompanied by not very muffled snickers. On top of this, some guys decided to use a more direct approach and complained—rather, glared down at me—from a distance too close for comfort.

I didn't know what to do with the machines. Professor Fitzsimmons hadn't said anything about mechanical problems. But by accident, while trying to fix one of them, I discovered that the plug was pulled out. Checking several others that wouldn't work at all revealed that they too had been disconnected. I finally realized that, at least in part, a concerted effort was being made to upset me.

I knew then that I had lost control and was in real trouble, but I hadn't the foggiest notion of what to do to regain any semblance of order. I had a terrible headache by this time and could hardly think with all these giants breathing down my neck. I guess I decided that the best thing that could happen would be for them to leave. Smiling and cajoling, I reminded them that if they quit horsing around, they'd finish and could leave early.

Appealing to their best self-interest didn't seem to help much, though, until someone actually finished and left. That seemed to be the catalyst and the turning point. Order, relatively speaking, then prevailed and the guys focused more on the problems than on hassling me. But what a terrible 45 minutes it was! When the lab was over, I immediately asked Professor Fitzsimmons for a transfer to another section. I swapped with Steve and got a section primarily from Human Ecology. That group happened to be mostly female.

After my trial by fire, I gradually began to feel more comfortable in the classroom and the challenge became making sure I understood the statistical concepts and how to solve the problems. This was more difficult than I had anticipated.

Professor Fitzsimmons had written the text, and it was different from the one I had used in college and the ones I reviewed over the summer. Sometimes I just didn't understand the answers on the "key" to the problem sets. Sitting in on the lectures didn't help. I couldn't afford to lose the T.A. job and by this time I had a commitment to my students, so I felt I couldn't let the department know how much trouble I was having. Usually Sarah Ward, one of my house-mates, helped me work the problems out. She was a Ph.D. in Urban Planning and had had a lot of stat work.

But one night, before my first lab of the week, nei-ther of us could get the right answer and match the "key." I couldn't wait until the next day to get the solution because the lab was at 8 A.M. I didn't know what to do. I couldn't go into the lab not knowing how to do the problem, yet I didn't have any way to find out how to do it. As it got later and later I got more and more desperate. Sarah finally went to bed and I was really all alone and didn't know where to turn. Finally, at 1 A.M., I decided to call Steve. He seemed the most approachable of the other T.A.s. Well, I woke both him and his roommates up, but he explained it to me and I could finally go to sleep.

The next morning at 10 A.M., just as the lab was breaking up, Steve came into the machine room. I thanked him again for his help. He grinned. I had swallowed my pride and taken a risk, but at least I started getting the help I needed.

Lynn Novak Describes George Perkins

The following are Lynn's recollections:

George Perkins was a sophomore in the Industrial Relations School, with a quiet, serious manner not usually found in the typical extroverted industrial re-lations student. About 5'6" tall, he had dark brown hair cut short and combed to the side, wore glasses, and always had on a neat shirt and a pair of slacks that contrasted sharply with the T-shirt-and-jeans uni-form the other three men in his lab—as well as most of the male population at Great Western—wore.

He was one of the first to arrive in the machine room on lab mornings and always sat in the first desk of the row immediately in front of mine. While many of the students drank coffee and joked with each other while trying to wake up waiting for the lab to

start, George always took out his stat book and re-viewed the reading assignment for the week. During the lab time when students were working on the problems and comparing answers, George would just turn to me to check the solution and ask any ques-tions, because our desks were so close. I don't think he knew many other people in the lab because they were mostly from Human Ecology, not Industrial Re-lations. He usually took the whole period to complete the problem set, and sometimes would stay over to the next lab (10 A.M. to noon) if there were calculators not being used.

George was extremely conscientious about doing his problem sets right and came up to the office to go over details all the time. For example, I remember one of his first office visits at the beginning of the semes-ter. He came in, put his books down carefully, and took out a notebook with a list of points he wanted to discuss. "I know you went over this in class, Miss Novak, but I want to make sure I understand the dif-ference between the mean, the median, and the mode. The mean is the average, the median is the 50th percentile, and the mode is the most frequent value. Is that right?"

I said, "That's right, George. Do you understand the formulas for calculating them?"

"I think so," he replied, "but I want to make sure. Can we work through these problems at the end of Chapter 2? I've already done them and would like to check them against the correct answers."

"Of course," I said and reached for the text. Half-way through the second problem I saw that he had made a simple arithmetic error and I pointed it out. "But that's not really anything to worry about, George. You didn't have a calculator when you were doing these and anyone can make a mistake, dividing with such large numbers. Besides, you used the right formula, put the right numbers in it, and understand why you were doing it that way. I think you really know what's important."

Dejectedly he answered, "I don't know, Miss No-vak. I did these extra problems and thought I had worked them through very carefully. I took a lot of time with them. I thought I had the answers exactly right. I just don't seem to have much of a knack for math."

"When was the last time you took a math course?" I asked.

"High school algebra, four years ago when I was a sophomore," he responded. "I didn't do too well in it and stopped taking any more math after that. I tried to get out of Stat 210, but the registrar's office told me that I need it to graduate in IR, and there's no way I can avoid it. Do you think I'll do OK? If I work hard?"

Trying to be encouraging, I said, "I can't see why not, although it's just the beginning of the course. You understand everything so far and seem to be willing to work hard, even do extra work, and that's a good sign. But remember, if you ever want to go over the problems or need to discuss anything you just don't quite understand in the course, feel free to come up. If you can't make it during conference hours, we can always schedule another time that's convenient for both of us. And don't worry about those math errors—you'll get more and more used to the numbers as time goes by."

As the semester went on, George came to Lynn's office almost every week. To her, it was apparent that he had a basic understanding of what the course was about, but also that he had to work hard for that understanding.

She recollected:

A week before his outburst in the lab session, when we were working on confidence intervals, he came to the office and said, "I think I've finally got down what a standard deviation is, but it keeps getting mixed up in my head, especially when I try to do problems. Now, it's the measure of how certain you are that a sample value is the true value, right?"

I said, "Well, standard deviation is the measure of the variability of individual observations from the mean." "And it can be used in hypothesis testing to see if a sample mean comes from a population with a certain hypothetical mean. And we use the confidence intervals, which are based on the standard deviation, to do the testing and give us a certain probability. You know, George, you keep telling me that you don't understand this, but it sounds like you do. You must, to answer your own questions the way you did."

George didn't look too reassured. He said, "It may sound like it, but if I do understand it why can't I do the problems better? Why do I keep making the same mistakes?" he asked plaintively. He pulled the last two labs out of his notebook and said, "I know the

final only has problems on it—not the definitions that I can memorize—and I just keep getting the labs wrong. Look at these! They have more red ink on them than pencil!"

"But you don't get the labs 'wrong,'" I insisted. "You make arithmetic mistakes, but everyone does that. Even when you attack a problem incorrectly, you always go back to it and make sure that you understand what you should have done. And that is the important thing—whether or not you do it perfectly right the first time isn't important. It's whether or not you understand it ultimately that counts."

He pushed his glasses up on his nose and paused before putting his lab exercises away. Then as he was picking up his books and coat, he said, "I'm getting tired of working so hard and not getting anywhere on this. It's frustrating. Completely frustrating! I know you're willing to help, but still, it doesn't get any easier and I put so much time into it that my other courses are suffering. I just can't afford that. Do you think I'm going to make it? Is it worth all this effort? What do you think?"

I hedged gently and said, "I don't know for sure, George, but I do know that you can do the problems similar to those on the exams when you relax and think them through without getting all tensed up. The numbers on the exams are easier to work with—they're smaller and divide evenly—because we don't want students to get all hung up on that when we're trying to see if they know the concepts. And we don't mark down for stupid math errors that result from trying to work too fast, so you don't need to worry about that. And I know you've been working hard. If you're on the borderline of a grade, that can only help. Besides, you're one of the few people that goes regularly to the lectures, reads the assignments, and attends lab as well! I'm sure you'll do fine!"

Lynn's Dilemma

Lynn told the researcher:

I still remember how shocked I was by George's furious speech—especially since I'd gone out of my way to be kind to him. As he stood there at my desk, all I could think was, "What's going on? What do I do now?"

Bay Area Graduate School of Management
(called Bay by its students) was a large, well-
reputed business school that conducted most
instruction by the case method, dividing its first-
year class of MBAs into approximately 10 sections
of 80 students each. Each section was assigned an
amphitheater-shaped classroom in which the students assembled daily at 8:30 for the first of three
hour-and-twenty-minute classes. The instructors
taught their courses by moving among the sections'
classrooms.

Included in the required first-year curriculum at
Bay were Organizational Psychology and Management, Business Economics, Comparative Political
Economy, Business English, Marketing, and Manufacturing Management.

That year, many instructors agreed that Section I,
of all the first-year groups, seemed to be the brightest, hardest working, and liveliest. Assistant Professor Ernie Budding, new to Bay that year, taught
the course Manufacturing Management (MM) to
Section I. He found teaching by the case method to
be exciting, and he especially enjoyed teaching Section I. Despite the technical nature of much of the
MM material, Ernie was quickly impressed with
Section I's desire to learn and its high level of preparation and participation. By second semester, however, he began to notice sluggishness in class participation and a widening gap between his
continued commitment to preparation and theirs.

This case details Ernie's perceptions of the section's deteriorating behavior through the year and
his various attempts to improve the situation.

The Instructor

Ernie Budding came to Bay with a brand new
Ph.D. in economics from Carnegie Tech. Teaching
MM, a required first-year course, to Section I was
his primary assignment. Ernie commented to the
case researcher: "I established rapport with Section
I very early in the first semester, and heard about
their excellent reputation from other instructors. I
was glad that we got along so well."

Ernie was 28 and unmarried when he began
teaching MM. He looked like one of the MBA students, except that he always wore a tie when teaching; the students usually dressed more casually. He
was enthusiastic, extremely energetic, and active—
always moving around the classroom when he
taught. Asked his favorite sports, he replied, "You
name it. Swimming, running, tennis, skiing, rock-

CASE

Ernie Budding (A)

*Abby Hansen wrote this case in collaboration with
C. Roland Christensen for the Developing Discussion
Leadership Skills Seminar. While the case is based on data
supplied by participants involved, all names and some peripheral facts have been disguised.*

HBS Case No. 9-381-038.

climbing. But I dislike competitive sports, probably because I'm so competitive by nature. I prefer to compete against myself." He described his family as "a whole bunch of high achievers," both in academics and the business world.

Ernie told the researcher that he chose Carnegie Tech for graduate work after he graduated from Berkeley because, as he put it, "I'm not instinctively quantitative, so I wanted the rigor that their program offered." He smiled and added:

> I'm not a masochist; I needed a rigorous program because, with my interest in organizations and their behavior, I would be labeled suspect if I didn't have quantitative skills. But I'm never willing to quantify things like human motivations. I created havoc at Carnegie Tech by always asking, "What's that number good for? What does it do?" It's a very theoretically oriented place, but I wrote my thesis on a rather practical subject. It's coming out this fall as a book, by the way.

When asked to describe his basic approach to teaching, Ernie replied:

> I have a concern for rigor. Of course, in and of itself rigor probably isn't a virtue, but deep down I feel dissatisfied about data that come to me with loose ends. Generally, I look for order and logic in the presentation of material. That doesn't necessarily require mathematics. T. S. Kuhn's *The Structure of Scientific Revolutions*, for example, is the most rigorous piece of analysis I've ever seen, and it isn't at all quantitative. Rigor is a matter of reasoning, accounting for everything in a problem.

Ernie attributed his decision to become a teacher to two major considerations: independence and potential influence. He said:

> I like doing what I want to do. I'd never be comfortable in a hierarchy because I wouldn't be any good at taking directions when I didn't think the directions made any sense. In the classroom, I can run it my way. Also, I consider teaching to be a way to bring human beings across. Manufacturing, for example, has a bearing on a variety of human issues. In one case, when we talked about the 20 years it took some guy to start a factory and the consequent personal toll that the start-up took, I was able to raise the

issue of the corporation's responsibility to this man. Moral issues often get ignored in business environments.

A Profile of Section I

[Ernie's overall evaluation of the section was glowing. The following is his own description.]

In general, they were a wonderful section, very highly motivated. If I warned them about a tough case and said, "You'd better plan on putting in five hours," they'd do more. Their preparation exceeded my recommendations. The section was balanced intellectually, but a few students stood out. Tom Selig and Barbara Reinhardt, for example, were so bright and articulate that the section perceived them as leaders almost immediately. Others stood out because of substantive preparation in their backgrounds: the engineers Jack Mannix, Mandy Farmer, Jeannette Bell, and Bill Sims, for example. Socially, Al Carpenter and Eric Schuyler were leaders. Arlene Allen, the educational representative, handled the students' complaints, so she had the closest communication with the faculty.

Section I performed extremely well as a group. The administration requires 15% to 20% Excellents and 10% to 15% Low Passes for the grading curve. I gave 19.8% Excellents with no trouble, but agonized over the 10.2% LPs because a few of these were marginal. They could have been considered higher.

The Course

[Ernie considered it significant that MM was the only course in the first-year curriculum with an interrupted schedule. Here is Ernie's own description of the course.]

We met for three months at the beginning of the term (September to November); then, except for one class meeting, we took a long break until late February, when we resumed a normal schedule. It's also worth noting that the material wasn't everyone's cup of tea. Most students come to Bay to specialize in finance or marketing, but MM is required. It was clear to me that many of the students, even the most brilliant, were uncomfortable with the material, for it teaches a way of thinking that was foreign to most of them. Inventory policy, aggregate planning, scheduling—few were familiar with these concepts. As a result, I was extremely directive, sharpening their focus and clarifying the details in every case.

Oddly enough, despite my own very theoretical background and complete lack of experience in manufacturing—I've never worked in a factory, for example—I found the material fascinating. In micro-economics you make the assumption that firms have inputs *a* and *b*. Then you apply a production function—a mathematical relationship—and get results *y* and *z*. Whatever actually happens between inputs and results occurs in a black box. For me, MM opened that box and showed what a production process really is. I certainly enjoyed teaching the course, and the feedback I got, in conferences and at some parties with the students, was excellent. In fact, some of them told me they considered me their best teacher.

First Semester ("When Things Went Well")

[In the following section, Ernie describes in his own words a typical early class.]

By the sixth case, the one on Sullivan Watch Company, I had memorized all the students' names and backgrounds. We were getting along well. I started by calling on one of my strongest students, Harris Pauley, who is very, very smart.

"Harris," I said, "tell me about the company."

"Well, they make watches."

"What kind of watches?"

"Well, digital watches."

I was at the left-hand board, which I used for facts about the company. I wrote down "digital watches," and asked, "What's special about that?"

"They use a certain kind of manufacturing process."

"Certain kind? What kind? What's it like to be on that line? How many people stand there working?"

"In total, you mean?"

"If that's what you want to tell me."

"Well, there are two or three at each station on the line, and. . . ."

"Two or three? Wait, let me write that on the board, too. Say, Jeannette, I notice you had your hand up a second ago. Did you have something to add?"

"Yes, a calculation. The exact time the watch took to go through the line."

"Great. What was that number?"

"The watch comes down the line in 20 minutes—"

"Wait. What does that tell us?"

"It means the whole assembly process takes 20 minutes."

I was getting at the difference between labor time—the actual work on the watch—and throughput time—the time the watch spent on the line, some of it just sitting. We were moving in the direction of talking about minimum possible labor time, in which there would be no idle time at all. There were lots of figures in this case, and we'd develop each part of the discussion for about 15 minutes. While I was at the board, I'd continually call on people, since I was able to remember whose hands had been up and didn't like to lose time while my back was turned and I was writing. I'd ask questions like, "What's throughput time?" "What's labor time?" "Describe the assembly process." "How are low-priced watches different from high-priced watches?"

I'd use the middle board for analysis, the left-hand one for basic facts about the company and market, and the right-hand board for recommendations. By now, we would have gotten to new ground where students didn't know quite what was coming next. It was a question of comparing two different manufacturing processes. They'd never done this before. At this point, I'd be going back to Harris fairly regularly, but other hands were going up continually and I went on questioning students quite closely.

Ernie's Choice of Teaching Style

[In the following section, Ernie explains his selection of a directive approach by citing the highly technical material in the early MM cases.]

The first semester focused on the nitty-gritty concepts like the nature of production methods, which can range from "job shops" to "continuous" processes. The early cases demanded simple algebra, but many students felt uncomfortable even with this, so I'd always ask, "Where did that calculation come from? How did you get that particular number?" My purpose was to have students clarify their answers for the whole class.

In the first eight to ten cases we discussed basics—materials, inventory, work force management, and capacity planning. I tried to get the students to realize that an understanding of production systems was important in a number of everyday contexts. A restaurant, for example, is a production process. I wanted them to see the relevance of the material to their lives.

Especially in the case of calculations, I wanted the section to understand each case as well as I did. I went slowly and asked, "Does everybody have that?" I guess it's possible that people nodded simply to avoid the embarrassment of admitting they didn't understand, but I was doing my best to get the explanations clearly laid out. I also wanted to give all the students a chance to participate because they're graded 50% on participation. I kept comments short, partly because I thought it less painful for them, if they were dead wrong, to embarrass themselves with a brief, rather than a long, comment.

I didn't take volunteers to start the cases, although once things were under way people volunteered freely and were recognized. I asked students to start the case "cold," without forewarning, because this opening allowed me to decide who had the best chance of making a good showing. I spent a great deal of time figuring out whom to call on, matching background with material. If the case involved the steel industry, I'd call on a guy who'd worked in a steel mill. I didn't mind at all the possibility that he might know much more than I did about steel. In fact, I'd have been upset if he didn't.

In the early cases I called on people with public speaking experience because I knew they'd be less nervous than the others. I'd start with general questions about the setting. After the student had started, I made it clear that this was his or her case to continue by frequent contributions throughout the rest of the discussion. I would usually cross-question the student closely to expose any faulty reasoning, so as not to confuse the class. Each lead speaker got about 10 or 15 minutes to dissect the case, aided by very specific questions from me, and then got the opportunity for additional comments later in class. I expected all students to prepare all cases, so I didn't think it necessary to warn them when they were going to be called on.

Going through the "blocks," as I call it, was another aspect of my teaching style. I generally organized my class notes in analytical blocks, and reviewed these notes right up until class. I'd bring the notes into class with me and toss them on the desk before beginning the case. I tried to get the class to go through those analytical blocks in order, because that was the most coherent sequence for the case. Although I didn't refer to my notes during the class, the blocks did govern my organization of the discussion. Actually, I only brought my notes into the classroom because, if a student were to come up after class and ask for a calculation I'd forgotten, I wanted to be able to furnish it right there on the spot. But some students later told me, "Wow, you're the only teacher who comes in and doesn't even refer to his notes. We're impressed!" That made me feel uncomfortable: it seemed as if I'd brought in the notes just to show that I didn't need to refer to them.

As for the "directive style," I guess that encompasses several things, including cold calls, cross-questioning, and going through the blocks in order. Frankly, as a new instructor, uncomfortable with new material, I found it easier to channel the discussion in areas I had prepared. I didn't feel competent enough to recognize a promising line of discussion in an area I hadn't prepared, let alone to ask relevant questions on the subject. Second, at the beginning anyway, the students gave me very positive feedback. They desired guidance, wanted to be led carefully through the technical intricacies of MM. Whatever its drawbacks, the directive style does make the reasoning process clear.

[Ernie's conclusion:]

I tried my best to prepare each case thoroughly. If the students did five hours' work, I did fifteen. It was my goal to learn the material thoroughly and help them understand things as well as I did.

Things Begin to Change

[Ernie continues his description as he recalls how things began to change.]

The first semester ended uneventfully. I taught the last class in my usual directive fashion and the section responded well, with high performance. My feedback at this point was gratifying, and I had high hopes for an equally good second semester. But I began to notice a slight difference in Section I's general attitude and performance when I met them briefly in January for a two-case module

that was part of a Combined Business Exercise in
which the whole first year participated. After that,
we didn't meet until late February, when MM resumed a normal schedule.

[In the second semester, a few benchmarks of
deterioration stood out to Ernie: the emergence of
game playing in class; the section's raucous behavior during a power failure; and Ernie's subsequent
speech to the class about maintaining standards.
Ernie continues with his recollections.]

Several trends emerged in the second semester.
MM's emphasis changed from quantitative analysis to strategic planning; the students had become
more confident and less willing to be led; and the
section had developed into a stronger social unit
with different operating modes in class. It took me
a while to notice the impact of these changes.

During MM's break in December and January,
other courses continued as usual. We did meet
once during this period, as part of the Combined
Business Exercise. As it happened, some students
told me that another instructor's cases had turned
out to be a disaster. I noticed a certain leaden
quality to my class as well, perhaps because of
outside factors, but, on the other hand, perhaps
because the section had changed style in the in-
terim and I hadn't. Also, I co-taught this unit with
Ted Kleber, whose subject is organizational psychology. Ted is practically my opposite number.
He's completely nondirective. At some points, he
simply removed himself from the students' line of
vision and let them talk with each other. I was
fascinated to see how well Section I performed under those conditions. Our unit was an unqualified
success. Of course, Ted's material, unlike MM,
lends itself to long, uninterrupted speeches by
students. But watching him gave me a hint at
some changes I might make in my own style.

When MM resumed its normal schedule, Section I's students had changed in several respects.
They had evolved several new modes of behavior,
both to amuse themselves and to offer help to
some slower members of the group. The "learning
curve game" illustrates the former, and "triage,"
the latter.

Buzzwords started to come up in the technology
unit, the first unit of the second term. For example, one day a student said, "The most important
consideration in this case is the product life cycle."

"What does product life cycle mean?" I asked.
He just hemmed and hawed. Buzzwords like
that—"learning curve," "sequential decision making," and "flexibility"—seemed to have a magical
appeal. As soon as the students learned them,
they started to use them indiscriminately. "Learning curve," for example, has a precise meaning.
With a doubling of cumulative output, costs per
unit decline a certain percentage because the
workers learn how to produce more efficiently.
But the concept must be applied carefully if it is to
have any usefulness as a management tool.

In one case, a student who had been having
some problems in the course said, "The company
should not go along with this process because
they're going to be overcommitted." As he used
it, with no explanation, "overcommitted" was just
a buzzword. Later, when he came to see me privately, I said, "There were three ways you could
have made that comment. An average way would
have been to say they should not go ahead because of x, y, and z other processes they're already
using. You could have named them. An excellent
way would have been to say, 'Because it's a
family-owned business, the scarce resource in this
firm is management talent, and that's why the additional processes would be overcommitting their
management.'" But simply saying "overcommitted" without further comment contributed little to
the discussion.

It was about this time that some students came
up and told me that the group actually had played
a "learning curve game" one day to see how many
buzzwords could be inserted into a class discussion. They had kept score. I was chagrined. I'd
certainly noticed buzzwords coming up, but the
idea of an organized game hadn't occurred to me.
I still think I should have picked up on it.

Triage was a different sort of strategy they used.
It took two forms. In one, the students decided
for themselves which courses they could let slip
and which they wanted to concentrate on. They
knew that each of them could get three Low
Passes without being screened out of the MBA
program, so they worked hardest where the probability of doing well existed. That eliminated MM
for many of them. Also, I learned from one student that the section had started to play triage as
a group. The brighter students, who were in no
danger of failing MM, had been asked to step
back in class discussion to give the weaker stu-

145

dents more class participation time so they could improve their grades. That meant the better ones were putting themselves at a disadvantage.

A Disquieting Episode: The Power Failure
[Ernie recalls the power failure.]

In the second week in April, there was a power failure in our building, and what happened afterwards showed me that the group's discipline and self-control had deteriorated. Twenty minutes into class the lights went out. I left the room to call maintenance to make sure that someone was aware of the problem. When I got back into the classroom, I was amazed to see that the students had unrolled a roll of toilet paper and draped every single seat in the classroom with it. They were stamping and clapping and yelling, "Tell us a ghost story!"

Now, even when I'd been extremely demanding, I'd always been ready to share a joke with the students. I'd only drawn the line at really bad taste. I said, "But I don't know any ghost stories."

"Then tell us a story," they shouted.

I'd been dragging in anecdotes all along, and I happened to have read a funny story, so I told it. "Once," I said, "at a Berkeley final exam in a large course, the proctor cleared the room and picked up all the exam books. About a half-hour after everyone had left, he noticed a student way in the back, still writing. He went up to the student and said, 'The exam's over. I can't accept your blue-book.' The student drew himself up tall and said, 'My dear fellow, do you know who I am?' 'No,' said the proctor, very unimpressed. 'Good,' said the student, and he jammed his bluebook into the middle of the pile of the others and ran out of the room."

The class laughed, but we finally did get back to order and finish the case that day. From that time on, though, "Tell us a story" became a favorite demand of the class.

It wasn't too long after this that I began to worry seriously about the way the class was slipping. The buzzword situation was bad, games seemed more important than cases, and we were beginning to lose rigor entirely. I decided to do something about the situation.

I knew that making a formal speech of reprimand would damage my excellent rapport with Section I. We had been getting along beautifully since the earliest classes of the first semester, and I like to be liked as much as anybody does. But the obvious drop in preparation and performance really upset me. I knew I had to do something. I agonized for a while about whether or not to make a formal speech.

After serious deliberation, Ernie Budding decided to deliver a formal reprimand to Section I. He recalled the speech as follows:

In the past few weeks I've noticed that your comments have become peppered with buzzwords. I can't count the number of times I've heard phrases like "ride the learning curve," "product life cycle," "flexibility," "dominant design," or "sequential decision making." There's nothing inherently wrong with those phrases. They all represent important concepts and are valuable tools of analysis. The problem lies in how you are using them. Don't just tell me that a company should pursue a "flexible" manufacturing strategy; tell me what that *means.* These phrases are without content if you don't tie them down to the particulars of a case. All companies can "ride the learning curve" to achieve lower costs through higher cumulative output. So what? Tell me *why* that is important for a particular company. Tell me *how* these cost reductions will be achieved. Otherwise, you really haven't said anything.

I raise this issue now because I think it is a special problem for Bay MBAs, particularly when they first enter the work force. By the time you leave here you will have absorbed an enormous number of concepts and a wide variety of buzzwords. The tendency of Bay graduates to use these phrases loosely, often as a *substitute* for hard analysis, only worsens the school's reputation for "blue-skying." I'd like to put a stop to that right now.

Another thing. In recent weeks the leadoff speakers have done a very poor job starting off the discussion. A leadoff is your chance to lay out a case, to walk other students through your analysis, and to work through a business problem logically from beginning to end. It serves a valuable educational purpose. Rather than making a few minor points and then reserving your major contributions for later in the class—as recent leadoff speakers have done—you should be prepared to start off with an organized presentation of the issues, backed by solid analysis.

OK, that pretty much covers it. Any questions?

[Ernie continues with his recollection.]

You could have heard a pin drop. It felt like a scolding, and they seemed as chastened as first- or second-graders. It was very uncomfortable for a

CASE

Ernie Budding (B)

Abby Hansen wrote this case in collaboration with
C. Roland Christensen *for the Developing Discussion
Leadership Skills Seminar. While the case is based on data
supplied from participants involved, all names and some
peripheral facts have been disguised.*

HBS Case No. 9-381-039.

few minutes, but when I called on one of the best students in the class to start off the case, he did a superb job. I ended the class by complimenting the section on how well they'd done that day, hoping that we would have no further problems that semester. I had felt extremely uncomfortable lecturing a section of adults as if I were their parent—after all, I was younger than some of the students—but I also felt I had a responsibility to uphold standards, and that was more important.

Afterwards, I collared six to a dozen students and asked them their reactions. Some said "It's about time somebody said something about buzzwords. We wanted to, but nobody would listen." Others said, "It's unreasonable to 'cold call' and expect students to lay the whole case out." That surprised me. I thought I had addressed one problem: the decline in the quality of section performance. Instead, I got reactions to two issues: the use of buzzwords and my policy of "cold calls" which held a student responsible for the case he or she started.

P rofessor Benjamin Cheever stared disbeliev-
ingly at the Marine colonel whose public
challenge had just interrupted a teaching
workshop Ben was leading for the faculty of a military institute. Nothing in his twenty years of teaching—eight using the case method—had prepared
Ben for a remark like this. He scanned the group
for reactions as the colonel's words echoed in his
ears: ". . . I am offended. Don't you think an apology is in order?"

Background

It was Friday morning. Ben Cheever, an economist and senior faculty member of Fairchild Graduate School of Organization and Management, had
sensed from the outset of this case discussion that
there would be difficulties getting the workshop
moving in the right direction. Along with two colleagues, Ben had traveled from New England to
Washington, D.C., to demonstrate case method
teaching in a two-day workshop for the faculty of
the Senior Commanding Officers' Executive Institute. Ben had come with only moderate expectations, but his instincts told him that this was, in
fact, shaping up as a particularly lackluster discussion. The group, which included, in his recollection,
"about 85% colonels and lieutenant colonels and
some majors, as well as civilian faculty members of
equivalent civil service rank," seemed wary, tentative, and unsure of how to proceed. This was particularly disheartening to Ben because his case—the
first of the workshop—had been preceded by a
rather long and thorough introduction, beginning
with a friendly welcome from the commanding general of the institute, an old friend of Ben's.

According to Ben, the general had given the faculty "a warm and humorous speech in which he
mentioned my military experience and the fact that
he had once worked for me. He told them that he
considered case method teaching something they
ought to know a bit about and that we were the
best." This introduction seemed auspicious to Ben,
and it was followed by "about 30 minutes of detailed
description of the case method by a colleague of
mine who not only knows the method extremely
well but also has a military background. He gave
the group an encouraging overview, and used many
military metaphors and references."

Nonetheless, Ben knew his efforts to make this
workshop succeed had two strikes against them.
First, the faculty at the institute was unlikely to

The Offended Colonel (A)

Abby Hansen wrote this case for the Developing Discussion Leadership Skills and Teaching by the Case Method
seminars. Data were furnished by the involved participants. All names and some peripheral facts have been disguised.

HBS Case No. 9-383-061.

include many dedicated teachers. Most of the staff were military officers who had attended the institute's programs, as Ben put it, "to get their tickets punched," and fulfill a requirement for promotion. Having done well in the programs, these participants had received invitations to remain and teach for a few years. Second, the teaching staff usually had Fridays free, but today many instructors in the large, half-filled auditorium had been volunteered by their supervisors to attend this workshop.

Inwardly, Ben acknowledged that in some sense he, too, had come mainly to "get his ticket punched." His major reason for traveling to the institute had been to test some cases he had just written under a government contract which stipulated that the new materials be taught in a variety of official environments. Nevertheless, he hoped to find in this group at least some potential enthusiasm for exploring the possibilities of the case method. Ben truly enjoyed teaching and welcomed the challenge to make this workshop a success under these less-than-promising circumstances.

As usual, Ben had adopted a breezy, informal approach during the session. In contrast to the military audience—some in uniform, others in rather conservative civilian clothing—he wore no tie. Ben also joked often, hoping to create a relaxed atmosphere in which lively participation could arise spontaneously. He had asked the institute's faculty to prepare for the class and then join him, first for a regular class discussion, and then to analyze their own performance, his teaching techniques, and the case itself, considered as a teaching vehicle.

The case dealt with a civilian appointee heading a government agency responsible for military research. Faced with information leaks and unresponsiveness in the agency, the case protagonist, Claude La Fleur, resorts to declaring a moratorium on all research. After sketching the situation and briefly reviewing a few details of setting, Ben addressed a general question to the group: "Well, what's bothering Claude La Fleur? Can someone start us off?" The members of the faculty looked around, each seeming curious to see who would volunteer, but not personally interested in doing so. Once the dis-

cussion did get started, the speakers in this group avoided disagreement with their colleagues, much to Ben's annoyance—thus causing an early consensus that Ben feared would close off many possible areas of analysis. Worse, however, was Ben's discomfort at realizing that the ascendant point of view happened to be one he considered off the mark. He began to feel the necessity of getting the group to produce some opposition to this stifling premature conclusion. To accomplish this, he chose to play devil's advocate. In the character of a hostile opponent, Ben responded to one participant's formulation of the majority view with a good-natured "Bullshit!"

The ploy succeeded because, after a laugh, a few proponents of minority views did then raise their hands to speak, but Ben felt it was still hard work to keep the discussion open. By 11:45 he was, like the rest of the participants, looking forward to lunch. The group had moved from the case discussion to the analysis of the morning's proceedings.

All participants had remained seated to speak, but when Ben called on one uniformed Marine Corps colonel at the very back of the room, the man leaned forward and stood up, glaring.

"Dr. Cheever," he said in a strained voice, "I'm wondering about something. Do you always use profanity when you teach? Or is it that you just feel you have to talk down to us servicemen?"

Ben felt everyone's gaze. As an Army veteran and former civilian employee at the Pentagon, as well as the son of a career military officer, he was taken aback by the colonel's statement. His surprise was clearly evident on his face.

"Why no," he said quickly, "I'm not talking down to anybody. This is the way I usually conduct my classes."

"Well, I just want you to know, Dr. Cheever, that I am offended. Besides"—the colonel gestured to the only woman, seated a few rows ahead of him— "there are ladies present. Don't you think an apology is in order, Professor?"

Ben looked at the woman, at the rest of the group, and back at the colonel. The room was silent. Ben wondered, "How do I respond to that?"

I t's difficult to spell. Hard to pronounce. Harder to define. It's hardest still to establish in a school. *Collegiality.* After a lifetime of residence in different sorts of schools, I am convinced that the nature of the relationships among the adults who inhabit a school has more to do with the school's quality and character, and with the accomplishment of its pupils, than any other factor. The success of a school depends upon interactions between teacher and teacher, teacher and administrator, and all school people and parents.

Yet, strangely, collegiality and the ideas it connotes have seldom shown up in the effective-schools literature of the past decade. It is not listed with such factors as strong leadership, emphasis on basic skills, and a clear sense of purpose, monitoring of academic progress, and an orderly school environment. Nor is collegiality part of the vocabulary of recent national studies of American education. It is recognized as neither part of the problem nor part of the solution.

I wonder why not. Most educators would probably agree that collegiality in a school is nice . . . but it's a soft and fuzzy notion at a time when schools need rigor and clarity. Collegiality is nice, but it's a frill when schools need to be pared to the basics. Collegiality is an adult notion when the lesson plan for schools should be prepared with students in mind.

I find that relationships among adults in schools—all schools, from preschools to graduate schools—take several forms.

One of them is described by a wonderful term from nursery school parlance, "parallel play." Two 3-year-olds are busily engaged in opposite corners of a sandbox. One has a shovel and bucket, one has a rake and hoe. At no time do they borrow each other's toys. They may inadvertently throw sand in each other's face from time to time, but they seldom interact. Although in close proximity, and having much to offer one another, each works and plays pretty much in isolation. This description serves remarkably well as a characterization of adult relationships in schools. Teachers and administrators develop subtle ways to influence the other group's domain, but they seldom venture there. A third-grade teacher on one side of the hall carefully respects the teaching space of the third-grade teacher on the other side. One principal in a system seldom visits the school of another. University professors, too, have been described as a group of isolated

READING

Sandboxes and Honeybees

ROLAND S. BARTH

HBS Case No. 8-388-111.

151

individuals connected by a common heating system and parking lot. We all seem to have an implied contract. Don't bother me in my work and I won't bother you. Yet, in schools, as in sandboxes, the price of doing things the way we want to—of having personal control over what we do—is isolation from others who might take our time and have us do things differently (and perhaps, better).

But, of course, not all adult relationships in schools are independent. I observe three different forms of interaction:

• *Adversarial Relationships.* Recently, a Boston-area school principal made a sage observation: "You know, we educators have drawn our wagons into a circle and trained our guns—on each other." When adults in school interact, all too often we attack one another. There's no dearth of enemies outside education, of course, but somehow we manage to create opponents under our own roofs.

A decade ago, Harry Levinson, author of *Organizational Diagnosis*, writing about the workplace of business, used the phrase "emotional toxicity" to describe unhealthy businesses. He observed that "psychotic" organizations, like many psychotic individuals, are characterized by a siege mentality, a feeling of being under constant attack. This mentality is also marked by preoccupation with self-preservation, constant scanning of the environment in search of potential threats, and a desire to avoid any close contact with others. It may be that adversarial relationships among adults in school make "parallel play" a welcome alternative.

• *Competitive Relationships.* The competition among adults in schools stems perhaps from a wish for *all those* in the school to succeed, or for the school to become better than others, but mostly it comes from a desire for *me* to excel.

Typically, competition takes the form of *withholding.* Most school people carry around extraordinary insights about their important work—about discipline, parental involvement, budgeting, child development, leadership, and curriculum. These hard-won insights certainly have as much value to the field as elegant research studies and national reports, but adults in schools have a strong reluctance to make these insights available to those who may be competitors for scarce resources and rec-

ognition—that is, almost everyone else. Nor does anyone want to be considered pretentious by professing this knowledge. Few teachers, for example, want to subject themselves to the criticism of their peers by standing up in a faculty meeting and sharing a good idea about grouping children or involving parents. Consequently, all the talk each day among teachers and parents and administrators notwithstanding, a taboo prevails in schools against school people sharing what they know with others. Kevin Ryan, author of *Don't Smile Until Christmas*, has referred to work in schools as an adult's "second most private activity." John I. Goodlad puts it more soberly in *A Place Called School*:

> The classroom cells in which teachers spend much of their time appear to be symbolic and predictive of their relative isolation from one another and from sources of ideas beyond their own background of experience.

How can a profession survive, let alone flourish, when its members are cut off from other and from the rich knowledge base upon which success and excellence depend? Not very well.

A day after watching the Boston Marathon from the top of Heartbreak Hill, I had the good fortune to sit on a plane beside one of the top finishers. I asked this young man how he did it. "How do you run and run fast for more than two hours, up and down hills, in the face of such extraordinary difficulties?" I expected him to emphasize competition or the pursuit of personal glory; instead, he observed thoughtfully that "I do it because of the crowds. The people along the side of the course. For 26 miles, everyone is cheering, giving me water, support, not interfering, keeping others from interfering, so I can run. I do it because everyone wants me to do it. I don't want to let them down."

Competition has its place, but we school people could well use some of these same *supportive* conditions as we struggle up our own hills. Instead, all too often we find along our course a society that values and supports the *product* of education far more than those committed to providing it.

• *Collegial Relationships.* The least common form of relationships among adults in schools and universities is one that is collegial, cooperative, and interdependent. Judith Warren Little, a researcher at the Far West Regional Laboratory in San Francisco, offers a good working definition of collegiality in schools. Collegiality, she says, is the presence of four specific behaviors. First, adults in schools *talk about the practice of teaching and learning* frequently, continuously, and in concrete and precise terms. Second, they *observe each other* teaching and administrating. These observations become the "practice" they can reflect upon and talk about. Third, they *work on the curriculum together* by planning, designing, researching, and evaluating it. Finally, they *teach each other* what they know about teaching, learning, and leading.

As obvious and logical and compelling as these ideas are, they find all too little following in schools.

We are all familiar with the enormous risks and costs associated with observing, communicating, sharing knowledge, and talking openly about the work we do. Yet somehow most good schools I've been in are ones where parallel play and adversarial and competitive relationships among adults have been transformed into cooperative, collegial ones. It is possible.

I am a beekeeper. I am looking out a window of a farmhouse in coastal Maine at three hives of Italian honeybees draped with a generous cloak of snow. Last summer, I robbed over a hundred pounds of honey from each of these colonies—more than enough to get family and friends (and bees) through the winter. I remember looking through this same window in August, pondering these remarkable little creatures and their complex social organization. In a hive of 60,000 insects, there are scouts always on the lookout in the fields for a new source of nectar. Fanners stand on the landing board during a hot day for hours at a time, beating their wings in order to circulate fresh air through the colony. Water carriers find a pond or stream and bring water back to help cool the hive and produce the honey. Nectar carriers bring in the raw material for the honey. Cappers seal the honeycomb in wax, and others mate with the queen and sustain the hive.

Observing these astonishing levels and examples of communication, sharing, and interdependence, I cannot help but compare the bees' little society with schools. Perhaps it is unfair to compare "lower-order" creatures with "higher" forms of life, but the comparison suggests to me just how much adversarial and competitive behavior dominates our schools, how little collegiality we see, and how much our schools suffer because of it.

On the one hand, it is a discouraging realization. But these little honeybees also suggest something else. They suggest just how great may be the power of cooperative behavior in the service of a common purpose. There is much we can learn from sandboxes and honeybees.

Section 4. Questioning, Listening, and Responding: The Key Skill Requirements

CASE

Assistant Professor Graham and Ms. Macomber (A)

This case was written by a member of the Developing Discussion Leadership Skills Seminar under the supervision of **C. Roland Christensen.** *While the case is based on data supplied by participants involved, all names and some peripheral facts have been disguised.*

HBS Case No. 9-379-020.

Professor Charles Graham glanced at the clock on his left. The hands on the wall were not encouraging. One hour and ten minutes into the class—only ten minutes to go—and the discussion had gone nowhere. Charles reluctantly concluded he would have to exercise the basic dictatorial prerogative of any instructor: he would have to tell the class how wrong they were.

Charles was starting out his second year of teaching and, as he told his New Dominion faculty colleagues, he had developed a sincere commitment to the case discussion teaching methods and philosophy. Charles was in his second week of teaching Quantitative Analysis and Operations Management (QAOM). He wanted to give that class every chance, but he had not foreseen that 80 intelligent persons might, individually and jointly, entirely miss the main point of the case. Charles disapproved of the practice of giving a pat "answer" to a case at the end of class; on the other hand, he could not conscientiously allow 80 apprentice managers to leave class thinking that the last hour passed for an adequate case analysis. Charles drew a slow breath; one more comment, he thought, and then they are in for it.

The hand Charles recognized was in the back row: it belonged to one of the women students, Janet Macomber. Janet was one of the younger students in the section, a graduate of the California Institute of Technology with an excellent academic record but with limited work experience. She looked nervous and started speaking softly and hesitantly. "Louder, please!" came from somewhere on the other side of the room.

Janet stopped, and started again in a stronger voice. "I'm sorry, but according to my analysis, the class's recommendations simply do not answer the company's problem—which is how to move work-in-process through the plant the best way possible."

"And just what is your analysis, Ms. Macomber?" Professor Graham asked.

"Well"—there was a note of apology in her voice—"when I was doing the case last night, I multiplied Exhibit 1 times Exhibit 2."

Charles did not want to appear amazed that someone had apparently cracked the case after all. He only wanted the class—each and every one of the other 79—to realize the import of Janet Macomber's words. He interrupted: "Let me understand, Ms. Macomber. You actually took Exhibit 1"—he held up the case opened to the exhibits—"and mul-

tiplied every number in Exhibit 1 times a number
in Exhibit 2?"

"Times the corresponding number. Yes, sir."

"And how long did that take you?" (Snickers
came from the side of the room.)

Janet Macomber appeared to be taken aback at
such a personal question. "Not too long," she answered, adding, as if to justify her computational
binge, "I used a calculator."

"And what exactly did you have, after you multiplied every number in Exhibit 1 times a corresponding number in Exhibit 2?"

"I had a matrix of the dollar-volume flow between
departments." Janet stopped. She was obviously
uncomfortable and ready to relinquish the floor. But
Charles was determined to expose her reasoning,
bit by bit.

"And what did you find . . . from this matrix?"

"I found that the flows were not all the same
[pause]. Some departments had a much greater flow
of work-in-process between them than others."

"And what did you conclude based on this observation?"

"I concluded that . . . if I were laying out the
plant . . . I would put the departments with the
most flow between them next to each other, lining
them up, and I would put the other departments
on the sides, or in other buildings, if I had to."

"Well, well." Charles looked around. The clock
on the wall showed that the class was already two
minutes overtime. There would be no chance to take
further comments from the class, and anyway it
might be more salutary for each individual to mull
singly over Janet Macomber's analysis. So as not to
end the class abruptly, Charles made a few extem-
pore remarks about how this case was related to
previous cases and to the course plan. He carefully
refrained from passing judgment on Janet's analysis
or on the preceding case discussion. Let 'em figure
it out themselves, he thought, now they have something to think about. All in all, Charles was quite
pleased with the way the class had turned out.

As he was leaving the room, Charles noted a
group clustered around Janet Macomber's top row
seat. There really is such a thing as section dynamics, he reflected. "When one of the class reasons
through a case, everyone learns. This case method
really works. What a break I had to start out my
career teaching with cases; it sure is a lot more fun
than lecturing."

CASE

Bill Jones (A)

At 2:20 P.M. Bill Jones concluded his class and made his way out through the swinging doors of the classroom, heading for his office. As he walked through the noisy corridor, he reflected, "In my eight years of teaching I don't think I have ever had to handle a more potentially explosive situation than I did this afternoon. Did I do the right thing?"

Background on Bill Jones

Bill Jones, a young associate professor at Metropolitan Business School, had been at the school for six years as a member of the Production and Operations Management faculty. An Arkansas native, Bill had received his doctorate in economics from the University of Texas. Prior to that Bill had received his bachelor's degree from Tulane University, where he had been a member of Phi Beta Kappa as well as a second-string quarterback for the varsity football team.

Immediately after receiving his doctorate he had been hired by Metropolitan to teach a first-year MBA course in Production and Operations Management. Although Bill had never been exposed to the case method of teaching before, he had become quite successful as a classroom teacher, consistently receiving high ratings from students in course surveys.

Bill spent four years teaching the first-year MBA course and two years teaching a second-year course on the Management of Nonprofit Organizations, which he had designed himself. Bill had become very interested in case method teaching and brought a great deal of enthusiasm to each class. He had a booming voice, a very dramatic style of teaching which he complemented with a quick wit.

In the spring Bill was asked by the chairman of his department to teach a new second-year MBA course called Labor and Production Policy. The department chairman would teach one section and Bill the other. Bill was somewhat apprehensive about teaching a new course, especially since he felt he had a meager background in labor relations. However, he did look forward to the challenge of teaching a different course and the opportunity to learn more about a new field. Bill spent most of the summer writing cases and preparing materials for the course, which was to be taught in the fall semester.

*This case was written by a member of the Teaching by the Case Method Seminar under the supervision of **C. Roland Christensen**. While the case is based on data supplied by **Bill Jones**, all names and some peripheral facts have been disguised.*

HBS Case No. 9-378-038.

The Labor and Production Policy Course

In October, as Bill Jones was about halfway through the semester, he set out to review course progress. First, he noted, enrollment had been very high: Bill had about 90 students in his section. The case material had proved to be very exciting and evoked a great deal of student discussion. During most classes Bill was unable to call on all of the students who wanted to participate. Bill felt that part of the excitement in his class was due to the fact that students had such diverse opinions and experiences with respect to labor relations. This diversity often sparked open conflict that produced exciting discussion sessions.

One of the section students who, in Bill's judgment, represented a somewhat radical point of view about labor policy was Dave Young. Dave was 27 years old and a graduate of the University of Wisconsin. After receiving his bachelor's degree with honors in economics, Dave had spent one year working in California with the United Farm Workers Union. After that he worked for two years in the California State Department of Labor as an assistant to the secretary.

Earlier in the semester Bill had asked students to submit a proposal for a paper topic. At that time Dave had come to Bill to discuss his ideas on writing a paper on participative management. Bill was impressed with Dave's intellectual ability, but he felt that his emotional intensity and aggressive manner often prevented him from successfully persuading others to accept his point of view.

In the course of the semester Bill found that many students came to his office to talk about career counseling. One such student was Paige Palmer. Paige was a graduate of a well-known Eastern women's college and had come directly to Metropolitan after receiving her bachelor's in art history. Although she had done well academically in the first year, many of her class comments were viewed as naive by some of her more experienced colleagues. They believed she was bright but lacked a certain "savvy" in her analysis of a case situation.

Bill felt that it was important to continue to encourage Paige to participate in class even though some of her classmates might rush to criticize and attack her point of view. There were 12 women in Bill's class of 90 students. Traditionally the production area had been viewed as "male domain," but increasingly women students had shown an interest in taking electives in this area. Bill felt that it was important for the women students to participate as actively as the men and to have their views heard, and he encouraged them to do so.

Another student with whom Bill had talked outside of class was Fred Wilkens. Fred had attended private schools, was an only child, and both of his parents were very active in professional work. He was a Stanford graduate in engineering, and after receiving his master's degree at that school he worked for Hewlett-Packard for two years prior to coming to the business school. He was basically a shy person, slightly built and studious in appearance. Fred was the only black student in Bill's section. Bill was concerned that Fred had not participated at all during the semester, although Fred seemed to be always prepared for class and had an excellent background in manufacturing. He had asked to see Fred after the student handed in an excellent paper on production planning earlier in the semester.

Fred told Bill during their meeting that he was primarily interested in leaving the manufacturing area to follow a career in finance. He confided to Bill that he had taken the Labor and Production Policy course primarily as an "easy" course so that he could devote the major part of his effort to his finance courses, which he found more difficult. Bill told Fred that he understood his reasoning, but that he hoped Fred would make an effort in the future to share some of his insights and experience with the other members of the Labor and Production Policy course. After this meeting Bill had been pleased to see that Fred had started contributing to class discussions.

The General Motors Case

In mid-October a case on the General Motors Corporation was assigned, dealing with a plant manager's decision to experiment with "stall" or "team" building of automobiles to replace the traditional assembly line method of production. The case made the point that after labor difficulties had forced the closing of a plant, General Motors began in earnest to re-evaluate some of its traditional labor policies. The company had found that younger workers were far more discontented with traditional production jobs than older workers and in general were also less productive.

One suggested remedy was to replace the monotonous tasks of the assembly line with a team-building concept. With "team build," four workers would be responsible for the final assembly of the car and each worker would be expected to learn all of the jobs associated with this phase of the production process. General Motors' top management chose an assembly plant to experiment with the team-build concept. The case described the labor force as being about 60 percent black, with almost all of the black workers under 40 years of age. The remaining older workers were mostly white.

The plant manager in the case had chosen four workers out of a pool of volunteers for the team-build experiment. He was primarily interested in determining how long it would take the team to begin working together harmoniously and how many production hours would be required to assemble a car using this method. Based on the results of this experiment, he would have to predict the total cost of assembly using the team-build method and then make a recommendation to top management on whether to expand the experiment, discontinue it, or convert the entire plant to team build.

During the first few months of the experiment the four workers involved in the project worked very hard to reduce the total amount of production time required for team-build assembly. The four workers, three black and one white, took a great deal of pride in their work and at one point asked the plant manager if they could put their pictures in the glove compartment of each car assembled, to inform the customer that they were personally responsible for the product.

While it was true that total production time kept decreasing as the workers discovered better methods or more efficient ways of doing things, still, the total cost for the assembly phase of the operations was considerably higher than for the traditional automated method. However, absenteeism had dropped drastically and quality had improved considerably.

The Class Discussion

Labor and Production Policy met at 1:00, right after lunch, and students begin filing into Bill Jones's class about ten minutes early. Bill was at the front of the room laying out his notes for the afternoon session while he talked and joked with students as they came in. He anticipated a lively discussion, particularly between Dave Young and Jim Casey, who had been a General Motors' employee and was fairly conservative.

Early student comments were directed toward the problem of determining the actual cost of the team-build method compared with traditional methods. One student offered the theory that as more and more cars were built using the team-build method, a "learning curve" effect would take place and eventually one could project that the cost would be driven down close to the assembly-line cost. After that comment Jim Casey, who sat in the middle section of the amphitheater, raised his hand. Bill knew that Jim was well regarded by his classmates as a bright and articulate spokesman. Also, because of his four years' experience with General Motors, he would often include in his class comments interesting anecdotes or helpful insights. Bill called on Jim, who said, "I think it is important to bear in mind that four people on one team-build project is a very limited sample on which to base long-run cost projections. After all, these four people have been hand-picked for this project, and even though their production time has been dramatically decreasing they are probably 'rate busters' anyway, and their performance in no way indicates how the average worker would perform under this system."

Bill Jones thought that Jim had raised a good point for discussion and he scanned the room looking for the next person to call on. Sitting in the back row by the door, Dave Young had been raising his hand continually and trying to get into the discussion. Bill decided to wait and not call on Dave at that point. In the front row, at his right side, Fred Wilkens was sitting with his notes spread out, but Fred's hand was not raised. Sitting next to Fred was Paige Palmer, who raised her hand immediately after Jim had finished speaking. Bill decided to call on Paige. Her reply: "Well, I disagree with Jim; I don't think the workers could be 'rate busters' because three of them are black, and . . ."

At that moment Fred Wilkens shot back in his seat so that his chair seat banged loudly; his fingers tensely gripped the desk. Most students looked down at their desks; others stared at Paige in disbelief. Paige did not finish her sentence; an icy silence prevailed in the room. Fred Wilkens put his head down for a moment. Then slowly he gathered his papers in a pile, ready to slide them into his attaché case, and half turned his chair seat as if to leave the classroom. Dave Young began to rock back and forth in his seat in an agitated manner.

I can't *believe* I'm expected to read this crap! It was never meant to be read by women anyway and I'm *sick* of them insisting on teaching it here! Men have been dominating women for thousands of years and I'm tired of being quiet and intellectual about it—I can't take it anymore! I mean these men *bound women's feet* so they wouldn't be able to escape the oppression of their lives!

Meryl Dorsey's voice was loud and shrill. Lisa Wheelwright, seated almost directly across from Meryl in the circle the discussion group had made with their chairs, was probably fifteen feet away from Meryl. Even at that distance, the voice felt almost painfully piercing in Lisa's ears. And Meryl's anger seemed to be amplified as her words reverberated through the drafty old Heritage University classroom.

"These men" were the patriarchs of Confucianist society. Lisa's discussion section for the *Scriptures and Classics* course had been talking about the hierarchy of values revealed in the Confucian *Analects:* family first, then the state, and then the gods. Another student, Joshua Larson, had just summed up one of the group's typically lively exchanges by noting that in the *Analects,* a son who lies to protect his father is virtuous because he honors the family before everything else.

"Yeah," Meryl had interjected in the sarcastic tone the others had begun to expect in ten weeks of classes, "especially because he honors his *father!*" When Lisa asked her to elaborate, Meryl had begun exasperatedly to point out that "family" really meant the father and all other males before women. Voice cracking partway through her sentence, she slapped her hands on her text, leaned back hard in her chair and gave full vent to her anger. Lisa thought she was overwhelmed by the force of the emotion. The more she tried to express it, the louder and harsher she became.

Dumbfounded by what seemed in part to be a personal attack, Lisa didn't know how to respond. Whatever she would say, she was conscious of the need to control herself, not to rise to Meryl's attack. She willed herself to stay calm and not to appear defensive. She made a point of avoiding jerky movements and forced herself to keep leaning forward and nodding at Meryl even though Meryl

CASE

Bound Feet (A)

Colleen Kaftan prepared this case under the supervision of *Louis B. Barnes* and *C. Roland Christensen* for the Developing Discussion Leadership Skills and Teaching by the Case Method seminars. While the case is based on data furnished by participants involved, all names and some perceptual facts have been disguised.

HBS Case No. 9-491-028.

seemed to be talking more to the ceiling than to Lisa or to anyone else. All the while, Lisa later recalled, her mind was racing at near panic speed:

> I kept thinking, oh my God I've got to stop her. I've got to get this class back. I don't want to subject the other students to this. I always encourage people to express their emotions in class, but she was *screaming* and not hearing anything but her own thoughts. Then my second thought—it came quickly—was I've got to help her. I've got to bring her back. If I can't get through to her now, I will lose her trust, her participation, her vote of solidarity forever. And if I don't do it right, I may lose some of the other students too.

Lisa Wheelwright and the Discussion Section

The *Scriptures and Classics* course, an elective attended by undergraduates as well as students from several of Heritage's graduate schools, was among the most popular of the Religion Department's offerings. The course was structured around the "Great Books" of religious thought. Students read one primary text per week, and the lectures placed the works in their historical and cultural context. No secondary texts were assigned; the smaller discussion sections aimed at exploring the students' own interpretations of the source material.

A 27-year-old fourth-year doctoral student specializing in Islam, Lisa had been leading discussion sections for the course since her first year in the program. Her own interest in the study of religions sprang not from any traditional religious affiliation, but rather from a fascination with the worlds people create and the meanings they assign to life. In the comparative approach, she saw—and encouraged students to see—a way of examining the assumptions and "truth claims" of various cultures without having to accept their precepts as "the truth." To understand a culture in that sense, she believed, meant that one would no longer be at its mercy, or dominated by it. Lisa's own heritage—mixed European and American Indian ancestry on both sides—and the encouragement of her mother, who raised her as a single parent, had given her ample opportunities to explore the philosophical universes created by diverse societies and their effects on individual members.

Most students appreciated Lisa's insistence on drawing out their emotional reactions as well as their intellectual responses to the course material. Twice she had received certificates for distinction in teaching. Among the faculty and her fellow discussion leaders, she was considered particularly creative in finding ways to meld present-day readers' sensibilities with the historical world views being studied. (For one memorable session on Islamic law, she brought in a bottle of whisky and threatened to drink a glass, thus putting her immortal soul in jeopardy unless the students, as "Islamic lawyers," could present arguments from the assigned texts that would convince her otherwise.)

In fact, Lisa found it so natural to put energy and enthusiasm into teaching that she sometimes wondered whether her own doctoral research was suffering as a result. For example, she did not have regular office hours because she found the office setting too formal and limited for students to express their real concerns. Instead, she gave her home phone number and told students they could call at any time of the day or night—relying on her answering machine to filter calls when she was busy or asleep. Contrary to her friends' expectations, she had rarely felt that a student abused her openness. Still, she was beginning to realize she had trouble putting her own work ahead of a student in obvious need of her time.

This semester Lisa had exercised an option few teaching fellows at Heritage knew was available: using class cards from the lecture group, she had handpicked Meryl and fifteen other students to compose an interesting, eclectic group whose members all had some creative leanings. So far, her experiment had been a wonderful success. Lisa thought of the group as her "all-time favorite" discussion section. Almost without exception, the time she had spent inside class and out with these students had been stimulating and rewarding.

There were several undergraduate students, including the 17-year-old sophomore Sascha Nichols, her friend Marie-Therese Lebel, and Peter Thomas, who were studying film and visual arts and seemed more mature than their years. Only a few of the undergrads seemed to be "typical" students for whom the course was just another step towards their degree. Others, like Vanessa James, a forceful government major who was absent that day, and even Ian Ivarsson, a shy, athletic sophomore interested in political science, seemed deeply involved in the subject.

Among the graduate students, there was a remarkable array of interests. Joshua Larson, a 24-year-old Jewish Buddhist studying architecture, was particularly interested in the use of space by members of various cultures. Bob Stone, a law student, wanted to learn about the historical underpinnings of modern legal thought. Mark Stevens, a young Lutheran minister enrolled at the Heritage Graduate School of Theology, was also a member of a punk rock band.

Meryl Dorsey and Deborah Glick, also graduate students in theology, had both returned to school after holding administrative jobs in school settings outside of Heritage. Thirty-four-year-old Meryl, whose fashionable clothes and slight frame made her look as young as the undergrads, nevertheless tended to bring in her "experience in the real world" to bolster the opinions she expressed in class. At least a decade older than Meryl, Deborah usually adopted a motherly role towards the other students. She often agreed with Meryl's strong statements about the unfairness of many religions towards women, but without the anger and vehemence that fueled Meryl's remarks.

The mix of personalities and passions had produced as lively and outspoken a group as Lisa had hoped for. From the earliest class sessions, she had worked hard to set a tone of openness and creativity, emphasizing repeatedly that the discussions were an opportunity to explore what the students themselves made of the text. When Marie-Therese Lebel mentioned, three weeks into the semester, that she felt intimidated by the force of Meryl's opinions, Lisa addressed the problem immediately in the next class session by announcing that some students thought the discussions had become too aggressive. Since then, the group had learned to monitor itself, teasing each other occasionally with remarks like, "Oh, oh! Not too aggressive, now . . ." and generally learning to appreciate each others' contributions. Lisa had recently noted with pleasure that virtually everyone in the class addressed everyone else directly, using first names.

The students' written work and their conversations out of class were also quite gratifying. Lisa had assigned three short papers or projects, to be presented in any form the students chose, provided they covered the basic elements of the text being considered. For the first assignment she had received a play, a critique, a short story, and (from

Joshua) a mockup of an architectural project. Meryl had handed in a very good, if traditional, academic paper. The second assignment was due today.

The Outburst

In a way, Lisa realized, she should have known Meryl would explode at some point. Throughout the semester Meryl had peppered the discussions with irritated remarks about patriarchal systems. She prefaced her comments with ironic non-sequiturs: "I *suppose* we could talk about the problem of women [in the culture being discussed], but of course that's nothing new. . . ." As the weeks passed, Lisa noticed a growing stridency to Meryl's tone in class, in the conversations that continued after class, and in phone conversations Meryl initiated once or twice a week.

In the course of those conversations, Meryl revealed that she had recently ended an unhappy relationship of several years with a man twenty years older than she. She also made frequent references to stormy exchanges with her father, a successful and (according to Meryl) overbearing attorney who had always dominated Meryl's mother and who now wanted to see Meryl enter a "traditional marriage—like theirs—a gentle homemaker with a nice man." Meryl hoped to meet a man who was "more intellectual." She wanted to complete her Master's degree and become a high school teacher.

Meryl and Lisa had agreed that, although both were only children, their experience with men as partners and father figures was very different. For one thing, Lisa's mother had always seemed to be a very strong character. For another, Lisa's step-father (who married Lisa's mother when Lisa was seventeen) and her fiance were both very gentle men. And Lisa had yet to experience the kind of chauvinism Meryl described from her professional experiences outside of academia. As a result, Meryl had recently told Lisa, "You just don't understand what men are like—what they have always been like."

That sentence flashed through Lisa's mind as she and the rest of the class tried to respond to Meryl's fury. On the one hand, it was encouraging to see that almost all of the students were taking Meryl seriously, showing real concern and trying to follow her arguments. (Everyone seemed to agree that their usual humorous remarks about aggression wouldn't work this time.) Only one or two undergraduate men had leaned back, seeming to disengage themselves. One was tapping his pen on his notebook. Another kept glancing at the clock, which showed another fifteen minutes left in the hour. What were they thinking as the others continued the discussion?

Lisa later remembered her own comments and those of other students immediately.

LISA: (trying to speak softly and calmly, in contrast to Meryl's tone): Well now, wait a minute. You're getting at a very interesting problem here. I mean, the status of women in the Confucian society.

JOSHUA: OK, I can see that's an issue. But what does it have to do with the son lying to protect the father?

MERYL: (calming somewhat, but speaking through clenched teeth): Because it's only the men who matter here! Women are nothing. They're not even *included* in the hierarchy! (Sascha, Deborah, and Joshua nod slowly in agreement; most of the others lean forward, listening intensely.)

LISA: Not included at all?

MERYL: (louder and faster again): I mean, for Christ's sake—they bound women's feet!

LISA: But Meryl, do you find that in the text anywhere?

MERYL: (more and more shrill, animated): Jesus Christ, they wouldn't even want me to read this!

LISA: Meryl, are you sure that Confucianism required foot binding? I mean, did you know that Confucianism began in the 6th century BCE, and that foot binding only began around the *12th* century *CE* under the Sung dynasty?

MARIE-THERESE: (softly): Yeah, I think it was usually only an upper-class phenomenon then, too.

IAN: (gamely): OK, I totally see your point, but maybe we *should* look at the text, and find a specific point to discuss . . . like a way to explain it, or understand it, or something . . .

MERYL: (slamming her hands on her book, and in her loudest, shrillest voice, speaking half at Ian, half at the ceiling): No! This has been going on from time immemorial! And if you're trying to explain it you're only going to reinforce it!

Ian sat back, looking stung. Watching him redden, Lisa thought, "This is just not working. What am I going to do?"

I 'll never forget that class on world hunger," Bob
Clarkson told the researcher. "I've never been
taken by surprise like that before."

Bob Clarkson was an assistant professor at the
Bay Area Graduate School of Business Administration (called Bay by most students). Bob's primary
academic assignment was teaching Sections I and II
of a required two-term first-year course called Comparative Political Economy (CPE) that dealt with
business-government issues in both a national and
international framework. Instructors taught their assigned sections for both terms. (There were 10 sections, each composed of 80 first-year MBA students
drawn from the United States as well as most re-
gions of the world.)

All classes, held in an amphitheater-shaped area
with instructors moving from one to another of their
own sections, were one hour and twenty minutes
in length and met at 8:30 A.M., 10:10 A.M., and 1:00
P.M., Monday through Friday.

Bob Clarkson

Bob Clarkson, now in his second year of teaching
at Bay, had taught economics for two years as a
teaching fellow at Berkeley. He received his Ph.D.
in comparative political economy halfway through
his first year at Bay. With that degree came an automatic promotion from instructor to assistant
professor, which, he said, made him feel more comfortable in his new professional role. Bob, a young-
looking, slim, 30-year-old of medium height, was
married, with two children. Experiencing the anxiety typical of younger professors, he asked himself:
Confronted by students who are in many cases
older than oneself, how does one maintain one's
authority in the classroom?

Bob commented:

> Students at Bay can be very forceful. In my first
> year there was a disturbing situation in which a
> group of them petitioned the dean to remove an in-
> structor they thought incompetent. I determined then
> and there that no such thing would ever happen to
> me. Fortunately, I had no trouble of that kind, but I
> felt quite defensive the first year, especially since I
> had begun the year as an instructor rather than as an
> assistant professor. Since then, my teaching style has
> relaxed quite a bit. I've learned to become less direc-
> tive; and I'm able to relinquish the reins of discussion
> to the students. I guess I'm feeling more secure, and

CASE

Class on World Hunger (A)

This case was written by **Abby Hansen** *in collaboration
with* **C. Roland Christensen** *for the Developing Discussion Leadership Skills Seminar. While the case is based on
data supplied by participants involved, all names and some
peripheral facts have been disguised.*

HBS Case No. 9-381-042.

[he smiled] maybe being a year older has something to do with it too.

I felt a need to maintain my distance from the students because of our close proximity in age. If I became overly familiar, the teacher/student line might be crossed. The next youngest professor teaching this course is 35; another is 38; others, 40 and over.

Bob also learned that teaching at a professionally oriented school like Bay demanded from its instructors perspectives very different from those he had gained in graduate school. He commented:

It's quite a contrast with my past experience. For example, in graduate school in economics, when we studied barriers to entry, it was from the other side. Here, it's how to raise and maintain them; in the economics department at Berkeley, the question was how to get rid of them. I was always interested in the interaction among management, economics, and public policy formulation and implementation, but from the public management point of view. I thought I'd be teaching in a school of public policy, so at first I was surprised when a professor at Bay I'd worked with said, "Why not come here?" The CPE course, once I learned about it, seemed a natural for me to teach.

I've since decided to try to make my career at Bay, although I realize it's unrealistic to be overconfident. Even in my two years here, I've seen faces come and go among the faculty. Fortunately, the case method style of teaching is excellent preparation for many other things. But, as for the difference between an academic graduate school like Berkeley and a professional, practical institution like Bay, I'm still trying to figure that out.

Bob's Second Year

I found my second year of teaching CPE much more enjoyable. I had gained familiarity with the material and felt more at ease teaching students older than I.

Bob taught CPE to Sections I and II of the first-year MBA program. Teaching Section I had turned out to be a real pleasure. "For some reason," he commented, "I got on their wave length quite early in the first semester."

They were well prepared and eager to contribute, the keenest, most engaged section I had taught so far.

By comparison, Section II lagged behind. They were eager to play pranks, prone to lateness, and tended to waste valuable class time with elaborate jokes. Section I, while lively, was generally issue oriented and energetic.

Interestingly enough, at the end of the year, when the students evaluated the teachers, I learned that Section I had rated me a 4.3 out of a possible 5, while II had rated me 3.5. I still wonder whether the whole educational experience—for me and the students— would have been better if I had somehow forged a better rapport with Section II; perhaps they might have performed better. Certainly, I tried to grade objectively, but it seemed that there really was a qualitative difference between the two groups. Perhaps my display of annoyance once at Section II's widespread lateness alienated the group and impaired my relationship with them. To me, effective teaching means keeping one's negative emotions in check for the sake of good class dynamics.

That isn't to say that you can or should avoid emotion in teaching. I don't think you can. In fact, case discussions at Bay are alive with all sorts of emotions—tension, excitement, humor, discovery, fear of failure, intimidation, sometimes resentment—I could go on. And this emotion emanates both from the students and from the instructor. A large part of the instructor's task is managing this emotion. That's probably the most difficult part of teaching here, especially for a young instructor. I think I still have a lot to learn in this regard. But one thing that I have learned is that it just does not pay to get angry at a section of Bay students.

To Bob, teaching was not merely a matter of obligation ("one of certain necessary conditions for advancement at Bay," as he put it). It was also a pleasure, and he felt he had a serious moral responsibility to help prepare leaders of world industry and government for extremely influential positions.

Bob's Teaching Style

Bob described his typical opening:

At the beginning of each case, I usually laid out the three main areas I had worked out according to my teaching plan. In the beginning of the year I tended to stick fairly close to my plan and also to intervene on particulars. When a student simply offered a fact without a hypothesis, or an unsupported conclusion, I would zero in and try to expose the fallacy either by pointing out a contradictory set of facts, or by suggesting an alternative hypothesis to explain the phenomenon in question. As the academic year progressed, however, I tended to avoid that for two reasons. Some of the students were offended by that approach—they seemed to take it personally—and it also robbed other students of an opportunity to correct their colleagues on their own initiative.

I also decided that it was better to let the students talk than to deliver material myself. "Air time," as they call the opportunity to speak in class, is an important factor in students' grades at Bay, and they compete for it. The opportunity cost of an instructor's intervention is lost time for student contribution. If it's managed properly, the students will do all the teacher's work in a lively discussion—bring up his points, expose each other's reasoning. As obvious as this is to me now, I didn't learn this until about 80 percent of the way through my first year here. There are many ways whereby you can have students intervene. Instead of correcting a student, I'd turn to someone else and say, "Joe, tell me why you don't agree with that," or I'd look for someone on whom I thought I might depend to supply a supporting remark to that argument, let the thing build, and then call on someone I knew would present a totally opposite position. I might simply refuse to let anyone take the opposite side until I thought the erroneous argument had been fully laid out.

When asked to describe how he currently ran his classes, Bob replied:

At the beginning of each class I'd go out to the center of the pit and—exactly at the appointed hour—open with introductory comments and describe the class agenda. Then I'd turn to a student and ask him or her to address the first study question. This was a standard beginning early in the course. We would discuss the economic situation confronting the government of *x*. Students would have a critical list of economic variables and we'd compare GNP growth rate, inflation, unemployment, productivity, and balance of payments data. At the beginning of the year, I wouldn't typically warn the first student contributor beforehand.

I called on people to start off the class and didn't accept volunteers. But about 40 percent of the way through the second year of teaching I stopped this.

Section dynamics had gotten more casual and, besides, it was a signal to them that I was satisfied with their general level of performance and didn't need to spur them. It signaled confidence. During the first year I taught I never took volunteers to open the class, and frankly, I don't think that worked out well.

The Incident

That Friday, Bob arrived about 10 minutes early for his session of CPE with Section I. It was 12:50 P.M. No teacher has a predictable year-long schedule at Bay, and Bob had drawn an unusual number of Friday afternoon sessions, but he didn't mind teaching that particular Friday afternoon class. He found the material fascinating because it was close to his own interests, and he also enjoyed Section I.

Bob recalled:

I was on my way to my desk in the pit [the center of the amphitheater] when one of my best students, Ian Kahn, stopped me. I was in a hurry to review a few points before the class started but I paused. "Did anyone tell you what's planned for today?" Ian asked. I said, "No, why?" Ian looked around, shrugged, and said, "Oh, nothing, except that the section's a bit rowdy, that's all." I didn't realize it then, but Ian's words were a warning.

As a few students began to straggle into the classroom, Bob carefully spread out his class notes on the desk and chatted with some of them as they entered the classroom. Amanda Brown paused to greet him on the way to her seat. He asked her how the class play had gone the night before. She responded that it had been a resounding success.

"One of the cast members [and a section member], Alec O'Reilly," she said, "did such a marvelous job last night that he got a standing ovation. Best of all for me, though, was the break the play gave us all from the grind of preparing cases. A whole bunch of us went out drinking afterwards."

As Amanda was speaking, a young man in a three-piece suit presented himself to Bob.

"Professor Clarkson," he said, "I'm Ken Call. Professor Friedman suggested I attend your class. I'm a prospective student. Would it be all right?"

Bob recalled:

I couldn't imagine why Professor Friedman, a senior colleague I hardly knew, had singled me out, but

I told Mr. Call he was certainly welcome to sit in. Call asked if I'd mind if he left at 2:00 for an appointment. Normally, I don't appreciate people coming late or leaving early but I decided to make an exception in this case and said, "I don't think it will be a problem. Maybe you can talk one of these guys into letting you sit near the back door so you can leave inconspicuously."

Then Bob walked up to the back row of seats to chat with Jack Law, the section's social director, who was usually an active participant in CPE discussion. He had invited the professor and his wife to join the section for a baseball outing May 9. Bob wanted to get the details straight and see if Jack had tickets for his youngsters, ages 6 and 4, as well.

"Sure," Jack replied. He seemed to be in a festive mood. "Bring the whole family. We've invited the dean, and he's bringing his kids, too. By the way"—Jack put on a baseball hat—"why don't you play softball with us this afternoon?"

Bob usually devoted his afternoons to work and student conferences. He smiled but shook his head. "Like to, but can't," he said. "Student appointments."

Bob's social interaction with Section I had been pleasant but usually limited to a fairly formal arrangement whereby eight students would sign up with the educational representative of the section for a lunch with Bob. The lunches were friendly and casual, and over half of the section took advantage of the opportunity. They had often invited Bob to their regular Friday afternoon beer busts as well, but he hadn't gone, nor had he played in the section's first Friday afternoon baseball game the previous week. At that time he had had other things to do, but, he explained, "I'm not sure I would have played even if I had been free. I wanted to maintain a little distance."

After speaking with Jack, Bob passed Ian and—to his subsequent chagrin—ignored his cryptic warning.

"How did you get stuck teaching a tough course like CPE on a Friday afternoon, anyway?" Ian asked.

"Just the luck of the draw," Bob replied.

"Well," Ian continued, "I don't think people really have their minds on the case today, what with the play last night. Eighteen people missed Finance this morning."

"Eighteen?" Bob raised his eyebrows with mock incredulity. "There'd better not be eighteen gone from class this afternoon!"

The Section's Mood

The second term was well under way, but the end from the students' point of view was nowhere in sight. The world hunger case was #36 in a syllabus that ran from #31 through #54. The CPE course had just completed a module on oil with a case on U.S. energy planning. The class discussion had been particularly encouraging to Bob. Students had grappled seriously with the important issues and political constraints that face a U.S. president who attempts to forge an energy strategy. In fact, the discussion had gone even better than Bob expected, given that it had taken place on his first day back in the classroom after the faculty had returned midterm exams and grades.

Bob considered the day's case, World Food Prospects and Policies, especially crucial, because it introduced a new module and therefore set the stage for the level of performance of the next three sessions and because he believed its underlying issue—widespread starvation in the Third World in the face of prosperity in the highly industrialized nations—to be morally significant.

Many first-year students were under substantial pressure at that point in the term because of a slightly unusual circumstance. Not only had they just received the results of their midterm exams in Finance, a subject many found quite difficult, but also, for some reason, the instructors of the Marketing area had delayed returning the March final exam grades until April. They had, in fact, just released the grades, along with an unusually high number of warning letters—30 percent. In the opinion of the first-year students, however, it was particularly upsetting for warning letters to be sent *after* the course was completely over and there was no longer any chance of improving one's performance.

"The first-year students," Bob commented, "had reached a peak of frustration, concern, and anxiety. Emotionally, they were exhausted. Like long-distance racers, they were hitting 'runner's wall' [near-paralyzing fatigue], but they knew it wasn't downhill yet. They couldn't quit. I had given my midterm after case #30. World hunger was #36, and my sections had just received their grades. Their performance on the exam was rather good, but some students discovered that they had fared far better in class participation than written work; that meant they had a lot of hard work ahead."

Section I Membership

Bob recalled:

Section I had shown itself to be gifted and mature, even by Bay standards. In discussions with other section instructors, I confirmed my judgment that this was an unusally capable group. Their discussions were almost always vital, with most of the section members participating. I had, in fact, found it difficult to award 10 percent Low Passes on the exam, along with only 20 percent Excellents. I respected the section as a whole and felt that they respected and liked me as well. There had been no crises and no particular tensions in our work together.

Among the students, Jack Law, the social director, was the most gregarious. It says something about him that he was the social director. He didn't like to be seen taking Bay too seriously; he didn't want to lose his personality to the school. Jack often wore a baseball hat in class, was very talkative, organized section athletic events, and tended to make jokes in class although he certainly wasn't a clown. His midterm grade was a Sat +.

Ian, a foreign student, had been a businessman in Japan, dealing with government agencies there. His performance in class had been outstanding. Another of my students, Frank Williams, had been in the Foreign Service, and he approached the material with a point of view similar to mine. Peter Barnes, an Oklahoman, had run for Congress and lost the Democratic primary by 100 votes.

Cynthia Andrews was the educational representative, a young woman Bob described as having "impressive maturity and the ability to understand both the social and intellectual aspects of the class." He found her to be "very motivated. She had come to me, for example, for outside reading on this particular case."

Elliott Farmer, who had participated adequately in class discussions, nonetheless had been given a Low Pass on the midterm. He had, Bob subsequently learned, a special interest in problems of world food distribution and famine relief. Just as some students study nuclear energy or the environment, Elliott made something of an intellectual hobby of the study of the world food situation. His interest in the case, therefore, was high. Martin

Harkness was an active Libertarian, prominent in the National Taxpayers' Union.

Amanda Brown was a bright, lively young woman who threw herself enthusiastically into the many social activities of the first-year class. She had mentioned to Clarkson a day or two before the world hunger case that she was working hard on the class play and therefore might not be as well prepared as usual.

As the Class Began

When Bob returned to the pit to review his notes, it was nearly time to start. Neil Salman waited by the desk with two more guests. "This is my wife Ellen and our friend Sara, who is thinking of applying here next year."

"Delighted to meet you," Bob said. "Neil, have you introduced your guests to the section?"

"Yes, I have."

"Fine, then. Why don't you take a seat in the top row?"

Bob turned to start the class as the second hand swept past 1:00. When he walked to the center of the pit he saw that Ian's prediction had been right. There were an unusually large number of students absent, including some of the section's best. And many students were not sitting in their usual places, a major departure from custom. Bob motioned to a student at the back to close the door.

The rest of this case is told in Bob's own words as he recalls how this particular class began.

I began with some irony, and said, "Well, I'm glad to see you all could make it." The section laughed. "We have a visitor," I said. "I'd like him to introduce himself."

The nicely dressed visitor in the back stood up and again it flashed through my mind to wonder why Professor Friedman had steered him to my class rather than someone else's. I hoped it might be because Friedman had heard something good about my teaching.

The class welcomed the visitor with a round of applause, and just then six more students came through the door at the back of class and waved at me on the way to their seats. The class attendance was turning out to be fairly normal after all.

I walked back to them. "Glad you could make it," I said, and they laughed a little sheepishly. "In a moment," I went on, "I'd like our friend Larry

Quirk to start the class." I gestured to Larry's empty seat and the section laughed. Then, after a pause, I turned to face the class and began my usual sort of introduction. "Today, we begin our three-day module on the world food problem. . . ."

Food Fight

Before I could finish my sentence, Jack leapt to his feet, bellowed "FOOD FIGHT!" and fired a roll directly at Larry Quirk's empty seat. The roll narrowly missed me. Immediately, students on all sides of the classroom began throwing rolls at each other. Bread materialized, it seemed, from every pocket and purse. The air was full of rolls. It must have been a carefully orchestrated prank. Students picked up rolls that fell near them and flung them out across the room and into the pit again, in several volleys. I retreated in shock and huddled behind the desk among the "bread-crumbs" to avoid the rolls that were still flying.

It was one of those times where you almost see your whole life passing before your eyes. I thought about the visitor, Ken Call. What would Friedman think when he told him about this? What would the other guests think? What should I do to uphold the reputation of the school—this supposed training ground for the future leaders of the world? On this of all days, when we're about to discuss famine and starvation, how can the section dare stage a food fight? What does this mean about their attitude toward the less developed world, those who go without nourishment while we in a place of power fling bread at each other?

A food fight at any time is bad enough, but here we were studying hunger, people who don't have enough to eat, and the students were throwing bread on the ground and at each other. There were rolls all over. The place looked like a pigsty. It seemed like an offense against the poor.

I was upset because I hadn't read Ian's signal, but most important, the symbolism also offended me. It looked as if everybody was involved. People had obviously brought a lot of rolls to toss. All you could see was rolls everywhere. I was so stunned I couldn't see individual faces. I wondered, what sort of a cabal have I stumbled onto? I also thought about Jack, who had heaved the first roll right at the seat to which I had pointed.

There I was, behind the desk with my blood pressure rising. I had been caught unawares. I was bothered by the surprise. I was bothered by the sym-

bolism. I was bothered by the awful embarrassment in front of guests, and I wondered how to manage this process. Should I get really mad and blow my stack, rap their knuckles? I happen to believe that it's always bad to get angry, but should I end the class and send everybody home? Should I excuse the section because it's Friday afternoon and they're under pressure, or take it as the tasteless joke it was and react? If I were to get upset it might do everyone damage, but is one sometimes, nevertheless, compelled to show anger at unacceptable student behavior? The answers just didn't come very easily or quickly, yet I knew that I was going to have to do something and soon.

"Is It Safe to Come Out Now?"

I came out from behind the desk where I had retreated to avoid the rolls. I didn't have a simmering, steaming look on my face. In fact, I appeared stunned—partly on purpose, but also because I felt really uncertain. It was an honest response, but I emphasized my shock, played upon it by shrugging broadly and looking blank. This must have seemed pretty comical, because my body language got a laugh. I felt good about that, since it meant that the roll-throwing had not been a personal insult to me. I had always had a good relationship with this section, and their laughter reinforced this. Still I wondered: should I point out that this section's behavior constitutes an extraordinarily tasteless and immature joke?

How to handle the situation? That was the question. I looked around, then looked directly at Jack Law, who had started it all, and asked, "Is it safe to come out now?" That got another laugh. I got the feeling that my classroom had turned into a Sigma Chi setting. We were all in a fraternity together. "Frankly," I went on, "I really don't know how to respond to this." I was fishing for a lifeline. I began slowly to focus on individuals, trying to pick out facial expressions that would give me some clues. Some faces, I noticed, were not laughing. Cynthia, for example, looked a little worried. Others appeared to be apprehensive, maybe even offended. Not everybody, it seemed, had been involved in the plot after all. I was still pretty upset, but I recalled a time when I had bawled out Section II, and I didn't want to engage in that sort of negative feedback again. "Can someone suggest where we should go from here?" I asked.

I wasn't even certain myself what I meant by the

question, but hands shot up. The section had interpreted my words as a new beginning to the case. Immediately, people looked prepared for a discussion—notably Elliott, who had received a Low Pass on the exam. He had been one of those who looked concerned.

Lots of thoughts rushed through my mind. What I was about to do had implications for the people in the group who hadn't partied the night before or even gone to the play. They hadn't been out drinking; they'd prepared this case. I realized I had a responsibility to them. The students who hadn't prepared would be only too happy if I were to say something like, "Oh what the heck, it's Friday—let's go play ball," and dismiss the section. They would have blown off their anxiety about their other classes and simultaneously avoided doing their work in my class. And I would, in effect, have joined the fraternity.

I saw on Elliott's face a look of "I want to avoid a Low Pass in this class; I have worked hard on this case, and I'm prepared. Give me an opportunity to show it." If I were to dismiss the class, I thought, it wouldn't be fair to him and others. Besides, I wanted to find out what Elliott had on his mind. He looked safe, and he had a very earnest look about him.

So I called on Elliott, and he gave the most beautiful evaluation of the case. He talked for 15 minutes, which was unusual. Typically, the lead-off person talks for a couple of minutes. Every word was a gem. He didn't refer to the food fight at all. He spoke of the obligation of those with place and power, raising the issue indirectly by saying, "World hunger is a problem for the rich as well as the poor." By the time he was done talking, people were ready to concentrate on the case.

It was the last class of a long week, but as Elliott spoke it might just as well have been Tuesday morning at 8:30. It turned out to be one of the best discussions we had had all year. We did go into the ethical issues relating to world hunger. People became very much involved—even those who hadn't prepared carefully. We talked about ideas rather than numbers; we got personally involved in the

matter, really identifying with the involved participants and being genuinely committed in our thinking.

When Elliott gave me his super response, I essentially forgave the section. His excellent presentation blocked the issue. All my anxiety dissipated. I didn't have to halt the class or deliver a tirade. I was lucky. I had called on Elliott because he looked serious and eager. Fortunately, he turned out really to have been the most prepared student in the section. The very case issues that were bothering me were bothering him. I ended up enjoying the class, thinking "This is the most improbable discussion I have ever had!"

Jack then raised his hand but I ignored him for a good long while, until I thought he was ready for serious contribution. I also noticed Cynthia looking very concerned. Afterwards she came over to me and asked, "Did you really think we were going to hit you?"

As the class ended, I considered making some joking reference to what had happened—"I was sort of worried about finishing the case today" or some such remark—but I concluded instead by thanking Elliott for his careful preparation. I passed out one or two other individual bouquets and then summarized the issues, being quite honestly complimentary. It was no longer "Animal House," it was the Bay Area Graduate School of Business Administration again.

As the students left the room a few came over to thank me for one of the best discussions of the whole year, but mostly they were just saying to each other, "Let's go play ball."

I went away feeling very strange, wondering about this peculiar experience. But I did have a sense of success in having had a good discussion in what had been a potentially disastrous environment. I must have done something right but I still had nagging doubts.

After that, the section went well. The section didn't play any other stunts. It was almost like a trial by fire. Once that critical incident was finessed, we went on to even better discussions. I never heard anything from Friedman nor from any of the guests.

CASE

Class on World Hunger (B)

This case was written by **Abby Hansen** in collaboration with **C. Roland Christensen** for the Developing Discussion Leadership Skills Seminar. While the case is based on data supplied by participants involved, all names and some peripheral facts have been disguised.

HBS Case No. 9-381-043.

In reflecting on his first two years of teaching at the Bay Area Graduate School of Business Administration, Bob Clarkson gave the following account to the case researcher:

A discussion leader has a problem of balancing discipline and order with the need for student freedom. You recall I spoke with you about my problem of late arrivals for Section II classes, which occurred the same year as Section I's food fight. The way I handled my annoyance at them, and what subsequently happened, taught me something. One 8:30 A.M. session with Section II—the morning before an exam in Managerial Economics—was particularly bad, and I was quite upset with them. Nearly half the class was absent when the discussion was supposed to begin. I remember turning to one of my better students and asking, "Where is everybody?"

"You might want to give it a minute or two," he replied. "At this time yesterday in the Manufacturing class, quite a few students were absent, but they came in a minute or two late."

I decided, based on his comment, to wait. One minute passed, then two. Only one or two additional students arrived. Then I started to get angry. I pursed my lips, put on a troubled look— furrowed brow, folded arms—and stared into space until five full minutes of silence had passed. You could feel the tension in the room.

Then I said, "I really want to address these remarks to those who aren't here, but perhaps you will be the conduits of my message." I spoke in measured tones. "An exam the next day in Managerial Economics is not a sufficient excuse to miss CPE," I said. "At the beginning of the term we talked about a contract. Your part is to be here, to be prepared, and to be on time, and if you can't do one or all of those things, to let me know about it in advance."

[Later, Bob told the researcher, he had second thoughts about that speech.]

It occurred to me, as I thought about that incident, that it was really a one-way sort of contract. I enunciated my terms at the beginning of the course, but I simply assumed they implicitly subscribed to the contract by having come to Bay. I realized all this later and decided it isn't a good idea to berate students for not living up to a one-sided contract. After all, a student could say, "I'm paying thousands of dollars for this, and if I decide I ought to miss a day of Clarkson's class to study for someone else's, that's my affair." In a sense, I now think it was unfair of me to get angry, and besides, the students reacted as if I had bawled them out like children. It was bad for class morale. It was very unpleasant. It showed me the cost side of getting mad and made me afraid of damaging the process of discussion with Section I when they staged that food fight.

Bob's Philosophy

His Teaching Experience

My teaching philosophy and style changed rather substantially from the first to the second year. The first year I was very influenced by Michel Crozier's *The Bureaucratic Phenomenon.* Crozier's theory of individual and group behavior in organizations holds that there is a relationship between power and uncertainty. Each group (or person) in an organization seeks to enlarge its discretionary area, and would retreat rather than submit. Being unpredictable can enhance one's power and one's hold on a discretionary area. During my first year, when I felt especially vulnerable—I hadn't yet completed my dissertation or attained professorial rank—I sought to maintain my authority in class by being unpredictable.

I tried to implement Crozier's theory so that the students wouldn't think they had my number, but I now think I was confused then about the proper role of an instructor at Bay.

In my second year at Bay, I started to run a less authoritarian-seeming class. I didn't time the agenda of my classes precisely, although I always started promptly, on the dot of the hour. I would introduce the case by saying that certain aspects seemed to be worth, say, 10 or 15 minutes, but I would let a discussion wander if it was good. When the discussion got too far from the point, I would sometimes stop the class 10 minutes early to make sure that something I thought was vital received coverage.

I did lecture at times like that, but I didn't do it often. Once, for example, I knew that a certain political analysis I had prepared would be very

important on an exam. The students in Section II, however, got off on a tangent talking about terrorism. I decided not to strong-arm them into following my prescribed pattern, and I let the discussion go on. But I did stop the class early and say, "Now this is pretty important, and I want to share my analysis with you." I then put my own diagram on the board and explained it.

I guess both my teaching philosophy and style have evolved over the past two years, too. My central theme now is that I want to manage a discussion rather than deliver my own thoughts. With an eager section you can just call on volunteers to bring out most points in a case. At Bay, we use the metaphor "discussion pastures" in talking about the case method. The instructor polices the fences of a pasture, but lets the cattle graze as they will, without letting the grass become grazed too closely in any one area. You can't cover more than three major areas per class. The teacher becomes a discussion manager, intervening only to move the fences and keep the pasture defined.

In graduate school, I was familiar with professors who had years of expertise to deliver, but that model, I found, didn't apply to the case method of teaching. I came to feel that a professor should be tinder for *discovery,* and that rapport with students was essential. As I gained confidence, I discarded Crozier's model and slowly came to seek consistency instead of inconsistency.

In a discussion of economic performance, for example, someone might say, "GNP is going up, but I think the crucial issue is moral." I'd say, "Fascinating observation, but let's lay out the facts first and then move in that direction." I would try to persuade the class that there's a logic to the agenda.

In a class where you simply lecture, the students' reactions to you are less important than in the case method. You could deliver a sermonette in a lecture class without negative impact, I suppose, but in a discussion class the students' attitude toward you can make or break the whole enterprise. The question that keeps coming back to me is: how do you uphold the standards of your school and the intellectual enterprise without becoming obnoxiously authoritarian so that you destroy or interrupt a delicate rapport?

READING

A Little Coffee to the Rescue

PETER KUGEL

When I first began teaching, I was invited to a workshop for new faculty. Like most people who teach at universities, I had spent a long time learning *what* to teach, but none learning *how* to teach it. Somehow, my university seemed to hope, a weekend spent with experienced members of its faculty would make up for that.

It took me more than a weekend to learn how to teach, but I did learn a few things at that workshop. One thing I learned is that I didn't learn much from speeches. My colleagues presented well-crafted lectures about the tools they used in the classroom. They told us how to use the blackboard well, how to show slides, how to make up tests. I enjoyed their presentations, but don't remember a thing they said.

One thing that I do remember happened at a coffee break. Finding myself alone, I turned to a mathematics professor standing nearby. He seemed quite old to me at the time, although he was younger then than I am now. I asked him what his favorite teaching tool was. "A cup of coffee," he said.

I drank coffee too, but I didn't think of it as a teaching tool. It helped to keep me awake, but that always seemed less of a problem for me than for my students. I asked him how he used it. "Well," he said, "I talk too much and too fast in the classroom. Students sometimes have trouble following me. So every once in a while, when I've said something I want my students to think about, I stop and take a sip of coffee. It lets what I've just said sink in."

The Cup Was Empty

When we were called to the next talk, he put down his cup and I noticed there had never been any coffee in it. I thought that was rather odd, and said so. "My doctor told me to stop drinking coffee," he explained. "So I use an empty cup. Doesn't make any difference."

I took a full cup of coffee with me to my next class that Monday morning long ago. It helped. My pauses, as I sipped, not only gave my students time to think about what I had said, but gave me time to think about what I was going to say next. I began to use my pauses to look around the room to see how my students were reacting to what I had just said. When I saw their attention wander, I tried to bring them back. When I saw them puzzled over some concept that I thought I had explained, I gave

HBS Case No. 1-389-122.

another example. My lectures became less organized and less brilliant, but my students seemed to understand me better. And my courses became more popular.

Eventually I had to cut down on coffee too, and so I started taking an empty cup to class. Now I don't even bring the cup. I find that pausing comes naturally to me. I stop, from time to time, to think about where I am, where my students are and where we are going.

When I started teaching, I thought only about what my students thought of me. I planned jokes, clever presentations and ways to demonstrate my erudition. Now I tend not to care so much what my students think of me, and to think more about the students, the course and the subject. I tend to think more about the big picture.

The ability to see the big picture seems to come with age. I remember when my children first started playing soccer. At first they could see only the ball. They chased after it, wherever it went. Then, as they grew older, they began to see the playing field as a whole, and they started to play their positions. They waited for the ball to come to them. As they grew older yet, they began to think about the whole game, to think about their team and to develop strategies.

Perhaps it was just that they had improved their mastery of the technical skills and could think about putting their skills together, much as people who have learned the mechanics of driving can focus on driving as a whole, instead of thinking about braking or shifting gears. Or, perhaps, they had just grown older and more mature.

Whatever it is, my children became better soccer players and, with time, I think I became a better teacher. I find that, as I get older, it becomes easier and easier to stop and think about what I am doing as I am doing it. It's easier for me to think about the whole picture. I still remember how my parents used to look at scenery, and how I wondered what they were looking at. They seemed to see forests, where I saw only trees or, more often, leaves. Now I see the scenery, and my children don't.

I've found that older people talk more slowly and pause more often. I like to think that it's not just that their thinking has slowed up (although mine has), but because they think more about what they are saying. Perhaps we choose older people as our leaders, at least in part, because they have the ability to think about the big picture.

Another Workshop

A few years after that workshop that was supposed to introduce me to teaching, I was invited to another. This time I was one of the experienced members of our faculty, and I was supposed to tell my younger colleagues how to teach. When the other speakers explained the proper uses of computers, slide projectors and videotapes, I explained the uses of coffee cups.

My friend the mathematics professor was there too. We talked again at a coffee break. I reminded him of our conversation, so long ago, and told him that I was now drinking less coffee too. I boasted that I no longer took a cup with me because I no longer needed it. But I told him that it had helped, and I thanked him for suggesting it.

I was thinking about all this the other day when a colleague told me about a new professor in her department. His teaching was not going well, she said. Although his research was exciting and he knew his subject well, he was doing badly in the classroom. Was there anything I could do to help? I thought there might be. I walked to his office, and knocked on the door. "Do you have time for a cup of coffee?" I said.

CASE

That Discussion Just Fell Apart

That discussion just fell apart! Not in any neatly bounded period of time or because of a simple mistake on my part. That would have been easy. If one line of questions doesn't involve the students, you can usually stop, shift, and rebuild; ten minutes downtime isn't crucial. And simple factual errors can be corrected without much trouble.

"No such luck that day! Slowly, with increasing agony on everyone's part, the discussion died. The imagery that flashed through my mind was that of a spring-driven alarm clock slowly winding down. So it was with Section A. As the section chatter decreased, a sort of academic coma settled over the entire group; the 'blahs' were the order of the day. First I was frustrated, then I became downright angry. I had spent an extraordinary amount of time preparing this case and knew it cold, its strengths and imperfections. Why did this have to happen?

"As I reflect on the experience, I still am uncertain as to what went wrong and worse, what I might have done to rescue the discussion. Thank heavens this doesn't happen often and rarely to this degree. But, I do get periods of discussion time in a number of my classes where nothing much seems to be happening. It is a phenomenon in discussion teaching which I don't fully understand."

The Instructor

Frank Taylor, on tenure track at Metropolitan, was speaking with the researcher about a frustrating problem he had experienced in the spring of his third year of teaching Corporate Strategic Planning (CSP), a required first-year MBA class. The difficult session had occurred midway through the semester.

Frank, the researcher learned, had an excellent reputation as an effective case teacher at Metropolitan. Students spoke of his teaching style as blending discipline with freedom for section exploration of ideas of significance to them. His high standards for case preparation and classroom contribution were well known. Frank enjoyed teaching and research and had few concerns about his next tenure review, scheduled within the next few years.

The Section

Frank mentioned that Section A of CSP had impressed him as courteous, cooperative, and competent, displaying a quality he valued highly; the students listened to each other. This helped him to lead an effective discussion since individual student

*This case was written by **Abby Hansen** in collaboration with members of the Teaching by the Case Method Seminar as the basis for class discussion rather than to illustrate either effective or ineffective handling of an administrative situation. Data were furnished by the involved participants. All names and some peripheral facts have been disguised.*

HBS Case No. 9-383-039.

Section 5. The Critical Instructional Choice: Guidance vs. Control

C A S E
That Discussion Just Fell Apart

comments were usually related to previous speakers' contributions and could be integrated into Frank's broad teaching framework for the day. Even if the lead students' comments were general in nature, section discipline was such that the group could push on into a situational analysis and then circle back to basic principles. Frank had, in fact, adapted this format of working from the general to the specific, back to the general as his standard approach with the section.

Within his section, Frank noted several subgroups. There were a half-dozen students whose statements qualified as gospel in any class. These individuals had industrial experience and could also synthesize and present case issues succinctly. Bob Parker, Tom Corelli, and Jack Jimson were in this group. Tom usually sat to the instructor's right, near the front of the classroom. There were the number-crunchers, most of whom were strongly academically oriented. Elliot Parker and Art Samuels were the leaders of that group; they sat side by side. There was a "run of the mill" group who could always say something sensible. These included the Section Student Academic Representative, Andreas Pappas. There was also a "contentious" group, whose members not only argued, but usually presented their points unpleasantly. When these students spoke, the others often tuned out. Finally, there was a group Frank described as "long-winded and BS-y."

Frank knew the class rather well at this point in the semester, and he had learned how to manage discussions so that no particular group monopolized the floor. In general, he believed section dynamics were good.

Preparing for Class

"My class preparation followed a pretty standard pattern. I worked through my own case analysis and then bundled it into a series of 'blocks' which I hoped constituted appropriate discussion modules. By appropriate I mean they gave the student enough room for inquiry along the lines of his or her interest and yet provided for some rough structural guidelines for the class discussion.

"In Addison Meats I ended up with four modules. Block One was a detailing of the various stages in the production cycle from feeder lots to the preparation of cuts of meat for the ultimate consumer (production strategy was crucial to this case); Block Two was an examination of the economics of meat

production and the cost position of major competitors; Block Three was an examination of the strategic alternatives open to Addison Meats; and Block Four focused on the implementation of the strategy chosen by the class.

"I ended up investing a lot more time than usual in preparing this case. I had had experience with Addison the previous year and it hadn't gone too well. It's a long (19 pages) and complicated case: there is a good bit of industry-specific terminology and lots of cost data in numerous exhibits to be worked over. What made the analysis quite tough was that the data from one exhibit were difficult to relate to data from other exhibits. All in all, the case was a dull one, too, but it did have valuable learning possibilities. A case discussion can be win, lose, or draw; this year I was at least hoping for a draw.

"As usual, I gave lots of attention to the selection of the lead-off student. I graded 50% on classroom contribution and opening up a case provided a student with a one-chance opportunity to demonstrate competence. At this point, there were only thirteen more cases to teach in the semester. Thirty students had not yet opened a case. Of these thirty, several were extremely good at CSP. I knew from their comments in previous classes, that they could give us an excellent kickoff. These students were, in fact, so good, that I had decided not to ask them to open any case. Even if they blew it, they were so good that it probably wouldn't affect their grades. Their earlier in-class comments had been stellar; they had nothing to gain from me calling on them.

"On the other hand, there were some students whose work on the midterm exam has been marginal and who were reluctant to speak in class. I worried about these people. Some of them were probably destined to receive a Low Pass in the course; others might be capable of improvement, given the right incentive and encouragement. Also in the pool of potential lead speakers were some students who seemed to be participating adequately but who might really shine if given a chance to lead off. Some of these were foreign students who had language difficulty but seemingly followed the sense of the discussion. Others were simply shy."

Frank found that as the academic year progressed, the quality of his students' opening remarks had been remarkably consistent. He commented:

"The 'raw material' for lead-offs does get worse and worse, but the weaker students tend to prepare more and more as they realize they need to do a good case opening if they're called on. They often outdo themselves.

"The night before, I had about ten students in mind as possible lead speakers. I reviewed their class cards (which give personal and professional background information) trying to sort out who might best benefit from opening up Addison. The list soon narrowed to four. Sylvia Michaels, whom I would describe as 'bland' had spoken perhaps twice in class, but as a rule remained silent. I considered her a potential Low Pass, but thought she might do a good job in this discussion. Her background was in finance, so I predicted she wouldn't have trouble with numbers. I put her card down and picked up another. Jean Delagarde, a 'frenetic Frenchman,' had difficulties with the English language. He had had problems in CSP first semester, and had asked me to call on him more in class. And he needed an opportunity to do well to raise his grade. Another possibility was Tom Corelli. He was fluent and intelligent and a class leader. I knew he would do an excellent job.

"The fourth candidate I considered was Neil Hafner. Neil, who came from an academic family, clearly was a person of potential. I drew this conclusion from conversations with him following class when he showed me his class notes. His midterm examination had been good, and there were inklings of high quality in his classroom work. But he seemed tentative and diffident, often apologizing for his in-class comments despite their good content. 'I'm not sure, but maybe this idea fits in somewhere,' he would say, and then present quite an intelligent point.

"I decided against Sylvia because I thought calling on her would probably serve little purpose. Some students, I thought, needed a kick to start them off, but others simply didn't intend to speak in class. I read her as the second type. As for Jean, I feared he would further confuse the already confusing Addison case. I rejected the idea of asking Tom to begin because that might look like showing off for our expected guest, Professor Sanford. Sanford, I knew, was going to visit the Addison class as a part of my promotion process.

"So I finally zeroed in on Neil. I knew he had had experience in the commodities business and hoped he would do a good job and bolster his own self-confidence."

The Class Opens

"As usual, I got to the classroom at 8:20, ten minutes early; I liked to be there to greet the students and to look over my notes for the final time. One of the early arrivals was Professor Ralph Sanford, a senior professor in my area. Since he had visited my class before, he asked not to be introduced again. I didn't feel any undue anxiety over his presence, but I'm not immune to tension. I like teaching at Metropolitan and wanted to make it my career.

"Standing behind the instructor's desk, I watched the students as they came in. One of the first was Neil Hafner. He bounded down the steps from the back of the room, sporting a great, wide grin, and carrying a large, black book.

"'Frank,' he bubbled, 'I'm really excited about this case.' He held out the book and I read the gold letters on the spine, 'Economic Analysis of the Meat Processing Industry, by Neil Hafner.' 'It's my senior honors thesis,' he explained.

"Neil then took his seat and immediately began to talk with the student beside him. I must admit to a twinge of uncertainty. Should I go ahead with my plan to lead off with Neil? Would he kill the case with over-preparation? My stomach growled. But after a few seconds reflection, I said, 'Neil, I'm going to ask you to lead off the class today.'

"'Great!' was the reply."

The Discussion Begins

"The classroom was full now and the students sat quietly waiting for the discussion to begin.

"'Neil,' I said, 'would you please tell us what decision you think Addison Meats should make concerning its future strategy and why?'

"My opening question lined up directly with the organization of the Addison case. That case history ended with a statement of three strategic alternatives open to company management: should the company continue its present strategy of shipping carcass beef to food chains, or should the company move to the new boxed beef system, whereby the carcass was cut up into basic consumer cuts at the packing house—thereby reducing the shipment of waste meats to the food distributor, or should it combine these two approaches? I was hoping for a good class; little did I know.

Section 5. The Critical Instructional Choice: Guidance vs. Control

CASE
That Discussion Just Fell Apart

"Neil turned to his section mates with a smoothing wave of his hand and said, 'Okay—sit back. I've got this in hand.' There was a subdued moan and an undercurrent of 'Oh, no. . . .'

"'Addison should go into boxed beef—Alternative Two,' he said, 'but before I tell you why, we need to understand the industry in detail.'

"I stood at the chalkboard, eraser in left hand, chalk in right, facing the class and thought: 'Wonderful! For teaching purposes, we do need to understand the flow of beef production from beginning to end. Last year the class never got the stages straight, e.g., what competitors handle which step in the chain from farmer to food store and that is crucial to understanding the case. I'm glad I picked Neil.'

"Neil then launched a description of the whole meat-processing industry in painstaking detail. As I recall, his first five minutes were a summary of his thesis detailing trends in meat packing and distribution. 'This could go on forever,' I thought, and it did seem to.

"'Neil, why don't you just walk us through the meat production process *briefly*,' I interrupted.

"'Sure,' he replied, but then he launched into an even more detailed and increasingly tedious description.

"I didn't cut Neil off then because I had given lead speakers a full ten or fifteen minutes of air time to present their ideas. So Neil continued to outline the meat production process, breaking it into twelve steps. From my point of view, six would have been ideal for discussion purposes.

"'Meat production starts with the cattle in pens and ends with packaged beef on the retail shelf,' Neil began, and named his dozen stages.

"'Could we get this to a broader level?' I asked.

"'Sure. The cattle go to the slaughterhouse and get their heads chopped off. The blood gushes all over the . . .'

"I raised my hand in mock protest as the class laughed with pained expressions on their faces. 'Please, Neil, let's keep the gory details to a minimum. Could we have more about the distribution strategy?'

"'Okay,' Neil said, and presented what I considered a good description. 'What's important,' he said 'is what are the key stages in this process and what firms compete in each specific stage.'

"'Wonderful! I thought. This is what the class

needs to build a good discussion. The length of the slaughtering knives and blood gushing on the floor isn't important.

"'I'd like to tell you now what was going on in the rest of the industry,' Neil was saying.

"I was beginning to wonder; 'How can I suppress this fellow? Should I suppress him when I've never seen him so enthusiastic?'

"At this point, there began to be a good bit of paper rustling and faces were registering boredom.

"Neil droned on, describing the competitive situation. 'An important development in this was the entry of James Meat Co.,' he said. 'The history of James Meat is as follows . . .' It must all have come from his thesis. The case included a passing reference to the company, but Neil pressed on to give its whole history.

"By now, there were a few hands up and so I interrupted. 'Okay, Neil, tell us what you think Addison should do.'

"'They have three alternatives,' Neil said.

"I thought, 'This is where he should have started.'

"'Can you summarize your position in a few sentences?'

"'Yes,' said Neil, and he did."

An Uncertain Beginning

"Neil's disquisition must have lasted a minimum of twenty minutes; it seemed like an eternity. When he finally stopped, the discussion began.

"Andreas commented, 'We don't have any numbers.' Elliot raised his hand and I recognized him with the introduction, 'I'll bet you can help us on that dimension.' Elliot did present a few calculations based on case data.

"Immediately Gary, one of the more 'contentious' section members, interrupted, 'I don't know where in the world you got those numbers, Elliot. They're cockeyed—totally off the wall—and won't help us one bit. And furthermore, Neil's last argument just doesn't make any sense at all.'

"I didn't see any hands at this point. I stood at the chalkboard thinking, 'I wish Gary hadn't said that and worse, in such a strident way.' The numbers seemed right to me, though I did recognize that these case data came from the real world—they were incomplete, partially inaccurate and capable of proving different conclusions. 'Oh well,' I thought, 'the numbers aren't super critical; besides, it doesn't feel to me as if more than five students have worked them through.'

"The class dragged on. Discussion was repetitive with students continuing to comment about alternatives that had already been well aired. Worse, the section simply didn't seem to be listening. Students would 'hear' a comment, raise their hands and say 'Yes, but I think,' and simply state another argument or restate a previous point. I began to realize that things were bad. There was, of course, some intelligent and thoughtful commentary, but darned little.

"At that point, I became interruptive, trying to stem the tide of BS; my questions became increasingly pointed and directive. What does that mean in terms of Gary's analyses, or, how does that calculation relate to Bill's numbers? But there wasn't any engagement. Comments were scattershot.

"And there was Neil. He sat waving his arm in the air. I ignored him. His response was to keep right at it, supporting one arm with his other hand and signalling his eagerness to participate. At one point well into the class, he interrupted, 'Can I say something, please?' 'Yes,' I replied, 'be *brief.*' Neil then went on to elaborate a point with facts no students possibly could have deduced from the case. The class looked angry. Later, Neil stage-whispered some postdate of the case into the discussion. The introduction of this current information killed one promising discussion lead."

Down the Tubes

"The combination of all of this made me so darned angry; the discussion was going 'down the tubes!' My reaction was to look for a Joan of Arc, one of my steady contributors, who might rescue the discussion, but none appeared available.

"The section mood now was one of increasing hostility. The discussion pace slowed down even more; there were perceptibly longer and longer lapses between each student's comments. Most of these comments were addressed to me, not to fellow students. On the sidelines, doodling on note pads seemed to be the students' principal activity. Individual students' contributions really stretched out; they became mini-speeches, and they were diffuse! I just couldn't sharpen them up. Worse, most of the 'speeches' were at a uniform level of generality with few specifics, for examples, or references to exhibits or text in the case mentioned.

"The clock eventually crept toward the 9:50 closing point. I made a few comments about the substantive aspects of the case problem and indicated where data were missing or hadn't been used in our evaluation of Addison's strategic alternatives. Then I noted the next day's case assignment and said I hoped that tomorrow's discussion would be better.

"For a change, no students gathered around my desk after class. I slowly picked up my papers and headed for my buddy, Bob Ryan's office. We worked over the events of the past class. 'How,' I asked Bob, 'do I handle a situation like this if it occurs again? I'm sure it will!'"

Rough day," was about all Nick Maitland could think to say to Professor Rowe when he caught up with him at the water fountain. Quite surprised by Rowe's abrupt exit from class, Nick (a Ph.D. candidate at Farwestern Graduate School of Business and an observer in the class) had followed him out of the classroom and down the hall.

"Yeah! If a bar were around, I'd buy us a drink." Professor Rowe was really "dragging," shaking his head as they continued to walk down the hall. "I just don't understand it. Here it is, almost the middle of the year, and this class is terrible." The frustration so evident a few moments before in class was returning to his voice. "They don't prepare, don't show any interest. As a class they just don't seem to have developed any effectiveness in discussing a case. I don't know, Nick. What do you think? What do I do?"

"Well, the last few classes before the holiday didn't go well and there certainly wasn't much happening there today," Nick replied. "But I have a hard time assessing the situation. The cases are long, the subject matter is complicated and difficult, and perhaps many of the students just don't have enough analytical background to handle it. On the other hand, those students who do have strong backgrounds don't seem to be helping much." Nick felt he wasn't shedding much light on the problem.

Rowe's shoulders were still drooping and he seemed more discouraged now than angry. "Look, every year there are students who have to struggle with this stuff because their analytical backgrounds aren't that strong. I think it's an important and exciting part of my job to work with them, but what bothers me most here is that this group just doesn't seem to be making an honest effort."

The Incident on December 1

It was Wednesday, the third day of classes after the four-day Thanksgiving break, but the first post-holiday meeting of Planning in Complex Systems (PCS). Professor Douglas Rowe was teaching the International Trading Co. (D) case to his first-year section at one o'clock. (The (A), (B), and (C) cases had been taught during the three preceding classes.) It was not long before it became obvious that this class was not going well. Professor Rowe surveyed the room at the beginning of class and noted that a dozen students were absent. As he began the class, members of the section seemed

*This case was written by **Gale D. Merseth** under the supervision of **C. Roland Christensen** for the Developing Discussion Leadership Skills Seminar. While the case is based on data supplied by participants involved, all names and some peripheral facts have been disguised.*

HBS Case No. 9-378-035.

CASE

We're Just Wasting Our Time

179

restless and uninvolved. One of the first students he called on declined to participate, acknowledging that he was unprepared. No one was volunteering, and Rowe tried several lines of questioning without results.

"How does this company's strategy compare with that of Northstar?" (Northstar was a case they had studied earlier in this course.) Several students tried to respond, but their comments were obviously shallow and most missed the point.

It was like pulling teeth. In another attempt to get things going, Rowe moved to the chalkboard and talked briefly about several key elements in the case. He returned to the center of the amphitheater classroom and said, "This company's strategy represented a great economic success story. How did they do it? What's their comparative advantage?" Still no one volunteered. He stood facing the right-hand side of the class. "Dave, do you understand comparative advantage?" Dave shook his head. The professor started working his way down the row. "Marie?" "No, I'm afraid I really don't." Rowe tried again, "How about you, Jack?" Still nothing.

By now, Doug Rowe was angry. "In all the years I've been teaching, I've never seen a class as poorly prepared as this one. We're just wasting our time. If you can't do better than this you'll have to get somebody else to teach this section." With that Professor Rowe gathered up his papers, threw his coat over his shoulder, and left the classroom. It was 1:20 P.M.

MBA Core Program

Three aspects of the first-year core program at Farwestern's Graduate School of Business (GSB) are worthy of special mention: pedagogy, scheduling, and the importance of the sections. The use of cases dominates the pedagogy of the program. Readings, exercises, lectures (really lecturettes), and other forms of teaching would best be thought of as supplementary to the case method rather than as equal partners with it.

Courses in the Core Program are scheduled in free-form fashion so that their content relates to and builds upon one another rather than being fitted into a more rigid quarter or semester system. The effect of this scheduling arrangement is that some courses begin in September and others at various times from November to March. Some courses are compressed into two months while others extend to five. In fact, some courses run for a few months,

stop for a time, and finish up later in the year. Students typically have three 80-minute classes per day.

Each of the sections has an enrollment of approximately 65–70 students. Because sectionmates take all of their classes together for a year, the section becomes the dominant social, as well as educational, unit in Farwestern's GSB. Members of a section tend to develop strong relationships with one another, and the section develops distinctive behavior norms. Students tend to become quite conscious of the behavior and norms of their section and think of it as unique and having its own "personality." Each section elects a representative to the program-wide Education Committee of the Graduate Student Council.

The Course

Planning in Complex Systems (PCS) was considered by all to be a difficult course. It dealt with complicated problems, and few students had had experience in the field prior to enrolling at Farwestern. Several earlier versions of the course had proved unsuccessful and were scrapped. The current course had been significantly revised several years earlier by some of Professor Rowe's colleagues. According to a statement of course goals by the teaching group, they felt that they were now at a point where they had a course concept and a set of teaching materials which allowed them to help their students effectively develop "basic technical skills . . . (and) . . . minimum levels of knowledge, skills, and attitudes for generalists in this field." The course relied heavily on cases in planning developed for the course and a set of readings that gave students necessary background in the techniques, models, and theory of planning. Cases and readings tended to be long compared with those assigned in other first-year courses. For example, the cases in the International Trading series averaged about 30 pages of text and 10 pages of exhibits each. The (D) case, assigned for the first class after Thanksgiving, contained 33 pages of text and 8 pages of exhibits.

The Professor

Douglas Rowe had been a member of the Farwestern faculty for approximately 20 years. He had taught both first- and second-year courses in the MBA Program and had studied planning problems extensively. Since joining the PCS teaching group,

Section 5. The Critical Instructional Choice: Guidance vs. Control

CASE
We're Just Wasting Our Time

he had contributed significantly to the thinking of his colleagues concerning the course content and presentation. This year in particular he had looked forward to his teaching assignment because he felt confident about the current state of the course; the teaching materials were in good shape and the pieces of the course seemed to fit together well. Beyond that, he had noted from the information provided to the faculty by members of their sections that several Section IIIers seemed to have strong backgrounds in planning, and he hoped they would be good resource people for the class.

By the time PCS began in November, Professor Rowe had talked with two colleagues teaching other courses to Section III, and they had both expressed their disappointment with the preparation level of the section. However, these instructors had not expressed their displeasure directly to the section.

At the beginning of the course, Professor Rowe had talked with Section III about the goals of the course and what he hoped they would learn. He noted the importance of effort on their part because the materials tended to be long and the subject complicated. In the early classes, he took great care to go slowly over points that were especially important or difficult, pausing often to ask students if they understood. He emphasized the importance of understanding case facts, relating them to one another, and developing an integrated understanding.

During the second week of the course, he had returned to the matter of his expectations for the class: "Your part of the bargain is to be prepared; my part of the bargain is to make a useful learning experience out of it."

By the time the Thanksgiving break rolled around he was particularly disappointed in the work of the section. Discussions in class were going badly, and it appeared that most students were not putting in sufficient effort to be adequately prepared. Another problem was also apparent: in the second class before the holiday break, 15 students were absent and the day before Thanksgiving, attendance had dropped to 40 out of 65.

Nick Maitland's Interview with Jim Catterson

As a part of his doctoral program, Nick Maitland was sitting in on classes taught by experienced case-method teachers. He had spent some time discussing with Professor Rowe the outline of the course

and how Rowe would approach the teaching. Several months after the December 1 incident, Nick talked with Jim Catterson, one of the student leaders in Section III. (A few weeks after the December 1 incident, Catterson had been elected the section's representative to the Education Committee.)

Maitland began by explaining his reason for the interview: "As you know, Jim, I'm a doctoral candidate here in Management Planning and Theory. Part of our work focuses on the teaching process itself, and that is why I've been sitting in on your class. Professor Rowe has agreed that the incident with your section might make a good case for use with people studying case-method teaching. You know—what really happened? What did Rowe do and why? Might he have handled it differently? The standard case-method approach. So, if you could give me some of your impressions, it would be a big help. Could you tell me some of the things going on in Section III at the time, and your impressions of the incident?"

Jim Catterson was thoughtful, but animated and eager to talk about "the incident."

JIM: I'll never forget that day. It was incredible. I can still see Doug Rowe standing in front of the right-hand section of the class. He had asked several people the same question, and they all said they weren't able to comment on it. He was furious; he threw his papers on the desk. He said people weren't prepared. He said he would not teach another class like that one and, in fact, he said somebody else would have to teach the class if we couldn't do better. Then he stormed out of the room.

We all sort of sat there stunned for a minute; then people started getting really angry. You know—saying "What right does he have to just walk out?" and that sort of thing. Some people turned to the ed rep and he said, "Well, Rowe's probably right." Then people were really mad.

NICK: What things were going on in Section III at that time?

JIM: Lots of things. First of all other teachers we had at the time were terrible! We had—I'm going to very candid with you and I'll use names—Professor Roger Williams for Business Information Systems. He's very famous, but he never prepared the cases. If you asked him a question, he couldn't answer it. He talked all the time. He never wrote on the chalkboard. He just looked for particular words, not for your ideas. That's not the way you teach here.

In Finance, we had Irv Kincaid who is still at the school but not teaching in the MBA Program anymore. He's a very nice guy and, as a matter of fact, he's brilliant. But he just could not teach by the case method. He couldn't get it into his head how to approach people. He was too far above everybody; he assumed he knew everything and we didn't know anything.

Then we had Francis Gress for Marketing Management. He had just been informed that he was not being rehired—didn't get tenure.

So the day that Doug Rowe walked out, all of these things were happening at once. One teacher didn't care because he wasn't rehired, another teacher couldn't teach, and a third teacher was terrible. That particular day, December 1, we had Finance and Marketing in the morning, and they were just terrible classes. No one was participating anymore. Everyone was saying, "Why are we spending *thousands* of dollars to come here? We're getting crap right now." It was just terrible! Doug didn't understand that and he walked out. He thought it was that we weren't preparing for his class, but it was actually a much, much larger problem than that. It was that the whole case method wasn't working. Our group had just fallen apart.

NICK: Had it been working better earlier in the year?

JIM [*his face brightening up*]: Oh, it was great. In the beginning of the year we were a tremendous section. In fact we were said by some instructors to be "too rambunctious." People wouldn't raise their hands, they'd just jump right in. Everybody had something to say. There'd be 20 hands up at a time.

What happened was that our faculty coordinator[1] in the fall, Professor Bob Waggonier, said that we were too rambunctious and that we had to be more rigorous. He really clobbered somebody in class. The person said a really dumb thing in class and Waggonier said members of the section should have jumped in and criticized him for the statement. That quieted things down a lot.

Also, earlier in the year we had Professor Richard Hagey, who is an excellent professor but a bit of a manipulator. So, a lot of people in the class didn't like him—a majority didn't. I did, but a lot of people really didn't like him at all. They felt he was manipulating the class.

Little by little, these teachers began to pull out of us a lot of the real zip that we came in with. So, by the time Doug Rowe started teaching, things had fallen apart. And by the time the Thanksgiving break came around, people were just dead. There was no interest. Does that answer the question?

NICK: Do you have any feeling as to why as experienced a teacher as Doug Rowe, starting to teach his course several months into the school year, could get nearly a month into his course without being sensitive to the things you've described?

JIM: The reasons are somewhat . . . well, they're very interesting. First of all, Doug Rowe is an extremely sensitive individual. He's probably the most perceptive individual I've met here. So, the fact that it took *him* a month to get into it was very interesting. The reasons? One, his course had some fairly serious problems, not our year but the year before. He had played such a major role in designing the course that he was very heavily invested in it personally. He felt he was on the line. So this year he was very sensitive to what was happening to the course as a whole but not very sensitive to what was happening in our section.

Then, he came in the first day of class in November and he didn't really go through a synopsis of what the course was about. He said something like, "We're going to have some hard cases in the beginning of the course but it will even up. You can take a look at the syllabus— the list of cases—and see what we'll be covering. I think that's all I want to say about the course for right now, so let's just start with the first case." He didn't go through what we would have considered the basics of what the course was to be built on, didn't really give us any background. We expected some sort of an outline. Then he could have said, "Even if you don't understand it right now, as we go along you'll see it fit together."

He was very sensitive to what was going on in other first-year sections, was very "into"

---

1. A senior faculty member who offered informal, administrative, and academic leadership for a section's teaching group.

Section 5. The Critical Instructional Choice: Guidance vs.
Control

CASE
We're Just Wasting Our Time

what was going on with other teachers teaching the same course: What was going on? How were new teachers doing? That sort of thing. He spent lots of time with teachers in other sections who were having a particularly hard time of it. It's a hard course to teach. Consequently, he

simply must not have had time to ask the other teachers of Section III about their perceptions of how we were doing. Plus, when he first started teaching us, our section was still decent. It wasn't until the end of the month that we went right down the tubes.

The Section Just Took Over: A Student's Reflections

'll never forget that class as long as I live! There was Associate Professor Kenneth Webster; we thought he was the case method instructor *par excellence*, the professor who was always in perfect control—simply nonplussed—just out of it! The section simply took the class discussion away from him. He was left up front, standing by the instructor's desk, just watching the parade go by. At that time, it was just an interesting episode to talk about at the weekend beer party. But now, as I'm about to start out teaching myself, I keep thinking about the class; it poses so many tough questions for me.

Nobody ever came late to Professor Webster's 8:30 A.M. Marketing Policy class. Besides being a key first-semester MBA course, many of us were almost intimidated by the highly polished "performance" of the professor. He was able to needle students into corners, only to lead them out again when the time was ripe by getting someone to dredge up the three numbers in Exhibit 2 which "cracked the case." His sense of timing in a case discussion was flawless, although he was never seen glancing at the clock; the class myth attributed part of his mystique to his having eyes in the back of his head. Professor Webster was always "on top" of the discussion, leading us through the relevant and the obscure to the climax and his brilliant five-minute windup. His smooth performance was always given in one of Southeastern's few amphitheater classrooms with their left, right, and center subsections of seats.

I was in the classroom a bit early that day. Webster came in and, as usual, removed his coat and carefully arranged the mechanical chalkboard so that only his class discussion outline could be seen by the students as they came in. He then stood taking a last look at his carefully prepared notes, finally putting them in a neat stack at one side of the instructor's table. Once class started, at least in those early weeks of the course, I could never remember him using those notes; he must have memorized an outline of the case as he would have done it. He had told us in his introductory speech for the course that he worked to combine class discussion freedom with a logical, scientific, and disciplined approach to marketing problems and solutions.

The case for this particular day concerned the marketing of birth control pills in an underdeveloped country by a large, multinational drug company. The issues ranged from problems of pricing,

C. Roland Christensen wrote this case from data supplied by a member of the Developing Discussion Leadership Skills Seminar. All names and some peripheral facts have been disguised.

HBS Case No. 9-379-007.

Section 5. The Critical Instructional Choice: Guidance vs. Control

C A S E
The Section Just Took Over: A Student's Reflections

to distribution of the product to diverse market segments in terms of literacy, income levels, and physician contact. Side issues included overcoming possible parochial government resistance to the "invasion" of local markets by a foreign company, and the powerful resistance of the Catholic Church, the country's dominant religion, to the distribution of such a product. It was the first case we had involving the kind of complicated product-market situation.

The case began with a mediocre "kickoff" performance by the first student called on: many of the distinctions between marketing sophisticated products in underdeveloped versus highly industrialized nations were missed. Contributions were slow in coming, perhaps indicating less than adequate overall class preparation. Webster kept slugging away, I thought, with the objective of getting more meat on the bones of his visible board class outline before revealing the "muscle" hidden on the board beneath. His disappointment, however, was clearly visible in his frequent gazing around the room during student comments, and in a lack of continuity between his questions and student comments.

Just about halfway through the session, Kay Woodward raised her hand—one of the only times she had done so during the semester. I didn't know her well, but I gathered she had not had business experience. But a member of one of the small "study groups" in the section told me not to mistake her quietness for an absence of feeling or a lack of depth of conviction on social issues. Was she right! She brought everyone up short!

"I think," Kay said, "we are avoiding the most important issues presented by this case, and that's discouraging to me if I am to believe that we are the leaders of tomorrow. This company's marketing plan should strike everyone's conscience as being highly unethical, even immoral. I read the case last night and thought I was studying a chapter out of *The Ugly American*. Here is this huge drug company, restricted in its own country from distributing the pill without careful medical supervision, pushing wholesale distribution of a hazardous drug to illiterates under the guise of doing them a favor. The only favor being done is to the stockholders of the company. Not only are the long-term effects of the drug acknowledged to be potentially dangerous, but the drug is also forbidden by the religious authority of the country. This is a gross example of

the exploitation of women—endangering their health and encouraging them to defy their religious beliefs—all done in the pursuit of Almighty Profits."

Bob Kinney—I believe he had been in the investment business for a number of years—wheeled his seat around and without even looking at Professor Webster shot back as soon as Kay finished: "Well, that's not really the main issue here. That kind of problem is a personal one for you, and not what I'd really like to have to listen to in class. I didn't come here to learn what I'd missed in Sunday School. . . ."

Wow, did that create an explosion. Almost everyone got in the act. There were students on the left side arguing with students on the right side of the room, plus at least several dozen neighbor-to-neighbor private discussions going on at once. The arguments, as far as I can remember, were all over the place. The only "quiet" part of the room was the first few rows of the center section. Students there just seemed half bored and half irritated.

With about 20 minutes remaining, Harry Jones, an older member of the section and a former divinity school student, came into the act. From his seat toward the rear of the center section, he took over: "I disagree with Bob Kinney and I don't think his response to Kay was fair. We should discuss the ethics of this issue. You have to consider ethical issues in the real world, and that's what we're here for, to learn how to handle these problems within the organizations we will be working for. I think the drug companies have suffered from a moral lapse in many instances; I have a big question in my mind about the way they influence doctors with their armies of salesmen. My brother is a doctor and when he graduated from med school, he and all his classmates received boxfuls of drug samples and instruments from the drug and instrument manufacturers. I don't like the idea that my doctor is prescribing a drug to me because some guy is a good salesman—a better word for it might be 'pusher'. . . ."

The class pace slowed and Professor Webster, who had made several attempts to bring the class back to "normal" operating patterns, held up his hands and stepped forward. The room slowly became quiet. Focusing his eyes on the back wall of the classroom he said, "Kay's question is not appropriate to discuss in marketing class. You all have the opportunity to air your views privately with each other outside the class. Now, let us get back to how you would approach *the* problem of the case—how should the company distribute this product. Peter, what would you do?"

The discussion resumed on a subdued note. At the end of class, Professor Webster gave a summary of the marketing issues involved in the case and the problems they presented to the company. No further "social-ethical" questions were raised in his marketing course that semester.

Kurt Jacobs, 31, married, of German nationality with a student visa, had been a "quiet" member of the Business Policy's Section A for the first eight weeks of the course's 13-week term. Kurt, one of the older members of the section, was tall, thin, angular of face, and solemn of demeanor. In Metropolitan's amphitheater-type classroom, he sat in the front row, aisle seat. Although the seat next to his was assigned to another student, it was rarely occupied. The seat directly behind Kurt was one of the two seats in the 100-seat room not assigned to any section member; it was occasionally used by visitors.

Since the classroom contributions were important to the section's overall learning experience, all faculty members encouraged this activity. Individual student reinforcement was provided via the assignment of 50 percent of the course grade to classroom work. A section member could make "alternative arrangements" with his instructor (for example, the submission of a number of written reports) if there were medical or psychological extenuating circumstances preventing classroom contribution.

Professor Brett, a senior, well-respected member of the faculty, as part of this effort, had become concerned about Kurt's silence during the early weeks of the course. His first step in dealing with the situation had been a personal, handwritten note attached to a course report that was being returned to Kurt at the end of the fourth week of the semester. In sum, the note complimented Kurt on his excellent report, reminded him of the importance of classroom contribution, noted that Kurt had not spoken yet in class, and suggested that perhaps professor and student should discuss the situation.

Kurt's response was immediate. He scheduled a 10:00 A.M. Monday appointment with Professor Brett. After Ms. Ash, Professor Brett's secretary, had noted his arrival, Kurt entered the office and asked if he might sit down. Coming quickly to the note attached to his report, he explained that he did come to each class with the case well prepared and that he did follow the classroom dialogue closely. Both of those observations seemed accurate to Professor Brett; he had often noticed handwritten pages of analysis at Kurt's classroom desk. Kurt continued:

> Professor, I do not feel comfortable talking in large groups. This case method teaching is so different from the Technical Institute in Germany and my

CASE

Kurt Jacobs

This case was written by **C. Roland Christensen** *for the Developing Discussion Leadership Skills Seminar. While the case is based on data supplied by participants involved, all names and some peripheral facts have been disguised.*

HBS Case No. 9-376-094.

industrial experience involved only small-staff group work.

Professor, I don't like to talk either unless I have something *worthwhile* to say. Some members of your section just talk because it is required or they want to please you. Perhaps we need less talking and more thoughtful, constructive reflection. There is so much rubbish, just rubbish, in all classes here—yours too.

Professor, I *will talk* in class when I have worthwhile points to make which might help students in the section to learn. Not talking in class hurt my first year's grades; it may happen again during my second year, but that is all right with me. When my experience and background make it relevant, I will contribute! Then I will help the section to learn. They are very young!

Professor, my next class starts in a few minutes and I do not like to be late to class! Please excuse me.

Kurt then abruptly left Professor Brett's office.

During the next weeks, Kurt continued his established class routines. His desk top always seemed crowded with handwritten case analysis notes and calculations to which he referred. He checked these as points were made in classroom discussion. His only visible personal involvement came when questions arose involving the ethics and morality of corporate and personal decisions.

In the ensuing weeks, Professor Brett gained some additional information about Kurt Jacobs. Kurt, he noted, did not appear to participate in the social "chit-chat" of the section before or after class. His relationships with other section members were courteous and formal, being limited primarily to social conventions. Professor Brett on several occasions did see Kurt checking his notes after class with another section member, Bob Anderson. Anderson, 31, had been an engineering supervisor before attending Metropolitan. The Student Association representative for Section A mentioned that both men were active members of a university religious club that met on a regular basis, and both lived in the same married students' housing development.

The student representative also mentioned an incident that had occurred the previous year at a first-year section social event, one of the few attended by Kurt. It involved Millicent Wyeth, who was currently a member of Business Policy Section A. "Mil," described by the student representative as "liberated," had been engaged by Kurt in a discussion of the appropriate societal role of women. Cit-

ing biblical sources, he had sought to convince Millicent that the proper role for women was the "traditional" one. The student reported that Ms. Wyeth had responded in a extremely spirited way; her most restrained suggestion had been that Kurt ought to at least try to crawl back into the Dark Ages.

The cases scheduled for the first class day of the ninth week were Heublein (A) and (B). The cases involved an analysis of Heublein's success in the vodka market, with key discussion questions focused on whether Heublein should move into new fields. Specifically, should it buy a beer company?

Class discussion for the first 50 minutes could, at best, be described as dull, Brett thought. The class did cover the basic areas of the case, but the students seemed to be going through a required exercise with little interest and zero excitement. Yawns increased, doodling became the order of the day, and two "back benchers" started to read the *Times*.

Approximately 30 minutes before the end of the class, Mike Healey, a recognized academic leader of the section, entered the discussion. Noting that he had experience in the industry, he summarized Heublein's strategy, noted major areas such as Scotch and bourbon into which the company might expand, gave a financial analysis which indicated the company's ability to finance these moves, and then presented a series of recommendations to senior management that directly followed his diagnosis. The presentation was impressive to the section, and Healey's demeanor and tone of voice indicated personal involvement and conviction.

Mike's contributions were followed by a series of useful questions and comments by other section members, which indicated at least modest case preparation and some interest in Heublein's strategic problems. The section seemed to agree that the company should expand its line of liquors and buy the beer company with which they were negotiating. The "back benchers" put down their newspapers and the section pace seemed to pick up a bit—though it still seemed to Professor Brett to be tedious.

As the pros and cons of Mike's recommendations were being debated, Tom Mooney, Mike's roommate and sidekick, broke into the discussion. Tom's section role had often been that of "the jester" although certainly not "the buffoon." On several occasions Tom's wit and perspicacity had turned routine discussions into sparkling, high-interest,

Section 5. The Critical Instructional Choice: Guidance vs. Control

CASE
Kurt Jacobs

productive class sessions. Professor Brett assumed Tom was again trying to increase the fun and interest level of the section discussion.

"Mike is too darn conventional! This company really needs some jazz—some new thinking." With a hint of merriment in his voice, he proposed a series of recommendations. "Let's expand our present markets. Why not put vodka in square bottles for the over-50-year-olds," he said, looking at the professor. "And we can start working to lower the drinking age—get teenagers to drink beer—the demographics are super. Why—why not have beer-flavored baby foods? And then there is the women's market. Why not break down hard liquor television advertising restraints—if we can sponsor 'soaps' on the tube—look at the potential!"

Other section members joined what Professor Brett perceived to be "the game" with a series of nontraditional recommendations. One student suggested diversification in marijuana and another reinforced Tom's comment about the women's afternoon cocktail market by saying that liquor could change the entire concept of mother's milk.

"No! No! This is sickening." Kurt Jacobs was standing. He walked slowly into the open area of the classroom amphitheater, his face flushed, his arms close to his body, his fists clenched; he turned and faced the section.

No! No! What are you doing? Why are we spending our time discussing the debauchery of the young—the degradation of motherhood? Are there no limits? Is there nothing we will not do? Do you not know that your words break His injunction to love, to help those less fortunate, to honor your mothers?

Is this professional education? Is this education for leadership—to entice the young into self-abuse—to destroy family life? It is wrong. It is a sin!

What does this discussion tell us about ourselves? Are you proud of it? What do your comments tell us about this school? I am ashamed of this discussion . . .

"Professor . . ." Kurt turned and looked at Professor Brett, who was standing near the chalkboard. The remainder of the sentence did not follow.

To Professor Brett the room seemed frozen: no sound, no movement. His mind raced through Kurt's comments. It seemed as if the contribution had lasted for hours, instead of the reality of a minute or so. He could at best remember the major points of Kurt's comments, none of the multitude of biblical references. Brett's eyes swept the room; his throat muscles seemed set in concrete. Kurt remained standing.

"Professor," he said again.

*This case was a collaborative effort of a member of the Developing Discussion Leadership Skills Seminar and **C. Roland Christensen.** While the case is based on data supplied by participants involved, all names and some peripheral facts have been disguised.*

HBS Case No. 9-380-016.

CASE

Trevor Jones

I n my book, you're one son of a bitch!" Bob Smith, heretofore our section's model of discipline, consideration, and moderation, was speaking. Bob's face was flushed, his eyes angry. He seemed to hurl his words at Professor Vinceberg. The class waited expectantly.

The Organizational Behavior Course

Organizational Behavior, or OB as it was called, was a required first-year course at New Dominion's Graduate School of Business. Dealing with the human problems of administration, OB was one of the shorter class modules in the two-year MBA program; it was allocated only 30 sessions instead of the usual 50 classes.

OB classes started up just after Christmas vacation. Therefore, OB professors, along with those teaching the Business and Government course, were faced with sections that had worked together for four months and had formed their own social organization and discussion norms.

OB cases usually included only a modest amount of quantitative data, if any. For many students, Professor Vinceberg believed, these "human" cases came as a welcome relief from "number-crunching" courses such as Finance and Operations Management. But he was also aware that some students thought OB was not a real, hard-core MBA course. Their attitude seemed to be that there was too much *feeling* and not enough *hard facts* for OB to be taken too seriously. He knew that some of his colleagues were having disciplinary problems with their sections.

Al Vinceberg: Background

Al Vinceberg's academic training had been in sociology. Before joining New Dominion's Graduate School of Business faculty, Al had done research in the business sphere. He found this type of research most stimulating and had continued those efforts during his five years on New Dominion's faculty. Many of Al's faculty associates concentrated on investigating psychological problems and group dynamics issues within organizations. Al, however, preferred to study overall organizational structures and was an expert on matrix organization problems.

Al indicated in conversations with colleagues that he had mixed feelings about his teaching assignments at New Dominion. He found case teaching to be a stimulating experience that fit well with his own vigorous approach to any task. He enjoyed the

Section 5. The Critical Instructional Choice: Guidance vs. Control

CASE
Trevor Jones

dialectic of class discussion and the clash of personalities so often accompanying it. He said, however, that he sometimes became impatient with the elementary nature of the first-year OB course and that he wished he could share with his students the intricacies of the sophisticated forms of organization with which he was researching and living in the real world.

Al's Teaching Style

Al's teaching style, as described by one of the informal leaders of the section, was "blunt, aggressive and demanding, but with a vein of good humor." This section member's description continues in his own words in the following paragraphs.

He evidently saw himself as embodying a gutsy, down-to-earth approach to people and to the organizational problems described in the cases he taught. In class, he showed that he respected and liked those who intended to see the case situation the way he did. In return, many students admired and respected him for his "no nonsense" outlook, and his ratings on student polls were good.

Vinceberg was very tall, and with his long strides and his loud voice he easily dominated the classroom. During class he would pace restlessly in the front of the room, as well as up and down the aisles between the blocks of seats. He liked to rest one foot on the instructor's table as if it were a low stool, and he seemed to enjoy striking vigorous shirt-sleeve poses at the chalkboard.

Vinceberg had strong ideas about what his students should know. He would often interrupt class discussion to summarize and give lectures on points he felt to be important. Lots of my sectionmates welcomed this approach, especially those who found OB's "soft" psychological and sociological concepts difficult to grasp. In keeping with his tough-minded approach, Vinceberg felt important to get across to the section the gritty realities of everyday, blue-collar work life. I think he may have come from that background himself. Anyway, he often commented on this subject and in one of our early course sessions, he read aloud extracts from Studs Terkel's book *Working,* including a lengthy piece full of oaths and profanity.

And, he clearly believed in the importance of classroom contributions for he announced at the beginning of the course that 70 percent of the course grade would rest on class performance and 30 percent on the final exams. In most of the other courses it was 50/50.

His teaching style was hard to describe—you really had to experience it to understand. Sometimes he tended to shape and guide the class discussion to the point where—well, you know how it works—you knew what he wanted you to say and you went right along. Other times he was confrontational. He put you in a position where your ego was involved, and you had to defend your position well. Also, I often felt that with his forceful manner he was "broadcasting with too loud a signal"; it drowned out much of the individual student responses. Yet, he could listen and understand.

He always tried to deal with us each as individuals. He referred to our backgrounds and interests. I got the feeling he liked us and liked our section. Yet we never felt close to him. I didn't ever feel like just going to his office for a chat, and I don't think others did either.

The Section

Like all New Dominion sections, students had been assigned carefully, so that each group had a balance of students of different ages, sexes, management interests and experiences, and geographical backgrounds. More than 10 percent of the students came from overseas. The school considered this heterogeneity a valuable enrichment of the learning experience.

As described by its educational representative,[1] the section was "a most interesting agglomeration. There was, naturally, plenty of rivalry among its members, but the general atmosphere was friendly and tolerant. We weren't a 'dog-eat-dog' section like many of the others. Individual differences were respected and even encouraged." The following paragraphs contain the ed rep's further description, in his own words, of the section and its members.

Surely there were no hard and fast lines dividing up the section. People just fell into the obvious social groupings: those from the same living halls, geographical areas, or business interests. There was quite a strong awareness that nobody had a monopoly on the truth. Midwesterners were

---

1. A student-selected member of the group, who, with colleagues from other sections, represents student interests on New Dominion faculty-student committees.

keen to hear what foreign students had to say about particular issues. Female students listened to the CPAs. All the students knew they would get a hearing from their associates.

As one would expect, the male, white, conservative group was large. Typical of these students was Bob Smith, a stocky, ex-Navy submarine officer and graduate of Kansas State, who was one of the "senior citizens" group. He knew what he wanted to do: to run his own business. And he wasn't afraid to state his mind. We sometimes jokingly called him "Mr. Middle America."

A more unusual student was Trevor Jones from Wales. Trevor was younger (25 years old), came from a working class background, had achieved a first-class honors degree in economics, and then spent two years in banking. Trevor seemed to get along with the rest of the section outside of class, though socially he preferred to mix primarily with those from the U.K. and the Commonwealth. The fascinating thing about Trevor was his academic conduct; he never spoke in class. This, of course, put him in a very disadvantageous position in terms of grades.

I talked with Trevor many times. In appearance and speech you certainly knew he wasn't Oxbridge. He had a burning desire to succeed at New Dominion. He felt that it would put a seal of approval on his career-to-date and free him for good from any social origin slurs.

The fact that he didn't talk in class was not, we believed, that he lacked ability or strongly held opinions. As he explained his position to his friends, he felt quite unable to put forward or defend his views in class because, in his opinion, the rough-and-tumble of case discussion was completely unreal and, therefore, irrelevant. It was confined within a set of artificial nonbusiness rules; a good student classroom "operating technique" was most of what was needed to ensure success. By participating, he said, one was agreeing to be judged according to this undignified and juvenile code of conduct, and therefore one would inevitably end up making a fool of himself. It also encouraged people to grab the maximum amount of "air time," run off at the mouth, and rarely listen to what other people were saying. Trevor said he always followed the case discussions attentively and said he learned a lot from them. I noted, however, that he was sometimes scathingly critical of his fellow students and teachers when

he felt they made themselves look ridiculous in class.

Naturally, it was necessary for Trevor to explain his point of view toward class participation to his instructors. At the beginning of each course, therefore, Trevor would see the new professor in his office and explain his situation. Invariably teachers never called on him in class and graded him solely on his written work. Trevor said he had been to see Professor Vinceberg and thought they had developed a good understanding. During their conversation they had discussed the attitudes of shop floor workers, and Trevor had mentioned some of the experiences of his father who worked in one of the Welsh plants of the declining British steel industry.

The Situation

The following is another section member's own description of the situation.

That was a class never to be forgotten; an experience that still gets talked about at our class get-togethers.

It was our sixth session; the beginning of our third week. The case concerned the use of various formal manager evaluation techniques to select personnel for dismissal during a period of company retrenchment. In addition, we had to grapple with the social and personality problems of carrying out such a drastic and unpleasant operation in a small, close-knit southern community, where the company was the sole employer and where it had a long-standing reputation for taking a personal, even a paternal, interest in its employees.

That day Al Vinceberg, as usual, strode into class, stripped off his jacket, and rolled up his sleeves in the vigorous mode he had used since our first session. He quickly established order in the room; we had just finished our first class.

I was never sure whether or not Vinceberg used a formal, planned call-list; he would always just call on someone to start off. That day he immediately called on Trevor Jones to "lay out the case." A ripple of surprise ran around the section. I watched Trevor closely. Trevor looked up quizzically at Al who, by this time, had his back to him as he paced toward the other side of the room. Then Trevor glanced around, took a deep breath, and started. He spoke disjointedly for about five

Section 5. The Critical Instructional Choice: Guidance vs. Control

CASE
Trevor Jones

minutes without coming to grips with the main issues of the case. When he finished, Al turned to the rest of the class and said, "Well, you're his colleagues; what sort of job do you think he did?" He paused; the class looked puzzled. Vinceberg went on, "How would you evaluate Trevor? Has he done a good job or a bad job?"

"Hands up for those people who thought he did not do a good job," Al continued. About two-thirds of the class hesitantly raised their hands. "How many think Trevor did a good job?" The rest of the class put up their hands, a bit quicker this time. Al stopped his pacing, wheeled on Trevor Jones, who sat three-quarters of the way toward the back in the center section of seats. "Your colleagues don't think you've done an adequate job. You're fired!"

The silence was frightening. We waited! Trevor started slowly to gather his papers together. He appeared stunned and surely was humiliated. He glanced up, looked around the class, and then at Vinceberg again. Then he carefully and deliberately pressed his briefcase shut, stood up, struggled along the row of occupied seats, and exited by the rear door.

Vinceberg continued with the case, seemingly unconcerned. He called on another student for an opinion on the case issues. He paced up and down the front of the room as usual, listening to the student. The door at the back of the class remained closed. A few minutes passed by, and suddenly Al was taking the steps three at a time from the front of the room toward the door, and he disappeared into the corridor. The student who had been speaking stopped. The section just sat silent for the few minutes Al was outside the classroom. He returned alone and called on the student to continue his contribution. When that student finished he called on another. Nobody raised a hand to volunteer. The level of tension in the section was overpowering.

Suddenly Vinceberg stopped. "I don't think we can continue like this. We're all a bit on edge at what's happened. I'm going to break for a few minutes and get myself a cup of coffee. We'll start the class all over again at 10:15."

When Vinceberg left the room everyone seemed to burst into conversation at once. One of Trevor's close friends, a quiet New Zealander, got up and went out in search of Trevor.

Al soon returned with a cup of coffee and began the class again. The discussion was sluggish. The section refused to make any voluntary contributions, and it seemed to me that the tension was rising rapidly again. Al stopped pacing up and down. Surely he must have felt the hostility but struggled on for a few more minutes. Then he stopped.

"We still haven't gotten over our bad start to the class today. I think we should discuss what happened and get our thoughts out in the open. That way we can clear the air. I confess that I did not intend this to happen like this. I didn't think Trevor would react the way he did. I realize I may have blown it with all of you. I'm very keen that that should not happen. Until now I think we've had an excellent relationship. Please help me."

The words were barely out of his mouth when Bob Smith burst out, "I'll tell you what I think. As far as I'm concerned you're nothing but a son of a bitch for doing what you did. You know what Trevor is like. You know he doesn't talk in class. Calling on him like that was wrong. And what came after was worse—much worse. In my book you're one son of a bitch."

Vinceberg appeared stunned. Bob Smith had always been one of Vinceberg's "stars," one of the section who appreciated his teaching program a great deal.

The entire section seemed to me to radiate hostility toward Vinceberg. Here we had had such a fine section working atmosphere and good relationships with all our faculty. Now that had blown. What a mess!

READING

Barn Raising: Collaborative Group Process in Seminars

DON McCORMICK

MICHAEL KAHN

Reprinted from *EXCHANGE: The Organizational Behavior Teaching Journal,* Volume VII, Number 4, pages 16–20.

HBS Case No. 8-386-025.

In the classrooms of higher education, the seminar is a puzzling phenomenon. Most teachers understand what to do with a lecture and, usually, what causes its success or failure. But the seminar is another matter. Most instructors aren't sure what a good one ought to look like, and, even if we did know, how to accomplish that. The problem is both technical and attitudinal. It seems intuitively clear that a seminar ought not to be a question-and-answer session, though often it is. Conversely, the implication is that it should be conversation among the students in which the participation is widespread and the teacher is just another participant, or else in some way a facilitator of the discussion. But what sort of conversation? Experience teaches that when it is not a question-and-answer session, it is either aimless drifting ("just a bull session" in the students' words) or an argument.

"Well," the reader might ask, "what's wrong with a good argument? It keeps people on their toes, forces them to have prepared and punishes those who haven't thought through their ideas. A boxing match is fast and aggressive or it is dull. Isn't that true of an intellectual conversation, as well?" This paper will take the position that the boxing match is not the best possible model for a seminar. "But," our reader might reasonably object, "for two hundred years the European and American tradition of education has been that students must be challenged to sharpen their thinking. They must continually test the validity of their ideas by exposing them in combat. The classroom is a dueling school in which one's most basic weapons are sharpened for the battle of life."

We would like to suggest:

1. The classroom battle is not a good way to teach thinking.
2. Even if it were, it makes idea-conversation so unpleasant that students do their best to avoid it, in college and afterwards.
3. It is a significant contribution to the building of a society of contention and enmity.
4. And, as an alternative, there is another way to talk about ideas which obviates those difficulties.

The model we are about to offer is not a boxing match but rather a group of builders constructing a building together or a group of artists fabricating a creation together. Anyone who believes the old aphorism that no work of art was ever made by a committee has never attended a good jam session.

Section 5. The Critical Instructional Choice: Guidance vs. Control

READING
Barn Raising: Collaborative Group Process in Seminars
McCORMICK and KAHN

It is not hard to imagine why the fight model has clung so in American education. For one thing, it has had the support of much of academic psychology. The motivation psychologists have taught for many years that moderate arousal is good for performance and that the *source* of the arousal is irrelevant. While acknowledging that *a lot of fear* or anger would paralyze the student, psychologists have steadfastly maintained that a little bit of adrenaline is what keeps things alive and that moderate amounts of fear and anger are perfectly acceptable ways of generating it. In the old rat labs of Yale and Iowa all drives were the same and could be added and subtracted from each other. That tradition has died hard. The truth of the matter is that there is absolutely no evidence that fear or anger *in any quantity* enhances complex mental activity and there is plenty of evidence that it interferes with it. There is no question but that moderate arousal is necessary to keep the students awake. But it matters considerably *which* drive generates that arousal. If fear and anger are not useful, what would do? Well, the breaking down of old cognitive structures is arousing; so is the excitement of working at an intellectual task; so is the joy of building a structure with collaborators.

Football coaches are apt to get a lineman angry before a game; all he has to do is beat hell out of the guy across from him. But coaches have cause for concern if the *quarterback* is angry. The quarterback needs all his smarts; he cannot afford the functional cortical damage caused by the mid-brain firing off the fear and anger signals. So we are going to offer here a collaborative model for the seminar.

Before describing how to go about setting up a more effective seminar, we will quote from an earlier paper which describes three dysfunctional kinds of seminar and then describe our fourth model. The four are:

> . . . the *Free-for-All*, the *Beauty Contest*, the *Distinguished House Tour*, and the *Barn-Raising*. We think they go in that order toward being progressively freer from our cultural liabilities, and consequently, that they go in that order toward being progressively richer styles of intellectual conversation.
>
> *Free-For-All*—In this seminar there is a prize to be won, whether it's the instructor's approval or one's self esteem. There is no other goal but to win. If fighting fair won't win, then one fights in whatever way will win. One

wins not simply by looking smart, but by looking smarter. Thus, important as it is to look smart, it is equally important to make the others look dumb.

> *Beauty Contest*—This is the seminar in which each idea is paraded in all its finery, seeking admiration. When it has been displayed, its sponsor withdraws to think up the next idea, paying little attention to the next contestant. Thus, each person's ideas bear little or no relation to anyone else's.
>
> *Distinguished House Tour*—The model for this seminar is a tour which takes you to a series of stately homes. The first might be a good example of Edwardian architecture and furniture. The hosts have spruced it up for your visit; they show you through, explain it, and answer your questions. Then you get back into the bus and go look at another house. Perhaps a good example of Georgian architecture.

Similarly, the Distinguished House Tour seminar begins with one member advancing an idea. The other students spend some time exploring that idea as they might an interesting house. They ask questions and look for inconsistencies, trying hard to understand the conception. When they have a good grasp of it, someone offers another idea and the seminar members explore that. Just as gracious hosts don't compare houses or claim one is better, each idea is thought to be interesting in its own right. This is a high form of discourse and can produce a good seminar. It also has some problems.

In our early work we had thought that the Distinguished House Tour was the most advanced seminar. It is, after all, the Socratic dialogue. Socrates invites a friend to adopt a position and then incisively questions that position. Gradually, we learned from our own experience what Socrates' students may well have learned from theirs: defending or explaining a position is lonely and stressful. When one is trying to explore a new thought, the pressure of the group probing for problems or inconsistencies is at best like a trial and at worst like an inquisition. We began by observing that the young and the shy, far from feeling encouraged, quickly retreated in the face of this exploration, however friendly and polite it might have been. Later, we saw that it was not just the inexperienced; there are few people, even those who enjoy fencing, who find that this position enhances the development of a thought. In most Socratic dialogues, we realized, Socrates emerges one-up and everyone else comes out looking a little foolish.

That discovery led us to our next step.

Barn Raising—In frontier America when a family needed a barn but had limited labor and other resources, the entire community gathered to help them build the barn. The host family described the kind of barn it had in mind and picked the site. The community then pitched in and built it. Neighbors would suggest changes and improvements as they built.

This seminar begins with a member telling the group ideas which might be newly formed and not yet thought out. Then the community gathers to build the barn, to put together that idea. As I hear you say the original idea, it may be something I "disagree" with or something I've never thought about before; but now it becomes my project, and I set about helping you build it, helping us build it. *After you've offered the idea, you have no more responsibility for developing it, defending it, or explaining it than anybody else in the group.* If I have a problem with that idea, the problem belongs to the whole seminar, not just to you. You are not the lonely defender of that idea but part of a task force whose job is to develop it to its fullest potential, to make the best possible case for it. It is not your idea anymore; it belongs to the seminar. The energy which might have gone into conflict, or into polite challenge-and-defense, now is directed toward a common goal.

One advantage of the Barn Raising seminar turned out to be that people don't come out of the seminars holding their original ideas. Social psychologists' work on persuasion has made it clear that an effect of argument is to entrench the original ideas all the more firmly (Hoveland, Janis Kelley, 1953). In contrast, one of the most effective methods of helping someone to unfreeze an old attitude or idea is to ask that person to make the case for an unfamiliar or unwelcome position (Nels, Helmreich, and Aronson, 1969). Thus, students, building on colleagues' ideas, maximize the chances of freeing their own flexibility and creativity.

It is not easy at first to discuss ideas in this way. Two problems quickly arise. First, we all tend toward intellectual conservatism (Festinger, 1957). Letting go of an idea can be quite wrenching.

Second, it is often difficult to acknowledge peers

as teachers. We are raised to believe that the person who teaches is one-up and the one who accepts that teaching is one-down. It takes some time to learn the particular gratification of giving another the ungrudging, even admiring, acknowledgment that he or she has taught me something.

It should be made clear that the freedom to build ideas in this way depends on the crucial difference between idea-groups and groups required to make a decision. In the early stages of conversation, a decision-group can learn much from Barn-Raising. But, eventually, mutually exclusive alternatives must be recognized as such. That fact serves to underline the major freedom provided by idea-groups. It is ironic how rigidly trained we have been to squander that freedom and argue ideas as though we believed a decision had to be made. Is Hamlet mad or not? The world will little note which decision we reach. But we will long remember whether we have explored the question in a way calculated to enrich our understanding of the play and our relationship with each other (Kahn, 1981).

We learned in Barn-Raising that when a seminar develops a point of view about anything, another point of view is likely to emerge which seems at first hopelessly contradictory to the first. In doing this work we have come to see the world as composed of an endless collection of dilemmas. In our culture what we typically do (and most academic discussions are no exception) is deny the pain of the dilemma by assuming that one horn or the other must be wrong. We then set up an argument—my horn against yours. The undesirable consequences of this way of defining differences are clear. First, it is very hard to think during combat. Second, it makes winning more important than understanding or analysis; and third, it forces us into a greatly oversimplified view of the issue when its complexity may be its greatest beauty. So, in our seminars, we learned to try to identify and preserve the dilemmas rather than allow them to deteriorate into debate.

But what do you do with them, beyond merely preserving them? It seemed to us that the thing to do was to try to convert them not to debate, but rather to dialectic. Dialectic consists of two posed, potential antagonists (thesis and antithesis) which come together and give birth to the synthesis. It also leads discussants to collaboration, instead of struggle, with each other.

The goal of the seminars we facilitate is to have

Section 5. The Critical Instructional Choice: Guidance vs. Control

READING
Barn Raising: Collaborative Group Process in Seminars
McCORMICK and KAHN

as much Barn-Raising and as few beauty contests and free-for-alls as possible. So how is that to be done?

Preparing the Students

We begin by asking the students to read a paper on Barn-Raising (Kahn, 1974). This paper offers the attitude of collaborative idea-conversation and teaches the general concepts of Barn-Raising. It also sets two guidelines for the student preparing for a seminar. The reading must be done—all of it, carefully and on time. There is no way to play this game if everyone is not familiar with the material to be discussed. In reading it, we give participants the following task: "Read the material looking for a question about it which you can offer the seminar. Choose the question you would most like to ask a very wise person who had read this material. Choose the question that seems to you to put the material in the widest possible perspective."

In addition to asking students to prepare by reading this paper, we have found it useful (and fun) to introduce the concept with a nonverbal experience designed to illustrate the principles of the four kinds of seminars. The exercise goes as follows:

1. "Divide up into pairs. Now, with your right hand, make the most beautiful hand sculpture you can, and with your left hand, screw up your partner's." (Let them continue for a minute or two or until it gets rowdy.) "OK. Now stop and quietly reflect on how that was for you. What feelings did it evoke?"
2. "Now, with both hands, make the most beautiful hand sculpture you can, but don't get caught peeking at your partner's. You might, though, *sneak* a peek to see if it is better." (Allow this to continue for a minute or two, then ask them to reflect on it.)
3. "Now, one of you, with both hands, make the most beautiful hand sculpture you can. The other person should explore it and examine it." (Let this continue for a minute and then have them reverse roles. When both have completed, have them reflect quietly.)
4. "Finally, make the most beautiful four-hand sculpture you can." (Let this continue for a couple of minutes, then ask them to reflect on how this is different.)

5. "Now talk to your partner about the different experiences for a couple of minutes."

Following the discussion, we have a general discussion with the pairs sharing their experience (paying particular attention to what they have learned about their own attitudes in doing these exercises). This exercise nicely complements the aforementioned paper as a way to introduce the seminar.

The Seminar

We begin every session with a brief "check-in" round, asking everyone to say a few words about how they're feeling and what is occupying them. We have found this very useful for ice-breaking. Then we ask everyone to read her or his question, with all of us writing down each question as we hear it read. The students know that one of them will be randomly picked to choose the question; thus writing them down is necessary. Also it focuses attention on the process and makes each student feel a certain welcome respect as the entire class writes down his/her question. And finally the questions prove useful later in the seminar as the developing discussion casts them in a new light.

Then the seminar leader randomly picks one of the students to choose a question. We remind them that we will undoubtedly touch on many of the questions in the course of the discussion so choosing one is not a life-or-death matter. When the question is chosen, its author is given the optional opportunity to say anything more about it. Then the question no longer belongs to that person who is not to be questioned about it. Any questions are now to be addressed to the group.

The seminar then proceeds by trying to find as many rich and varied ways as possible to answer the question. (This is the same basic format we use for subsequent class sessions.)

The Interventions

The task of the leader in a Barn-Raising seminar is to teach these new modes without putting down students. One thing that has helped us with this is to remind ourselves that the other ways of talking are deeply ingrained in the culture, that unlearning them requires some major resocialization, and that, for all our experience, we ourselves still talk in the old ways a good deal more than we wish we did. All of this tends to make us very tolerant. Thus we try hard never to imply there's a better way without suggesting what it might be.

There are several principles of intervening in this kind of seminar:

1. The instructor must intervene, and intervene a good deal at first. Eventually the leader can wither away, but until students have a considerable amount of experience with Barn-Raising they need an active, intervening leader. We have tried merely distributing the paper on Barn-Raising, but nothing changed, in spite of their all being very excited about the idea in principle. It isn't enough to read about a new behavior you wish to learn. We all need considerable guidance in learning these new behaviors.

2. The seminar leader has to keep her eye on the ball. This means remembering the original question and keeping track of how the conversation relates to it and when the tangents are getting too far from it. You can remind your seminar that they are building a coherent structure either by asking, "Could we take a moment here and see how this relates to the question?" or by actually doing some relating yourself: "We've been talking for some time about the price Oedipus pays for pursuing the truth. Our question is about the price Jocasta pays. I wonder if they're related."

3. Avoid battles by reminding the student that each remark belongs to the entire seminar and need not be defended by the person who voiced it. Suppose Jack is building a case for Marx's theory of history. Jill interjects, "How can you *say* that, when Weber showed that capitalism followed Protestantism rather than the other way around, as Marx would have said?" At that point you might say, "I would like to interrupt here. Before you answer, Jack, I would like you to consider, Jill, how it would work if you were to take responsibility for that question rather than putting the responsibility on Jack? Perhaps you could explain the Weber criticism to the group and see if we can somehow integrate it into Jack's ideas. Jack's support of Marx isn't his to defend once he's said it. It belongs to us all, yourself included." Hopefully this will short-circuit the attack and defense cycle of traditional seminars.

4. Watch for the chance to identify dilemmas. A very useful technique when two sides of a question square off for a debate is to suggest that the entire group build first one side and then the other. Whichever side a student was on originally, she joins with the others in building each side in turn. When both arguments have been well-built it is a fascinating exercise in group intelligence to try to build a superordinate picture which includes the best from both sides, i.e., to formulate the synthesis.

5. Try to keep the focus off you. It is usually enough to remind the group that you feel uncomfortable when most remarks are addressed to you instead of the group at large.

6. See if you can find ways of including the quiet people without increasing their discomfort. We sometimes say straight out, "Bill, I wonder how you're feeling about the discussion. We haven't heard from you." But at other times an approach that encourages without so directly putting the spotlight on the person is useful. ("Bill, you seem very engrossed in the discussion. I hope when you think it's appropriate, that you will jump in.")

7. As you approach the end of the allotted time in that class period, it is a good idea to spend the final minutes reviewing the content to see how the question was dealt with. This gives a final and often very useful chance to discover connections between the main question and what had previously looked like tangents. It also gives the seminar a chance to view the structure they have built, and, perhaps, to admire it. Then after that content review, it is useful to finish with a process review. How did this seminar work? How did we like it? What do we want to do differently next time? What did we discover that was particularly useful?

The Barn-Raising seminar is not merely a form of classroom learning. It can be a way of making every conversation an educational experience; a contributor to harmony and good feeling without leaving unwanted residues of frustration and irritation. And isn't *that* what learning in academia should be all about?

Introduction

Many instructors unwittingly behave in ways which not only frustrate their own goals, but also actively discourage significant (as opposed to rote) student learning. The relationship between certain behaviors of teachers as perceived by their students and the quality and quantity of students' learning, motivation, and student-teacher communication is amply documented in the research literature (Amidon and Hough, 1967; Flanders, 1970). In this author's experience observing teachers' behaviors in elementary, secondary, and university classrooms, both in person and on videotape, certain non-facilitating behaviors have become vivid through their very repetition.

At issue is the relationship between intent and actions: what teachers do and how they do it delivers more of an impact than what they say. Within the body of this paper, six common non-facilitating teacher-behaviors will be defined, exemplified, and discussed. These are the following: (1) insufficient wait-time, (2) the rapid-reward, (3) the programmed answer, (4) non-specific feedback questions, (5) teacher ego-stroking and classroom climate, and (6) fixation at a low level of questioning. Implicit in these discussions will be the means by which changes in behaviors can be affected.

Six Non-Facilitating Behaviors

Insufficient "Wait-Time." "Wait-Time" is the amount of time after the initial question has been posed before the teacher answers it himself; repeats, rephrases, or adds further information to the question; or accepts an answer from a student.

More than just a few seconds are a necessary prerequisite for mental information-processing. (Moriber, 1971; Rowe, 1974). When the teacher becomes a non-stop talker, filling every possible silence with his voice, what chance do students have either to think over what is being said, formulate intelligent responses, or ask for clarification?

Mental information-processing may be accompanied by verbal analysis or proceed in silence. It does seem logical, therefore, if the facilitation of students' learning is one of paramount importance, that teachers allow for individual differences in learning style by providing a modicum of quiet time for thinking as well as opportunities for verbal responses.

READING

Six Common Non-Facilitating Teaching Behaviors

SONDRA M. NAPELL

HBS Case No. 8-389-104.

Students who note that the instructor answers a preponderance of his own questions without waiting for a response soon grow dependent upon the teacher to do their thinking for them. In like manner, an answer too rapidly accepted has the effect of cutting off further information-processing and analysis by the rest of the class. We may attest verbally to our aim of encouraging independent thinkers, but unless we consciously work to expand our wait-time, we will have rhetoric with little resultant change in behavior.

Rowe (1974) reported that when teachers were trained to increase their wait-time from one second to 3–5 seconds, several changes occurred in students' behaviors: length and number of unsolicited but appropriate responses increased; failures to respond decreased; and the incidence of student-to-student comparisons of data increased. Instructors who are interested in repeating this experiment in their own classrooms can measure their wait-times ("one, one-thousand, two, one-thousand") and then deliberately expand these periods of silence-for-thinking both after a question is posed and after an answer has been given. Sharing the concept of wait-time for thinking with the students often enables the teacher to maximize his efforts and gives the class an insight into learning skills.

THE RAPID-REWARD. What is the effect on students' processing of information and analysis of data when an instructor says to the first respondent to his question: "Right, good?" As if to assure that further thinking will be terminated, the teacher proceeds to reword, repeat, and exemplify the answer or goes on to the next topic. Learning being a highly individualistic process, people learn at different rates and in varying ways. Rapid acceptance of a correct answer favors the faster thinker/speaker who has completed his thought processes; those in mid-thought are terminated prematurely.

A variation on this theme is the softly voiced, hesitant answer of the student seated nearest the instructor. Because many students commonly respond softly to the teacher if he is within close proximity, an awareness of the consequences of this behavior is crucial. Many a student seated out of earshot has become frustrated, bewildered or lost interest when a softly voiced, difficult to hear answer is rapidly rewarded. To ameliorate this situation, encourage student-to-student dialogue, discussion, and peer critiquing of each other's ideas.

The following are suggested: extended silent time after an answer is proffered; a questioning glance around at other students tacitly requesting comment; a question to those in the rear, "What is your analysis of what was just said?" and, most important, physical movement of the teacher from place to place about the room in order that as many students as possible enjoy close proximity to the instructor, "front row seats," at one time or another during the class duration.

THE PROGRAMMED ANSWER. The following are examples taken verbatim from classroom dialogues and best exemplify this third pattern.

1. "What are some of the enemies of the praying mantis? Cats kill them don't they? How about other animals? Or insects?"
2. "What thoughts have you about impeachment? Do you think the proceedings are too lengthy? That partisan politics play too great a role? Is there enough evidence?"
3. "What reasons do you have to use that formula? Was it suggested in the homework chapter? Have you ever used it before? Or seen it used in this context?"
4. "What happens when we add the sums of the rows? Do we get skewed results?"
5. "Look at this shrub and tell me, what observations can you make? Do you see dead stems? Are they damaged from insect feedings?"

The programmed answer not only deprives the respondent of expressing his own thoughts by steering him toward the answers that the questioner expects, but also conveys the message that there is really little interest in what he thinks or says. While the reasons offered by those who make a practice of this pattern are usually altruistic (i.e., "Silence after the posing of a question is embarrassing to the student"; "I feel impelled to help out by suggesting clues"), one needs to ask himself honestly: "Is it I or the student who is uncomfortable after a second or two of silence?"; "Do I have confidence in the student's ability to think about the question and formulate a response?" and, more important, "Am I interested in what the student has to say or in determining which of my answers he prefers?" While programming can be an effective tool when one desires to guide students' thinking, suggest possibilities, or model logical thought processes, it

Section 5. The Critical Instructional Choice: Guidance vs. Control

READING
Six Common Non-Facilitating Teaching Behaviors NAPELL

is important to be aware of its limiting effect in opening up a wide variety of possible ideas. It is via the latter route than an instructor can demonstrate his interest in the students' ideas and himself model inquisitive learning behavior. A willingness to listen helps create in the classroom a community of learners in place of an authoritative, superordinate-subordinate relationship between teacher and class.

NON-SPECIFIC FEEDBACK QUESTIONS. Many instructors feel justified in assuming that their students have no questions if no one responds when they ask, "Are there any questions? Do you all understand?" Purportedly designed to give the instructor information as to the clarity and comprehensibility of his presentation, these questions usually fail to solicit feedback. Why? We can isolate several possibilities, two of which are the nature of students and the nature of the questions.

What type of student will (bravely) call attention to his own ignorance when the question is posed to a class: "Does everyone understand?" Interestingly enough, it was a student who suggested that those who do respond comprehend most of the concept, lesson, problem, etc., and need only a minor point made clear. Others, whose lack of understanding is more comprehensive, whose confusion is more widespread, may be too intimidated to call attention in such a public way to their situations. Often the latter are so confused they cannot think of questions to ask. Yet these are the ones who most need our assistance. How can we determine what it is they do and do not understand?

Contrast the following pairs of questions:

1. "Who doesn't understand this?"
2. "Marx's concept, 'the withering away of the state' can be a difficult one to grasp. Let's try to summarize together some definitions of what this means."
3. "Does anybody have any questions?"
4. "Let's think of some other examples now of situations in which this principle is applicable."
5. "Does everybody see how I got this answer?"
6. "Why did I substitute the value of (theta) in this equation?"
7. "Who wants me to go over this explanation again?"
8. "What conclusions can we generalize from this graph?"

The teacher needs to ask himself, "What is it important for the students to say or do in order that I be able to determine the extent of their understanding?" He can then formulate and pose one or several specific questions which will give a more comprehensive sounding of the class's problems and questions.

THE TEACHER'S EGO-STROKING AND CLASSROOM CLIMATE. Think of the effects on students' willingness to respond to teacher-posed questions when statements such as the following are made:

1. "Since I have already explained this several times already, you all should know what is the effect of an increased demand upon this supply curve."
2. "Obviously when you use this formula you'll get ———?"
3. (After having listened to several students' answers) "The real answer is this ———."
4. "Does everybody understand the explanation I just gave? It should be clear by now."
5. "O.K. Now rephrase your answer the way you think I would say it."

Students need to feel that it is psychologically "safe" to participate, to try out ideas, to be wrong as well as right. The teacher's behavior is a most important determinant in the establishment of a safe or comfortable climate. Learning, an active process, requires that the learner interact with ideas and materials. Constant teacher-talk, feeling compelled to comment on each student idea, deciding to be the final arbiter in decision-making processes, interrupting, controlling, intimidating either through expertise, or the threat of grades—these are but some of the behaviors which prevent students from engaging in the active processes needed for significant (as distinguished from "rote") learning to take place. It is interesting to note the increased levels of student participation when instructors do not conceal the fact of their ignorance, when they sometimes hesitate about certain questions or information, when their responses are dictated more by an honest desire to assist the students than to demonstrate the extent of their own knowledge.

A few of the possible behaviors which can encourage the establishment of an environment conducive to participation are the teacher's remembering and referring to students' ideas, yielding to class members during a discussion, acknowledging his own fallibility, framing open-ended questions which provide for expressions of opinion and personal interpretations of data, accepting the students' right to be wrong as well as right, encouraging joint determination of goals and procedures when feasible (i.e., "How can I help you best to learn this material?"), sharing the responsibility for learning with the learners (i.e., permitting students to answer their peers' questions; freeing oneself from the burden of thinking that what isn't covered in the class, the student cannot learn elsewhere; encouraging group presentations of the material to be covered, etc.), and soliciting student participation in their own learning evaluation such as feed-in of test questions and joint correction of examinations.

FIXATION AT A LOW LEVEL OF QUESTIONING. Bloom (1956) has postulated that cognition operates on ascending levels of complexity. One begins with knowledge, or informational details, and moves upward through comprehension, analysis, and synthesis, to evaluation. Questioning can be a central feature in promoting the development of conceptual abilities, analytical techniques, and the synthesis of ideas. Skillful teachers use questions to guide thinking as well as test for comprehension. Too often however, as illustrated by this sixth recurring pattern, teachers' questions become fixated at the informational level, requiring of students only that they recall bits and pieces of rote-memorized data: information-level questions. For example:

1. What is the formula for finding the force between two charges?
2. What are the years usually ascribed to the writing of the Bible?
3. What is the definition of "quantity demanded?"

One-word or short-phrase answers, those capable of being sung out in unison, constitute the preponderance of question-and-answer dialogues in many classrooms and necessitate little interrelating of material, sequencing of thoughts, analyzing of data. While a solid base of factual information in learning is clearly important, fixating students' thinking at

this level discourages the development of the more complex intellectual skills. Questions such as those listed below encourage the students to use informational knowledge in order to analyze concepts, synthesize complex relationships, and evaluate the new data:

1. Describe some possible effects on the demand curve of a rent control law.
2. What would happen if we inserted a metal conductor in between the moving charge and the current?
3. Why must the information in Table One change when we consider these new data?

Being conscious of the levels of questions one is asking and attempting to structure the questions toward analysis, synthesis, and evaluation can do much to combat a fixation at the informational level of thinking.

Conclusion

If asked to formulate the goals of the educational process, would not most teachers include the nourishment of intellectual curiosity, encouragement of independent learners, development of people able to engage in the more complex thinking processes? Yet instructors' behaviors such as the six described in this paper militate against the achievement of these goals.

Those who sincerely desire to examine and analyze their own teaching behaviors face a problem—the evanescence and multiple-dimensional aspects of the teaching-learning relationship. Capturing the classroom behaviors of teachers and students on closed-circuit television with instant-replay features offers one solution. Utilizing such criteria as the six patterns described in this paper—insufficient wait-time, the rapid reward, the programmed answer, non-specific feedback questions, the teacher's ego-stroking and classroom climate, and fixation at a low level of questioning—teachers can analyze their own behaviors and examine the effects of these on student learning. Such self-analysis can be the beginning of behavior change.

Section 6. The Case Discussion Leader in Action: Operational Challenges and Opportunities

Mr. Costello, I'm so glad you're at home! I'm calling from Philadelphia! You know that paper I was supposed to have in to you last week? I found out why it never got there. The Federal Express truck apparently caught on fire, and all the contents were destroyed.

Mark Costello sighed. Cecelia Lawrence, a student in his first-year Rhetoric class was continuing her pattern of late papers. But a truck fire! Mark thought he had heard it all in a dozen years of teaching, but this took the cake.

"Hello, hello, Mr. Costello!" Cecelia's voice interrupted, "what should we do?"

The Institution

Kensington University, a prestigious institution, took particular pride in its Rhetoric program, a compulsory one-semester course for all entering students. Although the Rhetoric faculty were not members of a department per se (but rather of a program) the courses carry full academic credit.

The Instructor

Mark Costello had been a teacher for over twelve years. His appointment to teach a section of Rhetoric to first-year students at Kensington followed several years of teaching seniors at nearby Baxter College, also a select institution. During his first term at Kensington, Mark continued to teach a section of seniors at Baxter.

Although new to the Rhetoric program, Mark was well acquainted with Kensington. He was described by colleagues at both Baxter and Kensington as a bright, articulate, and friendly individual who got along exceptionally well with coworkers and students. A tall, athletic-looking man, he always wore a jacket and tie to class. Mark was an advanced doctoral student in another department at Kensington and had held a variety of research, administrative, and teaching fellow positions at the university. He had gotten to know the director of the Rhetoric program quite well while a student in one of his courses the previous year.

Mark consistently received very high reviews from his students and colleagues at Baxter. Although he had begun at Baxter by teaching first-year English, he was later asked to teach a senior-level seminar in Prose Writing. Mark taught that seminar for several consecutive years; occasionally

*This case was prepared by **Marina McCarthy,** under the supervision of **C. Roland Christensen,** for the Developing Discussion Leadership Skills and Teaching by the Case Method seminars. While the case is based on data furnished by participants involved, all names and some peripheral facts have been disguised.*

HBS Case No. 9-387-207.

CASE

The Puzzling Student (A)

he also taught a freshman section. Since he found the seminar model he used with the Baxter seniors so successful, Mark decided to try it out with the freshmen. They did equally well.

Most of the students in Mark's senior seminar at Baxter were English majors, but some were from other liberal arts disciplines, as well as from the schools of Social Work and Education. Of the eight sections of Prose Writing in the Baxter English department, Mark's class was always the first to fill up at registration. Since the class was an elective, anyone in the college could sign up, but the class usually was "closed" the first day of registration.

In August Mark looked forward to his new assignment with some trepidation:

> Since Kensington's admission process is more competitive than Baxter's . . . I expect the quality of the student writing will be very high. I wonder if I'll have anything to teach them!

The Course

Mark decided to teach his Rhetoric class at Kensington as he had at Baxter. He was given a Monday/Wednesday afternoon time slot and was pleased to learn that his class would include only 14–15 students.

> I encourage class participation and discussion in my classes. The setup at Kensington is ideal. Often at Baxter I had to hunt all over campus for a decent room, but here it's standard that the Rhetoric department gets first bid on the seminar rooms. Since I have students take turns being responsible for leading the discussion of the weekly readings, and I require a lot of peer editing—a method whereby students work in pairs critiquing each other's work—the seminar room is a perfect setting.

> Students are required to turn in a weekly writing submission to my faculty mailbox by Friday at 5:00 P.M. They are expected to attend a weekly writing conference every Monday—that gives me the weekend before to read and react to all the "final submissions." I give suggested topics for direction, but students are free to pick their own. My rationale *here* is that student writing tends to be best when the topic is self-generated rather than assigned.

> During the Monday one-to-one conference is a time when the student and I go over the Friday final submission; I guess it's like a tutoring session. Students generally sign up for the most convenient appoint-

ment slot for them at class the previous Wednesday. Generally I am available all day Monday from 8:30 A.M. until the dinner hour.

> Although other members of the Rhetoric faculty meet students 4–5 times during a term, I end up seeing each student every week (12 times). Many of my colleagues tend to write lengthy word-processed "letters" to the students critiquing their work; however, I find that briefer, written critiques in conjunction with a weekly one-to-one conference are far more effective. Students often "read into" the written comments more than need be. Written critiques often come across as more negative than intended. I feel that one-to-one conferences are much more effective, although tremendously time consuming. I still give students a paragraph or two of written reaction, but I try to save most of the critique for the weekly conference—where we can both discuss the student's paper.

> I have found scheduling three conferences per hour is about right. Seniors at Baxter were eager to have someone to talk with about their job search or graduate school plans, and freshmen just seem to crave adult attention. Although first-year students at Kensington have a tremendous support system built into their residential and advising programs, they still seem to need someone to take an interest in them.

> I feel helping a student see opportunities for improvement in a one-to-one conference, and working together to polish up a piece is more productive than giving a grade. Consequently I don't grade weekly submissions. In my writing classes, I emphasize learning to revise one's own work. I feel this is the most critical tool I can give my students. We accomplish this with peer editing in class and in one-to-one conferences.

> For about a half hour during class on Wednesdays, I have students exchange their weekly rough drafts and critique each other's work. One has to build trust into such an activity, and I usually begin the term by having the group critique something I have written. This modeling gives them an idea of how to accept and give criticism. To help them get started, I also give them a checklist of things to look for. Students find this feature of the course to be one of the most helpful. Peer editing of rough drafts gives students an opportunity to get feedback before handing in their final submission on Friday afternoon. It also gives students a chance to see how their *peers* write—not just how Hemingway and Austen write. Students inevitably compare themselves with published authors. This is discouraging for them yet understandable . . .

they never see how other eighteen-year-olds write. Further, helping others helps students learn to help themselves. To follow the student's progress each week, I request that a rough draft (or drafts) be attached to the Friday submissions.

As far as grading is concerned, I evaluate students with a letter grade only at mid-term and at the end of the semester. For a mid-term grade, I ask students to select one piece that they have submitted during the term and to revise it for a grade. I also have one, in-class, "open book, open notes" essay test on the readings, along with a short quiz on the first half of Strunk and White's *Elements of Style*. For the essays, students are asked several questions related to style, structure, point of view, audience, and other writing techniques.

My grading system works like this:	%
Papers - (average of mid-term and final papers)	50%
Participation -	25%
Tests - (average of mid-term and final tests)	25%

I also explain that my emphasis on classroom participation means attendance is critical.

The First Two Classes

After several days of faculty orientation at Kensington, Mark was somewhat surprised by the "hard-line" attitude of the Rhetoric department. The director "wanted to see more Cs," and one of the assistant directors insisted that all the freshmen "toe the line." Mark hoped there wouldn't be a conflict in philosophies.

Although I agree with the department's philosophy of the importance of revisions—"writing is a process of rewriting"—I don't agree with their philosophy on grading. I feel no particular need to give Cs to appear tough, and have no problem giving all As and Bs. The director and his assistants sound like they have a "don't take any prisoners" attitude. Their standards are high and uncompromising.

In my several years at Kensington, I've heard that freshmen compare the Rhetoric program to boot camp. It's a rite of passage. To me, intimidation has no relation to academic rigor. I refuse to teach out of fear.

Mark's class list consisted of twelve first-year students and two sophomores, transfer students who had to take the required first-year Rhetoric course.

Most of the first class meeting was spent with introductions—of me, of the individual students in the class, and of the course. I explained course expectations—the organization of the classes, weekly submissions and conferences, and the readings.

I was pleased with the first class and was glad to see the students were "just average kids." I dismissed my fears that there would be nothing I could teach them. The writing samples they had brought to class were hardly stellar. In fact, when I got home that night I was amazed that some of the poorest writing had come from students who had graduated from some of the most prestigious prep schools in the country.

At the second class meeting, another student appeared. A sophomore, Cecelia Lawrence, asked to join the class. I saw no objection and was rather intrigued that she had gone out of her way to find the class and present herself. Besides, I'm used to larger classes at Baxter.

I returned to the Rhetoric office after the second class meeting and handed in my revised class list to Amanda Hayford, the administrative assistant. Since she seemed somewhat distressed, I asked if there was anything wrong. Amanda just sighed, and told me that "students—especially sophomores should know better . . . they are not supposed to sign themselves into courses like this. Class assignments are done here at the Rhetoric office." Amanda and I agreed, however, since the class had already met twice, that Cecelia remain in the class.

Cecelia Lawrence

Although Mark's initial one-to-one conference with Cecelia Lawrence was basically a rehash of the first class—administrative matters and course expectations—subsequent conferences gave him a better opportunity to get to know Cecelia and her background.

Cecelia Lawrence was a sophomore who had come to Kensington from an exclusive preparatory school in Philadelphia. She had apparently had a difficult freshman year. Her father had died of cancer, and she had suffered from a serious blood disorder. Cecelia did not finish several of her first-year courses, including Rhetoric.

Cecelia's family was a legacy at Kensington. Several of her great-uncles and grandfathers had been prominent in national politics. The Lawrence family was very fond of Kensington, a great supporter of the educational efforts of the school, and most generous in the school's development campaigns. In fact, Mark Costello's office was housed in Lawrence Hall.

Cecelia lived in one of the most exclusive dormitories on campus, one with a reputation for being elitist. Cecelia and Mark walked across campus together one afternoon after class—he to his office, and she to her dormitory. Mark joked with Cecelia, asking her if she was related to the Lawrences of Lawrence Hall. Cecelia matter-of-factly explained that her family was one and the same.

Mark enjoyed having Cecelia as a student.

I noticed that though she was very talkative in conference, she seemed a bit detached from the rest of her classmates. She was always pleasant, but did not mix much with either of the two sophomores or any of the freshmen. Although the class had clicked quite nicely, Cecelia was somewhat of an outsider.

Mid-October/Mid-Term

Mark was pleased with the way his course was progressing. The students seemed to be adjusting well to Kensington and to their classes. Having weekly conferences enabled him to get to know his students quickly. The Rhetoric class was a very diverse one, despite Kensington's image as a "waspy school for the wealthy and well connected."

Cecelia's Progress

I noticed that right after mid-term, Cecelia was beginning to miss a class now and then. She had done well on her mid-term exam—receiving a 96%—on the essay/quiz component, and a B+ on her graded submission. I wanted to nip in the bud what could evolve into an attendance problem, and brought it up at our next conference in early November.

I reminded Cecelia that success in the course depended on participation and that since her attendance was slacking off, this could seriously affect her grade. I further explained that by missing classes she was also missing the opportunity to edit and revise her work with her classmates. Since the course stressed the value of revision, I tried to explain how critical it was that she improve her attendance at both class and conferences.

Cecelia was very apologetic. She explained to me

that she was a bit overwhelmed lately by a variety of out-of-town family obligations. Apparently, there had been a Lawrence Park dedication in Philadelphia the previous weekend. Cecelia's mother had felt that one of her children should be in attendance, and since Cecelia's brother was in school on the West Coast, Cecelia felt an obligation to attend. Because the ceremonies continued through late Sunday night, Cecelia was unable to make her Monday classes, and missed Rhetoric.

Cecelia hoped that she wouldn't be missing any more classes, though she explained that she had just learned that her uncle had contracted the same cancer that killed her father the previous year. Her uncle had apparently taken on the role of head of the Lawrence family since her father's death. She explained, though somewhat vaguely, that this development might necessitate more frequent and lengthy trips to Philadelphia.

I got the sense from our conversation that she was sincerely concerned and that she would make every effort to come to both class and conferences. I asked her to keep me informed.

Continued Deterioration

Mark had hoped their talk would solve the problem. Unfortunately Cecelia's performance continued to deteriorate. In mid-November, he observed:

Cecelia is a very likable person—*when* she's around, that is. I soon noticed, however, that she was missing far too many appointments. This was in part due to missed classes—she had no opportunity to sign up for a conference.

If Cecelia scheduled an appointment, she came. I guess she felt a personal commitment. Sometimes she didn't come at the right time, but was always able to reschedule for later in the day.

Cecelia's papers generally came in, although late and usually just the "final submission." Again, I tried to explain that a final draft was one of the goals of the course—editing, revising, and conferencing were critical to the writing process. "Getting a paper in" was not enough. I wanted to see her rough drafts—the process she went through. I wanted her to work on revising, on editing. I even mentioned how it was a departmental goal for students, not just a personal one.

I complimented Cecelia on her mid-term paper, which had undergone several revisions, and on her in-class exam, but emphasized that "she was slipping" and that I was very concerned.

At the next class to which she came—I believe it was just before the Thanksgiving break—I asked her to stay after for a few minutes. Again, she was very apologetic. She reiterated her interest in the class and how it was run—and again expressed her disappointment that she was not able to attend more often. She was, as usual, somewhat vague about both family obligations and her uncle who was dying of cancer in Philadelphia.

She said she understood my concerns, and I again got the impression that she would make a concerted effort to attend class and weekly writing conferences faithfully.

Meanwhile, I was unsuccessful in reaching Cecelia's designated advisor in her residence hall. He failed to return my phone calls. Finally, late one afternoon, just as I was about to leave my office, I decided to try his number one last time. Cecelia's advisor was in, and took my call. He seemed familiar with her history and her situation. His initial "ah, yes" had an exasperated tone to it, and made me think Cecelia's case was not high on his list of priorities. I also got the sense I was not the only instructor who called him about Cecelia. He said he would track her down and check into the matter.

Cecelia came to see me within several days of that conversation. When I asked her if her advisor had contacted her she replied yes, but said that she had intended to come to see me anyway.

Again, Cecelia intended to "get her act together," and I was to expect her in class that Wednesday with a final submission to follow on Friday at 5:00 P.M. I was pleased to see her in class on Wednesday and to receive her paper two days later.

Jim Roberts' Visit

In early December, Jim Roberts, one of the assistant directors of the Rhetoric program, observed Mark's class. Classroom observations were routine for new faculty, so Mark had known ahead of time that Jim was coming. Afterwards, while discussing the class with Mark, Jim asked if anyone was absent. Since Cecelia had not been present, Mark commented that although he enjoyed Cecelia, she had missed several classes lately and that he was concerned.

I explained that Cecelia was a sophomore and why she was repeating Rhetoric. I also mentioned her family obligations and her uncle's cancer.

Much to my surprise, Jim backed off the usual department party line. I expected to hear "flunk her . . ." but instead Jim began to rationalize passing her: "Well, she's probably been through some rough times. She already took the course last year . . . I'd do everything I could if I were you to make sure she passes."

I wondered if Cecelia's "lineage" didn't have something to do with Jim's recommendation. I must admit I, too, am a lifelong Lawrence fan—I'm sure Cecelia's family has had an effect on how I interact with her, either on the conscious or unconscious level.

The Situation Worsens

Cecelia continued her practice of handing in just her final submissions, often at odd hours when Mark was not in his office.

Cecelia would either slip her paper under my door or leave it in my box. Sometimes it would be postmarked from Philadelphia.

Cecelia was always pleasant and agreeable. Her manner was cooperative. Her follow-through was another story. She would promise that a paper would be in the next day, only to send it special delivery several days later.

Cecelia frequently sent notes along with her submissions. She would volunteer writing an extra paper "to make up for the classes I missed and the trouble I have probably caused you." She wanted to write an extra paper on her father and "how he waited for her brother to say 'hi' one last time." Cecelia didn't want this paper to be a "regular class one," however: "it still hurts too much to be read by another student." She was worried it might come across as a "sob story."

By the second week of December, for all intents and purposes, Cecelia had disappeared. Meanwhile her designated advisor in her residence hall failed again to return my calls. Finally one of his assistants did get back to me. She seemed more willing to help.

Cecelia came by the next day. I explained to her that the final exam was in a week and that her final paper (a research paper—for a grade) was due on the same day. I impressed upon her that if she missed the exam and/or did not hand in her paper that she would fail the course. I explained that although at mid-term she was doing well, her current participation grade was "failing." She had missed several classes in which we had already critiqued rough drafts of the class's research papers. I further explained how missing conferences was also a disadvantage—not getting help along the way. I just wasn't sure she could get a strong research paper done in a week.

Although Cecelia appeared to appreciate and understand my concern, she didn't show up on exam day. She wrote me a note that she had the flu and was in Philadelphia.

We made arrangements for a make-up exam to be taken in my office for the following week, and in the meantime she sent me her research paper. I contacted her immediately to let her know that her paper was a "good start" but needed a lot of work especially since it was without *any* citations.

Cecelia came to take her exam December 22 without her paper. She asked for another extension. I told her I could hold off the registrar until January 3, but no later.

Do I Give Her Another Chance?

It was now January 3, and no research paper had appeared. Mark had difficulty accepting Cecelia's story that it had been destroyed in a truck fire.

For the past ten to twelve days he had been in constant contact with another member of the class, who was taken suddenly and seriously ill on one of the last days of the term. Robbie Haratunian had apparently contracted a rare virus that had paralyzed both his legs. His parents flew to Kensington to be with him at the university hospital and stayed there through the holidays.

Despite Robbie's sudden illness, he asked his advisor to contact me and to let me know his paper might be a few days late. Of course, I sent word not to worry and made a point of calling him myself to take the pressure off. Throughout the holidays, I spoke with Robbie several times. Despite my insistence that he not concentrate on his school work but rather on getting well, he told me that he didn't want to get behind in any of his subjects.

Because of the holidays, there is no one left in the department with whom I feel comfortable discussing Cecelia. Further, I am not terribly well disposed to her situation anymore, especially given how Robbie has struggled despite a very grim situation.

Should I stall the registrar while I wait for Cecelia yet once again to send the promised xerox copy? Should I go ahead and calculate her grade without the research paper? She did take the final exam. Maybe her grade will be passing after all. My options are limited. The Rhetoric program does not allow incompletes. Either I pass her or I fail her.

Brad Park taught a sophomore tutorial for the Political Science Department at Wellhaven University, a large and prestigious research university located in the Pacific Northwest. The sophomore Political Science tutorial was a course required of all new departmental majors. The course introduced sophomores to the issues and modes of thought that were considered central to the department's concept of political science.

Each week a different topic was raised for discussion. Examples included religious liberties, equality under the law, different visions of democracy, and foreign policy. Six to eight students and a graduate student tutor gathered each week for two hours to discuss the readings that were assigned to go along with these topic discussions. Twenty percent of a student's grade was based on class participation. The rest was based on five short papers written on topics assigned by the tutor. The tutors met weekly as a group with two professors to talk about teaching issues that grew out of the discussion topics and the reading materials. The curriculum was the same for each tutorial class, although tutors usually varied in their individual teaching approaches.

During this period, Wellhaven was actively recruiting students of color and students from other countries. The school's administration and faculty were also committed to newly expanded teaching and scholarship efforts in the areas of diversity and multicultural understanding. The faculty of some departments, including those in Political Science, had also discussed among themselves the challenges faced in teaching students of different backgrounds, cultures, and expectations. According to Brad Park:

> On the one hand, I was told to treat women and students of color the same as everyone else. On the other, I was told to be sensitive to their differences—to their ways of learning and speaking, to their histories and their cultures. But how was I to do both?

Brad Park

Brad Park was a fourth-year graduate student at Wellhaven. He entered graduate school directly after receiving his BA from the Vanderbilt University. Brad reported to the casewriter:

> I come from Georgia and went to Vanderbilt where I was the most liberal person among the people I

CASE

An Earthquake Had Started (A)

Lee Warren prepared this case in consultation with *C. Roland Christensen* and *Louis B. Barnes* for use in the Discussion Skills Leadership Seminar. Data were furnished by involved participants. All names and some peripheral facts have been disguised.

Derek Bok Center for Teaching and Learning, Harvard University. Case No. 1.

knew. Strangely enough, here I'm one of the most conservative. Southerness does play a role in how I teach in the sense that I'm pretty sensitive to the stereotyping about southerners which holds that: a) you're stupid or b) you're a racist. However, sometimes that can work to my benefit. When I speak in a southern accent and say something intelligent, they think "Gosh! How wonderful!" But even that bugs me.

Brad began teaching in his third year at Wellhaven, working with two tutorial sections each term. He generally received very high teaching evaluations. Students commented that Brad had a nice personality, did a good job of getting people to talk without letting some people dominate, and did a great job of presenting interesting ideas. As a result, Brad was nominated for the Political Science Department's teaching award one year. In the term following the incident described in this case, he was made one of six Assistant Tutors to advise undergraduate students on courses and requirements, signing study cards, and talking with new majors about the department.

During this semester, both of Brad's tutorial groups met in some informal seminar rooms in one of the student living units. Both groups included a few students who lived in the same dormitories and knew each other outside as well as in class. Because of this and because of the informal class setting, the tutorials tended to have a casual atmosphere that enhanced the discussion. Brad felt that this informality greatly helped his classes arrive at productive discussion levels early in the semester.

The Students

Brad Park described one of his tutorial classes and some of the students in it.

We sat at a long rectangular table. Tracy generally sat at one end. To her right was Mary and then David. To her left was Sam and then me and then William. On the day of the earthquake incident, there were only five students in class, although normally there were six. One had a schedule conflict and went to my other section.

Tracy Hall was the best student in that section. Part of what made her successful in class was that she was a forceful, dynamic person. At the beginning of the semester, I was really happy I had her in the section.

She had a very bright disposition, always did the readings, her papers were well written and thoughtful, and she ended up with an A− in the course. She was always well prepared, and usually would volunteer when others weren't talking. I think I too frequently called on her, because I could count on her to keep the conversation going, to bring up a good point.

Tracy was the only black woman in the tutorial group of six. I think she came from Louisiana. I realized in the first couple of weeks that she was a member of a fundamentalist religious movement. During religious liberties week, we had been discussing school prayer cases. The last case we looked at was a Supreme Court decision preventing Louisiana schools from teaching creationism in science classes. The dissenting opinion said that the court was setting up its own religion of secular humanism. Tracy was in support of that dissenting opinion. It was clear throughout that week that she had deeply held Christian beliefs.

During the semester there were a couple of other times when I thought Tracy disagreed with the conversation and how I led it. For example, one week we discussed court cases on equality. One case was the Bakke case on reverse discrimination. I could tell during this discussion that Tracy was opposed to the class even considering the position that affirmative action wasn't good. I got more and more wary of Tracy and she seemed to sour on the class as the semester went on.

Brad went on to describe some of the other students in the tutorial group:

The most distinguishing characteristic of the rest of the class was its passivity. They were willing to talk, but Tracy was the most forceful person in the class. Initially in class I relied on Tracy at points when I needed a student comment. But by the time this incident happened late in the semester, I was relying on Sam.

Sam Beatty was a middle-of-the-road student. He tried hard and always rewrote his papers. He was the only one who was both local (he came from Portland, I think) and from a blue-collar family. He tended to be antagonistic to what you would call politically correct statements made by the other students. But he was not very combative. Looking back, if I had to pick a favorite, it would be Sam. He was friendly and outgoing and also a good student—not so much that he was brilliant, but he would work very hard and when he hadn't done his work, he would be up front about it.

By way of contrast, William Taylor, also black, got the worst grade in this section. He rarely did the reading and would try to bullshit his way a lot of times. He often tried to talk his way out of not having done the reading or having thought about it. William was from San Diego—a factor once when he skipped class to go on a recruiting trip. He missed class and a paper and came in afterwards and said he had been out of town. I didn't penalize him, but it was an indication of him not showing enough courtesy to tell me he would miss class.

David Eisenmann was from San Francisco and I assumed he was Jewish. He had a sardonic personality. He was taciturn, especially at first, laconic, wary, unwilling to volunteer much. But he became more and more open and warmer as the semester went on. I responded to that.

Mary Johnson was the only other woman in the section. She did real well in the class. She was not one to volunteer a lot of comments. But when discussions were set up so that it was her turn to speak, or I would ask her a question, she was always well prepared and her comments were to the point. She didn't seem self-conscious, but was a quiet person naturally.

This was a more difficult group than the other one I had that semester. For one thing, it met later in the afternoon, from four to six. And at times, the students' personalities made it difficult to get a conversation going. I always encourage people to talk directly to each other, especially on opinion questions, by asking one student what he or she thinks of another's argument. I had to pull conversation out of this section more than most, but it wasn't the most taciturn I've had. My subjective impression during the term was that the other section, which was more easy going and substantially more talkative, picked up things quicker and easier; but the grades at the end of the semester were the same.

Brad also talked about his objectives as a teacher:

My style of teaching was this: at the beginning of the year, I told students I might call on them to give their opinion, especially if things are dragging. I wouldn't try to burn them or test them to see if they did the reading. I asked general thought questions rather than questions about a specific reading. Not

what did de Toqueville say about individualism, but what do you think about fighting a war to prevent genocide. I would ask for opinions. And I encouraged students to talk with each other, not just with me.

Each week I handed out a list of discussion questions to look at when doing the reading. Often I assigned one of the discussion questions to one of the students, especially early in the semester when we are reading the Federalist papers, de Toqueville, John Stuart Mill, or things like that.

When we did court cases, which we did for a fair number of weeks, it was very helpful to assign the plaintiff or defendant role to specific people. They knew a week ahead of time that they would have to take the lead in presenting arguments. The feedback I've had was real positive. They enjoyed playing those roles. Sometimes they could step out of their own personality and express other views. There was a danger in this if students got too caught up in facts and didn't see the larger issues or paid all their attention to just that one case and didn't read the other material. But if you kept an eye out for the dangers, the role playing was a nice change for a couple of weeks.

I bent over backwards in tutorials to try to get arguments going on issues we were talking about. If most of the section agreed that affirmative action was a bad thing, I'd argue that it was a good thing. I think I argued both sides of the fence on almost all issues of race and sex. It had to come out after twelve meetings what my own political views were, but I tried to be as neutral as possible, and balance out the views of the section.

The Earthquake Day

Brad recalled the events of that day:

The incident happened late in the term and late in that week's two-hour session. All five students had been active that day. The topic was one that people could talk about even if they hadn't done the reading. The first half of the class was devoted to the problems and advantages a democracy, in particular the United States, had in formulating an effective foreign policy. How did it handle accountability? Did more authoritarian governments have an advantage over democracies when it came to maintaining secrecy or speedy decision making? Or did democracies have an advantage because they came up with policies created by a wide swath of people who were then already behind the policies they'd created?

Then we talked about Congress vs. the administration. Who had control? Who should take the lead? What were the advantages and disadvantages of each position?

One of the areas I liked to discuss in the tutorial came at the end of that class: when is a country, the United States in particular, justified in going to war? The first answers to the question usually revolved around national security or self-defense. These came out quickly. So I asked them, "How do you define national security? What does it entail?" And after that I asked, "Is there anything you would fight for other than self-defense?" We read John Kennedy's inaugural: "Pay any price, bear any burden to bring democracy. . . ." and we read Woodrow Wilson saying the same things. "What are the non-national security reasons that justify war? What moral concerns lead a country to declare war?"

I started by asking if a differing political system is reason enough to go to war.

"No, no," they said, "that is not justification enough."

What about slavery? Some said yes, some said no.

Then some said that there was no moral reason for going to war: "Who are we to tell another country what to do?"

So I asked them about genocide. "What about the holocaust? It's fairly clear the United States didn't enter the war because of the holocaust. The information became available when we were already in the war.

But let's assume we did know, would it be a just cause?"

One student said, "Yes."

I called on Tracy. "What do you think? Was the holocaust a just cause for war?"

"No, I don't think that's a reason to go to war."

"Why not?"

"Because they weren't Christians."

It felt like an earthquake had started. I paused.

"What do you mean?"

"In the first place, I'm not sure it happened like they say it did, and in the second place, I'm sure they had their reasons."

Stunned silence.

It seemed very clear to me that the "they" was referring to Jews in the first case and Germans in the second. After that comment it seemed like an hour while a number of things went through my head. I thought: Oh my God, this is awful. What do I do? Do I argue with her, and say, "Yes, the holocaust really did happen and it was a bad thing"? Man, this really isn't an argument I want to have. When you have an argument with someone who thinks the earth is flat, you can get into a lot of trouble, because they are well versed in pseudo facts and you might not have facts at your fingertips. I was looking around the room at other students, mouths open, looking at Tracy. "Geez, I can't just let this slide by."

There were still 15 minutes left in the class. Nobody said anything. It seemed to me that the silence was the worst thing going on, so I just said a long, drawn out "Ohhh Kayyy."

CASE

Bob Lunt (A)

Martha Elliot, a new assistant professor at the San Francisco Bay Area Graduate School of Social Policy, sat in her office on a gray January afternoon fuming inwardly as she pulled out Bob Lunt's bluebook for the final exam in Financial Management 220. For the fifth time that day she reread the most hostile of the few paragraphs he had scrawled instead of answering the exam question:

> Martha,
>
> What stops me from actually performing the task I see called for is my sheer unwillingness to play with numbers, my sense that in realities outside the classroom, numbers comprise a game rather than part of a publicly shared form of objective inquiry. I am simply not going to do what I'm told (prepare numbers to substantiate the department head's viewpoint), but my guess is that the Hospital Director is right.
>
> Bob

That was the most infuriating part. Feeling thwarted and angry, Martha wondered why Bob had wanted to ruin the otherwise successful first semester of her brand-new tenure track job at Bay. She had been thrilled and flattered at the invitation to teach full time in the same institution that had just granted her a doctorate in public sector management. But from the first week of term, she recalled, Bob Lunt had seemed to signal trouble. He was 10 or 15 years older than most of the other students, and she'd worried about whether he would fit in. Nevertheless, as the semester had progressed, he'd been so quiet—friendly, even, in response to her unfailing politeness—that she had gradually forgotten her worries about him. Now this insulting performance was the upshot of the way she'd handled him. She had been feeling quite pleased with the course and her teaching—especially because the dean himself had mentioned hearing "rave reviews" from students. Did Bob's refusal to answer the final exam question mean she'd failed after all? How on earth could she grade this so-called exam? Clearly she'd have to respond in some fashion. But how?

Background

Martha Elliot was twenty-nine years old, single, and the holder of a new doctorate in public sector management from Bay, where the School of Social

*This case was written by **Abby Hansen** in collaboration with a member of the Developing Discussion Leadership Skills Seminar. Data were furnished by involved participants. All names and some peripheral facts have been disguised.*

HBS Case No. 9-382-054.

Policy and Research enjoyed the same excellent reputation as the rest of the prestigious institution. The School of Social Policy prepared students for general management positions in public and private non-profit organizations, with heavy emphasis on health care professions. Most students in the program were between the ages of twenty-four and thirty.

Bob Lunt's background was unusual. In his late thirties and the holder of a Ph.D. in literature, he was a former professor of English at San Francisco State College who had decided to change careers. Martha had heard that Bob left the college in a huff when his promotion from associate to full professor (with attendant salary raise) had been tabled for a year. She didn't know precisely why he had enrolled in the School of Social Policy. His class card in F.M. 220 simply stated, "interested in Health Care Administration since days in Army Medical Corps." As Martha recalled the whole semester's worth of experiences with Bob, she realized she actually knew very little about him.

F.M. 220, a counterpart to Management Control[1] as taught in other management programs, posed a formidable challenge to many first-semester students in the School of Social Policy because it was heavily quantitative. It posed a challenge to Martha, too, not only because she prided herself on being able to humanize the numbers for her students, but also because F.M. 220 was her first full course responsibility. While completing her doctoral research, she had occasionally filled in for instructors and once team-taught a course, but F.M. 220 was her first solo effort. It was her task to teach new students basic financial and cost accounting concepts in order to enable them to understand and prepare financial statements, cost reports, and budgets.

The class met three days a week, from nine to ten-thirty A.M. but Martha scheduled extra review sessions and long office hours. She graded 50% on class participation and 50% on written work. Bay's grading policy allowed only three options: Excellent, Satisfactory, and Low Pass (equivalent to failure).

---

1. Management Control concentrates on how a manager ensures that an organization's resources are used efficiently and effectively. The course includes techniques for constructing and analyzing financial statements and cost data, alternatives for reducing costs or increasing revenues, and ways of motivating employees to share the organization's goals and objectives.

The Semester

Martha thought back on the events of the semester, aware that, despite the dean's comment about "rave reviews," there had been problems in the course. Within the first few weeks she had noticed that, instead of the learning unit she was trying to forge from the group, there were several factions. There had been an assertive "back-row mafia," generally quiet during the number-crunching but ready to jump into the overall analysis with hard-nosed management recommendations. Opposed to that contingent had been a front-row group that offered numerical solutions to everything. This group knew accounting rules but was less inclined than the back-row types to make decisions. Lastly, scattered throughout the midsection of the room, there had been the less active participants—some quite competent but shy, others simply quiet and apparently unsure of the material.

And then there was Bob Lunt. He usually sat at the back of the room near the door. Soft spoken, polite and, above all, almost floridly articulate, he had seemed to Martha from the very first a different type of person from the rest of the students. The others lacked his experience and extensive training in the humanities. In the early weeks of the semester, Lunt had appeared interested in the class material. He listened intently, occasionally contributing well-taken points. He always arrived early for class and, after depositing his books at his desk, returned to the hall for a cigarette. Martha also came early but she had no opportunity to stop and chat with Bob because she usually found herself engaged in conversation by the "number-crunchers" from the front row by the time she passed Bob in the hall. The front-row group was aggressive; its members besieged her with questions about classwork and gossip about public sector jobs as she entered the classroom, unpacked her briefcase, and spread her papers and books out on her desk. She did, however, make sure always to greet Bob cordially as he stood there smoking. He, in turn, always responded to greetings with a courtly nod.

After class, Bob left immediately for the library. Martha thought he seemed congenial with his classmates, but she gathered that he had neither joined a study group nor allied himself with any of the factions of the class. This aloofness, she reflected, might be due to the age difference between him and his fellow students.

From the beginning of the semester, Martha worked to push students to break with their old roles and think about new ways to attack managerial problems. Once the insecure students had quelled their anxieties about quantitative analysis, they had become interested, even excited, in what they were learning. Martha held optional review sessions once a week, and her office hours on Mondays and Wednesdays were always booked solid. Bob Lunt attended neither.

Toward the middle of the term Martha found that, as students began to know each other better, a mutual respect had developed among them. The factions were giving way to some general class camaraderie. After a few students sent Martha notes expressing their pleasure with the course, and a few others offered compliments in person, Martha began to feel proud of her performance in the first undertaking of her professional academic career.

Her elation was, however, far from absolute. As the class jelled into a cooperative unit, Bob Lunt seemed to become less and less involved with the group. He began slumping low in his seat, cynically or disdainfully observing proceedings from the sidelines, and participating only very occasionally. Shortly after midsemester, he began to deliver his infrequent comments in loud, argumentative tones, as if they were short outbursts of anger rather than discussion points. Martha was annoyed, but since the outbursts didn't seem to be directed at anyone in particular she decided not to challenge Bob about his worsening attitude. She didn't want to risk her solid rapport with the rest of the class, and she assumed that, since Bob's problems were probably personal and had nothing to do with the course, she really shouldn't interfere.

There had been one class, however, in which Lunt became very vocal. The discussion concerned the tuition policy for a large state university. The class talked about the implications of state subsidy of selected organizations in an industry and traced the control system established by public funding. This time Bob argued hard against comparing private and public universities when some of the students drew conclusions based on analogies to Bay. The class had ended with more issues raised and fewer resolved than usual, but Martha felt it had been a useful exercise.

A few days later, when she was sitting in the cafeteria, Bob Lunt surprised her by coming up to ask if he might join her. He had been thinking, he said, about the tuition policy case, and he wanted to discuss his perspective. He talked for half an hour—with Martha asking pointed questions to draw him out—about the pressures and problems of teaching in a public university that was accountable to the state legislature and, therefore, to voting trends. Such an institution, he claimed, was low in financial security, morale, and general academic freedom. He spoke intensely, and his parting words were, "Martha, you just can't imagine how different it is from Bay. You're so insulated here."

Martha left the cafeteria feeling that his points had fairly little to do with the case they'd done in class but she was glad they had talked because it seemed that she had finally achieved some rapport with Bob Lunt. Whatever the cause of his defensive behavior in class, she now believed he really wasn't out to make trouble for her.

The Final Exam

Martha distributed the F.M. 220 final—a take-home exam—at the last class. She was surprised to notice that Bob Lunt was absent from class for the first time that semester. Later in the day she passed him in the hall and he said, "Sorry I wasn't in class this morning but, uh, well, I just wanted to live differently." Martha asked if he'd gotten his copy of the exam. He said that another student had picked one up for him.

The exam consisted of a balance sheet for "Godard Hospital," and a case describing the desire of the department head (Dr. Parker) to keep an expensive dialysis unit open at the hospital. Dr. Parker had to present his argument to the hospital director (Dr. Leavitt) who thought the unit too costly to run. The students' task was to present an analysis, complete with figures and their own recommendations, in memorandum form.

Martha expected heavily quantitative analyses and was prepared to be flexible about recommendations that differed from hers—as long as the students showed mastery of the financial and cost accounting concepts they had worked with all semester.

Bob Lunt's exam—tantrum, really—took her completely by surprise. What to do now? (See Exhibits 1 and 2.)

Exhibit 1
BOB LUNT (A)

TO: Financial Management Students
FROM: Martha Elliot
DATE: January 15, 1980
SUBJECT: Final Exam

Exam: Godard Hospital

Please prepare a memorandum for the department head (Dr. Parker) to use in his next meeting with the hospital director (Dr. Leavitt) concerning the proposal to phase down or close the hospital's dialysis unit.

Your memo should not exceed two pages double-spaced and a one-page exhibit if necessary.

It is due on January 17, and should be left with Margaret Farrell, Room 320.

Exhibit 2
BOB LUNT (A)

Bob Lunt's Note to Martha Elliot

To make assumptions clear, let me say what stops me from actually performing the task I see called for: my sheer unwillingness to play with numbers, my sense that in realities outside of rooms with greenboards and chalk, numbers comprise a game rather than part of a publicly shared form of objective inquiry (that happens to words, too); my unwillingness to do what I'm told, prepare materials in effect for substantiating the department head's viewpoint for my guess is that the hospital director is right.

From Parker's viewpoint—assuming he and Leavitt stand at my unsophisticated plateau of accounting—it might be argued that each treatment now costs $124. Parker ought to hedge, as my wording does, because other figures can be calculated. Parker might also take issue with Godard's cost allocations, although—again to put things on Parker's behalf for a moment—this could backfire. One salary figure shows allocation by hours of service and presumably stands for the consulting nephrologists' pay; this in turn suggests Parker's salary is carried

in line 12, making him a beneficiary of the allocation system. (There is something disingenuous about keeping physicians' wages out of the cost center and listing underlings' wages in it.) Parker's best case would show that Godard's costs per treatment resulted in revenue from Medicare comprising at least 80% of the costs. The retrospective figures could be used for projecting costs at volume diminished to start-up and emergency treatments exclusively, in order to show revenues at 80% of those projected costs, though I suspect that the cut variable and semivariable expenses would not yet yield the figure that Parker needs. In sum, Parker's memo must tacitly discredit Godard's current allocation system or the clinic's competing definitions of cost or both. Parker might also try foreseeing and preempting Godard's plans for the space and staff made available by shutting down the renal unit, though this would be tantamount in the memo to throwing in the towel.

The quest to ascertain costs is unarguable, but it carries with it the problematic relationship of revenues. The revenues are determined by Medicare policy, not by Godard's costs; and Godard's billing is not determined by its costs (by whatever definition) but by a judgment combining costs with knowledge of what will be paid for, probably with a stress on what will be paid for. Leavitt may be right, even if simplistic and reductive: it is incredible that a department running at 100% one year and 50% the next isn't going to cost more and produce less revenue, even though volume fluctuations alone cannot explain cost differences not changing cost-revenue relationships. So short of recasting the assumptions governing Godard's internal accounting and short of recasting the entire pricing-payment scheme for dialysis retreatment, inquiry seeking to ascertain costs and revenue is uninteresting.

It makes good sense to keep people who are dependent upon dialysis out of hospitals. The key to the financial success of Godard's renal unit is the unlikely chance of that unit's becoming the exclusive resource in its region for treatment start-up. Since there are clinics charging Medicare significantly less for treatment than Godard, shut down Godard's renal unit and let clinics hire Parker to worry about start-up and back-up services. His salary won't drive the clinic's charges up beyond our ability to pay.

Martin Davis, M.D., age 65—Kendricks Professor of Endocrinology at Farwestern University Medical School—sat in his office ignoring the beautiful Pacific sunset outside his window. He frowned down at a student evaluation form on his desk and wrote "Kenneth Holmes" after "Name of Student." Then he paused.

Kenneth had been in Martin's discussion section of the second-year endocrinology course. (At Farwestern Med, all first- and second-year courses were taught in small group discussions, augmented by lectures and lab sessions.) Instructors were required to grade students' final course exams and also to write several paragraphs assessing their learning styles, problem-solving abilities, personal development, and interpersonal skills. Filling out most evaluation forms was a straightforward task.

But the prospect of filling out Kenneth's form was giving Martin a headache. In his twenty-five years of teaching endocrinology (the past five leading discussion groups), Martin had never encountered a student with more unsettling behavior. Kenneth had sat silent for the first discussion and then—after a pep talk from Martin about participation—launched a series of outbursts and complaints so disruptive that the other students reacted by trying to ignore him. Finally, after swearing that he couldn't learn endocrinology in this setting, Kenneth had earned a solid High Pass on the course exam. Grading Kenneth was easy—he *had* managed to learn the course content. But how to evaluate his behavior in words?

Martin agonized over the blank form. A bad evaluation could trigger anything from an official review to suspension. Martin wanted to do the right thing—for Kenneth, the school, and the profession. But what was the right thing? He stared at the empty spaces on the page so long that they seemed to stare back.

Farwestern School of Medicine

Founded a century ago in some of the most beautiful countryside in California, Farwestern University included a liberal arts college and seven graduate and professional schools. All had outstanding reputations; all were highly competitive.

Martin reported, "Five years ago, the Med School instituted an experimental curriculum and pedagogy that highlight group problem-solving discussions in the first two years. Basically, the whole class—about 150 students—assembles for lectures

CASE

"The Blank Page" (A)

*This case was researched and written by **Abby Hansen** for the Developing Discussion Leadership Skills Seminar. Data were furnished by involved participants. All names, places, and some peripheral facts have been disguised. The School of Public Health gratefully acknowledges a grant from President Bok of Harvard University in support of the case development project.*

Harvard School of Public Health, Case No. 2.

217

on various subjects each morning, then breaks into assigned discussion groups of 7 to 12. Each group has an instructor who is either a physician or a Ph.D. and often a specialist in the field of the course.

"The point of the program is to humanize the study of medicine, foster independent initiative in learning, and prepare students for the teamwork of real medical practice. The new pedagogy stresses the learning process over memorization and introduces group problem-solving right from the start. It also aims to provide closer contact with faculty than is possible in an exclusively lecture-based curriculum.

"Students rotate through a variety of discussion groups, so they get to work with most of their classmates during the first two years of the program. By the second year—which is when I encountered this group—most groups have already worked together and established behavioral norms. This means that we instructors are the 'new kids on the block' when we meet our students."

The Course

The curriculum was divided into courses of various lengths. Some of the shortest units lasted only a month. Endocrine pathophysiology, a second-year course, was one of these. Martin said, "In the endocrine course, students consider the origins of diseases of endocrine glands. The subject is complex and the material is confusing by any standards.

"This discussion group met in February, when students were also taking two other courses, which dealt with interviewing patients, performing physical examinations, reviewing lab studies, and understanding some of the psychological effects of illness." We met four days a week, after a group lecture. Discussions lasted for an hour and a half.

"On the first day, all of the students received problem sets and long, detailed explanatory notes about the subject matter. The course head was a textbook author, and the notes approximated an edition of his text."

The Teaching Approach

Martin described a typical discussion, "Students come to class with assigned discussion problems that they have worked on the night before. In class, they advance hypotheses about the problems, challenge one another in a positive way, expose flaws in reasoning, and learn from their failures as well

as their successes. As they cover various parts of a problem, we instructors hand out sheets of further information or extensions of the problem.

Before beginning his new teaching assignment, Martin took a brief workshop with a senior adviser from the School's Instructional Development Group, who suggested that the teachers' job was, basically, to keep out of the students' way.

"Instructors' teaching styles vary. We're still in the experimental stages. Some teachers try to direct the discussion, but I subscribe to the idea that we are there as supervisors, mainly to bear witness, with our presence, to the importance of what the students are doing as they learn to teach one another and themselves. This appeals to me because I take it as a matter of faith that, if you get people to invest in their own learning process, the skills they master and the gratification of that process will persist at a time when they're on their own."

The idea of discussion teaching also appealed to Martin because, "I had done a lot of lecturing and really detested it. In fact, it seemed like a lost cause. I found working with small groups of students far more rewarding. As a young student, I very nearly quit medical school because I thought that lectures were the death of the mind. I was rescued by a faculty member who put me into his lab and inspired what turned into two decades of research for me. The richness of close contact with a faculty member was crucial for me."

The Students

Martin "got this group in February, by which time they had already taken two discussion courses together. I asked them to fill out information sheets with their backgrounds, academic plans, goals for the course, and any special information that they might want me to know about them."

This group included:

Beth Kovell—"a no-nonsense, liberally educated, 'Berkeley type.' Beth was a warm, unconventional person. She had been a cellular and molecular biology major. She was quite wound up during this course because her brother had just been diagnosed with acute leukemia, and she was waiting to be genetically matched as a potential bone marrow donor."

Elliott Strickland—"a dental student (dental students take the first two years of classes with the medical students at Farwestern). He was relatively financially deprived, a graduate in biology from Adelphi College. He tended to be very earnest, not the brightest of students, but never dominating."

Linda Chen—"Linda was born in Taiwan, but came to the United States as a child. She was a Stanford bioscience major, smart and a little withdrawn. She didn't plunge into discussions, but she was always well prepared and ready to supply factual answers."

Fran Bennett—"Fran was a U. Cal., Irvine, biology major who planned to go into surgery. This surprised me a bit because, unlike many of the women students at Farwestern Medical School, she wore traditionally 'feminine' clothing, makeup, and jewelry to class—and surgery, unfortunately, still tends to be 'macho' and is often a center for sexual harassment. I would call her smart, but not brilliant. She was an active discussion participant."

Jeff Porter—"A chemistry major from the University of Chicago, Jeff was probably the best prepared, best organized student in the group. Everyone deferred to him for answers to difficult conceptual or factual questions. He was modest and diffident, but not withdrawn—just careful not to swamp the group."

Luke Vinelli—"A Yale College bio. major, headed toward genetics, Luke was smart and well prepared. He wasn't quite the honed intellect that Jeff was, but he participated in the give-and-take of the group. He was also an athlete."

Owen McNulty—"Owen had been a Holy Cross bio. major and done graduate work at Columbia University in philosophy of science. He didn't have as whiz-bang, incisive a mind as Jeff or Luke. He was more of a follower, but an active participant."

Kenneth Holmes—"Kenneth was a *summa cum laude* bioscience major from the University of Virginia who was also a filmmaker. He was about six feet tall, nice-looking, and with a normal voice timbre. He dressed informally but not inappropriately. I later learned, off the record, that the admissions committee had given him their very highest rating. He was what they called a 'gasper'—his record was so good, it made them gasp."

Kenneth's Behavior in Class

Martin recalled, "We met in a wedge-shaped room with blackboards on two sides and the door at the apex of the triangle. The eight students and I sat at a conference table with nine seats, and I always arrived early and sat in a different place, mainly to boggle their attempts to stake out regular turf.

"These students came directly from a lecture that took place in another building. They didn't all arrive together. Fran, Beth, Linda, Owen, Luke, Elliott, and Jeff came in a group, chatting and laughing, and Kenneth arrived a few minutes later, alone.

"At our first meeting, I introduced myself and told them that they had a chit from me, as it were, for trivial facts: if the discussion seemed stalled on a particular point of information, they could ask me for it. But I reserved the right to declare it nontrivial and ask them to look it up. I told them that I wasn't much into grading, but I would try to offer observations to help them improve their performance when we met individually at mid-course. I also told them to feel free to challenge these observations.

"Then I said, 'Let's get started. Who wants to read the first problem?' I've found that reading a problem out loud in class helps focus students' attention and lower their anxieties. Beth raised her hand and read the first part of the problem for the day. It dealt with processes that encourage and inhibit hormone production.

"As soon as Beth finished, Luke chimed in, 'The point seems to be how a hormonal system is regulated. It looks as if the hormone produces a substance that prevents the release of more of that same hormone. The question is, where in the process does that happen, and which hormone is being released?'

"Owen looked puzzled, 'Hormone regulation seems like a really sloppy process.'

"Jeff wrapped it up, 'I wouldn't call it sloppy—just loose. And that's good. It promotes stability in the body because the system isn't so tight that it's disturbed by outside influences, like episodes of illness.'"

Martin commented, "I could tell that the group had accepted Jeff's comment because they went on to the rest of the problem, which had multiple parts and was semiquantitative. Their discussion applied concepts that they had heard in the morning's lecture. All this was fine. But after an hour, it was clear that—while Fran, Luke, Owen, Beth, Elliott, Jeff, and Linda were challenging one another and building hypotheses cooperatively, in a lively way, without getting hung up—Kenneth had said absolutely nothing. He just sat there, expressionless and almost motionless. I couldn't read him at all. His notes lay open on the table in front of him, but he wrote nothing. I assumed that his silence meant that he was either unprepared or confused and embarrassed to ask the group for help. I wasn't about to single him out in public by asking him a direct question. But I was concerned.

"The other students left together, and I caught Kenneth at the doorway and said, 'Kenneth, I noticed that you didn't say anything today. Did you feel unprepared or ill at ease with the material, or is there some other reason that I should know about?'" I was expecting him to give some excuse for not having been prepared.

"But instead, he said, 'The group asked me not to talk in class.'

"This was unheard of. I was so flabbergasted that I just waited, hoping for more information. I didn't want to press him. When he volunteered nothing further, I said, 'Kenneth, I consider you to be a citizen of this discussion group. If you don't contribute, you're shortchanging yourself and your fellow students. I urge you to speak in class.'

"In the next session, the class revisited the process that it had looked at in the previous session, using the example of pituitary hormones. I greeted the students by name as they entered. Kenneth came in last. Then Beth, in her no-nonsense way, said, 'Okay, let's get started,' and read the first part of the day's discussion problem. All I recall is that the other students asked appropriate questions and gave useful answers. Then Owen launched onto a long tangent, rehashing material from the text that was irrelevant to the problem at hand. The others listened politely, but Kenneth started shifting in his seat and then rocking back and forth. Finally, he pushed his chair far back and leaned forward to put his elbows on the table. His whole body looked tense, and he interrupted Owen in mid-sentence.

"Kenneth said, 'Hold it, hold it—stop! This is all garbage. Let's get this discussion going. We're talking about a cascade. The HPT has capillaries going to the AP. The CRF gets to the AP that way and stimulates ACTH release, which boosts the release of glucocorticoid—'"

Martin explained, "This was a really off-the-wall contribution, and it went on for nearly a minute. Not only had Kenneth interrupted, fairly violently,

but—in five years of discussion-leading in this curriculum—I had never heard a student use abbreviations this way. His terminology was inscrutable; his manner was domineering; and his interruption was a put-down to Owen and everyone else. The others exchanged 'there he goes again' looks while Kenneth spoke. He ended by picking up his syllabus, slapping it down on the table with a startling 'bang,' and saying, 'Okay, that's the real basis for how hormones work. Now we can get on with this discussion.'

"My response was amazement. Nobody spoke for about fifteen seconds. Then Beth took control again. She said, 'Well, is everybody happy with Owen's suggestion?' The discussion picked up where it had left off before Kenneth's interruption. The others ignored everything Kenneth had said while they exposed Owen's comments as irrelevant. But now there were long pauses between contributions. People seemed to be laboring to fill the silence, whereas before they had joined in eagerly and competed for 'air time,' like a typical, enthusiastic group. Kenneth said nothing further, but his contribution had squeezed the life out of the discussion, and the group had lost time and missed some important points as a result.

"Alarm bells were ringing in my head. I had called this monster out of the cave by explicitly asking Kenneth to become more active in the discussion. Now how was I going to deal with him? I could point out, then and there, that the discussion had gone nowhere and ask how the group felt about that and what they would suggest be done. But that might encourage them to tear Kenneth apart, and I felt responsible for having urged him to contribute. Second, I could temporize and see how the group handled the problem by itself. Third, I could wait one more session to see if this was an idiosyncratic event or part of a pattern, and then talk to Kenneth privately.

"Kenneth missed the next discussion, and the class went better: discussion was animated, spontaneous, and focused. This suggested that there was a pattern; Kenneth's participation really did throw cold water on the group's discussion process. I was even more worried. Kenneth came to the next session. The class was discussing a complex interaction of primary and secondary hormonal factors. Some features of this material simply aren't understood yet.

"Fran said, 'Dr. Davis, could you summarize the

effects of all the hormones that raise blood sugar for us?' I thought that this was a reasonable use of class time, so I obliged.

"As I was speaking, Kenneth kept shifting in his seat, with an increasingly pained expression. He turned directly to me and interrupted—

"'Oh, come on! You're saying that high blood sugar stimulates insulin release and there are at least four independent hormones that increase blood sugar. I can't think about four things at once. I have to see things one at a time, in black and white, but you're making things muddy and gray. I can't learn this way and I don't think anybody can!'

"His outburst violated just about every rule, stated and unstated, of the group. I felt attacked: by saying that he couldn't learn this way, he seemed to be implying that I wasn't teaching properly. I sat up straight and kept my voice even when I replied, 'I have two obligations to you. One is not to tell you garbage. The other is to try to help you to understand some things that are inherently complicated. Maybe I haven't done a very good job of the second, but I have tried not to load you up with garbage. Now, I suggest that we move on to the next point of this meeting.'"

In Office Hours

"I always issue a general invitation to my students: they are welcome to schedule private conferences to discuss the material. Kenneth did so, several times, and he repeated his comment about not being able to learn it because I talked in grays. In class, he kept addressing direct factual questions to me and complaining—often in a loud, angry voice—when I sidestepped and told the group to look it up. He interrupted other people and criticized them for not phrasing information in a way that he could understand.

"I telephoned Sy Bridger, who I knew had taught this group in the previous semester, and said, 'Sy, one of the students in this group seems to be having the following problems. Can you tell me, did anything like this come up in your course?' Sy said, 'Well, as a matter of fact, yes, it was the same way.'

"That made me consider removing Kenneth from the group and just continuing our conferences, but that would have subverted the discussion process. I still hoped—ever more faintly—that the group might work things out over time."

Martin concluded, "I enjoyed the other students

in this group, as I almost always do. As the course came to an end, I even became somewhat hardened to Kenneth. My feelings of inadequacy as a teacher eased up a bit as I realized that his criticism of the way in which I presented information reflected his rigidity, not my failure to address him properly.

"A week before the final exam, Kenneth came to my office, looking very distraught, and said, 'Remember I said I couldn't learn this stuff, and maybe nobody could? Well, I was right: I'm going to flub this exam.' I didn't take the bait about the impossibility of learning this way, but I offered to spend as much time as the two of us could spare to respond to his questions. I said that he would have to define what he didn't know.

"We spent a couple of hours reviewing the major elements of the course. He could barely sit still, seemed extremely frustrated, pessimistic, and obsessed with the need for clarity. He asked questions like, 'Just tell me, does the ACTH hormone increase cortisol production or not? Period.' When I answered, 'Yes, *but . . .,*' he flung up his hands."

The Exam

"It was a one-and-a-half hour exam: forty-five minutes of multiple choice questions and two essays. All of it corresponded in content and style to the problems that we had done during the course. A multiple choice question might give quantitative data about a patient's blood chemistries, list four possible explanations for these results, and ask the students to mark the one that did not correspond to these numerical values. An essay question might say something like, 'Briefly describe the hormonal regulation of the serum calcium concentration. Identify those components most vulnerable to regulatory malfunction in the presence of altered diet, altered sun exposure, kidney failure, and certain widely available medications.' The questions focused on course content.

"The course director, who had written the text, had had a great deal of input into the exam, and the students had also been allowed to study copies of previous exams as part of their preparation. It was meant as a relatively easy exercise to sift out the students having real difficulties, not to spotlight the 'stars.'

"There were four grades—Honors, High Pass, Pass, and Fail. In a group of eight, one would expect one or two High Passes, an Honors grade only every few years, and virtually no Fails. We instructors were responsible for submitting our students' exam grades and evaluation forms. As a rule, neither presented an unusual challenge."

Martin "graded my students' exams personally, leaving Kenneth's for last. I was surprised that he had earned a High Pass. To me, this just showed how pressured and vulnerable he was. But stress is the norm in medical school; *lack* of vulnerability gets people through. I saw him as trying to control the way information flowed to him, shutting it off when it didn't fit his pattern, and expressing his frustration in angry outbursts that upset his colleagues. This worried me because physicians can't control how information comes to them, particularly when it comes from patients. And they spend a lot of time on problem-solving teams."

The Evaluation Form

Martin summarized some unspoken rules regarding evaluation forms. "A good evaluation would be something like, 'Y has a sound and detailed knowledge of the preclinical sciences, which she can usually call on in a relevant context to shed understanding on the diseases of the endocrine glands. Her ability to contribute pertinent information at useful junctures enhanced the quality of this group's discussion.' If you write something like, 'X's background in the preclinical sciences seems to me to be less sound than I would hope for in a student going into the third year, but her trajectory in this course was completely satisfactory and she was able to go back over the preclinical material and improve her contributions,' you've said, 'This student is okay and should continue, but we can probably rule out stardom.' Downright bad evaluations are extremely rare.

"Students read their evaluation forms. They're meant to help them identify areas for improvement, if that is indicated. And they may also be cited in letters of recommendation for residencies—although third- and fourth-year evaluations carry more weight than those from the first two years of the program. As a rule, evaluation forms do not quote students' words directly or give detailed de-

scriptions of their behavior. That sort of documentation is a red flag to those who read it.

"Evaluations go to the course directors, who may refer them to the academic dean if they see a problem. The academic dean may then further refer them to the dean of students. If there is sufficient cause for concern, the course director and the two deans then meet as a committee to determine whether there is a problem that calls for some response.

"If the problem is behavioral, they may set up counseling. Or they may ask the student to take a year off, with an agreed-on plan of activities for that year. Very rarely, if the pattern seems serious and prolonged, they may ask the individual to withdraw and not expect to be considered for readmission for X years. There is no option to tell a particular student, 'We'll give you your M.D. if you pass all your courses, but you must promise to spend the rest of your life in the lab and stay away from patients.'"

Martin Confronts the Blank Page

Martin "spent a couple of nights agonizing over what to write about Kenneth. Given his High Pass, I could have said something moderately critical but otherwise unremarkable, and let him sail on. But I thought that would be irresponsible. I had seen enough of him in action to be quite worried. On the other hand, I had no wish to write anything that would force him into some kind of obligatory program based just on what I had seen. My experience with Kenneth was insufficient for such a judgment, and it wasn't my job to make one, at any rate. Still, it seemed to me that someone in authority ought to take a good look at the big picture."

The evaluation form had three headings followed by spaces big enough for ten to fifteen lines. The headings were: "Learning Style," "Problem-Solving and Critical Thought," and "Personal Development and Interpersonal Skills."

Today was the final deadline for filing evaluations. Martin took a deep breath and picked up his pen.

W alter Faber, professor of German at Lindhurst College in suburban Chicago, grimaced as he recalled German 204, "Post-
War German Culture":

It felt like one protracted struggle with an upsetting
student, but actually the whole course was frustrating. It was my first year back after a sabbatical—I had
really enjoyed the world of ideas and a fruitful research trip to a German archive. At the beginning of
the second semester, I was still elated, full of energy
and enthusiasm for my subject. But German 204
brought me down to earth.

The Instructor

Walter Faber, 42, was a tenured associate professor of German who had steadily climbed the academic ladder at Lindhurst since receiving his Ph.D.
from the University of Michigan. He and his wife,
Elizabeth, an associate professor of art history at the
University of Chicago, lived near the campus with
their two young daughters. Tall and fair-haired,
Walter tended to conservative dress, and colleagues
described him with phrases like "a man of propri-
ety" and "a gentleman."

Although born and raised in Minnesota, Walter
was often mistaken for a German. His accent was
native because he had learned the language at the
age of twelve, when his family had spent a year in
Austria. Altogether, Walter had spent four years
studying in Germany. He tried to return at least
every other year for research and to keep his language skills sharp.

An innovative teacher, Walter frequently incor-
porated music, historical and sociological texts, and
films into his syllabi, and he had co-taught interdis-
ciplinary courses with colleagues in the music department. His departmental colleagues, by contrast,
tended to assign purely literary readings, like novels, plays, and poems. Students often wrote Walter
letters of appreciation, and many kept in touch after
graduation.

The Institution

Red brick buildings, neatly landscaped grounds,
and a solid endowment did little to dispel Lindhurst
College's "preppy" reputation. Founded in the
1880s by Protestant ministers, the college was now
extremely heterogeneous. Thirty percent of its 2,300
students were on scholarships. There was an ag-

CASE

Herr Faber's New Course (A)

Harvard Graduate School of Education Case No. 4.

gressive and successful minority recruitment program. And a high proportion of the students were foreign nationals. Still, the Lindhurst culture retained traces of old-fashioned formality. Students addressed their instructors as Mr., Mrs., or Ms. while instructors called students by their first names. "On campus," Walter commented, "I answer to the name Herr Faber."

The Lindhurst faculty numbered about 180, with 60 percent tenured. The departments of Economics, Political Science, Art History, and Music had particularly strong reputations. Among the foreign languages, Spanish and French enjoyed the greatest popularity, but the institution also offered Italian, Chinese, Japanese, Hebrew, and Russian.

Walter commented:

German is a small department: four tenured professors and one part-time instructor. Compared to Economics—which numbers about 20—we're minuscule. And size is power in a college like Lindhurst. If you have high course enrollments, the administration gives you money to hire extra teachers. But if your enrollments decline too far, the administration takes your teaching positions away and awards them to the bigger departments. This process directly threatens instructors like me. If a department loses a position—say, when a senior colleague retires—the remaining instructors have to absorb that colleague's work load. This might mean that they have to spend less time teaching what they like, and more time on administrative duties. As it happens, one of my colleagues is very near retirement, so this is on all our minds.

Walter went on:

In our department, we have even more reason to scratch our heads over student enrollments, particularly in upper-level courses that require a real command of the German language. Most Lindhurst students find German more difficult than, say, French or Spanish. So beyond the first- and second-year courses, our enrollments really thin out. The magic number is five. If you get fewer than that, the Dean cancels your course.

The Course

Walter described his new course:

I designed German 204 to appeal to students who

spoke German, were interested in the country, and welcomed real intellectual stimulation. The inspiration came from a course that a former student of mine took during her junior year abroad at the University of Munich. Its materials included excerpts from political speeches, cabaret songs, radio broadcasts, editorials, book reviews, all sorts of things. I thought they looked fantastic, so I adapted the course design to our milieu by choosing simpler texts and writing up lots of explanatory materials. I kept the mixed-media format and assigned audiotapes, videotapes, journal entries—one written in Berlin in 1945—and a famous essay by some psychologists about the German "inability to mourn." My colleagues couldn't really help me develop the course because none of them had ever taught anything like it.

The class met from 2:50 to 4 P.M. on Tuesdays and Thursdays in a typical ivy-covered building with long echoing corridors. The classroom had been renovated in the 1960s, with fluorescent lights, linoleum, a big chalkboard, and movable desk chairs with orange plastic seats. I pulled these into a circle, with my desk chair in front of the big teacher's desk so that I sat, as it were, at the head of the circle, near the board. I wanted to be able to jump up to write vocabulary words or key ideas as they came up in discussion.

He continued his description:

The format was eclectic. Sometimes I would open with a fifteen-minute mini-lecture. Sometimes I would begin directly with discussion questions. Sometimes a student would open with a report, which we would then discuss. I always came prepared with questions to help the students grapple with the material and to encourage their advanced conversational skills. I tried to strike a balance between letting them speak spontaneously and interrupting to correct their grammar.

The students wrote one brief paper each week in German. I treated the papers as drafts, corrected them, and handed them back to be rewritten for a grade. The whole course took place in German, naturally.

Walter had spent a lot of time preparing German 204:

I worked like a madman during the fall semester—reading a lot of work by German intellectuals on issues of German culture and identity. And I put a lot of energy into remedying my own lack of familiarity

with East Germany. After about a hundred hours of
background reading in the library, I put eight books—
three in English, as I recall—on reserve as recommended reading.

He reported a final detail of his course description,
"The course catalog said, 'prerequisite: seven se-
mesters of German or permission of the instructor.'
The last phrase proved to be my undoing."

The Students

Walter talked about his students:

Most of the students in the course—eight at first,
three more than the minimum—ranged from adequately to extremely well prepared. There was a student from Togo, whose first language was French.
She had studied at a Goethe Institute [a language and
culture institute for foreigners run by the German
government]. And three of the students were bilingual Americans, each with one German parent. Two
of the group had studied in Germany and done a lot
of course work at Lindhurst. Three were freshmen;
four were seniors. All of them had taken the equivalent of seven semesters of German, either in college
or preparatory school.

And then there was my problem student—a junior
named Elaine Rogers. Her father was an American
business executive and her mother was Mexican. The
family had lived mainly in Spanish-speaking countries
in South and Central America while Elaine was growing up. All her schooling had been in Spanish, and
her English was far from idiomatic. But her German
was much, much worse. In a small department,
teachers hear each other's complaints about students,
and *everybody* who taught Elaine had a tale of woe
about her. Plenty of Spanish-speaking students have
done well in our courses, so that wasn't the problem.
Some teachers said she simply didn't seem to do the
work. She wasn't a German major—I think she was
planning to go into business or banking—but some
German-speaker in her background had become a role
model for her, and she kept turning up in our department.

At the beginning of a term, my office door is always open. I saw Elaine in the outer room of the department, where students often wait to see instructors, and I thought, 'Oh, oh, some teacher's in
trouble.' I didn't think she was coming to see me because I was teaching an advanced course. She
couldn't possibly have the prerequisites.

Walter continued:

My heart sank when she walked straight into my
office and said, "Hello, Herr Faber, I would like your
permission to take German 204." Instead of saying,
"Absolutely not," or something else final, I cleared
my throat. "I don't think you've had seven semesters
of German, have you?" "Only three. But I am so interested in this course," she answered. "Well, that's
always nice to hear, but the readings are very difficult
and there's a lot of writing and conversation." "I can
do all this," she replied.

"I don't remember seeing you around the department last semester. Did you take German?," I asked. I
knew she hadn't taken any since last year. Elaine responded, "No, no. I realize my grammar is a small bit
rusted. But I will get it back." "I don't want you to
put yourself in a difficult position," I said. "The other
students have more German than you do *and* they're
in practice because they've all been taking German
right along." "No problem. I will just study more.
This subject is my interest," she insisted. "I'll have to
think this over," I said. "Can you come back tomorrow?"

Walter went on,

The moment Elaine left the department, I rushed
into my colleague Ursula Wagener's office. Ursula
had taught Elaine two years earlier. She groaned at
the mention of her name. "Oh, God, she's back? I
don't know what her problem is, but she certainly
didn't perform in my class. I think I gave her a C−."
"So should I bar her from 204?," I asked. Ursula
paused, then said, "Hey, I'm not going to tell you to
keep a student out of an upper-level course. We're
breaking our backs to get students *into* them. If she's
so enthusiastic, maybe she'll apply herself this time."
I left Ursula's office undecided. Elaine came back to
see me the next day.

"Well, I've decided to let you try," I said. "But you
really have to study more. You'll never get through
this course without that extra effort you spoke of."
Elaine nodded. "You won't be disappointed," she
said.

The First Day

Walter remembered the first class meeting of this
course:

Lindhurst courses usually open with directions: so

many papers, so many pages, no extensions. I did that sort of introduction and then asked questions like, "What else are you studying this semester?" and "What do you want to get from this course?" I wanted their answers and also to get them conversing and thinking in German. Their German was fine, but they didn't have much to say about the course yet—after all, it had just begun. I told them my goals for them: that they would expand their vocabularies sufficiently to discuss contemporary cultural and political issues, that they would learn facts about German history and society, and that they would be able to speak and write cogently about some dominant neuroses in this complicated, troubling culture.

He smiled and said,

> After that, I launched into my brilliant opening. I played the German national anthem—what Americans call "Deutschland, Deutschland, über Alles"—and distributed copies of the original and revised, postwar versions of the words. Then I played Haydn's String Quartet opus 76, which is the music of the national anthem, and a wonderful contemporary cabaret ballad about the singer's affection for the music and horror at its hideous historical associations. As I recall, my presentation went right up to the end of the hour—music always takes a lot of time.

To Mid-Semester

Walter proceeded to talk about the progress of the class,

> After a couple of weeks, I realized that Elaine had attended only about half of our meetings and turned in fewer than half of the written assignments. The other students were attending regularly and turning in all their work. But the course was going only medium well. I felt disappointed with the students' conceptual grasp of the texts.
>
> Somewhere around the third week, I got so worried that I turned one of our class meetings into an open gripe session. I surprised the class by asking them to tell me—in English—how they felt about the course and what they might like to change. Elaine was absent that day, as I recall. The seven others asked me to integrate the background readings into my lectures—I had just put them on reserve in the library as background readings. They also wanted weekly tests on vocabulary and the readings, and more films.
>
> It took me hours to redesign the rest of the course.

I found some films, wrote out new vocabulary lists, wrote exercises using the library materials, and made up content quizzes. But I think it paid off, at least a bit, because the core group of students liked the course better after that, and their participation got somewhat livelier.

About a week later, however, one of the strongest students—a near-native speaker of German—dropped 204 to switch into a course in the French department. Lindhurst students have a month to change courses and still get credit. After that, they can drop a course even on the day of the final exam but they lose the credit. I didn't speak to the student who switched out of 204, but I supposed that she had just gotten bored. Maybe my 'mid-course correction' made things too easy for her. Or maybe she just hated 204. At any rate, her departure cast a chill over the remaining students' participation. I worked harder and harder to spark discussions. It was difficult to get more than one-line answers. My frustrated efforts to give them a forum in which to show what they were learning began to suggest that maybe they weren't learning, despite their efforts and mine. Their halting contributions seemed to betray a silent struggle with the material.

My frustration grew as the weeks wore on. Twice a week I faced a semicircle of stony faces. And they looked pained when I asked a question like, "Let's summarize some main points in the first paragraph of this speech. Lee, could you help us—maybe you marked some places in your text?" Lee would hem and haw. The others would look away—embarrassed for Lee, I assume, and thankful that I hadn't called on them.

But Elaine didn't share much of their discomfort: she was absent half the time. Nor did she come to my office. When she showed up in class, her attempts to speak German made the other students roll their eyes. She was the only one in the class who would lapse into English. Sometimes she lapsed into Spanish. Once I asked her about a text describing a German woman: "What is the reaction of this woman to the government of her country?" Elaine said, in German, "His reaction—." I corrected, *Her* reaction." She repeated, "Her reaction were—." I corrected, "Was." "Was," she said, and then switched to English: "I can't go on." She didn't look upset, but the others did. By now they were really squirming, and any conversational momentum we had previously gathered had dissipated. I was grinding my teeth, and so were they.

Herr Faber Writes a Note

Finally, Walter took some action. He explained,

Shortly before mid-semester—around the sixth week—I sent Elaine a note:

'You have missed seven out of thirteen classes in German 204, failed to hand in five assignments, and earned such poor grades to date that I am advising you to drop the course. I wish you success in your future studies.

Sincerely, Walter Faber'

That brought her to my office. "I don't see the problem with my participation," she said. My jaw dropped. "I beg your pardon—you're absent half the time, you don't turn in the work, you barely speak in discussions, and your language competency doesn't begin to meet the course standards. Those are the problems." "They don't matter. I'm doing as well in this course as I want to. I have no intention of dropping it. Maybe you are not satisfied with my work, but I have my own standards," she replied.

I was dumbfounded. In my years at Lindhurst I'd only asked one or two students to drop courses before, but they had complied immediately and that had been that. Elaine's open defiance not only shocked me, it intensified my feeling that she didn't belong in this course. My silent reaction to her words was something like, "Why you little brat. . . ."

Walter went on,

I answered Elaine in measured tones: "The course standards are objective—students attend class meetings, do the reading, turn in written work on time, prepare reports, and join the discussions with language competency equivalent to seven semesters of German. All the others are meeting those standards. If you expect credit, so must you." I thought this recital would drive her right out of the course. I was

wrong. Elaine answered, "All right. I will do all that, and make up the work I owe you, Herr Faber."

Walter frowned,

I was furious. I wanted her to leave the course, but I had somehow given her a way to hang on by her fingernails. Dealing with this total non-starter didn't appeal to me one bit—it was hard enough to redesign the course for the others, who were working very hard. But there it was: if Elaine could somehow manage to turn in all the work, I didn't know how to justify depriving her of course credit. I said, "Then you'll bring in all the written work you've missed *and* come prepared to speak in class next Tuesday?" "Yes, all of that. I will be there," she said.

He shook his head,

Of course she didn't come on Tuesday. She showed up on Thursday though, and I asked her to discuss a particularly difficult point in the reading assignment. She simply said—in English—"I haven't read it." The others looked pained but said nothing. That was the lowest of all the low points in the course.

Wrapping up his rueful look back at German 204, Walter noted,

At Lindhurst there's a form called the "Instructor's Drop," which you can use to expel a student from a course at any point during the semester. You just send the form to the Registrar, and the student gets no credit for the course. I sent Elaine a note threatening to use this form to expel her from 204 because her dismal performance couldn't possibly earn course credit. I told her that she would be able to spare herself a "no credit" on her permanent record if she dropped the course herself. I really thought this note would make her drop the course to save face.

READING

Angels on a Pin

ALEXANDER CALANDRA

HBS Case No. 8-384-180.

Some time ago, I received a call from a colleague who asked if I would be the referee on the grading of an examination question. He was about to give a student a zero for his answer to a physics question, while the student claimed he should receive a perfect score and would if the system were not set up against the student. The instructor and the student agreed to submit this to an impartial arbiter, and I was selected.

I went to my colleague's office and read the examination question: "Show how it is possible to determine the height of a tall building with the aid of a barometer."

The student answered, "Take the barometer to the top of the building. Attach a long rope to it, lower the barometer to the street, and then bring it up, measuring the length of the rope. The length of the rope is the height of the building."

I pointed out that the student really had a strong case for full credit, since he had answered the question completely and correctly. On the other hand, if full credit were given, it could well contribute to a high grade for the student in his physics course. A high grade is supposed to certify competence in physics, but the answer did not confirm this. I suggested that the student have another try at answering the question. I was not surprised that my colleague agreed, but I was surprised that the student did.

I gave the student six minutes to answer the question, with the warning that his answer should show some knowledge of physics. At the end of five minutes, he had not written anything. I asked if he wished to give up, but he said no. He had many answers to this problem; he was just thinking of the best one. I excused myself for interrupting him, and asked him to please go on. In the next minute, he dashed off his answer which read:

"Take the barometer to the top of the building, and lean over the edge of the roof. Drop the barometer, timing its fall with a stopwatch. Then using the formula $S = \frac{1}{2} att$. calculate the height of the building."

At this point, I asked my colleague if he would give up. He conceded, and gave the student almost full credit.

In leaving my colleague's office, I recalled that the student had said he had other answers to the problem, so I asked him what they were. "Oh yes," said the student. "There are many ways of getting the height of a tall building with the aid of a barometer. For example, you could take the barometer out on a sunny day and measure the height of the barometer, the length of its shadow, and the length of the shadow of the building, and by the use of the simple proportion, determine the height of the building."

"Fine," I said. "And the others?"

"Yes." said the student. "There is a very basic measurement method that you will like. In this method, you take the barometer and begin to walk up the stairs. As you climb the stairs, you mark off the length of the barometer along the wall. You then count the number of marks, and this will give you the height of the building in barometer units. A very direct method."

"Of course, if you want a more sophisticated method, you can tie the barometer to the end of a string, swing it on a pendulum, and determine the value of the 'g' at the street level and at the top of the building. From the difference between the two values of 'g' the height of the building can, in principle, be calculated."

Finally, he concluded, there are many other ways of solving the problem. "Probably the best," he said, "is to take the barometer to the basement and knock on the superintendent's door. When the superintendent answers you speak to him as follows: 'Mr. Superintendent, here I have a fine barometer, if you will tell me the height of the building, I will give you this barometer.'"

At this point, I asked the student if he really did not know the conventional answer to this question. He admitted that he did, but said that he was fed up with the high school and college instructors trying to teach him how to think, to use the "scientific method," and to explore the deep inner logic of the subject in a pedantic way, as often done in the new mathematics, rather than teaching him the structure of the subject. With this in mind, I decided to revive scholasticism as an academic lark and challenge the Sputnik-panicked classrooms of America.

READING

Should I Fail Her?

MAX L. WATERS

HBS Case No. 8-389-121.

Midterm and the spring sun were renewing life as evidenced by the lawn sitting and class skipping. Missing again was the student occupying the third seat in the row by the window. She was an attractive student who performed well—at least until the sun seemed to be more inviting than class.

My first reaction after her several absences was that she was another Southern Californian, who after finding her man, was just going to ride out the term and then get married. However, because her performance was so good before the recent changes, I decided to visit with her before sending in a failing grade. Opportunity came unexpectedly when she passed by the open door as I was reviewing a set of papers.

Instead of the temptation to accuse and allow the usual justification speech, I asked, "You were doing so well until a few weeks ago. What has happened?"

Hesitantly, she recounted the events of the semester. "I wrote to a friend for the entire two years he was on a mission for the Church. He came home and didn't even call or come to see me. I've heard that he is engaged."

"That would upset me," I thought.

She went on. "And we have just learned that my brother has to get married." Her voice broke.

My thoughts turned into feelings. With her family's religious background, that must hurt.

Then Jill concluded, "Mom is in the hospital 50 miles north of here and I sit with her each night." Then she said more softly, "She has terminal cancer—and the doctor says she can't live more than a few weeks. Dad can't come and help because he has to take care of my younger brothers and sisters and the farm in Nevada."

Suddenly the class contract seemed totally irrelevant. I was grateful that I had spent some time with Jill before administering what at first seemed to be well-deserved justice. I closed my office at the end of that day thinking, "For the rest of my life, people will always be more important than programs—or schedules."

That was 22 years ago. I can still feel the emotions of that day and what Jill did to change my entire academic experience.

W alt Holland leaned back in his chair, re-
thinking the disturbing conversation he
had just had with a first-year student.
After listening to Tina Patride for almost two hours,
Walt was still uncertain just what had happened.
Clearly, however, Tina believed she had been sex-
ually harassed by one of his colleagues. "I'm angry,"
she had said. "Very angry! Mr. Spilletti is constantly
staring at me—at my chest. He makes me feel very
uncomfortable. I just had to talk with someone!"

Walt's reflective moment was interrupted by Jean
Chang, a longtime colleague and trusted advisor.
"What's wrong?" she asked. "You look like you've
received a distressing note from your editor!"

"Come in, Jean," he said. "I need your counsel
on this one. It involves an alleged case of sexual
harassment. But is it? The whole situation is murky
and I frankly don't know what to do."

The Institution/The Course

Midwest College (MWC), a prestigious institution
of higher learning, prided itself on its Composition
Seminar (CS), an intense year-long course for first-
year students. CS had a more favorable teacher/
student ratio (1:15) than many first-year classes at
MWC and students could elect to take sections ca-
tering to different disciplines—e.g., science writing,
fiction writing, or history writing. Classes generally
met twice a week in a small seminar room. Students
were encouraged to interact both with the instructor
and with one another. In addition, students generally met regularly with their instructors during office hours, usually about six times a term.

Walt Holland

Walt Holland, the head of the CS program, had
previously taught literature and writing at West
Coast University, where he had received his Ph.D.
Since sections were small he was responsible for
recruiting and supervising almost 30 instructors.
Some of the teachers were employed on a part-time
basis; one or two were advanced doctoral students;
others were writers or journalists who taught on the
side.

For the most part Walt had been very pleased
with the instructional staff. He had let a few ineffective teachers go over the years, but he generally
felt very positive about the caliber of his associates.
Instructors were offered contracts on a yearly re-
newable basis, and he had a great deal of flexibility
in dealing with marginal staff.

CASE

The Thin Grey Line (A)

*This case was written by **Marina McCarthy,** in collabora-
tion with **C. Roland Christensen** for the Developing
Discussion Leadership Skills and Teaching by the Case
Method seminars.*

HBS Case No. 9-387-201.

What Now?

Walt described his dilemma to Jean Chang. Tina Patrides had come to him on the advice of Nancy Dienstag, the coordinator of Women's Affairs. The student complained that her CS instructor stared at her, making her feel very uncomfortable.

> Tina is demanding *action*. Though she is not accusing Bob Spilletti of sexual harassment per se, she wants me to *do something*. She said that she had had a similar experience before. I didn't ask her what specifically happened, but when I tried to understand the when and where, she just said, "high school."
>
> According to Tina, Bob frequently talks a great deal about sexuality in class. She also feels this to be inappropriate. You know, Jean, Tina is a *very* thin young woman—beyond slender . . . extremely thin. Quite frankly, she has a boyish figure.

Walt leaned forward and continued.

> Last year, another student, Sandra Harris, came to see me. I still have the impression that she really dropped by because I was an old family friend. I had known her since she was a little girl—her parents and I were very close. I used to stay with them whenever I was in town on business.
>
> About halfway into our conversation, Sandra brought up her CS instructor—Bob Spilletti. She said how uncomfortable she felt around him. According to Sandra, he praised her excessively in class. She thought he called on her too frequently and gave her too much attention, both during class and afterward. She didn't like being singled out. Sandra said he "set me up on a pedestal." Apparently in a student conference he told her she should put more sex in her fiction. All this made Sandra feel *very* ill at ease. She was not angry, though, just uncomfortable. She told me she was getting an A in the class but she didn't feel as though she really deserved it. She felt it was a gift—not earned.
>
> Sandra seemed troubled when she brought this up with me. She knew I was Bob's supervisor. I recall asking Sandra a whole series of questions—not unlike those I asked Tina this afternoon: "Did he touch you? Did he ask you to meet with him?" I wanted to know if he ever hinted at a date. "Did he ask to see you at night? Did he ask you to go for a drink? Alcohol? Coffee?" Bob apparently never made such advances to either Sandra or Tina.

> Though Sandra said others in the class were aware of her situation, she asked me not to mention any of this to Bob while she was still a student in his class. I did, however, speak with Nancy Dienstag, with whom I had suggested Sandra visit after she and I talked. Nancy and I went over the information Sandra had given us and concluded that there were no grounds for charging Bob with sexual harassment. Since I have always had the highest professional and personal opinion of Nancy, I felt confident about our conclusions.
>
> The upshot was that we couldn't find anything conclusive. There may have been "vibrations" in the class, but that was not enough.
>
> I did speak with Bob after the semester was over, without using Sandra's name. Bob was shocked and said he had no idea that he was offending anyone. He was distraught that he had caused a student any pain or discomfort.

Walt abruptly stood up, stuffed his hands in his pockets, and began to pace:

> I think Tina's situation warrants a different approach, however. She is angry and is demanding action. *"Do something!"* she said, "I feel like he is going to rip off my blouse!"
>
> Jean, I told her that she needed to be more specific. I told her I couldn't lynch someone because they made someone feel uncomfortable. We have a procedure on sexual harassment here at MWC but not a policy per se. Anyway, Tina is not lodging an official complaint . . . she is complaining but not accusing—there is a distinction.
>
> Bob is a clumsy person. His wife is the first to admit this. He has an awkward manner and an awful sense of timing. The other day he barged in on a conference I was having with another instructor who was visibly distraught. He was very insensitive—no, clumsy. His style alienates the other faculty members. Colleagues make themselves scarce when he appears in the corridors or the xerox room.
>
> I'm troubled about what to do. Bob is a good writer. He's smart and loves to work with students on their writing. His comments to students are exceptional and his evaluations show that he is very helpful to his students. He has not abused his privilege of choosing his own course materials. I have examined the texts he has chosen for the class and they are standard literature anthologies.
>
> What do you think, Jean?

Sylvia Nevins, associate professor of history at Farwestern College of the Liberal Arts, was living in New York for a year to research a new book. She had never taught night school before, but when an offer came from Downtown University Extension School to teach a course called "The American Family, An Historical Overview," she accepted, delighted with the extra income. The course met once a week from 8 to 10 P.M. She dedicated part of the time to students' "family history" reports, part to lectures, and part to discussions in which she encouraged them to participate as much as possible. The material, as indicated in the course description, included issues like sex, birth control, abortion, and other matters central to the family. She had taught the course before and assumed that, like her, the students found these matters worthy of serious intellectual consideration. Sylvia had, however, never taught such a heterogeneous group: young people pursuing B.A. degrees at night while working days, and retirees—some quite elderly—taking courses for intellectual stimulation.

Sylvia tried to strike a note of informality as she began the course. She invited students to participate—even to interrupt her lectures, if they had questions or comments. Then she embarked on her typical pattern: an hour's lecture, then a break, then a class discussion. The first three meetings went well. On the fourth evening, however, Sylvia encountered a surprise. She had spent the first half of the class lecturing on the practical implications of Victorian notions of "true womanhood" and "manliness," using one historian's concept of "The Politics of Impregnation" as a central theme. She wrote the term on the board, with bibliography, and referred to it throughout her lecture. As the discussion began, one older man, who generally kept silent, raised his hand. "Yes?" Sylvia said, expectantly. "Professor Nevins," he said, in a strained voice. "I really do have to tell you I find that term very offensive!" He was glaring. Sylvia thought: Ouch! What he really means is that he finds *me* offensive for discussing impregnation in class!

Sylvia was shocked and a bit insulted. Given the subject matter of the course, what had he expected: no references to sexuality? Was he objecting to the term *impregnation* or to the fact that she, a woman, referred to sex in public? She wanted to deflect his comment somehow. But how? Ask the whole group if they were offended? Apologize and be done with it? Thank him for his forthrightness?

Sylvia stood there, perplexed.

CASE

A Night School Episode (A)

Abby Hansen *wrote this case from material submitted by* ***Elaine Tyler May*** *for the Developing Discussion Leadership Skills and the Teaching by the Case Method seminars. Data were furnished by the involved participants. All names and some peripheral facts have been disguised.*

HBS Case No. 9-384-085.

233

CASE

The Blooper of the Week (A)

I can't believe this. How humiliated she must feel!" Heart pounding, mouth feeling as dry as cotton, Nancy O'Donnell looked from the red-faced student in the pit of the amphitheater to the students directly across the room, and tried to think above the uproar in Section C. Jen Jacobsen had just been singled out by her classmates to receive the "blooper of the week" award. She was clearly surprised to have "won," and seemed mortified by the attention. "I should do something," thought Nancy. "But what?"

The session had started out innocently enough. It was an early fall tradition at Heritage Graduate School of Management: on the second Friday of the school year, as many section faculty as possible joined their first-year students for general introductions. Some instructors, including Nancy, had not yet met the students because their courses were scheduled to begin later in the year.

Nancy was eager to get started on her second year of teaching at Heritage, and like the other professors she had arrived a few minutes early for the meeting with Section C. Faculty Chairman Peter Koslowski had motioned for them to come into the amphitheater classroom while the section proceeded with its routine announcements. They crossed the room to take the few available seats, most of which were in the lowermost tier—the "worm deck," as it was known among students who generally preferred to sit higher and farther away from the central pit. Nancy was at the far right, in the third chair from the aisle closest to the instructor's table in the pit. Now she felt trapped there as she witnessed Jen Jacobsen's ordeal.

Teaching at Heritage

Just a few minutes earlier, crossing the campus to greet these ninety-five new first-year students, Nancy had been struck by the high spirits and nervous energy that filled the air at the start of every academic year. This year, she realized, she did not quite share the sense of newness and uncertainty the way she had in her earliest days on Heritage's O.B. (Organizational Behavior) faculty.

Beyond learning about the Heritage "culture," she had also learned a great deal about herself during her first year of classroom experience. The oldest of six children, Nancy had attended college at a women's college in her Indiana home town. After one year, she transferred to Indiana University to complete a B.A. in English.

Colleen Kaftan prepared this case under the supervision of Louis B. Barnes as the basis for class discussion rather than to illustrate either effective or ineffective handling of an administrative situation.

HBS Case No. 9-390-143.

After graduating, Nancy spent two years in Afghanistan as a Peace Corps volunteer—perhaps the strongest of her experiences in learning to respect another culture while also sensing its need to adapt to modern realities. She returned to the U.S. to study for a Master's in Communication at Penn State, then went on to the University of Michigan for a doctorate in Organizational Behavior.

Not until her last year in the Ph.D. program did she consider teaching at a business school. On the urging of her thesis chairman, she interviewed for an Organizational Behavior position that was open at Heritage. She sat in on a first-year class (taught by a woman who would be a colleague in the O.B. area) and was impressed by the intelligence and energy of the participants in the classroom.

Heritage's reputation as a "male bastion" was slowly giving way. The institution had made a public commitment to include more females and minorities in the corps of professors and students. By the time Nancy arrived, there were thirty women (only one of whom had tenure) on the 120-member faculty, and 27% of the students were women. Minorities and foreign students also added to the diversity on campus.

Nancy found it exhilarating to be part of Heritage while its dominant culture was evolving to meet changes in its social environment. She was pleased at the thought of joining a school that was a powerful force in shaping values among students—over 800 of them a year—whose influence would be widely felt throughout their active careers. As such, it was a good place for a faculty member to make a difference in the way people thought about and behaved in their relationships at work. Nancy aspired to be that sort of faculty member—synthesizing what was valuable in Heritage's established culture with new facets that would produce the more flexible, adaptive managers that she felt the future required.

Section Dynamics

Section C looked as diverse as last year's groups had been, Nancy reflected as she studied the faces in the classroom. One advantage of Heritage's specially constructed classrooms was that every student could see every other—an element many considered critical to the school's famous case method of teaching. The classroom was a section's home throughout the first year. (Already, Nancy noticed, Section

C had adorned the carpeted walls with colorful notices and messages.)

Case discussions were often lively, provocative, and engaging. Heritage's faculty valued class participation and worked hard at orchestrating the wide range of voices striving to be heard at every session (students' grades depended significantly on their contributions in class). As a result, even the shyest participants usually learned to express themselves in fairly large groups of people. Even the brashest learned something about listening.

Students found the process both intimidating and exhilarating. Heritage's high admissions standards and the professional track records of its graduates lent a certain mystique—some called it arrogance—to the Heritage student body. In the first part of the year, it was not unusual for new students to feel challenged (and, in many cases, frightened) as they never had been before.

Many informal practices, some spontaneous and others passed down from year to year, helped the sections weather the early tensions and anxieties. Regular meetings, social events, the election of section officers, and the open, confrontive class discussions themselves all tended to break down (and—on occasion—to create) barriers among students. Each section invariably developed its unique "personality" as its members progressed together through these activities and slogged through their daily work load. Sectionmates often became friends for life. At a minimum, they all knew each other well by the end of their first year.

Section C had probably already begun the long, slow process of forging its own norms. Today's meeting would extend the fledgling sense of community to include almost all of the ten faculty members assigned to teach the group at some point during the year. Three of the professors had already met the section the previous week. Some would not start their courses until much later in the year. Others, like Nancy, would hold their first class sessions the following week. On this Friday afternoon, though, the entire group was to meet together for the first time.

The Faculty Group

Despite her relative newness at Heritage, Nancy was by no means the most junior member of Section C's faculty for the year. Half the teaching group was new to Heritage; none of the others had tenure. Of the other two women, Marilyn Adams (the only other Peace Corps veteran on Heritage's faculty, Nancy had heard) had just been promoted to Associate Professor in Production Management. Ellen Franklin, the third woman in the group, was a first-year lecturer in Management Communication.

Faculty Chairman Peter Koslowski, an associate professor of Marketing, had also chaired one of the sections Nancy taught the previous year. She admired his approach to developing a section and, as he put it, "stretching them to new heights." Unlike some of his colleagues, Peter believed that faculty should be encouraging rather than taking a "boot camp" approach with the students. He did not adhere to the philosophy Nancy had heard other professors espouse, that Heritage should simulate "jungle-like" experiences to prepare students for the jungle of business practices. Nancy found Peter extraordinarily competent as a teacher and section chair, and she looked forward to working with him again this year.

The section faculty had met briefly just before the beginning of the semester to discuss the norms they wanted to encourage for the students. They quickly settled on questions such as tardiness, absence, preparation, and classroom demeanor. In general, they agreed that students should adopt the rules and conventions (other than dress, which was casual for students) that would be appropriate for a business meeting. Peter Koslowski had already communicated this policy at the section's very first meeting.

Nancy's First Year

In Nancy's first year at Heritage, she had been assigned to teach two sections, as were most faculty members in the first-year curriculum. The O.B. course ran from September through late November, and Nancy had been able to reflect on her first teaching experience during the spring and summer.

The two sections had been very different in character, as colleagues had suggested they would be even though the administration tried to assemble a representative mix in every section. One group seemed slow and hesitant, requiring a great effort on Nancy's part to push the discussion along. The other was surprisingly agile and forceful in its ability to move forward with minimal guidance from Nancy. In fact, Nancy remembered, one student from the second group had come in to suggest she work them even harder:

He asked me if I wanted some feedback about how the section was going. Of course I said yes. He told me that most of the people in the section liked the O.B. class, but that they wanted to get more out of it. He said there was so much brainpower in that classroom that, when they got to working well together, they were like a fine-tuned Ferrari. And he said I was driving them like a Ford. At first I was embarrassed, but then I realized he was exactly right. It was my first year and they *were* very smart. I was thrilled to have that energy in the classroom, but I was still learning about the school, the course, the case method and everything else. So I guess I erred on the side of conservatism.

Another comment came from a female student after the course had ended, and caused Nancy great concern:

She said the women from the "Ferrari" section were very upset with me—they thought I showed favoritism to the men, that I didn't call on women as much, and that's why none of them got the highest grades on the course. I was shocked, and even more so when I looked up the record and found that she was right about the grade distribution. I hadn't paid any attention to gender when I submitted the grades, so I checked on my other section's records to see if I'd been harder on women there too. I was relieved to see that the women were proportionately represented across the grading curve there. But I did spend a lot of time during the spring and summer thinking about that Ferrari section.

Students at Heritage had the opportunity to evaluate all their professors, and Nancy had received ratings that were significantly lower from her "Ferrari" section than from her other first-year group. A senior colleague explained that such a disparity sometimes meant the faculty member had done something during the semester to interfere with the section's idea of how it should be functioning. Nancy wondered if her "something" was the time she had pointed out, at the end of one class, that part of that day's progress had resulted from somebody's breaking the section's own agreed-upon norms by interrupting the discussion without raising his hand:

I suggested that the students could consider how to be more creative about making important contributions without being too bound up by rules. I told them I thought their norms were generally constructive but could sometimes lead to less desirable outcomes.

Nancy had also been surprised—as were many of her colleagues from the academic disciplines—by the implicit norms about sexual humor among the Heritage student body. Catcalls to "welcome" female visitors, snide remarks about "aggressive women" when the protagonist of a case was female, jokes and innuendos were, Nancy suspected, vestiges from the days when there were only male students. Nancy thought she was not alone in feeling that such behavior might prevent women from acting as equal partners in the educational endeavor—just as racist, ethnic, and homophobic humor blocked other groups from full and open participation.

Section C's Meeting

Peter Koslowski, having finished teaching Section C's last class of the week, stepped aside as a student came down into the pit to make announcements. By the time Nancy and the other faculty members came in, the section had reached its final agenda item: the blooper of the week award.

Almost every section used some form of an award ritual as a humorous way of learning openness, humility, and willingness to laugh at one's most embarrassing (or, in rare cases, one's most triumphant) moments. Some sections issued regular "shark awards" for the most aggressive comment made in the classroom. Others gave "hog awards" for students who talked too much. (A colleague had recently told Nancy about a student who called winning the "hog award" one of the most embarrassing but valuable lessons he had learned during his whole first year.)

The case method lent itself well to such awards. Students made, and heard, hundreds of comments during the week. Some were cogent and insightful: at best, a student's observation or recommendation could move the whole class to a higher level of understanding. At worst, a comment could force the section off on a useless tangent or cause the discussion to fall flat. Somewhere in between were the "bloopers," often hilarious, usually unintentionally so.

Most of Heritage's faculty considered humor an important element in the classroom. Sometimes a

"blooper" could imprint a lesson indelibly on students' minds. Sometimes it could derail an important discussion. Sometimes it simply served as "comic relief"—an outlet for the nervous energy in the room.

The Blooper

"We have three more candidates," the student M.C. was saying. "First, Jamie Bartlett in the Best Excuse category. Jamie brought 'My little brother ate my homework' into the New Age with his 'I ran all the numbers on my computer, but the printer's broken.'"

Groans and catcalls came from all over the room. Jamie stood up in the sky deck and bowed, apparently rather pleased at the attention. Nancy had the impression that Jamie and the M.C. were already fairly close friends.

"Next we have an old favorite: 'Fire the incompetent fool.' But Giancarlo Danzi says it with such a nice Italian accent! And how was he supposed to know that this incompetent fool went on to become chairman of the company?"

More hoots and scattered applause. Giancarlo, looking somewhat embarrassed, raised his hand from one of the seats near the door.

"Last, but certainly not least, Jen Jacobsen's *extremely* personal marketing strategy: 'I would bend over *backwards* to satisfy a customer . . .'" As if to exaggerate the innuendo, he leaned back until he was nearly lying on the instructor's table, grinning at Jen the whole time.

Sheer bedlam engulfed Section C. Students were pounding on their tables, stamping their feet, whistling, and chanting, "Jen! Jen! Jen!" There was clearly no real contest for this week's blooper award.

Feeling the blood rush to her own cheeks, Nancy watched a scarlet-faced Jen Jacobsen make her way to the pit. A tall, long-haired young woman from the Midwest, Jen was one of two Section C students Nancy had met at a reception for incoming women students the previous spring. Nancy flashed back on that meeting and remembered finding Jen bright, likable, and happy to be coming to Heritage. Jen expressed some concern that her background in advertising might not have developed strong quantitative skills. Nancy recalled responding with encouragement, and the two agreed that Heritage was an exciting place to be.

Dressed in the usual student garb—jeans, a loose

sweater, and sneakers—Jen somehow looked younger than she had in the business suit she had worn to the reception. Seeing her in this predicament reminded Nancy of other amorphous impressions and feelings from their meeting: How would this sweet-faced student with the girlish voice be treated at Heritage? How would she react? Would she have the self-confidence to weather what many considered to be a very tough experience? Would her appearance and her openness set her up for the kind of challenges to her competence that some women found difficult to overcome?

As Jen came down for her award, Nancy watched the reactions of the students in the opposite wing. Some were obviously very engaged in the moment. Most of the men looked relaxed and exuberant. Several women did too, but not all. Some looked uneasy, as did many of the foreign students. The man in the seat closest to Jen's had an expression of wry disbelief on his face. Was he disgusted? Embarrassed? If so, by what? The faculty presence? Would he have joined in more enthusiastically if only the students had been there?

"You know what the prize is," shouted the announcer over the din. "You get Section C's beautiful travelling trophy for a whole week." He handed her a pewter loving cup, and then pulled out a large bottle of beer.

"But first,"—splashing the beer into the cup—"you have to chug this beer." Gamely, still blushing, Jen raised the cup to her mouth. But the crowd had other ideas.

"On the desk! On the desk!" Hands clapped and feet stomped in rhythm with the chant. Nancy saw Jen hesitate as she looked over towards the desk.

Nancy felt terrible. For a split second she considered walking out. But the door was on the opposite side of the pit. There was no way to leave without walking right past Jen. The section would surely develop all sorts of interpretations and reactions to such a visible move.

"They don't know me," Nancy thought. "If I express my disapproval in some way, will they rush to judgment, write me off as a fanatic, and therefore shut off all the learnings I am so eager to lead them toward?"

Nancy glanced around to see what the other two women professors were doing. Marilyn Adams was behind her, so far to the right that Nancy couldn't see her face. Ellen Franklin sat directly across the pit from Nancy, gazing back at her from the worm deck there.

P eter Morgan couldn't understand why Cindy
had raised her hand and held it up throughout his summary of the case.

> I was confused as to why she had had her arm up
> during my entire summary. That was rude enough,
> but now she has escalated things. She is demanding
> what amounts to a public apology—for what?

The Institution

The Graduate School of Management at Northcentral University was a large, well-respected institution that aimed to prepare students for leadership
positions in industry. It emphasized practice rather
than theory, relying primarily on the case method
of instruction. Classes were conducted in amphitheater-shaped classrooms designed to encourage
student-to-student dialogue. In their first year, all
MBA students took a set program of courses. Students were organized into sections, each of which
took all its classes together, in its own classroom.
In their second year, students could take electives,
and no longer had all their classes with the same
section.

The Instructor

Although Peter Morgan studied chemical engineering as an undergraduate, he concentrated in
sociology when he pursued a doctorate at Columbia
University. He was an imposing person with an
authoritative voice, a prominent, thick, greying
moustache, wire-rimmed glasses, and was always
impeccably dressed. Peter described himself to the
researcher as a "basically serious person with a
clever sense of humor."

> Academically, I have a strong intellectual interest in
> organizations and strategic planning.
>
> Personally, I have a peculiar sense of humor that
> sometimes is on the edge of being caustic, though I
> usually don't intend it to be that way. When students
> write comments at the end of the semester, about
> 80% say that I'm "really funny and clever," but a
> number chastise me for taking verbal advantage of
> people. I've never been able to remember jokes.
> There are some people who have a file system of
> great jokes, not me, however. I am verbally very
> quick, though sometimes I put my foot in my mouth.
> But I've learned, even though sometimes I still let
> myself go.

CASE

Peter Morgan (A)

Marina McCarthy prepared this case under the supervision of *C. Roland Christensen* for the Developing Discussion Leadership Skills and Teaching by the Case Method
seminars. All names and some peripheral details have been
disguised.

HBS Case No. 9-389-089.

I was a child of the '60s—a pony-tailed hippie, a flower child, the whole bit. I must admit, however, that I don't get fired up and indignant over social and political issues any more. I'm married, have four kids, and basically have a different perspective—perhaps due to the passage of time, perhaps due to my academic interests in organizations and change.

Peter had originally been invited to teach in Northcentral's Human Relations department. After teaching a required first-year course for several years, he was asked to teach a section of the only required (nonelective) second-year course, Strategy and Policy (S and P). Peter appreciated this opportunity to change departments since his intellectual interest was in the relationship between strategy, structure, and systems in organizations. "Teaching S and P was a perfect opportunity to try my hand at integrating theory and practice," he observed.

The Course

Strategy and Policy was an integrative course that built on Northcentral's required first-year curriculum. It presupposed a basic understanding of marketing, finance and control, production, and organizational behavior. In practice, however, Peter explained, "the course has a bit of an identity crisis."

I guess there has been a wide range of faculty opinions as to what constitutes an integrative experience. The curriculum varies almost from section to section —each syllabus is different, reflecting instructors' favorite cases.

S and P sections were not the same as those of the first year; that is, students were reshuffled. As always, Northcentral's policy was to maintain a balanced composition of students in each section: about 25% women and 15% minority and international students.

The Section

Peter taught back-to-back S and P classes from 8:30 to 9:50 and from 10:00 to 11:20 A.M. He had difficulty "getting a handle on the personality" of his second section, he recalled:

The class wasn't bad, yet it wasn't great. S and P was the section's last class for the morning. Most of the students had had an earlier class, but they were all free after mine until 1:30 P.M.

S and P clearly wasn't as important to them as their electives. They were just going through the motions. I found myself unconsciously apologizing to them for having to take another compulsory course after a full year of lockstep requirements: "You know this is really important material and you *should* be taking it— even though you don't want to be here." Not many of the students in the class knew each other, and they didn't make much of an effort to get to know one another. My impression is that they hung out with students they knew from the previous year.

My relationship with the section could be described as somewhat distant and removed. We weren't having a great time together, yet we weren't having a terrible time either. Some of them were good sports about a course that they basically thought was a waste of time.

The Hewlett-Packard Paper

At the beginning of S and P, students were assigned a paper to be handed in at the end of September. They were asked to analyze a one-page description of a problem involving Hewlett-Packard Company and to develop a plan of action. "We began this way in an attempt to get the students to see the challenges of the course concepts," Peter explained. "We thought the paper would get the class enthusiastic. It's discouraging to have students sit in your class not wanting to be there."

The Incident, Day One:

One of the two major cases discussed in week ten of the course was *Werner Apparel*, about a Swiss clothing conglomerate. Peter described the case, which had been written in the mid-1970s:

The protagonist in the case was Fritz Bol, a Swiss national. In *Werner Apparel (A)*, Fritz was asked to investigate the company's Northern European market and to concentrate on the Stockholm branch office. While he was there, the home office wired him and told him to plan on staying for several more weeks. Fritz was disappointed. He wanted to get back to corporate headquarters in Zurich, where the action was. He was worried he'd lose visibility.

At that point in the class discussion I saw a chance to lighten things up. With a straight face, but the most subtle of smirks I said, "I can think of a lot of reasons why a person would want to spend a lot of time in Sweden!"

There were a lot of giggles and tittering. The group took whatever they wanted from my comment; but I clearly intended to make a sexual innuendo. The class was of an age to understand the "anything goes" association with Sweden. I plunged in to liven things up. It worked!

That was pretty much the end of the class. We had analyzed the (A) case to my satisfaction, and I don't remember much more discussion after that. Perhaps I made some comments as I handed out the (B) case for the next day but otherwise class was over.

Immediately after class three students came up to my desk—a bit odd because second-year MBAs don't tend to hang around and talk with the professor, especially in a required course. The most vocal of the three students had gone to the University of Wisconsin. The other two had completed their undergraduate work at Wheaton and Bennington. The University of Wisconsin woman was the most aggressive, and politically liberal. On the basis of class participation at that stage, she seemed the smartest of the three. She was clearly the spokesperson for the group. The woman from Wheaton was hard to describe. The Bennington woman was quieter and acted more feminine. Whereas most students tended to prefer the unisex uniform of jeans and a sweater, she was more Bohemian in her style of dress. She often wore floppy hats, even in class.

The woman from Wisconsin said they were unhappy about the case because they thought it was sexist. One of their complaints was that women were referred to as girls throughout the case—for example, "pattern girls." I could understand their concerns but reminded them that the case has been written in the 1970s. "The kind of language that was being used at the time the case was written may be inappropriate now, but does one keep rewriting teaching materials to suit contemporary values?"

Another objection had to do with a reference to the protagonist's wife packing his suitcase in preparation for his trip to Sweden. They didn't like seeing her portrayed as the "little lady" who stayed at home. Again I agreed this might be disturbing, but pointed out that in fact that's what his wife did—pack his suitcase. "What about case-writing integrity?" I also noted that the case alternately used "ladies," "girls," *and* "women" when describing its new lines of skirts and dresses.

The three women elaborated on their concerns. They emphasized that the role of women in Werner Apparel was particularly irritating since women are rarely mentioned in MBA cases. Again I said they had a legitimate point, but I explained how difficult it was to get cases with women protagonists.

Throughout the discussion, the woman from Wisconsin was doing most of the talking. The other two were providing moral support. The woman from Bennington was adding to the discussion here and there, but the woman from Wheaton said nothing. The tone of our conversation was fairly civil and friendly, certainly not hostile.

As the conversation continued, I began to gather my papers and moved from behind my desk around to the left. I put my papers in my teaching folder, and we started to work our way out of the classroom and down the hall. We parted ways at my office door. It all ended on a neutral, pleasant note.

In retrospect they probably were looking for a hip young professor who was ready to take up a cause. That's not me. I tend to look at such things from a more institutional point of view. Students just don't understand how a university works, what its long-term needs are. They are not very sympathetic to things such as the promotion process.

I'll bet they thought I was intellectualizing the whole issue. They probably left thinking I was not firmly committed to the feminist movement. Reading between the lines, they may have heard, "You don't know how complicated life is, girls!"

After Lunch

Later the same day, Cindy, the student from Wheaton, knocked on my office door and asked if I "had a minute."

Cindy was about 26 or 27 years old, and had been an investment banker. She began by expressing her concern about her overdue Hewlett-Packard paper—it still wasn't in. I had written her a note. I assumed from the way our conversation was going that her late paper was the purpose of her visit.

Cindy had previously told me that she was ill. She certainly didn't look healthy. Her class participation was quite low, perhaps partly because of her health. Clearly, she didn't stand out as one of the better students in the section.

I sensed that Cindy was uptight that afternoon. We talked about the paper for about five minutes, and I tried to allay her concerns. She really did not look well.

Then Cindy said, "You know there is another

thing. I would like to say once again that the case today offended me. I appreciated hashing out some of the stuff after class, but one of the reasons I'm so sensitive is that I had a finance professor last year who was just horrible. He was very sexist. He upset me a lot so I'm extremely sensitive to these issues."

I replied that it was unfortunate that he had antagonized her, but also observed that perhaps she was a bit sensitive now. I said I was sorry, but reiterated that, since *Werner Apparel* had been written way back in the '70s, I didn't think this was such a big deal.

Our whole conversation was sort of low-key. It was pleasant, no tension, no strain. Now understand that we're not the best of friends—I'm not one of her favorite professors and she's not one of my favorite students. I did learn, however, that she was interested in doing doctoral work. Then she added, "By the way, I just wanted to say that the sexist comment you made in class didn't make matters any better."

I was a bit taken aback. "What sexist comment?"

She told me that she found my remark about staying on an extra few weeks in Sweden offensive. I said, "Well, I'm sorry you feel that way. I don't see that as a sexist comment. One could say that it is a comment that had sexual innuendo in it. That may be offensive to you, but I don't see it as a sexist comment per se."

Cindy didn't argue with that. She said, "Well, O.K., fine." We chatted a little bit more. It was a civil, reasonable conversation. That was it—end of discussion. She didn't push me further. Her whole visit couldn't have lasted more than 15–20 minutes.

Day Two

Peter had carefully prepared for the *Werner Apparel (B)* and *(C)* discussion, paying special attention as usual to his closing comments.

I devote a great deal of thought to my summaries. They give me the opportunity to show the class that there is content to this material. I like to discuss concepts and theories about organizations. I like to draw relationships among variables. I feel certain things need to be covered.

I want students to find class enjoyable and get something out of it. Prepared summary comments are important to me. It's sort of my own intellectual agenda in which I communicate that there is more content—even theory—to this course, despite what they believe! I always give them my opinions, my prepared summaries, and try to link them to the class discussion.

I get wrapped up in delivering my message, which is probably more interesting to me than to them. In their reviews, only a small percentage of students said they found my prepared comments at the end of class very useful in pulling things together. Even if they don't think it's super interesting, I do. They can give me five minutes at the end of class!

The discussion that day was so-so. It's rough to analyze in great detail what Fritz did to turn the branch around. Everyone talked about how well he had done. That's not academically stimulating.

In academia things are so compartmentalized. You have OB people worrying about structure, and Control people worrying about systems, and S and P people talking about strategy. The reality is that all these things are managed simultaneously in organizations. *Werner Apparel* is a terrific case with all the integration a Northcentral case should have. There are markets, people, competition, structure, systems.

The Last Few Minutes

Peter described the class discussion of *Werner Apparel (B)* and *(C)* as uneventful.

It was very clinical, just a rehash of what Fritz did to turn the outfit around. Fritz was a superstar and it's all a success story. In neither the case nor the class discussion was there was any mention of girls or wives packing suitcases. Everything was straightforward, and the protagonist ends up helping the home office turn a healthy profit.

When I noticed that we had around five minutes of class time left, I cleared my throat and gave typical signals that I was beginning my summary. The section settled down—except for Cindy, who raised her arm in a "stiff" salute manner. She kept it up as I continued to give my closing comments.

I tried to ignore Cindy's hand, but it was not easy. As I gave my rap about structure and systems and processes, I could still see her out of the corner of my eye. It was quite a struggle to present the general theoretical issues of the case and to link them to things that people said in the discussion. Sections tend to blur when you have back-to-back classes. I was struggling to remember who said what while trying to ignore Cindy's ramrod arm. She had a very determined look. I continued my remarks, telling the class what happened at Werner in the '80s, and then went on to the theoretical points: "These are the major points I think we should be thinking about . . ."

I had a lot on my mind. I also wanted to announce what we were going to do the next day. Yet I was confused. Cindy hadn't talked in class more than once all year. I hadn't a clue as to what this was all about, and I found her behavior very rude.

When I had almost finished what I wanted to say, I noticed the women from Wisconsin and Bennington both motioning toward Cindy, signaling that I should call on her!

It was then about 11:19. I said, "I'd like to talk about what we'll be doing tomorrow, but before we do that, apparently Cindy has something to say." I wasn't too concerned about what she was going to say, but rather that I had only one minute left. The tone of my comment was mildly ironic, slightly dry. Cindy sat forward in her seat. She had a very determined, prim, almost steely look on her face. She said: "As a woman of Swedish descent I would just like to say how offended I was by the comment you made in class yesterday suggesting that the protagonist should stay in Sweden because he would get easy sex or free sex from Swedish women. I came by your office yesterday afternoon to try to discuss this with you and since I was not able to get any satisfaction from you there, I want to bring it up in a public forum. I hope everybody in the section will support me on this issue."

I was in shock, astonished! I felt I had been sandbagged, and now we were out of time! I thought Cindy's presentation was *so* different from what actually happened the day before in my office. Cindy's version made it sound as if she came to my office and said, Professor Morgan, I'm a Swedish woman, and I resented your implication that Swedish women will go to bed with whoever happens to be in town at the time. I want an apology. Her tone further implied that I said something like, Tough luck, sweetie. I'm not going to apologize.

I was angry. Here she had come to my office because she hadn't finished her HP paper, compounded with her continuing story about being really sick. I had to listen to her complain about her first-year Finance professor—which I didn't have anything to do with—and then, only in a tangential way at the end of the discussion does she bring up my remark, which I explained was not sexist.

I had told Cindy that at worst my remark had a sexual innuendo . . . and that was in the eye of the beholder. I fully intended to imply that things were pretty free and easy in Sweden, but it's free and easy for both men and women . . . with drugs as well as sex.

We had had the discussion; she took my explanation and said it was fine. I thought it was a closed book. I hadn't given any of this a moment's thought until now. Could she have gone home and thought some more about it and gotten angry at me? How did she decide I was slandering the virtue of Swedish women? This was really an extraordinary misrepresentation of what happened in my office.

I stood there oblivious to the rest of the class. I was internally focused, trying to process this whole thing at full RPM capacity. I did notice a deathly quiet in the room.

CASE

"Am I Going to Have to Do This by Myself?": Diversity and the Discussion Teacher (A)

*This case was researched and written by **Abby Hansen** for the Developing Discussion Leadership Skills and Teaching by the Case Method seminars. The case is based on data contributed by the involved participants; all names, places, and some peripheral facts have been disguised.*

Harvard Graduate School of Education Case No. 5.

Marian Blanchard, a new assistant professor at Farwestern University Graduate School of Education, recalled a discussion class in her "Sociolinguistics and Education" course that made a root canal operation seem easy by comparison.

Marian defined Sociolinguistics as "research on the way language helps define people's social identities." What better resource for teaching such material than an international, polyglot student group? And that's just what Marian had: 20 men and 25 women ranging in age from their twenties to their fifties, from virtually every continent on the globe. The seven Japanese students in the group seemed to be a particularly promising source of linguistic examples for discussion; many scholarly articles in the field focused on prominent examples from the Japanese language.

"Unfortunately," Marian recalled, "what appeared to be the greatest potential resource for this course—diversity—turned out to be just the opposite."

The Instructor

A slim, dark-haired 40-year-old, Marian wore casual skirts and blouses and simple jewelry when she taught. She lived with her husband—an environmental economist—and two children in an 'ordinary' neighborhood near the Farwestern campus. Marian had two Farwestern degrees: a recent Ph.D. in Developmental Psychology from the School of Education and a B.A. in History, which she had received in the 1970s. She recalled, "In the late 1960s and early 1970s, the Civil Rights movement, violence in the cities, the Vietnam War, and Farwestern's treatment of tenants in university-owned real estate were formative issues for me and my friends. I helped organize the Students Alliance for Social Justice, which held a sit-in in the Dean's office to protest against campus military recruiting. In the summers, I baby-sat in a nearby housing project so that tenants could attend welfare rights meetings."

After college, Marian taught English for five years in public high schools in Oakland, California. Then she returned to Farwestern for a Ph.D. Her research topic, "The Development of Literacy in Low-Income Adolescents," grew out of her high school teaching.

Farwestern School of Education

The Ed School bustled with students of every age and description from all over the world. Its administrative structure was complex: a mixture of academic departments, institutes, committees, subcommittees, and certificate-granting programs. Culturally, it resembled a mini-UN. The sidewalks around its central building, a high-rise from the 1970s, boasted a higher concentration of saris, turbans, and dashikis than most other enclaves of the Farwestern campus. Other academic institutions preached the ideal of cultural diversity, but the Ed School practiced it.

The Course

According to Marian, the course applied sociolinguistic concepts to education, and Marian had a free hand in its design. She explained, "I tried to include writings about the home languages of the class participants, and to accommodate their interests as well as some of my own. I also tried to address the interests of the youngest master's degree candidates—kids right out of U.S. colleges who were going to teach in inner-city high schools the next semester."

She described the course as "a banquet of theories and examples," and noted that some of the subtopics—"like 'Black English in the Classroom,' 'Bilingual Education,' and the social implications of male and female speech patterns in a variety of cultures"—inspired intense feelings and even open arguments among some of the students.

The Student Group

The subject matter of this course—comparative language and culture—attracted an even more highly diverse student population than the normal yeasty Ed School mix. "There was no common denominator in this group. About 45 percent of the students were probably less comfortable speaking English than some other language. About 25 percent were doctoral candidates, and the rest were in a whole range of different master's programs. Some of the students were taking the course simply out of personal interest. Others needed it for degree credit or professional preparation. In the doctoral group, many students were working on sociolinguistics, developmental psychology, and language-learning. Many of the students from Asia, Africa, and Latin America were already professors of language or sociology. Some were government administrators responsible for education or language policy [political decisions about the language of instruction]."

Marian recalled, "45 students were crammed into a discussion classroom meant to hold 35. The students represented about eight main language groups, every social class imaginable, ages from twenty to over fifty, career interests from 'don't know yet' to 'Assistant Minister of Education,' and academic ranks from undergraduate to senior professor. This was a really mixed bag."

Marian described a few of the students to suggest the ethnic richness of the group, "Ana Luisa Guillem, a 45-year-old Brazilian professor getting a Ph.D. in sociology; Oscar Barreda, a 29-year-old Yale graduate in the master's in teaching program, who was 'sick of teaching rich white preppies,' and wanted to be a bilingual education teacher in Harlem, where he had grown up; Sara Stowell, a Liberian high school teacher getting a master's degree; Ashok Veendayan, a college administrator from New Delhi getting a Ph.D. in developmental psychology; Vonelle Dugan, an elementary school principal from Ohio getting a Ph.D. in language policy; Marielena Suarez, a Mexican-American from Texas who had studied psychology at Princeton and now wanted a Ph.D. in developmental psychology; Sese Bakema, a professor of Linguistics from Nairobi, doing postdoctoral research on an exchange fellowship; and Peace Corps returnee Lee Ann Carver, who had spent five years in Senegal."

It was difficult to generalize about these students, even by home language. There were Portuguese-speakers from Brazil and Portugal; Spanish-speakers from Ecuador, Mexico, Puerto Rico, Spain, and New York City; trilingual women from Switzerland and the Netherlands; Chinese-speakers from Taiwan, Sichuan, and Hong Kong; Arabic-speakers from North Africa and several Middle Eastern countries, French-speakers from Canada, France, and Zaire; and English-speakers from Kenya, Liberia, South Africa, and Australia. Even the American-born English-speakers included people of different cultural and educational backgrounds and widely diverse career goals. The only cohesive unit among the language groups was the seven Japanese students. They often sat together, and none of them tended to speak in class without formal preparation.

Marian had spent a lot of time discussing these students' work with them outside of the class. She described them, "Junko Takeda was a 28-year-old woman who worked for a Japanese company in employee relations teaching English. She was getting a master's in bilingual education. Kiyoko Yamaguchi was a married woman here with her husband, a professor of engineering who was visiting Farwestern on a fellowship. She was getting a master's in teaching and wanted to supervise teachers of second-language pedagogy. Mitsue Harada was a 32-year-old single English teacher here for five years. She was getting a Ph.D. in sociology. The men were Akira Kawahara, a 30-year-old English teacher from a Japanese college, studying for an M.A. Akira had just married an American woman. And Yoshio Kono, who taught Japanese at Farwestern and was getting a certificate in bilingual education, which carries little weight here, but means something in Japan. The youngest Japanese student, Matsuo Kurokawa, was a 25-year-old English teacher, at Farwestern to improve his English and get a master's in teaching. And the highest-status man—the oldest and most advanced in his career—was my dissertation advisee Nobuo Shimoda. Nobuo, in his early forties, was in the United States with his wife and two teenage kids. He was a college teacher getting his doctorate in educational sociology. He had lived in New York and California for about five years and his English was excellent. I had spent a lot of time talking with Nobuo, and we had often discussed the subject of 'women's language' in Japanese."

Marian observed, "The U.S. and Canadian students argued the most, and the most enthusiastically. Their whole education had prepared them to speak in academic settings. The European-trained students would join in too, but not as often. So would the Africans. But the Asians rarely did."

How Marian Taught This Group

Acutely aware of the differences among her students' accustomed participation styles and the wide range of proficiency with spoken English in the class, Marian attempted to accommodate this diversity with a varied teaching format. Sometimes—at the request of those less fluent in English—she opened class with a mini-lecture summarizing points from the assigned readings and explaining some of the more technical terms. In discussions, she paid attention to the frequency with which people contributed and the topics that either attracted or discouraged them. To "make things more equal" for those with less confidence with spoken English—who "often spent a whole night struggling

through an article that took an English-speaker an hour to read"—Marian sometimes showed research videotapes in class and asked students to comment extemporaneously. Another technique—particularly useful with the Japanese students, she found— was to warn students about some upcoming discussion topic about a week in advance, and ask them to prepare a contribution that they might read in class.

But the core of this course was group discussion, which Marian thought important to foster self-confidence, independent thought, and cooperative learning. Discussions often focused on linguistic examples from the languages represented in the class. Marian would call for examples from the class, recognize students' raised hands, and write their contributions on the board as accurately as she could. She explained, "I wrote key words in context to help those less proficient with spoken English."

A Particularly Frustrating Discussion

About three weeks into the fall semester, in mid-October, the assigned topic was the special characteristics of "women's language," which Marian described as, "of high interest to everyone in the class." Marian recalled, "The assigned articles gave examples from all sorts of languages, but Japanese is particularly rich in words, phrases, and formulations of politeness that only women use, so the literature frequently cites examples from Japanese. The language is changing rapidly, as more women are working outside the home. This means that they may speak differently with friends and business associates, for example, so it's particularly interesting to look at the social implications. Obviously the Japanese students were an ideal resource for this discussion. Not only were they all from Japan, but Kiyoko, Mitsue, and Junko were writing short course papers on women's language, and Nobuo was doing a dissertation chapter on the subject."

Marian set the scene: "We were in a small, U-shaped amphitheater-style classroom with a flat area in the focal point of the U and a blackboard on the wall. I would stand in front of the board or pace around, and turn to write comments on the board when students contributed them. The room was completely full. Students tended to sit with others who shared their home language. The European and English-speaking students clustered towards the front of the U, and the Japanese students usu-

Section 6. The Case Discussion Leader in Action:
Operational Challenges and Opportunities

CASE
"Am I Going to Have to Do This by Myself?": Diversity
and the Discussion Teacher

ally sat together in the top row. That's where they were that day.

"After I introduced the topic of women's speech, I asked for examples from the students' home languages and cultures. As I expected, the Westerners got into the discussion first. They were experienced at speaking English, and their academic cultures included discussion teaching. Each time I got a contribution, I turned my back to the group and wrote on the blackboard as fast as I could. I wrote small and tried to get all the words onto the board.

"I was getting lots of contributions from the Europeans and Americans. Things like 'women speak in softer voices' or 'women use more endearments.' I knew it would take some work to get the Japanese students into this. In Japan, students don't tend to talk in class. They typically just listen and take notes. But the Japanese students were the best resource for this topic, and I knew that they were prepared.

"I said something like, 'Okay, some more examples about women and language?' Then I looked up at that back row—particularly at Nobuo, my advisee. Not more than two days before this class, in a conversation in my office, he had mentioned several examples of women's language in Japanese.

Sara Blaine, a Liberian student, said, 'In Liberia, people say that women talk too much.'

"I wrote, 'Liberia—people say women talk too much,' and said, 'Anyone else?'

"Martha Sweeney, a Peace Corps returnee, said, 'In Zaire, you hear people say that women should be modest in how they use language.'

"I wrote, 'Zaire—women should use language modestly.'

"Kim Peters, a young American B.A. from Cornell, said, 'In the United States, people say that women never get to the point.'

"I kept writing. Ana Luisa, a Portuguese Ph.D. candidate in educational sociology, said, 'In Portuguese, women use lots of diminutive, like teeny tiny little bit.'

"I wrote, 'Portuguese, diminutive—teeny tiny little bit.'

"More contributions came. The two Chinese speakers, Mei Lieu, an older, married woman from Taiwan, and Hsiu Lin, a young, single English teacher from Hong Kong, gave me examples. By this time I was writing in a big cloud of chalk dust and still waiting for the Japanese students. Not one of them had made eye contact with me.

"The rest of the class kept feeding me material. I wrote fast and kept turning my head to look back at the group. They were pretty animated, particularly the Americans. There was laughter among speakers of various languages. I could hear a few little side discussions. I assumed that people were mentioning little phrases women used in their languages and laughing about them.

"The silence of the Japanese-speakers didn't surprise me. I had expected to get some contributions easily and have to work harder for others. I turned and said, 'How about some of the other languages and cultures that are represented in this room?' This time I really stared at the Japanese students, and especially at Nobuo.

"Isabel DeArruiz, a Spanish woman, said, 'In Spain, it is considered okay for a man to be assertive, but if a woman is assertive they call her a 'bitch.'

"I wrote, 'Spain—okay for men to be assertive; if women are, they are called 'bitch.'

"Alicia, a Dutch woman, said, 'In my culture, women are more careful about how they construct sentences.'

"I jotted down, 'Dutch—women more careful with sentence construction.'

"Then I got some comments from other Peace Corps returnees who had been in sub-Saharan Africa. Once, when I turned around, I managed to make eye contact with Nobuo. He knew my agenda. We had spoken about this topic. He looked down. I turned back to the board and looked at what I had.

"I said, 'These examples are great. Let's keep going.' Nobody said anything. I faced the class: 'One of the things we talked about last week was the difference in men's and women's politeness strategies in Japanese. Can someone with firsthand experience with the Japanese language please give us some examples?'

"I thought this would do it. I was wrong. There was silence for a good fifteen seconds—and you know how long fifteen seconds of silence can seem in a discussion class. I tried again: 'One of the things I'm thinking of is specific grammatical constructions that stereotypically only women use in Japan.' This was the subject of Nobuo's dissertation chapter. Fifteen more seconds of silence.

"Finally, Esther Proctor, an American woman who had lived in Japan, said something like, 'Japanese women have a set of syllables they use to end sentences, I think. . . .' Then Esther trailed off and looked—imploringly, I thought—at the row of Japanese students and Nobuo in particular.

"I thought, *'Nobuo, help!* Am I going to have to do this whole thing by myself?'

"I was pretty desperate by then, so I did something that I knew was a high-stakes strategy—the most directive possible—in Japan. I looked directly at some of the Japanese students and 'nominated' them—called them by name. I looked at the women and said, 'Junko, Mitsue, Kiyoko—I *know* you all have examples. Could you expand on Esther's contribution?'

"Junko and Kiyoko turned deep red. Mitsue giggled behind her hand. Nobuo finally opened his mouth and said something almost completely inaudible and elliptical. I couldn't even write it on the board.

"'Okay,' I said, 'let's take the examples we've got on the board and start looking for commonalities.' I looked around the room—not at the Japanese students this time—and people's hands started to go up.

"The discussion moved into the theoretical part and, as I had expected, the U.S. students dominated the rest of the time—about fifteen minutes. They got into a pretty aggressive women-versus-men argument about who was to blame for women's lower social status.

"The Japanese students sat silent through the rest of the hour. I can't remember ever having worked so hard for so little in a class."

O n the Friday before a local holiday, Kho Tanaka, a native Japanese, first-year MBA student at Metropolitan Graduate School of Business, opened his mailbox to find a large brown envelope. It was his Business Writing paper which the instructor had returned with grades and comments. As Kho opened the envelope, he felt relief mingled with anxiety: relief because the long weekend meant his first few days of relaxation since coming to the school, and anxiety because he understood that the feedback on the paper amounted to an evaluation of his first six weeks' performance. It had taken him nearly two full days to write the paper. Success at Metropolitan meant an enormous amount to Kho. It was his whole life at the moment. His heart beat fast as he opened the envelope.

Several notes written in red caught his eye. Worried, he flipped through the rest and found more notes and underlines. On the last page there was a short paragraph. The red ink said:

> Kho! I'm reacting strongly to your paper. It's too wordy, too long, awfully wishy-washy, and I can't understand some of your sentences. Also, your logic is cowardly. Be more assertive!

Kho felt as if he were falling. The instructor's comments had turned his world to hell. He wanted to talk to someone, but his apartment mate—a Japanese doctoral student at Metropolitan with whom he got along cordially—was out of town. He called another Japanese student, with whom he had had dinner a few times the previous August, but he was also out. Kho, feeling worse and worse, reread the awful comments and tried to encourage himself with some glasses of Scotch. Deeply depressed, he wondered:

> After this disgrace, how can I ever raise my hand and talk in class? Is it going to be possible for me to graduate from Metropolitan with my level of English?

Japanese Background

Kho Tanaka, 31 years old, married with a wife and two small daughters living in Tokyo, had never lived abroad before coming to study at Metropolitan. He had come to the U.S. alone because, as he explained:

> My first daughter goes to pre-school in Tokyo, which will end in December. I don't want to separate

CASE

Kho Tanaka

This case was written by a member of the Teaching by the Case Method Seminar for the Developing Discussion Leadership Skills Seminar. While the case is based on data supplied by Kho Tanaka, all names and some peripheral facts have been disguised.

HBS Case No. 9-381-127.

her from good friends until that time. And I thought I could study very hard without being bothered by my family. Formally, the company program that sent me here does not permit students to take their families abroad with them.

Kho had been an able rugby player at his high school and college in Japan. There his physical strength had made great contributions to the teams. He felt that training and playing games had also developed his powers of concentration so that he could devote his heart and soul toward a goal. The teamwork also helped him learn to be sensitive and pay attention to other people's opinions and feelings. Right after graduation from college, Kho joined the large Japanese metal manufacturer that was now sponsoring him at Metropolitan. When he decided to join the company he thought:

> Metal manufacturing sounds rough and unpolished. But I feel people in the company are noble-minded and have capacity. I believe I can work together with this sort of people, even if the company should face bankruptcy. I love this company.

Every year the company's Overseas Education Program (OEP) sent junior managers to graduate institutes all over the world. The program was administered by the Human Resources Management Department, which also transferred people from department to department for the purposes of education, training, and promotion. Junior members of the company perceived the OEP as part of the job rotation program. Foreign language competence was not a prerequisite for the OEP. If a candidate lacked fluency, the company sponsored his or her language training. In preparation for his studies, Kho had taken an eight-week, full-time language course at an English school in Tokyo.

Kho described his view of the OEP:

> Officially speaking, the company requires me just to develop a broad, international business sense. I applied to several well-known American business schools, but the company said nothing about my applications. They just gave me time and money for study. *Accidentally* I was accepted by Metropolitan.
>
> I have neither a formal obligation nor an explicit contract to get an MBA degree from Metropolitan. It would be no problem, from this point of view, if I failed. But, I think there is a Western cultural point of

view that honors the importance of an implied contract.

> As a Japanese, I feel pressed to complete the MBA program successfully. No one from my company has failed in an American graduate school. I don't want to be an exception. If I failed, I would wonder how to explain how I spent the money. It would shame the name of my company.

Kho's Campus Life

Before coming to Metropolitan, Kho spent a delightful summer on the campus of a university in a midwestern state studying English. He enjoyed the university's international program, made many friends, and went walking and hiking in the mountains. He learned how to order breakfast at restaurants and drove around the countryside.

In the fall, however, Kho encountered very difficult days at Metropolitan. The daily case assignments were far beyond his reading capacity. Every case had unfamiliar American products and business practices. Class discussions went too fast for him. And the performance evaluation policy of the school threatened him.

Kho's daily life had only four basic ingredients: preparing the next day's cases, attending classes, eating, and sleeping. There was no substantial difference between weekdays and weekends, although he slept a bit longer and felt free of the pressure of class participation on weekends.

Kho described how he prepared for the next day's cases:

> I simply do everything given to me, but [now] I am suspicious that you need a strategy to study. Until now I have not thought of such a strategy, neither in high school nor college. I simply did quite well by doing everything given to me.

Typically, Kho started the next day's three cases right after classes ended, at about 2:30 in the afternoon. He needed approximately two hours to read each case. After reading, he made notes for analyses and recommendations. Then he continued the analyses until he felt satisfied with his work. Usually he prepared the cases plus one or two readings for the next day's classes. It was usually between 2:00 and 3:00 in the morning before he went to bed. At the beginning of the fall semester Kho had joined an informal study group with three American sectionmates. The group met at 9:00 in the evening for one or one-and-a-half hours. Kho made maximum, but unsuccessful, efforts to finish reading the cases by 9:00 and participate in the study group. But the American sectionmates spoke too fast for him to follow their arguments, and he rarely could complete the cases in time to be prepared to struggle to keep up with them. He withdrew after three sessions and started having telephone meetings every midnight—in Japanese—with another Japanese MBA student.

In the apartment Kho and his roommate divided housekeeping tasks: the roommate cooked during the week and Kho cooked on weekends. For a while, dinnertime was a short but relaxed break when they talked about Japan and Japanese management. But the unfairness of their labor allocation gradually became a psychological burden to Kho. He felt he should cook more frequently. Finally, they agreed to eat independently. Kho's mealtimes became irregular; he simply ate sandwiches when he felt hungry.

In class he concentrated on listening. He commented:

> I can follow when the class discusses an issue of which I thought the night before. But of unanticipated issues I can sense almost nothing. After class I feel regret. In order to clarify what was discussed I often consult another Japanese student in my section whose English is far better than mine, but I feel that on my own I have learned nothing.
>
> I can participate in class three or four times a week. I feel relieved when I raise my hand and the instructor calls on me and I speak. But the general quality of comments is far beyond me. When I prepare a case at night I sometimes practice speaking a comment for the next class. But my spoken English is so poor. I am busy preparing cases, and I can go without speaking English from morning to midnight.
>
> When I meet my instructors at their offices to talk about myself, I have to try to make myself understood. Being silent in class helps nothing. They all say to me: try to speak more!

An American sectionmate sitting next to Kho commented:

> Kho adds an awful lot to the class. It's just terrific finding out about other cultures. Initially, I tried asking people to clarify some comments in the class so Kho could better understand them. At least at first, some students were using polysyllabic, multiphrasic terms to impress the rest of the class. I would only understand about half of them myself! I'm sure Kho couldn't understand any of them. I put my own comments in short-syllabled words and tried to speak clearly for Kho's benefit. But I was getting negative feedback from the class. You have to speak in two- or three-syllable words. Vocabulary is an important part of the experience here.
>
> Frequently Kho will ask me to clarify questions during class, and I'll make sure he understands the ideas, but I can remember one or two times when I said, "Kho, forget it. I'll tell you later!" I know it's rough for him, but I can't afford to miss the ideas either.

Because the Metropolitan administration strongly advised the first-year foreign students to take the special English course on Saturday mornings, Kho had to attend the class. He talked about the English course:

> Frankly speaking, the English course doesn't help me. I can understand because the instructor speaks slowly, and I know the vocabulary the instructor uses. But I can't follow the case discussions. European students speak much faster than I do. I know, also, that Saturday is the only day for the English course, but it's hard for me to take the time.

After the English class Kho prepared Business Writing home assignments, which took a long time for him—almost one full day for each short paper. When he did not have a home assignment he wrote ungraded voluntary papers both to improve his writing skills and to communicate with his instructors. He worked all the time at Metropolitan.

Kho's academic week ended Friday night and began again on Saturday morning.

Instructors' Points of View

Two instructors commented on Kho and the other foreign students in the class. Instructor *A* said:

> I'm very conscious of difficulties foreign students have here. Cases take longer to read. They don't know people here, and they don't know the culture. Many of the cases are culture-bound, which means not only is there a reading problem, but then there is

a problem of knowing what "catch-22" means, for example.

For several classes, Kho didn't say anything and didn't raise his hand. I started to get worried about it. But he began to talk to me after class and to show me his analyses. And I tried to encourage him to speak in class. Still, he was very shy about his English. I think especially that things went too quickly in the classroom for him to keep up. I guess also there is some fear that if he starts something in class I would then ask him questions and he wouldn't be able to answer. So, you know, that's a risk.

Six cases had ended before Kho spoke up—probably three weeks. That's a long time. I was very, very worried about it and noticed, as I looked at his class card, that his birthday was coming soon. I saw that it was also another student's birthday, and that day I said, in class, "Kho, Bill—Happy Birthday!" Then the class sang "Happy Birthday." I think it was kind of breaking the ice. He finally raised his hand in class, and I called on him right away.

Another instructor commented:

I have a general problem in the first year in that Japanese students coming to class are not high participants or contributors. Then, from my point of view, there is always the problem: is this a language or a cultural difficulty? It's always hard to know which of these is operating.

An instructor fears only silence from Japanese students. He or she doesn't know the cause of that silence, so the instructor will ask a question of the Japanese student. The problem is that the student may not be able to follow the instructor. Then you get into a kind of impasse where neither one can understand the other. We tend to back away. I think that is a mutually defeating kind of problem. The instructor doesn't want to embarrass the student, and the student doesn't want to be embarrassed. The problem is, how do you change that pattern?

Writing up a paper to substitute for class participation isn't the same. The rules of the school talk about bias. If you're supposed to contribute in class, and I make special circumstances, then everyone is going to have some sort of special circumstance. So, that's a hard one in the first year. In the second year you can be more flexible.

After Kho Read the Business Writing Instructor's Comments

Kho sat at his desk with his red-marked Business Writing paper staring up at him. Shame and disgrace seemed to threaten him from every page. He thought: I can't understand what is taught in class; this means I am close to failure.

It was fall in New England, but Kho had no psychological room to enjoy the beautiful foliage or the clear sky outside the apartment. His mind was dulled by accumulated fatigue, physical and mental. He had been experiencing increasing difficulty falling asleep at night, and he felt as though he couldn't keep his ears sharp enough to follow class discussion because he was so tired. The smile left his face. Kho felt depressed at the enormous effort he was making for such a poor return. Midterm exams were coming up in five weeks. Kho wondered how he would reallocate his time to make room for exam preparation. He muttered to himself:

How can I possibly accomplish my tasks here? My English is too big a handicap. I'm so tired I can hardly read my cases. This year is looking like a total failure. I fear I will disgrace my company and myself. What can I do?

Section 7. Ethical Dilemmas and the Case Discussion Process

For a moment Catharine Webb thought Charles Campbell was trying to get her attention. He and three other Jesuit brothers, whispering among themselves, had distracted her as she listened to another student seated across from them in the discussion group circle. When she turned to glance back at Charles, though, she realized he wasn't even making eye contact. His gaze fell several inches lower; following it, Catharine looked down and realized, with a shock, that she had forgotten to take off the huge "Pro-Choice" button she'd bought at a rally earlier that afternoon.

The other student, Sarah Jacobs, went on talking as Catharine raced through her feelings about having exposed a strongly held personal belief in a classroom setting. Outside of class, she was quite active in political causes—as evidenced in part by the number of bumper and window stickers displayed on her car. Nevertheless, she had long considered it important to refrain from imposing (or even stating) her political opinions while teaching, so that students could develop their own ideas without fear of evaluation from the powerful instructor's role.

Now, inadvertently, she had broken her own rule, and had done so in front of a group for whom she thought the abortion issue was likely to carry a powerful charge. Charles had noticed the button—perhaps that was why he had been so uncharacteristically quiet during the first fifteen minutes of the discussion—and had obviously pointed it out to his three closest classmates. Most likely the twelve other students had seen it too, but Catharine wasn't sure how each one of them would react.

Only three weeks into her first experience in teaching at a graduate divinity school, Catharine already felt optimistic about the fairly lively rapport that had emerged in the discussion group despite a sharp divergence in students' backgrounds and their reasons for taking the course. She considered herself a veteran teacher, but this particular situation was new for her, and the group seemed to be developing better than she had expected.

Two years earlier, she had entered the doctoral program in Religion at Pacific Memorial University after twenty years of teaching in urban high schools while running her own graphic design studio. (A severe allergy had forced her to abandon her design activities.) Until now, all her teaching assignments at Pacific Memorial had been part of the core courses for undergraduates in the Department of Religion.

CASE

Message Intended and Message Received

Colleen Kaftan prepared this case under the supervision of *Louis B. Barnes* as the basis for class discussion rather than to illustrate either effective or ineffective handling of an administrative situation.

HBS Case No. 9-391-040.

This semester, for the first time, she had agreed to lead a discussion group for the course entitled "Images as Text in the History of Christianity" at the Pacific Memorial Graduate School of Divinity. A few undergrads from the Faculty of Arts and Sciences had enrolled, but the majority of students were pursuing graduate degrees in divinity.

The distinction was an important one for Catharine: most of the undergrads in the core courses were studying religion as part of their secular education. By contrast, many Divinity School students considered religious faith and adherence to a particular denomination's beliefs as essential to their training. Catharine felt certain that Charles and his fellow Jesuits, who were guest students cross-registered at Pacific Memorial from a neighboring Catholic seminary, would hold the latter view.

Catharine herself fell clearly in the first camp. Her interest in the course material was purely historical, secular, and academic. In fact, she had nearly turned down the teaching fellowship for the course, fearing she would be unprepared to meet the needs of students seeking a religious point of view. The professor, a world-renowned scholar with a liberal feminist approach like Catharine's own, had convinced her to take the job.

Professor Andersen was widely respected for her work on the power of imagery in the history of religion. The framework for her studies—and for the course—compared "the message intended and the message received" in religious imagery. Today's discussion, for example, centered on the different "messages" assigned to stained glass windows in the Holy Roman Empire and after the Reformation. As Sarah Jacobs—a Protestant Divinity student— was pointing out, the Catholics used stained glass windows to illustrate the doctrine of the virgin birth, because the sun came through the glass images without breaking the glass.

Sarah seemed deeply engrossed in her attempt to understand a medieval craftsman's impressions on seeing the windows of Chartres Cathedral for the first time. It was the sort of discussion that Charles usually joined with enthusiasm—even dominated on occasion—taking visible pleasure in being able to explain the Catholic perspective to his classmates. Catharine thought it was also Charles' way of overcoming his fairly obvious insecurity in the academic setting. From the earliest class sessions, Catharine had sensed that Charles had a strong need for approval. Several times in class he had mentioned that

he wanted to go beyond his previous experience— "just an eighth grade teacher"—to teach at higher levels once he received his master's degree. Thinking that he might need extra encouragement, Catharine had tried to be supportive when he talked in class, even if she found his contribution somewhat marginal to the discussion.

A warm, generous 47-year-old, Catharine had a strong sense of her own value system and its place in her role as a teacher. On the one hand, she found that her own political beliefs fit fairly easily with the Divinity School's prevailing reputation as a center of radical leftist feminist activism (although in recent years there had been a noticeable upsurge in fundamentalist thought). On the other hand, as a self-proclaimed "radical relativist," Catharine thought it was important to foster an environment in which students felt free to develop their own ideas about the subject matter. So far, according to many class members she'd known over the years, she had been successful in that endeavor.

She cared deeply about students as individuals and worked hard to create an atmosphere that was open, sensitive, and respectful of all views and opinions they wanted to voice in her classroom. Having returned to graduate studies herself after a long absence from academia, she believed she understood some of the uncertainties students like Charles might be experiencing.

Years of teaching in inner city high schools had impressed upon her the enormous power teachers could wield over students, not just through the evaluation and grading process but also because of the fragile emotions inherent in the web of classroom relationships. As a result, she had developed an almost automatic tendency to support the underdog in class discussions, to help the less articulate learn to express and explore ideas.

In this situation, Catharine realized, Charles and the other Jesuits could easily represent the underdog. She thought it very likely that the Jesuits' stance on abortion would clash with the prevailing view among other section members.

Catharine could already be sure of several students' reaction to the message on her button. A few of the undergraduate women had worn similar buttons to class. One man had pasted a pro-choice bumper sticker to the backpack he carried every day. The most vocal member of the group, a 45-year-old radical feminist lesbian, often intimidated the undergrads with her forcefully expressed opinions, but on this issue Catharine was quite certain they would agree in principle if not in the intensity of their arguments.

Among the graduate students, there were a few whose opinions Catharine was unable to discern. For example, Maria Fierro, a Maryknoll nun who always sat near the four Jesuits, had been participating as actively in the discussion as usual, seemingly unfazed by Catharine's button. Was she offended? Did she agree with the "Pro-Choice" message? Sarah Jacobs and her husband—who usually sat on the other side of the circle—were both studying for the ministry with the intention of returning to their conservative (Sarah called it "austere") Protestant parish in Nova Scotia. Both were searching for ways of integrating a liberal viewpoint with the traditions of their background. How would they view Catharine's unintended personal statement?

Charles' fellow Jesuits had all spent time in Third-World ministry assignments. One of them, back in the United States only a month after several years in the Sudan, seemed to Catharine almost overwhelmed by "re-entry shock" and had rarely spoken so far in class. The two others had spent shorter periods in Central America; both were quiet but articulate when they did contribute to the discussions. Until today, Charles had been one of the most active participators in the group.

Catharine took the whispering as a sign of dismay from the Jesuits, and from Charles above all. She had only a split second to decide whether and how to respond. Should she acknowledge the button, make a comment to reassure Charles (and risk singling him out among his fellow students), perhaps make a joke about "message intended and message received?" Should she ignore Charles' reaction, try to remove the button discreetly, and let the discussion continue uninterrupted? She had not even intended to send a message. What message were the students receiving?

CASE

"When the Cat's Away" (A)

This case was developed and written by **Abby Hansen** for the Developing Discussion Leadership Skills Seminar. Data were furnished by involved participants. All names and places and some peripheral facts have been disguised. The School of Public Health gratefully acknowledges a grant from President Bok of Harvard University in his support of the case development project.

Harvard School of Public Health Case No. 3.

Professor Gregory Lewis, M.D., an epidemiologist at the Farwestern University School of Public Health, in California, sat in his office with a jazz tape playing softly in the background. "That's what I listen to while I work," he said, smiling. A lanky 50-year-old with sandy hair and a low-key demeanor, Greg wore an open-collared shirt and chino slacks. On the office wall, photographs of mothers and children in desert landscapes reflected his many years in Africa working with problems of famine and diseases of infancy. A small Ashanti statuette stood watch over the papers on his desk. In the next office, his administrative assistant, Cathy St. Claire, helped a group of graduate students pack a trunk with conference materials to take on the evening flight to Zaire. Between phone calls from Lagos and Bangkok, Greg told the researcher about a classroom incident that disturbed him greatly.

"A few years ago, when I had to leave town for a conference, I asked Sylvia Hall, a distinguished 70-year-old emeritus faculty member of this school, to be a guest speaker in a course I was giving on international health policy. Sylvia had a lot to tell this group of students: not only was she a founder of the international community health movement, but she also used to co-teach this course. She happens to come from a politically liberal South African family, to have been among the first anti-apartheid activists, and to have given up her South African citizenship for political reasons. She is also an old friend of mine, someone for whom I have enormous respect.

"When I got back to campus, Cathy told me that several students had come to the office saying that a member of the class had interrupted Sylvia so relentlessly that she couldn't finish her sentences. Finally, to top it all off, this student had said, 'I'm not going to listen to a white South African!' and walked out. It was the next to the last week of the course, and the students hadn't acted this way when I was there. I could hardly believe it.

"I asked other students in the class about the incident when I ran into them around campus, and they told the same story. I was furious. The more I think about it, the more important it seems. There was a great deal at stake."

Farwestern School of Public Health (SPH)

Established a century ago amid some of California's most beautiful countryside, Farwestern University included a well-known liberal arts college and eight graduate and professional schools. Among the SPH faculty were specialists in various branches of medicine, sociology, statistics, politics, and health policy, and its student body had a high proportion of "mid-careers" (doctors, health care administrators, social workers, lawyers, and others) as well as recent college graduates. While the majority of students returned to their own countries, some became, like Sylvia Hall, political exiles. About 40 percent of the students were women. Many came from developing countries. "Cultural diversity" was more than a slogan at the SPH.

The Course

International Health was a popular subject at the school. Greg's course, "Policy and Program Issues in International Health," tended to be heavily subscribed because it provided an introduction to this field, and also because of Greg's outstanding reputation as a researcher, practitioner, and instructor. The course met for two months in the fall semester.

This year there were 45 students—"A big group for this school," Greg commented. "I taught the course without an assistant, except Cathy. We met Tuesdays and Thursdays, from 8:30 to 10:30 A.M. for an hour lecture, followed by a half-hour discussion. Our room was the worst lecture hall at the school: Revere Auditorium." Revere was known to many as "the crypt"—a cavernous underground amphitheater, similar in style to the U.N. General Assembly auditorium, but with the eeriness that fluorescent light produces in a windowless space. Its long, curved banks of seats could hold about two hundred people. To students sitting in the back rows, a speaker on the podium could seem small and distant.

"In this class," Greg continued, "students sat in little clusters—some down front near the stage, a few in groups in the middle, several way at the back."

The Students

Greg discussed the composition of the group, "Just a few students right out of college. The rest were mid-careers, mostly seasoned health care workers: M.D.'s, nurses, social workers, people with experience in the Peace Corps or other programs. The majority were from countries other than the United States. Their median age was about 31."

He described some students in the group:

"There was Chukwuma Akeke, M.D., a 45-year-old Nigerian internist who had headed an immunization program for the districts of his country. He was here for a two-year program on a World Health Organization fellowship. Everyone in the class called him 'Chuck.' And Greta Morris, a 29-year-old American Peace Corps returnee, had been the staff assistant in a maternal and child health care project near Kinshasa in Zaire. Eva Kowalska was a 35-year-old pediatrician from Poland who had run a regional health program. Chanok Kim, a Korean woman in her thirties, was a public health nurse. Frank Liu was a Taiwanese pediatrician in his late thirties. Maria Gonzalez was about 30, an epidemiologist from Mexico specializing in AIDS. And Scott Zaleski and Jennifer Mataleno, both Americans in their early twenties, were right out of college and interested in epidemiology."

Cathy added, "That year there was a student in the program who was just a really angry person— Claude Durelle, a French doctor who had worked in Mozambique for many years. He complained constantly—we were teaching about viral diseases and he wanted to learn about parasitic diseases; faculty members weren't accessible enough; the program was too narrow. Claude attracted a little circle of protestors. One of them was an Indian student named Jay Narayan, who had been working in a clinic in Kenya."

Cathy continued, "At the beginning of the year Jay was wonderful—sweet, soft-spoken, very polite. But then Claude and his bunch of rebels brainwashed him, and he started nitpicking. He would come into the office with groundless complaints. Once he showed up without an appointment and asked to see Greg. I said that Greg wasn't in the office, and Jay complained, 'It's impossible to see professors around here!' I told him that all he had to do was schedule an appointment. But he never did. That was typical: Jay ignored the rules and griped when his behavior didn't get results."

Greg remembered Jay as "always somewhat hostile in style. There's no question that many of our students are dissatisfied with the way health care is delivered in their home countries and elsewhere, and they feel that changes should be made. But the kind of anger that Jay expressed was unusual."

How the Class Went Before This Incident

"At our first meeting in September," Greg recalled, "I introduced myself, gave my office hours, and said, 'This is a lecture and discussion course. We're here to discuss the practice of international public health. We're not looking for right answers; we're here to explore various approaches to problems.' I went on to say that a third of the grade would be for class participation and that I would call on people even if they hadn't asked to participate if I really wanted to hear from them.

"At that meeting, I handed out and collected brief Student Profile Forms that just asked for degree program, department, country, profession, experience, and area of interest. I used this information to make up teams for group projects. It was my goal to vary the groups by country of origin, experience, gender, age, and the like so that people could add to one another's experiences. I didn't want a whole team of anthropologists, for example. And the forms also gave me ideas about whose experience could be useful when we discussed specific topics.

"In the six weeks we had had before I left town, this class was lively. People contributed their experiences. There's no way you can understand what it's like to work in the deserts of Ethiopia in a famine unless you've done it. Since most of the people in this group had done this sort of thing, we were able to speak on a fairly advanced level.

"People raised their hands to be recognized, and I called on them by name or by nodding at them. I made sure that they addressed each other's points. I'm very good at running a class, moving discussion around, making sure everybody contributes and no one dominates. People are free to disagree, but I don't let anyone overrun the class. When people had said their piece in this class, I would respond with, 'That's an interesting idea—why don't we go with that for a while?' Then I would turn to a classmate and say, 'Maria, how does this fit with what you said earlier today?,' or 'Eva, you directed a similar program in Poland. What was your experience?'"

Sylvia Hall's Guest Speech

Greg recalled, "I called Sylvia at the beginning of the semester and asked if she could come in and tell this class about her career in community health care: particularly her experience in South Africa's rural areas among people suffering the effects of apartheid. I told her the date and time—it was a Thursday, in the next to the last week of the course. I was delighted when she accepted my invitation. She had co-taught this course and guest-lectured in

it before. Part of the material dealt with historical changes in international health, and she had lived these changes. She was a wonderful resource. I reminded her of the format: about 55 minutes of lecture, a brief break, and a half-hour discussion. It was all familiar; she had done it before.

"On the Tuesday before her visit, I told the class that I would have to be away for one meeting and that Sylvia Hall would be the guest speaker. I said that she was a distinguished emeritus faculty member of this institution, originally from South Africa, who had been a founder of the international community health movement. I mentioned that she had left South Africa because of her opposition to apartheid. As it happens, she knew Nelson Mandela, had been an ANC supporter years before it became chic, and belonged to a family that has been very active in the anti-apartheid movement. But I didn't go into this much detail."

Cathy added, "Sylvia is about 5'6", gray-haired, very distinguished looking. She always wears slacks. There's nothing grandmotherly about her—she looks like someone who's been around. She has a slight accent, and speaks slowly, succinctly, and clearly. Her stories about South Africa are wonderful; you could listen to her all afternoon."

Greg said, "I left town on Wednesday, confident that Sylvia's lecture would go well. But when I got back to the school on Friday, Cathy said that several students had dropped by and mentioned that Jay Narayan had interrupted Sylvia so continually that she hadn't been able to give her talk."

Cathy commented, "Chuck Akeke stopped by the office on Thursday morning, right after Sylvia's lecture. He asked for an appointment with Greg to talk about something in the course. He didn't refer to the lecture. I asked how it had gone, and he said, 'Didn't anyone mention what happened to Sylvia Hall?' I said, 'No, I haven't heard anything.' Chuck said, 'Jay was very disruptive. He argued with everything she said and twisted her points. He really didn't let her talk. I felt horrible.' I asked, 'Did she say something that was offensive to Jay?' Chuck said, 'No. We couldn't understand what his problem was. He was creating an argument. He was terribly rude.'"

A few other students drifted into Cathy's office and told similar stories about the lecture. Maria Gonzalez said, "Jay didn't raise his hand, he just made rude comments and didn't let Sylvia Hall finish her sentences. It was terrible."

Cathy commented, "I knew that Claude Durelle was in that class and I asked people whether he had said anything during Sylvia's lecture. I got the impression that he had backed Jay up on some of his points, but when he saw that Jay was going after Sylvia hammer and tongs, he just sat back and let it happen. Jay had been the real problem. Greta came into my office Friday morning and I asked her about the lecture. She told the story in even more detail. Not only did Jay interrupt Sylvia and prevent her from answering his interruptions, he finally said, 'This is useless. I'm not going to listen to a white South African!' and walked out. At that point several others, including an African-American, none of whom had spoken, walked out with Jay."

Greg added, "I heard Cathy's reports and got a few more from students whom I questioned when I met them in the hall. As I pieced it together, it seemed that there had been dead silence for a few minutes after Jay left. Then Sylvia told the class that she understood people's hatred of the South African regime—she herself had suffered from it—but this class was to be a presentation of public health program development.

"I was perturbed because I had told the class who Sylvia was and what she had accomplished. It was the worst form of bad manners to treat a woman of her age and stature like that. It was wrong for Jay to impugn her right to speak, and I don't think he would have disagreed with her if he *had* heard what she had to say."

Greg's Response

Greg continued, "I called Sylvia that evening. She said, 'Yes, some of the students objected to hearing from a white South African. I'm only sorry they didn't hear what I had to say—but it's OK, I've seen much worse.' I felt guilty, as well as angry. If I had been there, this wouldn't have happened. I wouldn't have let Jay heckle Sylvia. I would have responded to his first hostile question with, 'Interesting point but, Sylvia, why don't you finish what you were saying?'

"Students were upset. I was upset. I had to deal with this right away, in the next class. But all I had was hearsay. I didn't know quite what to do."

Bob Thompson (A)

This case was written by **William Davidson** under the supervision of **C. Roland Christensen** for the Developing Discussion Leadership Skills Seminar. All names and some peripheral facts have been disguised.

HBS Case No. 9-379-004.

Bob Thompson, just returned from Christmas vacation, began to sort through the accumulated mail on his desk. He was in good spirits, not only because of two great weeks of skiing but because his "first go" at teaching had been most successful. The students had given him a standing ovation after his last class; he knew from reading exams and papers that the students had learned a great deal; and it seemed that several interesting job offers were in the developmental stage. Even the drab, cramped office, with its dirty windows overlooking an industrial district, couldn't dampen his spirits.

His meditation on success was interrupted by a loud knock on the door. Without any response on Bob's part, the door opened and Toby Bona appeared. Recalling the incident, Bob explained:

> Toby was tall, at least 6'4", muscular, and handsome. Golly, he was tall—standing on my toes I wouldn't come up to his chest. And his voice was booming—obviously he was very distraught.
>
> "I've got to talk to you, Thompson. It's very important," Toby said. "You see, I won't graduate unless I get at least a B+ in your class. I had hoped to go home (Nigeria) before Christmas, but I've been waiting to see you. Can't you increase my grade to at least a B+? You must!"
>
> My feelings did a flip-flop. Why did this have to come now? I don't want to ruin a really great sendoff to my teaching career. What now?

Background

Bob Thompson had been appointed a lecturer in Urban University's MBA program to teach a second-year course in International Finance. Bob's own experience in both teaching and the subject matter had been very limited, but senior faculty at the school had enough confidence in him to take a risk with an unproven instructor. The head of the international business department told Bob that a full-time position might be available the following year, and Bob was interested in the opportunity. Bob had worked very hard in preparation for the course, and by the time fall semester began, he felt prepared to teach the course, but "was I nervous!"

The course began on a very positive note. After the introductory session, enrollment increased from 39 to 61 students. Many of the students were foreigners with experience in international finance, and lively class discussions were enriched by their comments.

At the end of the third week of class, Bob had smoothed out some of the roughness in his teaching technique and was beginning to settle into a systematic approach to his teaching assignment. He also was getting to know the students on a personal basis, and this added stimulation to class sessions and made the whole process more fun.

The Fifth Week of Class

According to Bob:

It must have been midweek in the fifth week of class and I was explaining a very tricky international banking instrument. In the middle of my explanation, a very tall black man entered the classroom and stood by my instructor's desk. He was wearing tight blue jeans and a striped rugby jersey.

Somewhat taken aback, I mumbled, "You don't look familiar!" "Neither do you," the man replied, walked back to an empty seat, sat down, and pulled out a student notebook, preparing to take notes. I laughed and the class followed suit. I just went back to my explanation.

After class, the student came up and introduced himself as Toby Bona. I recalled the name from my registration list and asked Toby why he hadn't been in class or in touch with me. Toby replied that his case had been under review by the Academic Review Board and that he was not allowed to attend class during this process. The board had just approved his appeal and so he wanted to "start in." Toby noted that it was important for him to do well in class and promised that he would work very hard.

I was sympathetic but uncertain and told Toby so; the term was already a third completed. Toby replied that the timing wasn't his fault but the Review Board's, and that he wouldn't be able to get into any courses except for those for which he was registered. I told Toby to call the following day. Meanwhile, I went to check out Toby's story with the registrar's office.

When told of the situation, the registrar replied: "Ah, yes—Mr. Bona. I'm sorry you're involved in that one. He should have graduated last semester, but his grades were deficient. In fact, he received

the only *F* I've seen here in many years. The Academic Review Board had suspended him after last semester. It was only after Toby returned and registered for this semester that his case was put again before the board. The board was very reluctant to let him enroll this semester, but they have decided to give him another chance. I must add that it is entirely up to you whether to allow him to enroll in your course."

Bob left feeling somewhat confused. He resolved to settle the issue by giving Toby the exam that the class had taken the previous week. He called Toby, gave him all the assignments, and told him to be in his office at 3:00 P.M. that Friday to take an exam. After that Bob would decide about admitting him into the course.

On Friday morning, Bob received a call from Toby, who said that he had come down with pneumonia and couldn't take the exam that day. Bob rescheduled the exam for the following Tuesday.

Toby missed class on Monday, but did arrive to take the exam in Bob's office on Tuesday afternoon. Bob told Toby he had an hour and a half to complete the exam. After 45 minutes, Toby handed in the exam and said he would be in class the following day. Bob explained:

In retrospect, I must admit to some uncertainty as to the wisdom of allowing Toby to take the course. Later one student came up and asked, "Are you really going to let him enroll?" I had told Toby he would have to be very active in classroom discussion work, and he certainly was. He had a bad habit of speaking before he was acknowledged, although his comments were usually relevant. Toby sure wasn't a "business type," either. I did notice an undercurrent of resentment against Toby, but I wasn't sure whether this might have originated from previous contact or from the current class.

Toby did work hard and his writing skills were better than some of the other foreign students. His performance on the final exam was in the bottom third of the class, but not below my minimum standards for the course. Toby's term paper, a diatribe against U.S.-based multinational enterprises' activities in less-developed countries, showed some thought and a great deal of effort, although much of the reasoning was immature.

I felt that my grading process was just and efficient. I had 15 grading points (one for each week of the semester) and a personal knowledge of each student with which to 'fine-tune' borderline cases. I made out the final grade (including class work and written work) on a blind basis and then combined grades and names. I was pleased with the outcome; class performance was so excellent I felt a $B+$ median was appropriate. The grading curve was approximately this: 15%, A; 20%, $A-$; 20%, $B+$; 25%, B; 20%, $B-$.

The $B-$ pool was not strong. In retrospect there should have been three Cs. Two students were foreign students, admission mistakes. Four just hadn't worked and didn't have the right attitude. Two were men who had had previous academic problems, and one of them had had trouble with his midterm. He stuck at it, however, and earned his $B-$.

I gave Toby a $B-$. I just scratched the first five weeks and calculated his grade on the other ten points alone. Toby scored below the class median on all of his assignments.

Toby's Request

After interrupting Bob in his office, Toby explained that unless his grade average reached a certain level he could not graduate. He said that in the previous semester he had had a "personality conflict" with one professor. That professor's grade, an F, meant that Toby's overall grade average had dropped substantially. "I need a $B+$, Professor," Toby repeated with intensity.

Bob questioned Toby about his other courses. He said that he had received two Bs and a $B-$. "Couldn't these grades be changed?" Bob continued. Toby, however, indicated "no hope," since one grade had already been raised and he had talked to the other two professors without any luck.

After Toby finished speaking, Bob Thompson swung back in his chair and reflected to himself. With the benefit of a doubt, I might change a grade one level—but two?

acism!" Susan Roper gestured as if to push
the word away. "This incident occurred a
year ago, but I still shake when I recall it. If
there's anything I have spent my life battling, it's
racial prejudice. And the thought of its having
cropped up in my classroom sickens me."

Sue was a 38-year-old lecturer in Spanish at
Greenwood College for Women in Lancaster, Connecticut. An outgoing woman with long, dark hair
and a ready smile, she was beloved by students and
colleagues alike and had won several national teaching awards. She and her husband, Jed Henry (a
composer-in-residence and professor of music theory at nearby Lancaster Community College), lived
with their two young daughters in a rambling house
near the Greenwood campus.

Sue's office was cluttered with Spanish books,
posters, shawls, sombreros, toys, and other audio-
visual aids as well as piles of photocopied materials
for her classes, and stacks of notes for a literary
project. It was usually populated by numerous students, fellow teachers, and friends. Speaking with
the researcher in private, Sue tapped a pencil ner-
vously on the stack of homework papers atop her
desk.

"I never thought such a thing could happen in
my classroom," she said. "I consciously model values as well as teach language and literature. It's my
conviction that teachers shouldn't shy away from
moral issues in class, so I don't hesitate to reveal
myself. I refer to the kids and Jed, and I talk about
the importance of families and the need for acceptance in society. I always assumed that my openness
would automatically make something so vile, so
pernicious as racism impossible in my classroom.
Was I wrong! When this incident happened, I felt
as if my world had just collapsed!"

The School

Greenwood College for Women had a pleasant,
landscaped campus near enough to Yale University
to permit cross-registration and regular travel on a
shuttle bus. Founded in 1887, the college enjoyed
an outstanding academic reputation. Though predominantly white and middle class, it had made
significant efforts to recruit minority students. Although 74 of Greenwood's 800 students were officially classified as minorities, most people still
thought of the college as homogeneous—"a typical
New England women's school."

CASE

I Felt as If My World Had Just Collapsed! (A)

Abby Hansen and *Joy Renjilian-Burgy* prepared this
case in collaboration with *C. Roland Christensen* for the
Developing Discussion Leadership Skills Seminar. Although based on data supplied by participants involved, all
names and some peripheral facts have been disguised.

HBS Case No. 9-383-171.

The Instructor

Sue and her husband Jed were both active in several civil rights organizations. They had worked with the Lancaster Upward Bound Program, and Sue was treasurer of the Mayor's Human Rights Commission, secretary of the Greenwood Community Action Commission, and a founder of CREATE (Citizens for Racial Equality in American Teaching and Education)—a national group promoting unbiased educational materials in elementary schools. Sue had completed all but her dissertation for a Yale Ph.D. and brought over fifteen years of teaching experience to her lectureship at Greenwood. Over the years she had taught in Ivy League, state, and single-sex colleges as well as public and private secondary schools. Travel in Spain and Central and South America, in addition to numerous encounters with American black students and colleagues, had sharpened her sensitivity to prejudice and strengthened her commitment to social justice. She was a highly respected teacher at Greenwood, particularly well known for innovative reading lists, creative lesson plans, and effective classroom techniques.

The Course

Spanish 257, "Advanced Conversation," met on Mondays, Wednesdays, and Fridays for an hour. The course required demonstrated proficiency in spoken Spanish, coupled with the ability to read and write sophisticated prose constructions. Many students took the course in the third or fourth year. According to Sue, "The composition of this group, like many of mine, was about 30% black—five students in a class of fifteen. Of all foreign languages, Spanish seems to attract the most minority students at Greenwood. Also, many black students tend to take my classes." Sue devised many assignments to get the students to speak Spanish, both in class and outside. One of her favorites was the so-called "minidrama," in which each student wrote a two-character dialogue and then worked with another student to memorize and perform one of their scripts for the whole class. Pairing the students for this exercise gave Sue the opportunity to encourage strangers to work together. The class met in a conventional classroom with movable desk-chairs. Sue urged her students to arrange their chairs in informal groupings and to vary their seating arrangements in order to sit beside different people.

The Students

Despite Greenwood's reputation for homogeneity, conservatism, and a certain affluence, over 35% of the students were receiving some sort of scholarship aid and working part time. There were also many foreign students, as well as feminists, nonconformists, and eccentrics in their ranks. In her class, Sue recalled no particularly unusual young women, however. "This group was very much like most I've had at Greenwood," she reported. "There was the same racial composition, too. Of the black students, there were some from professional families and others from the working class. Of the nonblacks, there were no obvious problems. I recall them as pleasant, competent, and basically cooperative."

The Incident

[In the following section, Sue recalls in her own words the events leading up to the incident.]

It was a Friday in the third week in October. Classes had been in session for over a month. We had gotten about forty minutes into the hour and were finishing a discussion of the reading assignment from the previous day. I had begun to prepare the students for their next task—the minidrama—for which they had already written their scripts and brought them to class. I intended, as usual, to use the exercise to strengthen language acquisition skills and to develop public presence. It's also important to get people to talk to each other in a conversation course. I try to break up cliques in order to help people expand their horizons and maybe even form new friendships. At the very least, they can experience new and different conversational styles.

For one team, I paired Carrie Draper—a rather quiet, white girl from Ohio, a sophomore interested in European Art History—with Sarah Hawley, a black girl from Washington, D.C., who had declared her major as Economics. Sarah was a junior. Both girls had shown strong language skills. I picked them as a team simply because I hadn't previously seen them speaking together.

"Carrie," I began—all this was in Spanish, of course—"would you please sit beside Sarah so

Section 7. Ethical Dilemmas and the Case Discussion
Process

CASE
I Felt as If My World Had Just Collapsed! (A)

you two can read each other's dramas and choose which you'll memorize to perform for the rest of the class next Monday? Please remember to include simple props in your planning and preparation." I was giving my standard speech—I always mention props, for example—so I don't think I looked very intently at Carrie as I stood before the class. Then I went right on and turned to Sarah, saying, "Sarah, would you please take out your minidrama and get ready to work with Carrie?" It was only then that I realized that Carrie hadn't budged. Instead of getting up to go sit beside Sarah, as students usually do, she had simply turned her face directly to me. She avoided Sarah's gaze and said, "I'm sorry, I'm not going to work with Sarah. I mean, I can't work with Sarah.

We're . . . we're not in the same dormitory." (In Spanish, "No voy a trabajar con Sarah.")

In all my years of teaching, never before had a student refused to work with another in class. This was a stunning slap in the face to Sarah and a shock to me. I was so horrified I felt positively sick. I stiffened and flushed. Some students had obviously heard Carrie, because I noticed that they looked stricken and embarrassed. No one dared look at Sarah. My body felt hot, and my hands felt icy as they somehow rose before me in a robot-like gesture that was very uncharacteristic for me. I don't think I focused clearly on the class's reaction, because I was so utterly taken aback. But I vividly remember feeling them watch me to see what I'd do.

READING

Teaching and Teachers: Three Views

HAIM G. GINOTT

SOPHIE FREUD

NEIL POSTMAN

As the sun's rays pass through a prism and diffuse into a radiance of separate colors, so too the teaching profession generates teachers with varying views. Here are three hues from that spectrum. From Dr. Haim G. Ginott, noted child psychologist, comes this view:

I have come to a frightening conclusion. I am the decisive element in the classroom. It is my personal approach that creates the climate. It is my daily mood that makes the weather. As a teacher I possess tremendous power to make a child's life miserable or joyous. I can be a tool of humor, hurt or heal. In all situations it is my response that decides whether a crisis will be escalated or de-escalated, and a child humanized or de-humanized.

Many teaching problems will be solved in the next decade. There will be new learning environments and new means of instruction. One function, however, will always remain with the teacher: to create the emotional climate for learning. No machine, sophisticated as it may be, can do this job.[1]

From Sophie Freud, granddaughter of Sigmund Freud and professor of Social Work at Simmons College, comes another view:

Teachers are in an exposed position, scrutinized and judged daily by hundreds of students. There are days when I grow weary of performing, entertaining, and filling up others' emptiness. There are days when I tire of offering stimulation, encouragement, and comfort, and of being the target of my students' unresolved parental loves and hates. But curiously, as the years go by, those days grow fewer, perhaps because along with being more open, I have also become more detached. I used to get angry at students who did not meet my standards, and positively disliked and scorned them. With greater wisdom I have become less narcissistically engaged, both in my praise and criticism. I had to relearn the same lesson that motherhood taught me. Students, like children, must learn and achieve for themselves, not for their teachers. I must take care that my love and concern for my students, like motherly love and concern, does not become a prison. Sarton (1961) made this dilemma the subject of one of her early novels; it is one familiar to

1. Haim G. Ginott, *Teacher and Child* (New York: Collier Books, 1993).

266

women teachers. The teacher role implies distance,
authority, evaluation, and objectivity, as well as
warmth and nurturance.[2]

From Neil Postman, author and professor of English education at New York University, comes still
another view:

In spite of our attempts to make teaching into a science, in spite of our attempts to invent teacher-proof
materials, and even in spite of our attempt to create
'relevant new curricula,' one simple fact makes all of
this ambition quite unnecessary. It is as follows: when
a student perceives a teacher to be an authentic,
warm and curious person, the student learns. When
the student does not perceive the teacher as such a
person the student does not learn. There is almost no
way to get around this fact, although technological

people such as ourselves try very hard to. We believe
in experts and expertise, and we tend not to trust any
activity that does not involve a complex technique.
And yet, increasing the complexity of the act of teaching has not really made much difference, for there is
always that simple fact that teaching is the art of
being human and of communicating that humanness
to others. Why is this so difficult for us to accept?
Why do we trust our machines, our equations and
our formulas more than we trust our humanity? Why
do we think that a curriculum can do something that
a person cannot? Our failure to place affection and
empathy at the center of the education process says
something very grave about us, and I do not think it
will be of much value for us to persevere unless we
can learn to love our technology less and ourselves
more.[3]

2. Sophie Freud, "The Passion and Challenge of Teaching" in
Harvard Educational Review 50, no. 1 (1980):10. Copyright © by
the President and Fellows of Harvard College.

3. Excerpted from an article that first appeared in *Sensorsheet*, a
publication of the Earth Science Educational Program in Boulder, Colorado, and later appeared in *Media Ecology Review*,
published at the NYU School of Education.

Section 8. Some Wider Questions

CASE

Who Should Teach? (A)

The summer session was coming to an end, and the campus was caught up in the panic of papers and exams. The day was clear and dry, with a hint of approaching autumn. Kensington University's Christine Smith, new director of Kensington's Master's Program for beginning teachers, was seated at the desk in her third floor office. She paused for a moment before resuming her account of the previous weeks to the researcher. Suddenly she leaned forward in her chair as if to emphasize the frustration of her situation.

> Paul Warburton has been a real problem to his MA peer group, and to the "coach" of that group, Ellen Bailey. Now he is presenting me with an incredible dilemma. I wonder if he is fit for the classroom. Should Paul be asked to leave the program . . . or what? Who guards the gates? Who should teach?

Case Organization

This case is divided into three sections. The "A" case describes Kensington University, outlines its program for teacher training, and introduces three key individuals: Christine Smith, director of the Master's Program; Ellen Bailey, one of the six Master teachers supervising the entering MA group; and Paul Warburton, a newly enrolled student. The "A" case also details the situation from the perspective of Ellen and Christine. The "B" case presents Paul's point of view of the same events. "C" is Paul's update several months later.

Kensington University

Located in northern New England, Kensington University was a small, highly selective private institution with a strong undergraduate curriculum and a well-respected graduate and professional school program. Kensington emphasized its dedication to teaching, extensive personal contact between professors and students, and the diversity of its student body. Kensington students came from each of the fifty states and an equal number of foreign countries. Kensington offered one of the more prominent fifth-year teaching programs on the East Coast.

The MA Program

Kensington's Education Department had expanded during the past several years. It included both elementary and secondary teaching programs,

*This case was written by **Marina McCarthy**, in collaboration with **C. Roland Christensen** for the Developing Discussion Leadership Skills and Teaching by the Case Method seminars. While the case is based on data furnished by participants involved, all names and some peripheral facts have been disguised.*

HBS Case No. 9-387-139.

as well as doctoral programs in school administration and curriculum.

MA students generally had academically superior undergraduate records and outstanding references. They came from varied backgrounds: some were recent graduates, others Peace Corps volunteers; several had been tutors in either public or private schools; a few were lawyers or counselors; and some already had teaching experience.

The MA curriculum involved three principal activities. The 12-month program began in mid-June with Kensington's Summer Academy Program, which served approximately 200 high school students from the surrounding area. The 27 newly arrived MAs constituted the faculty of the Summer Academy, under the guidance of the Kensington faculty. They were responsible for developing its four-week curriculum, teaching groups of 20 high school students on a day-to-day basis, and evaluating their own progress. The MAs were coached by six Master teachers, often alums of Kensington's MA Program.

During the academic year, the MAs took half of their courses in the Education Department and half in the department of their subject area specialty—English, History, Mathematics, etc. A critical component of the academic year program was the apprenticeship with a "supervising teacher" in a local school system. During either the fall or spring term, an MA taught a minimum of two classes per day under the guidance of a supervising teacher.

Almost everyone at Kensington's Education Department was on a first-name basis—faculty, staff, and students. The department was headquartered in a huge brick colonial house close to the center of campus. A regular afternoon volleyball game symbolized the closeness and collegiality of the program.

Christine Smith

Before coming to Kensington, Christine Smith worked in a somewhat similar teaching program at Northwest University (NWU). Her current appointment at Kensington involved both administration and teaching. Christine was one of the newest members of the department.

I took a year off after my junior year at NWU to enlist in a voluntary group. I was very interested in issues of social justice. I worked as a teacher in a Job Corps Center. I returned to school for my senior year and, following graduation, went to graduate school in government and public policy. I worked in state-level government for five years but soon became quite disillusioned with trying to make changes within an entrenched bureaucracy.

I decided to go back to NWU and become a high school government teacher. I finished the MA program and got a job teaching 4/5 time at a nearby school. Several of my professors, however, advised me to pursue a doctorate. Although I loved teaching, I'm glad I was counseled into the Ph.D. program. It gave me an opportunity to think about teaching and issues surrounding teaching—a luxury one doesn't have when teaching four or five classes a day with thirty or more students in each class.

My doctoral program was in teacher education, specifically curriculum development. While I completed my coursework and worked on my dissertation, I taught part-time and substituted at nearby public, private, and parochial schools. My thesis is on how teachers make decisions about what to teach and how to teach it.

Looking out her office window at the nearby volleyball game, Christine's eyes sparkled:

Several of us (faculty) like to play volleyball with the students. It is an inclusive sport, not like football. It gives me a chance to socialize with the students. Ann Jackson, the only black student in the program, started the volleyball tradition and got the Ed Department involved in a summer league. Paul Warburton got us in the Kensington Intramural Program and is now the keeper of the equipment and the one who makes sure we all show up. His enthusiasm is infectious.

Ellen Bailey

Described by a colleague as "energetic and charismatic, a real dynamo in the classroom—someone who gets along well with everyone, both students and staff," Ellen Bailey was one of three Master teachers supervising the Social Studies MAs at Kensington's Summer Academy. Because she was new to her job, Christine Smith was particularly pleased that Ellen was returning for a second summer. They quickly formed a close working relationship.

A relatively recent Kensington MA, Ellen had taught for two years at a local secondary school. Her interest in teaching began during her senior year of high school, which she spent in a progressive Alternative Learning Program (ALP).

> The structure of the traditional school was stifling for me. I had read John Holt's works the summer after my junior year and was particularly impressed with *Schools Without Failure*. I eventually decided to attend St. John's in Annapolis, Maryland, a nontraditional college that stressed integration, not "class switching." I had so many fantastic role models at St. John's, discussion was stressed, not teacher-centered activities. Since there were no letter grades, students worked for an education, not grades. I really feel strongly that teachers need to encourage active learning, not just lecture at students. Coming to Kensington for my MA was important. Finally someone agreed with me when I said, "The Emperor has no clothes!" Teachers need to reform education, but first they need to be dissatisfied with the present structure.

Although Ellen was a relatively new teacher, her principal granted her request to work with a Kensington MA during the spring term. "We've never let a nontenured (less than three years experience) teacher take on a student teacher before," said the principal, but "Ellen is an exception."

Paul Warburton

An incoming MA, Paul Warburton was a recent graduate of a small midwestern college. He was fifth of six children; two of his siblings were currently teaching, and one had formerly taught. Christine Smith believed that Paul was "brilliant in history and social studies, and wants to be a teacher more than anything else in the world."

Normally proportioned, Paul was short in stature (under 4 feet tall). His attire was "standard Kensington," complete with suede vest, tweed cap, and navy backpack. Intense and earnest, he approached every task, from ordering a hamburger to organizing a volleyball game, with determination. His greatest passions, he said, were photography, volleyball, and teaching.

Paul described how he had come to Kensington:

> I have wanted to be a teacher for as long as I can remember, but by my senior year I wondered if I could do it. I began to fill out an MA application but my senior thesis got in the way.
>
> Then I didn't have any luck in getting a teaching

job. I was turned down at a private school and encountered several discouraging placement agencies. Several of the teacher agencies told me point-blank that my shortness was an issue. They were worried about discipline. I know I can be a good teacher; I can be very arrogant about this. With agencies where my shortness was not brought up, I could tell it was still an issue with them. I know! It's like when people talk louder to blind people.

> I decided to take a clerical job for a year and then apply to Kensington. I knew the MA would be a good choice for me. My brother had completed the program here several years ago and spoke highly of it. I looked forward to the summer; but now there are problems.

Ellen Bailey

Late June

Ellen Bailey recalled her orientation day with the new MA group.

> It was an exceptionally muggy morning and I was preparing the MA groups for their first teaching session at the Summer Academy. As in previous summers, the program provided for groups of three MAs to teach a section of the high schoolers alternately and occasionally team teach. I asked for a volunteer from each group to go first. Paul jumped at the chance; he seemed so confident. We met after class to arrange a time the next day so I could go over his lesson plans.
>
> Paul seemed at ease with his handicap. In fact, his shortness seemed as irrelevant as Greg's blond hair. Paul seemed so together—so at ease . . . so adjusted to his handicap. I thought that he must have received tremendous guidance and support growing up.
>
> That's why I was so surprised when Paul came unprepared to our subsequent meeting to discuss his lesson plan. He had no notes . . . nothing. The purpose of our meeting had been clear—or so I thought. We were to discuss what and how he was going to teach on his "first day." I scheduled another appointment for the following day, but he didn't show up. Finally I got a call from him that evening at 10:00 P.M. He was still having difficulty with his lesson plan, but we managed to discuss it briefly over the phone.
>
> Soon I began to see through Paul's veneer. He was unpredictable, disorganized, and incessantly argumentative. My positive initial impressions gradually eroded.

Early July

When I assigned the social studies MAs into groups of three, I thought Paul, Greg, and Joanne would make a good match; but Greg and Joanne came to me a week later, and complained that working with Paul was "unbearable." We required the MA's to work together, not only to encourage them to exchange ideas but also to provide a support system. That Paul couldn't get along with Greg and Joanne, such laid-back people, really concerned me.

Paul's manner toward both his fellow students and staff continued to deteriorate. I consulted with two other Master teachers, Dick and Bart. They had also noted Paul's abrupt manner but thought the situation was manageable. I was beginning to have doubts.

Meanwhile, Paul's teaching had not advanced since his first few classes. He did have good rapport with his students. He made them feel special—he would tell them "You're in *my* group." But meanwhile, Greg and Joanne were experimenting. They tried different methods with their classes: group work, independent work, role-playing, simulations, debates . . . Paul just lectured and engaged in an occasional Socratic style of questioning. He was simply not making as much progress as Greg and Joanne.

Paul became increasingly difficult. In the second week we were using a particular classroom for one of Christine's "Methods" seminars. The chairs were all plastic with dipped seats. Because Paul's feet did not touch the ground, he kept sliding. When he complained I said I would get a wooden "left-handed" chair (I noticed he was also left-handed) as soon as possible. There was a day's delay . . . I didn't have my keys to the supply room with me. At any rate, he hit the ceiling and said his "needs weren't being accommodated." He refused to understand why he wasn't attended to right away. Ironically, the previous day we tried to adjust the overhead projector for him and he just told us to forget it—he wouldn't use it. You know, Paul never really talked about being short . . . except he did mention it in the journal that he kept for Christine's class. He used to write how certain things bothered him.

Paul was unable to engage in a constructive critique of his teaching. He was lacking in tact when dealing with others and too defensive when the shoe was on the other foot. At the mildest criticism he would gruffly respond, "I was *going* to do that." He felt an incessant need to justify everything. When critiquing others, he would snap, "I have a problem with that."

Because of him, we instituted a new MA rule. No one in the groups could respond to *any* feedback being given about their own classes—either positive or negative. They were free to have an *inner* dialogue (including all sorts of nasty things about those giving the critique). This ground rule had to be implemented because of Paul. In the three years I have been associated with the Kensington program, we had never had to resort to such a method.

Mid-July

Another week passed. Greg and Joanne came to see me on Friday afternoon. They no longer wanted to remain in the same group with Paul.

I decided immediately to keep them "apart" for the weekend and let everybody cool off. The next decision: how do I tell Paul? I decided the best way was to wait for him outside the department office at the end of the day.

We strolled together toward the Graduate Hall, where Paul lived. When I asked him please not to work with Greg and Joanne over the weekend, he really became unglued. He was so distraught and kept insisting that he never had had any interpersonal problems before. I had my doubts.

I wanted to console him—but how? Height was an issue: I didn't want to treat him like a little boy. He just kept walking around the courtyard—so very, very, undone.

I asked him if he could talk to his parents. He said emphatically, "No." I asked if there was anyone else he could talk with. No. I finally remembered he was friendly with Brad, an MA who also lived in the dorm and went with Paul to Brad's room, How far does my obligation to you last? It's 7:30! On the way down the corridor, Paul told me he thought none of the other students liked him. I learned that he spent hours working over his lessons. He wouldn't take time out or even eat dinner with the others. Later that night, about ten o'clock, Paul called me. He had regained his composure and offered both his thanks and apologies.

I met with Christine first thing Monday at the Coffee House and recounted my Friday night experience. Paul is unfit for the classroom: he is simply not mature. I am concerned. What will teaching do to him? I also question what he would do to the profession. He thinks only his classroom work is important. Teachers are evaluated not only on their classroom performances, but also on their relationships with their colleagues and the larger community.

From my point of view, Paul had made no progress in his teaching since the first day. His comment earlier in the summer still haunts me. "I like teaching because I like to be the center of attention."

Christine Smith

The Ball's in My Court

After meeting with Ellen at the Coffee House, Christine took the long route back to the office.

I tried to sort out my own thoughts about Paul. I thought about my own "Methods" class, of which he was a member. His progress was a bit slower than the others'. It was hard to pry him loose from his need to lecture—to have total control of his class, to be the focal point. Paul was also having interpersonal difficulties with the other students in my class. People were continually giving him breaks, however. He knew it and began to demand it. Whenever he came into one of the offices, he insisted that you find time for him. He came to my home at 8:00 P.M. one evening, demanding to be let into the Ed. Department. He had forgotten an assignment that was due for class the next day. He had an "I've got to have what I want now" attitude. I firmly told him it was too late but that I would be happy to meet him first thing in the morning. I felt *some* of his problems were clearly related to his handicap, but not all.

Was it time to intervene? Paul has become quite demanding of Ellen and me and increasingly domineering with his fellow students. His behavior was affecting the morale of the entire group.

Christine met with Ellen again the next day, this time along with the other two Master teachers—Dick and Bart.

Dick and Bart had expressed optimism about Paul's situation. Dick was the one who had disagreed most with Ellen's grim assessment at our last staff meeting.

I arranged for Paul to work with Dick instead of Ellen for the remainder of the week. By Friday, however, Dick was fit to be tied. I was so discouraged. Earlier Dick had suggested that if I was in a bind, he would consider taking Paul on as a student teacher for either the fall or spring term. Now, Dick was brief

and to the point: "No way!" Placing Paul in a student teaching assignment was going to be very difficult.

Paul seemed to be living from one crisis to another—whether it be lesson plans, writing a paper, or securing an apartment for September. One afternoon, after he cited a list of problems (common to *all* MA's), I questioned his complaints. "But I have special needs," he retorted. "My problems are special." I then looked up from the papers I was sorting and asked, "Why?" Paul looked at his feet, "Maybe you're right," he responded. I thought I had achieved a breakthrough and hoped he was more aware of how he was "using" his handicap in self-defeating ways.

Paul had been particularly hard on Joanne. It never entered his mind that she might have problems. Yet Joanne is enduring a very distressful summer. Her mother had been deserted and decided to move into Joanne's apartment. This had been a terrific burden for Joanne, yet she remained composed throughout the summer, having only told me what her home life was like. Twice she came away crying after interactions with Paul.

Should Paul be allowed to teach? That is the question. This is a moral as well as professional dilemma. In one sense students can learn from him—how to overcome handicaps and obstacles in life. He could inspire them. On the other hand, teaching could be detrimental to both Paul and the profession.

I felt I couldn't ask him to leave the program. Ellen's assessment was that he could probably complete the MA program but was unfit to teach.

I was worried about finding Paul a student teaching placement. One last time I asked Dick and Bart, both private school teachers, if they would consider taking Paul on as a student teacher during the academic year. Both declined. After considerable reflection, I saw three alternatives.

One was to require counseling as a prerequisite to student teaching; another was to recommend he transfer to the Ph.D. program in history in the college of arts and sciences. A third alternative was to have him leave the program in August. The status quo was unacceptable. It couldn't go on.

If Paul did not agree to go to counseling and won't consider the Ph.D. route, as a department we decided we would have to brainstorm alternatives. The bottom line was that we were ready to initiate proceedings to let Paul go.

The following day I had a meeting with Paul to discuss his lesson plans. I brought up the subject of a

Ph.D. in history and asked if he'd ever considered it. He said that as much as he loved history, his burning desire was to be a high school history teacher.

I really felt we were up against the wall. Paul was not going to be deterred easily.

My Decision

Christine spent the better part of the weekend mulling over the alternatives.

I decided to require that Paul complete a successful semester of counseling as a prerequisite to student teaching. Since it is arbitrary whether MAs student teach in the spring or fall term, the arrangement could be a private one between Paul and the department. I double-checked protocol and procedures with the dean and the counseling staff and secured the support of the department chair. I felt that Paul needed help—not just so he could secure a student teaching assignment, but also to help him get along with people.

* * *

Christine Smith and Ellen Bailey

Christine described a meeting she and Ellen had with Paul at the close of the summer session.

Ellen, Paul, and I met in my office. A dreary afternoon did nothing to lighten up the somber atmosphere. Although only scheduled for a half-hour, our meeting continued for an hour and forty-five minutes.

Ellen and I spent the first twenty minutes explaining our concerns with Paul's behavior. We told him

that he was too aggressive to work with other people. We confronted him on his behavior, particularly with his peers. We explained that he was very insensitive to people who did not appear to him to be "hurting," and did not even entertain that others might have problems, perhaps even a handicap—though not a visible one. I told him that we felt if he wanted to stay in the program he needed to go to counseling.

Paul was stunned. His response was one of shock. He remarked, "How can you infringe on someone's personal business to this extent?" Initially he was furious with me, then with Ellen. Then he looked devastated.

Basically, we explained to him that good teachers get along with people, and how important it is for pupils rather than teachers to be the center of attention. Since we appeared to have reached an impasse, I attempted to convince Paul that my intent was not to "get him" but rather to help.

Paul kept resisting, however. He wouldn't listen. We were both frustrated. I then told Paul that none of the Master teachers would take him on as a student teacher—which at this point was true. We had hoped we wouldn't have to tell him this, but it finally drove our point home. I added, "I thought you would be grateful with the counseling option. We were at the point of asking you to withdraw from the program, but I believe in you." Paul then seemed convinced of the severity of the situation.

Finally I told Paul that I had gone to counseling while in Oregon. Ellen later said she thought this was the turning point of the meeting.

Paul got up to leave and pursed his lips. "Between now and September, I will have to convince myself that counseling will work." As he reached for the door, he turned to Ellen and me and said, "I'm incredibly disappointed."

Who Should Teach? (B)

This case was written by **Marina McCarthy,** in collaboration with **C. Roland Christensen** for the Developing Discussion Leadership Skills and Teaching by the Case Method seminars. While the case is based on data furnished by participants involved, all names and some peripheral facts have been disguised.

HBS Case No. 9-387-140.

Paul Warburton

After a mix-up in orders, lunch finally arrived. Smiling, Paul thanked the waiter and turned to the researcher. "It's been a disruptive summer; quite a disruptive summer," he said, leaning forward and speaking softly. "I was almost asked to leave the program."

A Tough Summer

These last few months have been tough! As I look at the problems, I see them in two ways. Some were personal and some were common to all MAs in the program.

I had taken a year off after graduation, and had come to rely on a paycheck. Coming to Kensington at the beginning of June I had no stipend, no fellowship, no income. Despite the year off, I was still burned out by my undergraduate experience. I was in a brand-new community and had no new friends. I also had a problem with self-discipline, something I have been plagued with for some time. I am a perfectionist and a procrastinator. When writing term papers, I grapple with ideas and want my finished product to be the best. I subsequently agonize over papers and often hand them in late. My undergraduate transcript unfortunately reflects many tardy papers.

On the other hand, we all had the same inhuman reading list and were pressured by time. Most of us wanted to spend *all* our time preparing lessons for classes. There is an inherent tension—an ambiguity switching hats every day from teacher to student. Also, one year is such a transient and fleeting block of time—unlike the undergraduate years. Time is limited and most graduate students have a life outside of their graduate experience. The intensity and pressure of the summer component cannot be overemphasized. The summer component was exhausting.

They told me that teaching was not my problem . . . working in my small group and absorbing criticism was. I enjoyed teaching my classes and had good rapport with my students. I just didn't want to experiment in what seemed to be a different teaching method every other day. I resisted Ellen's constant prodding to vary my techniques. Some of the suggestions were just not for me. I wanted to have some credit for knowing enough to make that decision. I thought it best to teach to my strengths and adapt other modes of instruction when I became more accustomed to the classroom. Ultimately we have to decide what's best for us as teachers.

Ellen and Christine were very concerned about my behavior. It seemed all I did was further convince them that they were right! Everything was snowballing, escalating. . . . They would tell me that I had to work on my attitude and way of working, and I would quickly say, "I see . . . but . . ." Unfortunately they saw this as being stubborn, defensive, and a symptom of not listening. I just didn't want them to think I hadn't thought about it. You know, I really think the summer might have worked out if I was in a different group.

Ellen's view was that I was the cause of the summer problem. I told her early on that Greg and Joanne and I were not a good match. I could tell we were not going to get along and was particularly concerned about Joanne. I mentioned this to Ellen. Though part of her job was group management, all she said was, "You'll have to!" I frequently asked to change groups but she ignored me. Then later on, it became my fault when the group wasn't working out.

Greg and Joanne were quiet—yet passive/aggressive. Greg was laid-back, but not because he was shy. Not to be stereotypical . . . but he was a former Peace Corps volunteer. Joanne, on the other hand, was quiet and timid. She was one of the youngest in our cohort. In group meetings, I misinterpreted Greg and Joanne's silence. I thought they had nothing to say. Given the opportunity, I'll fill silence! I later learned that Joanne and Greg felt overrun by me. But they never said anything to me. I never knew anything was wrong. When I heard they went to Ellen, I felt threatened and defensive. I guess my reactions were natural, but not necessarily good.

I'm willing to take Christine and Ellen's assessment. I know I'm aggressive, but it's a question of degree. Without being conceited, I strive for excellence, maybe perfection. My first class this summer was great. I taught the U.S. Constitution and tried to introduce the class to Locke, Jefferson, and Machiavelli as people. I was over the head of some of them, but I wanted to have something for them to reach for.

I know Christine and Ellen are only saying what they think is best . . . requiring me to go to counseling in order to student teach. But the bottom line is that they are the teachers and I am the student—despite how much Kensington encourages teacher/student interaction. The emphasis on addressing everyone by first name around here is deceptive. There's not enough distance. Life isn't as "liberal" as it appears here. I'm a romantic idealist, but there is a cynical streak a mile wide down my back.

Paul Reflects

Glancing up from his cheeseburger, Paul paused and smiled.

Ms. Lincoln used to tease me about taking my "worry pills." I was the fourth Warburton that she taught. Interest, caring, firmness—those qualities are very important to me in describing a good teacher. They are qualities that would sum up both Ms. Lincoln and Mr. Smith—my high school teachers. The classrooms themselves were not memorable; the classes are hard to recollect. What was important to me was their interest in me, their availability to students after school. This was important given my background.

A long time ago—as a child—the doctor told me that I would always be short. In junior high, however, reality was a bit starker. My friends were very helpful. . . . My parents, however, chose the path of least resistance and basically behaved as if nothing was different. My sister, Janet, who is also short, was bitter about this. She was angry that when she eventually went out into the world, people started treating her differently. I, on the other hand, do not hold a grudge. I'm glad my parents let me think anything was possible. When I was having trouble with those placement agencies, my father told me there will always be three kinds of people in this world; one will give you no chances because you are short; the second will go out of their way because you are short; and the third will take you for what you are.

Although I'm officially handicapped, I really don't see myself as such. For example, a few years ago I used to skip items in the supermarket if they were out of my reach. Now I ask someone for assistance.

Years ago there was little social concern for disadvantaged people . . . for different people. We needed reforms badly, especially after the Civil War. But today it is excessive. I'm a liberal—I have a social conscience . . . but I guess I'm tired of labels. "Physically challenged" instead of "handi-capped" is ambiguous, cutesy. It takes the sting out of it. It's more for the person who's saying it. We have such a quest to ensure that no one is offended. I'm more an advocate of saying what you mean.

I remember one time when an acquaintance of mine at Middletown and I were waiting for a vol-leyball game to begin. She turned to me and asked, "Are the rest of your family dwarfs?" I turned upside down inside, and chose not to an-swer her. Clearly, she had wanted to ask for some time. I'm not a dwarf. I don't like it when people ask if I have any midget friends.

You know, I love volleyball. I organized it at Middletown and I was the catalyst here at Ken-sington. I'm good at it, but it bothers me when someone praises me. The tone is very important. "That was a great return, Paul!" ("for someone who is short") I can hear it in their voice.

Christine has told me she sees me in a constant struggle with my shortness—part denial and part seeking special treatment. She often tells me (or implies) that she doesn't think I'm really very ac-cepting of my height. But I know I am. I wouldn't want to walk into a classroom and have people pretend I wasn't short!

Christine has told me several times that she thought I'd be a good role model in an inner city school—"look at me—I've overcome obstacles too!" I don't agree. I could be a good role model anywhere. I want to be challenged, but not by an inner city setting. My weakness is that I probably prefer honors classes. Perhaps I belong in a pri-vate school. I just don't want to be a full-time dis-ciplinarian. I know more about myself and what I want to do as a result of this summer's experi-ence.

You know, I really value friends and friend-ship—soulmates. Bouncing ideas off of friends is very important to me. That was a missing link last summer.

Lunch was over and Paul toyed with the straw in his iced tea. He then looked up.

At that last meeting they told me I needed counseling. I told them, "You have a lot of nerve making a personal decision." But it was an ultima-tum. I've been angry these past weeks. Through-out the rest of August, my family and friends were a great help. Initially, they all agreed with my assessment of the situation—that the ultima-tum to go to counseling wasn't fair. Gradually, however, one of my brothers and one of my sis-ters emerged as "unsympathetic." They thought I should view counseling as a positive experience. I truly felt persecuted on all fronts. I saw my goals crumbling before me. My sister, April, who teaches in a Quaker private school has many of the same qualities as I do. She said that she didn't initially see the negative effects of her bluntness. She cautioned me to be more sensitive. Not every-one sees conflict as a productive learning experi-ence.

I'm not a quitter. I have made a 100% commit-ment to teaching; to hell with them. You just couldn't understand how great I felt after my first class last summer. I was two feet off the ground. The student teaching experience is very important to me. I really question the required counseling . . . what will it accomplish?

The narrow path from Uvarovka village to the school had been completely covered with snow during the night, and only the barely perceptible pattern of light and shadow on its uneven surface revealed its course. The young schoolteacher stepped cautiously, ready to draw back her foot at once if the shadows proved treacherous.

It was no more than half a kilometer to the school, and the teacher had merely tied a woolen kerchief round her head and thrown her short fur coat over her shoulders. The cold was fierce, however, and fitful gusts of wind showered her with snow from head to foot. But the twenty-four-year-old teacher did not mind it. She even enjoyed the stinging sensation in her cheeks and the momentary cold touch of the wind. Averting her face from the gusts, she was amused to see the small imprints her pointed overshoes left behind, like the tracks of some forest creature.

The fresh, sunlit January morning filled her with happy thoughts. She had come here only two years ago, straight out of college, and already she was considered the district's best teacher of Russian. In Uvarovka itself, in Kuzminki, in Black Gully Village, in the peat settlement, and at the stud farm, everywhere they knew her and called her Anna Vasilyevna, adding the patronymic to show their respect.

The sun rose over the serrated outline of the distant woods and the long shadows on the snow grew a deeper blue, making faraway objects merge with those nearby—the top of the church belfry reached up to the porch of the village soviet, the pines across the river came up the slope of the nearer bank, the wind gauge at the school meteorological station whirled in the middle of the field, right at Anna's feet.

A man was coming across the field. What if he won't step off the path? Anna thought with mock apprehension. The path was too narrow for two people, and stepping aside meant sinking knee-deep into the snow. She knew, of course, that there wasn't a man in the district who would not go out of his way to let the Uvarovka schoolteacher pass.

As they drew closer Anna recognized the man as Frolov, one of the workers at the stud farm.

"Good morning, Anna Vasilyevna," said Frolov, and he raised his fur hat over his shapely, short-cropped head.

"Come on now, put that hat on! What are you thinking in this cold!"

CASE

Winter Oak

YURI NAGIBIN

Reprinted from the *Atlantic Monthly,* September 1979.

HBS Case No. 2-394-220.

Probably Frolov had no intention of keeping his hat off, but after the teacher's words he took his time about putting it on again. A short sheepskin coat fitted his trim, muscular body. In one hand he held a thin, snakelike whip, which he kept smacking against his high felt boots.

"How is my Lyosha behaving? Up to any mischief?" he asked conversationally.

"All my children are up to mischief; it's quite normal as long as they don't overdo it," replied Anna, savoring her pedagogical wisdom.

Frolov smiled.

"No fear of him overdoing it. He's a quiet one. Takes after his father."

He stepped off the path and immediately sank up to his knees, which made him look no taller than a twelve-year-old boy. Anna nodded to him graciously and hurried on.

The school, a two-story brick building with wide, frost-painted windows, stood a little off the highway, behind a low fence. In the morning light its walls threw a reddish tint on the surrounding snow. Children from all over the district came to it—from nearby villages, from the stud farm, the oil workers' sanatorium, and even the far-off peat settlement. Caps, kerchiefs, hats, hoods, and bonnets flocked to the school along the highway from both directions.

"Good morning, Anna Vasilyevna!"

From some the familiar greeting sounded in clear and ringing voices, from others it was muffled and barely audible, coming through thick scarves and shawls that swathed the young faces up to the eyes.

*   *   *

Anna's first lesson was to the twelve- and thirteen-year-olds in five-A form. She entered the classroom as the last peal of the bell was announcing the beginning of the class. The children rose, greeted her, and sat down at their desks. But it took some time for them to quiet down. Desk tops banged, benches creaked, somebody sighed heavily, evidently unwilling to switch off the carefree morning mood.

"We shall continue to study parts of speech today."

Now they became perfectly quiet. The sounds of a truck slowly rumbling along the slippery highway could distinctly be heard in the room.

Anna remembered how nervous she had been about this lesson last year. She had kept repeating to herself, like a schoolgirl before an exam, the textbook definition of a noun. And how foolishly afraid she had been that they would not understand!

She smiled at those memories, adjusted a pin in her heavy knot of hair, and sensing confidence coursing like blood itself through her body, she began speaking in a calm, even voice: "A noun is a word that denotes a subject—that is, a person, thing, or quality. A subject in grammar is anything about which you can ask the question What is it? or Who is it? For instance: Who is it?—a pupil. What is it?—a book."

"May I come in?"

A small figure in battered felt boots covered with melting snowflakes stood in the open doorway. The round, wind-reddened face glowed as if it would burst; the eyebrows were white with frost.

"Late again, Savushkin." Like most young teachers, Anna enjoyed being strict, but now an almost plaintive note sounded in her voice.

Considering the matter settled, Savushkin quickly slid into his place. Anna saw him shove his oilcloth schoolbag into the desk and, without turning his head, ask something of the boy next to him.

Savushkin's unpunctuality annoyed Anna; it somehow spoiled the fine opening of the day for her. The geography teacher, a small, dried-up old woman, very much like a night moth, had once complained to Anna about Savushkin's often being late to lessons. She complained about other things, too—the children's inattentiveness, their much too boisterous behavior. "Those first morning lessons are so trying," she said. They may be, for incompetent teachers who don't know how to hold the interest of their pupils, thought Anna disdainfully, and offered to change hours with the older woman. She felt a prick of conscience now: the old teacher had doubtless sensed the challenge in Anna's magnanimous offer.

"Is everything clear?" she asked the class.

"Yes!" chorused the children.

"Very well. Then give me some examples."

There was a short silence and then someone said haltingly, "Cat."

"Correct," said Anna, recalling that last year, too, "cat" had been the first example.

After that examples poured in like a stream: window . . . table . . . house . . . highway. . . .

"Correct," Anna assured them. The children were excited.

It amazed Anna to see such joy at the discovery

of a new aspect in long-familiar words. At first the choice of examples embraced only the most everyday, tangible things: cart, tractor, pail, nest. . . . From the back desk a fat boy called Vasya kept repeating in his thin voice, "Chicken, chicken, chicken."

But then someone said hesitantly, "Town."

"Good," encouraged Anna.

"Street . . . victory . . . poem . . . play. . . ."

"Well, that's enough," said Anna. "I can see you understand it."

The voices died down reluctantly; only fat Vasya's "chicken" still came from the back of the room. And then suddenly, as if awakened out of his sleep, Savushkin stood up behind his desk and shouted eagerly, "Winter oak!"

The children laughed.

"Quiet, please!" Anna brought her palm down hard on the table.

"Winter oak!" repeated Savushkin, heedless of the laughter around him or of Anna's order. There was something peculiar in his manner. The words seemed to have burst out like a confession, like some glorious secret which could not remain unshared.

Annoyed and uncomprehending, Anna asked, barely controlling her irritation, "Why 'winter oak'? 'Oak' is enough."

"An oak is nothing. A winter oak, there's a noun for you."

"Sit down, Savushkin. That's what coming in late leads to. Oak is a noun, and what the word 'winter' is in this case we have not studied yet. You will come to the teachers' room during the long recess."

"Now you'll catch it," whispered somebody behind Savushkin.

Savushkin sat down smiling to himself, not in the least put out by the teacher's strict tone. A difficult boy, thought Anna.

The lesson continued.

*   *   *

"Sit down," said Anna when Savushkin entered the teachers' room. With evident pleasure the boy sank into a soft armchair and rocked a few times on its springs.

"Will you please tell me why you are always late for school?"

"I really don't know, Anna Vasilyevna," he said with a gesture of surprise. "I leave home an hour before school."

It seemed that even in trifling matters like this, truth was not easily to be established. There were many children who lived much farther away from school, yet none of them needed more than an hour to get there on time.

"You live in Kuzminki, don't you?"

"No, I live on the sanatorium premises."

"Aren't you ashamed, then, to tell me you leave home an hour before school? Why, it's fifteen minutes from the sanatorium to the highway, and no more than half an hour's walk down the highway!"

"But I don't never go down the highway. I take a shortcut through the forest," Savushkin said earnestly.

"Don't ever go," Anna corrected him mechanically. Why did children have to lie? she thought unhappily. Why couldn't Savushkin tell her simply, "I'm sorry, Anna Vasilyevna, I stopped to play snowballs with the kids," or something else equally straightforward. But the boy said no more and just looked at her out of his large gray eyes, as if wondering what else she would want of him.

"That's not very good, Savushkin. I'll have to talk to your parents about it."

"There's only my mother, Anna Vasilyevna," Savushkin said softly.

Anna blushed. She remembered the boy's mother, the "shower nurse," as her son called her. A withered, tired-looking woman who worked at the sanatorium's hydrotherapy section. From continuous contact with hot water, her hands, limp and white, looked as if they were made of cotton. After her husband had been killed in the war, she remained alone to bring up four children as best she could. She certainly had enough worry without being bothered about her son's conduct. But all the same they had to meet.

"I'll have to see your mother, then," said Anna.

"Please do, Anna Vasilyevna. She'll be so glad to see you."

"I doubt that. What shift does she work on?"

"The second. She goes to work at three."

"Very well then. I finish at two. We'll go together right after school is over."

*   *   *

Savushkin led Anna Vasilyevna along the path that started at the back of the school. As soon as they entered the forest and the heavy, snowladen spruce branches closed behind them, they found themselves in a different, enchanted world of peace and quiet. Now and then magpies and crows flew from tree to tree, shaking the spreading branches, knocking off dry pine cones, and occasionally breaking off a brittle twig. But the sounds were shortlived and muffled.

Everything around was white. Only high up against the blue sky the dainty lacework of the tall birch trees stood out as if sketched in with India ink.

The path followed a frozen brook, sometimes right down along the bank, sometimes climbing up a steep rise. Occasionally the trees fell back, revealing a sunlit clearing crisscrossed with hares' tracks that looked like a watch chain pattern. There were larger tracks too, shaped like clover. They led away into the densest part of the woods.

"Elks' tracks," said Savushkin, following the direction of Anna's gaze. "Don't be afraid," he added, reading an unspoken question in her eyes.

"Have you ever seen one?" asked Anna.

"An elk? No. No such luck," sighed Savushkin, "I've seen elk droppings, though."

"What?"

"Dung," Savushkin explained, embarrassed.

Diving under a twisted willow, the path ran down to the brook again. Parts of the brook's surface were covered with a thick layer of snow; in other parts, its icy armor lay clear and sparkling, and there were spots where unfrozen water stood out in dark blotches like evil eyes.

"Why hasn't it frozen there?" Anna asked.

"Warm springs. Look, you can see one coming up right there."

Bending over the clear water, Anna saw a thin, quivering thread which rose up from the bottom of the stream and burst into tiny bubbles before reaching the surface. It looked like a lily of the valley with a fragile stem and tiny white flowers.

"Plenty of these springs here," Savushkin explained eagerly; "that's why the brook never freezes over completely."

They came to another unfrozen stretch, with pitch-black but transparent water.

Anna threw a handful of snow into it. The snow did not melt, but grew bulkier at once and sank, spreading out in the water like some jellied greenish weeds. This pleased her so much that she started knocking the snow into the water, trying to push off bigger lumps which took on especially fancy shapes. Carried away by the game, she did not

notice Savushkin go on ahead. He perched up on a low tree branch hanging right over the brook and sat waiting for her. A thin layer of ice covered the surface of the brook there, and light, fleeting shadows kept moving over it.

"Look how thin the ice is; you can see the water flowing underneath," said Anna, coming up to the boy.

"Oh, no, Anna Vasilyevna, it's the branch I'm sitting on. It sways and the shadows it throws over the ice sway with it."

Anna blushed. It looked as if she had better hold her tongue here, in the woods.

Savushkin trod on ahead, bending slightly and throwing keen glances around. Anna followed behind.

The winding path led them on and on. There seemed to be no end to all those trees and huge snowdrifts, to that enchanted silence and sunspeckled twilight.

Suddenly a bluish-white patch gleamed ahead. The trees grew sparser. The path rounded a nut bush, and a vast clearing flooded with sunlight opened up before their eyes. In the middle of the clearing, in sparkling white raiment, stood an old oak, tall and majestic like a cathedral. Its branches spread far out over the clearing, and snow nestling in the cracks of the bark made its gigantic trunk look as if inlaid with silver. It had not shed its dried foliage and was now covered to the very crown with snow-capped leaves.

"The winter oak!" gasped Anna. She reverently approached the tree and halted under its glittering branches.

Unaware of the tumult in his teacher's heart, Savushkin busied himself with something at the foot of the trunk, treating the magnificent tree with the familiarity of a long-standing friendship.

"Come here, Anna Vasilyevna," he called. "Look!"

He pushed aside a large clump of snow with earth and old grass clinging to its underside. A little ball plastered with decayed leaves lay in the hollow below. The skeleton-like remnants of the leaves were pierced with sharply pointed needles.

"A hedgehog!" cried Anna.

"See how well he hid himself?" And Savushkin carefully restored the protective covering of earth and snow over the immobile hedgehog. Then he dug at another spot and revealed a tiny cave with icicles hanging at its opening. It was occupied by a brown frog, its tightly stretched skin shiny as if lacquered.

Savushkin touched the frog. It made no movement.

"Isn't he a sly one?" remarked Savushkin. "Pretending he's dead. But just watch him leap as soon as the sun warms him up a bit."

He guided Anna on through the world he knew so well. There were numerous other tenants in and around the oak: bugs, lizards, insects. Some hid among the roots, others in the deep cracks of the bark. Thin, withered, apparently lifeless, they hibernated there all through the winter. The powerful tree accumulated in itself a store of vital warmth, and those poor creatures could not wish for a better shelter. Fascinated, Anna watched this hidden forest life, so little known to her.

"Oh, oh, Mother'll be at work by now!" came Savushkin's anxious voice.

Anna looked at her watch. A quarter past three. She felt trapped. Ashamed for her human frailties and inwardly begging forgiveness of the oak, she said, "Well, Savushkin, this only proves that a shortcut is not always the best way to choose. You'll have to go along the highway from now on."

Savushkin looked down and did not reply.

Heavens! thought Anna, isn't this the clearest proof of my incompetence!

The morning lesson flashed through her mind. How dull and lifeless her explanations were, how utterly devoid of feeling. And she was teaching the children their native language, so beautiful, so rich in shades, color, and meaning! An experienced teacher, indeed! She'd taken no more than a few faltering steps along the path that might well require a whole lifetime to cover. And how is one not

to swerve aside but follow the correct path? Yet the joy with which her pupils shouted familiar words, a joy she had not fully appreciated or shared, told her now that she had not strayed too hopelessly after all.

"Thank you, Savushkin, for the lovely walk," she said. "I didn't mean what I just told you. Of course you can take the forest path to school."

"Thank you, Anna Vasilyevna." Savushkin blushed with pleasure. He wanted to promise his teacher then and there that he would never be late again, but hesitated, because he was afraid he might not keep his promise. He only raised his collar and, pulling down his hat, said, "I'll walk you back to school."

"No, don't, I can find the way myself."

He looked at her in some doubt, then picked up a long stick, broke off its thinner end, and offered it to Anna. "Take this," he said. "If an elk comes your way, just hit him on the back and he'll run for all he's worth. Though better not hit him, just wave the stick at him. He might get angry, you know, and leave the woods for good."

"Don't worry, I shan't hit him," she promised.

She took a few steps back, then stopped and turned to take one last look at the winter oak, tinged with pink by the setting sun. A small dark figure stood at the foot of the trunk. Savushkin did not go home. He stayed to guard his teacher's way, even if from a distance.

And suddenly Anna knew that the most wonderful being in that forest was not the winter oak but this small boy in battered felt boots and patched clothes, the son of a "shower nurse" and a soldier killed in the war.

She waved to him and went on her way.

PART III

Improving Current Practice:
Reflection and Reappraisal

Next Steps: Writing Cases for Your Own Teaching Seminars

Why Write Your Own Teaching Cases?

If experience is the best teacher, what better way to learn about the totality of case method instruction than by writing a teaching case? The potential benefits of this venture include increased sensitivity to all teaching documents, enhanced effectiveness in preparation skills, and the production of materials that help blur the artificial distinction between the seminar room and the world "out there." Cases that reflect a seminar group's daily realities tend to spark high interest. When an instructor comments, "This could have happened to me," the energy level of the whole discussion rises. Like lightning, cases can really sizzle when they strike close to home.

For those intimidated by the idea of writing, let me offer reassurance: writing is a craft. Anyone literate can learn to write better. The basic research, design, and writing skills that I will sketch here may not earn you a Pulitzer Prize, but they can help you produce serviceable cases. The creative act of writing—getting words from your mind to the page—will always enfold a core of mystery. But experienced writers can articulate what they do well enough to advise and teach one another, because writing always involves some version of a basic process. You begin with a compelling idea and a vision of the shape it will take. Then you gather data, cull, and organize the data to fit an emerging pattern; search for words and images to capture your thoughts and impressions; and revise and revise (and revise) to make your vision ever clearer to readers.

Many first-time case authors have, to their pleasant surprise, written wonderful teaching documents—sometimes classics. Beginners, therefore, take heart: however untested your writing abilities, you have a better chance of doing a good job than you may think. In this endeavor, neophytes have a somewhat paradoxical advantage over more experienced colleagues: they think more like readers than writers. This perspective can lend early case-writing efforts an accessibility that veteran case writers struggle to recapture.

Another incentive to writing cases lies in the unique opportunity that case authors often have to witness at least a few of their readers' reactions firsthand. By either leading or observing seminars in which participants discuss your cases, you can road test your products, feel how they handle at cruising speed, and rebuild them if necessary. (When the discussion really zooms, you can sit back and enjoy the ride, with a discreet smile at having constructed such an effective vehicle.) Good reading is a measure of good writing. It's one thing to know that human experience can suggest myriad interpretations, and another to hear a group of reasonable people construct widely different interpretations of events that you thought you knew "cold." In cases that describe teachers in the classroom, even a superficially straightforward question, "And just what is your analysis, Ms. Macomber?" or sympathetic offer, "If you didn't have a chance to study the lesson last night, Jack, just tell me and I won't call on you," can provoke diametrically opposed interpretations. A disciplined and reflective group exploration of your case can show nuances and meanings of which you were unaware. Such revelations can humble as well as enlighten a case author, but they show the power of a written portrait of human experience.

I suspect that, however much instructors and discussion participants learn from a case discussion, the researcher-author learns even more. The interview process gives the researcher unique access to "backstage" information about the story, which, by definition, embodies some principle or way of thinking worth studying. And who but the researcher gets to talk with the teachers and students who participated in the events, sense their personalities, hear the shadings in their voices, and come as close as anyone can, through conversation, to walking a mile in their moccasins? I compare the process of selecting case data to film editing; many wonderful scenes in case drafts end up, sacrificed to brevity or coherence of pattern, on the "cutting room floor," but the researcher-writer sees them all.

The benefits of case writing tend to spill over and create ripples of improvement in a whole institution. The case writers draw strength from the workout that research and writing give the decision-making muscles. And the process of hearing other practitioners describe challenging moments in their professional lives, and capturing those moments in orderly, readable words, can hardly help but enhance teachers' appreciation of the complex decisions that others made to produce *their* cases. Such respect, in turn, raises the likelihood that instructors who write teaching cases will respect and reflect on the details in other people's stories, prepare for class with care and sensitivity, and model these qualities for their students. The net effect: greater learning for all.

Even more benefits emerge when instructors take yet a further step and teach material, "of, by, and for" their own institution *in situ*. Running such a venture takes planning, intellectual and emotional commitment, organizational resources, and a substantial investment of time. But teaching seminars in which the materials give the faculty time to focus and reflect on their own institutional challenges can trigger profound cultural changes. They take the chill off the impersonality of research institutions by fostering alliances across disciplines—a phenomenon largely absent from much of current academia, where specialization isolates instructors, even from other instructors in the same field. When economists, art historians, epidemiologists, and statisticians see their own teaching problems mirrored in another teacher's experiences, alienation begins to give way to appreciation. Participants get support, advice, and respect from a group of professionals who focus on current and common teaching problems. An even more obvious benefit is that participants in a teaching seminar tend to improve as instructors—a nice result for students and the institution as a whole. Everybody wins.

Before You Start: The "Buddy System"

It is virtually essential to enlist a friendly, respected colleague as a sounding board in the case development and writing process. Not an editor, full coauthor, or supervisor, but a helper and coach to act as a "reality check" when you lose perspective on the material (a phase that I, for one, have never figured out how to skip). As a writer, I know only two remedies for loss of objectivity: the disinterested perspective of someone other than yourself and the well-known potion, tincture of time. Putting your work aside and out of mind for several weeks can make it read like someone else's writing (always easier to evaluate than your own). But if you don't have a few weeks to spare, a friend's clear-eyed advice can help sharpen your vision of your work.

From the beginning, it is useful to know that the end product of the case development process isn't the document that you write, but the learning that it will stimulate. The case is an intermediate product, the means by which readers teach themselves and discussion groups teach one another. For student-readers to learn something practical from a case, it must convey truth. But how? With how much detail? In what format? With what tone?

A case writer's need for a sounding board begins when the research begins and ends with the final edited version. A disinterested reader (or listener) can help you distinguish foreground from background issues, plan questions to ask interview subjects, sort through the growing mass of data as you collect it, and (most important) evaluate your drafts for readability. It's never pleasant to hear a friendly critic say, "Interesting material, but I don't see how it fits into this case," or "I just can't understand this paragraph," but the experience of facing and overcoming these challenges—with a focused, clear piece of writing—can exhilarate.

One way in which your sounding board can help you focus on the end product is by going through the mental exercise of preparing the case-in-process as if he or she were going to teach it tomorrow. Does it invite the reader in? Can one read it with reasonable ease? Does it contradict itself? Do some elements overwhelm and obscure others? Is something missing? Have *you*, the author, missed a crucial point? Your colleague's detached analysis may save you from tossing a diamond away in your disciplined search for gold.

I recommend that the collaboration be an unequal partnership. The case writer bears final responsibility for researching, composing, and polishing the case. The sounding board agrees to listen, read, and comment. I have found that a partnership of two is workable. In case development, it's not "the more the merrier," but "the more the muddier." The writer does the hands-on work and puts in the larger share of the time. The sounding board spends far fewer hours on the project, although these can mount up. One way to repay a colleague for helpful criticism is to swap roles and act as his or her sounding board for a future project.

What Makes a Good Case?

My opinions on the elements of a good case reflect my personal taste. I favor teaching cases that make it both fun and fascinating for students to apply their inductive skills—reasoning from particulars to general statements in a Sherlock Holmes style. (With one major difference, I hasten to note: cases portray real events, which stubbornly resist yielding one single, neat, logical solution.) The cases that I like best give students ample details from which to select the ones that they consider significant. The students then speculate about patterns and meanings that the details might suggest, extrapolate actions that case characters might take, based on these patterns of meaning, and challenge one another's hypotheses. Seminar participants' whole experience of cases—reading, studying, and discussing them—yields rules of thumb and general principles that apply to their work lives.

Effective cases portray real people in moments of decision, faced with a need to take action and accept its consequences. Cases need to present enough material for student-readers to make imaginative reconstructions of the world in which the case events took place. This means that the writer should collect and reproduce data about context (physical, emotional, and cultural) as well as characters (teachers, students, administrators, and others), dialogue, and actions. The objective is to find a provocative, puzzling story and recreate it for your readers.

When cases come to life in readers' imaginations, they portray characters "in the round," with voices that ring true even though important details have been disguised for confidentiality. *All* of my teaching cases are disguised, but aim at portraying essential characteristics "from the life." Voice is one of those essentials, because people's characteristic phrasings, cadences, pauses, and hesitations give important clues to their ways of thinking. When cases convey these affective elements, they function as a "second-best" alternative to apprenticeship. A good case gives a reader a long look over the shoulder of a practitioner at work. I hope the following suggestions will help practitioners develop cases like this.

Evaluating Potential Material

The statement that good teaching cases convey real-life experiences has two important implications for evaluating potential material: (1) someone must have had an experience worth studying, and (2) that person must be able and willing to devote the time and energy necessary to relate and reconstruct the experience in interviews with the case writer. The germs of good cases—"leads," like news leads or the tips that help detectives crack *their* cases—come from interview subjects sensitive to the "who," "how," and "where," as well as the "what," in their lives. When an instructor has had some puzzling or intriguing teaching experience from which other instructors might learn, or when the experience, stripped to its essentials, recurs commonly in the profession, you may well be looking at a good case lead. For example, most teachers face unprepared, hostile, or bored students, demands to change grades that the students considered unfair, instances of possible plagiarism, domineering or shy students, and classes in which everybody (teacher included) has a hard time staying awake.

The case subject need not be a teacher. Sometimes a student or observer of an arresting incident has an enlightening tale. Find out if the subject can recount how the events unfolded, not just the outcome. And make sure that the subject understands that the process of getting complete information may take more time than either of you realizes at the outset. (In my experience, good case material *always* does.)

I cannot pretend to account for all the elements that make good case material, but I have noticed these general characteristics:

1. It is possible to see the story as a web of decisions that will lead to consequences.
2. The decisions involve a protagonist (not always the teacher) who must analyze a situation, identify alternative courses of action, and do something—usually under pressure.
3. The story takes place in a complex context (a school, an organization, a society) with characteristics that other settings share.
4. A few key players, or observant witnesses, are available to provide their points of view. They not only see things differently from the protagonist, but may present completely different accounts of the same events. Sometimes their goals and agendas are the opposite of the protagonist's. (A typical example: a teacher who wants to enthrall students with the beauty of her subject, while the students just want to pass the course.)
5. As the prospective case writer—aided by his or her sounding board—steps back to consider the material, it presents *one* broadly applicable theme. Even though several issues and subissues come into play, you can imagine where this case might fit into a syllabus. (One good way to identify this issue is to brainstorm about possible subtitles. The major theme of my case called, "Am I Going to Have to Do This by Myself?"—the difficulty of getting Japanese students to participate in a U.S.-style free-for-all discussion class—didn't emerge clearly until I thought of

subtitling the case, "Diversity and the Discussion Teacher.")
6. The story has one major decision point. Several minor forks in the path, and a resolution that reveals the road taken, may follow. But one can imagine the material being packaged into a rich chunk of data, leading to one complex, intriguing moment (the end of the "A" case). The purpose of this design is to present the discussion group with enough questions to pack a discussion of an hour and a half or more with useful considerations.
7. The events perplex and irritate the character who experienced them. They stick in the mind like grit in oysters, and shells of conjecture grow around them. "How could I have handled this better? What went wrong? Why didn't I see this coming? What can I do to prevent this from happening again?" Some of the best case stories have marinated, mentally, for years before being written.
8. When analyzed, the case events yield common rules of thumb that can apply to a variety of similar situations. Perceiving and learning from the fundamental lessons in a case situation may take time and require focused questioning and guidance from a discussion leader. But the best teaching cases show human nature pulsing under the skin of surface events.

Data Collection

Using Yourself as a Case Subject

If you have had a "juicy" experience that might make a good case, and if you can mentally reconstruct the "who," "when," "where," and "what" with reasonable objectivity, perhaps you should be your first interview subject. One advantage to writing about your own experiences is the relative ease of getting an appointment. Another involves a basic ingredient in the researcher-subject relationship: cooperation. Case subjects must trust interviewers well enough to relax and confide in them. Self-interviewers can, presumably, skip the trust-building stage. Even so, it is never easy to recall and recapture (in words that others can understand) what you saw, heard, and felt at critical moments. And people who recall their own difficult experiences often tend to throw excessively negative light on their own actions. Your sounding board's objectivity can help you evaluate the material, decide whether it is likely to yield broadly applicable learning for other teachers, and determine if you treat yourself as fairly as you would a respected colleague.

One way to gain perspective on your own experience is to regard yourself as another person. Imagine yourself from the outside, as a case character, and then describe that character's actions, feelings, and thoughts in the "as told to" mode. Envision a finished case about Instructor X, who tried to accomplish something and encountered disturbing obstacles. To expedite the process of interviewing yourself for a case, I suggest that you create a disguise early in the process to put some imaginative distance between the real you and the character you are now trying to describe. In general, a case disguise changes a character's name and key elements in his or her physical description, family, academic discipline, course, and teaching institution. It also changes all students' names and descriptions. I recommend minor displacements that preserve vital aspects (personal traits like shyness or extroversion, age, kind of academic training, general character of family background) but add up to a genuine disguise. In my opinion, an effective case disguise, however elaborate, preserves the essence of what happened.

Try to describe your disguised case character on paper. What aspects of yourself can you identify and present for others to appreciate and interpret? What details might serve as clues to the way you live, work, and think? Is there something telling about the way you dress? Are some beliefs essential to how you conduct yourself and evaluate others? What details about how and where you live, your family, and your background are relevant to this case? How do you express yourself in words? What did you say in the key case episodes? In recollecting dialogue, it is helpful to say it out loud or reconstruct it with a colleague. If you think best "on your feet," try writing interview questions and answering them into a tape recorder. As always, your sounding board's reactions to your self-descriptions and the material that you recall will prove invaluable in helping you find balance.

Gathering Case Material from Other People

It seems fairly obvious that, while you may be a marvelous first-case subject, you are unlikely to have encountered enough teaching problems to supply material for a whole string of cases. Most case writers get their data from interviews with other people—a process that involves a network of interrelated challenges. What is most basic is that the relationship between you and your interview subjects must rest on a foundation of trust. By confiding details of a puzzling, dramatic, or troubling event, your colleague is giving you a gift, a piece of his or her life. Let him or her know that you intend to treat it with respect and, above all, will do your best to prevent the gift from causing problems for the giver (or anyone described in the story). I have found it helpful to tell interview subjects how and where the case under development might be used.

The best interview subjects are not only candid but also tough-minded. They can depict themselves in unflattering circumstances with balance and a degree of humor. They have good recall, powers of observation, and enough adventurous spirit to risk being direct with you. For people unfamiliar with the case study method, I have explained that the sole objective of writing the story is to educate, never to cause problems. Sometimes, in recounting their own actions, teachers unintentionally portray themselves in ways that others may interpret as insensitive. Particularly when challenged unexpectedly in class, teachers often react awkwardly. I make it clear that I will disguise all material and delete potentially troublesome elements.

The case writer's responsibility is to help seminar groups (or individual student-readers) see broadly useful lessons in stories that portray characters in difficult situations. No one has much to gain by taking an unsympathetic, purely negative approach to a case character's predicament. Seminar groups that never get past blaming a character for his or her problems fail to appreciate the most useful aspects of the story: the underlying factors that created the situation in the first place, and ways in which they might evaluate their own practices to detect the ominous presence of similar factors. Seminar groups that look for actions, attitudes, and assumptions that they have in common with the case character tend to learn. As a case researcher and writer, your job is to collect material that will enable readers and students of the case to view the main characters' vulnerabilities with empathetic understanding.

Part of your contract with your interview subjects, then, is to observe a version of the Hippocratic oath: Do no harm. Remember that, in the case characters' positions and given their circumstances and the information that they had at the time, most of us would have done at least as poorly, if not worse. Your sincere desire should be to ground your relationship with your interview subjects in *fairness*. If they don't trust you, they will never speak honestly, spontaneously, or give you any "good stuff" for your case—and the product will suffer accordingly.

It takes a great deal of intellectual and emotional energy to muster and maintain the balance of rapport and intellectual detachment needed to grasp and convey someone else's experience. All case writers face and must conquer the temptation to project their personal interpretations, tastes, and emotional reactions onto the material. I have no surefire method for fighting this tendency, but listening carefully and keeping your records of interview subjects' remarks scrupulously distinct from your reactions can help. At times, I have drawn a line down the page of my interview notepad and written my interview subject's words on one side and my own (shorthand) reactions on the other.

It is also helpful to offer sources the opportunity to review their own comments—at a late-draft stage, after eliminating problematic material and disguising key elements. I show subjects only their own material. And I always let major sources know that the case will not be published without their signed release. When interview subjects understand that they are active participants with control over the process, they tend to relax and cooperate.

Being human, interview subjects are unique. But I have noticed a few underlying similarities that suggest some basic types of subjects who might require certain responses. My typology is one example; many others are possible. After you gain experience as an interviewer and case writer, you may want to develop your own.

1. The Resister. Some interview subjects participate at the behest of their superiors. Others present some information readily, but become shy when the interviewer asks probing questions. Whatever the source of the interviewee's reluctance, the writer will find that setting an explicit contract of behavior is invaluable. Reassuring an interviewee that the case will be not be released without a suitable disguise, that he or she will have the right to review it before publication, or that it will not be published until some stipulated time can often overcome potential blocks.

2. The Paper Doll. Some interviewees want to co-operate, but in conversation (perhaps about uncomfortable moments of decision), they speak stiffly. Their words are flat and without "juice." One technique to overcome this problem is to ask that the interviewee go over an episode several times—requesting more detail each time. "What did he say then?" "What did you think?" For the first several iterations, you may get analysis instead of story. I suggest that you keep asking simple, factual questions and back away from the "whys." Questions that call for analysis steer the interview subject's thoughts away from the guts of the story—and that's where the energy is.

3. The Fountain. Some interviewees can drench the case writer with their loquaciousness. They enjoy the attention, have near-total recall, and love to talk. In these situations, I suggest focusing on distinct threads in their conversation—aspects that you think you can use in the case. Try to concentrate on these and let the rest of the stream flow by. When the informant wanders off the topic, interrupt gently with a remark like, "Could we get back to that later? Right now, can you remember what Constance said right after you asked her to come up and write her question on the board?"

4. The Specialist. This species of interviewee is so imbued with a particular subject that he or she repeatedly shies away from talking about teaching it and launches into a lesson instead. Such instructors keep trying to turn the interviewer into a student. When your goal is to collect case material, not learn the teacher's particular discipline, this type of interviewee can lure you far off course (especially if you find the subject interesting and feel tempted to play student for a while). Again I suggest saying something like, "I'd love to learn more about this, but right now, can you tell me how the class reacted when you sprang that pop quiz on them?" Your task is to gather information about the *teaching* process, not the content.

5. The Innocent. Occasionally, case subjects become so involved in telling their stories that they provide too much personal information—intimate details about themselves, families, or students. Academics can be open and candid. Sometimes they fail to see potential problems that airing such material might raise in class. The ethics of case writing dictate that the writer give

thought to such sensitivities, even if the case interview subjects do not. It is the writer's job to protect sources and make every reasonable attempt to ensure that their stories will appear only in a form and a venue that cannot hurt them. Given the choice between writing a juicy case that might embarrass an interview subject and writing no case at all, drop the case.

6. The Painted Window. Some academics have so indelibly acquired the habit of analyzing that they have lost the ability to reconstruct the data on which they based their assessments. They remind me of painted shop windows: there may be a lot going on behind the surface, but you can't see it. Packaged insights like, "Jeremy behaved inappropriately when his opinion was questioned in class," do not make good case material. As an interviewer, you hope that a subject can reconstruct dialogue and action—something more like, "Jeremy jumped up and shook his fist at Seth when Seth said, 'Look, Jeremy, shouting doesn't prove nuclear power is unsafe.'" It isn't unusual for academics to answer an opening question— "What happened?"—with an analytical pronouncement. But if your interview subject answers a probing question—"Can you *reconstruct* what actually happened?"—with, "I just did," and offers similar replies to a few more attempts at prying the story open, your chances of seeing beyond that painted window are probably slim.

I have no goof-proof recipe for successful interviewing. But some leads are colder than others, and a preliminary conversation with prospective interview subjects will show if they can reconstitute and articulate experiences. When you actually interview your subjects, listening for patterns, looking ahead to next questions, and trying to get the essence of their dialogue constitute quite a complex job. I suggest noting their most memorable words—the ones that strike *you*—on paper. (I prefer note taking to tape recording because it forces me to pluck key words and phrases from the stream of dialogue as I listen. Note taking fatigues the hand muscles, but sharpens the attention and powers of discernment.)

In first interviews, after setting a few ground rules, get a sense of context. Ask not only about the instructor, but about the institution, the course, the student group, and individual students in the core incidents. I make impressionistic notes about

aspects of the subject's general appearance— phrases like "warm smile," "sits up very straight," "put feet on desk," "casual attire," "low voice," "paces when talks," "taps pencil on notepad," and the like. I try to reserve judgment and make sure not to include details that might give offense. It's one thing to write, "Professor Blake Parker—thirty-two years old, 5'10" tall, black-haired and hazel-eyed, liked to teach in jeans and cowboy boots," and another thing to say, "Blake Parker's casual attire undercut his attempts to develop a professional image." You may believe this, but, in case writing, it is your student-readers' job, not yours, to make a judgment call about Blake—and some of them may not agree with you.

One way to avoid giving offense is to ask interview subjects to describe themselves. Using the disguise name, ask something like, "Bearing in mind that our case character, Professor Carpenter, isn't you, but has your essential characteristics, tell me what she looks like. Where is she from? What course is she teaching? Who is in the class?" Promising subjects often warm to such creative opportunities. They get into the case development process, and their material perks up. As their conversation gains momentum, you, the case writer, must listen, mentally predict further questions, and decide which of many possible paths you will explore. To keep on track, it is helpful to have an idea, however hazy, of the finished case.

In all case interviews, you should listen not only for data, but also for patterns. What themes are emerging as you listen? Try to think about where this conversation might lead, and use your developing sense of direction to formulate the next questions. Insofar as we listen for patterns and try to see where they lead, we case researchers behave like discussion leaders: we attempt to make sense of an unscripted, unplanned flow of questions and responses without controlling, second-guessing, or annihilating its spontaneity. Good interviews, like good discussion classes, raise many questions and settle none. But neither should be chaotic. Both have to get somewhere. A good interview should reveal some aspects of the finished case.

Working with the Material

Some very practical considerations govern how you accumulate, shape, and develop case data. Most of the cases I have written were tailored to a specific teaching format: a class session of about an hour and a half, with the first hour devoted to a few introductory remarks or links to previous sessions, and then a good, long look at the issues, actions, and problems that the bulk of the case story raises for this group. Cases that fit this format open with a series of episodes that lead a central character to a dramatic decision point. I generally label this first segment (A) and often (but not always) follow it with a (B) which reveals what the protagonist did and what response his or her action triggered. Sometimes the (B) section plunges the case character deeper into hot water and leads to (C), (D), and even (E) segments. Often, the last segment of a case presents the protagonist's own "lessons learned" with the wisdom (or, at least, the distance) of hindsight.

As a rule, the seminar group spends the first hour identifying key players in the story, laying out alternative actions that they might take, producing some analysis of how things got to this (usually sorry) state in the first place, and formulating predictions about what happened next. All of this implies that the raw material to support such a discussion exists in the (A) case.

In interviewing case subjects, my familiarity with this format leads me to listen for a major "case break" and imagine it as the ending of the (A) segment. Then I mentally categorize further pieces of the story into potential (B), (C), and other segments. As I listen, I try to keep the case subject's analytical observations (and my own) separate from his or her retelling of the events. I also try to take notes that will enable me to produce a case calibrated to the sophistication of the intended student audience, its expertise at case analysis, the anticipated position of the case in a curriculum, and the general teaching objectives.

All of these considerations are on my mind—and that of my sounding board—during the whole case development process. But they come to the fore when I plan my interviews. Case researchers need to develop increasingly sharp focus as they interview and re-interview subjects. The better your appreciation of the core issues in the case, the more focused your questions will be—and I have yet to meet a case subject with unlimited time (or patience) for interviews.

I do not mean to suggest that only one format will work. On the contrary, good teaching cases come in many sizes, shapes, and styles. There is no perfect pattern that, cut along the dotted line, will

always yield a case of professional caliber. For that matter, I regard any one-size-fits-all pattern for cases with suspicion because case writing includes an element of artistry and will therefore always resist standardization. There are one-page cases that raise such provocative, pervasive issues that they easily support an hour and a half of discussion and leave seminar participants still talking at the end of the class. Other cases run to ten- or twenty-page (A) segments, with briefer (but sometimes still fairly lengthy) follow-ups. I try to cut all segments after (A) to a page or less, so they can be distributed, read, and discussed in a single class session. But not all cases follow this pattern.

As a rule, I hand out the (A) case before class, for students to read, reread, and reflect on. It should provide food for a good, chewy discussion—ideally one that raises many issues and gets people emotionally as well as intellectually involved in probing their implications. The (A) case gives readers what they need to understand the nature of the situation, what's at stake for the characters, their challenges, and some inkling of why they did what they did and said what they said. Intriguing (A) cases tend to end with a "cliffhanger." One measure of the success of an (A) case is the interest that a discussion group appears to have in the case character's fate. If you leave a protagonist hanging off a cliff and nobody cares, it's a pretty fair indication that you have more rewriting to do.

As a case writer, your purpose is to construct a document that will not only involve your readers, but stimulate discussion on a reasonably predictable set of topics. Surprises can occur, but in general, you have some control over the way students will respond to your document because the conventions of case study dictate that discussion should spring from specific case details. How would you like students to work with this material? What details would you like to see treated as clues to some underlying process or general rules? Listen for these details as you interview and review your notes. And be sure to include them in your case drafts.

In practice, I have found that the case development process calls on different qualities, attitudes, and skills at different times. Even during the course of a single interview, the researcher's reactions can fluctuate. As your subject tells one anecdote, you may identify intensely—"Yes, yes, in your place, I'd have done exactly the same thing." At other times, still writing attentively, you may feel detached or even confused—"Now why on earth did you react like that?" Case researchers cannot check their personalities and opinions at the door when they gather material or assess it—another good reason to enlist your sounding board's help early and often.

At times, despite your best efforts to keep subjects focused, the material that you anticipated will simply not emerge from the interviews. A variety of pressures can blunt your realization (or willingness to admit) that your material just won't make a usable case. Again, your sounding board's helpful reactions to your interview notes can alert you when this happens. Sometimes when you listen to your interview subject again, you may see a different, perhaps better, case taking shape. For example, a case originally about a teacher's efforts to integrate a socially difficult student into a discussion group eventually focused on the baffling task of how to fill out the student's official evaluation form. Another interview process to develop a case about an instructor's regret for "shutting down" a talkative student—by dismissing his question in class—yielded a case on a far more topical problem: how to get students from very different cultural and linguistic backgrounds to join a large group discussion in a U.S.-style classroom.

It is helpful to give cases rough working titles that capture some flavor of their central issues, even during the interview process. It is also essential to jettison and replace these titles when the case material develops in an unforeseen direction. I called one case "The Square Peg," until my sounding board suggested that it had less to do with helping a discussion section group deal with an abrasive member than with the instructor's perplexity about how to describe the "square peg" for an official evaluation. The case came into sharp focus only after I changed its title to "The Blank Page." While reviewing another case, which knit together several different plot strands, an early reader commented that my working title, "How Shall I Grade Them?," had the potential to confuse readers by making them look for a single, pervasive concern with grading. In fact, the case contained many intriguing teaching problems, and I renamed it after its main character, "Anna Winters," to encourage readers to broaden their sights.

Sometimes case interview data pile up but refuse to yield clear issues. At times like this, chaos threatens. If you and your sounding board are rea-

sonably certain that the research process is going nowhere, you should be prepared to drop the project. A corollary to this is that it is wise to pursue more than one case lead at a time, so you always have a spare.

A Few Suggestions about Writing Style

Cases can take many different tones. Some are extended conversations, for example, the questions and answers of a researcher and an interview subject, or a reported classroom dialogue. Some are narratives; mini-histories told in classic "omniscient narrator" style and interspersed with quotations. Some present multiple perspectives (the "Rashomon" or *Alexandria Quartet* type). Others—the "I am a Camera" variety—stick to one character's viewpoint. Some describe people's thoughts and feelings; others give only externally observable data. Some have a clinical, antiseptic tone; others—emotive, experiential, full of dialogue and description—use techniques of fiction and drama so readers "play" the episodes in their minds like movies. I prefer this last type because I have seen cases like this trigger intellectual and emotional involvement in discussion groups, and I have faith that the union of intellect and feeling characterizes productive learning.

Tone stems from diction, by which I mean the kind of words used. Is the vocabulary casual or formal? Are there many descriptive words? What kinds of verbs are used? Does the writer take the reader into his or her confidence and speak like a friend—or is there a cool, scientific cast to the words? All of these considerations become important in the writing process because they determine the feel of the finished document.

As far as case length, I agree with Shakespeare's Polonius: "brevity is the soul of wit." Unfortunately, like Polonius, I achieve this goal less often than I would like. Particularly in the early stages of a teaching seminar, very short cases (a few pages) keep the barriers to participation low and give the discussion leader class time to make introductions and help the group begin to form a collaborative working relationship. Later in a seminar, longer cases can give participants scope to explore, stretch, and probe for deep meanings. But overwriting is a far more common flaw than underwriting. (One recalls a famous apology for a long letter attributed to Voltaire—he hadn't had the time to make it shorter.) Early interview notes and case drafts tend to swell, and the writer must sweat to raise their muscle-to-fat ratio.

Like any creative activity, writing always includes an element of mystery, but certain aspects, or stages, seem to characterize it. Whatever one does to transfer impressions and ideas from inside one's head to the page, takes physical effort. The process often involves a degree of anxiety—and commensurate relief when the words are finally "out there." Many writers stop at this point. Having found verbal equivalents for their ideas and impressions, they think they've finished the job, but they're only half right. As countless unreadable reports, memoranda, business letters, and even published articles and books attest, the whole task involves making the material accessible to the *reader*. Think how a student-reader will see (hear, feel, and even taste) your words. What will he or she link them with? What thoughts and analyses might they trigger? This part of the writing process is as essential as the effort of crystallizing and encoding your own thoughts.

It can be helpful to picture your audience as you write. How old are these people? How academically advanced? How experienced with case study? How much time will they have to prepare this case for discussion? I recommend that you write for people as intelligent, busy, fatigued, humorous, irritable, emotional, curious, well-intentioned, and generally *human* as you are, even if they may be younger, less academically advanced, or from different backgrounds. Try to put yourself in their circumstances. What would a quick skim of this manuscript yield for you? What words or phrases would grab you? What would you underline, come back to, puzzle over? What would get under your skin?

As a writer, you cannot really control your readers' reactions. But you do have the power to include some details and discard others. And you can place some information prominently (at the beginning or ends of subsections, for example, or in subtitles). Your decisions about what facts to include, how to phrase them, and how to order them within the pattern of your case all guide your readers. As you write, imagine what your readers might think as they read. How are you going to grab and hold their attention until you're done telling your story?

To lure readers into your prose, involve as many of their senses as you can. Appealing to intellect alone can make for dry reading and listless discussions. Include alliteration and assonance so that readers hear melodious cadences in their minds. Few people forget a title like *Pride and Prejudice.* But what if Jane Austen had called her novel *Inflated Self-Perception of Status and Biased Assessment of Members of Other Social Units?* It is also useful to vary the length and syntax of sentences, using first a short one, then a longer one, then, perhaps, a fragment. Like this. Check to see if most of your paragraphs begin with participial phrases or the same words or phrases. Repetition dulls the mind. Also, it is usually effective to put important details at the beginning or end of paragraphs because many readers skim the middle portion.

In my experience, many effective tools for crafting lively cases come from fiction and drama. As Robert Coles points out in *The Call of Stories*, we learn the most enduring lessons from the tales of human life. Even though cases should depict events that really happened, the techniques of fiction writing have a paradoxical power to render reality in a form that someone who wasn't there can grasp. (The British novelist E. M. Forster observed, "We ask of fiction that it shall be true." To me, the remark should be taken not at face value, but rather as a useful hint about the value of fiction technique in portraying reality.)

Natural dialogue catches readers' attention. Seminar participants often cite it, dwell on it, and interpret it in class. Neophyte writers tend to clutter reconstructed conversations with intrusive attributive phrases and unnecessary adverbs. Consider, for example, the following:

"Hello, Paul, I'm surprised to see you," said Professor Julia Rose in a wary voice.

"Why, did you think I'd left school?," Paul replied.

"Please come in and sit down," she invited.

"I'll stand," he said, leaning against the doorway.

"What's on your mind?," Julia inquired.

"That F you gave me. I'll be suspended if I flunk this course. You've got to give me at least a C," Paul demanded.

"That's quite impossible," said Julia, getting angry, "You didn't do the work and everybody else did."

How would this dialogue read without the interpretive cues?

Throughout the whole case development process, from data collection to final editing, the observations of your sounding board can help you remember your readers and point you back to the main path when you stray. When you begin to get lost in excess data and blur the distinction between foreground and background issues (the ever-present "forest and trees" problem), your "buddy" can rescue you. It is possible, but much more difficult and time-consuming, to rescue yourself. But whatever your working situation, you will find it useful to keep a mental map of the case story. Into what central line of decisions and outcomes do all of its episodes flow, like tributaries into a river? What are its most salient themes, issues, questions, problems? What is this case "about"?

Farther down the Path

These brief remarks merely open the topic of case development and writing. Those who undertake the adventure will quickly discover its intricacies, frustrations, illuminations, and joys. Those who develop a series of cases may become so engrossed in the process that they take the next natural step and form their own case writing-teaching seminars. This experience involves many challenges—administrative, organizational, intellectual, and pedagogical. But, as I have noted, its benefits achieve and far exceed "consciousness raising." A home-grown seminar can foster true community in a seminar group by showing its members that they belong to a fellowship of teachers, and that they all have something to teach, and learn from, their colleagues. In addition to elevating the general level of effective instruction at an institution, this discovery helps enhance respect for the craft of teaching, as well as for its practitioners. Perhaps most important, it can encourage broad cultural evolution away from isolation toward creative cooperation, humaneness, and warmth.

READING

The Uses of Videotape Replay

CATHERINE G. KRUPNICK

Our traditional regime for preparing college-level teachers is curiously empty at its center. College and university teachers are carefully trained in research skills, in the arts of writing books and articles, and even in the folkways of academic administration. Paradoxically, however, they seldom receive instruction in the one activity that is at the core of their profession, namely, classroom teaching.

Beginners at the craft of college teaching usually face three problems: they lack experience, training for classroom communication, and a source of reliable feedback on their performance. Moreover, these problems are not restricted to beginners. Even experienced teachers face the same difficulties whenever they switch from one course or student population to another. Closely examined, the causes of these difficulties appear rooted in the current traditions of higher education. But before proceeding to discuss causes, it is important to state the good news. There is a quick and fairly easy solution available, which takes the form of establishing a video-replay-based service for teachers.

Such a service is simple to understand and implement. It employs an advisor (sometimes a professional who is a veteran college teacher—often a peer volunteer) and a videotape of the subject-teacher's own classroom situation. Its strengths are that it provides reliable and detailed data for teachers who wish to work on their teaching, and it provides a situation conducive to the serious discussion of classroom teaching. Taken in combination, these factors ameliorate many of the causes of ineffective teaching.

Insufficient training in classroom communication, lack of closely examined experience, and a paucity of feedback have several causes. One is that teachers are appointed to be professional "experts," and thus often find it awkward to ask their colleagues for fundamental advice. Even when they do request help, the specialization of college and university teachers by discipline obscures the common features of effective teaching that extends across fields. In addition, because college teachers spend relatively little time in the classroom (compared, for instance, with primary or secondary schoolteachers who gain a minimum of thirty hours of classroom experience per week), the rate at which college teachers learn their craft is comparatively slow. Finally, a third obstacle to acquiring the craft of college teaching is the confusing quality of feedback on one's own performance.

Most colleges and universities provide instructors little if any support or supervision by veteran teachers. Instructors are left, instead, to rely on end-of-semester evaluations which praise or denounce (too frequently with such vague phrases as "boring" or "interesting") after it is impossible to adjust one's teaching. And because their teacher-student contact hours are limited, most teachers feel they have scant opportunity to monitor students' progress. It is difficult to develop any skill without feedback, and teaching is no exception. What videotape replay services do—in teaching as in sports—is help teachers learn to monitor their environment and their performance within that environment.

Helping College and University Teachers in Classroom-Teaching Skills

The comments below are based on the author's work helping teachers become informed experts in their own craft. As advisor to and director of the Harvard Danforth Video Laboratory (now the Derek Bok Center for Teaching), a faculty development institution established in 1975, I spent thousands of hours talking with individuals who were watching videotape replays of their own classes. Since publication of the second edition of this book in 1987, I have continued practicing and teaching faculty development. It is a pleasure to note that the comments and suggestions offered below are still received as sound and helpful. A few changes have been made to clarify or update technical advice, but the program described is qualitatively the same as it was in 1985.

Indeed, both the program and protocol described below have made the transition from "experimental" to "established." Reasonable skepticism, borrowed rooms, and tentative support from the faculty gave way to enthusiasm, designated rooms, and generous support. Our equipment is ample and up-to-date. But facilities and hardware are unimportant compared with the provisions of an *in situ* tape and an empathic listening ear. These mainstays of our work will be described first.

The Video Solution: Facilitating the Process of Learning from Oneself

To learn classroom skills, teachers must have accurate data on what they do with students and on how individual students react. Often, teachers see the effects of subject matter on only the most active students. Thus even instructors with very keen memories find that videotape replays provide a highly informative account of classroom dynamics.

Providing Tapes

Providing instructors with a videotape record of their teaching is easy. The most basic pieces of equipment—a portable camera, omnidirectional microphone, and playback unit—are inexpensive and widely available at colleges and universities. Even amateurs can make useful tapes, as long as they remember four basic rules: first, *tape teachers and students in actual classroom settings*; second, *show teachers and students reacting to one another*; third, *focus on students' reactions to each other*; and finally, *less than 25% of what appears on screen will focus on the instructor*. Beyond these simple taping rules, any refinements that one can add should be regarded as extras. Of course, a zoom lens adds useful detail and a sound equalizer makes voices sound more pleasant. But nothing is as important as capturing the actual classroom interaction, for that is the data base which makes learning from tapes possible.

Providing Counseling; Framing the Consulting Session

Although videotape can be a wonderful tool, it does have the potential to do harm. The greatest danger attending videotape replay is that teachers who watch themselves on tape may come away from the experience feeling worse about themselves *and* their students.

We have found, however, that this disappointment seldom arises from the teacher's performance *per se*, since teachers already expect the worst on this count. Rather, video-induced despair is more likely to stem from the cosmetic distortions produced by the medium itself. Tapes made *in situ* usually exaggerate a person's weight and age, make receding hairlines recede further back, make voices sound somewhat high and flat, and magnify regional accents. Never mind how "objective" tape is supposed to be, it is neither realistic nor flattering. Worse still, it lacks television's liveliness; for the first few minutes of viewing, teachers may feel a hard-to-pinpoint sensory deprivation. The importance of warning clients about cosmetic disappointments before you even turn on the viewing monitor cannot be overestimated. Regardless of how sincere your clients are about examining their teaching, you must prepare them for the physical aspects of their image before you can get down to the business of analyzing their teaching. The first thing to keep in mind is this: *Never* let clients watch their own tapes by themselves! Without a trained professional to help them focus away from their distorted appearance, and on their class's behavior, even the most sincerely intentioned instructor is likely to come away having learned more about video images than about teaching.

Ordinarily, it takes twice as long to view a class tape as it does to tape it. This means that you should schedule a two-hour session for viewing a one-hour class. Usually, the best way to begin is by having the teacher state his or her objectives and concerns about a taped class, and then move on from the necessary preliminary warnings to actual plans—for example: "I'd like to warn you that videotape has 20/20 vision—it is capable of adding, say, 20 pounds and 20 years to the average teacher. Moreover, it distorts voices and accents, so please be prepared for an unrealistic depiction of your body and voice. What we will be watching is more like a home movie than television! Unless I warn you about this, it would be natural for you to wonder why your class lacks the technical liveliness we associate with television, and I don't want you to have to spend the next couple of hours wondering why your class lacks a certain undefinable something . . . Most teachers find they get used to it within a few minutes. Do you have any questions? . . . All right then, let's get an opening shot of you and your class starting up, and then you can introduce me to your students."

By focusing away from the teacher's physical person, the advisor helps the client focus on the classroom environment. In most cases, the teacher will accept this transition, although some need to pause and bemoan their poor posture or ask you if they are moving their hands "too much." Questions like this are not an impediment to your work, as long as you remember that the tape itself is the primary data base. Within a few viewings, responses such as "How would we be able to decide what 'too much' is?" will come naturally to you.

Beyond Framing: Seeing and Concluding

In most cases, teachers who watch their tapes closely will identify both the problems in their teaching and the requisite solutions, with only occasional prompting from their advisor. Given two hours to review sixty minutes of tape, both teacher and advisor will usually begin by discussing the teacher's overall objectives and then the objectives of an individual class session, then progress to the challenges posed by individual students, and, finally, end with a clearly delineated set of behavioral goals. Examples of behavioral goals might include facing the class while lecturing, looking around the class purposively, to encourage infrequent contributors, or intervening when a long-winded, dominant student begins to lecture the class.

The advisor should encourage the teacher to take the conversational lead. Sometimes, silence will result. (Of course, silence is easiest when two people feel at ease with each other. This ease will usually come naturally if you let the teacher take the conversational lead.) If, however, you find that a silence between you seems to be lasting forever, check your watch and count the seconds of silence. There will be fewer than you think! Most teachers will be eager to discuss their teaching with you; don't worry about keeping a conversation going. Your job is to keep the teacher's attention focused on the content of the tape, or on issues arising directly out of tape watching.

Many people find the hardest part of an advisor's job is maintaining a focused and nonjudgmental attitude. Keep in mind that it's far easier to give very general advice or to get drawn into a conversation about subject matter than to refrain and let the tape provide evidence. Remember also that teachers feel this temptation too, and it often gets in the way of their students' learning. Finally, keep in mind, also, Disraeli's maxim that "it's easier to criticize than to create."

There are likely to be many times during the course of a tape-viewing session when you will have strong opinions about how a teacher should have behaved or refrained from behaving. Again, your job is to maintain your silence until the teacher has asked for your opinion—or until the tape has demonstrated your point conclusively. For example, your observation that a given teacher speaks quickly and avoids eye contact with students is merely a criticism *until* the teacher has noticed the same thing and asked for confirmation, or *until* the tape shows several students losing the battle with rapid note taking. The creation of a worthwhile "advising" period lies in being willing to *confirm* observations and to help the teacher focus into a realistic plan of action. There are, however, additional considerations—role-modeling pointers, really—which you should keep in mind as well. The first of these is to refer to students by name whenever possible. Since the teacher has already introduced you to the students at the beginning ("framing") of the session, names are focal pieces of knowledge which you and your client share. If you refer to students by name, the teacher will feel comfortable in doing so too; the value of your tape-watching session will be doubled if this behavior is encouraged in the classroom.

Speak as specifically as possible; avoid generalizations. Rather than answering an inquiry (about, for example, whether a teacher is talking too fast and avoiding eye contact) with a simple "yes" or "no" or "compared with most teachers . . . ," direct your client's question to the evidence on tape. You might say, for instance, "Let's look to the tape and see what evidence we can find . . . It does seem that Doris and Mike look as if they're relaxed and keeping up, but the others *do* seem to be tensed up over their notebooks . . . Also, I notice those three in the back row in sweatshirts—Elizabeth and Lou and Toby—looking at each others' notebooks. Do you think *they're* behind?"

Third—and this has already been implied—keep your eyes on the tape at all times. When you and your client want to discuss a point, *put the tape on pause* and hold it there. Anything you do that underscores an interest in seeing and hearing the *whole class* imparts a feeling of respect for the teacher's endeavors.

Finally, remember that one of videotape's main advantages is its instant-replay capability. Many problems that arise during the class are rooted in events that happened earlier in the hour. You and the teacher with whom you're working will probably want to find those events which triggered the problem you're discussing. Sudden inattentiveness on the part of diligent students, for example, is frequently the result of something that the teacher or another student has said; find out if this is the case. And urge your teacher-client to suggest parts of the tape that should be reviewed in order to examine the roots of perplexing classroom behaviors.

Such diagnostic and prescriptive work, however, is not the whole story of a first two-hour session. The first session should also be considered an opportunity to accomplish something equally important—namely, to identify and reinforce the most positive aspects of the teacher's instructional behavior. Novice teachers, in particular, often have unrealistically low opinions of their own skills. Thus, your first viewing session should be aimed at realistic assessment. For example, many beginning

math teachers discover to their surprise and pleasure that they really do give clear answers to student questions, convey enthusiasm for elegant mathematical solutions, and outline class material effectively. The professional pride that beginning instructors can justifiably take in these areas of competence is a powerful inducement for them to invest in changing the less-satisfactory aspects of their classroom performance, such as an overly rapid pace of delivery, or infrequent use of students' names. By the end of your first viewing session with a teacher, the two of you should be able to state both the teacher's strengths and long-term improvement objectives as well as that teacher's immediate goals for change in the classroom.

Repeat the Experience

As important as these critical and reinforcing experiences of the first two-hour session are, however, they do not exhaust the potential of video-based consultation. Ideally, teachers will view themselves at least three times in the course of a semester. If they do, the review of a second classroom tape, made within a few weeks of the first one, will provide an opportunity to assess progress toward the teacher's target objectives, and to elaborate a second set of immediate goals. This is also an integral part of motivating the teacher to remain attentive to the lessons of the first tape-viewing session. Ordinarily, teachers leave the second session with a deepening understanding of their professional assets, an informed self-evaluation of their progress, and an expanded list of target objectives for future work. In addition, the second session also broadens the scope of the inquiry beyond the characteristics of the teacher's behavior to the fairly predictable behaviors of individual students in the classroom. It is at this time that many teachers consider the various ways in which particular students or classroom dynamics work to shape the presentation of material.

When a third or fourth viewing session can be arranged, it will sharpen your focus from the teacher's behavior to interaction between the teacher and the dynamics of the class. The third session may confirm earlier findings or provide new, sometimes contradictory, data. Either way, it will provide a new text for the analysis of classroom behaviors.

A third session is often scheduled after the teacher has shifted to new students and subject matter at the outset of a new semester. Far from being a disaster, such changes in class and subject matter provide an opportunity for the instructor to summarize the methodological lessons learned during the first two sessions, and generalize from them. By this time teachers are usually fairly fluent at articulating classroom problems and at generating lists of target objectives with minimal assistance from their advisors. Nevertheless, the opportunity to do so aloud is important because it builds self-confidence. In addition, the third session also gives teachers the opportunity to reflect for the first time upon all of the major variables in the craft of self-disciplined teaching, and all at once: teacher behavior, class dynamics, and subject matter. This permits teachers and advisors to explore more subtle craft issues, such as how to direct discussion by drawing on the strengths of individual students or how to assess the evolution of learning among various groups of students.

Three Examples

The following three examples[1] should help clarify the objectives and accomplishments of videotape replay sessions.

EXAMPLE NO. 1: Jesse Jensen, a teaching fellow with two years' previous experience, responding to the question "How can I help you with your classroom teaching?"

> I like teaching my sociology class, but I don't think I will by the end of the semester. I feel like things are about to go out of control. I worry about what part I should play in getting students to talk. Things go pretty well in the sense that we cover material during the hour—but it's October, we've been meeting for a month, and I'm beginning to realize that there are some smart people in the section of twenty students who hardly ever say anything. I don't want to call on people who don't have their hands raised, because that doesn't seem to be a good way to get the best answers; but I don't want the shyer students to get short-changed just because there are a couple of highly verbal pre-law types in the section. What should I do?

The advisor turned the question around by asking Jesse what he could see on the tape that suggested

a solution. Jesse, however, still found it hard to address the issue of imbalanced participation directly:

> Well, what I immediately think about is whether or not people can learn when they're intimidated. . . . I mean there have been many situations in graduate school where I've had nothing at all to contribute. I always hate being called on in a time like that.

The advisor's objective in this case was to direct the conversation to allow Jesse to realize that his confusion about teaching strategies was due—at least in part—to having insufficient information. (Usually a question like "Do you remember your response last time one of the shy students responded?" shifts the teacher's focus away from the immediate need for a solution to a broadly defined teaching problem toward a desire for more information.) At this juncture, the advisor suggested they continue playing the tape to see what new information could be gained.

Within minutes, Jesse noticed something about his teaching style that contributed to the uneven patterns of participation: when the highly verbal "pre-law" types talked, he listened silently and intently, even picking up a pencil to jot down notes on their contributions. But when more retiring students talked, they received a far different response. Almost as soon as they opened their mouths to talk, Jesse got to work "encouraging them" with short interruptions of "uh-huh, uh-huh, very good." Just as invariably, they took this as a signal to be brief; their contributions were shorter, and Jesse did not take notes on them. The teacher and advisor noticed another thing, as well: the students who sat directly flanking him *never* talked.

From these observations Jesse derived two hypotheses. First, the students who were interrupted by the teacher (regardless of how these interruptions were intended) were less likely to volunteer comments. And, second, there seemed to be an inverse relationship between being "out of sight" and a tendency toward participation. The benefit of having hypotheses based on solid evidence is that they suggest possibilities for experimentation. In this case, the experiment was simple: Jesse, the teacher, would change his seating so that he would sit directly across the table from the quieter students, and he would attempt to maintain fairly regular eye contact with each speaker. Also, he would

---

1. All three examples are disguised to protect the identity of involved participants.

make no verbal interruptions at all while any student was speaking. If these hunches proved to be correct, participation would even out.

Jesse and the advisor allowed a week to pass, taped another class, and—upon review—found that the experiment had succeeded. In the second viewing of the class, not only did two of the retiring students talk, but also, a third shy person (one who had formerly sat next to Jesse) contributed thoughtfully and at considerable length toward the end of the class.

Of course these conversational techniques were specifically suggested for one context—Jesse's sociology class. A sensitive teaching advisor will approach each new tape with the idea that a unique response might be necessary for this particular admixture of client and teaching situation.

It is often assumed that viewing tapes is a "hard business" and damaging to the ego, but that is rarely necessary. Recall that the teacher (Jesse) came to us with an uncomfortable dilemma: should he go against his instincts and put students on the spot? The viewing sessions resolved the dilemma and gave genuine cause for satisfaction. Of course, every class is unique, and many take a longer time than Jesse's to reach a happy conclusion.

EXAMPLE NO. 2: Sara, a lively young woman teaching Biochemistry at the medical school, asked to be taped because she was "just curious." According to her account, "I get pretty average ratings, but there are one or two complaints from students. Some of them say I'm boring and that I kill their interest. One of them even wrote [on an end-of-semester evaluation] that I reminded him—or her—of a corpse."

The tape-viewing session revealed a nearsighted teacher holding a single-spaced typed text close to her face, and reading it in a rapid monotone. Watching the videotape of herself made Sara visibly uncomfortable, and after several minutes she stared into her lap as the camera panned the students' bored faces. (Here was a client who needed careful handling.) Finally Sara turned to the advisor: "I do sound pretty deadly, don't I?"

ADVISOR: What do you mean by *deadly?*

TEACHER: [*with exasperation, but also more clarity*] Well, it sounds like I'm putting them to sleep, doesn't it?

ADVISOR: Do the students, in fact, ever fall asleep in class?

TEACHER: No—I mean yes—a few, the ones in the back row. But that's not the point. The point is that they all look dead to me, and I seem deadly to them. I don't know what to *do.* It's hard to think of reading my notes any other way, but the way things are going, the harder I prepare my notes, the less they seem to listen; they don't even answer my questions when I do try to get some reaction.

ADVISOR: Sara, let's find a spot on the tape where you do ask a question. [*The tape runs for several minutes.*]

TEACHER ON TAPE: In 1959 Janssen searching for a better analgesic agent developed the *butyrophenones.* Can anyone tell me the other name for butyrophenones? No? [*3-second pause*] All asleep? The other name—and this may be in the test, so you'd better listen—is *phenylbutylpiperidines.* I don't have time to spell it now, but you'll find it in the book.

TEACHER: I guess I didn't wait very long for that answer, but I was running late. That's the trouble with these classes. Too short to get through all my notes. Of course, now that I listen to myself, I'm not too fond of my note reading either. A lot of that stuff could be on a handout. The really interesting questions about clinical uses and side effects should be getting more attention.

ADVISOR: Would you consider lecturing from an outline instead of a full set of notes, Sara?

TEACHER: I'd lose the precision. Hmmm . . . What's the point of messing around with an outline?

ADVISOR: Well, for one thing your voice might probably sound more like it does now, so students would be less apt to, as you say, fall asleep. Secondly, you'd get a chance to walk around and look at students in the room. Eye contact has a number of advantages.

TEACHER: For instance?

ADVISOR: For instance, you could see if people were engaged in finding an answer to your question. Also, if you continue looking at a silent audience for four or more seconds, you *almost always* get an answer.

TEACHER: Yeh, I guess I know the answer to that. The real truth is that it's hard for me to do anything less than perfectly. But now that I see this lecture isn't working—I mean the students are right; I look like a corpse and I sound aggressive. But reading will be hard to give up. Perhaps I could try a phased withdrawal?

ADVISOR: Why not, Sara? Many teachers find it useful to try to change their classroom behavior in small increments.

The teacher and advisor then worked out a plan which involved a phased withdrawal from dependence on notes. During the next class Sara spoke from an outline for the first five minutes, and her outline included several probing clinical questions. A favorable student response could be seen on the second tape, and even more so on the third one. Sara pronounced herself "enormously cheered." By the end of the semester the mood of the class had changed dramatically; student evaluations placed Sara in the upper 20 percentile. Sara herself had this to say:

> You know, I admit I enjoy my class a lot more now. I feel good when they come up to me after class with questions—which hardly ever happened before—and when they say 'hi' in the halls. But you know [laughs], perfectionist that I am, I just can't shake my habit of going for quality, so I guess what I like best is that I'm . . . I can see that I'm teaching far more effectively. The students have totally changed. I can see they're really getting into the material!

EXAMPLE NO. 3: A 55-year-old senior professor in the social sciences called up the video lab one day to see if he could be taped. "My students have always responded well," he said. "But this semester they tell me that I should see myself on tape. I think something's up!"

That week he was taped during his seminar. Several days later he arrived for his viewing appointment. He was ten minutes late and—uncharacteristically—puffing on a cigarette. Within minutes of watching his tape, his face was beaming proudly: "By golly, I'm good!" he exclaimed. "No wonder they say all those great things about me. Those kids are really participating. I'm going to recommend this to all my teaching fellows. Young people need to feel good, too!"

Each of these cases illustrates a broad problem or situation that can be tackled efficiently through a video consultation, be it conversational dynamics,

preparation of outlines vs. notes, or the banishment of haunting self-doubts. All are grist for self-reflection; all are aided by reviewing a whole class episode on videotape.

Setting Up a Video Program

Establishing Counselor Credibility

The initial difficulty in setting up a video program is establishing your credibility. What people—all of us—commonly fear about video is that it will reveal some dark "truth" about ourselves: a confused unconscious, perhaps, or a frightened or fraudulent front. For better or worse, such revelations occur no more often in watching video than they do in real life, and watching oneself on video can almost always bring pleasant surprises. Still, initial offers to show teachers their own classroom teaching on tape are often met with apparent diffidence.

Besides the fears attending self-confrontation, potential clients will probably worry that their tapes will not be treated as confidential. This fear has many expressions, none of which are frivolous. No scholar wants to be held up to ridicule. No scholar wants to be evaluated behind his or her back. It is important to develop a firm policy: *Never show a teacher's tapes to anyone who was not in the class at the time of the taping, unless you have the teacher's written consent.* Publicize this policy before each taping, by announcing to the students:

> Hello, my name is _____ _____. I will be taping your class today so your teacher can have a chance to see himself [herself] teach. These tapes are the joint property of your teacher and the lab. They will not be used for an evaluation of your teacher or yourselves. If you would like to review today's class, please give us a call and we will make an appointment for you to see the tape.

Even if such fears were not a problem, clients would probably not beat down your doors during the first semester of your operation. Every new institution needs time to gain acceptance. But have patience; there's plenty to do while you wait to develop your client base.

Getting Your Equipment Ready

First, you need to get your equipment together. You will want to get a recording deck, a camera, one or more omnidirectional microphones (capable of picking up students' as well as teachers' voices clearly), and a playback unit. The playback unit includes a deck (you can actually use your recording deck for this function) and a monitor (a monitor is like a TV without channels). As mentioned previously, these need not be elegant, and they need not belong to you. As long as you can borrow functioning equipment and a private room for viewing on a regular basis, you will be in business. There's no need to worry about a permanent location until your operation shows signs of performing a necessary service.

Sponsoring Faculty Development Activities

It may seen impossible to establish a reputation for being helpful while you're waiting for people to get their classes taped, but it is not. There are several kinds of popular faculty development activities that will involve teachers in discussing their own teaching, and you can sponsor any or all of them. The first of these, which we call *microteaching*, is ideally suited for videotaping. It enlists a group of five or six teachers to deliver and critique a few minutes of a class lesson with their colleagues. Not only is this experience a good learning activity for instructors, but it also provides you, the advisor, with taping experience and an excellent vantage point from which to observe how various critical styles affect individual teachers. Though microteaching has a hypothetical and transitory quality that makes it inferior to real-class viewing, it can be a tremendously powerful tool if you insist that participants tape at least twice and then compare their "before" and "after" performances.

Another service that draws potential clients is a *teaching workshop*. Ordinarily these are seminar discussions targeted toward a single group, such as new faculty members or writing instructors who are interested in getting methodological tips on various aspects of the teacher's craft. Since workshop par-

ticipants do not require a promise of confidentiality, you can get administrators' help to target the potentially interested teachers. By calling people from this list, you will learn of topics that need addressing. Don't worry about being an expert. Think of yourself as an organizer or a conversational facilitator and your session will go well. Most teachers enjoy the chance to learn from colleagues almost as much as they appreciate having the advice itself. If you *do* have permission to show tapes of a real class or of a microteaching session, your workshop will have an immediate focus, but tapes are by no means necessary to lively and productive conversation.

A third service that you may want to offer is the *individual taping of a lecture practice session*. This activity, which consists of working through a lecture or a series of lectures until the client is totally satisfied with the finished product, is an excellent way for you to expose yourself to the various ways teachers plan their classes, and an equally good way for clients to ease into an enthusiasm for a live class taping.

Conclusion

Video-replay-based faculty consulting programs provide clients with the opportunity to gain a closer experience of, and insight into, their own teaching. Given the chance to watch a replay of one or more whole classes, instructors of all levels can learn to become competent experts on their own classroom teaching. Although the technical details of setting up a classroom taping laboratory are relatively simple, adjunct professional activities should be planned while the constituency for taping services grows and the advisors gain experience in being creative and nonjudgmental observers of teaching in many contexts. Within several semesters, advisors and faculty will be learning together about teaching, in the best way possible: unbiased reflection on directly observed experience.

Student Learning Beyond the Classroom: Implications for a Discussion Methods Teacher

Where Do Teachers Teach?

The cases and readings in *Teaching and the Case Method* deal primarily with teacher and student interactions within the classroom, a most obvious setting in which teaching and learning presumably take place. Except for homework, many of us convey that learning and teaching outside the classroom are somehow out of bounds. This belief may reflect some wishful thinking on our part, based on the hope that our classroom actions do indeed have all of the impact we want them to have. But does our obligation to student learning really end when the classroom empties? Or should it? What about our many contacts with students outside of class—in conversations, formal conferences, and casual meetings around campus? What responsibilities and opportunities do we have in these many and varied situations? Should we then be instructors, counsellors, directors, coaches, advisers, guides, or mentors, knowing that, at different times, we may be called on to be all of these? Is it possible that our emphasis on being a "teacher" overlooks *student* needs beyond the classroom—needs to develop knowledge, skills, and values peripheral to the immediate subject matter of the course in question? Should we attend to these?

Consider one account of how outside learning affected a group of adult students:

> In a university faculty seminar, the discussion turned to influences that had led each person to choose his or her own career path. The dominant catalyst for most of the 35 people present was an earlier teacher-mentor who had encouraged the student outside of the classroom. These out-of-class cheerleaders had played major roles in helping launch the younger protégés into their new careers.

Such impressive mentoring may be more than we can expect to provide to all students, but the example illustrates the power and durability that a teacher's influence can have—even outside of the classroom. If we grant that all teachers possess a potential for this kind of influence, another question arises: Do discussion teachers, more so than other teachers, have special obligations when it comes to working with students outside of the classroom? And, if so, what questions and approaches are most appropriate for these circumstances? Such questions are complex, and the answers to them will vary from teacher to teacher. But the considerations they raise have provided some of us with grist for both thought and conversation over the years. This essay hopes to explore some of these issues and their implications.

Student Expectations That Accompany Discussion Teaching

It seems fair to assume that a student's expectations of a teacher *outside of* the classroom will probably originate with the teacher's behavior *inside* the classroom. Most teachers provide these cues early in a course, and students extrapolate from them. We send messages about our expectations on everything from syllabi to grading standards and classroom decorum in the initial class sessions. Traditional teachers lean on lectures to establish their intellectual and positional authority. The messages delivered effectively create a knowledge and authority hierarchy within the class. In addition, the typical teacher's demeanor, age, reputation, academic status, physical position (i.e., standing at a lectern), and lectures send powerful signals about who is in control. Given these, students may well assume that any authority figure who provides incontestable classroom messages on grading practices and exam schedules must also be a source of knowledge and advice outside of class.

However, discussion teachers do something very different in class. Beyond a few basic logistics, they tend to shy away from delivering authoritative statements—or sometimes even opinions. As a rule, they encourage students to find their own way. Instead of giving their final judgments, they tend to ask further questions and raise new issues for discussion. In doing so, they convey more ambiguous out-of-class expectations for students. A discussion teacher's behavior in class may well contribute to these messages of ambiguity by encouraging such things as:

- Interactive exchanges aimed at involving most or all students in open dialogue with each other and with the teacher. In these discussions, the teacher dominates neither air time nor ideas. The powerful, but confusing, message that students may draw from this is that some teachers wish to share both learning and curiosity in the exploration of new ideas and knowledge.
- Frequent role reversals. The teacher often changes roles in these discussion dialogues, resembling an inquiring student while turning students into temporary teachers who are expected to argue for their own positions and opinions. The ambiguous implications are that students can teach; that teachers don't just expound but can also discover; and, most important, that questioning and listening are often more powerful pedagogical tools than assertions and answers.
- A tendency to resist giving authoritative opinions during discussions or even at the end of a class. This is particularly true when topics involve equivocal data and conflicting perceptions—a condition found in most real-life situations. As competing views are explored in discussion, learning and wisdom may come from students' comments and insights as often as from teachers' thoughts and summaries—although students may not immediately recognize the value of their peers' contributions.

One effect of this teaching approach is to blur the lines of authority. The instructor can no longer serve as the sole source of classroom wisdom and knowledge. Nor does the pattern of proactive teacher and passive student thrive in this setting. Interactive dialogue must replace instructor-dominated discourse as learning depends on mutual exploration more than on pedagogical persuasion.

As an instructor who tries to use these principles, I work hard at—and thoroughly enjoy—this approach to teaching. My MBA and executive classes tend to be fairly informal as I wander around the classroom and listen and talk during discussions. Early in the course, I make a practice of proclaiming to students that I've become very good over the years at asking "dumb" questions of smart students. I also find that such questions—theirs and mine—often move us beyond superficial assumptions toward deeper issues of opinion and insight.

The result is indeed a curious mixture of roles. With our large classes of from 50 to 90 students, I often feel like the conductor of a large orchestra who would prefer a seminar of chamber music. To be sure, there are musical scores (in the form of various cases, readings, or theory notes) available to everyone, but these permit us only to see the music, not to hear it. In addition, the musical scores are incomplete. They require improvisations and cadenzas from the players themselves. Though I am theoretically the director, neither I nor the students know exactly how the themes and variations will *sound* until after the discussion themes get under way. My role is to encourage and develop student contributions, to promote harmonies of purpose, and to discourage cacophony and chaos. As interdependent motifs emerge, students add new themes and variations. Some sound better than others to me, and the most melodic get higher grades—a matter of judgment, to be sure. Players who don't weave their own solos into richer contrapuntal combinations tend to suffer initially, and they need encouragement and opportunities for further practice. My major roles involve supporting the class process, asking questions, pulling emerging themes into connected discussions, rewarding those who seem to contribute to the collaboration, and alerting and assisting those who haven't gotten there yet.

The Discussion Teacher Outside of Class

So much for the discussion teacher's behavior in class. What about outside of class? How do our principles of in-class discussion relate to our relationship with students outside? Should we be the same people in class and elsewhere? My response, as a discussion methods teacher, is a paradoxical "Yes and No." Yes, I believe that we should remain true to the principles of open discussion and ambiguous guidance in almost all of our dealings with students. But no, we should not be rigid in form or substance. Our emphases will vary to fit the time, place, and particular student.

Let me give an example of how one such outside meeting helped to salvage some poor teaching on my part. The incident occurred in an undergraduate psychology seminar:

Bernice was a college senior and a psychology major in a 20-person class that relied heavily on student involvement and discussion. She claimed to have a strong academic record in psychology and professed to be knowledgeable about topic areas covered by the course. Possibly she was. We never really found out, for even her written work was erratic—sometimes quite strong and sometimes far off target. She tended to antagonize other students with a strong arbitrary manner and occasional harsh condemnations. When criticized, however, she interpreted other people's remarks as a total rejection of herself.

In this course, I initially told class members that they would be largely in charge of guiding the discussions on a range of course topics, and that I expected individuals and subgroups to take on this responsibility. Individual efforts at leadership were also subject

to peer feedback and evaluation. I tried to help the class explore and deepen its appreciation of these topics during discussion, often by asking questions. Although leadership roles rotated, Bernice's arbitrary efforts to control the class were typically rejected by the other students. When this happened, she became increasingly withdrawn and sullen in class. Her behavior tended to discourage further feedback from the other students.

Because of my earlier efforts to create a "contract," which drew discussion leadership and feedback largely from the students, I did nothing about Bernice until, in one of the last class sessions, she publicly rebuked me for being an ineffective teacher. The criticism was quickly challenged by other students who attacked Bernice instead. Some said that they had missed, and wanted, more of her professed expertise, but most assailed her for having missed the point of the course, for having been an arrogant noncontributor, and for being a rude, sulking class member.

Still, she was right. I had not been an adequate teacher for her. I could have done more during the course. Because of time constraints just after that particular class, I asked Bernice if she would like to discuss the problem further when we might find time to talk. That meeting finally occurred a few weeks later when she delivered her term paper to my office.

The obvious question was, How should I behave in this new outside-of-class context? We were no longer in the formal classroom setting with Bernice's fellow students. The power (to grade) was still in my hands at that point. Bernice had wanted stronger direction and leadership from me, though her own efforts to get it had raised wider problems in the class. She had, in her public rebuke, already graded me as a teacher. Should I now exercise my grading and evaluative powers—possibly to her detriment—in our office discussion?

This story may seem like an extreme case of a teacher abdicating control over a class. For me, though, it raised still more important questions about discussion teaching outside of the classroom. When teachers initiate a contract of sharing classroom control with students, *they must live with the consequences of that relationship both in and beyond the classroom.* The story illustrates how teachers can get trapped into learning contracts of their own making early in the term. It also highlights the question of who the discussion teacher *should be* outside: an irritated authority figure, a distant observer, a sympathetic friend, a disappointed parent surrogate, an encouraging coach? Should these meetings outside of class begin with and focus on what the teacher considers to be the relevant learning issues, or should the teacher let the student take the lead? When should the teacher initiate these outside contacts? More specifically, does a discussion teacher behave in one way with students in the office and another with those who crowd around the table at the front of the room after class asking questions or those who try to seek support for their own views outside? What about the meetings that a teacher has with students after the course is over and the grades are in?

Opinions will vary widely on these questions. However, the issues that I find most prevalent outside of class fall more or less into six areas:

- Students engage me in social and school-related chit chat, questions, compliments, or complaints.
- Students value the course and seek new understanding, extensions, or clarifications of course materials and contents. Where can they go from here, and how can I help them get there?
- Students come to talk because they are hurting, possibly because of prior feedback or a sense of futility in one or more classes. They want help in creating or rebuilding shaken confidence levels to gain more self-assurance, both within classroom discussions and outside.
- Students want more individual recognition in class or clues on how to do well in the course. They hope to make points with me as the instructor who still has control over their grade.
- Students want to discuss their sometimes thinly disguised disappointment in me because I am not providing the kind of clear-cut classroom leadership or answers they came for.
- I want to encourage or modify a student's approach to classroom discussions, sometimes based on what I hear and see in class, and sometimes based on what I hear and see from the student or others outside of class.

None of these is mutually exclusive. My guess is that in Bernice's case, all but the first and second were present during our discussion. At our meeting, after some initial bluster, she lapsed into a sad description of background experiences, anger, and disappointment in herself. We also reviewed our mutual disappointment in me and the class for not

finding ways to help her build the self-esteem that she so badly wanted. We talked more about her efforts to approach the future differently from the past. I was very honest with her and found that I liked the honest, struggling Bernice far more than I had the seemingly egotistical student. I wanted to help her.

But what happens in these out-of-class meetings? There are obvious choices available, but in my own case, rather than pursuing the traditional authority role of opinion giver, I tend to move from orchestra conductor toward the role of fellow musician. As initial questions and careful listening provide more focus and intensity, the dialogue becomes a concordant sonata of two people rather than my conducting a large class symphony. When tempted to regress into traditional authority patterns and give strong opinions, it helps to remember that one's outside-of-class role as a discussion teacher is an organic extension of the role in class: I am still trying to help a student go *even further* than before in the direction of curiosity and an honest exploration of choices, and sometimes the questions even become the leading questions. But the music is more like a muted piano and violin than a symphony.

The apparently small changes—outside instead of inside the classroom, after class instead of during class—require still further adjustments of roles and relationships. The biggest involves an even greater reduction of status differences and a search to become more focused on people and problems. The burden is on me, the teacher, to make the adjustments that move us from large group thinking to the narrower and sometimes more subtle accents required to help the student see and explore his or her problems and choices.

Discussion teachers who assume the lecturer-parent role outside of class will undercut the earlier expectations they may have set up in the discussion classroom. On the office stage, status differences may become both more obvious and more ambiguous, and the ambiguity can be employed to create a process of mutual exploration, particularly in the earlier stages of the discussion. The need is to build on classroom expectations of teacher-as-student, then become more problem-centered and conscious of choices in ways that help both students and teacher. Most important, discussion teachers who wish to help students outside of class in a manner that fits the contract and goals of discussion teaching must ensure that answers and action remain within the student's control and choice. If asked to express a preference, do so, but give equally honest weight to the importance of students being in charge of their own decisions. This sounds simpler than it is, especially when it comes to issues like personal standards, motivation, future actions, and life choices.

When teachers take responsibility for helping students define and diagnose problems and action choices, they often find that it takes considerable time and energy. This is because the teacher has chosen to become at least as much *student*-centered as topic- or discipline-centered. For many teachers, this is too much to ask in an academic world that demands that they be self-centered enough to publish in order not to perish. For others, attention to individual students detracts from their preferred emphasis on hard-nosed, objective rigor and content. For some of us, though, part of the challenge lies in the "soft" side of the process—subject neither to precise measures nor to clear directions. These can be roughly defined by the rather primitive rules of thumb examined below.

Some Discussion Methods Rules of Thumb for Outside of Class

For the instructor who takes on the responsibility of helping students learn outside of class, several rough ground rules might help. The first, and probably the most important, forms a basis for all of the others. The rules begin with the premise that instructors are genuinely interested in, and want to *care about*, their students collectively and individually. Such a premise—more emotional than intellectual—can pose a threat to instructors who use their intellects as academic armor against emotional ties with their students. For those who, by contrast, wish to build ties with students, it is necessary to begin in the classroom by listening to their ideas and opinions. Such teachers will also:

• *Signal an early interest in students as individuals and a willingness to meet with them singly or in small groups.*

If teachers signal a lack of interest in students, students will probably do the same, unless driven more by terror than respect. *Showing* interest, rather than just announcing it, means being in the classroom and available for conversations with students before every class and demonstrating a willingness to spend time with them after class. It requires making one's own appointments when possible, going beyond perfunctory office hours, meeting groups of students at lunch or informally, sometimes attending extracurricular events, and even wandering around lunchrooms and student lounges when time permits.

Another rule of thumb might be:

• *Try to discover what is important to individual students, whoever they may be or wherever they may come from. If we expect them to seek learning from us, we must demonstrate the very quality that we are trying to encourage in our students—a desire to communicate and to learn.*

Like the other ways of behaving, this one begins in class, but evolves outside. Learning is a trade-off experience that begins with individual actions but develops into norms of reciprocity that then become the currency of exchange for larger group-learning relationships. One person's behavior tends to beget similar behavior by another:

An outstanding medical school teacher confessed that, after many years of lecturing to his students, it dawned on him to learn each student's name in his classes, even though there were many of them. "It's hard work, but it makes all the difference in the world," he said. "The students really came alive. It now seems so obvious: they were just students before. Now they're people, and we talk differently. But I seem to be the only teacher around here who takes the trouble to do it."

However, names are only the beginning. Who *are* these individual students in terms of background, cultures, and experience? In this vein, students need the chance to become persons in their teachers' eyes and to exhibit, as well as gain, personal knowledge and experience. By learning about students' world perspectives and personalities outside of class, we teachers can gain in three ways. First, we gain knowledge of lives and events that we didn't know previously. Second, we can adapt our questions and responses more directly to students' outlook and experience. Finally, our interest in that particular person increases the likelihood of reciprocity—he or she will reciprocate and take interest in us and what we have to say. Once again, the pattern which sounds simple, is not. Mutual learning norms are often undermined by such factors as the layout of classrooms, course designs, teachers' priorities and pressures, institutional promotion policies, and academic rules and traditions. One way to promote mutual interest might be the following:

- *Reduce barriers of status and formality even more sharply outside of class than in class. Status formalities can block movement toward mutual learning, but teachers need to state their expectations on this score. In the same vein, teachers can also try to blur territorial distinctions.*

In class, my rule is to call students by their first names, try to learn as much as possible from the background data provided on class cards, and ask them to call me by my own nickname if they feel comfortable doing so. Most of them do. For students who find it important to maintain the status difference between professor and student (when, for example, this difference is an important part of their own cultural background), so be it. Some of these reservations disappear as time goes on, and degrees of trust increase. I like to make my own preferences clear, but leave the choice up to the students.

As I mentioned earlier, I also tend to move around the classroom a good deal and deliberately leave the "pit" in our amphitheater-shaped classrooms to walk, and sometimes sit, in the audience as students speak to one another. I will sometimes linger at the back of the room to encourage students to talk directly with each other and leave me out of the discussion altogether.

In my office, students and I sit in comfortable chairs or on a couch around an old coffee table, never on opposite sides of the desk or worktable. My door is not always open, but I ask students to make their appointments directly with me, if possible, so that I can get a rough sense of what their immediate concerns are before we meet. In addition, I try to make a point of introducing them by name to my secretary, whose warm acceptance furthers an atmosphere of personal acknowledgment.

- *Humor is wonderful, but most of it should be at the instructor's expense.*

Again, this begins in class, but it often serves as an ice breaker when students and instructor begin

to talk with each other privately. It becomes another form of role modeling. A teacher's sarcasm, cynicism, or anger tend to miscarry with students in and out of class. I learned this the hard way:

One year, early in my teaching experience, I was teaching a first-year MBA course in the spring semester, and I became impatient with students who seemed more interested in summer job searches than in class. On some days, absenteeism seemed too high and preparation too low. On one such day, a student made what I thought was an inane comment. In response, I suggested that, if he came to class more often, he might be able to make more worthy contributions.

A hush fell over the room. The class wasn't used to that kind of sarcastic remark from me. From then on, I lost many of the students in that class, because, in their eyes, I had bullied one of them—and probably not the worst offender at that. Worse yet, I didn't admit my error later on or try to recover the class in outside conversations. There were indeed ways in which that issue might have been discussed with students outside of class, even humorously. By now, I have developed a large storehouse of questions and a smaller storehouse of foot-in-mouth stories about professors like me. These stories not only reduce the status barriers, but they make it more acceptable for all of us in class to take ourselves less seriously.

- *Initiate interactions with students, both in person and in writing.*

Traditional ground rules suggest that lower-status people must go to higher-status people in the latter's territory for help. That is a rule worth breaking and bending more often than not.

Each semester, I tell the class that I would like to spend one or two lunch hours per week with anyone who would care to join me. The students work out a sign-up sheet for each week. We meet at a round table in the student cafeteria so that we can talk easily with each other. Most of these luncheons are special, not only because I get acquainted with students in more informal ways, but because some even talk *about themselves* that way for the first time. There are usually about eight students and me. If any students can't take part in one of these scheduled luncheons, I offer to set up others after the course is over. That doesn't happen very often, partly because the students want me to know them individually—before the course is over.

Even though most students are still on their best behavior at those times, the setting, circumstances, and questions differ from those in the classroom. I learn about personal ambitions, achievements, families, and problems. They learn more about me as a human being, I believe, than they can in the class setting.

In addition, written notes to students can be signals of concern and attention, even notes that might have a critical edge to them, like those questioning a student's class efforts. More welcome are the notes that convey appreciation or congratulations for jobs well done.

• *Work hard to remember and even write down a student's comments of particular interest to use and weave them into future discussions.*

Like so many other ground rules, this one, which applies both inside and outside of class, is hard work. In class, it may only involve bringing Student A back into discussing an issue that Student B has just commented on. Outside of class, in small groups, it may mean acting as moderator as well as contributor. With a single student, it means trying to recognize *that* person's individuality, even when it means challenging a point while accepting it. But whether the recognition comes in the classroom, the lunchroom, or in a note, it is a major reward to students when a teacher remembers, and accurately returns to, their earlier comments. It also helps us move from a person-centered discussion to a problem-centered one, as different comments blend into collective definitions of problems and diagnoses.

• *Show concern for the classroom's underrepresented students, whoever they may be. But along with appreciating the values of diversity, strive for unified goals and working achievements as well.*

It is a delicate balancing act, but both parts of this rule are critically important. In any classroom, there will be students who are underrepresented, be they women, Native Americans, people with special needs, older students, African Americans, gays and

lesbians, foreign students, or sometimes even straight white men or women from one region of the country or another. Sometimes we don't know how to deal with our own multiple identities, let alone the diverse attributes brought into class by others.

Sometimes some students—and faculty—feel, often justifiably, that they are being overlooked, excluded, or patronized by others in, or outside of, the classroom. At other times, they feel that they stand out, often uncomfortably. How do any of us behave under such circumstances? Sometimes we seek inclusion and wish to blend into the crowd. Other times, we struggle to assert our identity through distinctiveness. Still other times, we may reject the larger group in discouraged frustration because of our own past experiences. And to complicate matters even more, the same person—all of us—may exemplify all of these behaviors at different times. Being in the minority can sometimes be very lonely.

All the more reason for instructors to understand how they may react to, and influence, students whose experiences are different, a condition most certainly true when the instructor is in a minority. But all of us should have this kind of awareness. This can be helped by trying to be aware of who the underrepresented members are, and where they come from, and by being available for outside contacts with them in groups or individually if they wish. Encouraging their self-expression and independent contributions in ways in which they feel comfortable, both in and outside of class, can help, but instructors must also have some sense of their own comfort levels with diversity—and learn to expand them. That means a discussion teacher's repeated expressions of willingness to meet, work, and talk with anyone and everyone while espousing, and showing, an appreciation for both diversity and unity.

• *Seek an appropriate balance. Don't become too emotionally involved with individual students.*

In these days of societal abuses, emotional turmoil, family disruptions, and sexual harassment, any college or university teacher finds both temptation and risk inherent in the student-teacher relationship. This may be even more true for discussion methods teachers than others, because of the blurred topic and status lines that develop between teacher and student. Indeed, many of us do develop strong friendships with former students. The major problems, however, arise when a dependent student wants too much emotional commitment. At such times, a form of balanced objectivity is necessary. The teacher must assume a role that excludes favoritism. To the extent that teachers are available to one student, they must be available to all. To the extent that they try to help one, the same must be true for others. It is a difficult, but necessary, ground rule, because we all like some students more than others, and there will always be students whom we think we can help with their personal or professional problems. But the ground rule of balanced objectivity is crucial.

In Retrospect and Prospect

Teaching beyond the classroom begins within the classroom. But then what? For the lecturer or expository teacher, the pattern of explaining and expounding can continue after class or in the office as students continue to seek further knowledge and opinions from a teacher. The process typically tends to be teacher-centered in both arenas—inside and outside of the classroom. For the discussion teacher, a different kind of consistency is critical. Questions,

curiosity, and role ambiguities are the hallmarks of both in-class and out-of-class explorations. Choices rather than answers are the major goal, and the emphases are more on learning. than teaching. Rather than being teacher-centered, this process relies on the interactive relationship of teacher and student as they work together. The teacher's role still involves more questions than answers, more listening than talking—particularly in the early stages of the conversation—and more exploration than explanation. The process of learning beyond the classroom is thus an extension of the venture that students and teachers jointly begin within the classroom. It is indeed different for the discussion methods teacher than for others—more uncertain, more open-ended, more ambiguous, and potentially more frightening. But these are the same conditions that greet us when we take those first tentative steps into the classroom—and often for years afterward as well. In that sense, discussion methods outside of the classroom become a personal extension of what we are trying to create inside. Putting it all together *outside* is part of the excitement and joy of this particular art form. In that sense, student learning beyond the classroom can become teacher learning as well.

Leading Discussion in a Lecture Course: Some Maxims and an Exhortation

MARGARET M. GULLETTE

Lecturing feels lonely—there's the silence of extraterrestrial space out there. Once in a long while, a long way off, an extraterrestrial coughs, or drops a pen. As time passes, you may hear your own heart beating, but not theirs. It's like time spent in an anechoic chamber. You strive for bigger effects: your delivery gets broader, your joke lines more emphatic. Old hands at lecturing say they can "gauge" an audience, but it's a crude gauge. The more curious you are about the students' learning, the more oppressive lecturing becomes. "Are you *getting* it?" I heard a brilliant lecturer ask the 350 students in his class, after explaining a difficult concept. And then hearing his own frustration and futility, he asked, "Would someone phrase that more clearly for me?" There was a silence. He looked out briefly, as if in search of souls who had lost their way, and went on. How can you know whether they're getting it, or who is not?

Discussion, on the other hand, can feel lightweight, loose-jointed, like holding hands in zero gravity. The sense of weightlessness can overcome you—even if you're good enough at leading discussion so that your students are uninhibited and exploratory; even if you guide it subtly by the weight of a question or an inquiring gesture; even if you're sure that at each session they've learned three new ideas in the most unforgettable way, by discovering them and stating them themselves. The problem is that you get more ambitious—you want them to learn four, seven, nineteen new ideas. In one vivacious literature class, the leader had filled the board with the participants' best ideas about Virginia Woolf's *To the Lighthouse*. At the end, she gleefully drew a circle around their words and said: "And that's what an elegy is." But, simultaneously, she realized they did not know many of the moving elegies she wished they knew, or the early history of the genre and the current debate about genre.

What would relieve the discussion leader at such points—when class interest is high—would be to give a minilecture. What the lecturer mentioned above is craving, just at that point of his incomprehension, is an interval of class discussion. What they *both* need is the concept of the discussion-lecture format and some techniques for adjusting it to their own needs.

No other format makes as much sense as the mixed mode, pedagogically or (for most conscientious teachers) personally. It's got more zest and

READING
Leading Discussion in a Lecture Course:
Some Maxims and an Exhortation GULLETTE

variety than either discussion or lecture separately. We all know that listeners involved in strenuous cognitive activity have limited attention spans: in an hour-long lecture they need two or three changes (of topic, pace) or, at the least, breaks in the flow that enable them to stretch mentally and take a breath before the next lap. As lecturers, we summarize a unit then, or assert why the next topic matters; we help them tidy up their notes; we take a breath ourselves and start up with new vocal and intellectual energy. Long discussion classes, although much more flexible, also require some breaks—a sense of closure in one area, followed by what all can recognize as a new start. Some discussion leaders work on the half-hour rule; others feel that the first stint can last the longest, and thereafter the breaks need to come more rapidly; others break whenever the cognitive need appears to arise. In all cases, we are searching for a rhythm that matches that of student attention because without attention, there can be no learning.

Using discussion to break up lectures, or minilectures to break up discussion, is far more effective than either separately, however imaginative a lecturer or discussion leader may be. When you leave space for discussion, students who have been sedentary and quiescent up to that point can, figuratively or even literally, get up on their legs. Even those who don't speak are more alert—looking around, hearing new voices, trying to mold their thought to other points of view. (Some fade out, either following their own thought or catching the mental equivalent of forty winks.) When students actually stood in class, as we did in my childhood, it also improved their circulation and their sense of authority. But seated or standing, for a student to speak in a lecture class constitutes an event.

When you insert minilectures into discussion classes, where students have been moving forward with exhilaration together, they may be glad to rest on their pens for a moment, so to speak, letting the teacher work solo so they can organize their thoughts in relative tranquility for the next communal round.

The skilled discussion leader can easily introduce minilectures in her format. So here I particularly want to stress the importance of opening up the lecture mode to discussions. As teachers, the strongest argument for doing what we do or changing it may come from our belief in its impact on student learning. Educational theorists and re-

searchers agree that, to achieve certain kinds of learning, nothing beats discussion leading. When students participate, they become active. Speaking, as I said, is an event—rather a complex event. Until a student hears herself expounding or questioning, she may not know what she thinks. She may not know *that* she thinks, which is why speaking empowers future thinking and speaking. As soon as she has asserted something, even in the form of a question, she puts herself in the position of being able to criticize her own thought as well as the teacher's. In short, in saying as little as a single sentence, she becomes simultaneously a thinker and a critic, and—by the potential of her effect on others—an agent. The fact of an audience magnifies her discourse. As William James analyzes it, for each of us, when we speak in public, our expression "comes back to us. . . . We thus receive sensible news of our behavior and its results. We hear the words we have spoken . . . or read in the bystanders' eyes the success or failure of our conduct."[1] So important is this classroom magnification of discourse that James made a strong generalization out of it. According to him, there can be "no impression without expression." This would be my first maxim.

Those interested in empowerment believe that we empower people to some end. The event of speaking as an agent prefigures acting as an agent—exerting power in the outside world. If we believe this, then it will seem wrong that most students, even at elite institutions, do not discuss the material of their courses in any very valuable way (some students say, in *any* way) outside of class. Apparently, they need to learn *how* to talk about ideas, issues, ideologies, epistemology, process, ethics—they need to practice. For most of us, this kind of talking is one of the great pleasures of intellectual life. Our failure to teach it to our students (to those who do not already come to college as adept) should probably be considered one of the weaknesses of undergraduate education, as well as a serious loss to a democratic society. The remedy that is within our grasp is to provide them—while we have them—with more or better discussions.

Even if we agree that this constitutes a problem only practice can solve, discussion leading would still need to be energetically promoted, because

1. William James, *Talks to Teachers on Psychology*, edited by Frederick Burkhardt and Redson Bowers (Cambridge, Mass.: Harvard University Press, 1983), p. 32.

both the economics and the traditions of higher education make lecturing the dominant mode. What is a college "professor" if not a lecturer? (Indeed, this image is so ingrained that some dutiful souls have been known to lecture to classes of two or three.) Moreover, the more students one lecturer addresses, the more cost-effective the system is bound to be, according to an axiom that administrators like to repeat to one another. In higher education in the 1990s, accounting may govern everything, including pedagogy. Small-group discussion classes (15–20 students) may begin to seem fiscally irresponsible, a "luxury" we can't afford.

Colleges and universities differ so much in their governance that no strategies can be devised to promote discussion at large across the country. But as long as college teachers retain their classroom autonomy, we can address them at their level of commitment to the value of discussion. To those already convinced of its value, we can suggest *that most college teachers have classes small enough for discussion, that discussion can go on in classes that used to be thought too big for anything but lecturing, and that discussion can work in disciplines that have minimal traditions of using it.* To those who start out with the idea that the essence of teaching is lecturing, we need to expand the idea of the essence—by endowing discussion leading with utility, pleasure, and prestige. For the sake of both practitioners and those tempted to become practitioners, we can try to develop the most efficient ways to become expert.

Many excellent lecturers fear discussion. They're right to anticipate the problems—the students' and their own. These refer mainly to the chaos inherent in learning. Discussion models one main process of thought, which is the development from simplicity to something else. As learners, we typically begin a new topic with limited information, a single point of view, a dominant ideology that informs the content of our thought, and a sense that we are probably intuitively right and only need more support for what we believe. Class discussions, by pooling these simplicities, quickly disrupt them. Whatever the outcome of the discussion, up to the middle may be muddle. But there's no learning without this muddle (my second maxim). Class discussion only makes it public. Some discussion leaders initially appear to increase the confusion by quickly encouraging many different points of view. This is the stage at which the students should feel free to try out their relevant ideas. Few will talk long at

this stage, and no one will talk long if you say something like, "Let's get started by commenting in a few sentences on the following issue . . ." At this stage, the discussion leader may not be intervening at all. Many say they want to get a "global" view of student opinion. What they get may look at first like a crazy map.

Students need to walk through this newly chaotic terrain with excitement and high expectation. (It may be too early for pleasure.) They need to live through the proof that confusion is not the last stage in the process, and also get over their fear of change. "This is too hard for me." "This is too weird." "This is too dangerous." Part of the discussion leader's job is to explain the process to the students in advance. It's helpful during the very first class session, when the "contract" for the course is being declared and projected, to say that discussion will be a main mode of learning, that you have respect for their opinions, and that the class needs their contributions. I also like to say that discussion is more fun than lecturing—for me *and* for them. In classes small enough for you to know each speaker, participation can be used to elevate a grade; if you plan to use it this way, you should probably assure them that it cannot lower a grade. The first class is also the time to counter their own objections to discussion. These boil down to two. It's a waste of their time to listen to one another. They will state this objection openly because it flatters the professor. They won't state the next because it disparages them. They fear they can't talk out loud in a lecture class because competing with one another and with you is too intimidating.

This resistance is so crucial that if you cannot overcome it, the entire mode is closed to you. Having some discussion during that first session is the only answer. Do not be discouraged and, most of all, do not be discouraging. No expression without encouragement—this would be my third maxim. You can use the pre-discussion phase itself for nonverbal encouragement. You may also want to develop a different tone from the one in which you ordinarily lecture for the immediate pre-discussion stage. Some fine lecturers already talk in a natural, conversational manner—as if they were thinking things through again on their feet. Those who need to adapt are those who discourse so elegantly that their listeners despair of emulating them. A student who has two ideas and four tattered sentences that protect them is not likely to utter any of them after

READING
Leading Discussion in a Lecture Course:
Some Maxims and an Exhortation GULLETTE

listening for twenty minutes to your polished plat-form performance. You do not need to be an actor to develop a simpler, slower, more tentative pre-discussion speaking style. A lot of women are prac-ticing this way of speaking as a pedagogical device (without necessarily giving up other, more author-itative voices). A professor I know who does so says she was asked by a student in office hours, "Are you just hesitant, or are you a feminist?" The tone in which you ask the first question, when you come to ask the first question, is bound to affect the re-sponse rate and the quality of responses. A neutral tone implies safety, a playful one opens the game to everyone. The tone in which you make your first comment is also going to be a signal.

How long you wait before you jump in to com-ment (to judge) may be the most important signal you ever send. The time during which you wait is the time to use your repertory of interested, im-pressed, and pleased facial expressions—the facial expressions you exert successfully at dinner parties and job interviews throughout your adult life. One of the master teachers at Harvard, C. Roland Chris-tensen, lets at least two and sometimes many stu-dents make statements before uttering his first word. He limits himself to nodding with interest after each has finished. Or sometimes he simply says "thank you" to each. Being silent and looking thoughtful as the students begin to talk to one an-other may be the most useful thing you do in the first class. You can make it a regular practice. You may find it the most rewarding new technique you learn. For some lecturers, it may initially require a near-heroic effort of self-control: it is worth the ef-fort. It has a magical effect on the willingness of students to break that awful silence as your question lingers unanswered in the air.

Another powerful way to expand discussion later on in the semester, after good habits of participation have been inculcated, is to open the discussion sec-tion of the class by asking them to write two or three sentences on the topic or question you pose. Students can then be asked either to read their sen-tences or to give the gist of them. Teachers who have never tried this method are amazed at its ef-fectiveness. Even the shyest student will be as ready to contribute as the most fluent. (Some teachers feel that if they do this, they can call on students; others never call on students, no matter what.) Writing implies that the topic has seriousness and complex-ity; that the off-the-top-of-one's-head response is

not likely to be adequate. (Of course, you do not wish to convey such an idea early in the course when you are encouraging spontaneity.) Or you can organize the class into small after-class study groups: in class, some member of each group con-veys the essence of its discussion. This gives stu-dents additional practice, the ultimate goal.

As lecturers making the transition into discussion leaders, we may feel bewildered and even fright-ened by the first stage of discussion, while we are holding back and the crazy map is being con-structed. "The process is getting out of hand." "These ideological divisions are likely to explode." "What next?" Rectify a fact (which?), query a con-clusion (which?), summarize a debate (which?)? The direction of the class begins when we ask the first question—in effect, going down one of the roads on the crazy map and ignoring others. Different people have different tolerances for the stage of muddle. People who start from lecturing are used to being in control. Their goal may have to be that of forcing themselves to live with the muddle a little bit longer than they think is right. Some teachers feel they'll lose track of the other roads. You can jot down the directions you want to take later (it's flat-tering to the student to see you take a note after she speaks, especially if you say, "I want to come back to that"). Some teachers use a section of the board for jotting ideas they would like to pursue. A corollary advantage is that any road not taken by the end of the class remains on the board as a possibility for the next time.

The appearance of "error" may prove to be the real test of your gifts as a discussion leader. The possibility of your own error arises. There are times when you just don't know the answer to a factual question, or when you cannot summon a good, definitive brief response. If you have set an appro-priately generous and conversational tone, you will now be rewarded for it. To the fact seeker, you can respond with other relevant information and the promise that you'll look it up. To the seeker of final conclusions, you may offer a postponement of au-thoritativeness.

As for student errors, the response to them sep-arates the benefactors from the executioners. "How can a teacher permit error?" is the way the question used to be phrased. Postmodernism has made ask-ing it in horror more difficult—but it can still be asked, even by postmodern teachers, since the dim-inution of totalizing truths does not seem to have eliminated errors. So one of the crucial issues for discussion leaders is deciding how to handle them.

I think we would do well to try to prevent the situation from arising. The most effective way to do this is by loosening up our definition of error. There are various ways to do this, but one is by reminding ourselves ahead of time that they are *all* likely to be partly "wrong"—if nothing else, by being incomplete. If almost every utterance has some interest, by the same token, almost every utterance will have some error. Both halves of this theory encourage relaxation.

Some student will probably catch an egregious factual error. You may have to wait longer for the interpretation, or line of reasoning, or querying of assumptions that you are looking for. Another familiar situation is where several respondents crowd in the wrong direction, and you gather that the error is widely shared. Here, trying not to look disheartened, you might say openly, "I was trying to elicit something else, not [ ], but . . ." I once heard a leader wait as a group error emerged because it enabled her to guess the source of the bias and ask, "What's the single assumption behind every remark that has been made up to now?" Or, to elicit some particular point, you might want to rephrase an offending remark yourself, in a neutral tone. "Suppose I said that X = Y? What would you say to that?" A corrective tendency eventually appears. To clarify the difference between the old error and the new, shared understanding, you might want to ask the corrector, "Are you disagreeing with Joe's previous remark that X = Y?" Or you might want to leave Joe out, but highlight the corrector's emphasis by restating it, adding politely, "Am I capturing your reasoning? Is that a fair paraphrase?" The best discussion leaders, to my mind, are both bright and kind.

The discussion process can lead to the kinds of conclusions the teacher hopes for. But teachers need to set their goals. Some teachers hope for nothing more than for students to practice the kind of thinking a particular discipline calls for. At a high level of generality, deciding what kind of thinking we want them to do is not difficult. Very likely we want them to learn to present positions clearly and fully, to see objections to them, to answer the objections, and to evaluate and alter the positions that remain after these processes have been undergone. That leads to another maxim: no real discussion occurs without some level of conflict or, if you prefer, a

difference of ideas. If you believe that there is only one right answer to a particular problem, or one right approach, or that the answer should be simple and obvious, you probably cannot hope to vivify a discussion on that topic. Put positively: choose for discussion those issues where the debate is genuine, for you and for your students. Find the question you want to ask, and pose it dramatically.

The *tone* in which a teacher introduces conflict between ideas or responds to it affects the classroom atmosphere and student participation in discussion. For some teachers, their tone can only be a visceral, instinctual one. I met a teacher who liked to say, fiercely (quoting Milton's Moloch), "My sentence is for open War!" He justified his preference for discussions that contained highly emotional moments by arguing that they involved students more, focused the issues, became memorable. "Years hence, they'll remember the points that heated up because they mattered to somebody." The danger (again) is that some students are unprepared to handle new arguments couched in emotional language: it's too much for them. It may remind them of family feuds. Some teachers who like the *idea* of making their classes memorable in this way may be temperamentally unable to pull it off. Others may argue that civil conversation needs less—not more—emotion, or that their discipline as presently constituted is heated enough as it is. It is also true that the bigger the class, the more any emotion gets magnified. From time to time, teachers arrogate emotional expression to themselves while denying it to the students; this reinforces the hierarchy of power.

It is probably true that a class matters more to everyone if there is some rise in the intellectual temperature at some point, and that dispute sharpens points. A good teacher can plan this rise in temperature. In a small class, where you come to know the students well enough that you and they develop trust in the process, tapping emotion may become more possible as the semester progresses. You know the students' points of view: you can ask two of them whether they disagree, with some degree of security that they will. Personally, I like to work this stage with a safety net—not to suppress the emotion, but to look at it with some detachment. If passions emerge, I'm prepared to ask, "What is at stake here?" It's a good question to ask about discussion leading itself. After you and your students have worked through your assessments of risk, discussion leading will probably seem less per-

READING
Leading Discussion in a Lecture Course:
Some Maxims and an Exhortation GULLETTE

ilous to everyone, and precious precisely for its un-expected gains.

While I was at Harvard's Center for Teaching and Learning, I observed many teachers using the lecture-with-discussion format. The maxims of this paper are derived from the practices I admired, filtered through my own practice, theories, prefer-ences, and values. I kept noticing one recurrent feature. Invariably, skillful teachers chose to focus the discussion by giving the students a "document." They had made opening remarks that led right to the discussion, either giving the students new back-ground they needed to respond to, or reminding them of key factors. They were providing the con-text in which the question became an interesting, even dramatic one. And then they provided the document as a final cue.

In one extremely large Core class, a lecturer lured the students into reasoning about rights, with an introduction that could not have taken more than five minutes. "Our premise," he concluded, "has been that we have rights in our person" (he put his fist on his solar plexus), "in our labor, and in our property." He had written on the board:

Person – Labor – Property

This was his document. "Some people—libertar-ians—argue against taxation from this point of view, and say it is equivalent to forced labor, or to slavery. How can we break into this libertarian argument? Would someone want to challenge the argument at this lower level?" A student immediately began to give reasons why society had a counter-right to tax, and they were off. "Some people argue that" is a good way to pose a question because the students are arguing against an opponent who isn't (yet) there—in this case, the libertarian who thinks tax-ation is equivalent to slavery. Someone may then be asked to phrase the libertarian's rebuttal, and the conflict may become more personal.

This lecturer-turned-discussion-leader guided them closely: he paraphrased their reasoning or asked them to restate. He gave them labels for dis-tinctions he wanted them to know. He kept them on the track. He asked further leading questions—hard questions. He reminded them of arguments they had brought up in previous classes. He raised objections when they hadn't thought of them. He did each briefly, in scarcely more than a sentence each time, in what might be called an efficient tone. The result was that the students volunteering

tended to respond in a few sentences; they were probably those most comfortable with a rather high level of abstraction, and they certainly had great confidence in their verbal performance. This was, then, a discussion period high in control, high in clarity and structure (low in muddle), low in per-centage of participants, and low in incentives for the participation of the timid. But the class held over 500 students. To some degree, the teacher's decisions about tone and participation were con-strained by this fact as well as by his temperament and goals. The example proves, however, that high enrollments need be no absolute bar to discussion. My own belief is that a teacher with a different style could have risked more "incoherence" or "ineffi-ciency" (as he might put the risks) for the sake of other goals. Certainly, this remarkable instructor could, over time, change his goals.

In another class, well along in the semester, the document (again, brought out after no more than a ten-minute introduction) was a rather complicated chart of the "standard distribution of bridewealth" in a particular form of society. The students had received it at the end of the previous class. The teacher's first question was open-ended: "What did the chart make you think of?" But she had already closed off one kind of response by saying, "What I'm doing is giving the big picture. Don't get lost in details. Our theme is consensus in small commu-nities." In a small group (33 students), already fa-miliar with legal and anthropological discourse, her comments functioned to sharpen the students' con-tributions, restating points they made or asking "What if . . . ?" questions. Her corrections were usually presented as minor qualifications of positive contributions. "There are rules, yes—but not codes. So talking about 'rights' is both right and wrong." At one point she observed, "Better than I could have said it." Once she responded, "You're quite wrong," but her appreciative tone and the expla-nation that followed implied that this was an ex-pectable area of error, probably one that most of the class shared. Few discussion leaders will want to risk adding, "You're quite wrong" to their repertory of responses. "I'm glad you phrased that point of view because it gives me a chance to observe (or object) that . . ." could lead into the same explana-tion.

In 25 minutes of discussion, eight people spoke: five women and three men (a reasonable gender ratio, given the makeup of the class). Most received a follow-up question, which served to acknowledge the content of the remark, stretch the contributor intellectually, and mark the moment as an event. In the last 15 minutes, the teacher returned to the lecture format, but during this phase, too, she asked a question and waited long enough (seconds of real time) to elicit an answer. This class was moderately high in control but quite open to new ideas. A number of apparently heterogeneous topics were worked through. No muddle surfaced. The students addressed their responses directly to the professor. No issue was raised that might have generated sustained or emotional conflict.

In a third class, the document was a scene in a D. H. Lawrence novel that everyone was to have read and thought about. The teacher read a short essay he had written that explained an approach to the material through a number of details from the scene—details he quoted in full. The question that followed primed the students to reflect on the value of the approach. Many answered. (The class had 15 students, and I observed no skews in participation along gender lines.) But one immediate set of responses questioned the interpretation of various details (as he must have anticipated), and he worked with the students through several of those focuses of debate. While the conflict never became personalized or angry, a number of students responded to the Lawrence text in rather passionate ways, as they did to the interpretation that was offered. They talked directly to one another as well as to the teacher (as had not happened in the two earlier classes I described). He ended the discussion phase without a summary or last words, but he did restate a few of the students' ideas he liked, giving credit to them as he did so. He then returned to his essay and read the remainder. The discussion phase may have been high in muddle to some—at least initially—but he never seemed to have lost his "place," and he gave signs that he appreciated the wide range of the comments as well as their pertinency to the text. Certainly, the lack of conclusiveness would have taught something general about the reading of texts. There might have been some incongruity between his formal production of an essay and the students' willingness to participate, but in fact it proved no handicap. His own manner was extremely courteous.

Summaries of classes like these rarely satisfy the appetite they create: to provide enough complexity so that readers feel they have lived through a class and can draw their own conclusions about what to borrow for their own practice. I have rather simply examined three performances on the basis of the few measures that in an essay this brief seem to me primary. Creating maxims for discussion leading forces a teacher to decide what is important and generalizable in a format of fast-moving particulars. Depending on your point of view, maxims may serve you either as minimal guidelines or maximum enforcers of responsibility. For me, five are central. No impression without expression. No verbal expression without encouragement. No learning without muddle. No real discussion—and no engagement—without conflict. Conflict and focus come through the document.

Other teachers could, no doubt, construct more or do with fewer. This essay invites you to construct your own. But how you act on them remains entirely up to you. The format of mixing discussion with lecture leaves everyone with enormous freedom. There are some constraints. From what precedes, class size may appear to be the greatest. But in all circumstances, including huge classes, the format permits wide variations and permutation of temperament and approach—anyone can handle it. Everyone improves by doing it. For better or worse (I mean this to be encouraging), teachers do usually get the kind of class they are able to want.

Jeff Freeman, a Columbia Ph.D. in Modern European History, had taught for six years as a graduate student before coming to Southwestern University on tenure track. He considered himself tough but fair in the classroom and was moderately alarmed to learn that his first course, "European Constitutional History"—a required unit in the undergraduate liberal arts program—had a reputation for furnishing an easy B. The other six instructors in the course were an easygoing lot, and all had the authority to set policies independently. Jeff decided to steer his own course and be rigorous. To his pleasant surprise, his students seemed to react well to his teaching policies. They came prepared for the discussions he always held after his standard half-hour lectures.

But not Bob Crane. He attended only sporadically, never spoke in class, wrote a farce of a research paper, and neglected even to show up for the required class debate, which most students considered the high point of the course. When Bob's final exam proved no better than the rest of his work, Jeff had little trouble giving him a D.

A week later, in mid-November, Bob stormed into Jeff's office—his first appearance since the beginning of the semester, despite Jeff's frequent requests that they meet for a progress review.

"You can't do this to me, Mr. Freeman," Bob exploded. "I *deserve* a better grade than this."

"I don't see why," Jeff said. "You consistently fell at the bottom of the grading curve. I could have flunked you outright, but I thought you deserved some credit for at least submitting some written work." He proceeded to outline in detail Bob's many errors and failings in the course.

Bob changed tack. "Look, Mr. Freeman," he said. "You're making a mistake here. I absolutely have to have a C."

There seemed to be some threat behind this; Bob's dictatorial tone made Jeff furious. "Then you should have worked harder," he said coldly. "Now please stop wasting your time and mine. I think you should leave right now."

Bob left. A half hour later Jeff's telephone rang. "This is Matt Crane. Bob's my kid brother," said a loud voice. "We're not going to stand for this crap. What the hell kind of credentials do you have, to teach at a place like this anyway? We're going straight to the dean and get you fired!"

Jeff hung up, shaking with fury. Then the phone rang again. "That was immature, I know," Matt's

One Teacher's Nightmare (A)

Abby Hansen wrote this case for the Developing Discussion Leadership Skills and the Teaching by the Case Method seminars. Data were furnished by the involved participants. All names and some peripheral facts have been disguised.

HBS Case No. 9-384-063.

voice said. "I apologize. But it's like this: we're both on the football team, see? Bob's our star quarterback, and there are only two games left in the season. He's already on academic probation. If you don't give him a C, he'll be tossed off the team and out of our fraternity. This is really important!" Jeff was incensed. Football. Important? He had thought the issue was Constitutional History! "Your brother earned his D," he said. "Frankly, I doubt he even did the reading for the course. I don't see any reason to change the grade."

Matt's voice turned suddenly suave: "Well, look, Mr. Freeman. If he didn't do anything in your course, why can't you just give him a No Credit? That wouldn't pull down his average, and he could stay on the team. You don't know what that would mean to all of us. Can't you have a little compassion?"

Jeff hesitated. He was beginning to wonder how violently his standards clashed with the culture to which he had so recently come. He recalled an early academic meeting where a trustee had said, "We want a university our football team can be proud of!" Jeff had thought the statement funny at the time, but now he was inclined to wonder how important football really was at Southwestern.

It had not escaped Jeff's analytical mind that many Southwestern alumni who gave gigantic donations to the school based their allegiance on loyalty, not to the history department, but to the football team. Football was an obsession to many members of the Southwestern community. Was it possible, he wondered, that he had severely misjudged the whole value structure of the school? Had he placed expectations on Bob Crane that the situation did not, in fact, justify? In short, was there some sort of merit in Matt's argument?

Jeff clenched the receiver in his hand, muttered, "I'll see. Goodbye," and hung up. Then he sat alone in his office and stewed about this confrontation. What, he wondered, should he do? Submit to emotional extortion, or give the bastard the D he so richly deserved?

Slowly, Jeff Freeman's resolve crumbled. He boiled inwardly as he recalled Matt Crane's insulting tone, but as he revolved the issue in his mind, he began to see more and more merit in the fellow's argument. Football, Jeff knew, was a passion to many students at Southwestern. It happened to be a passion Jeff didn't share, but then most of the students didn't get excited about the Napoleonic Code. To each his own. Jeff began to think that, since football obviously meant the earth to this boneheaded Bob Crane, and nobody had elected Jeff Freeman Supreme Arbiter of Student Fate in Charge of Ruining Bob Crane's Life, he might as well go ahead and change the damned grade.

Feeling queasy, Jeff took out a Grade Change form and made the necessary pen strokes to keep Bob Crane on the football team. But part of him winced as he wrote "No Credit." He continued to feel uncomfortable with this decision.

CASE

One Teacher's Nightmare (B)

*This case was written by **Abby Hansen** for the Developing Discussion Leadership Skills and the Teaching by the Case Method seminars. Data were furnished by the involved participants. All names and some peripheral facts have been disguised.*

HBS Case No. 9-384-064.

This teaching note was prepared as an aid to instructors in the classroom use of the case series "One Teacher's Nightmare" (A) 9-384-063 and (B) 9-384-064.

HBS Case No. 5-384-088.

TEACHING NOTE

One Teacher's Nightmare

To start the discussion one might begin most dramatically with the point of decision: "What do you think Jeff ought to do?" There probably will be a range of responses: "He ought to change the grade and save his skin." "He ought to nail the jerk and report him and his brother to whatever academic disciplinary body exists for students." "He ought to consult the department chairman and the dean to discover what precedents exist in cases like this." "He ought to quit and go home to New York!" "He should start attending football games; he might learn to like them." Each answer—like the myriad other possible responses—could be used in one of two ways: the discussion leader could either probe for further elaborations on the same theme, or take another tack—call for other responses until a rather full range of possible responses for Jeff lay "on the table" for the group's further consideration. The group could then take up each path of reaction and its implications.

Each reaction to Jeff's range of opportunities brings with it a special set of implications and assumptions. "Jeff should change the grade" implies that (1) it is Jeff who is out of step, (2) Southwestern is a football school, (3) Constitutional History is not the be-all and end-all of life, (4) Jeff should learn to live in his new environment and play by the new rules. This is the course of adaptability.

"Jeff should stand firm and flunk the kid." This reaction implies an inflexible attitude: (1) the teacher has set policy, (2) most students have observed the teacher's wishes, (3) the maverick must suffer for his nonconformity, (4) it is Jeff's right to set whatever standards he thinks appropriate and his duty to maintain those standards, once set.

"He ought to get advice" implies a more sensible course of action. Paramount in this case is Jeff's newness and discomfort in an unfamiliar cultural climate. He seems to be trying to operate in a vacuum, all alone with his office telephone. Cultural adaptation requires contact with "the natives," and this Jeff appears to avoid. He would probably be well advised to seek advice from experienced colleagues—not, of course, abdicating the final responsibility of making his own decision. Jeff acts precipitously. He agonizes, squirms, ponders, relents, and reaches for the fatal pen to change Bob Crane's grade. All of this takes very little time. This researcher's opinion is that Jeff acted hastily and in the absence of potentially useful advice; but the issue of how he might have sought advice is worth exploring. How much time should he have invested in seeking advice? What sort of informant or advisor should he have sought?

The possible suggestion that Jeff "quit and go home" could be used, humorously, to set one pole of possibility. Jeff is an "alien," but need he remain so? What *are* the real differences between his devotion to scholarship and Southwestern's apparent devotion to moderate scholarship and passionate athletic participation?

The other extreme—in contrast to the cultural rejection of Southwestern's values—is complete capitulation. Could Jeff become a rah-rah, pennant-waving football fan, redesigning his courses for the convenience of the quarterbacks? The class will probably consider such overstated vision of adaptability with the derision it deserves. But positing the two scenarios of rejection versus acceptance of an unfamiliar cultural milieu and set of values might serve as a useful way to set the parameters of the discussion.

More fruitful—particularly as a means to help the participants plan their own early days in new courses—will be a discussion of Study Question 1:

1. How do you think this situation came about?

Here, the discussion leader might probe for an imaginative reconstruction of the way Jeff Freeman probably went about planning his course (alone, with his own notebooks open and glancing at the primary material, readings, and academic calendar). How else could he have done it—particularly given that there were norms already in operation and he was teaching in tandem with a staff of experienced instructors? Did Jeff bring this upon himself? In a way, yes. By failing to warn Bob Crane that he, Jeff, was *not* like the other easygoing teachers in the course, Jeff allowed Bob to live in a fool's paradise, confident that he could slide through the course with no effort and get a passing grade. Jeff should have set an explicit contract, allowed the students time to react to his proposals, and considered their counterproposals, if any, with real open-mindedness. Teaching a class is a two-way street.

2. Should Jeff change Bob's grade?

The question of whether Jeff ought to change the grade is less simple than it might appear. One is tempted, at first, to say, "Absolutely not!" Extortion like Matt's belligerent threats and subsequent whee-dling is repugnant; it incites one to resist merely by its impudence. There will very likely be a fairly outspoken faction in any discussion group who will argue for Jeff's need to stand firm. And they will have logic on their side. Jeff had the right to set his own standards. The other students managed to meet them. Why should Bob Crane receive a special dispensation because he's an "athlete" with a big brother? But there may be another faction in the class who take a different point of view: Jeff did not give adequate warning to Bob. Bob had no way of knowing, when he signed up for this section of the course, that this particular new instructor intended to break with the famous tradition of giving easy B's. Jeff had no one's approval for his unusually tough standards, and the option of giving Bob "No Credit" does, in fact, describe the situation with great accuracy. Bob did virtually no work; he is getting no credit for it. His penalty will be the necessity of making up the course—next time, presumably, by expending some more effort on his studies.

3. How do you think Jeff might have done things differently?

There are many things he could have done. He could have spent more time consulting the other instructors in the course about the ways in which they taught. Did they really let students get by without doing any work, or did they, perhaps, have ways to make the material more accessible, simpler to digest, more fun to work with? What sort of work *did* they consider acceptable? (He might have asked for samples of written work, with the grades they had received.) He might have met with some of his colleagues and tried to set group standards—perhaps a bit higher than the traditional ones, but less rigorous than his own—(compromised, in other words). Most important of all, he should have (1) warned his students that he had particularly stringent standards, (2) hoped they agreed with him that they would get more out of the course by following his guidelines for performance, and (3) wanted to hear their reactions and suggestions before setting final policy.

4. What larger issues does this case raise for you?

Here is the group's opportunity to present personal material. This researcher has encountered quite a few professors who have found themselves in situations reminiscent of Jeff Freeman's. Students do try to extort higher grades from professors—sometimes by belligerence, sometimes by veiled threats of bizarre behavior, depression, even elliptical allusions to suicide. How *should* the teacher react in these intensely uncomfortable situations? Whose well-being is paramount—the teacher's or the student's? Whose is the opportunity to grow, to learn? And what are the lessons implicit in these confrontations? The besetting problem of adjusting to an unfamiliar cultural milieu is another one that can profitably be discussed under this rubric. Academics tend to move a lot. It is not unusual for a career to start in California, continue in Texas, move on to Connecticut, and resume again somewhere in the deep South. What sort of resilience does this demand from the academic? How can he or she make these various moves with minimal psychological damage to all concerned? Again, the personal experiences of the participants will vary widely. If the proper atmosphere of trust and honesty has been established thus far in the discussion group, many useful, sympathetic, and heartening anecdotes may emerge—or many cautionary tales of errors committed, which will perhaps warn the listeners and help them avoid similar mistakes.

FINAL NOTE: Some role playing might be useful. Asking a participant to imagine the students' reactions to Jeff Freeman might open up some of the subtleties involved in this seemingly simple cultural confrontation. Most teachers will, most likely, instinctively side with Jeff. In fact, there is much to be learned by examining his situation through others' eyes. (For any teacher, the mental exercise of trying to think how the student might receive his or her teaching is always profitable!)

*   *   *

After the (B) case has been read:

1. What is your appraisal of Jeff Freeman's action?

One can either approve or disapprove of Jeff's capitulation. As we have seen, the discussion to this point will probably have succeeded in exposing subtleties not immediately apparent upon a first reading of the (A) case. One might feel initial moral outrage at Jeff for caving in under pressure. One might, despite this outrage, feel sympathy for his fear of reprisal if he should not change the grade. But cowardice isn't attractive, and the (B) case shows that Jeff felt queasy, uncomfortable, and sour. Clearly, he felt disappointment with himself for giving in.

But another point of view would be to approve of his action and chalk it up to *his* learning. Certainly, he could have seen this coming; he could, perhaps, even have prevented the actual confrontation by getting Bob Crane out of his section or warning him earlier in the term that he was heading for a D. But Jeff wasn't clairvoyant. Few of us are. By granting Bob the opportunity to stay on the team and in the fraternity, he was, perhaps, giving charity where it was not particularly well deserved, but the "No Credit" option has some appropriateness for this situation. Bob Crane will not emerge completely unscathed; he will have to take another course. And Jeff will have to give some careful consideration to what went wrong this time. One hopes he will consult some colleagues, accumulate further data on the institutional norms, and try to present his own expectations more clearly and honestly at the beginning of the next course he teaches.

Introduction

The editors of *Improving College and University Teaching* are pleased to present a remarkable and rare document. We are grateful for the generosity of Professor Selma Wassermann, of the Faculty of Education, Simon Fraser University, Burnaby, British Columbia, in sending it to us. Among Professor Wassermann's many research interests is the Italian Renaissance. While engaged in research on Michelangelo, she discovered papers which had been inadvertently attached to some discarded sketches. We believe that this revealing document will enlighten our readers on the perennial problem of tenure.

Lorenzo de Medici University
Memorandum

To: Sr. Michelangelo Buonarroti

From: Sr. H. Condivi, Chairman,
        Faculty Tenure Committee

Date: 18 August 1511

Dear Sr. Buonarroti:

The Tenure and Promotion Committee of the Faculty of Education deeply regrets that we are unable to recommend you for tenure.

We have given your case considerable thought and much discussion and while we think that your work has great promise, we feel that it is insufficiently scholarly to merit tenure at this time. The committee wishes to point to its recognition of your outstanding teaching capabilities—in particular, your work with young artists in a mentor capacity, your ability to inspire others, and your thoughtful and sensitive instruction.

However, in the area of scholarship, your performance has been found wanting. I refer specifically to the following:

(a) In the Faculty of Education, it is not important that you, yourself, be engaged in artistic endeavors. It is far more important that you spend time writing about how others should become artists. This you have failed to do.

(b) Your work, Michelangelo, is, I'm afraid, too clear, too unambiguous, and too straightforward. It is geared too much for the practitioner. Unfortunately, it is insufficiently obscure to be significant for academics.

Memorandum to Michelangelo: Tenure Denied

SELMA WASSERMANN

(c) While you have given us David, which is truly a thing of beauty, you did not, unfortunately, complete a review of the literature on sculpting. This indicates a grave shortcoming in your ability to do a critical analysis of scholarly sculpting.

(d) Finally, sir, your output is inordinately slow. It has been over three years since you have begun work on the Sistine Chapel and it is far from complete. Others in this faculty have generated dozens of manuscripts each year. You are a slow worker, Mike, and it is production here that counts.

We all like and admire you as a colleague—even though you do dress rather oddly and very unlike what is suitable for an academic, and there is frequently a lot of paint in your hair. If you were to move quickly to incorporate these suggestions, the committee believes you have a good chance to earn your tenure at the next hearings. After all, this is only your first consideration.

_____

Sr. H. Condivi,
Chairman

G ood teaching is an act of generosity, a whim of the wanton muse, a craft that *may* grow with practice, and always risky business. It is, to speak plainly, a maddening mystery. How can I explain the wild variety of teachers who have incited me to learn—from one whose lectures were tropical downpours that drowned out most other comments, to one who created an arid silence by walking into class and asking, "Any questions?"

Good teaching cannot be equated with technique. It comes from the integrity of the teacher, from his or her relation to subject and students, from the capricious chemistry of it all. A method that lights one class afire extinguishes another. An approach that bores one student changes another's life.

Faculty and administrators who encourage talk about teaching despite its vagaries, are treasures among us. Too many educators respond to the mystery either by privatizing teaching or promoting a technical "fix." The first group uses the variability of good teaching as an excuse to avoid discussing it in public—thus evading criticism or challenge. The second group tries to flatten the variations by insisting on the superiority of this or that method—thus evading the demands of subtlety. In both quarters, the far-ranging conversation that could illumine the mystery of good teaching has all but disappeared.

We misconstrue mystery when we think of it as a "black box," something opaque and impenetrable that we must either avoid or manipulate by main force. Mystery is a primal and powerful human experience that can neither be ignored nor reduced to formula. To learn from mystery, we must enter with all our faculties alert, ready to laugh as well as groan, able to "live the question" rather than demand a final answer. When we enter into mystery this way, we will find the mystery entering us, and our lives are challenged and changed.

Good teachers dwell in the mystery of good teaching until it dwells in them. As they explore it alone and with others, the insight and energy of mystery begins to inform and animate their work. They discover and develop methods of teaching that emerge from their own integrity—but they never reduce their teaching to technique.

I want to share a few reflections on the mystery of good classroom teaching, whether in large lecture halls or small seminars. I want to name some of its challenges, and suggest some responses, without treating it as a "problem to be solved." Only by

Good Teaching: A Matter of Living the Mystery

PARKER J. PALMER

HBS Case No. 8-390-152.

doing so, it seems to me, can we enlarge the community of discourse that might encourage more and more of us to teach well.

The Transaction Called Knowing

The knowledge we deal with in the classroom has not only a content, but also a characteristic way of imaging the transaction between the knower and the known. In the present "canonical" debate over *what* knowledge we should teach, more debate over *how* we gain knowledge would help if good teaching is our aim. (In fact, a hidden conflict among diverse modes of knowing continually confounds the debate over which texts merit full canonical status.)

The academy has been dominated by an objectivist image of knowing that holds the knower at arm's length from the known so that "subjective" biases will not distort our knowledge. This image of knowing is both reflected in and conveyed by our dominant mode of teaching, which, as Dewey said, turns education into a spectator sport. Students are kept in the grandstand so they can watch the pros play the knowledge game, but not interfere with its "objectivity."

Reformers have railed against this pedagogy. It makes learning passive and joyless, and it turns too many educated people into spectators of life itself. But many efforts at pedagogical reform have failed because the problem cannot be solved on the level of technique alone. The performer-spectator classroom is simply a faithful rendering of the objectivist epistemology. If the last word in knowing is to keep subjectivity at bay, then the last word in teaching will be to keep students off the field.

More engaging ways of teaching will take root only as we explore more engaged images of knowing—especially of "objective" knowing. Few of us want to throw out the Enlightenment baby with the objectivist bathwater. But we can no longer teach as if there were a reality "out there" that can be mirrored by logical-empirical propositions. This image of objectivity ignores the way reality is shaped by an interplay of knower and known, and it leads to teaching with no higher aim than making sure that students get the propositions straight.

The only objective knowledge we have is the provisional outcome of a complex transaction in which many subjectivities check and balance each other. It is a fluid process of observation and interpretation, of consensus and dissent, conducted within a far-flung community of seekers who agree upon certain

assumptions, rules, procedures—many of which are themselves up for debate. This, I think, is an image of objectivity that is faithful to the way we know. It is also an image that clarifies the goal of good teaching: to draw students into the process, the community, of knowing.

"To teach is to create a space in which the community of truth is practiced." That image of teaching has given me guidance in recent years, as has a related image of truth: "Truth is an eternal conversation about things that matter, conducted with passion and discipline." Good teaching, whatever its form, will help more and more people learn to speak and listen in the community of truth, to understand that truth is not in the conclusions so much as in the process of conversation itself, that if you want to be "in truth" you must be in the conversation.

I do not mean that every classroom must be turned into a discussion section. The "conversation" of truth can and must be internal as well as external—internally, it is called "critical thinking." That teacher of mine who walked in and asked, "Any questions?", created a space for external conversation. But the teacher who rained words had a way of arguing with himself that opened the subject up rather than shutting it down. His lectures created a space for debate within me, a debate that goes on to this day. Both of those good teachers knew that the relation of knower to known is not distanced and static, but interactive and evolving. They knew that objectivity at its best is a commitment to critical discourse.

On Content and "Covering the Field"

When conversation, internal or external, is named as one quality of good teaching, some teachers get nervous about the need to "cover the field." They feel obliged to deliver large numbers of facts that students simply must master, facts that neither require nor abide "conversation" of any sort—they are what they are. Of course, some of this reaction comes from confusing education with memorization, and some of it comes from forgetting that an educated person should know where "facts" come from. But some of it is well-placed. There *are* subjects that require students to master much factual material. How does good teaching deal with that demand?

Not best, I think, by nonstop lecturing, where our efforts to "cover the field" often do exactly that—they bury topics in a blizzard of information, obscuring them from the students' view. The fact-laden lecture is probably the least desirable way to get the facts across. Not only are students easily overwhelmed by all that data, but they are likely to get the facts wrong to boot. Far too many lecture courses resemble the "telephone game" where messages get mauled on their brief but perilous journey from speaker's mouth to listener's ear.

Surely the best way to deliver the facts is not with lectures, but on the printed page or computer screen where they can be read and read again, studied and reviewed. Perhaps it is not a sense of responsibility that leads to lectures burdened with facts. Perhaps it is a lethargy that keeps us from finding or creating the texts that could give our students the factual grounding they need.

When we deliver the facts on paper, we free the classroom for various exercises in generating facts, understanding facts, using facts, seeing through the facts—exercises that might draw our students into the community of truth. One such approach I call "teaching from the microcosm."

Every discipline is holographic. One can find small pieces of it that represent the whole. A critical episode in a novel, a particular historical event, a classic puzzle in science—any of these, properly approached, can be the grain of sand in which a world is revealed. In my own discipline, sociology, I once taught methods of social research, and I would spend up to two weeks taking students inside a single statistical table, a microcosm that discloses the basics I wanted them to learn.

Imagine a simple, four-cell table that correlates race (black, white) with income (high, low). The table stays on the board for six sessions while I lecture a little and ask a lot of questions, encouraging my students to respond not only to me, but to each other's answers. Can people really be divided into "black" and "white?" How—by observation or self-assignment? How reliable are the various ways of determining race? If race is really a continuum of traits, what is our warrant for using discrete categories? What are the consequences of doing so—for science, for persons, for society?

The questions go on and on as we turn to the concept of income, the general idea of concepts and indicators, modes of data collection and their validity, the logic of correlation, the social implications of such findings, the ethics of social research. Unlike the objectivist strategy of keeping students outside the subject as observers and manipulators, the mi-

crocosm approach brings them inside the subject as participants and co-creators of knowledge. After two weeks of dwelling critically in this simple table, many of my students were able to negotiate parts of the larger world of social inquiry and its findings.

The Autobiographical Connection

If it is important to get students inside a subject, it is equally important to get the subject inside the students. Objectivism, with its commitment to holding subjectivity at bay, employs a pedagogy that purposely bypasses the learner's life story. Objectivism regards autobiography as biased and parochial and hopes to replace it with "universal truth," as told through a particular discipline.

The challenge of racial and cultural minorities to higher education comes in part from their refusal to accept the validity of a "universal" tale that does not honor the particularities of their own stories. Feminists and black scholars, for example, compel those of us who promulgate universal truth to consider the possibility that our super-story has persisted less because of its persuasiveness than because of our political power. If there is a valid super-story, it will emerge only as the academy becomes what it is meant to be, but is not yet: a place of true pluralism where many stories can be told and heard in concert.

Of course, everyone's story is, in part, parochial and biased. But when we deal with that fact by ignoring autobiography, we create educated monsters who know much about the world's external workings but little about their inner selves. The authentically educated person is one who can both embrace and transcend the particularity of his or her story because it has been triangulated many times from the standpoints of other stories, other disciplines—a process that enriches the disciplines as well. When autobiography and an academic discipline are brought into "mutual irradiation" the result is a self illumined in the shadows where ignorance hides and a discipline warmed and made fit for human habitation.

By intersecting knowledge and autobiography we not only encourage intellectual humility and offer students self-understanding, we also make it more likely that the subject will be learned. When students do not see the connection between subject and self, the inducement to learn is very low. I know a geology professor whose students keep journals on the personal implications of each session to help them remember that the rocks they study are the rocks on which they live. I know a college where students are asked to explore the childhood roots of their vocational decisions (or confusions). In these ways, curiosity about the self can empower curiosity about the world.

When class size prohibits methods such as these, a teacher can help connect self and subject by giving away one of the academy's best-kept secrets: the major ideas at the heart of every discipline arose from the real life of a real person—not from the mind alone, but from the thinker's psyche, body, relationships, passions, political and social context. Objectivism tries to protect its fantasy of detached truth by presenting ideas as cut flowers, uprooted from their earthy origins. But good teachers help students see the persons behind the ideas, persons whose ideas often arose in response to some great suffering or hope that is with us still today.

We teachers can also show students how the ideas we care about are related to our own life stories. Many students will be surprised to learn that their teachers—separated from them by gaps of age and authority and vocation—even *have* lives. They will be even more surprised to learn that our intellectual interests arise from the larger lives we lead, that the two enrich each other. That, after all, is why many of us became scholars and teachers—and our teaching will become more vivid as we let the secret out.

Hearing Students into Speech

If good teaching depends on drawing students and their stories into the conversation called truth, then good teachers must deal with the fact that many students prefer to sit silently on the sidelines. Students have blocked interactive teaching at least as often as have faculty. Many of them do not want to suffer the conflict and ambiguity of external conversation, and some try to avoid inward debate for the same reason.

If we are to treat their condition, we need an accurate diagnosis. It is inaccurate, though common, to attribute most student speechlessness to laziness or stupidity—and that diagnosis usually leads to teaching that is more punitive than provocative. Instead, I suggest, the silence of many students is the result of disempowerment that leads to privatization. Students are often marginal to the society by virtue of their youth, their lack of a productive role, their dependency on the academy for

legitimation. Deprived of any sense of public place or power, they withdraw into the private realm where they keep their thoughts to themselves and, sometimes, *from* themselves.

"Hearing people into speech," is a phrase I first learned from the women's movement, and similar imagery can be found among blacks and liberation theologians. In those quarters, the diagnosis of speechlessness is not accusatory but compassionate; the silent one is understood as the victim of a system that denies his or her story, that ignores or punishes people who tell tales that threaten the standard version of truth.

The remedy is clear: establish settings where silenced voices can be heard into speech by people committed to serious listening. The classroom can be such a setting—if the teacher will work hard to gain credibility with students who have learned that silence is the safer way. Credibility comes as the teacher empathizes with the voiceless and with their struggle to speak and be heard.

There are many practical ways of "hearing people into speech." Teachers who must lecture much of the time can honor minority viewpoints on their subjects, giving minority students a sense that alternative voices can be spoken and heard. Even in the largest classes, it is not necessary to lecture all the time; some materials can be presented by questioning (as in the "microcosm" approach), and, if the questions are neither rhetorical nor catechetical, students will want to respond. When those responses come, teachers can hear people into speech by respecting their responses—which does not require assenting to false claims. The familiar problem of a few students speaking a lot while the majority remain mute can be controlled in many ways; I sometimes allow each student only three chances to speak, thus allowing the quieter ones to find an opening.

With smaller classes, when a divisive issue is up for debate and my students retreat into privatism, I sometimes give each of them a 3" x 5" card and ask that he or she write a few lines expressing a personal opinion on the issues. I collect the cards and redistribute them so that no one knows whose card he or she is holding. Then I ask each student to read that card aloud and take sixty seconds to agree or disagree with what it says. By the time we have gone around the group, the issue has been aired, diversity has been exposed, the unspeakable may have been spoken, and a foundation for real conversation has been laid.

"Hearing people into speech" is as pertinent to science as it is to social science and the humanities. Think, for example, of the gender stereotyping that has often discouraged women from pursuing scientific careers. If the work of such scientists as Barbara McClintock and her biographer, Evelyn Fox Keller, were more widely read in science courses, more women might be heard into scientific discourse. Or think of the implications of eugenics for some disenfranchised groups. Students who represent those groups must be helped to find their scientific voices lest they be speechless in the face of the next silent holocaust.

Conflict, Competition, and Consensus

Contrary to its reputation and self-image, the academy is a place where conflict is often privatized, not openly aired. If we practice the community of truth in our teaching, if we intersect our subjects with autobiography and hear more people into speech, we will experience more public conflict than the academy is accustomed to, or even appreciates. Our fear of public conflict is a major barrier to creating spaces where the community of truth can be practiced. If we want to remove that barrier, we must remind ourselves—and help our students to learn—that conflict can be a paradoxical path to health and harmony for persons and groups.

Many people regard conflict as terminal rather than creative because they have experienced it in settings that are competitive rather than consensual. In competition, the purpose of conflict is to determine which few will win at the expense of the many. In consensus, everyone can win through conflict as the clash of apparent opposites gives rise to fresh, fuller truth.

A consensual classroom assumes that truth requires many views and voices, much speaking and listening, a high tolerance for ambiguity in the midst of a tenacious community. Consensual truth is not the outcome of majority vote. It is a continuing revelation that comes as we air our differences in public, pay special heed to those who dissent, and seek deeper insight—whether the subject is a statistical table, a laboratory experiment, an episode in history, or an epic poem. Since consensual truth is the only truth we have, it is vital that students be brought into the process and into the conflict it contains.

Paradoxically, the most important thing a teacher can do to encourage classroom conflict is to make the classroom a hospitable space. Only under these conditions are students likely to do the hard things on which consensus-making depends—exposing one's ignorance, challenging another's facts or interpretations, claiming one's own truth publicly and making it vulnerable to the scrutiny of others. When the classroom is a hostile place, students either withdraw into privatism for safety or engage in public posturing to score points.

To give my students experience of conflict in a consensual setting, I sometimes use a simulation game. The game poses a problem that individuals first solve privately. Then small groups are turned loose on the problem after being given a simple set of conflict-consensus rules—e.g., "Present your views clearly, but listen to reactions before pressing your point." "Don't change your mind just to achieve harmony." "Avoid conflict-reducing techniques such as majority vote, coin flips, bargaining." "When stalemate comes, don't assume that some must win while others lose; seek a solution acceptable to all members." "Remember that consensus does not require that everyone love the solution, but only that no one be strongly opposed to it." The rules authorize and guide the very conflict that students want to avoid.

When the game is over, individual and group solutions are scored for accuracy. If a group has followed the rules, the group score is almost always better than the average of individual scores—and it is often better than the *best* individual score in the group. When these results are not achieved, it is often because the group failed to follow the rules. By playing the game, students learn that all of us together can be smarter than any one of us alone, if we allow for creative conflict. As the class goes on, this experience can be transferred from the simulated problem to the real problems we are studying.

In classes too large to permit corporate inquiry through conflict, lecturers can at least remind students where "the facts" come from. They come not from immutable authorities, but from very human communities that have sustained creative (and some noncreative) conflict for centuries, a conflict that continues even as we teach and learn the facts. A teacher whose class is too large to allow the outward conflict of a learning community can evoke the inward conflict called critical thinking.

The Nemesis of Evaluation

Any case for consensual teaching and learning can founder quickly on the shoals of grading. How can a teacher draw students into noncompetitive inquiry when the academy's system of evaluation seems to require competition?

The first step is firmly to reject the notion that grading on the curve, with its forced competition, has any educational merit, and to insist, instead, that if everyone receives an "A" that it might be the result of superb teaching and learning rather than sloppy standards. Another possibility is to allow each student to determine, within stated limits, what proportion of his or her grade will hinge on exams, papers, discussions, lab work, outside projects, etc. By allowing students to lead with their strengths rather than weaknesses, some of the anti-educational effects of competition are mitigated.

Teachers can give students a chance to have their work evaluated several times before it must be finished. Grading then becomes more a tool of learning and growth than a final judgment on the final product. But the largest leap a teacher can take beyond competition and toward consensus is to stop attaching grades exclusively to individuals and start assigning group tasks for which every member receives the same grade. When the academic reward system is used to make students rely on each other, the skills of consensus are more likely to be learned.

If teaching-and-learning is to become a corporate enterprise, students need a chance to evaluate teachers, too. I do not mean the kinds of evaluations that are collected on questionnaires and published as consumer guides. I mean the kind that can be conducted publicly at the end of every second or third class, a time of open reflection on how things are going (based on criteria that students help identify early in the course) so that mid-course corrections can be made. When a class knows that it will be asked periodically to assess its own progress, everyone—the teacher included—comes to class with more intention and wit, more sense of being in this together.

The Courage to Teach

The word "courage" comes from a root that means "heart," and I like to transpose the words. How can we develop and sustain, in ourselves and each other, the heart for good teaching (assuming that the mind is already available)? Good teaching requires courage—the courage to expose one's ignorance as well as insight, to invite contradiction as well as consent, to yield some control in order to empower the group, to evoke other people's lives as well as reveal one's own. Furthermore, good teaching sometimes goes unvalued by academic institutions, by the students for whom it is done, and even by those teachers who do it. Many of us "lose heart" in teaching. How shall we recover the courage that good teaching requires?

We need institutional support in response to that question—workshops and institutes on teaching, promotion and tenure policies that reward good teaching as handsomely as good research. But we need even more to do the inner work that good teaching demands. "Taking heart" to teach well is a profoundly inward process, and there is no technique or reward that will make it happen.

Taking heart means overcoming the fears that block good teaching and learning. Fear is a driving force behind objectivism, that mode of knowing that tries to distance us from life's awesome energies and put us in control. Fear is a driving force behind the kind of teaching that makes students into spectators, the pedagogy that tries to protect both teacher and subject from the give-and-take of community, from its rough-and-tumble. When our fears as teachers mingle and multiply with the fears inside our students, teaching and learning become mechanical, manipulative, lifeless. Fear, not ignorance, is the great enemy of education. Fear is what gives ignorance its power.

In its original meaning, a "professor" was not someone with esoteric knowledge and technique. Instead, the word referred to a person able to make a profession of faith in the midst of a dangerous world. All good teachers, I believe, have access to this confidence. It comes not from the ego, but from a soul-deep sense of being at home in the world despite its dangers. This is the authority by which good teachers teach. This is the gift they pass on to their students. Only when we take heart as professors can we "give heart" to our students—and that, finally, is what good teaching is all about.

Credits